AN
AMERICAN
SAGA

Juan Trippe
and His
Pan Am Empire

 Random House / New York

AN AMERICAN SAGA

ROBERT DALEY

Library of Congress cataloging in Publication Data

Daley, Robert.
An American Saga.

Bibliography: p.
Includes index.
1. Trippe, Juan Terry, 1899-
2. Aeronautics—United States—Biography.
3. Pan American World Airways, inc. I. Title.
TL540.T7D34   1980   387.7'092'4 [B]
ISBN 0-394-50223-X   79-4792

Manufactured in the United States of America

23456789

FIRST EDITION

For John C. Leslie

Contents

Part I
A YOUNG MAN PLANS

The Island

Topographically the island is singularly undistinguished, being a sandspit bent into the shape of a hairpin and barely awash in the heaving sea. Total land mass is only two and a half square miles, and mean elevation at high tide is twelve feet. The hairpin's long gaunt arms are in some places only a hundred yards wide.

As a type, it seems more suited to the Bahamas or the Florida Keys, where such islands swell up out of a shallow sand bottom and lie in clusters. People sail to them in pleasure boats for snorkeling or beach parties.

But this island is in a different sea. No one has ever sailed to it for a picnic and snorkeling is limited. Three-quarters of a mile offshore the water is 16,000 feet deep. The island is part of a mountain, all but the top twelve feet of which are underwater. It sits alone amid a million or more square miles of empty ocean.

It has no coves or inlets, and an unbroken reef encircles it as tightly as a wedding band. It has no harbor. There is no safe anchorage. Against the encircling reef on all but the calmest days pounds a constant surf. No vessel of whatever size has ever been able to approach very closely.

There is no way that anyone making a survey could ever have singled out this island saying, "Here's one of the world's important ones." It seems particularly unsuited to heroic events. There is no water—this is a true desert island. There is nothing to eat. Vegetation is extremely scant, amounting to only a few warped trees, some clumps of scaevola shrubs and tangled carpets of octopus vines which lie like hairpieces on the crowns of the dunes. These dunes are lumpy and uneven, having been rearranged many times over the years both by weather and by high explosives. Typhoons have struck every fifteen years or so. There is nothing to impede their growth, or to slow them down for hundreds upon hundreds of miles in all directions. When they strike, they scalp the dunes, and indeed the entire island, as if with razor blades. There is little shade here at the best of times. After each typhoon years go by before trees and bushes grow back—before shade itself reappears.

A beach rims the outside of the entire hairpin. It is composed partly of sand, partly of sharp coral rubble, and is no place for bare feet. One tramps it in sneakers. It seems immensely empty. One faces out into the northeast trade winds for a thousand miles. A good deal of military junk protrudes from the sand, most of it sharp-edged, all of it rusty. It competes with nature for attention, and will for some time more. Here are two concrete pillboxes. With beetle-browed eyes they still stare out over the sea, their mouths empty where the long cigars used to be. Both are canted to one side, whether by shellfire or erosion is by now impossible to say. Beyond them a rill of water laps against an upside-down, half-buried half-track. Theirs? Ours? Somebody's gravestone, anyway.

Ahead, half hidden in the scrub, still commanding 180 degrees of ocean, stands a great naval gun. Its eight-inch barrel looks burned out, as if from firing too many rounds too quickly. This was one of their guns, or so it is said today; no one is really sure. Its inch-thick carapace has been rusting for so long now that it has begun to peel in layers, like plywood.

The two arms of the hairpin, reaching out from the shoulders, seek to enclose a great round lagoon. They don't quite make it, but the encircling reef completes the job offshore and the lagoon is there, fully formed, limpid, placid, ablaze with tropical fish. All of it shimmers with color, from sapphire blue, where the water is deep, to the emerald green of the shallows, to opalescent white, where the water may be only inches deep. This is color more glorious and brilliant than the eye can absorb.

The lagoon dominates the island. This is partly because it alone is beautiful, and partly because it alone first brought men here. See that dark-blue patch underwater, that long straight channel across the center of the lagoon? College boys dredged that channel out in the summer of 1935, which is the year the island entered history.

Facing the lagoon on the inner side of the hairpin stand the island's buildings, all but a few boarded up, presumably forever. Most are quite old. They can be dated by their pockmarked foundations—modern man has learned to reckon age from bullet holes. Old or new, their architecture—what might be called twentieth-century military—is the same.

There used to be a 48-room hotel here too, built in a more luxurious style. It is gone now, along with nearly all it once represented. Poking around amid the weeds one can still discern its foundations. There used to be a pier out front as well, stretching out into the lagoon for a hundred yards, where the great flying boats used to tie up. It is possible to imagine the scene still: the wealthy passengers disembarking, walking up the pier toward the hotel veranda, where, after ten or more hours in the air, cool drinks awaited them. Today the pier is ruined; a few of its concrete pilings jut like broken teeth above the surface of the water.

Once the flying boats had been emptied, they could be taxied along the shore toward the service area nearby. Swimmers wearing goggles and the two-piece bathing costumes of the day would position a flatbed contraption under the hull. When all was ready, the immense flying boat would get winched up out of the lagoon via a sloping concrete ramp. Water would spill from it as if off a duck. Up on land it would rest there looking ungainly, far too clumsy to fly.

The underwater ramp is still intact. In a few places sand has drifted across it, but the concrete looks solid. It hasn't been used since the world it was built to serve ceased to exist. It is still known to the few current inhabitants of the island as the Pan Am ramp. Hardly any of them knows why.

Standing at the top of the ramp one can survey the entire lagoon. It is about a mile wide here. On it nothing moves. One can look across to the other spit of sand.

This is Wake Island in the middle of the empty Pacific. It was discovered, in effect, in the New York Public Library by Juan Trippe. For a brief time—only the blink of an eye as history is measured—it was one of the most famous places in the world.

Trippe

At the beginning Trippe was both a dreamer and a dare-devil, a youth with mind and heart literally in the clouds, and he could reasonably have expected to die either young or impoverished or both.

He was born on June 27, 1899, son of a New York investment banker. When he was about ten, his father took him to an air race over lower New York Bay. The Statue of Liberty was one of the turning pylons. The planes were open kites with pusher engines, and the boy could see the pilots manipulating feet and hands. He could see propeller blades flailing. On each lap the planes flew close over the heads of the awed crowd, and one plane crashed. On the way home the Trippe family car wouldn't start.

From then on young Trippe yearned to become an aviator. When he was about seventeen, his father sent him to Marconi School to learn Morse code, together with what little was known about radio at that time, because, although the Trippes were rich, the Puritan ethic prevailed in their household; their son would have to work for what he wanted. Radio first, then flight. So young Trippe learned radio, after which his father sent him to the private Curtiss Flying School in Miami. Soon he had about 100 minutes of dual flying under his belt—flying was counted in minutes in the summer of 1917.

That fall, having enrolled at Yale, he went out for freshman football and made the team as a guard, for he was a big hulking youth who could push other youths around. By then the United States had entered World

War I "to fight the Huns." Young Trippe wanted to fight the Huns too, as did most of his teammates, and once the season ended, almost the entire freshman squad quit college and joined the Marine Corps en masse; 1917 was a patriotic year.

Trippe's patriotism was more specific than most. The place he wanted to fight the Huns from was the air and when he discovered that the Marine Corps had no facilities for training him as a pilot, he managed to get himself transferred to the Navy, which did. He was sent to ground school at the Massachusetts Institute of Technology, and he soloed over Long Island, a twenty-minute flight in a Jenny. From there he was sent to Hampton Roads, Va., where he first flew flying boats, and then to Pensacola, Fla., where he volunteered for night flying, and for bombers, even though the romance and glamour of flying that year lay elsewhere. There were many heroes of the air battles of the Great War. All flew tiny pursuit planes. They engaged in dogfights high above France, and they fired their machine guns out through whirling propeller blades. Hardly any big bombers got into action at all; certainly Trippe never did, and his other new skills—radio, night flying—did not change the course of the war either. Planes of any description rarely flew at night, nor did they normally carry radios.

But Trippe was already obeying his own instincts, and moving in his own direction: bombers, night flying, radio. Though not yet nineteen, he was already thinking of after the war, of the time when he would become a man, and of the commercial possibilities of aviation.

Of course he enjoyed the training, as any youngster would have. He learned to machine-gun big wooden rowboats adrift in the sea, to make dead-stick landings into the wind, and he made a single parachute jump. He was once accused of zooming a Navy blimp with his bomber and, as punishment, was obliged to walk tours of the yard for two days with a pack full of bricks on his back. Upon graduation he and some others rolled about twenty cannonballs down a hill into the streets of the town, doing some damage.

The war ended there. Trippe went back to Yale, enamored of flying. He played guard again on the football team, rowed on the crew. He was six feet tall, and his weight was moving upward toward two hundred pounds. As a rich man's son he also played golf, and he became a superb golfer, with a handicap of five.

During his sophomore football season he was kicked in the spine in a pileup. His three bottom vertebrae had to be fused. It was one of the first times this operation was tried. Trippe spent three months in the hospital, and when he came out, his football and rowing days were over, and it would be a long time before he played golf again.

On Juan's twenty-first birthday his father died. The Trippe bank failed. Juan went back to Yale, where, while other students caroused, he founded and edited the *Yale Graphic,* a kind of general-interest college magazine. He was not then, and never became, a literary man. He was learning how to run a business, how to meet a payroll. It was not art that interested him, but bringing in advertising linage. He made a profit of a few thousand dollars, which went into the bank to gather interest alongside his small inheritance from his father.

During the long summer vacations he lived with his mother in New York, on East 76th Street, and he worked for Lee, Higginson and Company, the investment house. He worked as a runner, he worked in the cages. He learned how companies were organized, how funds were raised, what it meant to operate on margin. He learned the investment banking business, and it failed to excite him.

Back at Yale he studied principally business courses, accounting, engineering, transportation. He absorbed what interested him, and ignored what did not. Yale never counted him a brilliant student, but then Yale's norms were not Trippe's. He was well-bred, a gentleman. He was affable, polite and shy with girls. Even among his classmates, he was not one to assert himself. But he did have the ability to win long, persistent arguments. He would argue patiently until no one had any energy left to argue back. His classmates called him Wang, a corruption of Juan, the name he had been given in honor of his Aunt Juanita. Juan was a name he often hated. But he hated Wang more. He was also sometimes called Mummy because, except for the long arguments, he seldom spoke.

Flying was one of his few outlets. A great many war-surplus airplanes were being released to the public during those years. Trippe organized the Yale Flying Club, which bought a plane with two open cockpits. Trippe entered it in an intercollegiate air race against ten other planes representing that many other schools, most of them Ivy League. The race was to be held on Long Island around a four-cornered course, and the planes were supposed to fly about a hundred feet above the treetops. Trippe studied his plane. He thought that by changing the incidence of the dihedral he could make it fly faster; all his life he seemed to know more about the mechanics of flight than anyone gave him credit for. He was in third place at the first pylon. The second leg was down the Merrick Road for twelve miles to Amityville, and the Cornell, Princeton and Yale planes were flying neck and neck, ten feet apart and thirty feet above the road. The Yale plane (Trippe) dove to within ten feet of the ground at the pylon, got the inside position and took the lead. Two miles from the finish, Trippe took the lead for the final time, and brushing the treetops all the way, crossed the finish line six seconds ahead of the second-place plane. It was a heady moment for a youth who could no longer engage in the more athletic team sports that college crowds turned out to see.

When he graduated he was twenty-three, and he saw life as a rather more serious affair than did most of his classmates. The banker's son, all assumed, would become a banker, but Trippe refused. He was determined to make a business out of aviation. This was partly an intellectual decision, partly an emotional one. The only place where Trippe felt special was around airplanes. He was part of a small, select fraternity there. He was a pilot—though there was a certain devil-may-care glamour to the word which did not quite fit Trippe. Nonetheless he knew the adventure of flying. He understood the machine, and the mechanical laws that governed flight. He sensed where commercial aviation could go— not completely perhaps, but certainly more sharply than most other people did.

And so he determined to buy some planes and found an airline. His credentials were more considerable than they might have appeared. He had his inheritance from his father, plus access to the world of money in which his father had moved; among his own classmates were other young pilots, including William Vanderbilt and Cornelius Vanderbilt Whitney. William Rockefeller had lived across the street from him in Greenwich, Conn.; they had once climbed cherry trees together. These young men were connected to three of the biggest fortunes in the world.

Trippe also knew that seven war-surplus planes were about to be auctioned off at the Philadelphia Navy Yard—single-engined pontoon biplanes of the model designated 49-B. Trippe entered a bid of $500 apiece. This bid and all others were thrown out as too low, but when bids were called for again a month later the boy who would become the tycoon thought it over carefully, entered the same bid a second time—and got the planes.

Now to make them into an airline.

Most young men of Trippe's time—or any time—might not have bothered to organize a formal company just to sell airplane rides, for this took work and time, and it cost money in legal fees. Trippe, however, did organize a company. He capitalized it at $5,000, putting up half himself, selling stock for the other half, and incorporating as Long Island Airways. One of Trippe's partners was his uncle. Another was a boyhood friend, Dave Robbins, whose father owned the Robbins Conveyor Belt Company. Though Dave had been a World War I pilot and was no longer a child, Robbins Sr. was furious, and began bombarding young Trippe with angry letters. "I would prefer that you didn't encourage Bud to stay in the aviation business," one read.

The seven planes were in crates in Philadelphia, and they reached Rockaway Beach, where Trippe had rented an abandoned hangar, on seven railroad cars. Trippe and his pals began to assemble them, and then to test-fly them, and with that Long Island Airways was in business.

People, in 1922, sometimes ran through the streets after airplanes, congregating at the spot where the plane seemed likely to set down. They waited in lines to pay money to be taken aloft. A stunt or two by the hovering pilot, and the crowd was there, and the cash registers started ringing. This was especially true in summer at the beaches. There were potential customers sprawled on the hot sand from Coney Island to Fire Island. And behind the dunes there was plenty of still water on which pontoon planes could land.

Trippe did very little piloting himself. He was too busy trying to turn Long Island Airways into a business. He could hire men to fly—ex–military pilots were all around him clamoring for a chance to handle the controls. What could not be hired, at least not easily in 1922, were aviation-oriented young men willing to study the "art" for its business possibilities. This was what Trippe had to do himself, and he soon found it inordinately satisfying.

His planes had been built to carry two people only: one pilot and one passenger. The Oxx engine, though considered mighty for its day, could lift no more weight than that. Furthermore, with gas tanks built into the fuselage, there was no room for more than one passenger.

Two passengers would mean double the revenues, of course. It would mean more than that. A three-seater plane would mean carrying couples, something very few planes could do in 1922. It would mean commanding a bigger share of the beach business than any of his competitors. But how were two passengers to be crowded aboard? How was such a load to be lifted off the ground?

It was possible to buy French Hispano-Suiza 220 engines that provided more horsepower, and could lift more weight—theoretically, at least. However, their propellers were so big that if Trippe installed them in his Aeromarines, the props would cut the pontoons off. Besides, there would still be no room in the fuselage for the second passenger.

Trippe's dark brown eyes studied this machinery, his mind mulled over the possibilities, and he sought advice from every mechanic who crossed his path. At length he concluded that the Hisso engines could in fact be installed in his Aeromarines, and if the engines' reduction drive was removed, smaller propellers could be substituted for the big ones. The engines could then be revved up fast enough so that the original power would still be achieved and the pontoons would not get cut off. As for making space for an extra passenger, why not put the gas tanks on the outside of the fuselage? So he bought the Hisso engines and the smaller props, and he ordered these alterations carried out.

Able now to carry two passengers in the front cockpit, Trippe moved from the beaches into the charter business as his planes began carrying rich couples out to the Hamptons, or up to Newport, or down to Atlantic City—these were the important resorts that year.

In his spare time he began to haunt the New York Public Library, where he studied business tomes on railroads, on cross-country bus companies, on shipping lines. What laws regulated them? How much did it cost them to carry ten pounds of express freight, or a hundred pounds, or a thousand pounds from point A to point B? What was the elapsed time of such transport? How much might people be willing to pay if an airline could offer extra speed?

This last question, of vital importance to Trippe, interested almost no one else. In 1922 the airplane, when actually flying, was only slightly faster than crack trains or cross-country buses; it was much slower when its handicaps were considered—it could not fly at night or in bad weather, or land in the center of a city. It could beat ship travel, of course, but not over any considerable distance, for it had no range. Above all, it had almost no useful load.

None of these drawbacks dampened young Trippe's energy or drive. He was, in 1922, like an inventor. He was on to something and was sure of it, even if no one else was. He had just doubled the capacity of his current planes, and this seemed to him to prove that it would always be possible to make planes bigger, to double capacity again and again.

He had seven pilots and seven planes and he kept them in the air as much as possible. One day he hired out a plane to a newsreel company and flew it himself down Broadway below the level of the buildings, while his passenger ground out film. This stunt seems to have outraged New York, but there was no law against it. It was almost the last time Trippe himself would take part in what amounted to a boyhood prank. His boyhood was just about over.

He began contacting college friends whose fathers could provide letters of introduction to such companies as United Fruit, then one of the principal shippers of produce in the world, or the Pennsylvania Railroad. These letters opened doors to high officials who received him and patiently answered his questions, for he was very young, very serious, and of the same social stratum as themselves. He wanted to know their operating costs, terminal costs, carriage costs en route. He wanted to know if time and money could be saved by sending bills of lading and other such documents ahead of each shipment by airplane.

3

Colonial
Air Transport

At the downtown offices of the United Fruit Company one day he met the general manager for Honduras, who told him something of the geography of that part of Central America. Company ships docked at Tela on the coast, the man said, but official documents frequently had to be stamped in the capital, Tegucigalpa, which was some three days away by road on the other side of 9,000-foot-high mountains. Perhaps, Trippe suggested, United Fruit ought to charter one of his Aeromarines. The actual distance between the coast and the capital was only about a hundred miles by airplane. They could fly their documents up to the capital in an hour and a half.

An agreement was soon signed. United Fruit would secure flying rights and landing rights in Honduras, and possibly an airmail contract between Tela and Tegucigalpa. Long Island Airways would provide the plane and the pilot, and the two corporations—one new and tiny, the other old and gigantic—would divide the profits.

At twenty-three Trippe had just struck his first deal with a company bigger than his own, and his first deal in Latin America as well. He ordered one of the Aeromarines disassembled into several crates and loaded onto his flatbed trailer, and he himself jumped into the tow car, a Model-T laundry van so disreputable that his mother had forbidden him to park it in front of the house. The ride to the United Fruit Company's ship, which was moored to a pier on the lower West Side, began. The pilot sat beside Trippe, who meant to deliver plane and pilot simultaneously. He wanted to see them both loaded aboard ship. The only problem was that the laundry van lacked power. It staggered up each hill. It staggered up onto the deck of the Brooklyn Bridge also, and then on the downslope a terrible thing happened. The van and its trailer began to gather speed. Faster and faster they rolled. Trippe couldn't stop them. He had the brake pressed onto the floor, but the van and the trailer kept accelerating. At the bottom of the bridge came a right-angle turn. The laundry van made it around this turn, but not the trailer, which piled into the wall, spilling crates of airplane onto the road. Out jumped young Trippe and the pilot. Behind them traffic began to back up. Trippe was at his most persuasive as he explained to fuming drivers that these many crates represented an airplane on its way to Central America. An airplane? The word "airplane" excited everyone, and soon the stalled motorists were helping lift the crates back onto the trailer.

And so Long Island Airways began to operate in Honduras.

But by 1924 Trippe's business had begun to taper off. There were now far too many planes flocking to the beaches, far too many pilots able to carry wealthy passengers from New York out to resorts. Looking around him, he quickly found other spots where planes and pilots could be hired out. He sent two of each to Canada to service isolated logging companies, and others went off on private charters. They kept getting farther and farther away from Long Island, and several, including the one in Honduras, were wrecked. Those that remained Trippe managed to sell to the pilots flying them, until Long Island Airways had neither planes nor pilots, and ceased to exist.

Trippe was not unhappy. He had escaped with a small profit. He had faced payrolls. Pilots and mechanics had all been hungry by Friday, and some Fridays there had been no money, or very little money, in the till, and they had had to wait, and he had learned to think of having a reserve fund always on hand. He had acquired a good deal of economic data— what it cost to fly planes, to maintain them, what people were willing to pay to fly. Now, as he went forth to find new investors, to found a different kind of airline, he had cost data with him. He could talk about aviation, and he could talk about money as well.

What was his new venture to be?

An airline must have a route, he decided. It must have regular schedules. It must carry mail. The future of the airline business was in a substantial company, in big names, in big money. The Post Office certainly would never award an airmail contract to an airline like Long Island, capitalized at only $5,000, and a postal subsidy was essential if an airline was to survive long enough for passenger and freight traffic to build up.

In Europe, KLM and Lufthansa, heavily subsidized by their governments, already existed as airlines in embryonic form, and they kept more or less regular schedules. But in the United States Trippe's Long Island

Airways had been about as substantial as any "airline" that had yet been tried. As for the U.S. mail, it had begun to move by air just after World War I, first by the Army and then by the Post Office itself, which had conducted demonstration runs as far as the California coast. The pilots flew open-cockpit planes under Post Office contracts with the mailbags piled into the second cockpit, and they had begun now to fly at night. There were beacons akin to lighthouses at various points, fires were kept blazing at the bases of mountains to warn pilots away, and all pilots wore parachutes. Airmail in the early twenties was as perilous and primitive as the pony express, neither more nor less, and people learned to send duplicate letters by train. As a result, the idea had never really caught on. The system was underutilized, and there was some danger that the Post Office Department might soon decide to abandon it. When the Kelly bill was passed on February 2, 1925, giving the Post Office broad authority to contract with private parties for the carriage of mail by air, this was thought of in many quarters as the only viable means of saving an airmail system.

During the years following the collapse of Long Island Airways, Trippe founded a number of companies: Alaskan Air Transport, Buffalo Airlines, Eastern Air Transport, Colonial Air Transport and more, in each case bringing together groups of men, arranging financing, laying plans, in each case bidding for mail contracts.

Alaskan Air Transport started as one man, a pilot named Ben Eielson, and one plane, a surplus DH-4—plus an idea by Trippe. To Trippe the quickest future for aviation was in places where transportation was terrible, and nowhere was it worse than in Alaska where mail and passengers moved by dogsled. It took six weeks to cover a few hundred miles. The same passengers flying in the open cockpit of an Alaskan Air Transport airplane would get red noses, but at the end of a few hours they would be there. Mail would move at the same speed.

Trippe's idea extended further. From Alaska he planned to hop across to Siberia. The land bridge that had sunk beneath the sea eons ago would be replaced by Trippe's air bridge, and weeks could be cut off mail runs to Russia and Asia. A company with such a base would seem to have an unlimited future.

Trippe actually went to Seattle, where skis were installed on the plane. He saw it and Eielson off toward the frozen north, where the pilot competed with the dog teams for three months, flying south out of Fairbanks down the Kuskokwim River, touching all the small communities along its banks.

However, the dog-team drivers insisted that the law governing the so-called Star Route mail contracts made no mention of airplanes. Though Trippe went to Washington to argue with postal authorities for the right to carry mail, they ruled against him. He tried to get legislation written, but failed. He would get no mail, no subsidy, and therefore he had no viable airline. Eielson flew the plane home, and Alaskan Air Transport ceased to exist.

So Trippe incorporated Eastern Air Transport in Delaware on September 12, 1925. Its directors were Trippe; Lorillard Spencer, who was a World War I combat pilot of independent means; L. L. Odell, a transportation engineer with the consulting firm of Ford, Bacon and Davis; Robert Thach, a pilot from Trippe's squadron, now a lawyer; and Sherman Fairchild of the Fairchild Camera Company, who was interested in aviation chiefly as a means of selling his new aerial cameras. Two days later Eastern Air Transport submitted a bid signed by Trippe and Odell for the New York–Boston airmail contract, and Trippe went to Washington and began to lobby fiercely. Unfortunately, he was only twenty-six years old, and looked younger, and the mail in 1925 was serious business. Postal authorities were hoping to award their contracts to older, more weighty figures than Trippe.

There was a second company bidding for the New York–Boston route. It was called Colonial Airlines, and its investors came mostly from Connecticut and Massachusetts, as did its board of directors, which included some important financial and political figures, such as the incumbent governor of Connecticut, John Trumbull. Postal authorities seemed to like this group better, for on its board were no daredevil young aviators, and Trippe was advised to merge with this Colonial Airlines. On October 5 he changed the name of his own company to Colonial Air Transport, and two days later his Colonial and Governor Trumbull's Colonial merged.

At the last minute Trippe had bolstered his own board by adding young William Rockefeller, young Sonny Whitney and his great friend young John Hambleton, a World War I combat hero and son of a prominent Baltimore banker. Hurriedly Trippe now began to salvage what he could from the merger, and he managed to salvage a good deal, for he was bringing in money. First, though the surviving corporate structure was Governor Trumbull's, its name was changed to Colonial Air Transport, Trippe's corporate name, which perhaps made it appear to outsiders as if Trippe had done the swallowing up himself, rather than the other way around. Secondly, he got himself appointed managing director of the combined company. Thirdly, he argued that the combined board of directors, now comprising more than thirty men, was too swollen and unwieldy to exert control, and he suggested that a voting trust be appointed. This was done. Seven men were named: Trippe, Rockefeller and Hambleton from Trippe's group, and Howard Coonley, Irving Bullard, Harris Whittemore, Jr., and Governor Trumbull himself from Trumbull's group. Although this seemed to place actual control of the company with Governor Trumbull, Trippe saw clearly that if he wanted to control the company himself, he needed to win over only one opposition trustee. Furthermore, he was going to work full time at his job; these older men all had many other interests to distract them. So even without the voting trust it was going to be relatively easy to take Colonial Air Transport wherever he wanted it to go. Or so Trippe thought.

The moment the merger was signed, the Post Office awarded Air Mail Route No. 1, New York–Boston, to Colonial. This gave Colonial nominally the senior position in the United States. In fact, all of these first airmail contracts were awarded on the same day, and service was inaugurated on all of the others before Colonial's first flight the following year.

Upon winning the contract, Colonial had a corporation, but no planes, no employees, no route system, no landing fields. During the next nine months prior to Colonial's first flight on July 1, 1926, Trippe hired men, negotiated for aircraft, rented fields and planned for the future. The company roster swelled to twenty-one, "the most complete air-transport organization in the country," Trippe bragged. The rest of the brand-new airlines were happy with single-engined planes, but Trippe had ordered four trimotors, two of them Fokkers, two Fords. He called this "the largest order for commercial aircraft ever placed in the United States."

His board of directors, composed principally of middle-aged investors with no background in aviation, became quickly disenchanted with young Trippe. Not yet twenty-seven, he was committing them to expensive multiengined aircraft and they did not know why. Other companies were satisfied with open cockpits and single engines, were they not? There were as yet no planes flying, no revenues at all, but already the Fokker factory was dunning Colonial for first payment on the two trimotors under construction, and Colonial did not have the money.

In addition, Trippe was often out of the office and could not be found. Some days he was at the Fokker factory asking questions about the planes under construction. Other days he was in Washington, talking about aviation with anyone who would listen, including Commerce Secretary Herbert Hoover and even, on one occasion, President Coolidge.

The man he had most wanted to meet was the Pittsburgh congressman, Clyde Kelly, who had sponsored the first airmail bill and was now working on a foreign airmail bill. Trippe's college roommate had been Alan Scaife, son of a multimillionaire Pittsburgh industrialist, who had married the niece of Andrew Mellon. Mellon was the richest man in Pittsburgh and one of the richest men in the world. He was the richest constituent Kelly had. He also happened to be Secretary of the Treasury. Trippe went to Scaife, who introduced him to Mellon, to whom he explained his plans for commercial aviation. Mellon provided the introduction to Kelly, and now Trippe sat down and helped the congressman work out the details of his new bill.

Day after day also, Trippe waited at the dirt airfield in New Brunswick,

N.J., to watch the airmail planes come in from the other side of the continent, and when they landed he quizzed the pilots about their problems. There was much to learn, and he was learning all of it as fast as he could. One of the pilots he talked to was the young Charles Lindbergh. Lindbergh never remembered the meeting afterwards. Trippe did. Trippe forgot nothing.

Trippe took virtually no time for himself at all, and when invited to social events by his married friends, his "date" was often his sister.

As early as October 1925 Trippe was considering an airmail route from Key West to Havana—it is mentioned in one of his letters—and by December of that year he had persuaded Anthony Fokker to fly him down there in the first trimotored airliner ever seen in the United States. The bald little Dutchman, whose triplanes had been employed by Baron von Richthofen and his Flying Circus during World War I, had recently opened a factory in Teterboro, N. J., and was building the two Colonial planes there. This one, however, had been built in Holland, and had just arrived by ship. The place to take it, Trippe convinced Fokker, was to Havana on a barnstorming junket. This would attract favorable publicity for Fokker and his planes, Trippe promised, and would help Fokker's sales. Of course, it would also raise the stature of Colonial Air Transport, which was soon to be flying similar planes.

The flight took place during the final days of 1925. At the start there were four men aboard: Trippe, Fokker, mechanic Ken Boedecker and the pilot, a former Navy aviator named George Pond. At Baltimore the trimotor landed to pick up John and Peg Hambleton, and at the nearby naval air station the ship was shown to Navy officers, with Fokker boasting with particular pride of the ship's toilet—in 1925 a toilet aboard an airplane was a remarkable innovation.

The next day the plane continued south, running into rough weather somewhere between Atlanta and Augusta. Soon no one knew where they were, and as fuel ran lower it was decided to make a forced landing in a cotton field. Mrs. Hambleton was placed behind the rear cabin partition to protect her, and Pond bounced the plane down across the cotton rows. The passengers got out and continued to Augusta by car. When the plane had been radically lightened, Pond was able to get it airborne again, and to fly it to the Augusta airstrip, where his passengers rejoined him.

Such heroics as this attracted considerable press attention, but it went to Fokker and to Hambleton, who was the glamour boy of Trippe's group. Not only was Hambleton young, rich and handsome, but he had also won the Distinguished Service Cross in aerial combat over France. Trippe himself was scarcely mentioned. He had a way of shrinking into the background when reporters came around.

Even Peg Hambleton got more press than Trippe did, because, in a time when air travel was still thought to be terrifying, she was supposed to have fallen asleep in the air. She got off the "giant airship" at Tampa, and Hambleton deplaned at Miami, the last stop before Key West. The next to quit the flight was mechanic Boedecker, and he had reasons.

The Fokker was powered by three Wright J-4 engines, and these were designed to fly on aviation fuel. Aviation fuel in 1925 was hard to find, and so at each stop Fokker had been topping up his tanks with 50 percent automobile gas and 50 percent benzol. Boedecker, whose job was to watch the dials, had noted that the engines had begun heating up in flight. Oil temperature was especially high, and there was a bit of detonation in the engine. When Fokker informed him that the next stop was Havana, Boedecker replied, "Well, you can count one Wright mechanic missing."

"What's the matter, are you afraid to fly behind your own engines?" asked Fokker.

"No, I'm not afraid of the engines, but I am afraid of the automobile gasoline you are using, and I'm not flying over ninety miles of ocean behind anybody's engines with that kind of fuel."

"Those engines should operate on any kind of fuel," said Fokker.

"They were designed for high-test fuel," said Boedecker, who argued also with the pilot, Pond. The left engine's tachometer had broken down some days before, and Pond could not be bothered to get it fixed. "Anybody who knows anything about engines knows whether they are doing their stuff even without a tachometer," he said.

"Well, I can't tell if an engine is turning sixteen hundred or fifteen hundred RPM's without a tachometer," retorted Boedecker, "and if the RPM is one hundred low, something is wrong." With that, he refused to continue the flight. Trippe took no part in these arguments.

From Key West the Fokker took off for Havana, leaving Boedecker behind. His warnings at first appeared exaggerated, for the plane made the crossing successfully, landing at Campo Colombia, a military training field outside the city. There Trippe and Fokker put on a flying demonstration for President Gerardo Machado and other Cuban dignitaries. They showed off the ability of the Fokker F-7 to fly on two engines, or even on one. Machado was reported to be extremely impressed, and the next day Trippe made contact with a Havana lawyer who drew up for him what Trippe afterwards described as "a simple two- or three-page letter." Later this document, which was brought to Machado and signed by the appropriate official, proved extremely important, and not so simple. It appears to have accorded Trippe a variety of rights essential to any airline that wished to serve Havana, such as permission to use Campo Colombia as a landing field, the use of customs and immigration inspection facilities, possible tax exemptions and perhaps other concessions too. The essential point was that Trippe now, in December 1925, owned landing rights in Cuba, and Cuba not only was an important destination itself but it was also the gateway to the entire chain of Caribbean islands to the east and to the Yucatán Peninsula to the southwest.

All this Trippe did before his competitors back north were really aware of his existence.

And so the Fokker trimotor started back toward Florida. Again Boedecker's warnings had not been heeded, but there were no problems over open water. Landing on the golf course at Key West, pilot Pond refueled his plane with the same gasoline-benzol mixture as previously, after which he and his two passengers took to the air again, bound for Miami. But as they flew over the Keys the engines began to knock and to overheat, until finally the entire aircraft was vibrating. The left engine, the one with no tachometer, at length cut out entirely, and the plane began to settle toward the earth. The other two engines, choking on bad fuel, could not keep the Fokker aloft. But there was no place to land. The individual Keys were too small, too heavily forested or too snarled with mangroves. With no choices left him, Pond put the plane down on what he hoped was a mud flat, but which turned out to be a flattish reef barely awash. Both tires blew out. The plane skidded along on its rims, but came to a stop at last. The three shaken men climbed out. They were six hundred feet from the shore of Key Largo, and the tide gradually came in over their shoes.

A man came out in a rowboat to take them ashore, and they were marooned there until they lit a fire on the railroad track to stop the train. Once in Miami, Trippe and Fokker found Boedecker and sent him down to rescue the Fokker if he could. He managed to change the engines, planks were brought in and laid along the reef, the tires were replaced, and at length Pond managed to get it off and into the air.

4

Fired

Back in New York, Trippe found himself in trouble with his directors. The New York–Boston route they had invested so much money in was not yet even functioning, so what was young Trippe doing in Cuba? He had ordered these big trimotored planes; not only was there no money to pay for them, but also the Post Office airmail contract specifically called for the company to run single-engined planes. These were serious charges, and Trippe was obliged to answer them. "Chances of failure are increased at least ten to one if we are restricted to the use of single-engined ships," one letter read, "not to mention the greatly increased hazard and almost certain loss of life to our pilots."

Two weeks before Colonial was to start service, the Post Office began to insist that single-engined planes be used. To buy a fleet of them now might bankrupt the company, and certainly no funds would be left to pay for the trimotors. The situation—and possibly Trippe's neck—was saved when Dwight Morrow, one of the most respected financiers of the day, and later the father-in-law of Charles Lindbergh, went to Washington and persuaded authorities not to enforce the letter of the contract.

Of course the trimotors had not yet arrived, and practice flights from New York to Boston got under way in Fokker Universals, single-engined planes with a closed, four-passenger cabin. These planes operated totally at the mercy of whatever weather they might fly into, for the company was too poor to afford regular use of the long-distance telephone, which was the only quick way to send weather reports back and forth along the line. Nor was there any hangar for the aircraft, meaning that the weather would ravage their thin skins—dope-painted linen for the most part—even when on the ground.

All this time Trippe had been trying to raise more capital, for he had big ideas and wanted to expand. One prospect was Robert Wood Johnson, of Johnson and Johnson in New Brunswick, who listened to his arguments, reserved decision, then sent him a long letter outlining the following points: (1) the airplane as a means of transportation was not safe, not fast enough, and didn't carry enough payload; (2) air travel was not interesting to a large number of people; (3) an industry based on a government mail subsidy was uninteresting to capitalists such as himself; (4) as opposed to the railroads, which were more or less monopolies, the air would be open to competition for many years, if not indefinitely, meaning cutthroat prices and no profits; (5) eventually the government would regulate the airlines—again this was not interesting to capitalists. Saying that he didn't see any great need for immediate development of air transport, Johnson refused to invest in Trippe's airline.

Unfortunately, Trippe had begun to encounter one or another of these reasons in nearly every direction he turned, but he was persistent and thick-skinned. Shame was not part of his makeup. He always went armed with cost-analysis figures, and wherever possible he sought out as prospects only people who were pilots themselves or were already interested in aviation. Despite all this, the rejections came one upon the other.

Colonial Air Transport, still without the trimotors, commenced air-mail service between New York and Boston on July 1, 1926. Trippe was still running every detail of the operation himself, but dissatisfaction from the board of directors was increasing. Trippe's main problem, he judged, was that he seemed to the directors too young, and he decided to cure this by bringing in some middle-aged president, who would stand between himself and the board but who would be in all other respects a figurehead.

The man he settled on was a retired brigadier general named John F. O'Ryan. By October 1, 1926, with Trippe continuing as managing director and vice president, O'Ryan was on duty spreading exactly the aura of confidence and maturity Trippe had hoped for.

By then Trippe was urging the expansion of Colonial westward, first to Buffalo, and then to Chicago and California. In Buffalo, where a new airport had just been built and opened, Trippe was sure that capital could be raised, and so he headed there, together with his friend Bill Rockefeller, and W. B. Mayo, chief engineer of the Ford Motor Company, in a Ford trimotor.

Hardly anyone had ever flown over this terrain before. Once aloft it was important to keep an eye out for pastures and meadows that would make emergency landing fields, and when Trippe wrote his report later he listed every such field that passed below. He also noted certain factories, especially the General Electric factory, near Schenectady, and the American Locomotive Works. When his proposed Buffalo Airlines began operations, he wrote, it ought to be possible to solicit these factories for shipments by air of important documents.

The plane set down at Utica after 2 hours and 15 minutes of flight, and there refueled. Afterwards it followed the Erie Canal and the New York Central tracks to Syracuse, to Rochester and to Buffalo. Before landing, the pilot circled Niagara Falls. (A unique aerial view of the falls might lure plenty of customers to Buffalo Airlines, Trippe noted in his report.) The flight, including the refueling stop, had consumed 5 hours and 17 minutes.

Eleven days later Trippe started a second journey to Buffalo. This time the plane set down in Albany, where the mayor and other dignitaries made speeches, and a twenty-pound mail pouch was placed aboard. But the plane got only as far as Rochester before being forced down by bad weather. Trippe was trying to reach Buffalo to attend a gala dinner in honor of Major John Satterfield given by the Buffalo Chamber of Commerce. Satterfield, who ran one of Buffalo's biggest banks, was being cited for his work in developing Buffalo Airport. Trippe was hoping to persuade him to invest in Buffalo Airlines.

But in Rochester the rain poured down. Trippe secured a watchman for the plane, sent the pilot to a nearby hotel, caught a train into Buffalo with the mail pouch, and just made dinner. Following it, he went to Satterfield's house, and there the two men—the eager young airman and the middle-aged banker—discussed a New York–Buffalo–Chicago air route until dawn.

By November Trippe was writing Satterfield about a proposed meeting with Henry Ford, who by this time not only was building his own trimotor planes, but also had an air service from Detroit to Chicago and Cleveland. Established the year before, it carried company freight only, but it operated with the regularity and the reliability of a public carrier. Trippe was suggesting that Buffalo Airlines propose a joint operation with Ford. Buffalo Airlines would carry the mail from New York to Cleveland, where it would link up with Ford's airline.

Presently Trippe was back in Buffalo still again. Satterfield had got together a group for dinner: bankers, brokers, real estate operators, all of them apparently both interested in aviation and rich. To these men Trippe submitted a definite plan for financing Buffalo Airlines. The rest of his plan was even bigger. If he could raise altogether $1.5 million, he could bid for the New York–Chicago airmail contract and probably get it. Capitalization of Colonial at this time was $500,000. Buffalo backers would put up $500,000, he hoped, and an additional $500,000 could be raised in Cleveland and Chicago. The present Colonial investors would come up with the rest.

Up till now, each new airmail contract had been awarded by the Post Office not so much on the basis of low bid as on the basis of financial responsibility. Bid bonds of up to $500,000 were required. Postal officials were not interested in flying enthusiasts. They were as judicious as bankers. They wanted to see the financing.

Trippe traveled constantly—to Washington to confer with postal officials, to Boston, Baltimore and Buffalo to confer with bankers. He wrote scores of letters—to bankers about money, to politicians about bills.

He also wrote to airplane factories about building his newest ideas into Colonial's planes. One letter urged the Fokker factory to install a fuel-dumping arrangement. At the time of his Key Largo crash last winter, he wrote, it had occurred to him that the flight could have continued another fifty miles had it been possible to dump four or five hundred pounds of fuel. A second letter went to the Ford factory: he wanted sliding windows installed in their planes. By far the biggest factor in airsickness, he wrote, was the lack of clear fresh air. The Fokker had such sliding windows. When bumpy air was encountered, these were thrown wide open, and the extra-large heater that he had ordered installed in each of the planes was turned on full blast. Not one passenger, he wrote, including several women, had yet got sick.

Perhaps he concentrated on technical matters to take his mind off the rest of his life, which had suddenly gone very wrong. The money wasn't coming in. In addition, O'Ryan had begun ordering him around, had begun making decisions on his own even in Trippe's absence. The figurehead was refusing to behave like a figurehead, and Trippe was miserable. It was his airline, but this man O'Ryan was now thoroughly in the way. Trippe wanted to expand. O'Ryan wanted to get Colonial in the black first. O'Ryan even seems to have considered merging with National Air Transport, the only other airline of substance operating in the eastern United States.

"In view of the fact that I personally persuaded Messrs. Weicker, Rockefeller, Whitney, Fairchild, Hoyt and others to invest in the company, in the firm belief that its expansion would be laid out along lines most advantageous to the individual stockholders, I cannot agree to [O'Ryan's] policy," Trippe wrote Hambleton.

At one executive committee meeting Trippe charged that Colonial did not appear to have any definite policy or plan for the future. But the voices of older men were immediately raised against him, and the executive committee approved O'Ryan's policies in toto.

Trippe was silenced for the moment but not for long. He went to Boston and held quiet conversations with directors Howard Coonley and Irving Bullard. He was lobbying for support and at the same time trying to undermine O'Ryan. "I am so thoroughly and personally committed to the welfare of this company," he wrote Hambleton, "that I am going to stick, and five years from now I will turn back ten dollars for every single dollar invested, or bust in the attempt."

Bids for the New York–Chicago airmail contract opened on January 15, 1927. O'Ryan had decided to enter a bid after all, $2.13 per pound of mail carried, a figure Trippe opposed as too high. Apart from Colonial, there was only one other substantial bidder, National Air Transport. National later came in at $1.98, and Trippe either guessed at this figure, or had inside knowledge of it in advance. He kept driving for a lower bid, and at the last minute O'Ryan authorized him to enter Colonial's bid at $1.88. This should have given Colonial the New York–Chicago contract. Instead, all bids were thrown out on technicalities and the Post Office announced a two-month delay before the route would be readvertised.

As they waited, Trippe's relations with General O'Ryan deteriorated. "The present Colonial situation, to my mind, is discouraging," he wrote Coonley, who was president of the Walworth Company in Boston. Colonial was losing $8,000 a month, and was down to less than $100,000 of capital, Trippe noted. He was carrying on at no small personal sacrifice, and because he had interested many of his close personal friends in Colonial, would continue to do so, taking no salary at all if necessary, in order to get Colonial on its feet. But this could be done, his letter concluded, only if sound business principles were followed—which O'Ryan wasn't doing.

At last the New York–Chicago bids were reopened, but by then a mood of cutthroat competition prevailed among the bidders, and O'Ryan was caught up in it. He wanted to enter a bid so low that Colonial, if it won the contract, could not, according to Trippe, fulfill it without being ruined. "Very few men as yet understand the actual cost of conducting air transport operations," Trippe wrote one of his backers. "I believe it costs at least $1.34 per ship mile to operate trimotor airplanes and that under inefficient management the total cost would undoubtedly run to at least $2.00 per ship mile." He had made a bad mistake putting O'Ryan in as president, he said. Colonial now would almost certainly end badly. Twice in the course of this letter, Trippe asked that it be destroyed upon receipt.

An open break with O'Ryan became inevitable. On March 18, seven members of the executive committee passed a unanimous motion to the effect that Colonial's New York–Chicago bid should be decided upon by four men: General O'Ryan, Trippe, L. L. Odell and Tobe Freeman. But the next day O'Ryan called a second meeting. With Trippe and two of his supporters absent, a resolution was passed giving O'Ryan the sole right to decide the bid.

At once Trippe began to rally his supporters, but O'Ryan had supporters, too, including Governor Trumbull and most of the New England faction on the board of directors. A directors' meeting was held which not only ratified O'Ryan as chief executive of the company, but also became focused on the person of Trippe. A number of men demanded his resignation, and certain of them even threatened to withdraw their money if he stayed.

Trippe had one card to play—the voting trust which he had had the foresight to set up so many months before and whose existence everyone else seemed to have forgotten. He decided to call a meeting of the voting trust and overrule the board. Since Colonial was a Connecticut company, the voting trust was obliged to meet in Connecticut, and Trippe convoked it in the Greenwich railroad station after midnight on the day the New York–Chicago bids were to close. He needed four votes out of seven, including his own, and he got them. A few minutes later the milk train came through and the victorious Trippe and his supporters jumped on it. They dozed during the hour-long run back to New York, then drove across to Teterboro Airport in New Jersey and took off for Washington. It was not yet daylight. A company pilot, not Trippe, was at the controls. Trippe's old role was over forever and he realized it. He was a business executive now, not a pilot, and corporate risks were more exciting than any risks any birdman ever took.

After freshening up in a Washington hotel room, Trippe reached the Post Office just as it opened, beating the deadline and entering Colonial's bid at $1.68, as low as he thought he could go without ruining the company. He flashed the formal resolution signed in the Greenwich railroad station. It was all legal. Colonial's bid bonds would stay in to back this bid.

When news of what Trippe had done got back to Connecticut, and to Boston, O'Ryan and nearly everyone else were outraged. Lawyers were hired to study Trippe's voting-trust arrangement, after which a full meeting of the stockholders was called. There the lawyers presented their opinion that the voting trust, by which Trippe had overruled the board of directors, might not even be legal. If this was true, then Trippe's New York–Chicago bid was illegal also, and the Post Office would never award the contract to Colonial.

Whereupon Trippe proposed that it go to a vote of all the stockholders. Whose lead would Colonial follow? Trippe's? or O'Ryan's? Whichever side lost would be bought out by the other and would leave the company.

When Trippe's side lost by a percentage point it meant that he had, in effect, been forced out of the company. His investment was returned to him. He was told to take his still-undelivered Fokker trimotors with him, if he could pay for them, for Colonial didn't want them.

At the age of twenty-seven, he seemed again without a future and he was without a paying job. He had also, it seemed, lost his girl. Trippe had been courting Elizabeth Stettinius by then for about two years. She was five years younger than he. Her family, Hungarian in origin, had come to America around 1790, making hers a very old American family, though not as old as Trippe's, which went back to Henry Trippe, who settled in Maryland in 1663, and which counted war heroes from the days of the punitive expeditions against the Barbary pirates. A Lieutenant John Trippe had won the Congressional Medal of Honor during that action, and ever since there had been a destroyer or minesweeper in the U.S. Navy named the U.S.S. *Trippe.*

Betty Stettinius lived in a mansion in Locust Valley on the North Shore of Long Island, and played golf at the Piping Rock Country Club. It was her brother Edward who first brought Trippe home—the same Edward Stettinius who would become chairman of the board of U.S. Steel at the age of thirty-nine, and who would serve as Secretary of State under Roosevelt and Truman in 1944–45. Trippe, at the time he met Betty Stettinius, did not have much time for girls, but one day he found himself playing golf with her. She hit such a powerful drive off the third tee at Piping Rock that he turned to her and said, "Do you ever get into town on weekends?"

Betty's family was far wealthier than Trippe's had ever been, for her father had headed the Diamond Match Company and had become a partner in the J. P. Morgan Bank. When he died, he had left her a considerable trust fund. In a later age it might have been possible for the young couple to marry on the strength of this. But in the 1920's such an action for a young man of Trippe's station was not honorable, and therefore not conceivable. Trippe would have to show that he was man of substance, with a financially sound future, before Betty's brothers would allow her to marry him. And this he had not done. Instead he had continued to waste his energy on these foolish aviation projects, and so a family decision was made. Betty was sent abroad to forget her foolish affection for this unreliable young man.

5

A New Company

Trippe set to work at once to form a new company, once again persuading Whitney, Vanderbilt, Hambleton, Bill Rockefeller and the rest that there was a future in commercial aviation, and that he was the man to lead them to it. Most of these rich young men were far less serious than himself. "These fellows were all bankers," Trippe said later, "—or hoped to be bankers."

Trippe gathered together thirteen of them, and capitalized the new company at $300,000. It was incorporated on June 2, 1927, as the Aviation Corporation of America. Sonny Whitney, who had put up $49,000, was elected chairman. Bill Vanderbilt, John Hambleton and Bill Rockefeller put up $25,000 apiece and were elected president, vice president and treasurer, respectively. Trippe, having invested $25,000 also, was named managing director.

At once Trippe began looking around for somewhere to place that money. On July 12 he asked his brand-new board of directors to authorize him to submit bids for any airmail route he might select. This was agreed to. He was also authorized to invest in a newly formed New York corporation called Pan American Airways, Inc., which, even though it owned no planes and had very little money, seemed to have the inside track on the Key West–Havana mail contract soon to be awarded.

Pan American had come into existence in the following way.

Two years earlier, an Army Air Corps officer, Major Henry H. ("Hap") Arnold—as General Arnold he would command all American air forces during World War II—had been an intelligence officer stationed in Washington. For some time he had been reading intelligence reports about an airline recently established in Colombia known as SCADTA. Everything about SCADTA was German. Its capital, its pilots, its managing director, who was Peter Paul von Bauer, had all come from Germany shortly after World War I. According to Major Arnold's intelligence reports, Von Bauer intended to extend his airline up as far as the Panama Canal and—hopefully—into the United States. Germans at the Panama Canal? This had to be stopped. Arnold took a map and drew a sketch of an airline that would extend from Key West to Havana, across to Yucatán Peninsula, and down through British Honduras and Nicaragua to Panama. He then conferred with Major Carl Spaatz, and Major Jack Jouett. Later the three majors called in still another young Air Corps officer, John Montgomery. Together they drew up a prospectus for such an airline, decided it might make money and sent Montgomery to New York to find backers if he could.

The four officers called their project Pan American Airways. As soon as Montgomery could raise the necessary money, all four intended to resign from the Army. Arnold would become president and general manager of the airline, Spaatz its operating director, Jouett its personnel manager and Montgomery its field manager.

The first important backer lined up by Montgomery was Richard D. Bevier, a former naval officer with offices now in downtown New York. Bevier's business was supplying wholesale goods to U.S. Navy canteens all over the world. He was well connected, for his father-in-law was Lewis Pierson, an important New York banker. The second of Montgomery's backers was George Grant Mason, then twenty-three, who came from money, had attended all the right schools, and was part of what passed at the time for high society in New York. Mason, too, was close to an important banker, for he was about to marry the sister of Sloan Colt, and Colt would soon be named head of Bankers Trust.

At about the time that Mason and Captain Montgomery set off for Cuba to secure the requisite permissions and documents for their proposed airline, the three remaining Army officers became embroiled in the court-martial proceedings against General Billy Mitchell, who had accused the Army of treasonable neglect of air power. Mitchell was convicted. Arnold, Spaatz and Jouett received official reprimands, and with this cloud over their heads, felt they could not honorably resign from the Army. However, their names remained on the Pan American Airways prospectus, and the project went forward without them.

With Bevier now as president, Captain Montgomery as vice president, and Mason as secretary, Pan American was formally incorporated, and attempts were made to raise further money. Many promises were obtained and, on the strength of them, Montgomery and Mason journeyed to Cuba altogether three times. There they were accorded more promises and a few vague documents were signed, whereupon Mason got married, and fund-raising stopped while he disappeared for a month on his honeymoon.

Montgomery petitioned the Post Office to call for bids on the U.S. contract from Key West to Havana, and he represented Pan American Airways as a powerful force in modern aviation. On July 16, 1927, the contract was awarded to him. According to its terms, his planes had to be flying by October 19, and this was going to be difficult, because he didn't have any. When Bevier and Montgomery tried to call in their pledges, they found they had almost no money either.

A second company was interested in the Key West–Havana route. It was called Atlantic, Gulf and Caribbean Airways, Inc., and it had grown up out of the corpse of the now defunct Florida Airways.

Florida Airways had been founded by Reed Chambers, a famous World War I fighter pilot. Chambers, returning to civilian life, had gone into the securities business on the West Coast, but he continued to watch what was happening in aviation. In 1924 he watched Henry Ford begin manufacturing all-metal trimotor transport planes. The next year came the Kelly airmail bill. It looked to Chambers as if the time was ripe to make a business out of flying. He went to his best securities salesman, Virgil (Vic) Chenea, and in two nights' conversation in a Los Angeles hotel room talked Chenea into becoming his partner in the airline business.

Which airline business? Well, they would start one, and they looked over the list of Kelly bill routes as soon as it was published. Trippe in New York was studying the same list. Out of it, Trippe picked New York–Boston. Reed Chambers picked Atlanta–Tampa–Miami, and his reasons, as given in his prospectus, seemed good ones: mild weather and no fog; flat terrain useful for forced landings; a substantial time savings on the Miami–Tampa run to be effected by flying over the Everglades, instead of driving or sailing around them.

In addition, Florida was booming. Six thousand people, according to the headlines, were pouring into Miami every day. Florida Airways could not fail. Everybody in Florida was getting rich fast, and soon Chambers and Chenea would be among them.

And so they, too, went to New York to raise capital. They found Richard B. Hoyt, a partner in Hayden, Stone and Company, the Wall Street investment firm. Hoyt was then thirty-nine, and an important man in aviation, for it was he who had brought about the merger between Curtiss and Wright, the two most important manufacturers in American aviation, and he was now the Curtiss-Wright board chairman.

They found Percy Rockefeller. They found Eddie Rickenbacker, the ace of aces of World War I, the most famous American fighter pilot of all.

They went to Henry Ford, who granted them a $50,000 credit on the purchase of three Ford planes. In January 1926 these planes were at last ready to fly, and Florida Airways was ready to be born.

First the planes had to be ferried to Tampa, the company's operations base, and this meant refueling stops en route. At one of them, Nashville, the entire airline came to grief. Two of the three planes had already landed and were parked. The third pilot set down his machine, but he landed "long"—toward the middle of the runway. The runway was slightly hilly, and higher in the middle than at either end, and the pilot bounded over the hump and began to run downhill. In 1926 planes had no brakes. Once on the ground, they rolled until they rolled to a stop. The only means of steering was the rudder, which, unfortunately, was totally ineffective at taxiing speeds, unless a pilot gunned his engine, sending a blast of prop wash over the tail, but this made the airplane speed up, and it still had no brakes. The pilot of the third of Florida Airway's new planes, finding himself rolling downhill, unable to stop, and headed off the end of the runway, revved up his engine and turned his rudder full left. The prop wash turned him into the direction he wished to go, but too violently and straight toward a group of spectators. He revved up still again, holding the hard left lock, hoping to miss the spectators, and he did. What he did not miss was the other two parked planes. His wings and prop carved them up, and they carved him back.

With all three machines inoperable in Nashville, Florida Airways simply could not fly. An immense delay occurred while new wings were manufactured in Detroit, shipped down and riveted into place, and it was September, eight months later, before regular operations could begin. By spring of the next year, 1927, Florida Airways was bankrupt. Passenger business was almost nonexistent. Most major travel agents refused to sell air tickets. Passengers in the South were simply scared of climbing aboard these newfangled flying machines. No substantial mail loads ever developed either, for Chambers had made the mistake of bidding for a route that did not connect with any other. This meant that no loads were fed into him. Even locally only minimal time savings could be effected by sending mail via Florida Airways. Mail sent by trains—which ran all day and all night—was faster.

When Florida Airways collapsed, Chambers and Chenea took its corporate shell to New York and attempted to raise a million dollars in new capital in order to resurrect their airline with new routes and a new name. This time they meant to fly from Key West to Cuba to Yucatán to the Canal Zone. Their chief prospect was again Richard Hoyt, who was still willing to listen, partly because this new airline sounded more promising than the last one. Flying across large bodies of water meant competing against slow-moving ships, rather than against trains. If commercial aviation did have a future, then perhaps overseas was where it lay. In addition,

Hoyt's firm—Hayden, Stone—had important sugar interests in Cuba. This meant help in securing the necessary permits and documents there and perhaps even a Cuban airmail contract.

The new company, Atlantic, Gulf and Caribbean Airways, was incorporated in June 1927. Hoyt, looking for what he called "paper that could be taken to a bank," saw that Pan American Airways had such paper, the United States airmail contract to Havana. But when Hoyt attempted to absorb Pan American, he got nowhere.

So he went to see Trippe, whom he had met earlier that year. Trippe then had been interested in North Beach Field (New York's present LaGuardia Airport), which Hoyt, as board chairman of Curtiss-Wright, controlled. But they had not met since Trippe's withdrawal from Colonial. Hoyt's reasoning now was that Trippe, who had Rockefeller, Whitney, Vanderbilt and Hambleton money behind him, had also been to Cuba in an airplane and actually held paper—Cuban landing rights—that could be taken to a bank. Hoyt, as he went into the series of meetings that ensued, expected to swallow Trippe. Instead, Trippe swallowed Hoyt. Trippe was now twenty-eight, and Hoyt, the respected banker, nearly forty. But he won from Trippe only two concessions. If it proved possible to buy, or merge with, or otherwise take over Pan American Airways and its Key West–Havana mail contract, then the merged companies would become known as Atlantic, Gulf and Caribbean Airways, Hoyt's corporate name. In addition, the post of chairman of the board would be held open, and if all went well Hoyt might be elected to this post later. In the meantime, Trippe's group would own the controlling interest in the new company, and the president and general manager would be Juan T. Trippe.

In Florida, Chambers and Chenea waited anxiously to know what the future held. It held a wire from Hoyt asking them to come to New York for an urgent meeting at his office on Wall Street. There he told them that the only possible deal was a merger with Trippe's group. There was a long silent ride by taxi uptown to Trippe's little office on 42nd Street, where they waited a moment in an anteroom, and when the door opened, Chambers and Chenea shook hands for the first time with the big, apparently bland young man who was to be the chief.

6

First Flight

Attempting now to take over Pan American, Trippe entered into negotiations with the Bevier brothers, Richard and Kenneth. The Beviers were hardheaded businessmen. They were amenable to a merger, they said, and would consider accepting the Trippe group and the Hoyt group as minor partners.

When Trippe refused this offer, the Beviers suggested that each group should hold a one-third interest, with their group controlling the merged company. Trippe gave a gentle smile and shook his head.

A friend of Trippe's from those days later credited him with "an intuitive dreamlike sense of where aviation could go—a vision based on very little." He also had an intuitive, dreamlike sense of where any negotiation could go. He seemed to understand at once where the difference lay between what a man said he wanted and what he would settle for. As a negotiator, Trippe was incredibly persistent. He wore people down. He wore them out. He seemed innocent, kindly, bumbling, but he never backed off or conceded a point. In a gentle way he was absolutely obstinate. He would present his arguments, and if they were rejected, he would simply present them once more, often in exactly the same language. He never raised his voice or lost his temper. The same words and phrases kept appearing over and over again. If the negotiations were resumed a week later, or a month later, his opposition would hear the same record replayed. It was maddening, and it was incredibly effective.

In addition, he seemed to have learned very young, or to have been born already knowing, that the most successful negotiations were those that lasted longest, and he knew a hundred polite ways to stall. Negotiations with Trippe almost never went anyplace very fast, and now as the summer of 1927 dragged to a close, the Bevier brothers were in a state of increasing nervous tension. Their airmail contract bound them to begin service on October 19, a date they knew they couldn't make. If they missed it, the Post Office would withdraw the contract, which was the only thing they had that Trippe wanted.

Montgomery was sent back to Cuba a fourth time to try to secure documents that would impress Trippe and improve Pan American's bargaining position. On September 8 Montgomery cabled that he had obtained a mail contract from the Cuban government: four years at $150 per trip. He had also obtained a five-year contract from the Cuban Army for the use of Campo Colombia; he had signed a contract for the building of a hangar and machine shop in one corner of this field. These details failed to impress Trippe, or so it seemed to the Beviers, and they petitioned the Post Office for an extension past October 19.

On September 30 came the Post Office's answer: No extension. Pan American had nineteen days to go, and still no progress in these negotiations with Trippe.

At last the Beviers cracked, and a deal was hammered out. Control of the merged companies would rest with Trippe's Aviation Corporation of America, which would hold 45 percent of the stock. Atlantic, Gulf and Caribbean (Hoyt's group) would hold 35 percent and Pan American 19 percent. For his time and pains, 1 percent would go to Reed Chambers.

On October 11 Trippe, already president of Aviation Corporation, was elected president also of Atlantic, Gulf and Caribbean Airways, Inc., and two days later he was elected president and general manager of Pan American.

At twenty-eight he had emerged in full control, and he stood up and presented a detailed plan for the company's future activities. He proposed developing a route from Miami to Cuba to Yucatán that would extend down through Central America as far as the Panama Canal, and from there to Valparaiso, Chile; and a second route across Cuba to Puerto Rico, and from there down through the chain of Caribbean islands as far as Trinidad. He spelled out the concessions that would have to be secured in Cuba, Mexico, Costa Rica, Honduras, Guatemala, El Salvador, Peru, Chile, Venezuela. It was all exceedingly detailed, and also exceedingly visionary, and it all depended on fulfilling Pan American's Key West–Havana mail contract. There were six days to go.

At the Fokker factory in Hasbrouck Heights, N.J., Trippe had a pilot standing by, ready to test the first of the two trimotors to come off the assembly line. These were the planes Trippe had ordered for Colonial more than eighteen months before. The men were working overtime, but the plane was not complete. This hardly seemed to matter, because in

Key West there was no airport to receive it. The "airport" there was at present only a field strewn with rocks and pitted with deep holes. For two weeks—starting even before the merger—Trippe had had a ground crew at work trying to make runways, but the holes were swamp pits, and some seemed bottomless. Rubble from the leveling operation was dumped into them, but they never seemed to fill up. One took some four hundred loads of rubble before the desired mushroom was formed and the pit plugged. Four days before the deadline, two intersecting dirt runways, the longer of them about twenty-two hundred feet in length, were completed. Whereupon rain began to fall heavily. It turned into a deluge that lasted two days, and when the rain stopped, Key West "airport" was a swamp again. On October 17, less than forty-eight hours from the deadline, there was still no place in Key West to land an airplane.

In New Jersey, meanwhile, the first Fokker had been pushed out into the sunlight. It was given a few hours of abbreviated flight tests, and then flown to Miami, where it landed late on October 18. And there it sat. Lacking a landing field at Key West, it could go no farther. There was one day to go.

Trippe himself seems suddenly to have realized that he had stalled the negotiations too long. At stake was the mail contract itself, of course. At stake also was a $25,000 performance bond which had been posted by Bevier in accepting the contract. It had been Bevier's money during the negotiations. It was Trippe's now, and he rushed to Washington to beg, if he could, an extension from Post Office authorities. But he was refused.

Then he got an idea. A seaplane could land off Key West, and off Cuba too. If he could find a seaplane somewhere and charter it, the contract would be fulfilled.

Frantic and inordinately expensive long-distance phone calls began to be made to flying services and barnstormers in Jacksonville, Cincinnati, Chicago, New York and Boston, but no seaplane was found. By then the first mail pouches were already speeding down the East Coast aboard a train that would arrive in Key West just after dawn on October 19. Vans were ready to carry the mail to the Pan American plane, if one was there, or else to the Cuba-bound ferryboat as in the past.

For J. E. Whitbeck, Trippe's manager in Key West, only a few cities remained on the list to be called, one of them Miami, where he knew personally that no seaplanes were permanently based. On October 18 Whitbeck called a friend there, and the friend reported that a single-engined seaplane had landed at Miami on its way to Haiti. It had been leaking oil, but repairs had been completed, and the pilot, Cy Caldwell, was even now making final preparations to depart.

Caldwell was brought to the phone, but he listened unmoved to Whitbeck's pleas. The plane was not his, he said. He had no right to change his flight plan. He would like to help, but—

Whitbeck offered money. One of the figures later mentioned was $250, a fortune to the pilots of those days. Caldwell decided that he could change his flight plan, after all, and he landed at Key West just before dark.

The next morning he was at his plane by 7:00 A.M., and shortly after that seven sacks of mail—about thirty thousand letters—were loaded aboard. At exactly 8:04 A.M., Caldwell took off. Sixty-two minutes later he landed in Havana, the mail was off-loaded, and Caldwell kept on going. But he had earned his footnote in aviation history. He had saved a tycoon and an airline.

The official inauguration of the route took place on October 28. The Fokker trimotor, having reached Key West safely, took off from the newly smooth field with Huey Wells and Eddie Musick as pilots, carrying a load of mail weighing 772 pounds. The usable portion of the runway was only 1,600 feet long and only 15 feet wide, but the Fokker lifted off with no difficulty and reached Havana, where a heavy rain was falling, without incident.

Because of the rain, inaugural ceremonies took place at a downtown hotel; the Fokker was christened *General Machado,* after the Cuban dictator himself.

Thus was completed not only Pan American's first regularly scheduled flight, but also its first inaugural ceremony and its first airplane christening in honor of a foreign dignitary.

Betty Stettinius was in Paris when Trippe's telegram came: FIRST FLIGHT SUCCESSFUL.

Betty burst into tears.

7

Priester

Trippe had begun putting his personnel together before he even had an airline. The two pilots he had hired were diametric opposites. Musick was a meticulous, deliberate man who flew airplanes with a total lack of flamboyance; nonetheless, he went on to become the most famous airline pilot of all time. Wells was a flashy, happy-go-lucky individual who was still a barnstormer at heart. He was typical of many of the pilots of the day, and was very soon replaced.

Captain Whitbeck's title was "airport engineer." Whitbeck had been in charge of the Eastern Airmail Division when the government operated the airmail, and later he became the owner and manager of Hadley Field, the airmail's eastern terminus, in New Brunswick, N.J. He was said to have laid out and supervised the construction of more than eighty fields. In short, he was the best Trippe could get. He was also red-haired, stolid, rather humorless, and he wore a red goatee. The pilots ragged him from the start. They said his beard was pink, and from then on he was known throughout the aviation world as "Pink Whiskers."

Trippe had also hired a short, bald-headed Dutchman named Andre Priester, then thirty-six years old, and had given him the title of "chief engineer." Priester, who couldn't even speak proper English, took the title seriously and soon began to take over operating control of the airline, telling the pilots not only how to fly but how to behave. He made mechanics polish brass fittings that, being inside engine nacelles, could be seen by no one. He would fire a pilot for smoking, or a mechanic for a dirty toolbox. He introduced the idea that flying must be done with unlimited care, completely without regard to cost or effort. He demanded perfection.

For the men on the line, as soon as there was a line, Trippe was only a name. They never saw him. He was in New York, with big money behind him. Whereas Priester was there before their eyes. He was the man they worked for. Everything he said was retold by pilots, mechanics and airport personnel in what tried to be a Dutch accent. Even his written directives were translated into a Dutch accent and quoted up and down the line: "Der flying uff ninety miles uff vater iss no dchoke und iss not to be treated as such."

Priester was born in 1891 in Java, the third son of a provincial assistant governor. When biographical sketches appeared later, the rank of his father was usually elevated several degrees, and it was written that three rajahs had signed his birth certificate—since only a rajah had sufficient rank to attest to the birth of a governor's son. To this exaggeration were appended others: that Priester had graduated from the University of Leiden, and that he had once served as superintendent of KLM operations in Amsterdam.

When Andre was seventeen his father died of a heart attack, and his mother brought her family back to The Hague. He attended a technical high school, and afterwards studied at the Munich Institute of Technology and at the Zurich Polytechnicum, a famous engineering school. When World War I ended, he fell in love with airplanes and was determined to learn to fly. He did take lessons but never soloed.

Instead he got a job as assistant to the KLM station manager at the Amsterdam Airport. After several years, dissatisfied with the progress he was making, the thirty-four-year-old Priester decided to emigrate to America, which seemed to him the promised land for aviation. With business booming there, he would be sure to catch on somewhere, he convinced himself. But business was not booming, not yet; the year was 1925 and he was two to three years too early.

To avoid Ellis Island, he and his wife crossed second class; spending too much money. As they came ashore in New York Priester told his wife that henceforth they should speak to each other only in English. They were bound for Detroit, which had seemed to the little Dutchman to be the hub of aviation activity. At Grand Central they were shoved into the wrong train, with the result that they had to wait four hours on a station platform in the middle of the night for the right one. Their Dutch clothes were much too warm, and their luggage was an old-fashioned wicker trunk. In Detroit they looked so bedraggled that the hotel clerk made them pay for their room in advance. Overwhelmed by the distances, they rode around on street cars holding the map of the city in their hands. Prices were about two and a half times Holland's. They moved into a furnished room near a police station, and cars with sirens came and went all night.

In Detroit no one would hire Priester. His wife went to work in a hotel to keep them, and soon had charge of two floors. In desperation Priester contacted his countryman Anthony Fokker, whose factory had now opened up in New Jersey. Fokker sent him to Philadelphia to take a job as operations manager of an airline that was starting up there. To Priester's astonishment, being a foreigner in America worked miracles. In Philadelphia he was accepted at once as an expert on commercial aviation, which he was not.

The Philadelphia Exposition ran from July 6 to November 30, 1926, and because of it a company called the Philadelphia Rapid Transit Airline had come into existence. Under Priester's direction it began to run regular flights between Philadelphia and Washington at a cost of $15 per person one way, $25 for a 15-day round-trip ticket.

Priester ran his temporary airline exactly as he would run Pan American the following year. People could set their watches by his planes. There were no accidents. There were not even any incidents. Scheduled operations were maintained—on schedule—day after day.

In the operations manual that Priester immediately produced, the duties of pilot and flight mechanic were stipulated in great detail. Before takeoffs, pilots were ordered to check over airplanes for withdrawn nails or splits in the fabric, which were to be repaired with dope if discovered. Interior cleanliness was the responsibility of the flight mechanic, who was also "to assist the pilot in keeping a sharp lookout during poor weather conditions," and to tend to airsick passengers.

Pilots had been navigating via road maps for years. Priester furnished his pilots pictures of surface landmarks as well, the better to orient themselves if they got lost. The Dutchman's rules for landing and takeoff were especially strict. Outgoing planes were to be accompanied by attendants holding the wing tips and tails with hooks to prevent them from overturning during taxiing. As for incoming planes, as soon as one was sighted the field manager was to sound a siren, and the field crew was to rush with their wing hooks to the middle of the field. The pilot was to circle first around the field to check the wind direction and the position of the field crew. He was not to taxi his plane after landing until the field crew had fastened their hooks into place. The pilot was then to taxi as slowly as possible toward the hangar so that the field crew might at all times man their hooks.

Priester's job was of five months' duration, but he treated it as if it were his lifework. Comradeship, he wrote, was especially necessary if all of the difficulties of the company during the pioneer period were to be solved. Comradeship could be accomplished by (1) taking lunch together; (2) holding short meetings after daily flight service ended; (3) holding weekly dinners, after which a show might be seen.

But at the end of five months the exposition ended, and the airline shut down. Andre Priester was out of a job again. He went back to Detroit, and this time he found a job bucking rivets on the assembly line in the Ford plant. He was still there when a telegram came from Trippe. The name meant little to Priester. He had met Trippe, but had not recognized him as anyone special. He only vaguely remembered having seen him at the Fokker factory or perhaps at Teterboro Airport.

Trippe wanted to know if Priester would work out for him a complete and detailed operations and revenue estimate of "a proposed Southern Sea Airline." This was in February 1927. Trippe was still running Colonial at the time and his directors wanted nothing to do with any Southern Sea Airline.

Priester answered by return mail. The estimate would be written by himself in longhand, he wrote, because a hired stenographer might keep a copy of it. In the next paragraph he asked, "What is your price for it?"

Eight months later, as soon as Pan American's planes started to fly, Priester began writing another operations manual, and his directives remained in force long after the jokes about his English stopped. "All controls, especially throttles, will be operated smoothly and steadily," he wrote, "rather than hastily or impulsively, insofar as possible." Pilots, Priester knew, tended to be free spirits, for the air was a free place, the last on this earth. Airline flying demanded a new type of man, and Priester was the first in America to see this, and to preach it as doctrine.

In New York, Trippe's expenses were as minimal as he could keep them. The tiny airline with the momentous name operated out of a three-room office suite at 100 West 42nd Street. Trippe had one room, outside of which sat a Miss Swaggerty, who operated the telephone switchboard and also served as Trippe's secretary. Priester, who was not often there, had a desk in the second office, and there were two other desks arranged against the walls, one for director John Hambleton, the second for a Miss Ulrich, who was the airline's accounting department.

8

Key West

In Key West a terminal had to be built. Trippe allotted $2,500 to the job, and the result was little more than a shack. Something better could be built later, if the airline caught on, if any passengers ever turned up to be carried. A hangar to keep the planes out of the weather was more important, and so a substantial one was built out of steel and corrugated iron. It measured 90 feet by 100 feet. The airfield's principal physical feature was East Martello Tower, part of the ancient fort that once had dominated the island. Some of the rooms in the outer circle of the fort were rehabilitated for storage and as emergency repair shops. Most of the roofs over these rooms leaked. Since there was neither time nor money to repair these roofs properly, boiling asphalt was poured over them and swabbed down to make a seal.

To lose one of the planes now would very likely put the company out of business. Trippe gave orders that the load factor of the two Fokkers —a second plane, christened *General New* after Postmaster General Harry New, had since been delivered—should be restricted to a limit that would permit them to continue flight with two of the three engines out.

For the two months that remained of the year the mail was carried back and forth every day. Occasionally there was so much mail that both planes flew. There were no accidents, no forced landings. Not a single flight was missed. There was not even a single engine failure. Efficiency, Trippe bragged in his first "annual" report to the stockholders, was 100 percent. In November 19,496 pounds of U.S. mail was carried, and 877 pounds of Cuban mail. In December both figures rose—the U.S. mail to

26,513 pounds, and the Cuban mail to 1,492 pounds. Revenues for the first sixty-five days of service came to $29,575.49, which resulted in a net operating loss of only $1,712.57.

By January 16, 1928, Trippe was confident enough to order passenger service inaugurated, and he rode the train down from New York to board the first flight. The manifest listed him as John T. Trippe—certain of his employees did not yet know the boss's name. Though the day and flight were historic, and though he in effect owned the plane, he did not attempt to take the controls himself, for this would have been contrary to passenger interest. On a commercial flight, the passengers were entitled to professional pilots, he reasoned, and he remained in his wicker chair all the way to Havana.

He had had a four-page folder printed up that was more tourist brochure than schedule. "Travel the Comfortable Way" read the headline, and the text continued: "How many times have you stood on the deck of a steamer, tossing in a rough sea and enviously watched the gulls wheeling and dipping round the vessel? What swiftness and lightness, what ease, while you suffered the agony of the rolling and pitching of a spiteful sea. How you longed for the smooth, quick flight of the gulls." The folder equated the straits of Florida with the English Channel, which was "famous for its roughness." The steady Florida breeze was always at cross-purposes with the currents, and "those on the surface where wind and water meet, suffer aplenty."

There followed a description of the "large eight-passenger trimotor Fokkers" and a photo showed prospective passengers the accommodations they could expect: wide wicker chairs, sliding glass windows the length of the fuselage. The round-trip fare was $100, thirty pounds of baggage included. After making connections with the train from Miami and points north, the planes left Key West each morning at 8:00 A.M. The return flight left Havana at 3:45 P.M., arriving in Key West in time to connect with the same train northbound. But very few passengers turned up at first.

From John Hambleton's father-in-law, who headed the Atlantic Coast Railroad Line, Trippe got permission for a salesman to board the train up the line in the middle of the night. The salesman was Vic Chenea, who had once owned part of Florida Airways. His usual tactic was to find a sleeping-car conductor, give him rum, and learn the names and berth locations of Havana-bound passengers. Chenea then would accost these people in the washroom and launch into his sales pitch. Later Chenea was assigned to Havana, where he would lure prospects into bars and buy rum until they agreed to fly back to Florida—after which he would not only furnish the ticket or tickets, but also drive the prospects to the plane and push them aboard.

Priester was in Key West most of that winter and spring, for there were problems. Although Havana was only ninety miles away, in hazy or rainy weather the pilots often had difficulty finding it. They had no navigational aid except the compass, and they measured wind direction and wind velocity by judging the amount of foam on the peaks of the waves 1,500 or more feet below. Sometimes on the return trip they couldn't easily find Key West, and they learned to navigate by the color of the water. They knew from Coast Guard charts where the Gulf Stream ran, and where the bottom began to shelve upwards toward the Keys, and on a clear day there was a great deal of color variation in the water below. The Gulf Stream was gunmetal blue, and the water then became green, and after that, almost milky white over the shoals. This meant they were approaching the Keys, and they would try to discern Sand Key Light. The appearance of this lighthouse gave them their exact position, and they would follow the Keys home. Cuba to the south and the Keys' archipelago to the north—these seemed vast targets. Nobody expected a pilot to miss one of them completely and go down at sea, but Priester realized this could happen, and he worried about it. When a plane was due, he would pace the landing field in front of the hangar, and from time to time he could be heard to mutter, "Vere iss der plane?"

He could rely on Musick, whom he had known at Philadelphia Rapid Transit Airline. Musick and his wife had lived in the same apartment building as the Priesters. Musick had flown accurate schedules then, and still did. But there was only one Musick. Needing a second reliable pilot, Priester decided to hire Caspar Swinson, a pilot he had known in Detroit.

Swinson had learned to fly in the Army during World War I. When the war ended he went to work in a Detroit bank as a clerk, but he could not stay away from flying. Six months later he bought an interest in an airplane and began barnstorming. One day, although people were standing in line a block long, he cut the barnstorming short because he had a date with a girl in another town. A few minutes after he landed in the girl's town, people were standing in line there, too. But barnstorming got progressively less profitable—this was exactly what Trippe was finding on Long Island—and so Swinson joined the Ford Airline.

Priester, working on the Ford assembly line, had sought Swinson out, for he wanted to learn all he could about aviation, and he invited Swinson to his house for dinner many times. Now, needing a new pilot, Priester sent his friend a letter. It read only: "Please advise your schedule for joining Pan American Airways at Key West." That was all. Small talk or friendly greetings were not Priester's way.

It was May 21, 1928, before a third pilot arrived at Key West by train, accompanied by his wife and child. This was Robert H. Fatt. Born in Niagara Falls in 1895, Fatt was then thirty-three years old. He, too, had learned to fly in the Army. Later he was a pilot for National Air Transport on the Kansas City–Chicago run, where he was paid $450 a month, a lot of money in 1926. But he had learned to hate the winter flying in un-heated cockpits. One night, flying over Kansas, it was 32 degrees below zero up there, so cold that he had no feeling left in his hands on the controls of the airplane.

At that point he remembered having read about a new airline flying from Key West to Havana. He wrote to the airline's office in New York, outlining his experience: 3,500 hours in the air, including about 500 at night. He even went to New York to be interviewed for the job, and was told that his application was on file. When a contract at last came from Pan American, Fatt headed south with his family. Musick checked him out in the Fokker F-7—three takeoffs, three landings. This was the first time Fatt had ever handled the controls of a multiengined airplane. Musick carried him as copilot on two round trips to Havana. His total copilot time was 4 hours, 20 minutes. Then he was a Pan American captain.

Key West had once been the biggest city in Florida, but had been declining for decades. Now it was heavily Cuban. It lived off the shrimp boats and the cigar factories. Most of the Pan American peo-ple—the pilots and Priester when he was there—stayed at the La Con-cha, the only hotel in Key West with an elevator. The elevator was al-ways full of Cuban kids riding up and down in it. In the evening there was nothing to do. There was no entertainment, no place even to stroll. The town did not even have enough fresh water, and tap water was brackish. But there were numerous places, despite prohibition, for drinking and carousing.

One day Priester called in his friend Swinson and said, "I'm going to haf to fire you for drinking."

"I don't drink that much," protested the pilot.

"It isn't how much you drink," said Priester, "but vere you drink."

For airline pilots new commandments applied. Swinson cut out drink-ing in public, and remained.

All three pilots considered the flying easy. They continued to make their landfalls as best they could—sometimes many miles off course—but this was normal. No pilot in the world could do better, or even hope to do better.

In New York Trippe was brooding about these same navigational problems. If they were indeed insoluble, then his airline could grow no bigger, and would be unable ever to span any larger sea than this one, except in the impractical way that Lindbergh had just done it—as a single isolated stunt.

Trippe, however, was confident that the problem could be over-come, and that the solution was radio. Ships navigated by radio, tak-ing fixes on specific shore-based radio stations, and if ships could do it, so could planes. However, radio sets of 1928 were enormous, weighing up to 1,400 pounds, a mass that no airplane in the foreseeable future would be able to lift off the ground and still have room for passengers and mail. What Trippe needed was someone who could build him miniature receivers and transmitters whose signals would nonetheless carry immense distances, and he arranged to meet with a man named Hugo Leuteritz.

9

Leuteritz

Radio at this time was only a slightly older, slightly more advanced art than aviation. Marconi had developed the first wireless telegraph in 1895. Voices had first been transmitted by radio in 1900, and by 1906 it was possible to broadcast phonograph music. During the first decade of the twentieth century Marconi sent a radio message across the Atlantic Ocean, and a steamship foundering in heavy seas radioed for help—and got it. Radio messages even influenced strategy in the Russo-Japanese War, the first use of radio as an adjunct of military slaughter.

By 1910 ham radio operators existed, and a thirteen-year-old boy in Brooklyn—Hugo Leuteritz—sometimes talked to them on a radio set he had made himself by winding a coil around an empty round oatmeal package.

The Germans had worked on radio navigation for ships before World War I, and the Telefunken Company had built a radio navigation device at Fire Island, an installation as big as a lighthouse. In the winter of 1916 Leuteritz even hiked out there across the ice on the bay to have a look at it.

The loop antenna in receiving sets came into existence about this time, principally as a means of saving space. Then it was discovered that signals seemed to come in stronger when the edge of the loop was pointed toward the transmitter. This led to the realization that the loop antenna could be used as a direction finder.

All this existed in vague form when, in February 1919, Leuteritz went to work for a newly formed company called RCA—the Radio Corporation of America. He was assigned to conduct experiments into the dark corners of radio in an old farmhouse near Lakewood, N. J. He was not yet twenty-two years old. Few RCA employees were any older.

Radio promised to be a profitable business one day, but nobody knew what direction this business might take. Among the possibilities was aviation. If one could communicate with ships at sea by wireless, then one ought to be able to communicate with aircraft as well. Toward the end of 1925 Leuteritz was detached from the farmhouse laboratory and ordered to make a survey of aviation as a potential market.

By this time various small airlines were in operation: National Air Transport, Pacific Air Transport, Pitcairn Airlines, Colonial Air Transport. Leuteritz contacted most of these lines and, as a passenger, flew some of the routes. The pilot would ride in one cockpit, and Leuteritz would ride in the other sitting on top of the mailbags. He was a tall, lanky young man, and most of his body protruded into the slipstream. A more urgent problem than communication, he realized very quickly, was navigation. When bad weather closed in, pilots immediately got lost. Trying to orient themselves, they would fly along railroad tracks, searching for a station with a name on it, wheels almost touching the roadbed. Riding half out of the cockpit, Leuteritz could see the danger better than the pilot could.

So he began to think about navigating by radio, and this led him to conduct certain experiments, some from the top of an 864-foot tower near Tuckerton, N.J. The tower offered a useful height from which to test the range of a signal beamed toward a ship at sea. Like many aviation pioneers, Leuteritz often seemed to outsiders absolutely fearless. Heights never scared him. Regularly he took his gear up the tower himself, 86 stories up an iron ladder toward a triangular platform on top that measured 24 inches to the side. Once when he was on top of the platform an electrical storm struck, and he was forced to clamber down swiftly because the tower seemed certain to attract lightning. It was a long climb down. Rain was falling in torrents. It was running down his sleeve and out his pants leg.

When all his experiments were complete, Leuteritz advised RCA that no market existed in aviation at present because no plane could afford to give up the weight and space that radio sets required. He recommended that RCA appropriate $25,000 for research into lightweight equipment. RCA turned this proposal down, commenting that the future of aviation was too uncertain for an investment of such magnitude.

During his survey, Leuteritz had contacted Colonial Airlines and had spoken to Trippe. He had met Fokker. He had even met Priester at the Fokker plant in New Jersey. But nobody wanted either radio or Leuteritz, who kept brooding.

Back at the RCA lab he built three experimental transmitters and two receivers. The small 10-watt transmitter was for single-engined planes. A trimotored airliner might possibly carry the bigger 100-watt set. The 300-watt monster was for dirigibles.

Now Leuteritz's problem became to get these radios onto aircraft somewhere, for he wanted to try them out, and he contacted every airline he could think of—Trippe had now left Colonial—but none was interested.

Around June 1927 Leuteritz was called to a meeting in a downtown office building. Present were Trippe, Fokker, John Hambleton and the Bevier brothers. Trippe wanted to know what radio could do, and what his costs would be if sets were used by his new airline. But he refused to tell Leuteritz where this airline meant to operate, nor over which distances. "We can't disclose that information," said Trippe. (Trippe was secretive even as a young man, and it would get worse.) "Because we are just forming the company."

Leuteritz displayed the proper eagerness. If he was to prove or disprove his theories, he had to find someone who was willing to give up space on an airplane. Trippe's new airline was the only nibble so far.

Some months later Trippe and Leuteritz met again. This time Trippe described the Key West–Havana route Pan American was already flying, and also those routes he hoped to fly soon—Havana to Puerto Rico, Puerto Rico down through the chain of islands. He asked Leuteritz to specify the kind of gear that was available and to submit proposed costs. More important, he gave the radioman permission to install his equipment in the Pan American Fokkers in Key West, and to conduct experiments there both on the ground and aloft.

On July 5, 1928, Leuteritz and his wife, Alice, arrived in Key West by train. Leuteritz, still working for RCA, had with him a considerable amount of electronic gear, and he went to work. The first thing he found was that static here in the tropics was so intense that no signal could cut through it. He was worried about static, and worried about weight. He had to find a range of frequencies that would cut through the static and at the same time find a means of focusing his signals. Lightweight sets would become possible the moment he could define his signals sharply enough to reduce the need for substantial power. He was not the only radioman who knew about ground waves and sky waves; what was new was that he needed them both. The ground wave covered the nearer distances, and the sky wave the more distant ones. But in between came areas where there was no signal at all. He was exploring frequencies every day, trying to find what he needed.

It was slow, painstaking work, and it was complicated by the need to improvise. He had his experimental transmitters, but like all radio gear of the time, they were too fragile to bolt down inside an airplane—they would be shaken to pieces. So Leuteritz suspended them on ladies' garters. Since there was no power source inside the plane, he improvised a windmill generator that he attached to a strut outside the cabin.

As planes went out on their normal runs to Havana, the mechanic aboard was supposed to hold the telegraph key down for a specified length of time at certain intervals so that Leuteritz in Key West could attempt to pick up the signal and make his readings. But the mechanics kept forgetting, for they had other jobs aloft, and they neither understood nor cared about radio. The pilots were even more negative. Said Fatt to Leuteritz: "I've thrown better radio equipment off my airplanes than you can build."

Leuteritz sent an SOS to New York, and a young radio engineer named F. W. Sullinger was sent down to help. From then on, one or the other flew to Havana and back every day; experiments were conducted on schedule both by telegraph and by voice; and Leuteritz began to zero in on the frequencies he needed.

On the morning of August 15 it was Leuteritz's turn to fly. Aboard the Fokker was a voice transmitter only. The plane's receiver had broken down the day before, and Sullinger was in the shop in the fort trying to fix it. Leuteritz's transmissions were being monitored in the operations shack by twenty-four-year-old Daniel Pippinger, an out-of-work dishwasher who would later become a Pan Am pilot.

At Havana the Fokker—it was the *General Machado*—was loaded with sixty pounds of Cuban mail, and two passengers, William Walton and Charles Norman Ageton, climbed on board. The pilot was Fatt, who took off for Key West at 3:55 P.M. Beside him sat flight mechanic Gus Alfonso, and in the cabin aft sat the two passengers and Leuteritz, who began transmitting five minutes after takeoff, reporting an altitude of 1,200 feet, a ground speed of 80 miles per hour and the weather. It was raining.

Regular transmissions came about fifteen minutes apart. Once Leuteritz stuck the microphone in Fatt's face and the pilot's voice was heard complaining that visibility was poor and the air bumpy. He was flying at 3,000 feet. The wind, he judged from the wave tops, which he could see occasionally, was out of the southeast. There were many clouds, and some were full of rain.

At 4:55, one hour out of Havana, the Fokker flew over a tramp steamer, Leuteritz radioed. They had not yet spotted Key West, he said.

In his next transmission fifteen minutes later Leuteritz noted that all five men on the plane were peering out windows looking for the Sand Key Light. They could not find it. No one was yet very worried. "We did not see Cuba this morning until we were about five miles from it," Leuteritz said. "We'll tell you when we see Sand Key Light, so stand by."

He began to transmit every five minutes. The import of all these messages was the same. Visibility was poor. There was no sign of Key West yet.

Two hours out of Havana Leuteritz radioed: "Have not sighted the Keys yet. Passed a steamer headed same direction we are. We ought to sight something very soon now."

Leuteritz kept radioing details: that Alfonso was peering around with binoculars, that their air speed, as they dropped down to 1,800 feet, was about 100 miles an hour.

Fatt, deciding that they must have missed the Keys to the east, turned northwest. Leuteritz radioed the change.

For some time Priester, in the operations shack, had been standing first at Pippinger's shoulder and then at Sullinger's, listening to these messages. There was no alarm in Leuteritz's voice, but there was plenty in that shack. The experimental loop direction finder that Leuteritz had rigged to the roof of the shack was primitive, but it was sufficient to show that Fatt had just turned away from the Florida peninsula and was heading out into the Gulf of Mexico. Priester ran out of the shack and found Swinson, whom he sent up in the other plane to look for Fatt.

Leuteritz, still transmitting, still did not sound particularly worried. At 6:16 P.M., 2 hours and 21 minutes out of Havana, he radioed another change of course. "Think we allowed too much for drift," he said. "When we get down to the last half-hour of gas, we'll look for a ship and land near it."

From then on Leuteritz transmitted every two minutes:

"Visibility poor, haven't sighted anything yet."

"Things running smoothly. Have not sighted anything yet."

"Air calm. No whitecaps on the water."

"Have not sighted anything yet. Don't excite anyone, as everything is running smoothly. We intend to sight something before long."

"Have not sighted anything yet. Gas getting low. We are doing everything we can. Getting the boats ready."

At Key West, Swinson was still out searching in wide circles. Visibility was as poor for him as for Fatt. Priester, listening to every word from Leuteritz, now had two planes up there. He was worried about them both.

At 6:52, 2 hours and 57 minutes out of Havana, Leuteritz began his final transmission. They had sighted a tanker below. "Putting a note in a bag," Leuteritz radioed, "getting ready to drop it to the ship."

The tanker was the *American Legionnaire.* It was in some way airing out its tanks, and fumes that were invisible from the air hung over its decks. Alfonso opened his window and fired down an emergency flare. This created panic on the tanker. All its hatches were emitting fumes, into which an airplane was shooting fiery things. The crewmen were worried not about the Fokker's plight but about their own. As the *General Machado* swooped low over their decks a second time, Alfonso threw out his message inside a shirt tied to the inertial starter crank: "If I am over 100 miles from land, make a lot of black smoke. If I am less than 100 miles from land, turn your ship towards land."

The crank handle landed in the water and sank.

Fatt was circling, peering down, waiting for a response. None came. His left engine quit. Immediately he leveled off, and the engine started again. But on his next turn the right engine quit, and after it the other two. The *General Machado,* out of gas, glided down toward the sea. Fatt was trying to land as close as possible to the tanker. In August 1928 few pilots knew what a fixed-gear airplane would do when it landed on water, particularly when a five- to six-foot sea was running. Would it flip onto its back?

The tail skid struck the wave tops. In the cabin Leuteritz was thrown headfirst into a bulkhead and knocked unconscious. A wall of water struck the plane. The escape hatch over Fatt's head burst open, and water came down on top of him. He struggled up through it onto the wing. Alfonso was already sitting on the wing, holding his head.

"Never mind your head," cried Fatt. "Let's get these people out."

When Leuteritz came to, the plane was full of water. He was floating in an air bubble at the front end of the cabin, and the escape hatch was aft. He sucked in air, dived and pulled himself along the netting which constituted the overhead rack. Suddenly he felt something under him. He thought it was one of the passengers, and hooked it with his feet.

From outside, Fatt had torn open the escape hatch. Up popped a spare tire, along with other junk, obstructing the hatch.

"Try to get the door open," Fatt yelled at Alfonso. The door was in the side of the fuselage, not far from the escape hatch in the ceiling. Alfonso got the door open, and Fatt shoved the tire down out of the escape hatch and out the door. One of the plane's wicker chairs floated up in its place. Fatt kicked it down and out the door as well. The next thing to pop out of the hatch was Leuteritz.

"How are you?" asked Fatt.

"I don't know, but I've got something hooked on my leg."

Alfonso dived down into the fuselage, and dragged out the passenger, Walton, who was unconscious. They laid him out on the wing. In a moment he came to and began weeping.

The plane carried an ax in its emergency closet, and Fatt, reaching down into the water, found it. He began chopping at the plywood top surface of the wing, trying to cut his way down into the front of the cabin where he imagined that the second passenger, Ageton, might be wedged. But Fatt was unable to break through. The ax kept bouncing off the plywood.

All four men were bleeding. Fatt and Alfonso had head injuries. Leuteritz had lost all sensation in his legs and imagined himself paralyzed from the waist down. He hoped he would die.

The Fokker was floating with its nose engine just beneath the surface. The boat from the tanker was banging against the plane. One of the sailors swam through the cabin, but could find no trace of the missing passenger. The sailor reported that the floor of the fuselage was smashed open. Ageton must have gone out through the bottom when the plane smacked down. In any case, he was gone.

The survivors were taken back to the tanker. The waves seemed mountainous, and the small boat was riding up and down the tall steel wall of the ship. Leuteritz could not move his legs. Fatt, a huge man, carried the tall skinny Leuteritz piggyback up the rope ladder onto the deck.

Meanwhile, Swinson in the second Fokker had been gone a long time. He had no radio gear aboard and there was no way to communicate with him. For all Priester knew, he was as lost as Fatt, and would never find his way back. Fearing he had lost both planes, Priester ordered gasoline fires lit along the runway, and in the gathering darkness flames rose toward the sky that he hoped Swinson might see and home in on. Swinson, flying back, did see the flames; he landed safely, and when he had jumped down onto the ground, Priester, always so dignified and formal, rushed up and embraced him.

But Swinson had found no sign of the other plane. He and Priester stared at each other, their faces lit by the blazing fires.

By this time the tanker's captain had ordered a rope fastened to the nose engine of Fatt's Fokker. Although the plane in 1928 was counted as a "huge" airliner, the captain thought he could haul it up the side of his tanker, using its wheels to hold it off from the ship, and his winch began turning. But as the fuselage came free of the water, the engine mount let go, and the rest of the plane settled back onto the waves, where it floated on its wings. The Coast Guard sank it some days later.

A radiogram was sent from the ship to the Tropical Radio Station at Hialeah, and Priester was notified that his plane and one passenger were lost. A Coast Guard cutter was sent out to the tanker, and at three o'clock in the morning the four survivors were off-loaded and rushed to a hospital in the nearest town, which happened to be Tampa—Fatt had missed Key West by something like three hundred miles.

When the cutter docked the next morning, reporters waited. "I have no statement to make," Fatt told them as he came off the gangway. "There will be an investigation by the Department of Commerce, and if it turns out I am to blame, I'll never fly an airplane again."

Press photographers moved forward. "No, no pictures," said Fatt, holding his hands in front of his face. A flashbulb exploded anyway. Fatt grabbed the camera with his left hand and broke the photographer's jaw with his right. Five policemen jumped him, and he tried to fight them off. Then he was in handcuffs.

A lawyer sent by Trippe turned up, Fatt was released, and the survivors were sent back to Key West by boat. When they landed, Priester was there on the pier.

"If it makes things any easier for the company," Fatt told him, "I will quit."

"Dere vill be an inwestigation," responded Priester. "If you are to blame, you vill be fired. If you are not to blame, you vill be our most waluable pilot, because you vill be der only vun who ever landed on der vater."

Later Fatt served as chief pilot on Pan American's Eastern Division for nine years.

In 1928 a crash like this caused headlines all over the world, and further undermined the public's already dim faith in commercial aviation. Trippe reacted by dropping the small public relations firm—specialists in aviation—that he had employed up to now, and addressing himself to Doremus & Co., the financial advertising subsidiary of the Dow Jones–Wall Street Journal group. Doremus had as clients most of the important financial houses. Trippe asked Doremus to take Pan American as a client. He wanted Doremus & Co. somehow to suppress the bad publicity, which, if it went unchecked, might destroy his company. He wanted Doremus to make Pan American sound as safe as a brokerage house.

There would be many crashes in the years to come, but this first crash was the worst, for it had shaken the confidence of everyone, Trippe included. At that, Trippe was luckier than he knew; he might have lost Leuteritz.

Doremus & Co. sent a young man named William Van Dusen. Trippe greeted him as the seventeenth Pan American employee, which he was not, since Doremus continued to pay him. Over the next weeks, mostly at night, Van Dusen and Trippe thought out what their public stance should be, and Van Dusen developed the philosophy that would guide him in the years to come. "The airplane was such a frightening thing," Van Dusen noted many years later, "that we had to go to any length to put the most attractive face on things, so as not to frighten off the politicians whose votes we needed, or the public. Stark survival necessitated some stratagems. Sometimes we had to invent. Our cause depended more on sympathetic understanding than it did on truth and the absolutes."

Despite the crash, Priester remained lukewarm about navigation by radio—it was a radical idea and it was still unproven—and the pilots were totally opposed to it. Leuteritz knew this, and he also knew that opposition to him and his theories would get worse. For he had decided that navigation would have to be done from the ground. It could not be done in the air at all with existing equipment. It would have to be done by someone sitting comfortably in a chair in a dry, warm, stable place. This meant that navigation would pass outside the pilot's control altogether, and it constituted the worst heresy of all: the pilot in the air would be obliged to take orders from someone else.

How could pilots, each one the captain of his ship, ever be made to accept such a notion? Leuteritz began to lobby gently, arguing with the pilots night after night on the porch of the La Concha Hotel. "We can correct your navigation by radio," he told them, "but you have to let us do it. You have a little engine fluctuation, and by the time you get your mind back to navigation, you are way off your course."

By now he had found exactly the sharply defined frequencies he needed. He had designed lightweight sets. In the hospital he had sketched a new direction-finding loop antenna of sufficient size to pinpoint the bearings of planes flying between Key West and Havana. The loop was again a masterpiece of improvisation—it was nothing but pieces of wood knocked together to frame a four-foot square, with hundreds of feet of wire wrapped around it. Needing a compass rose for this loop, Leuteritz had bought a tin pie plate in a ten-cent store, and had nailed this to a stand underneath the loop. But to calibrate it required test flights, and test flights meant cooperation from the pilots.

Fatt, despite having missed the entire peninsula of Florida, was still against navigation by radio, but Musick agreed to make the test flights —among all the pilots flying the embryonic airlines of the times, he appears to have been the only one who understood that the old days were gone, that flying now must change. He went out beyond Key West and lined himself up on landmarks as Leuteritz instructed, and transmitted signals while Leuteritz and Sullinger in the shack took bearings on him and calibrated their antenna. After that the two radiomen made flight charts for the area between Key West and Havana, a kind of grid map divided into five-mile squares. From then on it sufficed for the telegraph key—voice transmission had been abandoned as unreliable— to be held down long enough for the loop to be pointed out on the direct bearing of the signal. This gave the plane's heading, and it became possible to send corrections to the pilot—one dot for each square of the grid off course to the east, one dash for each square off course to the west. The next step was to determine distance from the loop as well as direction, and Leuteritz patiently explained to the pilots how, if they would fly brief tangent headings from time to time as instructed, a second directional fix could be made and their distance from Key West computed from it.

Still Swinson and Fatt remained unconvinced of the validity of navigation by radio—which shows not that they were stupid, but rather how revolutionary, in 1928, Leuteritz's ideas sounded.

With even Priester only half convinced, Leuteritz had to use all his tact just to make the pilots keep sending the signals he needed. He did not often send signals back to them, and he never ordered them to change course. The technical problems had been solved, but the political ones had not been, and he was trying to go slow.

One day "Cap" Swinson was up there nearing Cuba, but the signal that he had landed had not yet arrived. The door to the shack was open. Outside Priester paced anxiously up and down, calling from time to time, "Hugo, vere iss der airplane?"

"It's okay," Leuteritz said.

Priester entered the shack and stood at Leuteritz's shoulder, studying Leuteritz's chart. He saw that Swinson was going to make his landfall far east of Havana, and although Leuteritz sent him first four dots, and then five dots, Swinson's course did not change.

"Hugo, dot isn't possible. Dot's Swinson," said Priester, grasping the situation.

"Wait and see how long it takes him to get to Havana, and when he lands," said Leuteritz.

Swinson's bearings began to show that he had finally headed west toward Havana. But thirty minutes passed before he landed.

That evening Priester decided to confront Swinson with the chart, and he came to Leuteritz and demanded it.

But Leuteritz refused. The chart belonged to RCA, he said, not to Pan American.

Priester said, "I vant der chart."

"No, you'll go down there mad, and he'll say that these radio guys are spying on him. Handle this diplomatically," Leuteritz begged. "The pilots are already hostile to direction finding from the ground. Talk to him. Tell him that you noticed that his flight was overdue. Ask him if he had headwinds."

But diplomacy was not Priester's strong point. In an office that Pan American kept in the La Concha Hotel, the chief engineer told Swinson that he had missed Havana by sixty miles.

"How do you know?" retorted the pilot. "I know how I flew."

Priester summoned Leuteritz, and ordered him to produce the chart. Reluctantly Leuteritz did so, saying, "We are just trying to help you, Cap. We are just trying to see that what happened to Fatt doesn't happen to you."

Swinson stared at the floor, then said, "Okay, I guess you're right."

By the middle of September there was nothing further for Leuteritz to do in Key West, and he went back to New York, wrote his report for RCA, then went on a working vacation to the Berlin Air Show. Priester phoned repeatedly in his absence, and upon his return to New York, phoned again. "Mr. Trippe vants to see you for lunch today," said Priester.

At lunch Trippe came straight to the point. "Andre has told me about what happened at Key West. Andre will not be satisfied unless you take on the job of communications for Pan American Airways."

"Well—" said Leuteritz.

"Andre will have nobody else but you."

Leuteritz thought about it. "I have a good idea of what your requirements will be, but you have only a few airplanes. That's not enough to keep me busy. I have more ambition than that."

Trippe said, "We will have a big fleet of planes. We will fly to Latin America next year, and after that we will fly across the Atlantic, across the Pacific."

"What you are talking about is a gamble," said Leuteritz. "I know what I can do. But you don't know what you can do. I know that as far as radio is concerned, it can be done, but—"

After talking to his wife, Leuteritz arranged for a six-month leave of absence from RCA. He was willing to gamble six months, no more. Then he sat around waiting for Trippe to phone with a concrete offer. He was certainly not going to phone Trippe.

Presently Trippe did phone, and another luncheon was arranged. "I'm not going to discuss salary," said Leuteritz. "You know what I was getting from RCA. If at the end of six months you feel that I am entitled to more money, you handle it. There's only one thing I am interested in. Who is my boss?"

Trippe said, "Report directly to me."

So Hugo C. Leuteritz joined Pan American Airways. His office consisted of a chair beside Priester's desk. He was working out of his lap. But he was there, and all of Trippe's dreams for conquering the world became possible.

10

West Indian Aerial Express

Trippe's dreams had long since focused on South America. The problem had always been how to get there—fast—before someone else did. Trippe had needed navigation, but that was now in hand. He had needed machines, and had recently ordered brand-new twin-engined S-38 amphibians from Sikorsky. But he also needed not only landing concessions from foreign governments but men permanently stationed in the places where his planes would touch down, and these things were harder to come by. The best way to acquire both, and also the best insurance against competition was simply to take over, by whatever means proved available, companies that already existed en route.

To get to South America in a Fokker—or even in the new Sikorskys, once they were delivered—meant refueling every two to three hundred miles. There would have to be stops on nearly every island in the West Indies chain. But a company called West Indian Aerial Express was already there, and stood in Trippe's way.

West Indian Aerial Express operated, theoretically, from Cuba eastward across Haiti to the Dominican Republic and Puerto Rico, and sometimes even as far as the Virgin Islands. Its regular route spanned some 800 miles, including two overwater crossings, one of 50 miles between Santo Domingo and Puerto Rico, and the other of either 40 or 230 miles between Cuba and Haiti—the length depended on how brave the pilot felt, whether he chose to fly the direct route over two and a half hours of open water or to follow the coastline around to where the two islands

lay closest. In either case there would be up to nine stops during the two-
to three-day trip.

West Indian Aerial Express was more typical by far of the airlines of
the period than was Pan American, just as its founder, Basil Rowe, was
more typical of that era's aviators than was Juan Trippe.

Rowe, three and a half years older than Trippe, was born in Shand-
aken, N.Y., on February 10, 1896, and he figured to live in or near that
upstate village for the rest of his life. But in 1915 something happened
that changed all this. A barnstormer named Turk Adams landed in a
nearby pasture, and when the necessary crowd had collected, he took off
to stage an aerial exhibition. His plane soared aloft, gained altitude for
a few hundred feet, then settled into the treetops beyond the field. After
hanging there a moment, it plopped into the stream beneath. Among the
boys who rushed to help was Basil Rowe. He worked on the wreck all day
and into the night, and in return Adams taught him to fly.

Later Rowe became a famous air racer. He won the Aviation Town
and Country Trophy at the International Air Races in Dayton, the Allen
Hinkle Trophy at the National Air Congress in Wichita, the Glenn H.
Curtiss Trophy at the International Air Races in New York.

In between he barnstormed. But soon there were too many air meets,
too many barnstormers. Business got worse and worse. A pilot could
survive only if he could think up and bring off incredible stunts, and so
stunts became Rowe's forte. Once he swooped down under the middle
span of the Camden-Philadelphia Bridge, lifted up just over the brackish
water of the Delaware, and roared back into the air again. He did this with
a paying passenger aboard, and afterwards had to fight the customers off.
His stunts drove competitors to ruin. Another time he decided to fly
through an open dirigible hangar. As he approached the hangar he
checked to make sure the dirigible *Shenandoah* was moored to its mast
outside. It was, so Rowe pushed the stick forward and zoomed down into
the open end of the hangar. He was actually inside the hangar when he
suddenly became aware of a training blimp being towed into the other
end by a ground crew. Rowe made a U-turn and flew out of the hangar,
and never understood afterwards how he did it.

By 1926 he was thirty years old, and stunt flying for a living was very
nearly over. The crowds weren't there any more. He had to find someplace new, and he decided on the Caribbean. In the fall he and a pal, Bill
Wade, loaded two Wacos, two cars, spare motors and spare parts and
themselves aboard a ship to Puerto Rico.

Business was good there. No one had ever seen a plane before. The
people were poor, but willing to spend their life savings on the thrills
Rowe and Wade offered. There was one tremendous problem: contrary
to what Rowe had been told up North, the Caribbean was highly unsuited
to flying, for there was practically no level ground to land on, and every

forced landing therefore became an accident. "We got so that after a crash," Rowe said later, "we could pluck an airplane out of the trees, carry it to the field, repair and assemble it, and have it back in the air or in another clump of trees the following day."

At length Rowe and Wade found themselves in Barahona in the Dominican Republic. The barnstorming business was falling off even in this isolated spot, and so when the sugar planters spoke to Rowe about starting an airline that would connect them to the outside world, he listened.

West Indian Aerial Express was incorporated on June 20, 1927— about the same day that Trippe was incorporating the Aviation Corporation of America. A few of Rowe's stockholders, who put up $50,000 altogether, were Americans. Most were local businessmen.

The operations manager was Roscoe Dunten, who had been an engineer in an ice plant in San Juan when Rowe first landed there in October 1926. Fascinated by aviation, he had spent most of his afternoons at the baseball field that served Rowe and Wade as an airport, and most of his evenings in bars with Wade, a hard drinker.

With the company formed, Rowe went North to buy new aircraft. He came back flying a trimotored Keystone Pathfinder; he had also bought a Fairchild FC-2 pontoon monoplane, and had induced his friend Cy Caldwell to fly it down to Barahona for him—this was the flight that was interrupted briefly when Caldwell fulfilled Pan American's contract by flying the first mail to Havana.

Regular service by West Indian Aerial Express was inaugurated when an Australian pilot named Jenkins took off on a flight from Barahona to Port-au-Prince in one of the Wacos. This plane disappeared en route. The company's call for help was radioed to U.S. Marine Corps Observation Squadron 9 in Haiti, one of whose planes found it near a lake, forced down by engine failure and partially wrecked. After repairs were made, Jenkins took off, continued on to Port-au-Prince, and crashed there.

Barnstormers had flown only when the weather was fine. Airline pilots had to fly whether the weather was fine or not, and now West Indian Aerial Express pilots regularly experienced the jolt of flying into tropical rainstorms: "Like a solid curtain of water joining heaven and earth," was the way Rowe described one of them. In such rainstorms single-engined aircraft were more or less doomed. The engine would simply stop. The pilot would begin to glide down through rain toward terrain he could not see but knew to be either mountain or jungle. Multiengined planes flew a bit longer because, usually, the engines cut out only one at a time. Sometimes pilots would fly right through the rainstorm and out the other side in a silent glide, whereupon the engine or engines might or might not start up again.

These same tropical rains soaked landing fields to such softness that every takeoff became perilous. As the plane gathered speed, one wheel after another would sink into soft spots, and the machine would attempt to nose over. Meanwhile the wheels threw up mud and stones, which the propeller fired like bullets back toward the cockpit.

For seven months West Indian Aerial Express planes were flown more or less regularly in both directions between Santiago de Cuba and San Juan, Puerto Rico, usually at the rate of one scheduled flight a week. Often it took a week to get to the end of the line and turn around. If all went well and the round trip was completed in six days, then barnstorming rides were sold to the public on the seventh day.

The company had a sales agent in each town but no airport or terminal building or hangar facility of any kind. Its planes flew without radio, and most of the time the company was too broke even to send arrival, departure and weather information along the line by telegram. The San Juan baseball field, the principal airport and base of operations, was only slightly superior to similar fields in Santiago, in Santo Domingo and in Haiti. At other scheduled stops the pilots used whatever flat pastureland they could find.

The company had franchises for the carriage of passengers, mail and express on all three islands, except that no mail could be carried outward-bound from San Juan; this was U.S. mail and therefore controlled by U.S. Post Office authorities. For its services the company received $500 a month from the Dominican government and about $200 a month from Haiti. Of course, expenses were low, too, rent on the baseball field in San Juan coming to $10 per month.

The day came when West Indian Aerial Express found its credit for gasoline shut off. This misfortune was followed immediately by another: between Haiti and Santiago one of the trimotor's engines blew a cylinder and its propeller quit turning. Rowe was the pilot, and Dunten was with him. The plane staggered on as far as Santiago, the end of the line, where it was turned around, and the two men sold enough tickets to buy enough gasoline to take off with a load of passengers on two engines. They were trying to get back to Puerto Rico, where they had a spare engine waiting. At Port-au-Prince they talked an oil-company agent into loaning them enough gasoline to reach the Dominican Republic. Once there, they again begged for gas—enough to reach San Juan. They had made it home, a flight of roughly a thousand miles, more than ten hours in the air—all on two engines, and usually with seven or eight paying passengers aboard, staring out at the dead prop.

On March 8, 1928, the Foreign Air Mail Act became law. This permitted the Post Office to accept bids and award contracts for the carrying of international mail. Rowe, Dunten and their colleagues began to hope that if they could just hold on a few months longer, if they could just attract a bit more financing, then they could reasonably hope to win a U.S.

airmail contract, and to build their airline into a substantial moneymaker.

Foreign Air Mail Route No. 6 was advertised on May 31. It was to run eastward along the spine of Cuba across Haiti and the Dominican Republic to Puerto Rico—precisely their route.

Dunten went to New York to raise money. Only American-controlled companies could submit U.S. airmail bids and Dunten's stockholders were principally Latins. To get his bid in on time he had to raise American capital fast. On June 4 he made a proposal to Trippe, for he was trying to sell shares. It was somewhat akin to walking into the cave with the bear. Trippe offered to buy the whole company, but meant to put up no money at all. He would pay Dunten and the other West Indian shareholders with 7,000 shares of common stock in the Aviation Corporation holding company. A single share in the holding company was said to be worth $15. Trippe was offering Dunten not cash but paper having a book value of $105,000.

Dunten pointed out to Trippe that if he could in fact raise capital, and if his bid for the route was accepted by the Post Office, his company would be worth a good deal more than Trippe was offering. And if he didn't get the route, responded Trippe, it would be worth less.

On June 25, Trippe put his offer in writing. He gave Dunten three days to consider, concluding: "It is understood that this offer, unless accepted, expires at noon on Thursday, June 28, 1928."

In the next few days Dunten managed to raise $35,000 from American investors, with promises for three times that much if West Indian was awarded the airmail contract. The company's bid was thereupon submitted to the Post Office, $2 per mile, the maximum bid allowed by law, and the same bid that Trippe had just entered on behalf of Pan American. West Indian's major argument was that this was their route; they had now been flying it for seven months, they knew it intimately.

Slightly more than two weeks elapsed before the Post Office announced its decision. Dunten and his group appear merely to have waited this time out. Trippe, on the other hand, made contact with those men in Washington who counted in such matters. During the past three years he had managed to sell himself to them as the dominant young man in commercial aviation—the man, young as he was, with the answers. He had spent hours explaining aviation to them. There was something solid about young Trippe that older men responded to. Trippe was a businessman. His arguments were always direct, rather blunt—and solid.

Moreover, often in New York and at least once in Washington he was accompanied by Charles Lindbergh, the most famous young man in the world. Lindbergh that year was everybody's hero; his name opened every door, gave weight to every proposition. Even bureaucrats were in awe of him. Following his 1927 flight to Paris, Lindbergh had received hundreds of job offers. This was public knowledge. He could name his own terms.

But there he sat beside Trippe, nodding agreement to each of Trippe's arguments. Everyone had wanted him; Trippe had got him, and it made Trippe seem even more formidable.

Trippe had first met Lindbergh in 1926 at Teterboro Airfield in New Jersey. Lindbergh was then twenty-four years old and chief pilot for Robertson Aircraft Corp. on the No. 2 U.S. Domestic Air Mail Route. He was worried about aerial navigation, particularly in bad weather and at night. Trippe, managing director of Colonial Air Transport, and not much older, was worried about the same thing. Lindbergh, having landed at Teterboro, came over and introduced himself, and they began to talk about the ground triangular radio navigation equipment that Colonial was trying out. At least this was the way Trippe remembered it. Lindbergh afterwards had no recollection of meeting Trippe that early. They did meet several times the following spring, and at the last of these meetings Trippe arranged to contact Lindbergh on the day he returned from his proposed transatlantic flight.

According to Trippe, he next saw Lindbergh in the predawn of Friday, May 20, 1927. Lindbergh was about to take off on his attempt to reach Paris nonstop, and Trippe was among those who waited at Roosevelt Field, Long Island, to see him do it. Afterwards tens of thousands of people claimed to have been there. The actual number was about five hundred, and Lindbergh afterwards had no recollection that Trippe was among them.

It is possible that Trippe went there intending not only to speak to Lindbergh, but even to make tentative arrangements with him for the future, in case the flight was successful. Trippe's entire career was marked by astonishing foresight. It is possible that he intended to watch every takeoff all the rest of the month, not just Lindbergh's, because whoever might make it to Paris was going to be a valuable acquisition for any airline. It is also possible he simply could not bring himself to accost the preoccupied Lindbergh.

Instead, being a pilot himself, Trippe studied the field and saw that it was muddy. He studied Lindbergh's small plane and saw that it was terribly overloaded, with its 451 gallons of gasoline and 20 gallons of engine oil. He saw that Lindbergh was well down in it, seated in a wicker armchair, with extra fuel tanks built into the plane in front of his face where the windshield should have been. He knew that Lindbergh had a few sandwiches, two canteens of water and some emergency Army rations, but no drugs to keep himself awake, not even coffee. He knew that Lindbergh, at the time of his takeoff, had already been up five and a half hours. Calculating that it would take 35 to 40 hours to reach Paris, Trippe wondered how he would be able to keep himself awake that long.

But the first big danger was the takeoff. Trippe was worried about it. He saw the plane begin to roll, very slowly at first, then a little faster.

There was a gully in the middle of Roosevelt Field, and telephone wires at the end. The plane disappeared into the gully, then rose into the air. It cleared the telephone wires by about twenty feet. Then it was gone, and Trippe and the others went back to the city.

The flight to Paris was as risky a venture as existed in 1927. A number of aviators had already been killed. But the next evening came news that Lindbergh had landed safely at Le Bourget.

A month later Trippe watched the Lindbergh ticker-tape parade from a window of the Union Club. He had left Colonial, and Pan American had not yet entered the picture. He was a few days short of his twenty-eighth birthday, an ex-pilot, ex–airline executive. He was out of work and he had a date with Betty Stettinius that night—one of the last before she was sent abroad—but when he managed to get himself invited to Lindbergh's Commodore Hotel room for a fifteen-minute chat, he broke his date and rushed off to get as close as he could to the new national hero. His motive was business, not celebrity hunting.

Though other men clamored for Lindbergh's attention, Trippe managed to talk to him alone briefly. Lindbergh mentioned that offers were pouring in and he didn't know what to do. It was a cry from the heart, one young pilot to another. Trippe suggested he do nothing for at least a week. He himself had an offer to make, he added, but he had no intention of bargaining with Lindbergh directly, for Lindbergh was not a businessman. Lindbergh should get himself a lawyer. Trippe would not negotiate with Lindbergh except through his lawyer.

This meeting nearly terminated Trippe's engagement. Betty Stettinius, having been stood up, was at first in tears and then was furious. "Obviously, there are people you care about more than you do me," she told him when he made his belated appearance.

Trippe and Lindbergh met again about a week later in an apartment on 57th Street with Lindbergh's lawyer. They chatted casually for a few minutes, after which Trippe asked Lindbergh to leave the room.

"What's it all about?" the lawyer asked.

Trippe wanted Lindbergh associated with his new airline, which he expected would be formed by the end of the summer. It would be an international airline. It would go to the Caribbean first, then to South America and eventually around the world. He wanted Lindbergh associated with this airline in some technical capacity or other. Trippe was extremely persuasive, and an agreement in principle was hammered out that night, even though his airline did not yet exist and his prospects were far from sure.

It was understood that Lindbergh would fly off on his goodwill tour through all forty-eight states, as planned. After that he would swing down through Central America on a second goodwill tour, this one backed by the State Department. By the time he came back, Trippe's airline should be better defined. Details could be worked out then.

Now it was a year later. As Foreign Air Mail Route No. 6 came up for bids, Trippe in Washington talked quietly to all the men of influence he could reach, explaining—once again—how solidly organized his company was, how solidly financed, how solid the men were who sat on his board of directors. The company's technical adviser was Charles A. Lindbergh; probably it would be Lindbergh himself at the controls of the first plane—should Pan American win the contract—to fly over the new route. This would make headlines; the Post Office's judgment in having chosen Pan American would be applauded; and public confidence in the Post Office would rise to a new high.

Perhaps West Indian Aerial Express could do the job, too, Trippe conceded—if the Post Office wanted to take the gamble. Basil Rowe, Trippe's counterpart in West Indian Aerial Express, was a fine pilot, though no Lindbergh, of course. In addition, Trippe wondered if any one man could run an airline and also fly the planes. Rowe could be in the air or a thousand miles away when some problem arose, and then the problem couldn't be solved until the fellow got back to his desk. And if the U.S. mail was involved, that would make his absence really serious. West Indian had a lot of foreigners involved, too—maybe they could be trusted, maybe not. This last thought was getting very close to what would be—now and for a long time to come—Trippe's principal argument when trying to win new routes.

It was not his way, in conversations with officials, to slander his opposition. He didn't have to, or want to. It went against the grain both of his personality and of the role he had determined to play—he was a gentleman. In any case, his principal argument was something else entirely, and it was the most powerful possible one. "Let's do what's best for the country," he urged. "Whether Pan American gets the route, or some other company gets the route, is not what's important. What's important is that the country open service on the route before foreigners have a chance to get in there and take over. Let's get some company in there before it's too late."

In 1928—and indeed until well after World War II—patriotic sentiments, even patriotic platitudes, carried great weight. The person uttering them was not scorned but believed. The Washington bureaucrats considered Trippe sincere. They believed him. The route did seem vital to national interests, and if this was true, then it had best be awarded to someone the country could count on: Juan T. Trippe.

On July 14, 1928, it was announced that FAM No. 6 had been won by Pan American, and the Post Office revealed its reasons. Since both bids had been the same, Pan American had been selected over West Indian because it had already demonstrated on the Key West–Havana route that it could perform.

Dunten and his colleagues promptly protested the unfairness of the decision. Their company had been operating the route for seven months, whereas no Pan American plane had ever flown it. But their protest was ignored. Three weeks later they agreed to sell out to the Aviation Corporation of the Americas. "It was evident enough to me that someday a profitable airline would be operating between these islands," wrote Rowe later. "But I simply could not make anyone else see it. The men financing the corporation were unwilling to put any more money into it." Trippe, buying out West Indian Aerial Express, Inc., was still unwilling to pay cash; he would hand over stock certificates only. And he was no longer willing to pay 7,000 shares, as he had been two months earlier. This time he offered 5,008 shares—book value $75,120. This was roughly what the planes, spare engines and other gear belonging to West Indian were worth, according to an inventory prepared by Dunten. To this inventory Dunten, trying to raise the price, had attached a list of intangible assets: the company's leases on the few available landing fields; its general office in San Juan ("well known to the public by reason of the large amount of publicity we have put out," according to Dunten); its exemptions from Dominican Republic customs duty on planes and parts; its government connections; its goodwill.

"Intangible assets" Trippe declined to buy. His offer remained stuck at 5,008 shares. At length West Indian took it.

The line was kept open, but most of the passengers now were Trippe's men, principally Pink Whiskers and a financial expert named J. H. Johnston. It was their job to figure out what was there, and to advise Trippe in New York of what his future plans should be.

When the reports came in, Trippe made his decisions. Certain planes were sold. Certain "airports" were abandoned. The Pan American logo was overpainted onto what was left, and West Indian Aerial Express disappeared. Rowe, unlike some whom Trippe would best in the future, was neither a vindictive nor an introspective man. Instead of worrying about what might have been, he became a Pan American pilot, and remained one for most of three decades. Dunten could do no better with Trippe than to stay on as operations manager right where he was. Five years later, in a mood of black despair, he killed himself.

The complete FAM Route No. 6, which Trippe had just won, included much more than West Indian's terrain; it continued down the chain of islands to Trinidad, off the South American coast—1,930 miles in all. That same day Trippe had also won FAM Route No. 5, which extended down through seven Central American countries to the Canal Zone, about 2,074 miles in all. As soon as Pan American could open service on these routes, as soon as it could begin carrying eight hundred pounds of mail twice a week on both routes—on that day it would begin earning $2 per mile, according to the contracts. Trippe was able to do the arithmetic quickly enough, and so was everyone on Wall Street. Pan American would receive from the Post Office Department about $2.5 million a year—and the contracts were of ten years' duration, an important detail that Trippe, through Kelly, had managed to get written into the Foreign Air Mail Act.

Of course, neither route was open yet, and there were obstacles along both of them, but Wall Street was agog anyway. Two more of these Latin American mail contracts would be advertised for bids in 1929. It seemed clear now that Trippe would win both of them. This would bring him another $2.5 million in mail revenue—$5 million a year in all, beginning a few months hence. Pan American's mail revenue for 1928 would work out to only $160,000. But there would be $50 million coming in for mail alone over the next ten years just on these first routes.

Very soon Aviation Corporation of the Americas would prepare to offer new stock. Within months it would have $6 million in capital, and the $15 stock shares would be selling for $50, then $70, then finally, just before the stock market crash, for over $89, and Juan Trippe, who had taken most of his salary in stock, and who at one point owned 25 percent of the company, would become a multimillionaire.

Trippe and Betty Stettinius had at last set a wedding date. "Steer clear of that guy, he's a nut," Betty had heard repeatedly during the more than three years of their courtship. But there seemed no arguing with the future of Pan American now.

The wedding was one of the social events of the season. It took place at the bride's home at Locust Valley in a garden overlooking Long Island Sound, and it was attended by numerous financiers, socialites and other celebrities, including Junius Morgan of the Morgan Bank, the John W. Davises, the Russell Leffingwells, the William Ewings and even General "Black Jack" Pershing.

The bride and groom spent two days in the Catskills. There was no wedding trip, no honeymoon worth the name. Trippe was too busy. They would take their wedding trip in four months' time in Berlin, said the bridegroom to the bride, for a major air show would take place there, and in addition to a honeymoon he would be able to get a lot of business done that would profoundly affect the future of Pan American Airways.

With this promise Betty Stettinius Trippe, aged twenty-four, was forced to be content.

Trippe had decided to push south along three major trunk lines: (1) down the Caribbean islands along FAM No. 6, (2) from Cuba to Yucatán to Panama along FAM No. 5, and (3) from Brownsville, Texas, down through Mexico City to the Canal Zone along what he hoped would be FAM No. 8. In addition, he was planning a route from Miami to Nassau and two lines in South America itself—one down the west coast to Santiago, Chile, and the second down the east coast to Buenos Aires. A great many sovereign nations owned the airspace along these various routes;

landing and customs concessions would have to be procured. In some places airlines of one kind or another already existed, and these would surely attempt to block Pan American.

One by one each obstacle, beginning with each existing airline, had to be removed.

In Mexico there was an obstacle called Compañía Mexicana de Aviación. It had been founded in 1924 by four Americans, George L. Rihl, W. L. Mallory, Archie Piper and C. V. Schlaet, and it served principally the oil-rich Gulf coast near Tampico. Bandits infested the region, drawn by the oil payrolls. Oil workers were paid in gold dollars, and Compañía Mexicana's initial business was flying sacks of gold to outlying camps over the frustrated bandidos' heads.

The company's financial statements for 1925 showed expenses of $45,000 and income of only $10,000. The entire "fleet" of aircraft was valued at $5,000.

Rihl, having decided to expand his business into aerial mapping, needed both cameras and additional financing, so he went to New York and sold a 20 percent share to aerial-camera magnate Sherman Fairchild. At the same time he committed himself to purchase 31 percent of the stock, giving himself and Fairchild absolute control. However, according to Mexican law, the company remained a Mexican airline. This was important because only a Mexican airline could fly to, through or over the Republic of Mexico.

Trippe's negotiations for Mexicana had begun early in 1928; they were concluded January 16, 1929, and Rihl himself came into the Pan American organization as a vice president.

When the Post Office Department opened seven sealed bids for FAM No. 8 (Brownsville to Mexico to the Canal Zone), it was seen that Pan American had bid the legal maximum, $2 per mile for 800 pounds of mail. All six other bids were lower; nonetheless, none of these companies could be seriously considered for the route, for none could legally operate in Mexico. The only bidder who could was Pan American, owner of Compañía Mexicana.

In Peru an airline operated that was called Huff-Daland Dusters. Trippe bought it and renamed it Peruvian Airways. He organized another company in Santiago and named it Chilean Airways. In Colombia, SCADTA (the Colombo-German Aerial Transport Company) controlled all traffic rights. Founded in 1919, it had been run since 1922 by the Austrian aristocrat Dr. Peter Paul von Bauer. Trippe bought out Von Bauer for $1.1 million. The shares Von Bauer handed over were bearer certificates with no name on them. For political reasons the transaction was kept secret in Colombia. Von Bauer agreed to vote the shares he no longer owned at future SCADTA board meetings in whatever manner Trippe and/or Pan American stipulated. This secret deal would cause multiple problems later, but for the moment all was well.

There were other obstacles to Trippe's conquest of Latin America, and they would have to be dealt with presently. First it was necessary to consolidate some of the gains. FAM No. 5, Miami to Panama, was ready to be opened; Trippe assigned Lindbergh to be the pilot and ordered the hero to take off at dawn on February 4, 1929, on the first leg of the three-day, 2,000-mile flight.

A formal contract between Lindbergh and Pan American had been signed. Lindbergh would serve for four years as technical adviser to the airline. He would be paid a salary of $10,000 per year, plus options on 10,000 shares of Pan Am stock at $15 per share and on 30,000 additional shares at $30 per share—these options to remain open until June 30, 1933, six months past the end of the contract. Since Pan Am stock had already begun its meteoric rise, his options figured to make Lindbergh rich.

It was clear from the start that Trippe would get his money's worth. Two days before he was to open FAM No. 5, Lindbergh and his plane, a twin-engined Sikorsky S-38 amphibian, were at Miami Airport—and so were 50,000 people, all anxious to get close to him. Their cars jammed roads for a mile in all directions. The hero wore a dark suit and carried a linen aviator's helmet rolled up in his hand. Every time he stepped out of the hangar or out of the plane, the crowds surged forward. His four police bodyguards were barely able to keep people off him.

He made seven takeoffs and seven landings, each time with parties of distinguished Miamians aboard. This constituted more than enough drama to mesmerize the crowd, and it resulted in front-page headlines all over the country the next morning. Trippe was there. Once he was photographed standing with Lindbergh in front of the plane's whirling propeller blades. Otherwise press and public took little notice of him.

On February 4 Lindbergh was at Miami Airport at 5:15 A.M., and he ate a quick breakfast while standing in the hangar supervising the loading of the mailbags onto the plane. Although it was still dark, a crowd began to gather, and before long a thousand people stood watching, many of them in evening clothes. When the plane was moved out of the hangar into the open, the people surged toward it, but Lindbergh held up his hand and they fell back.

Takeoff was at 6:08 A.M. Three days later Lindbergh was in Cristobal, having produced crowds and headlines at every stop en route. The mail was delivered. FAM No. 5 was open.

From Cristobal, taking his job as technical adviser seriously, Lindbergh sent a telegram to Trippe in New York. He recommended multi-engined amphibious planes on the Miami–Honduras portion of the run, and trimotor landplanes the rest of the way south. Three amphibians and four trimotors would be required to service the route. The telegram, which was a long one, advised Trippe where airfields should be constructed, where radio equipment should be set up, and it even told where possible emergency fields were located.

Nine days and four thousand miles later Lindbergh arrived back in Miami, touching down early in the morning after the short final hop from Havana. Despite the hour, three thousand people had collected to watch what was—to Lindbergh—a routine landing.

Trippe in New York was busy with still another obstacle to his plans. From Colombia south along the west coast of South America, he had men working to secure the concessions Pan American needed, but these were being accorded either slowly or not at all. He was being blocked by W. R. Grace & Co., the giant conglomerate. Grace himself had roomed with Trippe's father in college, but this did not help. The company saw no reason why Pan American should be allowed to enter its domain at all, much less move mail and passengers faster than its ships did. The Grace Co. was a formidable opponent in 1929, for it dominated a substantial portion of all South American trade. It owned piers, warehouses, real estate and, most of all, ships. Its investments controlled South American banks and stock exchanges. Local politicians were in its debt.

It could not start a viable airline on its own, for Trippe controlled the bottleneck at Panama and landing rights in various countries, and more important, had already secured most of the applicable U.S. airmail contracts.

Trippe had understood at once that Pan American was still too weak to contest such power in South America. The Grace Co. could block him for too long a time, and he was in a hurry to take over all of South America before some other airline formed—he had heard of one being organized even now—that could compete against him.

And so he proposed a joint company, to be called Pan American–Grace Airways. Capitalization would be $1 million. The stock would be split fifty-fifty.

Grace men knew nothing about aviation, and would leave him alone, Trippe believed. Pan American–Grace would have no president, only a managing director, who was to be John McGregor, a Pan American man Trippe thought he could control. The new company, which came to be called Panagra, was incorporated on February 21, 1929, and on March 2, 1929, it duly won FAM No. 9, Panama to Chile, with provision to cross the Andes to Buenos Aires and Montevideo. At a time when no domestic airline had yet managed to span the United States, Trippe was now ready to push his planes out along ten thousand miles of routes. The Caribbean was his. He had only to work his way down the east coast of South America to encircle an entire continent, and this would be easy.

Or, at least, so he thought.

11

NYRBA

In the spring of 1929 a Navy flying-boat pilot named William Grooch went to New York to apply for a job as a Pan American pilot. He was received by chief engineer Andre Priester, whom he later described as "a small man, with eyes that appeared never to smile." Priester had the habit of contemplating a person or persons across the desk in absolute silence. The silence lasted. It was unnerving. Invariably people who did not know Priester sought to fill it with inane comments, to which Priester did not reply.

For several minutes Grooch endured Priester's silence. Suddenly Priester barked, "Vat iss your eggspeerience?"

Grooch, who had been a naval aviator for twelve years, replied that his questionnaire and references were in Priester's files. But the little Dutchman shook his head: "I vant you should talk to me."

Half an hour later Priester proposed a job as maintenance engineer, but Grooch declined, because he wanted to go on flying.

Priester shrugged. "Vell, dat iss all ve have yust now."

So Grooch went across the street to a new airline known as NYRBA —the New York, Rio, Buenos Aires Line. Its intentions were very big, and it was so new that its offices were nearly bare of furniture. There were not even partitions between the offices. Grooch was a cautious man, and though offered a job as operations manager and pilot there, he wanted to know who the men running NYRBA were. Among the names given to him he particularly recognized two: Dick Bevier and John Montgomery. He used to fly with Bevier at Rockaway Beach and Montgomery he remembered as a little cotton planter from Georgia in his class at Boston Tech. In the late twenties pilots still constituted a small select fraternity. Most of them knew each other.

What did surprise Grooch was to learn that the competition between NYRBA and Pan American, which was about to get under way, was something of a grudge fight. As Grooch understood it, wrongly, Bevier and Montgomery, who had started Pan American, had got kicked out by Wall Street interests.

The president of NYRBA, Grooch was told, was Ralph O'Neill, a muscularly built young man of medium height who had flown Nieuport pursuit planes over the western front during World War I, and had won three Distinguished Service Crosses for shooting down Germans. Now thirty-three, O'Neill was as aggressive, even as belligerent, as always, and grudge fights were fine with him.

In fact, NYRBA was O'Neill's idea. The idea had come to him in South America, for he had spent some time there as chief salesman for the Boeing Airplane Company. His job as salesman had dissolved when he flew his demonstrator Boeing into a mountain in Uruguay, demolishing the machine and nearly himself. Out of a job, he had begun to envisage a 7,800-mile airline extending from Buenos Aires to New York, with himself at the head of it. He would acquire traffic rights to serve some thirty cities in sixteen countries. He would set his airliners down every 250 miles to refuel and pick up passengers, making for a dawn-to-dusk run each day of about 1,000 miles; he would complete one round trip a week.

So he had come to New York to try to raise money, but the rumor spread that he had cracked his head open in his crash in Uruguay and had never got over it. In truth, he was a man who often talked too loud, and he had a quick temper.

At first no investor would back him. Then he found Jim Rand, chairman of Remington Rand, and after that, Bevier and Montgomery. Once he had lined up Reuben Fleet, head of Consolidated Aircraft, NYRBA began to seem a viable project, for Fleet would supply the planes—the same flying boats he regularly built for the Navy. And so NYRBA was incorporated on April 29, 1929. Stock began to be sold—in enormous amounts. NYRBA looked like a good thing, and during the next thirteen months investors poured into it some $6 million.

It was Grooch, the new operations manager, who now began to gather together the needed stable of flying-boat pilots, principally by raiding the Navy for former shipmates. But it was O'Neill himself, though president of the company, who flew south to make the survey flights that would open up the east coast of South America.

The first flight started out from Norfolk Naval Air Station on June 11, 1929. The plane was a Sikorsky S-38, the same type Lindbergh had flown to Panama four months earlier, which Pan American by now was flying regularly on many of its routes. The S-38 was a useful plane, if care was taken not to overload it, and if the weight of people, baggage and mail-bags was properly distributed.

But O'Neill was not always a careful man, and his S-38 was packed to capacity: full tanks, gear and baggage, seven people aboard. Normally during takeoff the S-38 sprayed tons of water back over itself, and the pilots were always blinded until the plane had been rocked up onto the step of the hull, when the spray would subside. But now, bearing a too heavy load, the S-38 plowed deep into the water and a deluge of spray poured back as high as the propellers, reducing the revs and chewing up the leading edges of the blades. After three attempts at takeoff, everyone aboard was soaked to the skin and sloshing around in sea water. With reporters, cameramen and a crowd watching from shore, O'Neill taxied farther out into open water while crew and passengers bailed, and at last the plane gained the air, though not before the props had taken another beating and all hands another drenching.

At Havana some days later, in hot, still air, on water surrounded by mountains, much the same thing occurred. The plane failed to rise to the hull step in two attempts, so O'Neill ordered his copilot to taxi out to the harbor mouth—straight into six-foot waves. There the plane did get airborne, but its props again became pitted and scored, and from then on, all the way south, they had to be filed down smooth before each takeoff. To save weight, O'Neill even ordered his retractable landing gear removed and left behind—the amphibian became permanently a sea-plane only, and he came close to jettisoning his radio, which weighed six hundred pounds (lightweight sets such as Leuteritz had by now installed in all Pan American planes were still not commercially available). O'Neill was still doing most of the flying himself. He was at the controls when the battered S-38 at last reached Rio, and he felt so good that he could not resist power-diving the Copacabana Palace Hotel.

On August 29, 1929, NYRBA opened service between Buenos Aires and Montevideo, and six weeks later its Ford trimotors began crossing the 20,000-foot-high Andes twice a week between Buenos Aires and Santiago. Of course, the Fords would not climb to 20,000 feet, but the pilots had discovered a pass 4,000 feet lower down and they crossed there. They sailed along over the pampas, which was flat between Buenos Aires and Mendoza at the foot of the Andes, and then the mountains rose straight up and the Fords with them, and they crossed snow and ice through the roughest air any of the pilots had ever encountered. It was tough on passengers, but lasted only an hour. The planes carried oxygen cylinders with a tube for each chair. Passengers learned to take a whiff whenever they ran short of breath.

But NYRBA pushed out no farther north that year. O'Neill had made

THE PAN AM SYSTEM—1929

0 — 500 — 1000
Scale in Miles

UNITED STATES

MEXICO

Tampa
Brownsville
GULF OF MEXICO
Havana
Tampico
Mérida La Fé
Mexico City
Tuxpan
Vera Cruz
Carmen
Minatitlán
S. Gerónimo

Miami
Nassau
Camaguey
CUBA
Santiago
Cozumel Isl.
Port-au-Prince
Santo Domingo
San Juan
HAITI

Belize
Tela
Tegucigalpa
Barranquilla
Guatemala City
Managua
San José
Puntarenas
Cristobal
David

CENTRAL AMERICA

COLOMBIA

ECUADOR

PACIFIC OCEAN

Lima
PERU

Curaçao
Cartagena
Maracay
VENEZUELA

Guadeloupe
Martinique
Port of Spain
Georgetown
Paramaribo
Cayenne

GUIANA

ATLANTIC OCEAN

BRAZIL

SOUTH AMERICA

Pará
Maranhão
Natal
Pernambuco
Bahia

BOLIVIA

Victoria

Santos
Rio de Janeiro

——— Routes in Operation, July 1929
- - - Under mail contract and
       in course of organization
········· Routes under survey

CHILE

San Juan
Córdoba
Valparaíso
Santiago
Rosario
Buenos Aires
ARGENTINA

Pôrto Alegre
Rio Grande do Sul
URUGUAY
Montevideo

the astonishing decision to concentrate all of his efforts eight thousand miles from his ultimate destination, New York. He would work his way up stage by stage.

By contrast Panagra rapidly snaked down the length of the west coast of the continent as far as Santiago, and Pan American, with Charles Lindbergh again at the controls, inaugurated airmail service on FAM No. 6, from Puerto Rico as far south as Dutch Guiana—the first time the mail had ever been flown from the United States to the South American mainland. On this gala circus of a journey Lindbergh was accompanied by his new bride, Anne, and also by Betty and Juan Trippe.

Anne, as the flight started out from Florida, was dressed in a blue-silk traveling suit, and Lindbergh at the controls wore a gray business suit. Trippe's suit was a glaring tropical white. The aircraft's cabin was a bower of roses handed up out of the vast crowd during takeoff ceremonies, and they flew all day a thousand feet above the tropical sea, surrounded by the scent of flowers. NYRBA constituted the greatest threat to date both to Pan American and to Trippe personally, but this was not yet clear, and he was not yet worried. On the contrary, he seemed in an ebullient mood during the whole of the three-week, 9,000-mile flight. He was then thirty years old. Anne Lindbergh, newly married and only twenty-three, had the impression of "a great big bumbling bear of a man, very energetic, very vigorous, very young. He seemed younger than he was. He gave a sense of great good nature."

From San Juan south the route had not been flown before, meaning that the great Lindbergh was blazing still another trail through the sky —so people saw it in September 1929—and Trippe had made all necessary arrangements to share Lindbergh's exploit, and Pan Am's, with the world. At the Pan American base at Miami a representative of Doremus & Co. waited behind a typewriter, and after every routine radio telegraph report from the plane in the air he rapped out a new and flowery paragraph. This was mimeographed and distributed to the assembled reporters, who transmitted it at once to their papers. Thus the world learned that Anne Lindbergh was writing letters while aloft, that Betty Trippe was keeping a diary, that Juan Trippe was conducting business by radio with ground stations along the route, that the air in the cabin was delightfully cool, that Lindbergh "handles the plane masterfully." Each tramp steamer, each island that the plane crossed over was described in detail, but a radio silence of about five minutes preceded each landing—the radio aerial trailed behind in the slipstream and had to be reeled in each time—giving the world many anxious moments. Had Lindy made it safely down or not?

This was no easy junket, for the plane was aloft most of each day from dawn to dusk, the air was frequently bumpy, and there was usually nothing to eat on board. Lindbergh was flying the airmail now and a schedule had to be kept; refueling stops, though frequent, were not only short but most often were entirely taken up by dignitaries anxious to make speeches, and by mobs of ordinary people crowding as close as they could get. At every stop more flowers were presented, but rarely did anyone think of offering the hungry aviators food. Most times the flowers had to be left behind to save weight—weight in 1929 was that critical—and Betty Trippe worried constantly that this must seem rude to their hosts.

On the twenty-third the coast of South America came into view. There were occasional clearings in the jungle, straw huts and people looking up. Occasionally a wild beast stood stock-still, staring up at the low-flying plane, and once Lindbergh, having spied a flight of brilliant red birds, brought the plane over as close as he could get and cruised alongside them for some seconds.

Georgetown harbor, a scheduled refueling stop and a mail drop as well, was full of small boats, but according to the Doremus & Co. log, as distributed to the press, "Lindbergh slipped in with his usual grace." Flags flew everywhere. Whistles were tied down going full blast.

The ceremonies were cut somewhat short and the plane took off again, and for once there was food aboard. The Lindberghs and Trippes had a picnic lunch in the air, and Lindbergh delighted Betty Trippe by wiggling his ears and "acting like a kid." They flew on only a few hundred feet above the jungle, and saw birds with wingspreads of four to five feet and great flowering yellow and red trees. The beach in the distance was a lovely color of pink, so Lindbergh flew slightly off course to see what it was. It turned out to be a flock of young flamingos too young or too frightened to take to the air. At Paramaribo, which was, for the moment, the end of Pan American's line, they landed on the river just before sundown. The usual excited crowd waited on shore, and as the Lindberghs and the Trippes stepped onto the pier the cheers grew louder and the native women undid their great turban headdresses, each one a beautiful bandanna, and spread them out on the ground for the Trippes and Lindberghs to walk on—a carpet of bandannas down the pier and all the way across the square to the house where they were to stay.

That night there was a state dinner at Government House. Betty Trippe struggled to make conversation, but Lindbergh gave up, and from then on, wiggled his ears whenever Betty looked in his direction, all the while never cracking a smile, so that Betty could hardly keep from laughing. Although Paramaribo was then little more than a clearing in the jungle, there was a parade through the streets in flag- and flower-decorated cars. Lindbergh refused to ride in the lead car, which struck Betty Trippe as a bit childish, and when Trippe took his place, he was taken by most of the crowd for Lindbergh. Soldiers carried torches through the streets, and a brass band played a new composition called the "Lindbergh March."

In the morning everyone slept late except Trippe, who strode off to meet with the governor; he was in conference with Post Office officials most of the rest of the day.

The flight continued toward Venezuela. Lindbergh had with him an aerial camera and was anxious to take pictures. But this was difficult from the S-38 because of its rather odd construction. The fuselage of the plane was shaped like a shoe with the pilot at the top of the laces, and the passengers behind that. The "shoe," and the two engines as well, hung from the high straight wing by a series of struts; the tail surfaces rode on outriggers trailing behind the wing. From the pilot's compartment, visibility was good only straight ahead. In every other direction it was interrupted by struts, wings, engines and pontoons.

Unable to get the camera angles he wanted from the pilot's cockpit, Lindbergh crawled forward through the "shoe," opened a hatch at mid-instep and stood up in the slipstream with his clothes almost blowing off him. The plane was cruising at 1,500 feet at around 110 miles an hour. Apparently, this angle didn't suit Lindbergh either. To everyone's horror he stepped up out of the hatch and began to crawl forward over the toes of the "shoe" toward the forward compartment, where the anchor was stowed. He was not wearing a parachute. Balanced on hands and knees on top of the cowling in the wind, he at last stepped down into this compartment and shot his pictures. He then began to crawl back the way he had come, with the wind at his back threatening to blow him off. His new bride watched him crawl back inside and slip behind the controls again, but she said nothing, and a little later he set the plane down in Maracay.

There they were met by Preston Buford McGoodwin, who had been for seven years the American minister—then the equivalent of ambassador—to Venezuela; he was now Trippe's agent working to obtain political concessions so that Pan Am flights might land there regularly. McGoodwin brought the aviators to the presidential palace, where they were received by General Juan Vicente Gómez, the reigning dictator. In full view of the Trippes, of Anne and of the assembled dignitaries, the tiny dictator pulled Lindbergh down and kissed him on both cheeks. Said Trippe later, "It shocked Lindbergh something terrible."

The Maracay Airport was a short and bumpy dirt strip. Lindbergh, as was his habit before each takeoff, walked its entire length. There had been heavy rains the night before and it was deep with mud, and as the plane taxied toward takeoff it sank to its hubs. It had to be pulled out by a car. Finally Lindbergh got it airborne, and after setting his course for Curaçao, he took off his socks and hung them to dry on the strut outside the window. After a moment or two they blew away and everybody laughed. Two hours later came an official reception in Curaçao—crowds, massed bands and dignitaries—starring Lindbergh wearing no socks.

By 5:15 P.M. that day, low on fuel, Lindbergh was circling over Barranquilla, Colombia. An enormous crowd swarmed over the field, and it was impossible to land. A note was dropped—then several more—urging the police to clear the field. For forty-five minutes the plane circled. A final note was dropped: fuel was almost gone. The plane was circling only a few hundred feet above the crowd when suddenly both engines stopped turning. There was no sound now inside the plane. Then Lindbergh remarked calmly, "It's all right, I noted a lagoon earlier."

The lagoon was about two miles away. Lindbergh put the wide-winged amphibian into a shallow glide. The lagoon, as it came into view, was not straight. There was a sharp bend in the middle. In total silence Lindbergh glided toward the water. He just made it, and he got through the bend also, and the plane surged to a stop and began to rock gently. Inside the plane everyone laughed with relief. Then they sat again in silence in the gathering darkness.

Finally two dugout canoes approached the amphibian. In them were Indians—two grown men wearing G-strings, and many naked children. All the children were transferred to one of the canoes. The naked men suggested by signs that the passengers now climb down into the other.

"But these men have nothing on," said Trippe. "What about the girls?" The girls had just survived a traumatic forced landing but the straitlaced Trippe was worrying about their modesty.

Lindbergh had a revolver, which he now carried in his hand. Trippe got the snakebite antitoxin from the emergency supplies, and they clambered down into the dugout canoes. Moving through the darkness, Lindbergh and Trippe began to tease the two young women about being abducted by Indians, about imaginary alligators waiting to devour them.

They were paddled to the far end of the lagoon, where they flagged down a car. They drove out over a muddy trail to a road and then to the gates of the city, where a mad, cheering crowd waited under an illuminated sign whose lights read: WELCOME LINDY. The reception seemed endless—speeches, bouquets, the key to the city, warm champagne, perspiring officials making long speeches in fast Spanish. Another dinner and reception followed later, and it was past midnight before anybody got to bed.

With Lindbergh still behind the controls (Trippe never took them once the whole time), the flight continued up through Central America, setting down in Panama, Nicaragua, San Salvador, Guatemala City, Belize, Cozumel. In some of these places they were met by the new Pan American agent on the scene, and in all of them there were official receptions involving governors, presidents and dictators. These festivities were laid on for Lindbergh, not for Trippe or Pan American, but Lindbergh insisted that Trippe, as president of the company, belonged in the forefront rather than himself. There were many good-natured disputes about who should enter a car or room first, and in Panama Lindbergh stuck a pin through the eraser of a pencil and with this he jabbed Trippe in the behind at every doorway, making Trippe jump forward ahead of him. Lindbergh seems to have brought out a streak of playfulness even in Trippe, who got his own pin and eraser, and the battle was on. This playfulness continued in Nicaragua, where the couples were assigned connecting rooms, a big room for the Lindberghs, a small one for the Trippes. Lindbergh insisted that the Trippes take the big room. The Trippes refused. A pillow fight began between the two men, and they bashed each other until everyone was giggling hysterically. Finally the Trippes got the big room—because Lindbergh had won the pillow fight, according to Anne; because Lindbergh had begun to undress in the small room, according to Betty Trippe. They were two boys, Anne Lindbergh thought, having fun.

At each stop also, Trippe met with public officials, particularly from the Post Office. After spending all day in the air, he would sometimes stay up with these men half the night while his wife and his companions slept. He seemed to them a person of great physical strength. He never got tired.

"The Trippes have been such fun, and wear so well," Anne Lindbergh wrote at the time. "I think they're remarkable. The more I see of them, the more I think it. They both have such a wonderful sense of humor and are such a reassuring comfort in hot moments." But she also thought Juan Trippe somewhat prissy, and not only because after their forced landing he had been so worried about the nudity of their rescuers. She had noted also that although weight most times had been so critical that they could not even bring flowers on board, still Trippe had traveled the whole distance carrying clean sheets for his own and his wife's beds for each night.

Shortly after Trippe's return to New York, the threat from NYRBA began to loom large, for delivery was announced on the first Consolidated Commodore flying boat, the most advanced plane of the day. It had a 100-foot wingspan, was able to carry twenty-four passengers, could cruise at over 100 miles an hour and could fly some 650 miles without putting down to refuel. The Commodore was three times as much airplane as the Sikorsky S-38, Trippe's best, and Trippe not only didn't have any, he knew he couldn't get any. Reuben Fleet, the man who built them, had reserved them all for his own airline, NYRBA. The contest between Pan American and NYRBA had suddenly become unequal. If NYRBA once got those planes into operation all along their route system, Pan American over those same routes would not be able to compete.

O'Neill, staring up from the floor of the Buffalo, N.Y., factory at his first Commodore, was ecstatic. Each pontoon seemed as big as a six-passenger motorboat. The open cockpit, in which the pilots would sit, was high above his head, nestled into the bow. Behind it stretched the passenger cabin, and he climbed up a dozen steps to the hatch to peer inside. The center aisle was thickly carpeted. There were three compartments on each side of the aisle, the pairs of seats facing each other between the structural bulkheads. Gone were the wicker chairs of earlier airlines. These chairs had fabric upholstery, the air world's first.

Later O'Neill sent Grooch to the factory to oversee the completion and testing of the first plane.

When he got there, Grooch, unlike O'Neill, was not ecstatic at what he saw. He particularly didn't like the open cockpit. The factory's chief engineer told him that it was better—in a closed cockpit in the tropics the pilots would smother. What about sun and storms beating down on their heads? responded Grooch. The cockpit could, of course, be closed in, but, said the chief engineer stiffly, this would delay production.

During the next week Grooch submitted a list of changes he wanted made, and the chief engineer complained to O'Neill. O'Neill caught the first train to Buffalo, where he confronted Grooch and in his rough way demanded, "What the devil is going on here?"

For two hours Grooch showed him why the hull should be made stronger, the fittings heavier and the anchoring gear improved. O'Neill overruled him, saying, "We've got to make a showing. If she hangs together till we get to Buenos Aires we can afford to scrap her."

There were innumerable delays. Among them was the fact that the factory stood a mile from the Niagara River, where the Commodore was to be launched. The wingspread being 100 feet, the plane could not be hauled through the streets. It had to be carted to the river in sections and assembled on one of the piers.

Next O'Neill wanted Grooch to rush through tests so that President Hoover's wife could christen the plane in Washington at an elaborate ceremony that O'Neill had already arranged. NYRBA needed the publicity, O'Neill told Grooch, more than it needed any full range of tests.

And so the half-tested Commodore, with a Consolidated test pilot at the controls and Grooch in the copilot's seat, started south, landing for the night off Staten Island, despite heavy seas running there. The rough water lifted the plane and dropped it repeatedly against the concrete ramp, ripping open the hull. Grooch and O'Neill conferred by phone, and O'Neill ordered Grooch to reach Washington the next day no matter what, because the christening could not be put off. O'Neill said, "I don't care what it costs."

All night mechanics tried to hammer the twisted metal plates back into shape, but at dawn a dozen bad splits remained, and Grooch ordered his crew to boil twenty gallons of tar and pour it over the hull from the inside. This was done, and the plane reached Anacostia Naval Air Station, where a crowd of dignitaries, reporters and sight-seers waited for the ceremony to begin. This was O'Neill's big moment, and as Mrs. Hoover arrived he stepped forward to greet her, but secret service men pushed him back into the crowd. He was not allowed near the dais, which Mrs. Hoover now mounted, clinging to the arm of her escort—Juan Trippe. "I was seething in an incandescent fury," O'Neill wrote later. "I had witnessed an unbelievable masquerade that would remain engraved in my memory for the rest of my life." Trippe later denied this, and according to newspaper reports, O'Neill did make a speech during the ceremony.

For the next ten days a crew worked trying to repair the plane's damaged hull, but when tested, it still leaked, and more hot tar was poured in. O'Neill accepted delivery anyway, telling Grooch, "We can't afford to wait."

The plane was promptly jammed with passengers and gear for its trip to South America. The rear of the cabin was piled high with baggage, the plane was 1,000 pounds overloaded, and for five miles, with O'Neill and Grooch at the controls, it raced across the surface of the Anacostia River before picking up enough speed to get airborne. Its next two takeoffs were made into a stiff breeze successfully, but at Miami in a dead calm O'Neill and Grooch ran the bay three times before the Commodore could lift its load off the water.

At Havana O'Neill invited a dozen government officials for a courtesy flight, but twenty-five showed up. They all crowded on board. Grooch took them over the city, then ran into squalls. Havana harbor was obscured by heavy rain and filled with boats. In terrible visibility Grooch set the Commodore down just outside the harbor in the swells booming against Morro Castle. The overloaded plane smashed into the seas and its bottom sprang open. With water pouring in, Grooch drove it up onto the beach. The passengers were up to their knees in water screaming.

As soon as he got into dry clothes Grooch went to O'Neill's room. O'Neill was furious. He said, "We've had nothing but trouble with that ship since it left the factory."

It was their own fault, Grooch pointed out. "No ship with a patched bottom could stand the beating we've given this one. We've got to cut out the barnstorming and get the line into operation."

"Are you telling me how to run this show?" O'Neill demanded.

But a few minutes later, being a man of quick rages and equally quick reconciliations, O'Neill was buying Grooch a drink at the bar.

Later Grooch flew to South America alone and reported to the NYRBA office in Buenos Aires. The entire group of NYRBA employees, he discovered, had been waiting around for weeks for instructions. There was nothing to do and no one in charge. He was anxious to start operations, but a cable from O'Neill ordered him to defer everything until O'Neill himself arrived.

Nonetheless, as 1929 ended, O'Neill had four Sikorskys, one Commodore and three Fords working NYRBA's southern division; the Buenos Aires–Montevideo service was in full operation, and so was the Buenos Aires–Santiago run; the Buenos Aires–Rio section was about to open. However, there were problems. Although mail contracts had been signed with the Brazilian and Argentine governments, the U.S. Post Office had not yet even advertised for bids on the same routes, and a political scandal erupted that helped to delay indefinitely the award of any FAM contract to NYRBA. O'Neill, according to the U.S. press, had maligned Postmaster General Walter Brown to Brazilian government officials by charging that Brown had sold out to Trippe and Pan American.

O'Neill now spent all his time getting friendly government officials to sign statements assuring his board of directors, Postmaster General Brown and the world that he had never made any such statement, and he sent a cable to Jim Rand, his most important backer, which read in part: "Believe libel planted by Bill Summer, Coyote undercover representative here." Coyote was NYRBA code for Pan American. Summer had seemed to O'Neill to be a U.S. government employee. It was clear enough to most others that he worked for Pan American.

The second Commodore was delivered. Again O'Neill decided to help fly it south himself. At takeoff from Fortaleza, Brazil, the waves outside the harbor were so brutal that the right engine tore loose from its mount and the whirling prop carved through the cabin like a buzz saw.

That laid up Commodore No. 2 for a month. Commodore No. 3 reached Dutch Guiana, where a fuel line on the port side burst, causing a fire that destroyed the wing. Within two days a big new wing was on a steamer headed south, but the plane would be out of service till it got there.

At last all was ready for the first Buenos Aires–New York mail run. This was Argentine mail; O'Neill had no contract with the U.S. Post Office and no authority to carry even Argentine mail over U.S. territory. Takeoff was in the predawn darkness of February 19, 1930, O'Neill and L. C. Sullivan at the controls, and the flight very nearly ended at Pôrto Alegre, where Sullivan, after refueling, managed to nick a harbor buoy on takeoff, splitting open the hull and rupturing an oil line. Hours were lost before O'Neill and the mail, having transferred to an S-38 flown in by Grooch, continued north. The overnight stop was to be Santos. It was 9:00 P.M., pitch-dark and raining hard as Grooch prepared to land there. He intended to land in the bay because there were too many coffee steamers in the river, and he glided down across the city heading for a curved row of lights that marked the shore. But as he settled into the blackness at sixty miles an hour, the plane struck the face of an advancing wave and bounced high into the air. O'Neill grabbed for the controls screaming, "You're landing in the city, you've just hit a rooftop."

Grooch struck O'Neill's hand from the wheel and eased the plane down, banging it into a dozen similar shocks until it had lost enough speed to stay on the water. As he attempted to turn shoreward a wave crashed over the plane. According to Grooch, O'Neill kicked out the cockpit window on his side, thinking the plane had capsized. According to O'Neill, it was the impact that popped the window open. There were two passengers, who were frantic by this time. One drew a gun, shouting something in Portuguese. The flight mechanic rapped him over the head with a bottle.

After nearly capsizing several times, Grooch got the plane headed for shore and they shot forward on a comber, with O'Neill frantically cranking the wheels down so that when they hit the beach they would ride forward on the wheels. They did taxi out of the surf in this fashion, and the passengers jumped from the rear hatch and ran off into the darkness. O'Neill leaned over and vomited, then crawled into a taxi and departed for a hotel. Both lower wings were ruined, Grooch saw, and the wing-tip floats were crushed. Inside the cabin the mailbags were floating in water a foot deep. Grooch took the bags to the hotel, and spread the mail out to dry.

Pulling himself together, O'Neill began telephoning up and down the line, ordering that the nearest Sikorsky, which was in Rio, be flown to Santos to pick him up, and that a Commodore be held for him in reserve —clearly, he was willing to disrupt his entire line for this one big publicity flight. However, the Sikorsky in Rio could not take off. It was surrounded by harbor police because of an injunction obtained by a local company against NYRBA. There was still another NYRBA Sikorsky at Bahia. O'Neill ordered it to fly to Rio, but to land on the other side of the harbor so as to avoid the police. He then rented a limousine, drove all night to Rio with the mail, and boarded this second plane. It took off for Vitória into the dawn light with the harbor police launch speeding toward it.

At Vitória more mail was taken aboard, and the S-38 continued to Bahia, where, after refueling, the pilot, whose name was Clarence Woods, managed to steer it into the seawall on takeoff, wrecking it. Or, at least, O'Neill always blamed Woods afterwards. There were an astonishing number of mishaps on this flight, and in each case O'Neill found someone else to blame. Pilots, planes and terrain kept changing. They were variables. There were only two constants: the mailbags and O'Neill.

Climbing from the wreckage, O'Neill ordered in still another plane, and when it came he proceeded north directly over the jungle on a compass course, cutting off the coastal bulge and saving two and a half hours at the risk all day of setting the mail down in the trees. Eventually O'Neill did reach Miami in only six days' elapsed time, arriving February 25. But he never reached New York. At Miami the mail was taken away from him by U.S. postal authorities.

Along the route he had been greeted by newly hired executives sent down by his board of directors behind his back; he fired them all. At each stop he had been greeted also with rumors that he was through as president of NYRBA. At Miami, where two dozen landplane pilots had been assembled without his knowledge, O'Neill proved once and for all who the president of NYRBA was. According to the rumor that circulated, O'Neill lined up the pilots in the hall of the hotel and walked along poking each in the chest, saying "You're fired, you son of a bitch." He himself claimed that he only spoke quietly to each man in turn, explaining that only flying-boat pilots were needed by NYRBA, and that therefore their employ was necessarily terminated.

When he reached New York, O'Neill learned that Jim Rand had lost a fortune in the stock market crash, and as a result the Bevier faction had begun making all decisions with regard to NYRBA, including hiring the landplane pilots. O'Neill promptly presented Rand with an ultimatum: either O'Neill ran the airline or Bevier did.

Later O'Neill met with Bevier. "I haven't time to argue with you about a subject you know goddamn little about," O'Neill told him. "Just get this: if ever again you stick your dirty spoon in anything to do with our operation I'll ask the board to request your resignation based on the harm you've done already."

Bevier said, according to O'Neill, "Jesus Christ, you're the most arrogant guy I know."

Between Florida and Argentina regular eight-day service began. The southbound plane left Miami the same day that the northbound plane left Buenos Aires. The planes flew only by daylight, and the pilots turned over their loads to new flight crews at each overnight stop, remaining where they were to pick up the return load five days later.

Week after week NYRBA's mail went through on schedule, and cities along the line became enthusiastic.

12

The Mad Cutthroat Struggle

It was O'Neill's plan to run the airline like a railroad—eight divisions, each covering about 1,000 miles. Each division would have its own shops, planes and personnel. This called for double the amount of personnel and equipment actually needed, and each plane was idle five days a week, which was fine with O'Neill, who liked to point out that now the planes wouldn't wear out as quickly.

Trippe in New York held the opposite theory—that aircraft became obsolete very, very fast; and there was no sense saving them.

O'Neill planned docks and floats in each town, but none existed as yet. Planes arriving at way stations were met by the agent in a small boat or dugout canoe. Transferring passengers to and from planes was always risky. Gasoline in five-gallon tins was passed up to the mechanic on the top wing and poured into the tanks through a chamois-covered funnel. Floating service stations were promised. The few actually under construction would not be ready for months. Meanwhile, engines were beginning to need overhaul, hulls were beginning to develop leaks. Repairs to Commodores had to be made while planes were afloat because there were no facilities except at Buenos Aires for hauling them out of the water. At length mechanics began to cannibalize planes.

Publicly Trippe had given orders to Pan American ground personnel to extend every courtesy to NYRBA: "I asked all our fellows to help so we wouldn't be criticized." But it appears that in South America men working for Trippe sowed whatever trouble they could. For instance, the Argentine Post Office, probably at Pan Am's urging, suddenly ordered

NYRBA to fulfill the terms of its contract to get the mail to the United States in seven days, not eight, as regular schedules called for. In order to comply, O'Neill put the mail aboard 130-mph single-engined Fleetsters for the first leg of the journey. The Fleetsters would overtake the Commodores, which had left the day before, somewhere up the line. This device worked, and the mail got to Miami in seven days, but it was very expensive. Once, when the pursuing plane was delayed by bad weather, it reached Rio a full day behind the Commodore. There Grooch took up the chase. Starting at 4:00 A.M. the next morning, he covered 1,500 miles before landing in the dark and heavy rain at Pernambuco. But the Commodore was still four hundred miles ahead, and Grooch had to keep going. Delayed by bad weather, by freak tides that marooned him on a mudbank and by lengthy refueling stops, Grooch chased the Commodore for two more days. Flying back to Rio afterwards he felt depressed: "It all seemed like a mad, cutthroat struggle."

Confrontations between Pan Am and NYRBA were inevitable. They were not accompanied by fraternal spirit on either side. At first Pan American survey flights down the South American coast were allowed to use NYRBA facilities, but when Pan Am announced a weekly service to Rio, O'Neill warned that there would be no more assistance from NYRBA. Presently a Pan American plane, in trouble, was forced to land at a NYRBA base on a small inland lake at Montenegro, Brazil. There the NYRBA agent in charge trained a rifle on the pilot and ordered him to leave. The plane took off, but being almost out of gas, was forced to land at sea. Pan Am had to send a special plane to the rescue. In press reports this became known as the Battle of Montenegro.

All this time O'Neill's strategy never changed. He was still investing huge sums in route development in Brazil and Argentina, totally ignoring New York, where the money came from, and Washington, where the mail contracts came from. Apparently, all this money was to be recouped when NYRBA received FAM contract No. 10 from the U.S. Post Office Department. Unfortunately, Postmaster General Brown saw little merit to competitive bidding for foreign airmail contracts—so he later testified before Congress—and still less merit in giving NYRBA the Buenos Aires–Dutch Guiana contract when Pan Am already held the Dutch Guiana–Miami contract. NYRBA, as Brown saw it, was merely trying to use airmail pay to enter the peculiar terrain that Pan American and Juan Trippe had already staked out. Whatever the law stated about competitive bidding, Brown had become convinced that the interests of the United States could best be served by a single airline operating abroad. And as far as single airlines went, he was satisfied with Trippe's.

NYRBA had a further disability from the standpoint of the Post Office. It had committed itself to airmail contracts with South American governments at very low rates. For example, its contracts with Argentina and

Uruguay specified approximately $6.50 per pound; by contrast, Panagra's rate in countries on the west coast under FAM No. 9 was $22.50 per pound. Since, according to FAM contract terms, all money paid U.S. airlines for carrying foreign mail went to the U.S. Post Office to offset the U.S. subsidy, NYRBA's contracts with Argentina, Uruguay and the rest were disadvantageous to the U.S. Post Office, which had published a rate structure stipulating the much higher rates that Pan American was ready to charge, and that NYRBA now couldn't charge.

NYRBA was losing money at the rate of more than $400,000 a month. The company had started in 1930 with $662,000 cash on hand, and since then had sold stock for $1.4 million more, but by May 31 its cash balance was down to $16,000. It was virtually bankrupt, and the board met to consider what to do. At this meeting O'Neill made an impassioned speech describing future plans, future profits. The reaction was mixed; one director drawled, "But while the grass is growing the horse is starving." The directors wanted to sell out to Pan Am.

By mid-1930 Trippe was meeting regularly with William P. Mac-Cracken, Jr., the chairman of NYRBA. Together Trippe and MacCracken arranged to meet with Postmaster General Brown in his office, but O'Neill learned of the proposed meeting and intercepted the two men at breakfast at Washington's Mayflower Hotel. The following is O'Neill's account of what next took place.

Trippe was the first to recover his composure. According to O'Neill, he rose, smiled suavely and extended "a moist hand."

O'Neill announced bluntly that he intended to attend the meeting with Brown that morning, and he understood that Trippe would phone Brown in half an hour. "You can come along if it's all right with him," Trippe said.

But when O'Neill looked for Trippe and MacCracken half an hour later, there was no sign of either. They had gone off to see Brown without him. O'Neill concluded that "others" were selling his airline out from under him, and he was right.

Trippe insisted later that he never met O'Neill at all at that stage of the negotiations.

After meeting with Brown, who had absolute discretion in the advertising and granting of airmail contracts, Trippe and MacCracken recorded their findings in a memorandum which both signed. NYRBA at present was unable to return reasonable airmail revenues to the Post Office because of the burdensome contracts it had entered into with South American governments. On the other hand, if the U.S. contract went to Pan American, the NYRBA competition at lower rates would cut the Post Office's northbound mail revenues almost completely. Inasmuch as competition between Pan Am and NYRBA hurt principally the Post Office, Brown would make no advertisement of the east-coast South

American airmail contract until the competitive situation between the two companies had been eliminated. The final question hashed out with Brown, according to the memo, was whether the purchase of NYRBA by Pan Am would violate antitrust statutes. Brown stated that, on the contrary, he regarded some such agreement as mandatory.

Trippe went to Lewis Pierson, one of NYRBA's principal bankers. Trippe, as always, would pay for physical assets only. Intangible assets—goodwill, landing rights and the rest—didn't interest him. He was ready to offer one share of stock in Aviation Corporation of the Americas for 5.2 shares of NYRBA. This would work out to around $2 million—only one-third of the money already invested in NYRBA. That is, NYRBA investors would get paid back thirty-three cents on the dollar. Also, Trippe would pay only 50 percent of this price at closing and the rest after inventory of NYRBA's planes, hangars, gear and bank balance. Since NYRBA was losing money heavily, its value diminished every day. What Trippe's terms amounted to was unconditional surrender. The final details were worked out by Pierson and Trippe, who met on Pierson's yacht on Long Island Sound. Rand is supposed to have remarked that if the sale had been delayed two more weeks, he would have had to practically give the company away.

At the final meeting of the NYRBA board of directors, after a lawyer had read the merger contract, O'Neill asked to be heard. Rising to his feet, he stated, "We are being defeated by a scandalous maneuver of Walter Brown to eliminate competition for his favorite airline. I would like to expose these shenanigans and I believe the newspapers are ready to support us. To demonstrate the rooking we are getting, I would like to bring all our planes to Washington and anchor them on the Potomac. In other words, to display publicly the greatest and most modern fleet of transport airplanes in the world—all being sacrificed to the whims of interest of a shameless bureaucrat. It would smell to high heaven."

This produced vociferous protests. Someone shouted, "Let's wind it up! I call for a vote!"

On August 19, 1930, the company was sold to Pan Am. FAM Route No. 10 was advertised the next day, and Pan Am won it as the only bidder.

Thus perished NYRBA. The merger, said Trippe publicly, was the best thing for the mail, for U.S. aviation and for Pan American. Privately he said, "Those fellows were just damn dumb."

A good many NYRBA men simply switched teams, including John T. Shannon, who was to retire many years later as senior vice president of Operations at Pan Am; Humphrey W. Toomey, manager of the Africa–Orient Division during World War II; A. S. Galbraith, who rose to become vice president of Supply; and William Van Dusen, who had left Doremus to go with NYRBA as director of public relations, and who now returned to Pan Am with the same title.

Most of the pilots were taken on by Pan Am as well, and among them was Grooch, who went to New York to ask for a job even as NYRBA was collapsing. Vice President Rihl hired him and named a salary, and then sent him along to brief Priester about conditions in South America. Priester picked Grooch's brains for some time, then said, "Maybe ve meet again von day."

Grooch assured him that they probably would.

"Vy iss dat?" snapped Priester.

When Grooch explained that he had just been hired by Rihl, Priester's face hardened. "I vill see him about it."

The next day Grooch's job offer was withdrawn; Priester, though nominally only chief engineer, outranked Rihl. Priester in 1930 outranked everyone except Trippe himself, and it was he, not Rihl, who controlled who was hired or fired.

Grooch headed back for South America, but had got only as far as Trinidad when a plane from Miami landed. Aboard, among other Pan American officials, was Priester, who that evening came over to Grooch's table on the veranda of the hotel.

"I understand you haf bin to Brazil," said the little Dutchman.

He was bound for Brazil himself to survey NYRBA installations, and seemed to be groping for a way to open the conversation. When Grooch did not respond, Priester, who had sat down, began drumming his fingers on the tabletop. Then he said, "You know de vedder, de coast, de harbors, yes? Our pilots do not know dose harbors. I vant you should come with us tomorrow."

"Do I understand that you wish to employ my services?" said Grooch stiffly.

"I vant you should come with the company. Ve vill talk about your chob ven I haf had time to see things down dare."

Crossing the northern South American jungle, the Pan Am flying boat nearly ran out of gas—one engine actually stopped as its tank ran dry, and the plane barely reached Paramaribo. That night Priester again approached Grooch, for he had come to a decision about Grooch's "chob." "You vill be technical adwiser to the dewision, and you vill please see dat ve do not run out of gas some more." Later Priester instructed Grooch to train a certain company employee as an operations manager, saying, "Dis company vill grow pigger. Ve must train more mens."

Although it was Trippe who had begun to think of Pan American in naval terms, it was Priester, who, taking Trippe's ideas, first dressed pilots and crew members in naval-type uniforms with peaked caps—and he forbade them to stuff or twist these caps into the dashing, high-peaked shapes so dear to most aviators' hearts. He kept to himself, having decided that social contact with men under him was unwise, but he was always solicitous about the lower ranks, especially pilots. He was death on alcohol in airplanes and against drinking in general. He forbade smoking in uniform and in public. Discipline was paramount, and he could be inflexible. One plane made a forced landing near Camaquã, Brazil. Passengers and crew stood around while the plane was repaired, and one passenger shot a roll of movie film. Later this film was shown in a Miami hotel, and Priester happened to see it. It showed the pilot smoking. Priester fired him. Another time in Miami, Priester went on board a plane that had just landed and ordered the steward to pick up the newspapers and other such refuse. The steward protested that this wasn't his job. Priester said, "You haven't got a chob."

When displeased with a subordinate, he would bark, "Confidence is out." His English was still poor. He refused to answer telephones himself, and he avoided insofar as possible the company of men he did not know well. To subordinates in distant places he sometimes sent instructions couched in language that upset them completely. Sometimes they complained to Trippe. Other times they would gather together to assure themselves that Priester, because of problems with English, could not possibly have been aware of his letters' offensive tone. He once sent a postcard to his wife that read: "Best regards to you from your Andre."

At all of these isolated spots flying-boat floats had to be built in harbors and rivers; airports had to be hacked out of jungles. In many cases the available labor force was not only illiterate, but had never before seen machinery or tools. How were such people to be trained? Priester's way was to collect them, give them a bath, put them in white coveralls, tell them how important their work was, and then begin to train them to do it. But the first thing was to give them a bath and put them in white coveralls.

Priester had a way of inspiring people. To those who knew him well he was not a distant man at all but, rather, one imprisoned by his own lack of social grace. He cared very much about most of the people who worked for him, nearly all of whom sensed this. He demanded that his subordinates do a superior job, that they take pride in their work. He imposed himself on Pan American, and through Pan American on the entire airline industry.

The pilots now wore naval uniforms, but most were the same men as before, and the public was the same as before. This was a time when pilots still got tipped by passengers—one rich passenger regularly tipped Swinson $100 after trips to Havana, and it was possible to rent a Pan American airliner for $100 an hour. In the fall of 1929 a husband and wife chartered a Fokker out of Miami and stepped aboard accompanied by a doctor and a nurse. It was the woman's ambition to be the first to give birth aboard an airplane, and her baby was born over Biscayne Bay seven minutes after takeoff. Fatt was the pilot, and Pippinger, the ex–out-of-work dishwasher, the copilot. Another Pan Am plane was hired out of Port-au-Prince by Charles Patterson and Jeanette Bonell, who brought along a Methodist minister and nine friends and proceeded to get married at 7,000 feet, nineteen miles south of Jacmel Bay over the Caribbean Sea. The plane was aloft precisely fifty-nine minutes.

The pilots were individualists, who took Priester's discipline hard. One of them, a former Navy pilot named Shorty Clark, virtually refused to fly flying boats overland. He'd fly around an island, rather than across it, no matter what this added up to in extra distance, and when asked why, would reply, "I'm a sailor, not Tarzan of the apes." Where the Orinoco River emptied out of the Venezuelan jungle, jaguars often hunted the tidal flats. Pilot Ed Schultz sometimes pushed his window back and shot at them with a rifle. Schultz, also known as Graf Schultz or Germany Schultz, could bark like a dog. One Pan Am executive once shared a hotel room with Schultz at a way station. Schultz phoned his wife, and asked her to "put the dog on." Thereupon he barked to his dog for a while, and the dog barked back. Pilot Steve Bancroft had been a famous college football hero. He conceived a liking for snakes, and once wrapped a ten-foot boa constrictor around his middle to get it past customs in Miami. Bancroft had an apartment in Rio and for a while kept this snake or another in a box there. Bancroft would invite people in and serve drinks. The party would get convivial and more noisy, and the snake would slither out to see what was happening. The guests, it was reported, would sober up fast.

These were the men Priester had to cope with. He began to write operations manuals. His regulations were detailed and they were strict, and the early pilots fought them. In flight they were supposed to report checkpoints at regular intervals; one pilot liked to study his map until he had found obscure inlets or villages or mountaintops, then report these places as checkpoints rather than the major landmarks that were required. Back at the base this drove trackers crazy.

These same pilots still boasted of barnstorming bravery, and sometimes would keep going long after dark in order to make up a delay, even though in the early thirties night landings anywhere were fantastically dangerous. They would merely radio ahead for the station manager to put out flares in the harbor in rowboats, and when they took off again the next morning, the flight would be on schedule once more. With only a few people stationed at each stop, there was always tight teamwork. "Pan Am was like a religion then," said one old-time employee.

Customs men watched the pilots like hawks, and Bancroft once attempted to stride past carrying a gift-wrapped cigar box. "What's in the package?" asked a customs agent. Bancroft replied that the box contained horse droppings, and this was the truth, for Bancroft, a practical joker, was out for one of the best laughs yet. The customs man got angry, and demanded again, "What's in the box?" When Bancroft gave the same reply, the customs agent ripped off the wrapping and peered inside.

"See, what did I tell you," said Bancroft.

Pilots learned not to accumulate possessions. If an order came down from Priester transferring them to Trinidad, or Paramaribo, such an order could not be questioned. They packed their stuff and went. Mechanics, radio operators, ground personnel were the same. Leuteritz also was constantly on the move. One year he came home on January 3 and said to his wife, "We are leaving tomorrow for three or four weeks." They got back in May. Their Christmas tree was still standing in the house when they walked in the door. As the door slammed all the needles fell off the tree.

Planes and personnel got caught in revolutions. One broke out in Bahia, Brazil, the night that Priester, Leuteritz, Grooch and the others reached it on the survey flight of the NYRBA facilities. The shooting started about midnight, and the Pan Am men in their hotel stared out at a mob turning over trolley cars and setting things on fire. In the hotel they kept the lights out lest someone fire in at them. Buenos Aires, when they got there, was under martial law, and the flying boat took off with riflemen shooting at it. During the Cuban revolution the secretary of state and secret police chief, Dr. Orestes Ferrara, took refuge on a Pan Am flying boat in the harbor. The station manager, S. B. Kauffman, aged twenty-six, wanted Ferrara off the aircraft, but the Cuban, declining to depart, pulled a gun. Kauffman then ordered the airplane towed out to the overnight buoy, and arranged for it to wait there until passengers and their luggage could be loaded by launch. An emergency signal was arranged. If the captain, whose name was Leo Terletzky, saw Kauffman on shore waving a red flag, then he was to take off at once. A few minutes later the mob arrived on the pier, brandishing weapons. Kauffman ran up to the second floor and waved his red flag from a window. Out at the buoy Terletzky began starting his engines, a job that had to be done by hand. With one side started but the other side balking, Terletzky cast off from the buoy, and began making wide circles, trying to work his way out to sea any way, starter grinding. The aircraft was some distance out, but broadside now to the pier, when the mob began firing. Later nine bullet holes were counted in the plane, one about six inches from the captain's head. But Terletzky managed to take off and the Cuban police chief disembarked safely in Miami.

No aircraft, the pilots knew, had ever been built any bigger, faster, safer or more modern than the ones Pan Am assigned them. Nonetheless, flying was still in a primitive state, and the pilots seemed to sense this. Therefore, when the first four-engined flying boat came into service, it brought with it certain physical changes, to be sure, but more important, it brought changes that were profoundly emotional and psychological. It altered the infant airline industry forever.

The plane was the Sikorsky S-40, the first aircraft ever designed specifically to suit an airline's needs.

13

The First Clipper

The S-40 had been born in Trippe's head toward the end of 1928, when Pan American, which was scarcely a year old, flew a single 251-mile route, Miami to Havana. Somehow Trippe had guessed at the fantastic growth that was ahead, and to cope with it he had seen that a new plane would be required. Thus far not a single plane had been built to Pan Am's needs, or indeed to the needs of any airline. Even the great Commodore flying boats inherited from NYRBA had originally been conceived of as Navy patrol boats, not as airliners.

Trippe, from the autumn of 1928 on, had been thinking of something special, of a kind of flying luxury steamship, of an airliner specifically designed for Pan American. As a boy he had traveled to Europe on the great Cunard liners. He had been fascinated then, and was fascinated still, by the Cunard mystique, by the romance of shipboard life, and his ambition now became to run Pan American as a kind of nautical airline.

He knew he was condemned in any case to a fleet of flying boats, for all of the company's expansion so far had been to the backward countries south of the border where for the most part land airports simply did not exist, and could not be built except by Pan Am itself at prohibitive cost. Pan American, in Trippe's own words, was a seagoing proposition: flying boats.

The question became: What kind of flying boats?

Trippe, around Christmas 1928, seems to have met first with Lindbergh, and they discussed flying boats for hours. Both knew what types were available. So the discussion was not about what was available but, rather, about what was conceivable. How big, how fast, how luxurious. Next to be brought in on the discussions was Priester, and he began, as was his way, to stress not size or luxury but safety, fuel ratios, range, strength.

At this time the Sikorsky factory was well established in Bridgeport, Conn., and Igor Sikorsky himself was a famous man in aviation circles. Born May 25, 1889, in Kiev, in the Ukraine, he was the son of a physician and psychiatrist who had written some one hundred books. Young Igor's hobbies were electricity and chemistry, and as a youth he spent three years in the Naval Academy in St. Petersburg. Resigning in 1906 to study engineering, he soon began to work in the brand-new field of aeronautics. He tried first to design a helicopter, but the one he built would not fly. In 1910 he built his first conventional airplane, which would not fly either. He scrapped it and built another, which he flew for the first time on June 3, 1910, at an altitude of four feet. This plane, though it flew—sort of— would not turn, and soon crashed, but subsequent models built by Sikorsky became increasingly sophisticated, and during World War I he built four-engined bombers for the Russian Army.

Then came the Bolshevik revolution. Sikorsky fled to France, then to the United States, where he lived on eighty cents a day, giving lectures on astronomy and aviation to Russian immigrants. But he kept dreaming of building airplanes, big airplanes, and by 1923 he had found enough backers to form the Sikorsky Aero Engineering Corporation. One of his backers was Sergei Rachmaninoff, the composer, who subscribed $5,000.

His first plane crashed on its maiden flight. Virtually broke, Sikorsky coaxed more money out of his backers and built another. When this one was successful, Sikorsky decided to construct a plane for the first nonstop transatlantic flight, and when it was ready, René Fonck, the French World War I ace and possibly the most famous aviator in the world, crashed it on takeoff. Fonck survived, but two crewmen and the plane itself were incinerated.

So Sikorsky built still another model, and he tried to sell one of them to Juan Trippe, who decided it was too flimsy for a commercial enterprise as solid as Colonial Air Transport. Sikorsky boasted that the plane was actually extremely strong, and he invited Trippe along on a test flight to prove it. Sikorsky himself was at the controls, and he suddenly pulled the plane up into a loop. Later a shaken Trippe alighted mumbling, "He looped me." It was the only time in his life that Trippe ever looped in an airplane.

That plane was a failure, but the S-38 that followed was bought by the Navy, by Pan American and by NYRBA, and was a success everywhere it flew.

Now, having heard that Pan American wanted some sort of giant flying boat built, Sikorsky stepped forward and offered to build it. As a child of eleven, he said later, he had dreamed that he was walking along a narrow, luxuriously decorated passageway past walnut doors similar to an ocean liner's stateroom doors. The floor was carpeted, and the passageway was illuminated in a pleasant bluish light. He felt a slight vibration beneath his feet, and realized that he was on board not a ship but a "large flying ship in the air," and he continued to the end of the corridor where a door opened onto a decorated lounge. Then he woke up.

For Sikorsky it was enough to hear that Trippe was looking around for an ocean liner of the air. Even before bids were asked for, Sikorsky and his staff had written a kind of outline of what the new planes should be like.

Early in 1929 agreement between Pan American and Sikorsky was reached. Two giant four-engined airships, designated the S-40, could and would be built, the first in American aviation. A third was optioned. They would cost $125,000 each.

After that there were many more conferences. What Sikorsky most wanted to build was, basically, only a bigger, sleeker S-38 with two extra engines. Lindbergh was opposed to this. He wanted a more advanced aeronautical design. But that would take too long—time was of the essence—and Sikorsky's original concept of the S-40 stood. Like the S-38, the fuselage would hang beneath the wing by a forest of braces and struts. The tail surfaces would extend on outriggers back from the wing. But Lindbergh began to win points too. For one thing he wanted the cockpit up forward, because he hated the way the waves splashed back over the windscreen whenever he flew the long-nosed S-38 off the water.

One by one, design problems on the giant new flying boat were encountered and solved. The pontoons were so big that they constituted separate problems in themselves. Each eventually would hold 250 gallons of fuel, and another 540 gallons would go into wing tanks. In April 1929 water tests were conducted in Washington, D.C., at the Navy seaplane base there, and also on the Housatonic River, near the factory. A speedboat towed hull models and pontoon models behind it at 30 miles per hour for 200 hours, after which these same models, or others, were subjected to 300 hours of wind-tunnel tests.

It had been decided early on that the S-40 would be an amphibian, but the plane would weigh 58,000 pounds and no landing gear existed that could survive such weight coming down on top of it. So Cleo-spring shock absorbers, formerly used on boxcars, were acquired from a railroad yard. A rudder was needed for steering on water, and also a tail wheel, but tests showed that the wheel alone would be enough, for it could be levered like a rudder when in the water, and do the job there, too. The huge wing area was covered with 1,740 square feet of fabric, and the overall length of the flying boat was 76 feet 8 inches from the tip of its bow to the tip of its outrigger tail.

Production started in December 1929, but it was April 1931 before a tractor towed the first S-40 out of its hangar and flight tests were begun. Its four 575-hp Hornet engines began to turn over, driving the standard two-bladed props of the day—except that these standard props cut an arc 10 feet 6 inches in diameter. With a Sikorsky test pilot at the controls, the plane rose off Long Island Sound and climbed to its ceiling at 13,500 feet. Tests soon proved that it could cruise comfortably at 115 miles per hour. Maximum speed was 130. It had an absolute range of about 1,500 miles, and its range with a useful payload would be well over half of that.

Tests continued. On August 7, 1931, on one of the windiest days of the summer, the S-40 repeatedly landed and took off in heavy seas that deluged it in tons of water.

By this time Trippe had settled on a name for the giant plane. The walls of the den of his Long Island weekend home bore prints of the American clipper ships that had once crossed the oceans at the fastest speeds of the day. Trippe determined that henceforth all Pan Am airliners would be called Clippers, and the first of them would be called the *American Clipper*. Aboard, all would be as nautical as Trippe's men could make it. The pilot henceforth would be called captain, and the copilot would be called first officer. Speed would be reckoned in knots, and time according to bells. Walls and ceilings would be finished in walnut painted in a dark stain, and the fifty passengers would sit in Queen Anne chairs upholstered in blue and orange. The carpet would be blue, and the windows equipped with rope blinds. As aboard any ship, life rings would hang from the walls of the lounge.

On October 10, 1931, its tests completed, Basil Rowe flew the plane to the Anacostia Naval Air Station, where, two days later, Mrs. Hoover broke a bottle of Caribbean water against the bow. It was Columbus Day, and a modern caravel was about to begin its historic journeys. A crowd of twelve thousand people watched the christening, massed Navy and Marine Corps bands played the national anthem, and Trippe presided at microphones that broadcast the event over America's two major radio networks.

Only four years had passed since Pan American's first ninety-mile flight. At the beginning Trippe had sometimes shown uncertainty. He had not even been sure what to call his airline. There had been many meetings with public relations director Van Dusen. Trippe had wanted to change the name from Pan American to Aviation Corporation of the Americas. He himself wanted to be known as J. Terry Trippe. Van Dusen talked him out of both notions. He said that "pan" means all, and that's what the airline was—it served all the Americas. As for calling himself J. Terry Trippe, he ought instead to be capitalizing on the name Juan, for 200 million people south of the border were willing to imagine that "Juan" Trippe must be a Hispanic. Trippe protested that he didn't want to be taken for a Hispanic. He didn't even speak Spanish, and he certainly didn't have time to learn it now. Eventually he compromised. He became J. T. Trippe, and he hired a bilingual male secretary who, when required, could compose letters to South American presidents and dictators in flowery Spanish, to go out over Trippe's signature.

By the end of 1931, though still only thirty-two, Trippe had changed. He had begun to carry himself with the dignity of a much older man. He wore dark, conservative suits and smoked cigars, as if this would make him look older. When in conference with his peers or his director, he could be affable, almost charming. To others he often seemed distant, aloof. He answered questions absentmindedly, or not at all. Some of the people who worked for him were afraid of him. All showed him deference, except for Priester and Lindbergh, who, when they thought him wrong, told him so. He took it from Lindbergh. From Priester he did not like it one bit.

Although usually he acted alone, he pretended most times that he did not. In Washington he professed to represent his board of directors, and when he wished to disagree or hold to a strong position against Congress or the Post Office, he always put the blame on his board. He could stall forever, if necessary, simply by claiming that he was unable to get his board together.

Most often his board had no idea what he might be doing or not doing in Washington.

Conversely, when standing before his board, he would often claim that certain of his decisions had been mandated by the Postmaster General himself. Sometimes this was true. Sometimes it was Trippe's way of getting his board to cave in to his wishes. Pan American had just posted a profit for the first time—only $105,452 on total revenues of $7,913,587, but indubitably a profit, after only four years. A profit while expanding. A profit while opening new terminals and new routes. A profit while ordering new flying boats. His board appeared to have absolute confidence in him; and when he requested broader authority, it gave it to him —power of attorney to represent the company before the government and all administrative authorities in each and every country of the world. There could be no broader power of attorney than that.

When dealing with subordinates, he rarely told any man more than he needed to know. No one but himself had the total picture. He was in the habit during conferences of scrawling something on a pad and handing it across to someone saying, "This is what we are going to do next." On the page might be penned the name of an airport to be built, a sea to be crossed, a route to be surveyed—in any case, a vast project that was still secret except for the recipient and Trippe himself. To some extent his penchant for secrecy pervaded the entire company. Code books were sent out, and when communicating over open wires, station managers, pilots and the rest were ordered to put their messages in code. From time to time important visitors went out over the line, and when this happened, Trippe invariably sent letters along asking that every courtesy be extended to them. But simultaneously confidential memos would leave the president's office. These, signed by one or another of the young men who served as assistants to the president, would make clear exactly which courtesies Mr. Trippe wished extended, and which not. One, dated January 12, 1932, explained that the distinguished visitors were "to see the watch without having a good look at the works." Radio gear was not to be shown them, and "the usual information which we generally treat as confidential . . . likewise should not be made available."

Part II
THE
PACIFIC

14

The Next Step

On November 19, 1931, the four-engined S-40 flying boat took off from Miami on its maiden flight with paying passengers aboard. The destination was Panama, and for reasons to be seen, this was one of the most important flights in the history of aviation.

To assure headlines, the pilot again was Lindbergh, but there was a difference. The hero, now twenty-nine years old, was at the controls of a commercial flight for the first time, which made him subject to the authority of Andre Priester.

There were at this time about thirty-five pilots. Musick, Swinson, Fatt and Rowe held seniority over all the others, but not by much. Musick had been made chief pilot, and lived in Miami. Fatt and Swinson were ordered to take their turn on what was then called "foreign duty"—a year's permanent station at Trinidad. Both flatly refused to go. Both were told to go or get fired.

The big, bluff Fatt, after fighting hard, conceded, but Swinson stormed out cursing. On his next flight he shut down his radio shortly after takeoff. By the time he landed, a search-and-rescue operation had been mounted to look for him. On a later flight he boarded wearing overalls for a uniform. Other pilots also caused trouble. The constant engine noise would deafen them by middle age, some claimed. Constant high-altitude flying would shorten their lives. They appeared to believe this, and no one could prove it wasn't so. They talked of forming a union.

Priester, meanwhile, had ordered them to expand their knowledge in what seemed to them unrelated subjects. New pilots were assigned to work six months as mechanics to learn the aircraft before being allowed to fly. All pilots were forced to learn not only to operate the radio, but also to send and receive Morse code by wigwagging flags; they had to learn the names and locations of every sail on every type of sailing vessel, to recognize every signal flag in maritime use, to learn the symptoms and incubation periods of diseases such as bubonic plague.

Priester's checkout procedures for new aircraft were especially strict. At one point Swinson was ordered to check out Basil Rowe in the Commodore flying boat. Rowe balked. He was a better flying-boat pilot than Swinson, and had more hours in more kinds of boats than Swinson, he said. He was told that if he did not agree to being checked out by Swinson, then he could not fly the Commodore, nor any of the other big flying boats that were coming, either.

Two weeks passed before Rowe came to Swinson and said, "All right, let's get it over with," and he looked at Swinson's smug grin.

No pilot could command a new plane until he had made ten practice takeoffs and landings in it, Priester ruled. Did this rule apply even to the great Lindbergh? It did. Lindbergh arrived in Miami early, and prior to the first commercial flight of the S-40, he made his ten takeoffs and landings in a single day without protest. This so impressed other pilots up and down the system that at last they began to fall into line.

Other important events followed as soon as the S-40 was aloft, beginning with a hot meal, the first ever prepared in an American overwater aircraft galley. Until an airline learned to feed its passengers it could not take them very far in one jump. Service was by a uniformed steward. Passengers dined with heavy silverware off real tables draped with linen tablecloths.

More important still was a conversation that occurred during lunch, for Lindbergh had chosen to turn the controls over to copilot Rowe and to step back into the cabin to sit down opposite the number one paying passenger aboard, Igor Sikorsky himself. They began to talk about what in those days was always spoken of as "the next step." The next step meant the next plane off the drawing board. What was the next plane to be? Flying boat or landplane? How many engines? What would it be designed to do? Soon Lindbergh was making sketches on the back of Sikorsky's menu.

Lindbergh had been opposed to the plane they were riding in now— more opposed even than he had seemed, he admitted. He had wanted Sikorsky to build a really new airplane, something completely clean in design, with no external bracing, no outriggers, no fuselage hanging from the wing by struts, no engines stuffed amid the struts like wine bottles in a rack. All those struts and bracings only meant wind resistance to Lindbergh, and wind resistance meant loss of range and speed.

But the plane he had wanted, Sikorsky told him now, was two steps ahead in development, and Sikorsky had wanted to make one step at a time, because lives were at stake. They could not afford mistakes. They only had a certain amount of knowledge. They knew how to make this plane, the S-40. They didn't know how to make anything better. It was Priester who had seen this argument most clearly, and had thrown his vote behind Sikorsky's concept, Sikorsky said. But now we are ready for that next step. What is that next step going to be? They began to work it out. High above the Caribbean, while Sikorsky ate his hot lunch and Lindbergh drew on the menu, the S-42 was conceived.

Today's flight was to proceed south in short hops, stopping first at Cuba, then at Kingston, Jamaica, for the night. There Lindbergh and Sikorsky sat at dinner together at the hotel, and Lindbergh again made drawings on the menu—Sikorsky was to take these menus home, and show them to people from time to time for years. Lindbergh wanted something sleek, and he wanted provision made for refueling in the air, because the next plane ought to be able to go anywhere in the world. The critical overwater jump, he said, was San Francisco to Hawaii, which was about twenty-five hundred miles. There was none longer. So a plane that could fly nonstop for twenty-five hundred miles, Lindbergh said, was what was needed.

The next day's flight was from Kingston nonstop across six hundred miles of water to Barranquilla, Colombia, with a heavy payload aboard, the longest nonstop commercial flight ever attempted. There were no islands down there if trouble occurred. All day the S-40 flew high above the empty sea. Leuteritz's navigational aids were still unsophisticated, but they worked well enough, and the plane came in over Barranquilla on time, set down, and the passengers disembarked.

However advanced the aviation art in 1931, ground operations were primitive. Before proceeding to Panama, the plane was refueled by men on the wing pouring in gas by hand, and they spilled half a barrel of it down the wing and into the water. The passengers were standing on the pier smoking, and Lindbergh rushed among them calling, "Put out your cigarettes."

When the great Lindbergh gave orders, people obeyed. Instantly, the cigarettes began arcing out into the air, plopping down into the highly volatile film on the water. Fortunately, there was no fire or explosion. The cigarettes simply fizzled out.

Then, when it came time to take off, Lindbergh saw that four of his passengers were missing. He did what commercial pilots always did in those days. He sent men down the pier into the nearest saloons to find them.

But every night his discussions with Sikorsky continued. Mostly the two men talked theory, not fact. In 1931 there was still painfully little exact knowledge about the mechanics of flight. Even so, physicists had posted laws that controlled it. One law held that there was an exact limit somewhere to the possible future size of aircraft. The argument of the physicists was mathematical, the so-called rule of square and cubes. In squaring the size of any structure, including an airplane, one cubed its weight. Planes would get heavier faster than they could get bigger—much faster. At a certain point it would become impossible to get them off the ground, and that point had probably been reached.

Sikorsky didn't believe the physicists, nor did Lindbergh. They were in the grip of an idea that has captivated mankind from time to time all through the ages—that man is great enough to achieve anything he sets his heart on. They wanted to believe in an illimitable future.

At Kingston on the way home takeoff was delayed and it seemed possible that the S-40 would reach Miami in the dark. This would be dangerous. There were no lights on the water there, and none aboard the S-40 either. But Lindbergh took off, for he had made his calculations, and he judged they could make it.

He was wrong. It was fully dark when he circled over Biscayne Bay and he could see almost nothing. He did not even know the direction of the wind, and when he set down his S-40 full of passengers, it struck the water with a smack and began to porpoise. Then it swung hard to port, coming to an abrupt stop under a deluge of spray. The passengers had been flung around, and two went skidding across the floor, but no one was seriously hurt. Lindbergh apologized to Sikorsky as they left the plane, blaming himself for the rotten landing, but Sikorsky apologized to the hero, blaming the design of the plane. Then both men went off to New York, Sikorsky carrying his menus, having agreed to urge Trippe to start thinking about crossing the oceans, for they had convinced themselves over the last several days that a plane could be built to do it.

15

Staking Out the World

In New York there was no need to convince Trippe of anything, for he wished to cross the oceans more strongly, if possible, than either of them. But there were problems that were not mechanical in nature, problems of which they, perhaps, were unaware. Trippe had been working to solve these, mostly in secret, for some three years already. He was a man with no confidants—no one knew the details of what he was up to, and very few knew his long-range plans even in broad outline. His number one business philosophy seems always to have been this: Get in and get started before other people know what you are doing and can organize to stop you.

The ocean he wanted to cross first, and had been planning to cross since 1928, was the North Atlantic, because it was the busiest trade route in the world. He had begun his planning by gathering the latest statistics he could find. In 1925, out of about a million steamship passengers, a hundred and eighty thousand had crossed in first class, each one, Trippe judged, a potential customer if an airline could offer equal comfort and safety plus superior speed. In addition, ships had carried about 9 million pounds of precious merchandise (jewelry, art works, currency, precision instruments); about 28 million pounds of express packages, including cans of moving-picture film; and about 38 million pounds of letters and printed matter. This fraction of ship traffic suitable for air transport worked out to only eight-tenths of 1 percent but still added up to 75 million pounds. The potential profits were staggering.

Of course there were problems. Trippe saw them as geographical, financial and, most of all, diplomatic—and all were equally staggering. They could be overcome only by the most careful long-range planning imaginable. He began trying to solve the geographical problems first, and he went to the Public Library on 42nd Street and asked for maps of the North Atlantic detailed enough to show even the smallest known islands. Trippe was in some ways a studious man. New York's vast Grecian temple of a library was a place he understood. When he needed to know something he went straight there.

The maps given him showed that there were three logical air routes to Europe. The shortest was the so-called great circle that Lindbergh had flown the year before in *The Spirit of St. Louis,* but it contained an overwater jump between Newfoundland and Ireland of about eighteen hundred miles. *The Spirit of St. Louis* could make this because its payload consisted of about 150 pounds—a single six-foot-three-inch, 145-pound boy-man plus a few sandwiches; in addition, Lindbergh had happened to pick a day and a half of relatively good weather. Good weather, as any ship traveler could attest, was fairly rare in that part of the ocean.

The southern route, via Bermuda and the Azores to Lisbon, promised better weather, but the air distances overwater were enormous. In 1928 Trippe's Fokker trimotors were the most advanced airliners ever built, but one had recently run out of gas over the Gulf of Mexico after less than three hours of flight. The Fokker had an extreme range of under 300 miles. It would go down less than halfway to Bermuda, never mind the next two jumps—2,000 miles to the Azores, 1,000 more to Lisbon.

The extreme northern route, via Greenland, Iceland, the Faroe Islands and the Shetlands, attracted Trippe the most because it offered many places to refuel—an island chain all the way across. The biggest jump would be Greenland to Iceland, 496 miles, an impossible distance this year, though perhaps not next. Although the Arctic was renowned for howling gales, Trippe rated this as not insoluble. Trippe in 1928 was arrogant enough to rate nothing insoluble, and in October of that year, being twenty-nine years old and the proprietor of a 90-mile airline, he went to Europe—by boat, of course—requested audiences with air ministry and airline heads of Britain, France, Holland and Germany, and began negotiating for landing rights for Pan American in their countries. Although he obtained no concessions, at least he made them know who he was.

In Latin America he had been dealing and would continue to deal with rulers who had neither the means nor the ambition to mount airlines of their own and who, therefore, demanded no reciprocal rights. But the European countries each had a national airline; to be permitted to land abroad, Trippe would have to sign agreements with each of them. These negotiations could be begun at once, and had best be, since they were not going to be easy, and so Trippe, over the next several years, sometimes accompanied by his wife, spent literally months on ships, sailing to and from aviation conferences, meeting everyone who counted.

At last in New York, in November 1930, Trippe was able to enter into formal negotiations with Imperial Airways of Great Britain and Aéropostale of France for "development" of routes across the Atlantic. Most sessions took place in the Trippe apartment at 1111 Park Avenue—in French. The Frenchman, André Boilloux-Lafont, insisted upon it. Trippe could get by in French, for he had once had a French nurse, but it was hard, slow work. It was even harder and slower for George Woods-Humphery, managing director of Imperial, who had no useful command of French at all. Negotiations went on for three weeks, until, on November 21, all three men signed a tripartite agreement not to operate across the Atlantic except jointly with each other. Four specific destinations were mentioned: New York, Lisbon, Paris and London. What was odd in the agreement was the clause covering future traffic. Like a giant pie, it had already been cut up in unequal portions. The other two signees were speaking for their governments. Trippe was speaking for Trippe. Although the English controlled landing rights to England and Ireland, and although the French controlled the Azores through an exclusive agreement with Portugal, and although Trippe controlled nothing at all—not even, since he was not a government agency, New York—nonetheless he gave the French and the English a quarter of future transatlantic traffic each, and kept one half for himself. He was only thirty-one at the time. How did he accomplish this? The only answer seems to be that he accomplished such feats again and again over the years. Though he seemed artless, he got his own way almost always. No one, even those who watched him most closely, ever understood exactly how he did it. He seemed naïve. He seemed innocent, kindly, bumbling. But he wore people down. Observers kept returning to this: Trippe wore people down.

There was one other obvious truth. He usually held out for an advantage in case of some future contingency that others did not see clearly or did not believe would ever occur. Fifty percent of traffic was, at the moment, 50 percent of nothing. If he wanted it that badly, why not give it to him?

Trippe wanted everything badly, especially landing rights to Bermuda, first stop along the southern route to Europe. These had to be negotiated separately; and he won a fifty-fifty agreement with Imperial to divide flights there, a place neither could reach. Terrifically pleased, he formed New York Airways Inc. and prepared for service from New York to Atlantic City and Norfolk, Va. A hundred miles closer to Bermuda than New York, Norfolk would be the jumping-off point to Europe. He even flew to Norfolk himself in a floatplane to pick a spot for a transatlantic terminal.

Separate agreements were necessary also with Canada and Newfoundland on the northern route, and Trippe sent Alan Winslow, a former State Department diplomat, to obtain them. Within a month Winslow in Ottawa had won Canadian traffic rights as far as Halifax. Even as Winslow went on to Newfoundland to bargain for rights there, Trippe himself founded Boston & Maine Airways, Inc., and in Washington he bid for and won an airmail contract, FAM No. 12, from Boston to Halifax. Planes to fly this route came up from the Caribbean, and service was inaugurated almost at once, six flights a week.

Negotiations in Bermuda, Canada and Washington, the tripartite agreement—all this should have kept Trippe busy enough, but during these same months he also negotiated for and absorbed NYRBA while simultaneously pushing his Latin American network up to 18,029 route miles and 111 planes.

And even that was not all. It was now time—as Trippe measured time —to look toward Asia. He was already trying to stake out the world, and he went back to the Public Library to study more maps. Obviously, Asia could be reached via Alaska, and he determined to send an expedition in that direction as soon as possible. Could it also be reached via islands straight across the Pacific? The first maps told him no. Although west of Hawaii, by 1,300 miles, lay Midway, a cable station, this was followed by a gap all the way to Guam, a gap wider than the United States, wider than the entire North Atlantic, a gap for the planes of 1930 totaling more than a day in the air. It meant that the Pacific could not be crossed.

Trippe found he didn't believe the maps. There must be some tiny island the map makers had overlooked. There must be something. He could not believe 3,000 miles of ocean without something. There was one further place to look for the island he had to have, the logs of the clipper ships which during the previous century had plied the Pacific under sail, and now he approached the information desk and asked to see them. He knew about them because, ninety years before, his family had been in the clipper business. The handwritten documents that were given to him were brittle with age and even a pragmatist like the big burly Trippe succumbed, for a few minutes, to the romance they seemed to contain. Then he got down to business, searching for the island stepping-stone he sensed must be there. In a state of high excitement he found what he was looking for—mention of Wake Island. It lay approximately halfway between Midway and Guam—exactly where it had to be. It was all alone out there, a single tiny island. But a single island was all he needed. His inchoate dreams hardened. He would cross the Pacific via Wake.

Trippe's admirers credited him then and later with incredible foresight, claiming that he always knew in advance which direction to take and was never wrong. This is not accurate. He knew only that aviation was going very far very fast. He did not know exactly where or how, and neither did anyone else. The result was that, as he tried to cover every imaginable possibility, he was wrong many, many times. Nowhere is this more evident than in his somewhat frantic attempts—years before it was possible—to cross both oceans at once, and by all possible routes.

At the same time that he was considering routes he was also considering vehicles. A host of vivid and fantastic ideas had been advanced, any one of which, if it worked, might revolutionize the air-transport business. The Arctic routes were not necessarily closed to flying boats just because harbors to land in would be frozen solid each winter and filled with icebergs each spring; one could perhaps land, as Sikorsky had suggested, on shallow ponds scraped into the tundra and filled with Prestone. Nor were all the great water jumps necessarily too long. Already there existed Armstrong Seadrome Development Inc., a serious company backed by Du Pont and General Motors executives, which was proceeding with plans to anchor "seadromes" at sea. A "seadrome" was a floating-island airport.

The idea seems to have originated with E. R. Armstrong of Philadelphia, about 1925. Armstrong suggested that floating islands could be anchored every four hundred miles or so. For instance, eight might be needed to carry planes to Europe. To withstand storms, the islands should be light platforms on top of heavy bases. The 1,200-foot runways would be seventy feet above sea level, with more than 95 percent of the island underwater below the level of surface-wave disturbance. Planes, each carrying twenty-five passengers, would make each lap in three or four hours. While their plane was refueling, the passengers would dine in the hotels on the islands, or else transfer to a waiting plane to make an express crossing. By 1930 there were numerous other ideas. Trippe looked over all of them, and some he seriously considered. The French were said to be developing a six-engined plane, two of the six engines driving pusher propellers. The Germans had already developed the DO-X, a huge flying boat powered by twelve engines—too many, for it couldn't carry enough gas to feed them very long, and had no range.

But Lufthansa was working also on the concept of small transatlantic seaplanes so heavily loaded as to be unable to take off under their own power; they would be catapulted into the air. In mid-ocean these planes would land on the quiet water formed by a huge sail dragged behind a mother ship, be lifted aboard for refueling, and then recatapulted into the sky—this to be repeated all the way across the ocean. Catapults really slammed everybody in the back, and were unsuited for first-class passengers, who had to be cosseted. But perhaps existing catapults could be tamed, and in terms of mail, the plan would go into operation almost at once.

Trippe himself in June of 1931, five months before Lindbergh and Sikorsky made their drawings on the backs of S-40 menus, sent a letter to all six prominent U.S. aircraft manufacturers asking them to design him "a high-speed multimotored flying boat having a cruising range of 2,500 miles against 30-mile headwinds and providing accommodations for a crew of four together with at least 300 pounds of airmail." That seemed the reasonable limit of what he could hope for in 1931: range but no payload, a bit of mail but no passengers. However, four of the six manufacturers told him he was dreaming; the plane he wanted could not be built. But Sikorsky had agreed to study Trippe's demands, and so did the Glenn Martin Company of Baltimore, which built flying boats for the Navy, and Trippe waited to hear what they would propose.

Lindbergh now came forward with a plan to fly to China via Alaska. Trippe was enthusiastic, and promised every support. Lindbergh would be accompanied by his wife Anne, aged twenty-five, who had been taught Morse code by Leuteritz, and who would operate the standard Pan American sending-and-receiving radio telegraph during the flight. Obviously, this flight, which would carry the young couple over unknown areas of the globe, was hazardous, and Anne was just a slip of a girl, but when the danger to her was pointed out to Lindbergh, he merely smiled and said, "But she's crew."

On July 27, 1931, the Lindberghs would take off from College Point, Long Island. If their flight succeeded, then Russia and China were within Trippe's grasp, and he waited to hear what news the hero would bring back.

16

North
to the Orient

Lindbergh would head northwest across Canada toward
Point Barrow, Alaska, then southwest to China.

His flight, like all his other flights, was meticulously prepared. He
could have had his pick of any aircraft then flying, but he chose a Lockheed Sirius, a single-engined, low-winged, twin-float monoplane. There
were two cockpits with sliding glass canopies. The engine was a 600-hp
Cyclone swinging a two-bladed prop and there was enough fuel aboard,
most of it in the pontoons, for about two thousand miles.

Anne Lindbergh had been educated in the best schools. She had been
taught that her role in life was to be a "lady," to ornament the life of
whatever lucky man she chose for a husband. But now she spent weeks
learning not only Morse code but also where the oscillator plugged into
the set, and how it related to the power amplifier, for Pan Am radio gear
in 1931 had to be virtually assembled and disassembled each time one
wanted to send or receive a message. To change frequencies one inserted
a different transmitting coil, and the Sirius would carry six. A second set
of coils had to be worked into place in order to receive. She learned to
crank the trailing antenna in and out; it had a heavy ball weight on the
end, and had to be cranked out precise distances for each frequency. For
instance, 48 reel turns equaled 3,130 kilocycles. The radio operated on
400 volts, and she learned, each time she stuck her fingers in there, to
be prepared to be jolted nearly out of her seat.

At home the Lindberghs' living room was littered with equipment:
radio and navigation gear, personal clothing, emergency food, emer-

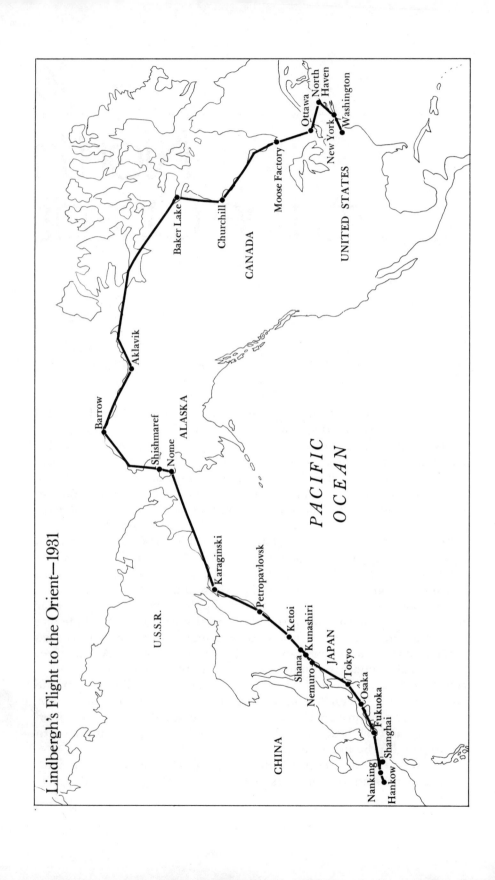

Lindbergh's Flight to the Orient—1931

gency items for forced landing at sea, and different ones for forced landing on land. Each piece was weighed many times on Anne's white baby scale. Not all could go. Which were most vital?

The usual vast crowd watched the first takeoff. Radio reporters spoke excitedly into microphones on stands. Then the Sirius, a black plane with bright orange wings, was speeding across Long Island Sound, while spray sluiced over the windshield, and hard water spanked the pontoons. The spanks came closer together, and then the plane was in the air.

After landing in Ottawa, the Lindberghs dined with the most notable Canadian aviators, meteorologists and explorers who could be assembled.

Fifteen hundred miles further northwest, the Lindberghs landed on Baker Lake and taxied up to the trading post. On shore waited a small group of Eskimos and a Royal Canadian Mountie in a red coat. In the damp muggy air mosquitoes swarmed around their faces and they ran inside the trading post. Dinner was fresh salmon trout—delicious to the visitors, but monotonous to the traders, who said they had not tasted fresh fruit in months. At this news the Lindberghs withdrew three plums, a pear and four beef sandwiches from their pockets. The traders cut the beef into equal portions, and passed it around. No one, to their knowledge, had ever eaten fresh beef this far north, they said.

At 7:00 p.m. on August 4 the Lindberghs took off again. It was already very cold, and they were flying still farther north. Below them was empty tundra with, here and there, caribou herds moving across it looking, to Anne, like the shadow of a cloud.

When the sun set, a green glow came over the world. All night the plane's vibration hummed through the soles of their feet, and it never got dark. They took turns flying and dozing. Once Anne was jolted awake when the engine quit—then came on again. Lindbergh had forgotten to switch to a full tank in time. At one settlement they landed at three o'clock in the morning, shut down the engine and listened to dogs howling in the white Arctic night.

So far so good; the route seemed viable, at least in summer, for whatever commercial airliners might one day follow them. At Point Barrow, Alaska, their northernmost point, they were to refuel, then turn south, but the yearly supply boat, with their fuel aboard, was locked in ice out beyond the horizon. They put on their heavy flying suits, though it was summer, and took off again, heading for Nome with what gas they had, flying rapidly out of the zone of permanent daylight. With Nome still ninety minutes ahead, darkness began to close in. From the front cockpit Lindbergh passed a note back to his wife: "What time does it get dark at Nome?"

Anne tried to radio Nome, but no message came back. Looking ahead past her husband's cockpit, she could see the exhaust flashes from the engine—it had got that dark.

Lindbergh and Anne passed more messages back and forth. The light would blink on first in one cockpit, then in the other. They could see a range of peaks ahead. They were flying directly into the darkness and into the mountains as well. Suddenly Lindbergh pulled the plane up, throttled down on the engine, and shouted back to his wife that they would have to land.

Land? Where? Lindbergh pointed to water below. They would have to land on unknown water in the dark.

Anne began frantically cranking in the antenna. Down, down they slanted toward what looked like a dim lagoon shining pale gray against the blackness. Lindbergh slapped the plane down on the water, and they skidded along waiting for rocks or floating logs to rip the pontoons off. This did not happen. With shore half a mile ahead, Lindbergh cut the engine, and in total silence climbed out onto a pontoon and threw over his anchor. It landed with a splash, but pulled out no rope. The water, Lindbergh saw with a shock, was only three feet deep. The couple crawled into the baggage compartment to sleep, while from Nome word went out to the world that the beloved couple was lost.

The next day in Nome they walked along the plank streets of the former gold-mining town, and then, after refueling, they flew across the Bering Sea to Karaginskiy Island, population 136, a fur station off the coast of Soviet Kamchatka. Furs hung everywhere—bear, red fox, ermine. They drank fresh milk, ate wild strawberries and tried to converse with people in Anne's weak French and their hosts' worse English.

On to Petropavlovsk. A hillside of houses with carved eaves above a beautiful harbor. They were lodged in a government building at the end of a hall decorated with portraits of Lenin and tractors. Their room contained three cots, including one for their nonexistent "mechanic." Two cots were separated from the third by a screen. On a table lay gifts: two razors and a bottle of perfume. Was this to be Trippe's route to Asia?

From the Russian coast they flew across toward the northernmost Japanese islands, intending to continue down the chain to Tokyo, but these high, harsh islands became suddenly enveloped by fog. Their radio crackled with signals—"Welcome to Japan"—but the fog was all around them. There was no way of going down low enough to find the sea without risking at the same time smacking into one of the islands. Lindbergh put on his linen helmet and goggles, pushed back his canopy and cranked his seat as high as it would go—signs Anne recognized as "the familiar buckling on of armor." He began diving toward holes in the fog that invariably closed before he reached them, causing him to soar for the sky once more. They were in terrible trouble until at last Lindbergh spied the peak of a volcano peeping above the clouds. He pointed the plane straight down its flank, plunging into the mist, into the dense fog, toboggaging straight down the slope, at the bottom of which was a sharp cliff. Below lay the water that Lindbergh had been hoping would be there. He dropped the plane onto it with a sharp smack. They were safe. They were still alive.

The next day's flying produced more fog, which produced another forced landing, Lindbergh setting the plane down in the lee of Shimushiru Island. It was raining. He taxied toward a fisherman's hut at the end of the bay. They were welcomed inside by an old man and a boy, who asked via signs if they wished to eat. Lindbergh declined, being afraid of contaminated food. But when the boy appeared with a string of fresh fish, Lindbergh realized how hungry he was. To communicate his change of heart, he drew a fish in profile on a piece of paper and showed this to the fisherman with one hand while pointing to his mouth with the other.

Some days later the Lindberghs flew from Osaka west across the Yellow Sea. China was signaled to them a hundred miles out when the sea turned brown for as far as their eyes could delimit from the tremendous outpouring of Yangtze River mud. The Yangtze, thirty-four hundred miles long, was in flood, and China when they came to it was a scene of ruin and desolation. When they overflew their destination, the walled city of Nanking, they saw that the river had totally encircled the walls.

Having volunteered to airlift doctors and medicines into the interior, Lindbergh flew up to Hinghwa; one doctor sat in the second cockpit and a second in the baggage compartment. As soon as the plane landed, river craft surrounded it, for these people were starving. People in outlying boats began running across intervening craft to get at the plane and whatever food might be aboard. People clung to the plane's wings, pontoons, tail surfaces. When they began to climb onto the pontoons, Lindbergh brandished his .38-caliber revolver. They started clambering aboard. Lindbergh fired high in one direction, spun sharply about and fired high in the other.

The mob fell back across the boats, then came on again. One of the doctors was hauling up the anchor. The plane began to blow downwind, clearing its own path. Lindbergh pressed the starter, the engine began roaring, and Lindbergh took off in the only direction open to him, the plane scooting across flooded fields and then rising—effortlessly, it seemed—into the air.

Lindbergh made contact with the commander of the British aircraft carrier *Hermes* and asked that their plane be lifted out of the turbulent Yangtze by derrick. The next morning, with Lindbergh and his wife already aboard, it was lowered back down again, but it was caught by the flood current and swept downstream with the derrick cable still attached. At the end of its leash the plane dipped its wing into the river. As the wing dug deep, Lindbergh and Anne dove for their lives, came up swimming, and were hauled aboard the carrier. So was the ruined Sirius, which came home, like them, on a steamship.

Some weeks later Lindbergh reported to Trippe. The route north to the Orient was feasible, he said. In winter planes could use skis. The main problem up there would be darkness. Airfields would have to be brightly lit during the perpetual winter night. Radio navigation would be vital, not only across the tundra but also down the vast Siberian shoreline where no one lived, where no lights showed, where few identifiable landmarks existed. But these were not insoluble problems, and the route could be flown right now.

Lindbergh was saying that Asia was wide open, and that meant Russia was wide open, because once reaching Siberia, an airman need only find the Trans-Siberian Railroad; he could follow its tracks all the way to Moscow.

Within a few months of Lindbergh's return Trippe had bought up two small aviation companies operating in Alaska and had merged them into a subsidiary incorporated as Pacific-Alaska Airways, and operations were begun over some two thousand miles of routes.

From then on data on flying conditions in Alaska began to reach New York regularly. Trippe meanwhile had begun negotiations with Amtorg, the Soviet government trading agency, for permission to operate an airline on Soviet territory, and before long he signed a contract that gave him the right to cross Siberia as far as Moscow. In exchange, Pan American agreed to build permanent hangars along the route and to train Russian pilots.

For Trippe a new empire was taking shape. He had Russia, or thought he did, and he began to cast covetous glances at China.

17

China Airways

He was not the first to do so. Clement M. Keys, arch rival of Trippe at this time, was already there. Born in Canada in 1877, Keys had graduated from Toronto University and had begun as a teacher of classics at Wridley College, in Ontario. Moving to New York two years later he became a reporter for the *Wall Street Journal,* and by 1906 he was railroad editor. Four years as financial editor of *World's Work* magazine followed. Then in 1911, at the age of thirty-four, he founded C. M. Keys & Co., an investment service that soon expanded into an investment bank, and he began to put money into aviation. In 1916 he accepted a nonsalaried vice presidency of the Glenn Curtiss Company. During the war years Curtiss boomed, producing 3,240 airplanes in 1918. The following year Curtiss produced only 147 and went $3.5 million into debt. So Keys bought the near-bankrupt company for $650,000 and nursed it through the lean years that preceded Lindbergh's flight to Paris. Keys often bragged that though he cut wages and laid off personnel, he never reduced the engineering budget by as much as a nickel.

Unlike Trippe, Keys was not an aviator, and he was not really interested in the air. He was a promoter. He was interested in floating stock, and in acquiring vast amounts of money. "Ten percent of aviation is in the air," he once said, "and ninety percent is on the ground."

He had studied the railroad barons of the previous century. He liked the notion of becoming an air baron.

It was Keys who had dominated National Air Transport, which, in winning the New York–Chicago airmail contract, had soundly thrashed young Trippe of Colonial Air Transport. It was Keys who dominated Trans-Continental Air Transport, which had joined with the Pennsylvania Railroad to speed passengers across the United States in forty-eight hours—flying by day, riding sleeper trains by night.

It was also Keys, who, in partnership with Clarence Dillon, another rich investment banker, had formed Intercontinent Aviation, Inc., as the corporate vehicle for the expansion of aviation projects throughout the world. In the wake of the Lindbergh flight aviation stocks boomed, and Keys, having raised $10 million, founded an internal airline in Cuba and an aircraft factory in Turkey; he negotiated with eleven governments in South America, Europe and Asia during 1928 alone.

Trippe, moving fast, was able to stay ahead of Keys in Latin America, though just barely. Elsewhere in the world it was another story, and it was again Keys who, in 1929, sent a group headed by Major William B. Robertson to start an airline in China.

The Chinese authorities appeared to want an airline. It was a country almost without railroads. Highways were the rivers, or else dirt tracks. But no sooner were contracts signed and China Airways founded than the mood changed. Company planes were barred from Chinese military airfields, and there were no other facilities unless the Americans built their own. A competing company was given the airmail route between Shanghai and Nanking. Maddening delays occurred as Chinese bureaucrats demanded bribes.

A member of Keys's group hurried back to New York to tell him that it might be impossible ever to operate a profitable airline in China. The millionaire fixed him with an icy glare. "If I want to invest a million dollars," said Keys coldly, "that's my business." This was the golden summer of 1929. Investors were pouring money into U.S. aviation stocks, whose market value had shot up to $1 billion, even though the gross output of the entire aviation industry at the time was only $90 million. Curtiss-Wright stock alone had risen to a value of $171.6 million. Keys sent enough money to China to begin building the airfields. He also sent over five Loening Air Yachts and a six-passenger amphibian, and on October 21 China Airways at last was able to open service. Three days later came Black Thursday. All stocks fell, but aircraft stocks nose-dived. Curtiss-Wright stock value dropped to $106 million.

In China problems continued. China Airways was carrying mail, but the minister of communications refused to hand over the postal receipts called for by the contract; a month later he tried to pay in promissory notes. When company president Ernest B. Price sought instructions from Keys, he got back a letter that read in part: "It is necessary to impress upon you the need for extreme conservatism and extreme economy." Clement Keys no longer had a million dollars to invest in China. The market crash had made it "utterly impossible" to raise additional funds, Keys wrote.

From then on, the self-styled successor to the railroad barons received nothing but bad news from China. China was racked by inflation, and the value of its money continued to fall. One of the Loenings crashed on takeoff, killing the pilot, copilot and two passengers. Two weeks later an aide to Chiang Kai-shek phoned the local agent at Hankow to reserve for the generalissimo and his party all six seats on the next flight to Nanking. Although it was scheduled to leave at 8:00 A.M., the aide asked that the plane be held for Chiang until nine. The American field manager, Ray Ott, sent the plane off at eight anyway. When Chiang turned up half an hour later and found the plane gone, he turned purple. He jailed the agent, he jailed Ott, and when the plane came back to pick him up, he jailed the pilot, and proceeded to Nanking on a gunboat. The next year came the most severe floods in China's history—the same floods Lindbergh found at the end of his flight over the Arctic. Civil war broke out. One plane crashed into Taishan Mountain killing the pilot, copilot and two passengers. Two others crashed in a single day in fog near Peking. Another plane was damaged when its pilot landed with gear down in the water.

Deficits soared. It seemed hopeless. Conducting airline business in China was akin to fighting a ground war in Asia against the Chinese Army. One could not win. Keys, his fortune nearly wiped out by the stock-market crash, relinquished control of Curtiss-Wright. The surviving directors, seeking to unload their Chinese investment, were looking for a sucker, someone who thought he could make a profit on an airline in China. They found Trippe easily enough.

One day during the course of negotiations, Lindbergh appeared in Trippe's office with a man named Harold M. Bixby, who wanted a job.

"I have nothing but debts and my friendship with Slim, here," Bixby told Trippe.

The St. Louis–born, Amherst-educated Bixby was then forty-two years old. He had gone into balloon training during World War I, and afterwards had bought a balloon for $50. This balloon became a familiar sight over St. Louis because Bixby used to drift around in it on Sunday afternoons. Later he bought an airplane, from which he took photographs of factories. Aerial photos excited everyone then, for they gave people a new and unfamiliar perspective of their world. Flying was Bixby's hobby. His business was banking. He had started as a clerk in the State National Bank and had risen to vice president. Hobby and business came together when Lindbergh arrived in St. Louis to raise money to build a plane for his proposed flight to Paris. Bixby was one of the first and most important backers Lindbergh acquired there, and the plane, when built, became *The Spirit of St. Louis.*

Later Bixby's bank sold bonds for an arena/exhibition hall; the project collapsed. Bixby, though not legally responsible, agreed to pay back investors' losses out of his own pocket. Trippe was tremendously impressed by this detail. He checked—and it was true. A man of such honor was exactly what he needed to run China Airways. And he bought out Curtiss-Wright's interest, and hired Bixby.

Bixby's appearance was unromantic. A tall man with a high forehead, he wore spectacles and a neat little mustache. He was a staid-looking banker in a conservative business suit. Trippe furnished him with a Pan American code book, and he sailed for the Orient. His first port of call was Japan, where he became deathly ill eating raw fish, and where the code book was stolen out of his hotel room. He wired this news to Trippe. At the price of thousands of dollars, the code was changed throughout the Pan Am system.

When he reached Shanghai, Bixby was still ill. Nonetheless he made a tour of inspection. The airport was five miles south of downtown. There was a small hangar, along with five Stinsons, four of which were out of commission, and five Loenings that seemed in good condition, although when he went for a ride in one he found the cabin noise so thunderous that he had to use cotton earplugs. He also had to tie his hat on aloft, he said later, even with the windows closed.

The airline's name had recently been changed to China National Aviation Corporation (CNAC). Six pilots were American, and one was German. The copilots were all Chinese. There were four American mechanics. Weather reports arrived by radio before takeoff, sometimes, but were unavailable in flight because there were no aircraft radios. The Stinson flew to Peking twice a week. The Loenings flew between Shanghai and Hankow daily except Monday, and made two round trips a week between Hankow and Chungking. This added up to fifty-five thousand route miles per month, but the airline was losing money at the rate of twenty-five cents per mile. There was not a single paved runway in the entire country.

And yet, Bixby thought, there was such a need for air travel in this country that CNAC ought to be making money. Perhaps all it needed was new routes—between Chungking and Chengtu, for instance. At present the Yangtze Valley route ended at Chunking, but Chengtu, a city of a million people, was only 170 miles further on, less than two hours by plane, whereas the "road" between the two cities was a 300-mile footpath across plains and mountains. Travelers who could afford it rode in chairs carried by bearers, or else in wheelbarrows—the journey took ten to fifteen days—and they were so regularly robbed by bandits that whenever possible they were accompanied by a bodyguard of soldiers. To survey this possible new air route, Bixby boarded a Stinson in Shanghai and started up the Yangtze to Chung-

king, 900 miles inland. It was to be a three-day trip. He was accompanied by holdover operations manager William Langhorne Bond. The pilot was Ernest Allison.

From the air Bixby saw that the hills were literally white with poppies. Opium, he realized, was the only product with high enough value concentrated in low enough bulk to stand the high transportation costs of China. Just above Ichang the little plane overflew an awesome, sixteen-mile-long gorge, in which the river surged past precipitous cliffs. In places the cliffs turned into fantastic rock battlements that Bixby thought looked like medieval castles. It was a breathtaking ride. "If flight over the gorges of the Yangtze fails to restore a man's sense of values, then he must indeed be an insufferable ass," Bixby wrote later.

Arriving at Chungking, he and Bond called on Marshal Liu Hsiang, the local warlord, to request permission to continue to Chengtu. They were given a breakfast of champagne and angel food cake, then ushered into the marshal's presence. He told them they could not proceed because Chengtu was under siege. But when Bixby insisted, Liu said okay, and he wired the attacking and defending generals not to fire upon the plane when it attempted to land.

It seemed worthwhile to wait for whatever responses Liu's telegrams might generate. When no word at all came back from Chengtu, Bixby decided to go on anyway, and he and Bond alternated with Allison as copilot. While waiting, Allison had studied three maps of this stage of their flight, all of them different. But at length Chengtu did appear. Allison circled over it, looking for a place to land. The only available field, he saw, was a military parade ground. It looked long enough, but it was blocked by a two-story building at one end and by a twenty-foot wall at the other. Also, it was crowded with soldiers carrying rifles, all peering upwards, none, as yet, firing. After much discussion within the plane Allison came down and landed, and the plane rolled to a stop. Immediately it was surrounded by soldiers with fixed bayonets. The three men climbed out nervously. At a command the soldiers presented arms: one of the bayonets speared through the wing, whose fabric popped like a gunshot, scaring the soldier, and the three Americans as well.

Meanwhile Pan Am's expedition to China had been put together from the Miami division. It was led by William Grooch, and it included a former German submarine commander named Paul Groeger, pilots George Rummel and Robert Gast, radio engineer Ivan Carlson and two radio operators, and chief mechanic Zigmund Soldinsky. These men had boarded a Danish freighter in late May in Savannah, Ga., and the ship also carried the two S-38 amphibians that constituted the rolling stock of the Pan American effort in China. For some days the freighter had beat its way down through the Caribbean Sea and then, having passed through the Panama Canal, had steered toward Shanghai. For those aboard, and also for the waiting Bixby, this constituted an exceedingly long trip. Under a contract left over from the Curtiss-Wright regime, CNAC had only until July 8, 1933, to open its Shanghai–Canton route. Bixby, waiting for the expedition's arrival, was counting the days.

At last on June 26 the ship docked at Shanghai. Grooch stepped off the gangway carrying a book called *The Qualities of Leadership,* which had been given to him in New York for shipboard reading by Priester. There were twelve days to go before the Shanghai–Canton deadline.

One of the S-38's was hurriedly assembled; Grooch test-flew it, then loaded Bixby and Bond aboard, and started toward Canton. The three men expected to pick up mail for the return trip, thus fulfilling the contract. But lacking navigational aids, Grooch was obliged to follow the ragged coastline south, which added hundreds of miles and turned the flight into a long one—about twelve hundred miles in all—necessitating overnight stops first at Foochow and then at Hong Kong. Before landing at Hong Kong, Grooch dragged the airfield. It looked solid to him, so next time around he set the plane down. The wheels ran smoothly for fifty feet, then broke through the runway crust and dug in. The plane came to a jarring stop with its tail in the air, its landing gear ruined and its nose bashed in. There goes the mail contract, thought Grooch.

Only a day was lost repairing the plane, however, but another day—July 7—vanished at Canton as Bixby sought to pick up the load of mail. The minister of communications, it seems, had ordered the mail withheld, for he wanted the Americans to grant financial "concessions" first.

In any case, there was no mail, which meant that the contract would be lost. Bixby searched out the local postmaster, a European, and persuaded him to hand over two bags of Shanghai-bound surface mail. Next day at dawn the two mailbags went aboard the S-38; Grooch, Bixby and Bond reached Shanghai by nightfall and delivered the mail. The contract was saved.

Or was it? There followed months of hard bargaining by Bixby as to who was to pay what, and how. The Chinese wanted 20 percent of gross passenger revenues and 40 percent of mail receipts. Bixby was appalled. If he signed such an agreement, and news got back to Latin America, then Pan American could expect the same financial demands to be made there. Literally millions of dollars were at stake on this one point.

Bixby was trying to learn Chinese ways and negotiate at the same time. He saw that he was expected to pay "cumshaw" at every turn. Everyone, from house servants to government ministers, expected it. The usual bribe was 2 percent, explained Bixby in letters to Trippe. More was stealing, less was to lose face. Trippe wrote back that if cumshaw was once paid, there would be no end to it; Bixby was to explain to the Chinese that aviation was a new and different business, and that Pan American was not better than other American companies already established in China who did pay cumshaw, but that it was merely different and could not do it. As always in negotiations, Trippe believed in stubbornness and in the passage of time. Bixby was to hold firm, to wait a few months, and to see what happened.

So Bixby stayed at the bargaining table. Eventually Pan American agreed to finance $200,000 worth of new flying equipment, to build a $25,000 hangar and to bear the entire cost of airline operations. A complicated system of loans, revenue sharing and mail subsidies was worked out, and the agreement was signed. No cumshaw was ever paid. Typical Trippe negotiating tactics had won again. The so-called inscrutable Chinese had proven no more inscrutable to Trippe than New York bankers.

The pilots of the first passenger flight from Shanghai to Canton were Rummel and William Ehmer, who wore their trim blue uniforms with white caps. There were seven passengers aboard the S-38 as it lifted off the Whang Poo River at 6:15 A.M. on November 24, 1933. But thirty minutes later Rummel ran into fog over Hangchow Bay, so he turned the plane around and returned to Shanghai. At 8:00 A.M. Rummel took off for the second time. But there was still fog over the bay, and as its tendrils began to swallow up the airplane Rummel lost sight of the water. From 1,500 feet he dropped down to 500, but visibility only worsened. The bay water was yellowish and muddy, the same color as the haze. At 200-feet altitude Rummel still could see nothing at all. He began a shallow turn to port, caught sight of a strip of beach, pulled back sharply on the yoke and plowed into the top of a hill in a climbing attitude, instead of head-on.

When Rummel neither landed nor reported in, Grooch took off to try to find him. What he found was a splash of yellow on a hillside. It was the upper wing. Circling, it seemed impossible to Grooch that anyone could have escaped alive, for the wings and tail were torn off, one pontoon was lying down the hillside, and the hull lay upside down.

Although most of the passengers were severely injured, no one was killed, and Rummel himself was not even badly hurt. One of the American mechanics remarked, "That guy Rummel sure used up all his luck this time."

The company struggled on with only one S-38. Every time it put down on one of the rivers, hundreds of sampans, their crews yelling in queer singsong, paddled madly to get alongside the plane, and several times pilots were obliged to fire flares at these boats to keep them away. In bad weather the pilots learned to pray for the sight of a pagoda peeping above the mist-covered rice fields. At least then they could tell more or less where they were. They began to long for the lighted beacons of the United States, for the radio beams of Pan American's Caribbean. The weather was often dismal: rain, fog, sleet, even a typhoon that damaged some of the planes on the ground; others merely broke down, and sometimes crews had to work all night to get a plane ready to take off again the next day.

The American dollar began to fall, and the prices in Shanghai, already exorbitant, became more so. The pilots were barely able to live on their salaries. None of the Americans liked China; to them it was a place of fetid odors, cluttered with filth and refuse. They hated even the restaurants—Grooch once wrote about spending half an hour "trying to solo a pair of chopsticks on various queer dishes."

Nothing was the way anyone had hoped it would be. Financial deficits continued to mount. The rathole that had swallowed up Keys now yawned beneath Bixby—and beneath Trippe. Bixby's wife and four daughters joined him in Shanghai; he was going to have to stay on there longer.

Instead of improving, things got worse. Grooch's wife and two sons, aged seven and five, leaped to their deaths from the top of a Shanghai apartment building. Evidently, the woman jumped while holding on firmly to two little hands. The remaining S-38 took off from Shanghai for Canton, and was never seen or heard from again. Searchers did find bits of wreckage that matched the missing amphibian, and the body of the pilot, Robert Gast, badly decomposed, was found floating in the bay several months later.

Bixby sailed to America to see Trippe before it was too late. But Trippe's gaze now was focused in another direction. He was not at the moment interested in China. Bixby waited weeks and saw Trippe for ten minutes. If CNAC was to be saved, Bixby would have to save it himself, and he sailed back to China.

18

Europe via Greenland

Trippe was concentrating on the Atlantic, and on Europe. Specifically, he was fixed on the Greenland–Iceland route, which, since it offered islands all the way across, was the only one that could possibly be flown with the planes that existed right now. Unfortunately, the Icelandic government had already accorded exclusive landing rights for the next seventy-five years to a company called Trans-American. Trippe went to Trans-American and bought these rights for $55,000.

He also called in and studied every Arctic report then extant. Some said the Greenland–Iceland route was feasible, some not. Ben Eielson and Hubert Wilkins had flown from Alaska to Spitzbergen, Norway, in 1928. A pilot named Parker Cramer had set out from Rockford, Ill., that same year bound for Stockholm. He got lost in Greenland, landed on the ice and walked out. Back home he refinanced a second attempt and reached Labrador, but was wrecked at anchor by drifting ice. In 1931 Cramer was back still again, bound this time for Denmark, and the newspapers followed his spectacular progress from island to island until he took off from the Shetlands on his last leg to Copenhagen and was never seen again.

These few flights constituted virtually all that was known of the region's flying conditions. Not much more was known of conditions on the ground, so Trippe, the year before, 1932, had sent two scientific expeditions to Greenland, one of them in conjunction with the University of Michigan, and had maintained them now for over a year. But information he was receiving was inconclusive. Somebody would have to go up there and actually fly the route, and this had best be Lindbergh. The hero's flight would answer all—or almost all—of Trippe's questions.

The earlier flight north to the Orient, Lindbergh later claimed, had been "conceived, organized and paid for" by himself—an exaggeration, for Pan American had helped with his arrangements, furnished his radio, profited from his data. This new flight north to Europe was much more under Trippe's control, and a cargo vessel called the *Jelling* was hired to sail along part of the way, carrying not only supplies and fuel but even a spare plane.

The Lindbergh baby, Charles Jr., had been kidnapped and killed in 1932. A new son, Jon, had since been born. Anne Lindbergh left the baby with her mother, climbed into the second cockpit as before, and took off behind her husband on a trip that ultimately lasted five months and ten days, and covered thirty thousand miles on four continents. Later she was to write of her cockpit as "my room."

The Lockheed Sirius, repaired at the factory after its misadventures in China, was again Lindbergh's vehicle. Its colors had changed slightly —it was now red and black.

The *Jelling* had sailed from Philadelphia on June 29, 1933, with a party headed by Major R. A. Logan, and gasoline supplies had been placed along the coast as far as Labrador for Lindbergh's use. The Lindberghs left New York ten days later, stopped at North Haven, Me., for twenty hours while Anne bade good-bye to her infant, then continued northward to Halifax, to St. John's, to Botwood and to Cartwright, Labrador, where they landed on July 14. The *Jelling* was waiting for them. So was bad weather, and they were stuck there a week before the overcast at last rolled back and a blue and lovely sky appeared overhead. The weather was perfect. Too perfect. There was no wind at all, and Lindbergh couldn't get the Lockheed off the water and into the air. The curse of seaplane flying: unruffled water stuck to pontoons like glue. Of course, the plane was heavily loaded; Lindbergh, who by his own lights took no chances ever, was carrying enough fuel to make it to Greenland and, in the event of bad weather there, all the way back to Cartwright.

Much was made of the fact that the Lindberghs flew without parachutes; to parachute down into the sea, or onto the Greenland ice cap, meant certain death anyway, he reasoned; their only chance was to get down with plane and emergency gear intact. Parachutes represented two or three extra gallons of fuel. Lindbergh wanted that weight in fuel.

The next morning, with some fuel off-loaded and with a slight breeze blowing, he managed to get the plane unglued and to rise into the air.

When they landed at Hebron, Labrador, mosquitoes swarmed around their faces, and they ran for the safety of the mission. The missionary family had had no fruit or beef in months. It was like the Alaska trip a second time. The Lindberghs handed over one banana and some sandwiches, and took off again. A few hours later they were flying over Greenland. Charles passed a note back to Anne. She opened it and read: "Every five minutes we save a day's walk."

For three weeks they flew back and forth over Greenland, once discovering an unmapped fjord extending inland more than a hundred miles. They flew alongside snow-capped mountains 12,300 feet high, and twice traversed the island's great interior ice cap.

They spent a week in Iceland, then flew on to the Faroes and the Shetlands, both of which they found wreathed in mist, and then to Denmark. The Faroes and the Shetlands got one day of their time, Copenhagen a week. After that they visited Norway, Sweden and Russia, where they landed on the Moskva River between two bridges, with people cheering from a grandstand on one bank and a park on the other. Other European countries followed in irregular succession. They spent three weeks in England, a week in France, three days in Switzerland. From Portugal Lindbergh steered the Sirius out to the Azores to look for water smooth enough to receive flying boats on a regular basis; he found no such water.

From there he flew south to the Cape Verde Islands two hundred miles off the coast of Africa, which was to be his jumping-off point for South America and home. This distance of two hundred miles was critical. From the Cape Verde Islands the Sirius could reach Brazil with a slight fuel reserve. From the African mainland it would arrive, if it arrived, with nearly dry tanks.

Certain arrangements, a fuel cache for one, had been made for the Lindberghs in advance. But the Cape Verde Islands were not a tourist resort, there was no hotel, and they were obliged to lodge in a private house. This presented problems, for the Lindberghs were fastidious people. When Anne reached for a limp towel hanging beside their host's sink, Charles hissed that she must not use it. She dried her face on her handkerchief. Their mattress proved infested with bugs. In darkness they sneaked back to their plane, crawled into the fuselage and slept on top of their baggage.

Worse than this, the wind sent great rollers into the unsheltered harbor, and they were told it blew this way for six months at a time. Because there was no possibility of getting off with a full fuel load in the face of such seas, they flew back to Africa, where there were no rollers, no wind at all. To take off for South America from here began to look equally impossible. With tanks full to the brim and the harbor like glass, the Sirius would not rise. They needed the help of a breeze and they waited a week before one came. In the predawn of December 6 Lindbergh at last coaxed the plane up into the darkness and pointed it toward South America some sixteen hours away. The little Lockheed was lifting 29 pounds to the square foot of wing surface—an incredible lift for the wing shapes of 1933. Within an hour Anne at the radio had raised Miami, 4,120 miles away, and from then on she was in regular communication with Pan Am operators up and down the Latin American coast, all of whom stayed at their keys throughout the night: Rio, Bahia, Fortaleza, Pará, George-town, San Juan, Miami. Reports were relayed to the company office in New York, were typed up and handed out to reporters hour by hour.

Thousands waited at Natal when Lindbergh set down the plane there. In some other parts of the world prayers of thanksgiving were said, but not all publicity was favorable. A number of editorial writers echoed *Time* magazine, which wondered if "interest accruing to the national welfare by his flights is worth the calamitous crash of principal which would accompany his death. He is worth keeping. One way to keep him is on the ground."

In New York Lindbergh put together a report of his findings: a sched-uled transatlantic service probably could be operated through Greenland and Iceland during summer with a high degree of regularity and without great difficulty. It could be done with seaplanes, without the need for extensive organization or preparation.

"As usual," he wrote, "in a country where little flying has been done, the difficulties have been greatly exaggerated. There is bad weather, strong winds and low temperatures, but by no means to the extent com-monly believed . . . From our observations and inquiries it seems that the weather improves with increasing latitude north of Newfoundland." He went on to sketch tentative routes across Greenland, suggesting that the coast be avoided—inland bases were more likely to be free of fog. He talked about wind, about glare off the ice cap, about haze that extended upwards like drifting snow as much as a thousand feet high. He talked of the airplane itself in highly technical terms: "Unusually high wind veloc-ities would make a high wing loading desirable for handling the plane on the ground or water. A full cantilever monoplane with flaps or other similar devices would probably meet the requirements of northern flying better than any other type. It is inherently less subject to winds when on the ground. It is more adaptable to the installation of flaps. The wing is less affected by the accumulation of ice and is more adapted to the installation of deicers."

Iceland, Lindbergh wrote, presented no problems. Conversely, the Faroe and Shetland islands would have to be overflown, for the weather was almost always terrible there. That meant Iceland to Europe in a single bound, not an easy prospect in 1933, but not impossible either. The new planes were coming, Lindbergh knew. The "next step," the S-42 that he had discussed with Sikorsky, would be flying early next year. Supposedly it would meet Trippe's specifications—just: a 2,500-mile range with a crew of four and 300 pounds of mail. Sikorsky claimed it would, anyway.

Behind it by about nine months would come the bigger and possibly better Martin flying boat for which Trippe had also contracted.

19

The Long-Range DF

In New York, or in the jungles of Brazil, or wherever he happened to be, Leuteritz, too, was trying to cross oceans. The Atlantic, in the early thirties, was the one he had been told to work on. He was trying to find a way to track an airplane all the way across.

His homemade loop direction finder had picked up signals under optimum climatic conditions at a range of up to 100 miles, and much less than this—30 miles or less—at dawn and dusk. This was adequate for the Key West–Havana route, and improved transmitters had extended its range enough so that it had sufficed when the terminal was moved back to Miami. Then had come the 600-mile jump from Jamaica to Barranquilla—navigation had to be precise not only because this distance was vast, but also because of major hazards at either end that a lost plane might fly into: the 14,000-foot Sierra Nevada de Santa Marta range east of Barranquilla and the 7,000-foot Blue Mountain Peak near Kingston.

For Leuteritz, 600 miles was the outer limit of his art. To force radio transmitters and receivers to operate in conjunction with the loop over any greater distance would require huge amounts of power. Transmitter, receiver and loop would swell to impossible size. In an airplane, how was such size to be accommodated, and where was such power to come from? It would all have to be paid for. In a new and struggling industry, where was the money to be found?

Leuteritz kept puzzling the thing over in his head. Where was he to find the power he needed? How was he to get more range plus the same or greater accuracy? How much money would Trippe be willing to give him? To all these problems a single solution kept presenting itself: higher frequencies. If he switched to higher frequencies, present power would suffice, range would be extended, accuracy would be improved, and costs would be minimal.

But unfortunately, this would make the simple loop antenna totally impractical. He would have to switch also to an entirely different direction-finding system, and no such ready-made system existed.

A man named Adcock, Leuteritz knew, had done experiments in England with an antenna strung between four telephone poles oriented to the four points of the compass, a system that came to be named after him. Adcock had worked only with normal frequencies, 500 to 900 kilocycles, and these were useless for long-range navigation. Nonetheless, perhaps his four-telephone-pole idea could in some way be adapted into the high and very high frequency ranges Leuteritz needed.

The radioman went to RCA and talked to engineers there. He wanted RCA to build an adcock, to conduct the necessary experiments, and also to foot the bill. He urged RCA to do it "for the good of aviation."

Several RCA engineers were assigned to do the job, and an adcock was erected out at the end of Long Island to pick up test signals from incoming aircraft. Later RCA built a second adcock in Miami, where more tests were conducted. The results were shown to Leuteritz who was unimpressed, and said so. He was an acerbic man. He said what he thought most times, and displeasure was something he seldom tried to hide. He told the RCA engineers that they had accomplished nothing, as far as his own needs were concerned.

Having decided to withdraw from the project, RCA offered to sell its calculations and drawings, but Leuteritz refused to buy. Pan Am would be throwing money away, he said.

Leuteritz then sent Trippe a memo offering to conduct his own research. To it he attached a request for capital appropriations of $10,000. As an executive Trippe could be extremely tightfisted. Requests for money he normally cut way down, but there was one exception, and it had existed from the beginning: Leuteritz. Most often Trippe accorded him exactly what he wanted; it made some other department heads furious.

Leuteritz took his $10,000 to Miami and sat down with Sullinger, whom he had brought into Pan Am as his chief assistant, to talk over ideas.

Human ears detect sound direction because each sound reaches one ear a fraction of a second before it reaches the other. In theory the adcock worked the same way. If a plane was coming in from the north, the pole on the north would receive a stronger signal than the other poles.

To the basic principle of the adcock Leuteritz had nothing to add. Instead, his ideas centered on higher frequencies and therefore shorter wavelengths, for it took less power to produce them, and they could be projected great distances. Because they were not bound to the earth's surface by gravity, they shot off into space, where they struck the Heaviside layer some 120 miles up, and bounded back to earth again.

Of course, the basic adcock had to be bent to Leuteritz's purposes. To each pole of the system a dipole would be attached, and in the center of the four poles would stand a shack housing a receiver for tuning purposes. The receiver would contain an instrument invented by Leuteritz and Sullinger for balancing the two opposite dipoles.

All the rest was experimentation. It was clandestine, and it lasted about four months. The spacing of the poles and dipoles had to be consistent with the frequency to be used, Leuteritz found. Finally he decided on two sets of poles, the outer ones about 500 feet apart, the inner ones only about 100 feet apart. This gave him two ranges of frequencies. The first would operate over distances of 500 to 700 miles. For planes passing beyond that range, different, higher frequencies would be used. Leuteritz was thinking in terms of a maximum direction-finding range of 1,200 miles. This would mean an effective range of twice that; the DF at takeoff would guide the plane halfway, where the destination DF would take over.

When basic research had been completed, Leuteritz, checking it out, arranged for radio operators aloft to transmit on certain frequencies at certain times. He also ordered night flights. In the early thirties this was asking pilots to risk their lives, and all but two pilots refused to do it. Even the two who agreed were not told why, nor was the operations manager. Leuteritz was protecting what he knew to be a business secret of the first magnitude.

Leuteritz was part scientist, part pioneer. He prided himself on being interested in cold data only. Nonetheless he was elated by the tests; they exceeded his expectations. Back in New York he drew Trippe aside after a staff meeting and said, "Juan, we have the DF. It is working. As far as navigation is concerned, we are ready to go. The only thing we have to do is make a survey off Nova Scotia and Greenland to find out what atmospheric conditions are up there." He began to talk to Trippe about wave propagation, about frequencies, about dipoles.

People who didn't understand radio sometimes couldn't understand Leuteritz. How much Trippe understood was never clear to him. He always credited Trippe with a fantastic memory, and also with an aloof quality that suited Leuteritz fine. It was Trippe's habit, Leuteritz believed, to find the best man for a given job, and then to leave him alone. In all the months that Leuteritz had been working on long-distance direction finding, Trippe had never once asked for a progress report. Trippe himself had been making full-scale plans to cross oceans. Millions of dollars had been invested with Sikorsky and Martin for new flying boats; millions more had been spent in Greenland, China, Alaska. Months had been spent in negotiations for landing rights, in personnel training, in feasibility studies. But Trippe could go nowhere without long-range direction finding, and he could not have been certain in advance that Leuteritz would be able to invent a workable system. Leuteritz, at the start of his experiments, had not been certain himself. He simply had had a feeling, an instinct, that a system existed, and that he could find it.

Leuteritz, when he looked back in later years, was amazed at Trippe's ability to construct long-range plans on top of systems that did not yet exist, to spend so much time and money on systems that were perhaps impossible and would never exist.

Leuteritz himself gave orders to his men to build the necessary units, and he began to decide where they should be installed. Driving out to the end of Long Island, he selected a field near East Hampton. He paced off the ground. He saw where the poles would be planted, visualized the control shack in the center, heard the planes overhead heading out over the ocean. This East Hampton station would control the first thousand miles or so of the flight—or the last thousand for returning planes—and another would be needed at Botwood in Newfoundland. A third he planned for Ireland near Foynes, close to the river on which the flying boats would land.

Trippe informed his board of directors that as soon as the new planes were ready, the company would cross the Atlantic.

20

A Switch to the Pacific

He was wrong.

For six years he had schemed. He had traveled, bargained, signed dozens of agreements, incorporated around ten new companies. When he had sent others to speak in his name they were the best available. Alan Winslow in Canada had been Yale '18 and captain of the crew just before Trippe's time, and had lost his left arm flying in the World War. John C. Cooper was a specialist on international air law, and had represented the United States on European commissions; he wore three-piece suits, rimless glasses, a gold watch chain, a gold Phi Beta Kappa key and a gold clip under the knot of his tie. Even more prestigious was Evan Young, former consul general in Halifax, former minister to Ecuador, Bolivia and the Dominican Republic.

Six years of scheming. Nearly every scheme had seemed at first to succeed; in reality every one had failed.

The tripartite agreement had fallen apart within four months of being signed. In Paris, Aéropostale had collapsed in a great scandal. This blocked the southern route to Europe because landing concessions in the Portuguese Azores remained with the defunct company.

Following his purchase of the $55,000 landing concession in Iceland, Trippe had imagined that both northern routes were open to him. They weren't. Both were blocked at Newfoundland, which was a dominion and enjoyed the same status as Canada, including sovereignty over its airspace. Winslow went there to negotiate. Suddenly antigovernment riots broke out. "Government routed by mob violence with prime minister and cabinet as refugees somewhere in backwoods," Winslow cabled. "My negotiations appear to be interrupted." This was one of the last messages received from the one-armed ex–war hero, who, for unknown reasons, plunged out of his hotel-room window some months later. Voting to give up its sovereignty, Newfoundland became a crown colony; if Trippe still wanted landing rights there, he would have to open new negotiations with the British government in London—negotiations that would probably consume years.

Toward Asia the view was equally gloomy. Pacific-Alaska Airways was losing money. It had now operated all of one winter. Sub-zero conditions had proven intolerable. For the moment Alaska was the route to nowhere. Trippe's contract across Siberia had proven useless also. Russia had refused to pay its war debts, and in retaliation the United States had withheld diplomatic recognition of the Bolshevik government. The State Department had asked Trippe to cancel his planned air route to Moscow. He had had to do it.

It was now mid-1934. Trippe had three Sikorsky S-42's and three Martin M-130's about to be delivered and he kept staring at his globe, at the broad Pacific. With the Atlantic closed and Alaska closed, there was no place to send those new planes except across the earth's widest ocean at its widest point. He would have to cross to China via Hawaii and Wake. Hawaii constituted the longest overwater jump in the world, and Wake represented one of the tiniest known targets. He didn't know if the new planes would have enough range to reach Hawaii, for they had not yet even been flown. He didn't know if navigators would be able to find Wake; aerial navigation that precise had never yet been tried. He didn't know a lot of things. If the plane made it to Hawaii, if the navigators found Wake, was there any place to land there? The next two stops would be Guam and the Philippines, where naval bases already existed. Compared with Hawaii and Wake, they looked easy.

In later publicity Van Dusen would tell the world that the Pacific venture was four years in the planning and that all decisions had been arrived at soberly. In fact the most important decision—to cross at all—was made by Trippe from one day to the next. He thought about it alone all one night and by morning had decided. Pan American would cross the Pacific. Reaching his office, he began giving orders. He looked serene and untroubled, but he was also as cagey as always and he revealed the future only in pieces, only on a need-to-know basis. He wanted a budget study, of course, and from the man who would sign it, C. H. "Dutch" Schildhauer, he wanted one thing more. He and Schildhauer faced each other across the desk; he wanted Schildhauer, he said, to go to Washington—on his own, so to speak—and find out all he could about those islands. He was to do it quietly. He was to research especially Midway and Wake. A flying boat, both knew, needed sheltered water. To plow into a rough sea in landing was to tear off an engine or a wing, and taking off from an open sea was impossible. Did sheltered water exist at Midway and Wake?

Trippe showed Schildhauer to the door. "Do it quietly," he repeated. "You don't need to bring our name into it."

Schildhauer went to Washington to the Navy Department, where he still had friends. He asked to see charts and reports on Midway and Wake, and they were given to him. There was ample data on Midway, which lay thirteen hundred miles west of Hawaii, for it had been a cable station since 1903. Midway, he saw, was a fairly typical Pacific atoll, and atolls were exactly what flying boats needed. Most of the islands of the world were what might be called nautical mountains. They rose steeply out of the sea, waves smashed against their coastlines, and only the biggest boasted sheltered harbors. But in much of the Pacific a different phenomenon had occurred: because of the depth of the water, islands were likely to be tiny, even barely awash, and around each would be a loosely fitting ring of coral. The water inside the coral ring became a lagoon, and lagoons, if of sufficient size, were something flying boats could land on.

Midway, Schildhauer saw, was not one island but two. The bigger was called Sand Island. It was roughly triangular in shape and roughly five miles around. The second island, Eastern, was about half that size. The coral ring surrounding them had a circumference of about twenty-five miles, thus enclosing a rather large lagoon. The charts showed that the coral rim was unbroken; no ship could get into the lagoon, and depth soundings therefore were not given. Nonetheless, in a lagoon that big, Schildhauer reasoned, surely a marine runway either existed or could be dredged. The cable station, Schildhauer read, was on Sand Island; a windmill there pumped up drinking water.

He turned to the file on Wake.

Supposedly Wake was visited by a Spanish galleon as early as 1568. In 1796 it was rediscovered by a British captain, William Wake, and in 1840 it was explored by U.S. Commodore Charles Wilkes and the painter-naturalist Titian Peale. In 1899 an American warship dropped anchor offshore; a ceremonial flag was raised above the dunes and a plaque was deposited in the sand that claimed Wake for the United States. The most recent expedition occurred in 1923, when a party of scientists from Yale University and the Bishop Museum of Honolulu landed there briefly from the U.S.S. *Tanager,* only to find that there was no water ashore, and that the island was as deserted as it had been all through history. Nonetheless, they charted the island—a chart that at the time interested no one; and Schildhauer studied this chart now. The lagoon was small and shallow. But perhaps it could be made to do. The island was, of course, extremely low in the water. Schildhauer had no way of knowing year-round weather conditions there, or even if such a low island remained afloat during great storms. There was no ship channel into the lagoon, and the depths immediately offshore were extreme. That meant rough water all around the island, which in turn meant that flying-boat operations, if the lagoon proved impractical, probably could not be conducted at all. There would be no lee side to this island. It was the lagoon or nothing.

Schildhauer sent a brief memo to Trippe. Hawaii, Midway, Guam and the Philippines looked okay. About Wake he was hopeful. That the feasibility of the route depended entirely upon Wake, Schildhauer well knew. Like Trippe, he had found between Midway and Guam no alternative refueling base. But he believed the Pacific crossable, his memo concluded —which perhaps only meant that he wanted to be part of crossing it.

Now Trippe sent to Washington to find out which department administered Wake. No one knew. Although letters passed between State and Navy, there was no firm answer. It had never been administered by anyone. There was nothing there to administer. Until now the tiny island had been useless.

21

The Public Decision

The Sikorsky S-42 was almost ready for test flights.

For two years in Trippe's office, on the fifty-eighth floor of the Chrysler Building, meeting had followed meeting. Sikorsky would come in and spread blueprints out on the desk. Trippe, Lindbergh and Priester, in their shirt-sleeves, would pore over them. For two years Priester and Lindbergh had kept pushing Sikorsky for more and more performance. Trippe, as was his way at such times, had kept silent. He never argued if someone else would do it for him.

To all these men there was nothing mysterious about flight. It was true that Lindbergh saw flight in mystical terms; but at the same time he saw it as something purely mechanical, and so did the others. The plane itself was a machine that operated according to mechanical laws. The air was as real a substance as earth or water, and it too conformed to mechanical laws.

Which meant that most problems were mechanical in nature, and could be solved mechanically.

Lindbergh had wanted the S-42's skin sleek as a baby's. This meant flush riveting. It meant engine nacelles buried in the wings, which had not been done in the past—and for good reason: when an engine broke down, its propeller continued to turn, windmilling, but as it windmilled it blocked off air from whatever was behind it. If the engine was in the nose or slung below the wing, then windmilling was acceptable, but if buried in the wing, that entire portion of wing behind it was no longer developing lift.

Lindbergh and Priester wanted the engines in the wings anyway. The solution to the windmilling problem was to invent and install propeller brakes. Could this be done? It could be and was.

Other radical ideas were adopted also. By designing a very long, thin wing, Sikorsky had gained much more lift. Could propeller blades be reshaped too? Would that increase the amount of air thrown back? They could and it did.

What about adjustable pitch propellers? Cars had at least three forward gears, but a plane only one. Adjustable pitch propellers had just been invented. They gave only two gears, the equivalent of low and high, but this alone was a huge advance. The blades took quick, small bites of air on takeoff, changing to huge gulps of air for easy cruising. Could such props be made huge enough for the S-42? Yes. It was no easy job, but it could be done.

The S-42 was test-flown by Lindbergh on August 1, 1934. With a full load under transport conditions the great new flying boat averaged 157.5 miles per hour over a 1,242-mile course. It set eight world records and, of course, made front-page headlines. Such a range would "cover the ocean trade routes," read a *New York Times* headline the next day, which wasn't true. The plane had an absolute range—with no passengers aboard—of about 2,540 miles, not enough to reach Hawaii safely. The first S-42 went into service in Latin America. The second went back to the factory to have its range stretched, if possible, and Trippe, still without a plane that could do the job, informed the Secretary of the Navy in a letter dated October 3, 1934, that Pan American was ready to fly the Pacific; he requested a five-year lease on Wake Island renewable for four additional five-year periods. Needing an airmail contract, needing to know the reaction of the Roosevelt administration to his plans, Trippe also sent a letter to Postmaster General James Farley. In it Trippe noted that Pan Am was preparing for the Pacific at a time when certain foreign airlines were making "aggressive" moves on that area from the other direction. This tone of patriotic fervor was typical of Trippe's method when dealing with the government: Pan American was willing to stand alone against the foreign hordes. Both then and later it was the type of argument that almost always produced results.

Farley answered by return mail. Not only was the Post Office Department "interested," said Farley, but so was the government generally. Both sides made the letters public. It was official: Pan American was about to cross the Pacific. Trippe now went quickly back to San Francisco. He had gone there several times already to try to establish an identity for himself and his company in the business community in California and Hawaii. For some reason new routes aroused strong passions, sometimes even in people not themselves competing for them. A new route required so many concessions and permits that it could be blocked easily enough.

Trippe wanted friends, not enemies, in San Francisco and Hawaii, and he wanted the most influential friends he could get: newspaper publishers, shipping executives. Now in November his special targets were Wallace Alexander, who was one of the richest and most influential men involved in Hawaii–California trade—he was also chairman of the Matson Line, which ran its ships from San Francisco to Hawaii—and Stanley Kennedy, president of the Matson subsidiary Inter-Island, which provided inter-island air and sea service. Pan American had always been a community effort, Trippe told them, and he wanted the Pacific Division to be similar. Therefore he was offering the two companies options on $500,000 of Pan Am stock, and if they took up at least half of this, then they would acquire an option on $1 million more, plus the right to name two directors to Pan Am's board. Of all the companies whose territory Trippe was invading, the Matson Line was the most important and best connected. He had somehow failed on the Atlantic; he had no intention now of failing on the Pacific.

And yet, as he contemplated the future, Trippe continued to brood about the island bases on which a Pacific route hinged. Back in his office, he sent once more for Schildhauer, and when the former flying-boat captain appeared, Trippe sent him to Hawaii to check out, as best he could, the proposed sites. Hawaii itself certainly. And Midway. And, most of all, Wake.

Schildhauer sailed to Honolulu on the *President Coolidge,* and made contact there with Stanley Kennedy. Among the men Trippe had been wooing, it was Kennedy he most feared, but the man was cordial to Schildhauer and helped him in many small ways.

Schildhauer was in luck. The S.S. *Dickinson,* which supplied the cable station on Midway, was about to sail with supplies for the winter. Schild-hauer booked passage. He was on Midway only a day and a half. He found that the two islands were separated by a channel: deep blue water that changed in the shallows to aquamarine. This channel was about a mile wide. Summer temperatures on Midway, he was told, rose to 85 degrees, but it was a cold place in winter.

The cable station was at the northeast end of Sand Island, and it was a kind of lush green enclave surrounded by thirty-year-old iron-wood trees planted there when the cable station was opened. These trees were now so high that they had had to be topped to allow the wind to get at the windmills. The southern end of Sand was fairly densely covered with magnolia; Schildhauer had to move along clearly defined paths. The entire island was rimmed with a beach of ex-tremely fine sand, and at the southeast end the coral reef was so close he could walk to it. On the northern end the reef was three miles away. Eastern Island did not interest him. It was covered with magno-lia also. Three or four ironwood trees stood up very high. It was inhabited, he learned, only by thousands of birds and by four donkeys, survivors of a herd bred many years ago.

Borrowing a transit from the cable superintendent, Schildhauer began surveying Sand Island. Frequently he got down on his knees to plot angles. The sand bothered him. It was glaringly white and so fine that it got into his clothes, his ears. He was always glad to return to the cable station. There was grass in front of the bungalow, and Hau trees and palms, various shrubs and gardens of pink geraniums, red hibiscus hedges and bougainvillaea vines. He listened to the eight or nine cable people praising their beach. Sometimes they found a seal lying on the shore, they said, or a turtle, or ray, or shark. Between August and April the water was too cold for swimming, they told him. The rest of the year it was just right, and the sand was cool on the hottest days. They went shelling a lot, and claimed that a hundred and fifty varieties of shells existed. Sometimes they went to the shack on Eastern Island for picnics.

Midway was a lonely place. Schildhauer was glad to leave. Sailing back to Hawaii he studied his figures. He had no further questions about Midway. A suitable base could easily be built and maintained on Midway.

It was Christmas, 1934, when Schildhauer sailed for California. From there he flew in stages to New York, where he handed over the results of his tour to Trippe. Hawaii was okay. Midway was okay. Wake was still a question mark, but he had learned of a Navy ammunition ship called the *Nitro* that was expected to sail from Guam to Honolulu early next year. Normally it carried an amphibian aboard, and Schildhauer had asked the Navy to order the *Nitro* to sail past Wake so that the pilot of the amphibian could photograph the island from the air. These photos might give a definite answer on Wake. Of course, it would be weeks before they would be made and months before they reached New York.

A man more prudent than Trippe would have waited for them, but Trippe could not afford to wait months. He could not afford to wait any time at all, and so he gave the orders that set into motion all the vast machinery connected with starting an air route out over nine thousand miles of ocean. He had gone too far to back down now.

22

Practice Flights

The expedition to Midway and Wake was put together by
L. L. Odell, the same Odell who had been Trippe's partner in Eastern Air
Transport in 1925, and who was now listed on the company masthead as
chief airport engineer. It was Odell's job to hire a cargo vessel, fill it with
the hundreds of thousands of items needed to build and maintain bases
on the two atolls, hire the men who would do the actual construction,
send them to sea, and then to supervise by radio from San Francisco the
work itself.

Odell began organizing on January 7, 1935. No detailed plans were
ever worked out by anyone, nearly every item being ordered on the basis
of simple penciled memoranda. Orders to manufacturers went out beginning about January 15. Pier 22 on the San Francisco Embarcadero was
rented as the assembly warehouse. Stacks of gear began to pile up in the
dim light. At length the freighter *North Haven* was brought in alongside
and winched closer and closer to the pier openings until its high black
sides rose up out of sight, and the warehouse became even darker.

The gear began to go aboard: food for a hundred and eighteen men
for four months; a quarter of a million gallons of aviation gasoline mostly
in fifty-five-gallon drums, forty great, long antenna masts with which to
construct Leuteritz's adcock direction finders on five islands; four landing
barges and four motor launches, two each for Midway and Wake; and all
of the tents, tractors, tanks, refrigerators, generators and prefabricated
buildings with which to construct two villages in the middle of the ocean.
Odell and his staff were trying to think of everything: forty-five books, ten

packs of playing cards, three dozen rubber heels. No one knew what would grow on either Midway or Wake; nonetheless the *North Haven* would carry seeds for royal palm, coconut and papaya, for beets, onions, radishes, spinach, tomatoes, cauliflower, cucumbers, peas, and for assorted flowers as well. It would be most of a year before either island could be resupplied, and so aboard the freighter went ink, chewing tobacco, shower compartments, pillowcases, coat hangers, eggbeaters, sugar bowls, six iced-tea spoons per island, pie tins, kitchen sinks, two tons of coal, ice-making machines.

According to drawings and written specifications, each compound would consist of prefabricated, one-story anti-vermin-treated wood structures built on posts three feet above grade: thirteen buildings, two windmills, a pile dock with a landing float attached. The buildings would have overhanging roofs to give maximum shade. Rainwater would be stored in steel cisterns and pumped with windmills to elevated tanks to obtain water pressure.

Meanwhile the Pacific Division was created—forty-one men were culled from the Eastern Division at Miami, and sent to man the San Francisco base under Clarence Young. Some moved through the dim pier looking out, past stacked stores, at the steep hull of the *North Haven* while their blood stirred and vague romantic longings filled their heads. Though they would not go out themselves, they were part of the adventure: mid-Pacific islands no one had ever heard of were to be colonized; an ocean was to be crossed. This ship would establish bases at what seemed then an incalculable distance out into the unknown.

Construction crews were hired, not depression laborers out of work, but eager college boys—the building of these bases was not a housing project. Besides, college boys were cheaper. Many came from the East, from the Ivy League colleges that had formed Trippe and so many of his associates.

All was ready. The *North Haven* awaited only orders from Trippe to set sail.

In New York Trippe coped with tremendous details. He still had no permission to use Wake—or Midway either. It wasn't even clear who could give it to him. He wanted the islands placed under the jurisdiction of the Navy, because he and his company had a better working relationship with the Navy than with any other department. In addition, if the islands were naval bases, then the Navy might improve them at no cost to Trippe; it might blast channels for him through the reefs into the Wake and Midway atolls; Navy ships and planes might be there to search in the event of an emergency. But to get Wake put under the Navy required a presidential order.

In Washington such an order was written and sent to the White House, where President Roosevelt signed it. Next, contracts to use Wake,

Midway and Guam as air bases were drawn up. With the *North Haven* waiting to sail, Trippe and Secretary of the Navy Claude Swanson signed them.

A revised budget had been prepared, and Trippe studied it. Total investment in aircraft and other flight equipment came to $1,910,000, including a crash reserve of $644,485. Revenue needed to cover expenses and provide a 6 percent return on investment came to $2.11 per mile— and the legal limit for airmail contracts at the moment was $2.00 per mile.

Trippe's bets were enormous, and he was hedging none of them. He had no airmail contract, and would lose money even if he got one at the maximum rate. Passengers might make up part of this deficit later, but there would be none for a year, perhaps longer. He was approving the investment of all this money when Wake Island—and the airplane itself —were still question marks. In addition, he still had no permission to land in the Philippine Islands or on the Asian mainland.

He might not even get the airmail contract because two other airline projects had recently sprung up. Stanley Kennedy, president of the Matson subsidiary Inter-Island, whose planes linked up the Hawaiian Islands, had just announced plans to start a new airline, or expand Inter-Island, to compete with Pan American on the route to China. Kennedy was a big man in Hawaii, and Matson was the biggest name in the whole Pacific— certainly far bigger than Pan American. A second newly formed company —South Seas Commercial—was in the running also. It had applied for government leases on Midway, Wake and Guam. South Seas seemed a serious venture, for it was backed by Donald Douglas, manufacturer of Douglas Aircraft, in collaboration with an Australian navigator named Harold Gatty. If either Inter-Island or South Seas got the transpacific airmail contract, then Trippe's new route would be a commercial disaster.

Could this happen? As far as airmail contracts were concerned, the Washington climate could hardly have been worse for Pan American. During the past year the so-called Black Investigation had focused on these lucrative Post Office contracts. Rarely, the Black Investigation had disclosed, had they been awarded on the basis of low bid. Instead, the Postmaster General had always favored the strongest, richest companies, and in 1930, at a so-called Spoils Conference called by Postmaster General Walter Brown, the airline map of the United States was drawn and routes allocated among the principal companies. Now, as a result of the Black Investigation, every single one of these domestic airmail contracts had recently been canceled. In the United States the Army was now flying the mail. Instinctively Trippe had known he should not attend the Spoils Conference and had not done so. Pan American's contracts had therefore not been canceled; in any case, there was no alternative carrier in Latin America. But the company had seemed tainted: to the general public it had seemed that Pan American, like the domestic airlines, was guilty of misconduct; unlike the domestic airlines, it had gone unpunished.

It was no longer the public's darling.

Congress now passed a $2 million appropriations bill for transpacific airmail. This prize the newcomers, Inter-Island and South Seas, could see and almost touch. In light of the recent scandals, they were going to have a good shot at it. Unlike the earlier days in the Caribbean, the contract would go to the lowest bidder. Trippe's friends in Washington were not going to be able to help him this time.

In Bridgeport, Conn., the range-stretched S-42 had come back from the Sikorsky factory. Its maximum range at birth had been about eighteen and a half hours in the air. Depending upon winds aloft, this worked out to more or less 2,500 miles. Now, with passenger fittings ripped out and replaced by cabin tanks holding 4,500 pounds of fuel, the plane's range had been extended by a safety reserve of about three hours—about 500 more miles. These cabin tanks were connected to the wings by tubes, and all that fuel would have to be pumped up to the wings in the air. The result was going to be a constant odor of raw gas inside the fuselage. Everybody noticed it at once and worried about it. Nonetheless, the plane was sent to Miami and a series of tests was begun to try to extend the maximum range even further. What were the best carburetor settings, altitudes, engine speeds for long-range cruising? Meters were installed so that fuel consumption could be accurately measured in flight. Automatic carburetors were designed and installed to provide a constantly accurate fuel flow. For the first time in the history of aviation long-range flight was being scientifically analyzed. Tables began to be printed up that showed optimum engine settings for optimum range at various altitudes and conditions. These were for the "guidance" of aircraft captains only. The captain was still God. Stretching the range of a flight was still heresy. To a pilot, stretching his range was stretching his luck, and most of those who watched the S-42 experiments over Miami day after day were instinctively hostile. Though not the chief test pilot, who was again Musick.

Now forty years old, Musick seemed the same quiet, meticulous man who had flown the first regularly scheduled commercial flight between Havana and Key West seven years before. The general public, which within a year would make Musick the most famous airman in the world after Lindbergh, had never heard of him. It was Musick, together with a young engineer named John Leslie, who did the work from which the technique for long-range cruising crystallized. It was clear that the engines should be turning slowly but laboring hard, like a truck crawling up a steep hill in high gear. But what was this optimum cruising speed, this optimum fuel mixture, this optimum altitude? At what point did a too lean mixture burn out engines? At what point did too much effort cause an engine to explode? Over the Caribbean the tests went on. In the cockpit Leslie stood at Musick's elbow, giving instructions, noting data on his clipboard. There were hours of flying with one engine shut down, with an engine off on either wing, with two engines off on a single wing. Always Leslie and Musick watched the fuel-consumption figures.

Possible emergency procedures were tried out also. A wind-operated pump transferred gas from cabin tanks to wing tanks. Suppose this pump broke down in mid-Pacific? Day after day crewmen practiced pumping the gas out to the wings by hand. There were frequent engine overhauls as well; wear was checked; minor but vital improvements were made.

On March 23, 1935, came the final fuel-consumption test. Theory was over, and Leslie stayed on the ground. At midafternoon, carrying a full crew and a full load of fuel, Musick lifted the S-42 off the water at Miami and headed straight out into the Atlantic. Windows were open because the men could smell fuel vapor. There was no heat in the cabin, and all were bundled up in sweaters and flying suits.

About two hours later the sun set behind the flying boat, and the sea below disappeared into darkness except for occasional white streaks of waves. Musick held the plane at 4,000 feet, at an airspeed of about 150 miles per hour. Musick and copilot Rod Sullivan were at the controls, watching the dimly lit bank of flight instruments. Radio officer W. T. Jarboe was in contact with the Miami direction finder. Engineering officer Vic Wright, crouched to the rear of the darkened cockpit, watched his engine instruments. A few paces aft was the chart room. There navigator Fred Noonan and junior flight officer Harry Canaday worked over the charts, plotting and replotting the position of the plane. No one aboard was at ease. All had brought picnic lunches and thermos flasks, but no one was eating. This was the first long-range flying-boat flight in the history of commercial aviation, and these men were sweating it out. The object was to fly this machine out to sea some 1,300 miles to the Virgin Islands, turn and come back, hitting specific checkpoints en route, and land safely again at Miami. It was a dress rehearsal for the San Francisco–Hawaii flight, and it was the only rehearsal the crew would have.

Six hours after takeoff, flying through cloud and light rain, a light was sighted blinking on the horizon. The startled Musick called navigator Noonan into the cockpit. Both men stared at the blinking light. Both thought they were looking at a lighthouse in the middle of the ocean where there was supposed to be none. The nearest island was Puerto Rico, several hundred miles south. Was the light Puerto Rico? Were they that far off course?

Aerial navigation was brand-new, and Noonan may have been the world's first professional aerial navigator. A merchant marine captain without a ship because of the depression, he had been found managing the Pan American station on Martinique, and had been given the job of training himself and others to find atolls in oceans. Celestial navigation from airplanes had been deemed in advance more accurate and more reliable than Leuteritz's long-range DF, which had not yet been tried out over vast ocean distances, nor even on an east–west axis, and which perhaps did not work. Or suppose it broke down in flight? Obviously, aerial celestial navigation was essential. Unfortunately, it was not easy to do. Normally a navigator used his sextant, with its system of mirrors, to pull the sun's or a star's image down to the horizon. He then measured the exact angle and referred it, together with the exact time of day, to printed tables which gave him his position. In the air these tables were falsified by the plane's altitude. In addition, from five or ten thousand feet up, there was often no sharp horizon to be seen. A new instrument had to be developed, and it was, but it was difficult to manage. The navigator worked with a bubble, as in a carpenter's level, and he now had to put a cross hair on this bubble and superimpose on it the star's image. But planes in flight vibrated, meaning that the bubble, the cross hair and the sun or star bounced around. Readings, it was learned, took a considerable time to make, and were often inaccurate. Noonan was learning always to take six or eight sights, to do his calculations at least twice, checking. But during the time this took, the pilot might fly fifty miles, perhaps more, in the wrong direction.

Now, six hours out in the empty Atlantic at night a lighthouse had been found blinking on the horizon. Captain Musick wanted an explanation from navigator Noonan.

The cockpit was crowded. Navigation was no casual matter, and all aboard stared at the blinking light.

Then it stopped blinking. After a heavy silence, Noonan started to laugh, for the explanation had just come to him. It was the planet Jupiter, he said, slowly lifting out of a shelf of low-lying cloud. But it made everyone realize how tenuous their lifeline was, how slim their confidence in their DF, in celestial fixes, in nighttime aerial navigation in general.

The cockpit was filled with the noise of embarrassed laughter.

The night wore on. It was very dark, and the interior of the plane got extremely cold. Before midnight Noonan came forward with still another fix. He had made star sights and matched them to the Miami radio DF. The plane was now one hundred miles due north of St. Thomas, and had reached its turning point. Musick began very slowly to bank the plane around.

On a northwest track the trade winds pushed them through what was left of the night. Musick held eight thousand feet, the plane's most economical cruising altitude, and when Wright shone his flashlight out the window on the props, he could almost count the blades as they swung around. Musick, running at specified reduced power, was stretching the fuel as far as it would go.

There were two bunks in the rear of the fuselage. In theory, each man was entitled to a rest period, but in fact no one got any rest. There were too many jobs to do, pumps to be switched on and off, star sights to be taken, bearings to be plotted, radio signals to send and receive, instruments to be monitored. The cabin fuel had to be pumped out to the wings evenly, keeping the eight wing tanks balanced.

All night the men worked. Dawn came. By then the S-42 was crossing the chain of the Bahamas. At breakfast time it crossed the Florida coastline, and then the entire peninsula passed beneath its wings and it headed out across the Gulf of Mexico. Another turn. Below now was Key West, and Musick gazed down at it, but said nothing. Instead, he turned the flying boat up the keys to Miami, came to Biscayne Bay, and calmly set down on the water. They had been aloft 17 hours 16 minutes, and had flown the equivalent of the ocean separating San Francisco from Hawaii.

This was enough for Trippe. He had a plane that could reach Hawaii; the only question mark left on the route to China was Wake Island, and he gave orders for the *North Haven* to set sail from San Francisco. Three days later it steamed out through the Golden Gate into the long Pacific swells. Even as it did so, Musick and his crew were winging toward San Francisco in their S-42. Because it could not make California nonstop, and because there was no body of water on which to land and refuel en route, it had headed south across Cuba, across the Gulf to a point south of Veracruz where Musick banked it into the west, gained altitude, and flew for two hundred miles across the mountainous spine of Mexico. On the other side of the narrowing continent he set the flying boat down in Acapulco harbor, where it was warped alongside a float. It was then dusk. A crew sent down from Mexico City swarmed over the engines, and refueling began by hand from drums in a boat. Canaday and Wright remained on board while the rest of the crew went ashore. Takeoff for San Francisco would be at dawn.

Noonan was a splendid navigator, the best available. He also liked parties. Musick knew this. It was one of the variables that Musick, as captain, had to contend with, and he took care always to room with Noonan on overnight hops, if he wished to be able to find him again in the morning. On this particular night, Noonan never got to bed. At dawn Musick went rushing about the town looking for him. Noonan, meanwhile, had decided to report directly to the dock, where a launch waited to take the crew out to the flying boat. In the predawn light he stepped off into what he thought was the launch. It wasn't. It was the shadow cast on the water by the dock. Fished out by his crewmates, he boarded the S-42 both drenched and sober.

A few minutes later a worried Musick was rowed out. "Has anyone seen Fred?" he demanded. "I can't find Fred."

At Alameda, across the bay from San Francisco, Pan American had established temporary headquarters. There, awaiting the arrival of the

S-42, a vast throng crowded the yacht basin; political officials waited in a roped-off enclosure.

Musick, who hated crowds and publicity, knew in advance what he faced, and he did not like it. After landing in the bay and taxiing up to the mooring buoy, he filed ashore with his crew, moving through the microphones and newsreel cameras. On the reviewing stand he listened self-consciously while notables praised him and his crew for the epic Pacific crossing they were soon to make. Musick himself was pushed to the microphones. He was always a taciturn man, even among friends. "Glad to be here," he said, and stepped back. Later, when he shouldered his way out through the crowd, people handed him autograph books and tried to shake his hand; the next morning his picture was on the front pages of newspapers. Then came requests to make speeches, to sponsor cigarettes, liquor, shaving cream. These piled up on his desk; he stared at them and did nothing.

New test flights began for Musick and his crew. Up and down the California coast they flew until they could identify every village, bay and lighthouse without reference to their charts. They practiced approaching Alameda from every possible angle, in every possible light. They flew out to sea, and homed back in on the DF radio beam.

23

To Hawaii Nonstop

Meanwhile the *North Haven* plowed toward Hawaii and the islands beyond. Cargo jammed corridors and decks. It was difficult to move about the ship. Men slept like coolies in bunks three tiers high. There were too many men aboard—a crew of 32, a construction force of 74, and 44 technicians—and they got in each other's way.

At Honolulu, where the ship stopped for three days, a ton of dynamite came aboard, together with still more passengers: a group of Chinese houseboys; a young man named Bill Mullahey who strode up the gangway wearing swim trunks and a straw hat, with a surfboard over his shoulder. At the rail one man turned to another and said, "Lord, what are we getting here?" Mullahey had once been on the Columbia University swimming team; now he was the expedition's underwater demolition expert, a job at which he was untried. But then, everyone else was untried also.

Out of Honolulu the *North Haven* pitched and wallowed for four more days. At last Midway Island showed: a pale smudge on the horizon.

The reef formed an unbroken noose around the two islands, and outward from the reef on all sides lay shoal water. The *North Haven* was obliged to drop anchor four miles out, and there it hung, alternately soaring and plunging in heavy seas while unloading proceeded. The two barges and two launches were dropped overboard, and the ship crashed into them each time it rolled. Responsibility for the cargo had rested with the *North Haven*'s owners to this point. It passed now to this gang of eager, untrained college boys. One by one the heavy items—tractors, diesel generators, the antenna masts—hung in the air over the barges. As the crane operators tried to time pitches and rolls, boys scampered about underneath to receive what was coming down. One of them got squeezed by a load, but was not badly hurt. Another had his fingers chopped off.

Approaching the reef was just as dangerous. There were two low spots over which water surged. The safer of the two held the transpacific cable, and could not be used. The lighters tugged the barges through the other by timing the surge so as to ride seas in over the jagged coral shelf.

Once ashore, every load had to be dragged by tractor on sleds through heavy sand. Winds were strong and the air cold. There was no shelter except tents, and at night millions of the so-called moaning birds flew overhead; their shrill, mournful cries kept almost everybody awake. By day these same birds hid in burrows in the sand, and into these burrows men constantly fell.

Midway also boasted an enormous congregation of gooney birds—the Laysan albatross. Pairs of these birds would face each other bowing, bobbing, scraping in some sort of ceremonial exchange. It was like watching humans. It was the best entertainment on the island, and almost the only one. The females laid one egg at a time directly upon the sand, and when the small bird hatched, it stayed there. If it moved even a yard away, its parents would refuse to recognize it when they came back from fishing. The soft-hearted college boys preceded tractors and sleds on foot, lifting the egg or small bird out of the way, and then replacing it after the tractor had passed by. It was enormously time-consuming.

Out at sea, standing on rafts lashed to the *North Haven,* watching heavy gear descend over their heads, these same boys were at all times ready to jump for their lives.

In San Francisco a new round of tests began. Musick took off with sealed orders, and when three hundred miles out to sea on a southwest course, he broke them open. He was ordered now to turn northward and intercept the Hawaii-bound steamer *Malolo,* which had left San Francisco at 4:00 P.M. the day before and was cruising at a speed of twenty knots.

Noonan, calculating fast, handed Musick his course. A short time later Musick dropped down through clouds, and there was the ship. He crossed over its smokestacks. Additional instructions came from Alameda by radio. Musick was to pull down his cockpit hood and fly blind back to Alameda by direction finder only. He was not to raise his hood until he entered the so-called cone of silence directly over the Alameda adcock. He did this, descended through clouds, oriented himself over San Francisco Bay, and landed. His crew was ebullient, and felt ready for the entire Pacific.

Musick himself had begun to study navigation. Night after night, on the roof of his apartment building, he got out his instruments and plotted the stars. Once he was surprised up there by cops with drawn guns investigating the report of a burglar.

San Francisco Bay was notorious for fog. Suppose the flying boat returned from Hawaii into fog—and with insufficient fuel to make it to an alternate landing site?

Blind landings were practiced. Shortly after takeoff, Musick pulled down his hood. At thirty-second intervals radio officer Jarboe received bearings from Alameda. This brought the flying boat inside the cone of silence, and from then on, navigation was by stopwatch. With Noonan at his elbow, Musick banked to the right, throttled back, and dropped his nose into a gentle glide. Theoretically he was now headed down the center of the south bay. Seven minutes precisely would take him to the still-unfinished San Francisco–Oakland Bay Bridge.

Noonan, watching his stopwatch, gave corrections. At an altitude of a thousand feet Musick crossed over the bridge, then swung back toward Alameda, twelve miles away. He dropped down toward the water. The plane spanked the water twice, then settled in for good. Musick cut his engines and threw up his curtains. Noonan clapped him on the back. Musick, however, was unimpressed. "All the way down I had the feeling we were going to smack that bridge right in the face," he said.

But they were as ready as they would ever be to fly to Hawaii and beyond. Headlines appeared: PAN AMERICAN CLIPPER POISED FOR PACIFIC FLIGHT.

There were those who considered such a flight suicidal. Still vivid was the 1927 Dole Race from San Francisco to Hawaii for a $25,000 prize. Seven aviators either crashed to their deaths or disappeared at sea. Since then a number of planes had reached Hawaii. A flotilla of Navy planes had made it the year before. But these were isolated stunts by daring individuals. Now Pan American was proposing not a stunt but a regular commercial route. To most "experts" of the time disaster seemed certain. Flying boats would go down at sea. Innocent passengers would be lost. The navies of the world would be mobilized to search for days or weeks. A death blow would be dealt to the prestige of America and American aviation.

To protest the proposed route, two members of Trippe's own board of directors had already resigned. Now Dr. George Lewis, chairman of the National Committee on Aeronautics, the United States' aeronautical research establishment, approached Trippe with a plan designed to save Trippe from himself, and to save Pan American's life. Dr. Lewis perhaps was speaking also for certain military and government officials. He considered Trippe's plans premature and dangerous, he told him. No flying boat, both knew, had ever made it to Hawaii before. Only one had come close, and it had drifted, fuel exhausted, for four days before being found near one of the tiny islands of the Hawaiian group. Probably Trippe wished to back out, said Dr. Lewis, but could not do so without losing face. He, Dr. Lewis, was willing to help: he would issue a public statement opposing the flights on the grounds that developments in aeronautics and in navigation did not yet permit them to be made safely.

Though Trippe was appalled, his face showed nothing. He could not afford any such statement by a man as prestigious as Lewis, and he began in his persistent quiet way to argue that his planes could fly the great distances involved, that they could navigate and find the mid-Pacific islands. Safety margins did exist. There was nothing to worry about.

Dr. Lewis went away.

But it was enough to make Trippe seek out Leuteritz, and he went to San Francisco, where the radioman had been camped for months setting up and calibrating his adcock direction finder. The two men had dinner at Trippe's hotel. The question was navigation, and finding those islands.

"Hugo," Trippe asked, "are you sure of your DF?"

Leuteritz, who could be irritatingly condescending at times, laughed. "Juan," he said, "you saw the results of the tests in Miami. We took accurate bearings from Miami on our planes flying up the Amazon River to Manáos twenty-two hundred miles away. We've been running experiments here for weeks. We've taken accurate bearings on Eastern's planes flying between New York and Miami. We've had them confirmed by Eastern. The DF works. You have nothing to worry about."

The two men nodded at each other. Leuteritz pushed back from the table. "Do you want to see for yourself? Come on out to Alameda with me right now."

Trippe shook his head. "No, I believe you."

Just before 4:00 P.M. on April 16, 1935, Musick prepared to take off for Honolulu for the first time. He would go that far only, then turn back; there was no place to land any further west. The *North Haven* was still unloading at Midway. Wake was still unexplored.

At San Francisco there was no takeoff ceremony, except that the ground crew crowded around. So did the five wives—Jarboe was not married—who had driven cross-country from Miami. No one admitted to fear, but everyone was tense.

Takeoff weather that afternoon was perfect. Musick, taxiing, made several lazy circles on the bay while his engines warmed up. Then he pushed forward the four overhead throttles. A layer of overcast lay just offshore. The S-42 clawed up through it, came out into the clear at six thousand feet, and headed west. About two hours later the sun turned red, and slipped down beneath the overcast. The sky flamed, then slowly went dark. The first stars appeared. Musick sent a message back to Alameda: "Sunset 6:39." It was the first ocean flight in history that people left behind could follow. Every half hour Musick radioed back progress reports.

Aboard the S-42 it began to get cold. Wright's uniform was a leather flying jacket over red-flannel pajamas and bedroom slippers. Most of the others wore fleece-lined boots and heavy flying suits.

There were steamships strung out below. Each was a checkpoint. All night Musick steered silently through darkness. All night he and his crew listened to the sounds of the plane's engines.

An hour before dawn they broke out of an overcast into starlight, and Noonan was able to take a fix. It showed them to be only about twenty miles off course. Musick throttled back and dropped down until far to the south he could make out the vague outline of Molokai. Then for the first time he smiled. "We can swim to port from here," he said to copilot Sullivan. For Musick this counted as a witty remark.

There had been only one crisis during the flight. The small propeller that operated the wind-driven fuel pump—it was mounted outside on the fuselage—broke off. Pieces of its blades pierced the skin of the plane and lodged inside. Someone could easily have been killed. The blades were dug out to be kept or given away as souvenirs; and the pump for the rest of the night had to be operated by hand.

About an hour out of Pearl Harbor Musick ordered his crew to clean up; they shaved with cold water. He was determined that they should look fresh when they came off the plane, and they did, stepping off smartly in their blue naval-type uniforms and white caps.

Four days later at 4:00 P.M. the S-42 rose from the waters of Pearl Harbor for the return flight. The plane again climbed up through overcast and came out into bright sunlight at seven thousand feet. Musick had only local weather forecasts that predicted adverse winds early in the flight. What he did not know was that he would be bucking powerful headwinds all the way across.

For weeks Pan Am meteorologist William Clover had been studying Pacific weather, but not a single synoptic weather chart of the Pacific was available. (Synoptic means that all local weather observations are made at the same time each day and the findings then are plotted on a single map.) Practically nothing was known of the general pattern of winds aloft between San Francisco and Hawaii because aircraft had never ventured out very far from either end of the route. The behavior of frontal systems was unknown also. There was regular ship traffic between California and Hawaii, and surface observations had been made for years but rarely at night, and never in the kind of detail that airplanes needed.

Like Musick, Noonan and the rest, Clover on the ground was trying to learn his part of the job of crossing oceans, but it was a job for which there were no teachers. Neither he nor Musick had any warning of the type of winds the home-bound flying boat was about to encounter.

Having climbed above the clouds, Musick throttled back to cruising speed, and hour after hour steered the plane along the course radioed to him by the adcocks at either end. The adcocks could give him direction only. They couldn't measure his ground speed, and headwinds against him were so violent that he wasn't making much progress at all, though he didn't know this at first. Not until the stars came out was Noonan able to get his first fix. It showed that the plane was considerably west of the point it ought to have reached by now. Further calculation put the flying boat's actual ground speed at only 96 miles per hour, and with this news everyone aboard became tense. If such winds continued, the fuel tanks would run dry long before they reached San Francisco.

All through the night, Noonan sought to calculate the plane's angle of drift, for this was the only way to monitor the strength and direction of the wind. To do so accurately required a fixed target on the ground; at sea at night of course there was none, but flares had been used as drift targets during the Caribbean test flights, and now Noonan repeatedly dropped flares out the window, then focused his instruments on them; as soon as day broke he began dropping chemical flasks overboard instead. They contained aluminum powder. A flask smashing on the water below spread a slick on the surface; Noonan focused his instruments on that.

During the second half of the flight he saw that the wind occasionally shifted to one beam or the other, but always it came back, blowing straight on the plane's nose—and hard, incredibly hard. The hours drained away. Their remaining fuel also. Engineer Wright had all four engines running at the lowest possible speed. At ten o'clock in the morning, after eighteen hours in the air, they were still five hundred miles from the California coast, still averaging under 100 miles per hour. Musick dropped down to an altitude of six hundred feet, hoping for milder winds close to the wave tops. He didn't find them, and presently climbed back to a more economical cruising altitude.

Trippe was in Washington for meetings with government officials. He came into Pan American's 15th Street office about 4:00 P.M. On a map on the wall the position of the plane in the air was being marked off hour by hour. Theoretically the plane ought to be landing in San Francisco about now, the end of an eighteen-hour flight, but the wall map showed it was still an alarming distance out to sea. Trippe sat there waiting for news. Presently it was dinnertime, but no one was hungry. Trippe watched the wall map. So did everyone else.

At a position calculated as two hours from the California coast the undercast thinned out, and for the first time since takeoff Musick could see the whole ocean below. Another aluminum flask was tossed over. The waves spread it out; it showed that a weak tailwind had developed, and for a while all aboard became cheerful. A short time later, as strong as ever, the headwind was back, beating at them. Engineer Wright was focused on his flickering instruments. He had the engines leaned down as far as he could, and he sat adjusting and readjusting the most minute settings, watching his gas gauges.

Soon there was only an hour's fuel left in the tanks, then only thirty minutes. The California coast was still not in sight. All of them sat there, waiting.

At Alameda the plane was five hours overdue. The wives still waited to greet their husbands. Finally Wright's wife, Ione, nerved herself up, found an engineer and asked how long the plane could stay in the air.

"About twenty-four hours," the man lied. Twenty-one and a half was the best anyone had ever calculated.

Mrs. Wright glanced at her watch. The minute hand was closing on twenty-four hours now.

"Don't worry, they'll make it," said the engineer.

Clouds that had hung low over San Francisco all day began to drift out to sea.

Off the coast Musick and copilot Sullivan, flying again through solid overcast, were peering intently out the narrow windshield. At 5:21 P.M. the plane broke into the clear, and suddenly they could see the line of hills shouldering down to the coast south of the city.

Musick steered toward San Francisco Bay. He came straight in. He could not afford to bank lest whatever gas was left splash away from the engines. The plane spanked down on the water and Musick taxied to the ramp, then cut the engines. For a moment all of them simply sat there. Then they got ashore and moved stiffly toward the embraces of their wives.

In Washington, a relieved Trippe and his men went out to dinner.

Engineer Wright remained behind to test the wing tanks with his gauge stick. He found them "just about damp on the bottom. I don't think we could have made it once around on the bay."

The plane had been in the air 23 hours and 41 minutes, and a lie was given out to the press by Van Dusen: Musick had been delayed only in part by headwinds; mostly the delay had been planned so that he could veer off course for observation purposes at various altitudes on a number of occasions.

24
Wake

By then, already a week behind schedule, the *North Haven* was steaming on toward Wake. It had left half its men and half its cargo behind, and now there was enough room on board to turn this part of the voyage almost into a pleasure cruise. The freighter made only about ten knots, and was at sea for five languorous days—five days of discussing Wake. What would they find there? Was the island high enough for a base to be built? Would the lagoon prove able to receive flying boats?

The chief engineer on Wake was to be Charlie Russell, a bald-headed man with a clipped accent and pretenses at being British. Unlike Midway, Wake was a tropical island, he instructed the boys. Take it from an old-timer—to stay healthy in the tropics was a difficult thing. He himself had lived in the tropics many years. Under no circumstances must they go bareheaded or bare-chested.

Wake, smaller and lower than they had expected, was upon them almost before they saw it. Time was lost trying to find a passage through the reef into the lagoon. There was none. Well, they had not really expected better, and so the *North Haven* hove to off the southwestern tip of the hairpin where there seemed to be a beach, and dropped anchor. The anchor never reached bottom. Other spots were tried, but the result was the same. The water was too deep. The anchor was floated in on a boat and snagged on the reef, and the freighter began to pull against it while standing out to sea.

Unloading began. As the two barges and the two launches were lowered, the sea was calm, the sky a serene brilliant blue, and it was very hot.

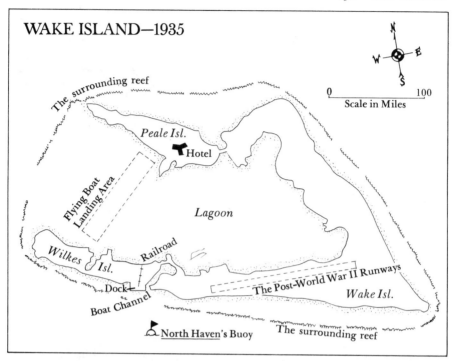

WAKE ISLAND—1935

The surrounding reef

Peale Isl.

Hotel

Flying Boat Landing Area

Lagoon

Wilkes Isl.

Railroad

Dock

Boat Channel

North Haven's Buoy

The surrounding reef

The Post-World War II Runways

Wake Isl.

0   100

Scale in Miles

A camera and binoculars slung around his neck, Russell appeared at the head of the ladder wearing Bermuda shorts and a pith helmet. As he went over the side the pith helmet tumbled into the sea, never to be seen again. Later he became so sunburned he could not move and had to be carried about the island.

There were islets at either point of the hairpin. They were separated from the main island by tiny channels. On the charts one was called Wilkes, the other Peale. Wilkes had been chosen as the place to build the compound, but the reconnoitering party sent ashore came back with bad news: clear evidence of flooding all over Wilkes. Across the lagoon, which was nearly a mile wide, the ground looked somewhat higher and the vegetation much more dense. Clearly, the place to build was on the other islet, Peale. However, prevailing winds struck the island on that side, meaning that if it tried to heave to over there, the *North Haven* would risk getting driven up onto the shore.

No, it would have to unload its three thousand tons of stores here on the Wilkes side, and then somehow they would have to be got across the lagoon to the Peale side.

So the first job was to get a barge, and a launch to tow it, into the lagoon through the thin channel between Wilkes and Wake, which at high tide was less than knee-deep. The barge, especially with a launch on its back, would not float through. It had to be pushed and dragged by forty young men for four hundred yards, scraping bottom the whole way.

A dock was built extending out across the reef into deeper water, and the other barge began to ferry supplies in from the *North Haven* to the dock. These barges measured 15 by 32 feet. On each trip the first barge had to be emptied at the dock and its contents slogged on shoulders four hundred yards across Wilkes to the lagoon to the waiting second barge. Until eliminated by a curious invention, it was this middle part of the job that was the time killer and the man killer. The invention was a railroad. The *North Haven* was scavenged for beams and girders that could serve as tracks and for bits of lumber, much of it from packing cases, that could serve as ties. Wheeled carts and flatbeds were constructed to serve as rolling stock. Once the railroad existed the idea was proposed that they incorporate as the Wilkes, Wake & Peale Railroad, Inc., so as to charge Pan American a stiff freight tariff. The railroad did not quite reach all the way across, and its only power was young men pushing. But it was better than carrying three thousand tons on shoulders. Once the railroad was built, spirits rose.

At length the *North Haven* was empty, or nearly so. Its anchor was floated out, and it steamed on toward Guam and Manila, now carrying little more than radio masts.

Abandoned on Wake, the boys watched it go, then sat down to count what they had. Clearly, there were not enough nails; they scrounged more out of packing cases. They had kegs of salted fish, but only two hundred gallons of fresh water, and already they were caked with salt and sweat and sand. It began to rain. They stood naked in the rain soaping up, at which point the rain abruptly shut off. Covered with lather, they stared up into what was once again a serene blue sky. Then, one by one, they walked into the lagoon to rinse off.

Bit by bit a village began to rise. Each building was staked out in advance, then the pilings went down, after which the prefabricated walls were lifted upright and held there while the noise of hammers ringing on nails sounded across the lagoon. In an earlier culture a church would have gone up first. Here it was the one-story, peaked-roof airline office; other buildings, as in medieval times, clustered around it tightly, taking sustenance from it. A patch of ground was cleared of bush and the antenna masts rose like crosses. Each night at 2:00 A.M. Wake's high priest of radio, G. E. Taylor, Leuteritz's acolyte, stood in the darkness shooting the North Star. The orientation of the DF had to be absolute.

Meanwhile the lagoon had been surveyed and the disturbing findings radioed to San Francisco. It was too short and too shallow. It could perhaps be made to serve, but the work would take months.

The problem was coral heads, many of which reached almost to the surface of the water. They had to be blasted out one by one or they would gut any flying boat that landed. Normally, flying boats seemed to skim down onto the water. But not all landings were perfect. They could also land with a tremendous crash, plunging deep before rising to the surface again. At rest a flying boat drew two feet of water, but the safety factor was six.

From San Francisco orders came back: Begin blasting those coral heads.

A man named George Kuhn, who had signed on as a plumber but was now foreman of the carpenters, each day floated out over the lagoon in the barge, measuring depths, putting markers down. He was followed by the beachboy, Mullahey, who at each marker would swim down looking for a hole or crevice in the upstanding coral head. Rising to the surface, he would call up to Kuhn for however many dynamite sticks he needed. The delicate business was to place them and to attach the detonator wires without setting off the charge. As soon as Mullahey had climbed up into the barge, Kuhn would fire the explosion. Then Mullahey would swim down to inspect the results. Sometimes one blast would do it, sometimes not. The channel to be cleared had to be one mile long and about three hundred yards wide. They kept count of the coral heads blasted: fifty, seventy-five, one hundred. Two months passed. Three. They were still barely halfway across the lagoon.

In New York Trippe had coral heads of his own to demolish if he could: principally the two companies threatening to initiate competing transpacific service. South Seas Commercial was the first of these to come to terms. About the time that the blasting on Wake started, Trippe bought out South Seas, bringing principal owner Donald Douglas on the Pan Am board of directors, and hiring Harold Gatty, Douglas's partner, then sending him off to Australia and New Zealand to set up future routes.

The more serious threat was Stanley Kennedy, president of the Matson satellite Inter-Island. These Matson people considered Hawaii and points west their personal property. Passions were inflamed, and had to be cooled before meaningful negotiations could begin. One friend willing to help Trippe was Roy Howard, chairman of the Scripps-Howard newspapers. On April 17, the same day as Musick's first flight to Hawaii, Howard wrote a letter to Earl Thacker, a prominent Hawaiian, asking Thacker to use his influence not to let local interests "crab" Trippe's efforts in the Pacific. "I don't know whether the Pan American crowd will ever make any money or not," Howard wrote. "Personally I rather doubt if Trippe makes any, because he's at heart a pioneer . . . I regard Trippe as one of the finest of the younger generation of Americans who are going to make this country a better one to live in and who are going to make a definite contribution to the welfare of their generation." Howard went on to outline Pan American's success in Latin America, its influence as a quasi-official arm of the United States government, and its qualifications for opening air travel over the Pacific; and he warned Thacker that any attempt to stop Trippe would incur ill will for the Hawaiian Islands in the power centers of the mainland. He himself, as a prominent newspaper publisher, would be watching the results very closely.

This letter landed heavily in Honolulu, and after a time Thacker wrote back: "You may assure your friend Trippe that every consideration and courtesy will be extended to him here in the islands."

When Trippe next met with the Matson people they were smiling, and on June 20 a series of agreements was signed. Weather data collected by Matson liners at sea would be supplied to Pan American. Inter-Island would become general agent for Pan American in Hawaii. Matson chairman Wallace Alexander would go on the Pan Am board of directors, and Trippe's previous offers to both Matson and Inter-Island were renewed: the option to buy $500,000 of Pan Am stock. Specifically this came to 13,750 shares at $37 per share, the approximate market value that day. Both companies, exercising their options the following year, netted big profits, for by then Pan Am stock was selling in the mid-50's.

For Trippe the way was now clear. The Post Office had promised to advertise for transpacific-airmail bids in two months' time; there would now be only one bidder.

Numerous other details occupied Trippe, who was trying to overlook nothing. Specifications and drawings of the structures to be built on Midway and Wake he sent to the director of Naval Intelligence—if he was dealing with a complacent government, then he meant to keep it that way. He was continually in Washington telling officials exactly what he was doing. When it became impossible to build the Wake base on low-lying Wilkes, Trippe so informed the Secretary of the Navy by letter, and he formally requested permission to use Peale instead. Perhaps he need not have bothered; there was no way the Secretary could find out which end of the island Trippe was using, and little likelihood that he cared. However, Trippe was taking no chances. He was a man who made major bets only. As a gambler he was willing to risk millions on each turn of the wheel, but on the slot-machine level he did not intend to risk a nickel.

Musick's second flight to Hawaii was delayed almost two months while engine modifications were carried out and tested, and while Midway readied itself to receive its first transpacific flying boat. On June 12 Musick took off from San Francisco, landing at Pearl Harbor the next morning following a routine eighteen-hour flight. After a day's rest he took off for Midway. He was so used to flying over the empty Pacific that he was surprised now to gaze down at a chain of reefs and islands extending northwest from Hawaii almost all the way. It was like flying in the Caribbean. There was no difficulty in finding Midway, nor in landing there. Nor were any difficulties encountered on the return flight to San

Francisco. But the major question still remained: What about Wake?

The *North Haven*, steaming from Manila back to San Francisco, stopped at Wake long enough to take off all but twelve men, the island's permanent complement; at Midway it took off more men, and it docked in San Francisco four months to the day after setting out. Its mission, Van Dusen told the press, had been completed.

Left behind on Wake, Mullahey and Kuhn went on blasting coral heads. Their score reached a hundred and fourteen, and they were not nearly finished.

Water level in the lagoon, it had been discovered, was fifteen inches higher than in the ocean outside. Was this normal? Suppose the lagoon level dropped just as a flying boat was due. How many more of these coral heads ought to be blasted?

Two months after the first flight to Midway, the major part of the Pacific was still uncrossed and the holdup was Wake. Trippe could wait no longer. The S-42 was sent winging west to Hawaii, and the first landing in Wake's history was scheduled for August 17.

To the dozen men marooned there this was exciting news. However, the marine runway was not complete. Two long lines of buoys were laid out anyway, delineating the best landing area, and its length and direction were radioed to San Francisco, as was the position of every buoy. Everyone on Wake realized that the lagoon was a bit short. In anything but optimum conditions it would be difficult to land a flying boat on the lagoon and get it stopped in time. In any case, the plane was coming.

For several days its imminent arrival dominated all conversation; to watch a flying boat come in would be the culmination of all they had worked for months to achieve. Certainly, they should greet the plane's crew with a celebration, but how, when there was little on the island to celebrate with?

On the morning of the seventeenth the baker baked a cake, and on top he scrawled with icing: "Welcome to Wake Island." A flagpole had been erected in front of the airline office. Now a pretty new flag was broken out.

The captain on this third Pacific survey flight was not Musick but his former copilot Rod Sullivan—Musick was in Baltimore, where the first Martin M-130 flying boat, one third bigger than the S-42 (and one third better, too, it was hoped), was completing its tests.

From Hawaii Sullivan took off in the S-42 carrying three tons of mail and supplies—mostly fresh food, and especially salads—for Wake and Midway personnel. It would be the last that men there would see of either for some months. Aboard also was a cage of canaries for Wake, hopefully intended to be breeding stock, anything to cheer up the men on the isolated atoll. Wake was so far out in the Pacific that it weighed on men's spirits; this was already recognized stateside. It was not going to be possible to keep personnel there more than six months at a time.

Landing at Midway, Sullivan found a concrete tennis court already in play, and a nine-hole golf course laid out in the sand. One played with red balls, and the principal hazards were hitting balls into the lagoons or down the bird holes. Inside the cable-company compound lay a grass baseball field, and there were upwards of a dozen cable people—including a woman, the manager's wife—to socialize with. Sand Island was in itself a bigger place than Wake, and there was also Eastern Island to row or swim to. Midway to Sullivan looked bearable. Wake he would find merely small.

After overnighting on Midway, Sullivan took off at dawn for Wake. Beyond Kure Island, scarcely forty miles from Midway, he looked down on nothing but water. No land, no rocks, no ships. An unbroken expanse of glittering sea stretched, endless, to the circular horizon. For twelve hundred miles his horizon remained unchanged, and he had the distinct sensation of being in suspended animation in the center of that ocean vastness for eight hours.

Sullivan had a heavy hand on the controls most times. Those who flew with him sometimes accused him of manhandling airplanes. He circled over the Wake lagoon staring down at coral heads. Each stood out clearly. He hadn't been told about this. He hadn't been told that the usable runway was this short. Now, in addition, a crosswind was blowing, and strongly. Sullivan was obliged to land directly down the marked channel, but it took him two tries to sideslip into it, and with the wind on his beam instead of head-on he landed fast. Everyone on the island stood on the shore watching him bring the flying boat in. He got the plane down okay, but barely got it stopped in time. When he taxied over to the ramp and stepped ashore, he was fuming. He said he wouldn't have made the flight if he had known how small the landing area was. Wake manager George Bicknell tried to calm him down, but he cursed all the way to the mess hall where the "Welcome to Wake Island" cake waited on a tray.

So much for the celebration.

Of course Sullivan mentioned none of this in the article he signed in the company magazine, which was written for him in glossy prose by a member of Van Dusen's public relations staff. "Crimson fire flooded the glassy surface of the ocean as we took off from the shelter of the Midway base at dawn today." The clouds were described as "towering battlements that dissolved into rainbow-silver mist as the Clipper flashed through. Coming out of these misty baths, the sun, sparkling on tiny drops of water, turned the great wing into a brilliantly glittering strip of jewels." This was the type of aviation literature people wanted to read in 1935. Romance was the thing, and Wake's first landing was "historic."

There was no room in articles for the ragged band of lonely men waving upwards, for a tense landing in a too short lagoon, nor for Sullivan's explosion of temper once ashore.

Sullivan flew away. It was Guam's turn to receive its first flight. Mullahey and Kuhn resumed blasting coral heads.

25

The China Clipper

In Baltimore on October 9, 1935, the first of the Martin M-130 flying boats was commissioned and handed over. This was the plane that presumably would carry the first mail all the way to China and, much later, the first passengers. A complete series of flight and surface-handling tests had already taken place, and now as Musick took the plane up over Baltimore and Washington, it was filled with political celebrities. These people wandered about the three cabins and the lounge—they tried out the broad armchairs, they stretched out on the two berths that were made up just as they would be on overnight flights to Hawaii, they listened to the "pullman-car quiet" of the cabins despite the roar outside of four 800-hp engines. They were impressed, as Trippe wanted them to be. The transpacific airmail contract was to be awarded twelve days later —not by the Postmaster General alone this time but by a special panel that would include the Attorney General and the Secretaries of State, Treasury, War and Navy. Impressing official Washington was what today's ceremony and flight was all about; Washington was being made to march to a scenario devised by Trippe. He wanted no slip-ups when the panel met, since the inaugural mail flight was already scheduled for the following month. There would be no other bidders, but the panel could decide not to award the contract at all.

The acceptance ceremony, though carried over national radio network hookups, had been mercifully brief. Glenn Martin himself was sick. Trippe couldn't wait for him, so L. C. Milburn, a Martin vice president, represented the company and spoke first, lauding "this great flying boat, the largest airliner ever developed in America . . . the first airliner in the world developed to carry swiftly and safely men and mail and merchandise across the oceans." Said Trippe in his turn: "This flying boat will be named the *China Clipper,* after her famous predecessor which carried the American flag and crossed the Pacific a hundred years ago."

Lindbergh was present, but he had not taken part in any of the test flights to date, nor did he fly the plane now. Pan American in its publicity had credited Lindbergh with being the guiding genius behind the plane, a claim the newspapers were only too happy to accept, but Lindbergh in 1935 had had other things on his mind. The sensational trial of the man charged with kidnapping and killing the infant Charles Lindbergh, Jr., had taken place some months before; all year Lindbergh and his wife had stood in the grisly spotlight, hounded by the press, until at last they had gone into hiding, avoiding all public appearances. Within a few weeks they would sail secretly to take up residence in England.

In fact the engineering genius behind the new flying boat had been Andre Priester. The Dutchman operated out of his New York office with a very small staff: Sanford Kauffman, Ed McVitty and one or two others. There ideas poured out of Priester in a steady stream, and he bombarded manufacturers with them. From Pratt and Whitney, the engine designers, he wanted better fuel consumption, and he got it. From Martin he wanted more and more safety features, and he got them too—a dual electrical system, a dual hydraulic system, extra bulkheads in the hull; he wanted a plane that would stay afloat even if it split its bottom open in an emergency landing. He had ideas for better engine cowlings that would conserve or release extra engine heat as required, and ideas for new wing flaps that would increase the plane's performance.

It was one thing to conceive an idea but another to transmit it, and Priester could not speak proper English. So he had devised a curious method. Once an idea had clarified in his mind he would call in Kauffman, McVitty or one of his other young assistants, explain what the idea was, and ask them to write it down for him. His letters and memos were written by these same young men, in the same way. Many went to Trippe, for Priester kept him informed, and usually they ended: "We are proceeding, unless advised to the contrary by you." On the whole, Trippe countermanded none of Priester's orders. Priester was riding high. He could do what he wanted.

Deciding that pilots needed special training to cope with ocean flying, he arranged for correspondence courses in basic and advanced mathematics, in engineering, economics, history, languages, meteorology and law, as well as in company and civil regulations. Henceforth no pilot could get promoted until the correspondence school said he was ready, and he would proceed upwards through new ranks Priester established, the highest of which was Master of Ocean Flying Boats.

It was Priester who decided on the so-called multiple-crew concept: apart from the steward, any man aboard any oceangoing flying boat ought to be fully qualified in at least two other skills apart from his own; as a result, later flying boats would sometimes cross oceans with five of the seven crewmen aboard certified as pilots. Still other ideas churned in the Dutchman's head, even a company pension plan, and he pushed almost all of them through.

On October 21 the airmail contract was awarded to the only bidder, and shortly after that, Musick flew the *China Clipper* from Baltimore to Miami, to Acapulco, to San Diego. There nineteen people came aboard, some of them reporters ("Thrill of danger lacking on luxurious airliner," one headline read the next day), and Musick flew calmly up the coast to San Francisco. The world was agog at what was about to happen—the beginning of regular service to the Orient—and five thousand people were waiting for him when he landed. They saw Musick and his crew as heroes, and the pilot was mobbed as he tried to get through to his car. As he bent to kiss his wife, cameras clicked; when he was asked to kiss her again he glared around with annoyance, and at home he muttered, "This publicity racket is getting me down." He said he felt like an ape in a cage.

Van Dusen had come out from New York to handle press requests. He found that the man people wanted to see, hear, touch was Musick. The pilot was obliged to sit for interviews, to make speeches at luncheons and receptions, but he was not at ease and did the job badly.

Nonetheless, facts about him began to appear. He was born in 1894 in St. Louis, but had grown up in Los Angeles. Smitten by aviation as a boy, he had built his first plane himself. It had bicycle wheels, a hand-carved propeller, and instead of linen fabric on the wings young Musick had used bed sheets. His first flight was scheduled to take off from a Los Angeles racetrack. It took three men on each wing to hold the plane down as Musick, wearing a turtleneck sweater, a football helmet and goggles, gunned his engine. As the plane rolled down the racetrack infield one wheel dived into a chuckhole. Then the plane went up onto its nose and disintegrated. Musick's pals found him sitting amid the wreckage, cursing.

Later he rode cars as a racing mechanic, pumping pressure into the gas tanks, pumping oil and grease to moving parts. He got drunk at twenty for the first and last time. Tongue-tied around girls, he avoided them.

When Glenn Martin opened an airplane factory in Los Angeles, Musick went to work there. Presently he became a mechanic at air shows, and pilots who watched him polish every turnbuckle found him so extremely precise they took to calling him "the jeweler." They also noticed that he kept a notebook on everything he heard. What they did not know was that he climbed into their empty planes at night, and imagined himself flying them.

Once he learned to fly, Musick began to learn tricks, but he learned them one at a time. The cemeteries, he reasoned, were full of pilots who had tried too much too soon. At night Musick had bad dreams about tailspins, then the number one killer of pilots. He decided he had to find a way to pull out of a tailspin, or he would never be sure of himself in the air. So he built a cardboard model plane and studied it. Soon he realized that once in a tailspin the role of various surfaces changed. Therefore, if—

Musick took his plane into the air, and once over a swamp, allowed himself to fall into a tailspin—if his calculations were wrong, the swamp might possibly save him. According to his theory, he should now push forward on the stick, and he did so, even though every instinct told him to pull back. He forced himself to push forward. Amazingly, the plane stopped spinning and went into a dive. Musick hauled it out of the dive, and threw it into another tailspin. Again he converted the tailspin to a dive. His theories worked.

He began to tour in air shows. Sometimes he was advertised as Monseer Mussick, the famous French flier; other times he was called "Daredevil Musick." On the Pacific coast he was a headliner. He had money, a car and fine clothes, but he still didn't know how to talk easily to girls, nor indeed to anyone he did not know.

War came. He became a civilian flying instructor for the Army, and then a marine lieutenant instructor in Miami. In 1919, when he was discharged, he joined Aeromarine, an "airline" that sent 75-mph flying boats across to Nassau, Bimini or Havana with the ordinary compass as the sole navigational aid. The other pilots called Musick "Uncle Ed" because he was so extremely cautious. He was twenty-six.

Aeromarine disbanded. When prohibition descended on the land, Musick began flying bootleg liquor, taking it from supply ships lying just beyond the twenty-mile limit, depositing it at prearranged points on the mainland. Those were bad years for pilots because barnstorming was just about over and serious airline jobs had not yet opened up. Musick was not the only pilot who earned his living flying bootleg rum. One weekend in New York he met a girl, Cleo Livingston, at a restaurant. The man Musick was with introduced him. She was so attractive he was stunned, and he had to force himself to talk to her.

He went to Miami for three months, but wrote frequently, signing his letters: "Sincerely, Ed." When he went north again, he pleaded with her to marry him. They eloped on August 14, 1924. Musick was thirty years old. The world had hardly heard of him, and the only talent he had was not much in demand. The dawn of commercial aviation, when he would go to work for operations manager Andre Priester of Philadelphia Rapid Transit Airline, was still two years away.

At noon on November 22, 1935, a luncheon in honor of Musick and his crew was given at San Francisco's Palace Hotel. Speeches lauding him and them were made by Postmaster General James Farley, by Angelo Rossi (mayor of San Francisco), by Frank Merriam (governor of California), by Pacific Division manager Clarence Young and by Trippe. Immediately afterwards Musick and his crew, together with many of the dignitaries, were taken aboard a motor launch and sped across San Francisco Bay to Alameda. There were crowds on the docks, crowds on the rooftops, and crowds aboard the many extra ferries that had been added on.

At Alameda the *China Clipper* was drawn up nose first to a dock that had been turned into a flag-draped reviewing stand, and it was full too. In the background a huge American flag measuring 122 by 70 feet was stretched upon the grass and guarded by a hundred and seventy boy scouts. Already bombs and rockets were bursting overhead. Sirens blared from boats in the bay.

The inaugural ceremony, which began at two-forty-five, one hour before scheduled takeoff, was broadcast live over CBS and NBC, and also over seven other networks in Europe, South America and the Orient.

For millions of people around the world it was the radio announcer who now set the scene: "We are here on the shores of historical San Francisco Bay, on the marine ramp of Pan American Airways' Pacific operating base. Around us surges a great crowd of interested, excited people, extending as far back over the airport as the eye can reach. Across the bay a hundred thousand people are watching and listening on the shores near the Golden Gate. In Hawaii are other thousands. On the five continents of the globe are millions who by the magic of radio are about to witness with us one of the most dramatic events in the history of our modern world. Within a few feet of our platform the *China Clipper,* studded with powerful engines, her great glistening whalelike hull resting gently in the water, stands ready. What drama is packed into the hold of this tremendous airliner, the largest ever developed in America, where the airplane was born, the most outstanding aircraft ever developed in the world; what years of pioneering have preceded her! Pan American Airways, the standard-bearer for America and American aviation in the international field, courageously began nearly five years of work which today will be climaxed in the inauguration of the first scheduled airmail service eight thousand miles across the world's greatest ocean to link America and the Orient."

Next Trippe stepped to the microphone. "It is significant and appropriate," he said, "that the first scheduled air service over a major ocean route is being started under the auspices of the American government, by an American company operating aircraft designed and built in the United States and in the charge of American captains and crews."

Postmaster General Farley then read a letter from the President that ended: "Even at this distance I thrill to the wonder of it all." Farley went on in his own words: "A personal letter will arrive in China within six days after leaving New York. I am proud that this history-making service was inaugurated during my administration of the Post Office Department. Each year brings new triumphs in American aviation, but it will be a long time before any of them overshadows the achievement which we acclaim today."

The announcer came back on: "All eyes now are on the *China Clipper,* riding at anchor just beyond our platform. What a thrilling sight she is! So confident, so sturdy. Her gleaming hull and wings glistening in the sunshine, her great engines ready to speed her on her way!

"Now seven uniformed figures, in navy blue, with white visor caps— Pan American's colors—are moving along the narrow catwalk to the front hatch of the giant airliner. There is little excitement about them. They are the flight officers of the *China Clipper*—the winged pioneers about to set out on an ocean's conquest.

"The first to go aboard is Rod Sullivan, who, as first officer, made the first flights to Hawaii and Midway Islands and, as captain of the Pan American *Clipper,* made the initial flights to Wake Island and Guam. Captain Sullivan is first officer of the *China Clipper.*

"Right behind him is another old-timer—a product of the old square-riggers and veteran of all Pan American Pacific flights: Fred Noonan, navigation officer of the *China Clipper.*

"Now George King, ocean pilot in training on his first actual Pacific crossing. He is second officer.

"Certainly, the *China Clipper* can't go wrong on the engineering department. Both the engineering officers, now going aboard, are Wright! — first engineering officer C. D. Wright and second engineering officer Victor Wright. They are not brothers, by the way. Right behind them goes William Jarboe, Jr., radio officer, another veteran of the Pacific survey flights. The last to step aboard is Pan American's veteran, Edwin C. Musick, captain of the *China Clipper.*

"Seven men in the crew. And what a crew! Five of those seven are transport pilots. Three of them are registered aeronautical engineers. Three of them are licensed radio officers. Two of them are master mariners, and two others have their navigators' papers. That will give you some idea of the preparation behind America's conquest of an ocean!"

It was now the turn of stations along the route to call in one by one: "Manila calling San Francisco . . . stand by for His Excellency, Manuel L. Quezon, President of the Commonwealth of the Philippines."

"From the other side of the world to you, Postmaster General Farley, and to you, Mr. Trippe," said Quezon, "the people of the East send greetings—across the breadth of this ocean which since the beginning has been a barrier separating the peoples of the East and the West. Today we await impatiently the arrival of the flying clipper ships that will, with incredible swiftness, finally sweep away that barrier of time and space forever. This bold project of Pan American Airways has, since its inception, fired the imagination of the peoples of the East. With hearts and minds thrilled by the meaning of this flight, the Commonwealth of the Philippines, the people of the Orient, await the coming of the clipper ships."

After Quezon, another voice came on: "This is Honolulu calling San Francisco . . . stand by for His Excellency Joseph P. Poindexter, governor of the Territory of Hawaii." Said Poindexter: "Here we are about to see the second of Hawaii's three dreams come true. The first, just thirty-seven years ago, saw these islands become a part of the United States of America. Today the second is about to change from the fancy of hope to the fact of achievement. Hawaii, no longer to be separated by two thousand miles of open sea, is to be but overnight from the mainland. Across the barrier of ocean, soon to be dissolved forever, we in the Hawaiian Islands pay tribute to you, Postmaster General Farley, and to you, Juan Trippe. We await the coming of the *China Clipper* with confidence and with thanksgiving. Her arrival will open a new chapter in the glorious history of this territory and will hasten the day when it will rise to its fullest stature—the third dream—of full statehood in the glorious union under the Stars and Stripes."

The announcer's voice returned: "The *China Clipper,* a beautiful sight resting on the quiet waters of Pan American's enclosed base here, is turned toward the opening in the breakwater. Ground crews stand at their posts, ready to cast off their lines at the captain's signal. By radio now Mr. Trippe will get the report from the *Clipper* and from the far-flung airway's bases across the vast Pacific to the other side of the world. Here is Mr. Trippe now, speaking to the *Clipper.*"

Trippe: *"China Clipper,* are you ready?"

"Pan American Airways *China Clipper,* Captain Musick, standing by for orders, sir."

Trippe: "Stand by, Captain Musick, for station reports."

Now, one by one, code signals came in from the other side of the world. From KNBF, Honolulu: "Pan American Airways ocean air base No. 1—Honolulu, Hawaii. Standing by for orders."

KNBH, Midway Islands: "Pan American Airways mid-ocean air base No. 2—Midway Islands. Standing by for orders."

KNBI, Wake Island: "Pan American Airways Trans-Pacific Airways No. 3—Wake Island. Standing by for orders."

KNBG, Guam: "Pan American Airways mid-ocean air base No. 4—Guam. Standing by for orders."

KZBQ, Manila: "Pan American Airways Trans-Pacific Air Terminal, Manila, Commonwealth of the Philippines. Ready and standing by, sir."

Trippe: "Stand by, all stations. Postmaster General Farley, I have the honor to report, sir, that the Trans-Pacific Airways is ready to inaugurate airmail service of the United States Post Office from the mainland across the Pacific to the Philippines, by way of Hawaii, Midway, Wake and Guam islands."

Farley: "Mr. Trippe, it is an honor and a privilege for me, as Postmaster General of the United States of America, to hereby order the inauguration of the first scheduled service on Foreign Airmail Route Number Fourteen at three-twenty-eight P.M., Pacific Standard Time, on this day which will forever mark a new chapter in the glorious history of our nation, a new era in world transportation, a new and binding bond that will link, for the first time in history, the peoples of the East and the West."

It remained now only for Trippe to order Musick to take off, and as he stepped to the microphone again there was much on his mind. The S-42 survey flights had reached Hawaii only four times, and once had barely made it back. Wake had been reached only twice, Guam only once, and Manila not at all. The great Martin flying boat in front of him had not yet crossed any part of the Pacific. Assuming that it reached all of the bases ahead of it, it would have to be serviced by men who had never seen it before. Would it reach them? To the Japanese government this flight constituted an intrusion of Japan's domain, and diplomatic protests had been lodged in Washington. In addition, only hours before, the FBI had arrested two Japanese nationals attempting to tamper with the long-range direction finder. The apparatus had since been thoroughly checked over. It appeared to be all right, but, of course, there was not yet any flying boat a thousand miles out to sea testing the strength of its signals.

Into the microphone Trippe said: "Captain Musick, you have your sailing orders. Cast off and depart for Manila in accordance therewith." With this command the international radio audience heard the *Clipper*'s engines increase to a roar. Then "The Star-Spangled Banner" blared.

Over San Francisco Bay twenty-two aerial bombs exploded in salute, the last two carrying small American flags attached to parachutes, which drifted gently down on the breeze. Hundreds of automobile horns honked. Ships' whistles and sirens screamed, and a fireboat offshore loosed streams of water from every hose. Thirty other planes circled overhead, and then, as the New York *Herald Tribune* reporter would write, "dropped down toward the Monarch as though they would shine in her glory, as though they were coming to see how an eagle flies."

The plane was heavily loaded not only with fuel but also with 1,837 pounds of mail—110,865 letters. Musick lifted it off the water easily enough, but it would not climb, and ahead of him was the Bay Bridge, which was then under construction. Below it hung cables, ropes and scaffolding. Musick had no choice but to fly directly under the bridge, and

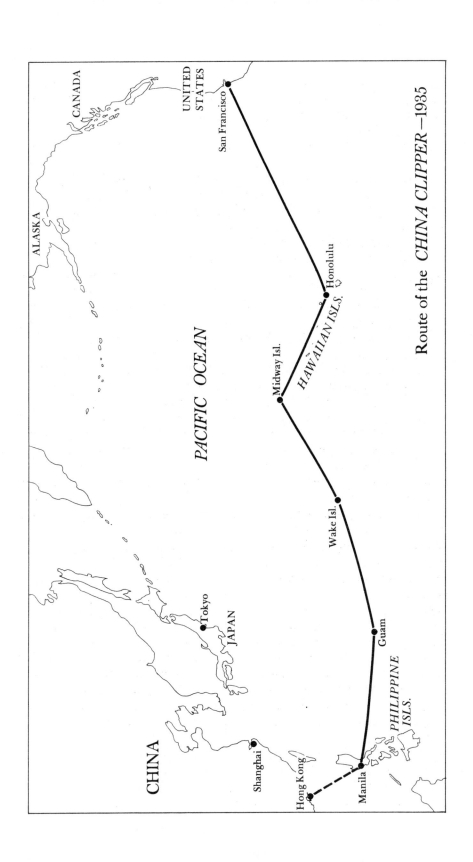

CANADA

UNITED
STATES

San Francisco

ALASKA

PACIFIC OCEAN

Honolulu

HAWAIIAN ISLS.

Midway Isl.

Wake Isl.

Guam

Tokyo

JAPAN

PHILIPPINE
ISLS.

CHINA

Shanghai

Hong Kong

Manila

Route of the *CHINA CLIPPER* — 1935

he did so—"We all ducked," said engineering officer Vic Wright later. Much of the flotilla of small planes, thinking this part of the scheduled show, calmly followed Musick through and out the other side. Nearly everyone thought the maneuver normal, but Trippe knew otherwise and he flinched, and division engineer John Leslie, then thirty years old, later blamed this takeoff for his prematurely white hair. Past thousands and thousands of schoolchildren lining the marina, Musick flew at rooftop height, then gained enough altitude to pass over the cables of the new Golden Gate Bridge which were just being strung at that time.

The multitude watched until the *China Clipper* became a speck in the distance and at last disappeared.

The reporters moved into the lobby of the Pan Am base, where a huge wall map had been hung. Every hour press agent Van Dusen came out of the operations room to draw a mark over the *Clipper*'s latest reported position. In actual fact Van Dusen was unable to make much sense of the bearings that were radioed back, and very soon gave up trying. Instead he simply marked off the map in regular sections every hour. His reasoning was entirely defensive. So many aviators had already disappeared between San Francisco and Hawaii that the general public more than half expected this flight to do the same. The purpose of Van Dusen's propanganda line had become to convince the world of the opposite: Pan American had the plane that could do it and crews that knew every foot of the way.

After each check mark, each briefing, Van Dusen would disappear back into the operations room, where his typewriter was set up, for he had work to do. Contracts had been signed with newspaper syndicates for by-line stories by all seven of the crewmen aboard, and it was Van Dusen who now busied himself turning out the stories. He kept his best material for the column that went out over the wires each day entitled: "Musick in the Air." Musick, who always in the past had answered reporters' questions in monosyllables, proved to be an exceedingly vivid columnist. In the morning papers of November 27, for instance, readers of his work learned that "the United States has a flourishing city at Wake Island." It bristled with a forest of orange-and-black radio masts, red roofs, white walls and a dozen buildings, walkways, garden windmills and watchtowers. "The Stars and Stripes floating at the top of a mast is a thrilling sight." Van Dusen, describing these things, had never seen any of them.

At Honolulu, and later at Manila, the true Musick stepped forward, and when reporters asked him to describe his epochal flight, he replied only that it was "without incident." Which it was, though the receptions at Honolulu and Manila were another thing—big in the first instance, gigantic in the second. Adjacent to the jetty in Manila, between two and three hundred thousand Filipinos waited for the *China Clipper* to arrive. Within a special enclosure waited two thousand prominent guests. The park across the street was jammed to overflowing with people. In nearby streets people hung from every rooftop, every window. A flotilla of military fighter planes had headed out to sea to escort the *Clipper* to its landfall and landing. It splashed down in an area marked off by a variety of boats, all flying flags and pennants. The crew disembarked at a dock through flower-covered arches. All the buildings around were decorated. Crowds around the palace made it difficult for Musick to present a letter from Roosevelt to Quezon, and it was necessary to restage this ceremony so that newsreel cameramen could record it.

Afterwards came an official reception, a banquet, and a ticker-tape parade through the joyous, decorated city. The mobs were so enthusiastic that they attempted to lift the car carrying Musick off its wheels and to carry it through the streets in their hands. It was such a tumultuous, spontaneous welcome that even Musick seems to have enjoyed it. In any case, in most of the photographs that were taken he is shown smiling.

Like it or not, by the time he set the *China Clipper* down on San Francisco Bay ending its return flight, Musick was a full-fledged hero. *Time* magazine gave him a cover story, and later he was awarded the Harmon Trophy, aviation's most prestigious, which had been won previously by only two other Americans, Charles Lindbergh and the late Wiley Post.

26

Life on the Atolls

The second Martin flying boat, the *Philippine Clipper*, was delivered—the third would be called the *Hawaii Clipper*—and by December planes were running through the islands once a week.

George Bicknell, Wake Island manager, got out of bed each day at four-thirty, got his men up at five, and then set up his theodolite for the 1800 hours G.M.T. upper-air observation. By a quarter past five there was usually enough daylight to start his balloon up into the upper air and to track it with his instrument. As soon as his observations were logged he sent them by radio to San Francisco.

Bicknell had only ten men working for him, and nothing was completed. The roofs all leaked, and the windows didn't fit properly, and at times rain came in over his desk as he worked on his weather reports. Gutters and downspouts that were supposed to lead into catch basins were not connected, meaning that all that fresh water was being lost after each storm. There was still no screening on the windows, and the flies were often bothersome. Bicknell, in his letters to the mainland, gave his return address as "The Isle of Capri," or else as "The Island of Lost Souls." He complained of cheap hardware already rusting, of cheap plumbing being ruined by salt water. "The amount of work done in this short time is remarkable," he wrote, "but I fear for the future and sometimes wonder if it would not have been more economical to have done a little better instead of going quite so fast."

Bicknell's men were all homesick. They dreamed about hot baths in fresh water, about soaking in suds so high they could hardly see through them. They longed to hear music, to read the new books, to see new faces. They were sex-starved, and when Schildhauer wired that they could each have a thirty-pound baggage allowance sent out from Honolulu, four of them wired back that they had pooled their allowance—Schildhauer should send in a 120-pound blonde. One of the boys had only recently been married; he walked about mooning for his bride—would she wait for him during his long stay on Wake? There was constant sickness, everything from skin fungus to a badly infected ear. The cook came down with tuberculosis and had to be returned. There was constant friction, particularly with the doctor, who considered himself to be on a higher plane than the others and constantly told them so. Often they hooted with derision, but at least partly they believed him, and so hated him fiercely. Bicknell called him tactless. Someone else promised to stay sick forever rather than crawl to that doctor for treatment. The doctor retorted he was there for major medical or surgical purposes, not first aid. Bicknell, furious, put him to work building his own medical shack and then painting it, and after that set him to work painting the dock to which the flying boats were moored when they arrived each week. No one was getting rich on Wake. Mullahey, who, at the risk of his life, had now been blasting coral heads for nine months, was earning only $100 a month.

Bicknell was in charge of loading the flying boats, but there was no scale on the island. He had to guess. He tried to overestimate everything that went on board. Nonetheless he was extremely worried each time the hatch cover finally slammed shut. Once when the flying boat came by the end of the dock still on the water, Bicknell was muttering to himself— maybe it was too heavily loaded to get off. When the plane at last lifted up, he was, he said, as limp as a dishrag.

A tropical storm struck, and the lagoon filled up over the level of the dock, which broke loose and floated away. The gasoline drums were floating across the lagoon also. Then the storm stopped, and all that water began to spill out over the reef. Dock and drums were moving toward the reef too, and had to be rescued by swimmers. But when, in December, Wake received its first celebrity—the Secretary of War came ashore—Bicknell was "so damn proud of this crowd that I nearly burst the buttons off my shirt."

On Midway the three big refrigerators were in Bill Newport's charge; they contained all of the island's perishable food, and food was a special worry—it came in only every six months. The first things Newport checked each morning were his refrigerators, and he checked them again the last thing before going to bed.

If the weekly flying boat was on time, it landed just before dusk. The Midway staff then swarmed over it. Usually by midnight the boat was ready to fly out again in the morning, although if something went wrong, the men worked all night. They also worked seven days a week, but every flying-boat captain as soon as he stepped ashore invariably joked that he was interrupting their fishing. All the captains had the same line. All thought it was funny.

Midway was where the newly hatched gooney birds scrambled toward the water. There about half learned to fly, and the other half died, either from drowning or from attacks by sharks. It left the men a disgusting job— to remove dead gooney birds from the beach before they began to stink. One day in came the sooty terns, thousands of them, hovering in clouds the size of city blocks. Abruptly they alighted, all of them, and began laying eggs. They were hatching eggs in the middle of every pathway, every road, and they squawked furiously at every man who walked by.

Musick's every flight was news, and it happened now that he aborted flights three times, the first time on takeoff when the plane struck a submerged object in San Francisco harbor and ripped its bottom open. There was talk of sabotage—the Japanese again—but nothing was ever proven. On another flight, Musick flew seven hundred miles out to sea, watching his dials all the way. He was a man who watched his dials always and believed what they told him, and he was not satisfied this day with engine performance; after he had turned back and landed, ten days were spent checking and rebuilding his engines.

His third aborted flight brought the so-called point of no return, a new concept only recently introduced into aviation, to the attention of the public. The point of no return varied on each flight, depending on the winds; theoretically, it was the exact halfway point—in flying time rather than in distance—between takeoff and destination. En route to Hawaii but bucking 30- to 40-mile headwinds, Musick had almost reached it— he was some 1,200 miles out to sea—when, abruptly, he turned around and went back to San Francisco. Weather forecasts ahead had warned him of 45- to 50-mile winds against him at Hawaii. He had practically brand-new engines on which there was only test-flight data on fuel consumption. He had calculated that the winds would add six hours to his flying time, equivalent to 900 more miles. Although the plane could probably make it—this was a Martin, not an S-42—Musick declined to take the chance. Tens of thousands of dollars were lost, but Musick shook his head doggedly. He did not care. In New York Trippe backed him up, saying, "The greatest courage sometimes is the courage to turn back."

It was enough to provoke another spate of articles about Musick—that he had flown more than two million miles without serious accident, that he had never suffered an injury and had never injured anyone else.

Priester flew out across the Pacific, bringing with him Charles Montieth, chief engineer for Boeing. The "next step" in flying boats was already out for bids—something bigger, faster, more capacious than the M-130, obviously—and Boeing seemed the likely winner. Priester invited

Montieth, therefore, to cross the Pacific in the Martin. He wanted the new Boeing designed strong and built strong. He wanted Montieth to see what Pacific conditions were.

Montieth at first had declined the invitation. A former M.I.T. professor, he was the author of the classic text on aerodynamics. A firsthand view of conditions was not necessary, he said—a firsthand view was redundant.

Priester, a stubborn man by nature, was by now used to getting his own way. If Boeing wanted the contract, then Montieth should cross the Pacific before work began, he said, and at length the professor conceded. But he soon wished he hadn't.

Between Guam and Manila the flying boat flew straight into a typhoon. It had been sailing along at eight thousand feet when it entered what appeared to be haze. A moment later the typhoon engulfed it. It was as if the plane was cruising underwater. It dropped like an elevator a thousand feet straight down and then soared almost as high, almost as fast. Rain drummed on it. Both pilots were gripping the yokes with all their strength. The sky outside had turned as dark as night. All four engines were at full power, but the altimeter showed that the plane was being forced steadily down toward the sea. At about five hundred feet the waves came into view below. The navigator threw out a drift flask. It showed that the plane, under full power, was being driven backwards. The captain, Mike La Porte, let it go in that direction and the flying boat was blown out the northern side of the typhoon into tumultuous but clearing air.

Priester and Montieth had stayed in the lounge throughout. During the whole of the typhoon Priester had sat calmly in his seat, strapped in, saying nothing. Montieth had swallowed his cigar, and in addition, his footprints were on the ceiling. When this was pointed out, everyone aboard laughed except Priester, who only smiled. He began to lecture Montieth about the new Boeing—"It must be strong, Montieth, strong, strong, strong," he said. When he stepped off the plane in Manila that evening, he was still thinking about the new Boeing, not about having survived a typhoon. "Dat vuz a gut eggsperience for Montieth," he told an assistant.

The next day the typhoon was due at Manila. Priester held a series of conferences. Where was the safest place to leave the flying boat, in the water or on land? On land it could be partially tied down, but debris might blow into it and the wind might turn it over. On the water it would swing into the wind, but suppose it dragged its mooring? Suppose other boats were driven into it? After talking the matter out, Priester ordered the plane left on the water, and he supervised the tying of planks onto the top of the wings to break the lift. He ordered the crew to remain aboard with the engines running. That night the typhoon struck, but when morning came the flying boat was still there in the harbor, unharmed.

The *North Haven* set out from San Francisco once again, this time with two complete hotels in its hold. Passenger service through Wake and Midway could not start until there was someplace for passengers to sleep. The hotels, designed by Delano & Aldrich, were to be, under the circumstances, elaborate: two wings built out from a central lobby, wide verandas, each room having a bathroom with hot-water shower. The *North Haven* was as jammed full as the last time, for it carried everything; Simmons beds, coat hangers, ashtrays, even cashiers' cages and materials for building aquariums—the hotel lobbies were to be decorated with brilliant fish native to each atoll.

The plan was to touch at Midway first, then at Wake, and the material in the hold was stowed accordingly, Wake on the bottom, Midway on top.

When the *North Haven* reached Midway, the winds were so high and the seas so rough that unloading the hotel was impossible. But the island desperately needed food, and it needed a new launch too, the old one having been lost shortly before.

There were still only two passages into the atoll. The Southeast Passage, very narrow and shallow, was the better, but it contained the cable. George Kuhn volunteered to try to bring the launch in through the cable passage before the cable manager saw what they were doing. It was loaded with all the food it could carry, and Kuhn and George Ferris waited outside the passage. The waves built higher and higher. The men were picking their crest, and when it came they sailed in through the passage over the reef.

They were taken off in a small boat, and the *North Haven* went on to Wake, still carrying both hotels, the Wake one on the bottom. The two weren't alike, and during four days at sea, men calculated which pieces of the Midway hotel could be used on Wake, and which pieces of the Wake hotel had to be snaked out from the bottom of the hold.

Off Wake the Pacific was rough even on the lee side. The ship was rolling heavily. At night it was obliged to pull back into the open sea, leaving its small craft behind. When the weather worsened, a barge dragged its anchor and gouged out its bottom on a reef. A launch went up in flames, severely burning the helmsman. But work continued. Day by day the hotel moved in pieces to shore and crossed the lagoon.

Afterwards the *North Haven* steamed back to Midway and unloaded there. When both hotels were ready, the inauguration of passenger service was scheduled, and new norms of personnel conduct were mandated in an edict that went out to the islands from San Francisco. Henceforth, when eating in the hotel dining rooms alongside passengers, all personnel would wear coats and ties at all times.

27

Trippe around the World

When one of the flying boats was on the bay at San Francisco, mobs trooped by to stare at it, hoping to touch it—a scene amazingly similar to one that would occur thirty-four years later when crowds would gather to stare at the space capsule back from the moon.

The first passenger flight all the way across the Pacific was still many months away. Tickets would not be cheap—$648 round trip to Honolulu, $1,438.20 round trip to Manila—but already hundreds of ticket requests were on file.

When the third Martin was commissioned, Musick flew it to Honolulu, where it was to be christened the *Hawaii Clipper*. Though this was his fifth trip to the islands, an escort of twenty planes from Wheeler Field led him to his landing, where three thousand people were waiting to greet him, including the governor of the territory and the mayor of Honolulu. The plane was christened by spilling coconut milk over her prow.

Meanwhile Trippe had an enormous problem to resolve. He still needed an Asian terminal for his line. The one he wanted was Hong Kong, where he could connect with planes of the China National Aviation Corporation—after which both lines might begin to make money. However, the British had so far refused to concede landing rights at Hong Kong. They were still protecting their "all-red route," even though they were as yet unable to fly it themselves.

Was there a way around this British intransigence? Trippe, who knew his geography, thought he saw one, and he sent a man named Richard Long to Lisbon to negotiate for the far less valuable landing rights to

Portuguese Macao. An enclave and trading post sixty miles farther south along the China coast, Macao had always been a kind of second-class Hong Kong. Long did conclude an agreement for Macao, one that, to the Portuguese, seemed to promise a new era of prosperity for their Asian enclave; Macao now might even supplant Hong Kong as the world's gateway to China.

Unfortunately for the Portuguese, Trippe had no interest in Macao or its prosperity. He had a keenly developed social sense, and would not accept the second class ever. Hong Kong was like an exclusive country club to which he had been denied membership. Trippe never sought to change the existing social order—only to join it. He intended now only to use Macao, briefly, to force admission to Hong Kong.

His plan was a devious one. Now that he held rights to Macao, he ignored Hong Kong altogether, for he was satisfied that boastful Macao businessmen would spread their good news—Pan American is coming to Macao—among colleagues there. He made no request for Hong Kong rights at all; he simply allowed time to pass. He was allowing Hong Kong businessmen, anxious to maintain the supremacy of Hong Kong, to become more and more nervous. Inevitably they began to pressure the British to offer Trippe those rights he had not asked for, and at length the offer was made, the papers signed, and Hong Kong opened itself to Trippe. Once again he had won. He had brought himself and his company to the edge of the Asian mainland.

Regular transpacific mail service by the three Martin flying boats had been conducted as far as Manila for eleven months. With Hong Kong ready and the island hotels ready, scheduled passenger service could be inaugurated, and this was announced for October 21, 1936. However, Trippe organized his own personal flight for the week before, and he invited a number of extremely influential people, most of them newspaper publishers, to join him.

Although the Martin flying boats supposedly could carry thirty-two passengers, the twenty-five hundred miles between the mainland and Hawaii required such an enormous amount of fuel that passenger capacity dropped to eight. Trippe and seven guests would fly the first leg; the remainder would proceed by steamship to Honolulu and join the flight there.

To identify the seven men who boarded the flying boat with Trippe in San Francisco is to identify Trippe's priorities at the time: the California senator William McAdoo, chairman of the Senate Commerce Committee; Wallace Alexander and William Roth, chairman and president, respectively, of the Matson Steamship Line; Sonny Whitney, the rich socialite who was the figurehead chairman of the Pan Am board of directors—and whom Trippe wished to keep a figurehead; Roy Howard, chairman of the Scripps-Howard newspapers; Paul Patterson, president of the

Baltimore *Sun;* and Amon Carter, publisher of the Fort Worth *Star Telegram.* Seven others, including Trippe's wife and two other wives, had boarded the S.S. *Lurline* out of San Francisco four days earlier, and they were standing on the ship's bridge at 5:00 A.M., with the pink glow of dawn coming up over the distant outline of Molokai, when a tiny dot appeared in the eastern sky. Presently they heard the roar of four engines, and as Captain John Tilton banked the flying boat over the *Lurline* Betty Trippe held her movie camera on it. It seemed to her the culmination of her husband's vision, his impossible dream come true, and tears of joy streamed down her face. Next to her stood James Stahlman, publisher of the Nashville *Banner,* and his eyes were damp too.

That morning Trippe made official calls on government people, but in the afternoon he took his wife surfing. A native had to hold Betty Trippe upright on her surfboard, but Trippe mastered surfing at once; the former football player rode in many times alone. That night a luau, a native feast, was given in honor of the Trippe party by Stanley Kennedy, who was now all smiles. The women were each wearing a night-blooming cereus, a great white flower eight inches across. The table was laden with tropical fruit, and the fifty guests dined on octopus, crab and roast pig while Hawaiian girls in grass skirts sang soft island songs and danced the hula. Stanley Kennedy made a touching speech about air travel and the future of Hawaii, and heaped lavish tributes upon Juan Trippe. Trippe in his turn spoke of all the men of his company who had made the Pacific route possible.

Although the dancing had gone on until 1:00 A.M., the passengers were called at 4:00 A.M., and driven, after a hasty breakfast, to Pearl Harbor. Then they were off the water bound for Midway. Betty Trippe, who had not seen the interior of a Clipper before, found it comfortable and luxurious, with a big central lounge wider than a pullman club car. Four berths were made up, which the passengers took turns using throughout the day. There were separate lavatories, one for ladies and one for men. Four copies of *Gone With the Wind,* the book everyone was reading that fall, had been placed on board. The noise was not bad, Betty Trippe found—she only had to raise her voice a little to be heard.

After ten hours the flying boat set down in the lagoon at Midway, and the guests were led into the hotel. Each room had its own private bath with hot and cold running water, and firm beds. Dinner was served by Chamorro boys in immaculate white uniforms. Trippe's picture hung on the wall of the administration building. The men, according to airport manager J. C. Boyle, had put it up of their own accord.

When the Clipper landed on Wake late the next afternoon, the crew insisted that Betty Trippe step ashore first, for this made her the first white woman to set foot on Wake, and probably the first woman ever. She walked to the little hotel on paths of crushed coral, between rows of newly planted tropical trees. It was hot enough, she thought, to blow your head off.

As the passengers sat down to breakfast next morning a mimeographed newspaper was handed around, and they read about the Spanish Civil War; about the presidential campaign—Governor Alf Landon vs. FDR; and about Mrs. Simpson, who denied that she would marry King Edward VIII following her divorce. The publishers had one complaint: there were no football scores. Thirty minutes after the dawn takeoff the plane's radio operator came into the cabin and handed over the requested scores, courtesy of Wake airport manager S. A. Saunders, who had radioed to San Francisco for them, and this seemed still another miracle to go with this miraculous flight.

At Guam, an existing naval base, the harbor was ringed with low cliffs. There was another hotel in the same style as on the two atolls, and the passengers sat in bamboo chairs on the porch, drank iced tea and looked out at the harbor through the palm trees. At four o'clock the next morning they were on their way again; taking off in the dark so as to reach Manila, eighteen hundred miles west, while it was still daylight. Nonetheless it was nearly dark when they landed, and as they stepped ashore they were greeted by a band, by photographers, by government officials dressed in immaculate white and by hundreds and hundreds of spectators. They were the first passengers to fly the Pacific, and as they were driven into Manila people lined the roads on either side to watch them go by.

There followed two days of parties and receptions, one in Malacañan Palace in the Trippes' honor given by President Quezon, and attended by about a hundred and fifty guests. A river ran beside the ballroom, and the Trippes danced under the stars, with the river lapping against the stone steps while natives in small boats drifted by, their inquisitive faces shining in the palace lights as they passed. The Trippes got to bed at twenty minutes after two, and were called forty minutes later for the usual dawn takeoff. Breakfast was at 3:30 A.M., a hilarious occasion, for some of the passengers were still high and all were exhausted, and their new Filipino friends, on the way home from the party, stopped to say goodbye. At the other end of the table sat Captain Tilton and the crew looking, in contrast, serious, rested, businesslike.

That day the flying boat landed at Hong Kong. This should have been a magic moment for Trippe—he had reached China—but he seems to have been too busy to savor it. Betty Trippe in her journal noted the harbor crowded with shipping, the great junks with their orange sails, the rickshaws, the odors of cooking. But for Trippe there were telegrams to answer, a radio broadcast to London to prepare, people to meet, arrangements to make. He ran so far behind schedule that he and Betty arrived late for dinner at the governor's mansion. The governor and his lady, Betty Trippe reported, were very understanding.

The next morning, accompanied by Harold Bixby, the Trippes flew north toward Peking in a six-passenger Douglas Dolphin floatplane belonging to CNAC, for Bixby meant to show Trippe how well Pan American's Chinese investment was now progressing. Following the disasters of 1934, Bixby had reorganized the company, putting William Langhorne Bond in charge, and bringing in better radio gear and new planes. CNAC had made a small profit in 1935, and might make another this year.

Over the next five days the Trippes flew about three thousand miles, covering all of the CNAC routes. Most mornings they would rise at 4:00 A.M. and be driven to the river or to the airfield. Sometimes there was difficulty getting the engine started in the damp cold and the Trippes would stand shivering, waiting. From the air they would peer down on tiny villages, each walled for protection against pirates and bandits. They landed to refuel on grass airfields or in muddy rivers surrounded by hundreds of junks. While Chinese mechanics worked on the plane they would be served tea and sandwiches, and look out at the otherwise primitive world of China. Almost always local Chinese officials were there to give them presents—lacquered cigarette cases, jade cuff links, soapstone carvings, exquisite embroidered handkerchiefs.

At Shanghai they dined with the mayor. The Chinese ladies wore iridescent nail polish on fingers and toes. On the menu were mandarin fish cooked in a ginger sauce, and shark's fins and pigeon's eggs in bird's-nest soup. The tiny wine cups were filled after every sip, so that it was impossible to know how much one had drunk. Steaming hot towels were passed with which to wipe greasy hands. At Peking, then called Peiping, Trippe took his wife for a rickshaw ride alone though the moonlit streets. At Nanking, the new capital, the Chinese minister of communications, General Yu, gave them a ceremonial "chow," at which a great deal of hot rice wine was drunk, and Yu, an exceptional artist of Chinese calligraphy, drew a testimonial to Trippe. Trippe was told that this was the highest compliment that could be paid him.

Then they were back in Hong Kong, where Trippe divulged to his wife his secret plan. Since he had meetings to conduct in Berlin, Paris, London and such places, it was pointless to fly back home across the Pacific. He and his wife would continue on across Asia. There would be more to his plan later, but this was all he was telling her at the moment. Secrecy with Trippe was a habit. He kept secrets even from his own wife.

And so at 11:00 A.M. on October 30 they left Hong Kong for London in an Imperial Airways four-engined landplane that took them five hundred miles across open sea to Tourane (later called Danang) in French Indochina at a noisy but comfortable eighty miles per hour. Landing in late afternoon, they drove into the city. They dined with the local Shell

Oil Company representative, then went alone for a romantic rickshaw ride along the river in the moonlight.

At dawn they took off for Penang, via Saigon, where the plane was refueled. At dinner with the resident Imperial Airways men, Betty Trippe nearly disgraced herself by falling asleep, but the indefatigable Juan kept the conversation going with no difficulty. The next morning they went on to Bangkok in another four-engined Imperial Airways plane. The Trippes were the only passengers. The plane seemed obsolete, both noisier and slower than comparable airliners being built now in America, and with a very small payload. The flight, which took ten hours, was their third all-day flight in a row. They went to a Buddhist temple and stared at shrines, and at 4:00 A.M. the next morning they were at the airport again, taking off with the first ray of daylight for Calcutta, another long and uneventful flight over barren country except near Rangoon, where they flew over the Golden Pagoda, a Buddhist temple built in A.D. 500. At Calcutta they visited the "Black Hole" and a Jain temple, where it was suggested that they take off their shoes and go in—when dirty slippers were offered to them, the Trippes refused. The filth and poverty were shocking, and the smells nauseating. They had a bottle of eau de cologne, with which they saturated their handkerchiefs. It was dark by the time they reached a burning ghat. Three bodies were being burned. The smell, the smoke, an old man vomiting, and the knowledge that she was seeing bodies being burned were more than Betty could stand, so she fled into the street. But Juan went closer, and claimed later that he saw the head of one of the corpses between the logs. Next day they flew to Delhi— another ten hours aloft. They had been flying now for eight straight days and so, the next morning, Trippe hired a guide and they set off to see the sights. Betty Trippe wanted to see the Taj Mahal, but it was four hours away by car—too far. Trippe, to please his wife, chartered a light plane, and they flew up in an hour. When the engine wouldn't start for the return, Trippe stood in front spinning the propeller by hand until it caught.

On they flew toward Europe, stopping for the night at Jodhpur. The British, Dutch and French air services all stopped there to refuel. The airport and hotel had been built by the Maharajah. The hotel was small —only large enough for the few passengers coming through by air. The Trippes were awakened at 3:00 A.M., and took off in the dark, the first night flying they had done in the East. At Karachi, where they stopped to refuel, they watched the KLM plane come in, an American Douglas airliner that made Baghdad in one day from Karachi. Imperial Airways required two days. To the Trippes, British equipment looked pathetic compared with the American.

Flying over the Arabian Sea, they saw many schools of sharks. The plane was refueled again near a place called Gwadar, where they lunched

in a tent in the desert while an Arab swished the ceiling fan to and fro
to cool them and keep the flies off their food. About 5:00 P.M. they landed
at Sharja, an Imperial Airways base, and slept in a fort surrounded by
barbed wire. The bedrooms were clean but tiny, and there was no plumbing or running water. Compared with this, Wake Island, with its Simmons
beds and private baths, seemed the heart of civilization.

At 5:00 A.M. they drank morning tea at Sharja; four hours later in a
tent on the desert at Bahrain they breakfasted on fish caught in the
Persian Gulf. At Baghdad, where they stopped for the night, the creamed
fish was lukewarm, there was a dead fly in the sauce, and the sheets on
the bed in their room were dirty.

They were awakened at 3:30 A.M. and took off in the dark, curling up
for more sleep as the plane flew across the northern Arabian Desert.
Later came the rugged hills of the Holy Land. They lunched in Gaza, and
three hours later were touching down at Alexandria.

Awakened in the dark the next day, they took off for Europe. Betty
Trippe was so tired that even dawn over the Mediterranean left her
unmoved. They were riding a flying boat that, with fifteen passengers
aboard, plodded along at 90 miles per hour, compared with 140 by the
China Clipper. They landed in Crete, where refueling took ten minutes,
then were off for Brindisi, and Rome. At Marseille, another refueling
stop, they looked over some French flying boats—mere kites compared
with the Clippers, the Trippes decided. Following the Rhone north, they
passed the *Graf Zeppelin,* looking like a clumsy caterpillar as it crept along
toward South America. At Paris, where they checked into the Ritz late in
the afternoon, it was raining, but they went out to dinner in a festive
mood, and ate foie gras with a good deal of wine. Betty passed the next
two days in the shops. Juan met with Air France officials.

From London, Imperial Airways officials drove them to Rochester to
look over the new flying boats being built at the Short Factory. One boat
was at anchor in the harbor, and they went aboard. It was all of six tons
smaller than the Martin, but the height of its ceiling was greater, creating
an impression of spaciousness. Also, more space was given to the galley
and the lavatories. But the result was extremely costly in terms of payload
and range. "Does it seem very much larger than your Clipper?" someone
asked smugly. The Trippes were polite and complimentary, but when
alone, decided that the superior British attitude in a highly competitive
field like aviation would eventually leave them far behind. Their flying
boats, though just now being delivered, were already obsolete compared
with the Pan Am Clippers.

At Seven Oaks the Trippes spent the night with the Lindberghs, who
had been living quietly in England for the past year in self-imposed exile.
In front of the fire after dinner, Charles and Juan discussed aviation.
Anne Lindbergh would have liked to have joined in, but was prevented

by Betty, who saw it as her job at such times to separate out the women, keeping them occupied so that their frivolous comments would not disturb whatever weighty subjects the men might be discussing. Anne Lindbergh had noticed this long ago, and would continue to notice it for many years to come. Sometimes it amused her; sometimes it left her mildly annoyed. Tonight she glanced across at Trippe from time to time. Listening with one ear, she realized that Trippe was almost ebullient; he was eager for the future. He had just come through many countries. He had seen the planes flying there. He had seen the ground facilities, and in some cases the aircraft factories. He was certain now he was way ahead not only of the British but of everyone else and he was happy.

It was in London that Trippe at last revealed to his wife the rest of his secret plan. They weren't going home by boat. Instead, they would fly across the South Atlantic by Zeppelin, thus becoming the first travelers ever to fly around the world by commercial aircraft.

On to Berlin, where Lufthansa officials greeted the Trippes with deep bows, hand-kissing and bouquets of flowers. More conferences. A luncheon in Trippe's honor. A meeting at the Air Ministry with Erhard Milch, second only to Göring in German aviation—Trippe was to have seen Göring himself, but the great man was away. The Air Ministry Building, a masterpiece of modern architecture, had automatic sliding steel windows operated at the touch of a button, making the building invulnerable to aerial attack. Trippe noted the frank discussion of war, the Germans' preparedness for war and the great emphasis on military aviation, and was alarmed.

Heinz Wronsky, Frankfurt head of the Zeppelin Company, met them for breakfast when they got off the train there. They had known Wronsky as a bright, ambitious youth in America. Now he was a conceited, opinionated man, and almost rude when discussing with Trippe the future of Zeppelins as opposed to heavier-than-air aircraft. When a man got angry in casual conversation, Trippe decided, it was usually because he knows his point was weak. There had been many fatal airship accidents already, and every country but Germany had given up such craft as too dangerous. Later that morning Betty Trippe went aboard the *Hindenburg* feeling as if she were entering a hospital for a necessary operation. Trippe himself, though convinced that the day of the slow, difficult Zeppelins was almost over, went aboard full of curiosity.

Even now three American reporters, racing against each other, were flying around the world on commercial aircraft in the opposite direction, claiming to be the first to do so, and filing stories to their syndicates every day. That Juan Trippe, the number one name in international aviation, was doing the same thing would have made even bigger headlines. It also would have reduced Trippe's journey to the level of a stunt. This was not the image Trippe wanted for himself, and so he and his wife were traveling now under assumed names. The Zeppelin's passenger list carried them as Mr. and Mrs. Brown.

At 8:00 A.M. some hundred and fifty soldiers pulling on a hundred and fifty ropes dragged the giant airship out of its shed. There were fifty-six passengers on board, who waved and shouted down to friends and family on the ground while the warmth of the early morning sun expanded the hydrogen gas and the airship slowly began to rise. At about six hundred feet the engines were started, and the *Hindenburg* moved slowly off toward South America. That day it crossed Germany and then much of France, and at twilight started out across the western Mediterranean. It moved noiselessly and its altitude never changed, and in the luxurious main lounge, which measured about 45 by 20 feet, the passengers sat in armchairs watching the countryside pass below. One deck down there was a small bar and smoking room. Because hydrogen gas was highly inflammable, smoking was permitted nowhere else. The dining room was as luxurious as the lounge, and the passengers were assigned cabins the size of compartments on a train, with upper and lower berths and no windows.

Just before setting out over the Atlantic, the *Hindenburg* hovered over the West African town of Bathurst while mail brought from Berlin by fast plane and destined for South America was taken aboard by rope. Then the Zeppelin was moving again, and the Trippes were invited forward to the captain's cabin, which was attached to the outside of the balloon near the nose. Holding a handrail, they walked a narrow gangway—the airship was over eight hundred feet long—looking down at the fabric of the balloon that if they fell they would no doubt plunge right through. Above them were the bags that held the hydrogen gas, and they walked past the great diesel-oil tanks that fueled the engines. In the forward cabin five men worked at guiding the ship across the ocean, one manipulating the elevators, another the rudder. On the third night out at sea they passed the *Graf Zeppelin,* the *Hindenburg*'s sister ship, coming home. Her lights were blinking in salute, and the moon shone on her elongated silver body. She looked like a fantastic fish in the sky, and it seemed to Betty Trippe as if they were living in an age to come, and not in the year 1936.

On the last night came the usual business found on shipboard before landing—the Trippes packed, tipped the stewards, paid their wine bill. At 3:30 A.M. they were awakened to see Rio lying below with a full moon shining on the water. Since the landing was scheduled for 6:00 A.M., they circled the city for two and a half hours. Under reduced power, the airship at last gradually descended until it hovered seventy-five feet above the airport. The ground crew—another hundred and fifty men—ran to attach ropes to a cable lowered from the Zeppelin. It took them about ninety minutes to secure the airship to its mast and then to pull it along a track into its hangar.

The Trippes were met by several of Pan Am's highest-ranking South

American officials, and almost immediately were taken to see the company's big new passenger station, which had just been completed and which could serve both flying boats and landplanes. For the rest of the day Trippe rushed from one business conference to another, taking time out only for a swim in the surf with his wife. The business conferences continued even after dinner, and in the end the Trippes got only three hours' sleep, boarding at dawn a Pan Am S-42 on the first leg of their flight north to Florida. At each overnight stop now they stayed in hotels built or else renovated by Pan American, sleeping on identical Simmons beds every night, tying up to refuel at every stop at identical Pan American barges. Their final hop was from Trinidad to Miami, eighteen hundred miles with intermediate stops at San Juan, San Pedro de Macorís, Santo Domingo and Port-au-Prince—a dawn-to-dusk ride that ended when they landed in the bay at Dinner Key, the company's new Miami base, and walked in under the long awning of the quarantine station to have their temperatures taken before public health authorities would allow them officially back into the United States. They came the rest of the way home via Eastern Airlines, having traveled altogether about thirty-six thousand miles in thirty-eight days of flying. Both the Trippes now had a new and far more vivid picture of the world than in the past. These feelings Juan Trippe never tried to articulate; he was not an articulate man, and so he had chosen during the last ten years to construct an airline and air routes that would speak for him. But Betty Trippe, once home, once having embraced her children, put her thoughts down on paper. What made the Chinese industrious and the Indians so slovenly? she asked. What made the Germans so aggressive and the British so complacent and self-satisfied? Was it climate, race or religion? Let us hope, she added, that the development of aviation around the world will bring more understanding of other countries' customs, and peace.

28

New Zealand

Trippe's trip around the world was a tourist success but a business failure. His negotiations in England, on which he had lavished most of eight days, had gained nothing. He was as far from crossing the Atlantic as ever. Britain claimed to be interested in joint service or none at all, but had no flying boat that could make it across—and from the look of things, would not have one for a good long time.

Trippe had hoped also to win the right to island-hop southwest from Hawaii to Australia and New Zealand. But these destinations, too, Britain had chosen to block. Australia and New Zealand, though sovereign, were thoroughly dominated portions of the British Empire in 1936, and Britain did not want Trippe landing in either place until it got rights to land in Hawaii in exchange. Imperial Airways was already running an eleven-day service between London and Australia; Hawaii was essential if Imperial hoped to continue either to the United States or to Canada. However, Hawaiian landing rights were impossible for Trippe to concede; he was not (whatever the British may have thought) an arm of the U.S. government.

And so: impasse.

Or was it? Trippe thought he saw a way to split Australia and New Zealand off from each other, and if this worked, then splitting them off from the mother country would follow. He would have his new routes, he would control the entire Pacific, and there would be nothing Britain could do about it. The plan he settled on was similar to, just as devious as, and even more risky than, the one by which he had squeezed out landing rights in Hong Kong, and he set it into motion by devising the routes he would need. Total distance to either destination was just over 6,000 miles—2,000 miles shorter than the route straight across to China. After Hawaii it would be necessary to make just two stops, and these he plotted out on a globe. The first would be 1,100 miles away at an atoll called Kingman Reef, and the second at Pago Pago in American Samoa.

The several islands of American Samoa had a population of about fifteen thousand, but Kingman Reef was uninhabited. It was also the tiniest target any oceangoing aircraft had ever elected to try to hit. It was smaller than Wake Island, smaller than most ships. It was 120 feet long and 90 feet wide—too small even to plant Leuteritz's adcock there. It was totally nude except for three small palm trees, and rose barely three feet above sea level at high water. It was, however, like Wake, a drowned mountain summit, and the reef that surrounded the tiny bit of sand also enclosed a big sheltered lagoon on which flying boats could land—if they could find it. Well, a ship could find it, and planes could home in on the ship.

As a solution to a problem, Kingman Reef, with a ship perpetually standing by, was preposterous. The "island" was too small and the ship too expensive. Nonetheless, Trippe by this time was in love with what he later called "creative pioneering," and a tanker named the *North Wind* was hired, loaded with aviation gasoline and radio direction-finding gear, and sent to anchor in the Kingman Reef lagoon.

Pago Pago was a much bigger place, and had a good harbor—for ships. The six Pan American technicians sent there rated this harbor only marginal for aircraft. It was almost entirely surrounded by 1,500-foot-high hills, which rose out of the water almost as sheer as cliffs. Nor was the harbor very big. Flying boats were going to have to drop in sharply, smacking the water hard. At takeoff, boats would have to leave the water quickly in a steep climbing bank. Nonetheless, it was the best available along that part of the route, and the technicians recommended it to Trippe, who ordered all necessary equipment—adcock, landing barge, marine runway, airline office—installed there. He was spending a great deal of money on a route that so far had no terminus: he still had no permission from Australia or New Zealand to land in either place.

Meanwhile an Imperial Air Conference had been called in New Zealand, and it was attended by officials representing the British, Australian and New Zealand governments. The British reiterated their demand that unlimited landing rights in Hawaii be obtained from the United States government before any similar rights were accorded to Pan American in Australia and New Zealand. Australia and New Zealand were urged to stay firm.

The results of this conference were communicated to Trippe, but his plan remained in place, he was still optimistic, and he went on spending money. He still saw a way—or thought he did—to separate the two former colonies from the mother country, and his idea was to drive in a wedge at the weakest point. This point, to Trippe, was New Zealand, and he sent Harold Gatty, late of the South Seas Commercial, back there to negotiate anew. Gatty's argument was to be that if the main South Pacific air route was established—whether by the British or the Americans—from Hawaï straight to Australia, then the country to suffer would be New Zealand. Its second-class status would be reaffirmed. From then on it would be a detour only. What Trippe was offering New Zealand was a chance to get in first. Pan American was ready to serve New Zealand right now. Why shouldn't New Zealand stand astride the main route? Why shouldn't New Zealand step into the mainstream of the world? Let Australia be the detour for a change. Direct communication by air between New Zealand and the United States would establish the supremacy of New Zealand overnight. What this could mean to the business and diplomatic community of New Zealand passed beyond all imagining.

On March 11, 1937, New Zealand conceded full commercial traffic rights to Pan American, and six days later Musick prepared to head there from San Francisco in a survey plane. The New Zealanders were amazed that the flight could start out so quickly, not realizing that all had been in readiness for weeks.

The rest of Trippe's plan was, as in the case of Hong Kong, simply to wait. Once his airline had reached New Zealand, pressure on Australia would be immense. Its business community would force the government to let him land, and if this did not happen, then Trippe had already conceived a ploy by which he would shame them into it. He would hire a yacht and announce publicly that his yacht was standing by to "speed" airmail and passengers from New Zealand to Australia on the last leg of their journey.

Apart from such creative thinking, the Pacific Division no longer excited Trippe very much. The Pacific had been crossed and the challenge was over. Others could run it, and he turned toward the Atlantic, where his energy was needed most. His executives realized this. Therefore, although the Pacific still had problems, these were no longer brought for decision to Trippe personally. Indeed, memos and letters about them now tended to refer to "New York," or to "the president," rather than mentioning Trippe by name: "You indicated yesterday that the president was unfavorably disposed toward our proposed expenditures," read one memo. Trippe was now in his late thirties. His hairline was beginning to recede. He was a little bulkier, a little less approachable than before. There was a hardness about him discernible to all. His devotion to his company seemed just that—a devotion not to the people who worked for it and him, but rather to the corporation itself, this thing that he had built and that he meant to throw around the world. Most memos about the

Pacific's problems were marked "Confidential," and some after being written were, on second thought, never sent. "Up to this time, we have received no definite information whatsoever from New York as to the availability of a fourth airplane for San Francisco–Manila service," wrote division engineer John Leslie to division manager Clarence Young. "We do not know when it will be available, what it will be, or indeed whether anything is yet on order . . . never in all of the hectic days of the Caribbean Division expansion were we in the situation where the loss or damage of one aircraft would completely disrupt all schedules . . . I must repeat with all the vigor at my command that we cannot continue this operation here safely or regularly without reserve aircraft and I must state my belief that New York owes it to us to advise us at the earliest possible moment what action they propose to take to provide us with adequate flying equipment."

A memo from operations manager Schildhauer read: "We have got to have more personnel." But Schildhauer himself was stripped from the Pacific Division and sent to fill the same job in the newly formed Atlantic Division, where no planes were yet flying. In June of 1937 Leslie wrote to E. W. McVitty, one of the bright young engineers in Priester's office in New York: "Now we have facing us the New Zealand operation, with such severe limitation upon personnel, flying equipment, and airport characteristics that it is going to take the utmost experience and discrimination to avoid a hazardous operation."

Musick's survey plane, as he took off for New Zealand for the first time, was an obsolescent S-42. Like its predecessor, on the route to China, it had had its insides ripped out and replaced by tubes, valves and extra tanks filled with fuel. Once again it was necessary to pump this cabin fuel out to the wings in flight. Once again there was the constant odor of raw gas inside the plane, and the crew flew bundled up with the windows open. Once again all aboard were aware that they were pushing their "art" to its outer limit. Many years later, navigator Harry Canaday remarked: "I wonder how we ever did this sort of thing. You wouldn't even begin to do it now—to take this sort of chance."

About halfway between San Francisco and Hawaii on this first New Zealand flight engineer Vic Wright suddenly stiffened: something was wrong, he didn't know what. He was monitoring his instruments in the cockpit, sitting just behind the pilots, Musick and Frank Briggs. The stainless-steel bow post mounted about five feet in front of the windshield always reflected the color of the engine exhausts. This flickering reflection was mainly blue. Normally there was a touch of yellow in it, and staring at it now, Wright realized that the yellow was gone. His eyes began darting from gauge to gauge until he discovered why: No. 1 engine, outboard on the port side, was running hot. He told Musick.

At this halfway point less than half its fuel had been expended. Musick decided to shut No. 1 engine down, and after that he decided to dump gas from his wing tanks, thus lightening the flying boat enough so that normal altitude and normal cruising speed could be maintained on three engines. The dump valves were opened. Hundreds of gallons of gasoline blew into the night sky, and the plane began to fly easier.

About five minutes passed before Canaday came forward from the chart room to report drops of gasoline on his chart table. This meant that some of the dumped gas had blown inside the plane.

Tension was immediate. If there was free gas inside the cabin, then at any instant a spark from one of the electrical circuits—radio, one of the pumps, even the cockpit instruments—might ignite the vapor and blow the plane apart. They were twelve hundred miles out in the Pacific riding a bomb that was waiting to explode.

Reaching up above his head, Wright pulled the master switch instantly. This shut off all electrical circuits except those in the engines. At the controls, Musick said nothing. He and Wright had flown together so long that an almost perfect understanding existed between them.

Radio officer T. R. Runnels came hurrying forward, squawking. His radio had just gone out.

Musick flew the plane on three engines through the night as Wright began pushing open additional windows. He ordered Runnels, Canaday and the others to do the same all the way back throughout the plane. After that he and junior officer William Holsenbeck moved through with pyrene extinguishers, flooding the bilges, the tail sections under the floor, and every other corner where they thought gas vapor might accumulate. After that, there was nothing to do but wait. The plane flew on with a miniature gale blowing through it.

A little later Wright moved through the plane sniffing hard. There was no gas vapor he could detect. Back in his place he threw in the main switch once more. The instrument lights, the pumps, the radio came back on.

The next day in Hawaii, with the plane safe on the water, Musick and Wright looked over the fuel-dumping ducts, which were flush with the bottom of the wing skin. Apart from advising San Francisco that structural changes seemed called for, there was nothing they could do. In any case, from the time of this first trip to New Zealand Musick knew what the danger was.

He took off for Kingman Reef, 1,100 miles away, the next leg of his journey. It was a fine, clear morning, but the weather soon changed. By afternoon he was flying through a driving rainstorm, and trying to find a patch of sand ahead that was not much bigger than a tennis court. Kingman Reef as a target was less than one-tenth the size of Wake, but the directional signals from the *North Wind* anchored in the lagoon came in loud and clear, and when Musick plunged down out of the overcast, there everything lay—the ship, the single dune, the lagoon; flying across the *North Wind*'s decks, he circled and landed.

Takeoff next dawn was normal, and by midafternoon the plane had flown 1,600 miles and was circling over the harbor of Pago Pago and Musick, looking down, was cursing. The bay, he saw, was extremely beautiful, but it had a narrow, reef-girt mouth that opened so directly into the path of the prevailing trade winds that the seas piled up there. Musick, circling, watched the ocean swells build into giant combers. There was no choice as far as landing was concerned. Musick would have to swoop down over the high steep hills, spank the water hard, and then sit there hoping the flying boat would come to a stop before it crashed into the rough water of the harbor entrance. It would be like landing in a teacup, Musick thought as he cursed. Most of the Clipper's gasoline was gone, meaning that it would land light. It would have a tendency, once on the water, to skim along rather than to settle. There was a very good chance that it would crash into those combers. Musick lined up his landing approach, and came in just over the hilltops at two thousand feet. The wing flaps were full down. At this angle he was going to use up too much of the bay before he struck the water, so he added power, pulled up the flaps and came around for a second try. This time he dove almost straight down the slope of the hills into the harbor, the trees just below his wings, pulling up at the last moment almost into a stall, and striking the water hard.

As soon as the flying boat had rocked to a stop, it was surrounded by outriggers and war canoes filled with half-naked Polynesians whose skin glistened with coconut oil. There was no hotel on the island. The crew was lodged in the governor's mansion, and there Musick waited four days for the perfect wind conditions that he felt he needed to get the flying boat safely out of Pago Pago harbor with enough gas on board to make Auckland 1,800 miles away.

Takeoff finally was at dawn. The crew had been paddled out to the flying boat in the dark in a war canoe by natives wearing skirtlike lava-lavas. Musick made two false starts across the bay before he was satisfied that he had picked the best line for his takeoff. After that he lifted the Clipper into the air in a steep climbing turn, and pointed his nose toward Auckland.

Musick ought to have been used to tumultuous receptions by now. He was not. At Auckland thirty thousand people waited to cheer him, and when he mounted the reviewing stand he was applauded for five solid minutes. Some of the people applauding had tears in their eyes, for it seemed to them that with a single stroke he had brought them into the mainstream of modern life. New Zealand was now only four days from San Francisco.

"We are glad to be here," Musick said into the microphone. It was his usual stiff speech, but it was enough. They cheered him again and again until finally his face broke into a kind of beatific grin, as if, standing there, he understood for the first time the magnitude of his achievement. Others could talk about bringing peoples together; he, a pilot, was doing it. He was offering these isolated New Zealanders the greatest gift of all: he was offering them the whole rest of the world. The love Musick saw on the faces below astonished him. Their new aeronautical station was almost ready. A short time later they would name its site in his honor: Musick Point, and this would astonish him too.

But when Musick landed at Pago Pago on the way home he was in an ugly mood again, for the harbor looked even tighter to him this time than the last. Tomorrow's dawn takeoff worried him in advance. Ordering his crew to off-load everything not absolutely necessary for the next leg to Kingman Reef, he stormed ashore. And he meant everything. It was the first and only time, Wright noted later, that he had ever seen Musick upset. Every souvenir that the men had picked up—the grass skirts, the sea shells, the hand-carved coconuts, the toy outrigger canoes—all of it he ordered left behind, even the sacks of spare parts the plane normally carried.

Next day at dawn he ordered safety harnesses attached, added full power to the stripped-down flying boat, and drove toward the huge breakers at the mouth of the harbor. The S-42 lifted off the water just in time.

In Florida, Bob Fatt was ordered to run fuel-dumping tests on a similar plane.

"What are we going to dump?" he asked.

"Why, gasoline," the operations manager told him.

"Not me. You'll have to find somebody else."

"Well, we have to do it. Who else are we going to find?"

"You have some sort of half-ass license yourself," Fatt told him bluntly. "Why don't you take it up and dump it?"

"I was only kidding. We're going to use diesel fuel."

"I'm going to try the stuff beforehand," said Fatt, "and if it burns, I don't fly it."

Fatt took a sample, a mixture of dye and diesel fuel, heated it, and put a match to it. It didn't burn, so he flew the test. The dye showed that dumped fuel came out of the vent hole in the bottom of the wing, flowed forward along the skin of the undersurface, then up over the leading edge back into the wind. Some of it also appeared to have been blown into hollow spaces inside the wing itself. The results of this test and others reached the Department of Commerce, which issued an order sealing all dump valves on commercial planes. However, this order did not apply to noncommercial flights, and Musick, as he left San Francisco for another survey flight to New Zealand, was perhaps not aware that it existed.

This was his third trip and therefore his fifth time at Pago Pago, whose harbor he hated. Although the S-42's cabin was as jammed as always with fuel tanks, he made an uneventful landing there, and the next day, January 11, 1938, he and his crew filed on board at dawn for the final 1,800-mile leg to Auckland. He was flying with a new crew—Canaday, Vic Wright and the others were not with him—and he moved up into the cockpit and began the same precise preparations that preceded every flight he made. Taking a rag, he wiped off first the yoke, throttles and other handles. After that he wiped off his seat. He was the most meticulous man most of his colleagues had ever known. They said he even loaned cigarettes meticulously: when he gave one of his cigarettes to a pal, he wanted the pal to take a match too, for there were twenty cigarettes in a pack and twenty matches in a book, and he wanted them to come out even. In a cockpit he was meticulous about his hands, about his trousers. His hands had to feel just right on the wheel, the crease had to feel just right on his legs, and until he was satisfied he would not take off.

He was forty-four years old. He liked to go to baseball games, prizefights and midget races, and to trim his wife's hair when he was home. But he was often gone a month at a time. He kept photos of the places he had been to, and he liked to buy his wife presents in exotic spots. He held ten world aviation records. He was the most famous transport pilot alive, and one of the only ones licensed to fly any type of aircraft.

About two hours out of Pago Pago that morning his plane exploded in the air.

An oil leak had developed in No. 4 engine. Musick radioed that he was returning to Pago Pago. A little later he radioed that he was signing off preparatory to dumping his fuel; there was no way he could land in that hated Pago Pago teacup fully loaded.

That was his last message.

A search was mobilized. About twelve miles off the island the Navy minesweeper *Avocet* late in the day came upon charred fragments of flying boat floating in an oil slick. Items recovered showed signs of an internal explosion, including a coat belonging to radio officer T. J. Findley, twenty-nine, which had holes blown through it; a wing emblem was the identifying mark on the coat. Trousers were found floating that had belonged to J. A. Brooks, thirty-eight, the assistant engineering officer, and these were identified by Brooks's tie clasp in the pocket, the clasp being bent. Pages from the engineering log were found, and the navigator's desk, with bits of his charts still attached. Many small wood fragments from the inside of the plane were recovered, one of the biggest being an entire drawer.

In New York Trippe called the loss of Musick and his crew an irreparable blow: "I feel that Captain Musick and his flight crew are entirely blameless. Radio reports from the plane prove that on this flight, as on all of his previous flights, he carefully followed the most conservative operating technique possible. Needless to say, everyone connected with Pan American Airways is grieved beyond expression at the untimely fate of Captain Musick and his splendid crew."

MUSICK, SIX OTHERS KILLED IN CLIPPER BLAZE headlined the San Francisco *News*. The disaster was front-page all over the world. It was more than a plane crash; the great Musick was dead. Grief seemed strongest and most personal in New Zealand, for he was not only a hero there but also a kind of beloved figure. A Musick memorial radio station was erected in his honor, and from that year on, New Zealand has awarded the Edwin C. Musick Trophy to "pioneers in advancing safety in aviation."

An article in *The New York Times* linked the cause of the explosion to static electricity. "Aviation engineers pointed out that the control of static electricity collected by moving vehicles had long been a mystery." Vic Wright thought that gas vapors had collected inside the wings after the fuel was dumped; Musick, preparing to land, would have lowered the flaps. The flap motor was in the tower that joined the wings to the hull, in an area where there might have been fumes or raw gas. Wright guessed that as Musick switched on the flap motor the whole thing just exploded.

In Florida Fatt said that Musick had dumped fuel to save the airplane; if he had landed heavy, his extra speed almost certainly would have taken him out through the harbor into the giant combers, wrecking the plane. Fatt himself would not have worried about the plane, he said, and he would not have dumped: "I would have said the hell with it."

A memorial ceremony was conducted at sea by the master of the ship *Matua* three days after the Clipper went down. Slowly the ship steamed within sight of the spot. Then at the clang of the telegraph on the bridge all movement ceased. The ship's company stood assembled on the deck as the captain read the burial service for those who die at sea. It was a gloriously sunny day, and on the hatches lay garlands of South Pacific flowers that filled the warm summer air with their fragrance. The hymn "Abide with Me" was sung as the wreaths were lowered into the glittering waters.

The official memorial service was held two weeks later in the City Hall rotunda in San Francisco. Mayor Angelo J. Rossi spoke the eulogy, the municipal orchestra played hymns, and invocations were given by a rabbi, a priest and a minister. Pan American was represented by acting division manager John Leslie; Trippe did not come out from New York.

By then the Department of Commerce had withdrawn its approval for the company to use Pago Pago, which meant that the New Zealand route was closed also, and service on it was suspended for more than a year while a new route was set up. This one passed via Canton Island, still another uninhabited, waterless atoll. The island itself was a narrow strip of land ranging in width from fifty yards to a third of a mile. Its vegetation amounted to not much more than eight coconut trees, but its lagoon measured 9 miles long by 3 miles wide. It took months of blasting coral heads before the lagoon was usable by flying boats, and more months before the necessary installations could be erected in the sand. All this work was authorized by Trippe at a cost of hundreds of thousands of additional dollars.

There had been an enormous public outcry following the Musick crash. Pan American and Trippe were accused of opening a new route to New Zealand which was neither necessary nor desirable, of pushing ahead with reckless disregard for human life, and for one purpose only, to forestall competition. Possibly the loudest of the voices belonged to Grover Loening, the disenchanted former Pan Am board member, who sent telegrams to members of the Washington press: "This accident brings into focus the monopolistic aims of this one company in a tragic blunder of overexpansion, underpreparation and overworking of its personnel and of its old equipment. I have been almost alone in insisting for years that the worst thing for our aviation industry and for our advancement in foreign air trade is to allow this company to grow any larger." Loening's words struck with heavy impact. He had been a pilot and aviation pioneer himself, and after that a successful aircraft manufacturer. Most important of all, he had been for many years a member of the Pan American board.

For a time a great storm centered on the personality of Trippe. Trippe ignored it. Hearings were held, articles appeared. Trippe ignored them also, and when, after several months, the weather at last cleared, it was seen that Trippe was still standing.

Six months after the Musick crash the *Hawaii Clipper,* carrying six passengers and a crew of nine, went down between Guam and Manila. The weather was rainy, but there was no reported trouble. The flying boat had been in regular communication with Pan Am radio stations. A routine signal had been received, followed by—nothing. The plane simply disappeared. It was never heard from again. An extensive search was mounted by aircraft and surface vessels, but no trace was ever found.

Almost immediately rumors were heard. Supposedly two Japanese gunmen had hidden in the tail, which explained why the plane had seemed to take off tail-heavy from Guam, remaining stuck to the water about twenty seconds longer than normal. In flight, after remaining hidden for some hours, the Japanese had come forward and hijacked the plane (the word "hijack" was not used in 1938 with regard to aircraft, and indeed the concept was unknown). The plane was then flown to Yokohama, where all aboard were killed. There was no lack of motives for such a hijacking: a Chinese passenger aboard was carrying a suitcase full of money for Chiang Kai-shek; the Japanese government had wanted the Pratt and Whitney engines to copy for their warplanes; Japanese nationals, who may or may not have been under official orders, had acted out of hatred of everything American. Everyone knew how much Japan resented and hated the penetration of what it considered its airspace. The famous aviatrix Amelia Earhart, attempting to fly around the world the year before, had disappeared, and the Japanese were supposed to have forced her down on an island and killed her too. There was much other precedent to base the rumors on. Had not the FBI arrested those two Japanese nationals trying to sabotage the DF as far back as 1935? More recently a Clipper had turned back when it proved impossible to pump fuel from bilge tanks to wing tanks. The plane had made it only to the Long Beach Naval Station, where battleships turned on their floodlights to illuminate a landing area. When maintenance crews found that a fuel feed line had been plugged with a cork, Japanese sabotage was immediately suspected, and the FBI had assigned two agents to investigate, one of whom had put on khaki coveralls and worked as a maintenance crewman for weeks.

Now the *Hawaii Clipper* had disappeared and rumor again blamed the Japanese. Trippe grasped this rumor eagerly. Whatever blame stuck to the hated Japs could then not stick also to Trippe himself, and he repeated the story, with many details, to many people.

For the first time he was in serious trouble with his board of directors. The year before, the Pacific Division had posted operating losses greater than expected—more than a half a million dollars. This year, 1938, these losses had only increased. Now, with the *Hawaii Clipper* down, the transpacific schedule to Manila and Hong Kong simply could not be maintained. The 8,000-mile distance was too vast for the two remaining Martin flying boats. They could not be turned around quickly enough.

Able to fly only 60 percent of its schedule, with losses running at $95,000 a month, the company had formally petitioned the Post Office Department for additional mail payments.

In Washington, on his board of directors, in his own entourage, voices muttered openly against Trippe. If he heard them it did not show. Certainly, he did not heed them. Instead, he plunged borrowed money into a new attempt to cross the Atlantic. The headlines, when they came, were nonetheless unexpected. They reported that Trippe had been ousted as the company's chief executive.

Part III
THE
ATLANTIC

29

The Obstacles

By the time he fell from power Trippe had invested uncounted man-hours—his own and others'—plus a million and a half dollars in out-of-pocket expenses, plus more than $4 million in new aircraft, all in attempts to cross the Atlantic. Despite these vast outlays, he had still not managed to push forth a single transatlantic commercial flight. Worse, it now seemed entirely possible that other national airlines would open scheduled service either before Pan American or to the exclusion of Pan American, or both.

Imperial Airways of Great Britain had been formed in 1924 by amalgamating a number of small airlines that had proliferated following World War I. A government subsidy of £1 million (then about $5 million) was promised. It would be spread over a ten-year period. All pilots and aircraft, it was stipulated, had to be British. A board of directors was named, with Sir Eric Geddes, the head of Dunlop Rubber, as part-time chairman. The rest of the board members were part time too, being men from the Air Ministry, the Foreign Office, the Dominions Office, the Colonial Office, the Post Office and the Treasury.

George Woods-Humphery was named managing director. Glasgow-born, Woods-Humphery had been trained as an engineer. During World War I he had risen to the rank of major in the Royal Flying Corps, and afterwards had gone to work for Handley-Page, the aircraft manufacturers. Eventually he ran their airline, one of those amalgamated into Imperial. He was a bit older than Trippe, worked just as hard, but was much more coldly and obviously a dictator. He lacked Trippe's outwardly amiable manner, Trippe's ability to convince people—temporarily, at least—that he was not a dictator at all.

Woods-Humphery, an aristocrat in an aristocratic country, refused until the end of the twenties to refer to pilots as captains. Instead, he treated them as chauffeurs, offered them £100 a year as a retainer, plus flying pay at the rate of fifteen shillings an hour—then about $3.75—not a bad wage. But the autocratic way in which he forced this down their throats provoked the first airline pilots' dispute in history. Once, when he entered an airport waiting room, he spotted a man lounging about whom he mistook for a pilot. He walked up and fired him. It was not a pilot but a passenger waiting for a plane.

Woods-Humphery was said to work sixteen hours a day. He believed in the supremacy of all things British. He also had a very British sense of fair play. Beginning in 1928 scores of letters passed back and forth between him and Trippe, and there were scores of transatlantic telephone calls as well. The letters and telephone summaries were masterpieces of good manners and good breeding. In one agreement that both men signed, the term "square deal" appeared, and this was to cause a good deal of trouble later.

From the beginning Imperial's direction was charted not so much by its own executives as by the whims of high government functionaries. The same type of government interference obtained in other European countries, and the governments bought this right with money. For instance, France's Aéropostale received over 80 percent of its revenues in direct government subsidies.

Trippe, at the beginning, differed from these competitors not so much in the size of his operations—he would soon outgrow them all—as in the one fundamental particular that would make all the difference. They were under pressure to link up capitals of far-flung empires. The French were trying to reach such places as Madagascar and Saigon while the Dutch needed to touch down in Indonesia. The British were aiming for India, Hong Kong and eventually Canada; however costly Canada might be, it must be attained because it was British, part of the "all-red route" that was so much to be desired. (In those days on most globes, certainly on English ones, the British Empire was marked in red.) The British, French, Dutch and German air routes were all mandated by duty, prestige, honor, glory—by political necessity. In international aviation in all the world, so it seemed, not one man was focused purely on profit except Trippe.

As early as 1932 Geddes and Woods-Humphery had begun to see this difference in purpose. Imperial's profit that year was £52,894, about $250,000. But it, like the airline itself, was stagnant. Pan Am's profit, despite the heavy costs of expansion, was $698,526. France had 269 aircraft employed in regular air transport, Germany 177, and Britain only

207 · The Obstacles

32. Pan Am's fleet had already reached 121. That same year Woods-Humphery noted: "It is little use grieving over the United States' aerial invasion of Canada whilst the United States is prepared to spend so much money on the development of commercial aviation and the British Empire is not." Geddes and Woods-Humphery were being dominated by government functionaries and at the same time intimidated by London journalists. In December 1932 the *Daily Telegraph* reported that Pan Am would soon cross the Atlantic via Bermuda in winter and Newfoundland in summer with flying boats carrying fifty passengers and several tons of mail—this was a reference to the S-42 and the Martin M-130. "The keels of the two air leviathans," the *Telegraph* added, "have been laid in great secrecy in factories in Bridgeport and Baltimore."

Well, there was no great secrecy in either place. Always in the past Trippe had answered Woods-Humphery's questions about American technical developments, but if the two new flying boats were secret, then this became a subject Woods-Humphery felt he could no longer approach. He was, after all, a well-bred man, and to probe into another fellow's business secrets was impolite. From then on, he culled most of his information from American aviation journals, and when these began to report progress on the so-called leviathans, Woods-Humphery became gloomy—projected ranges and payloads far exceeded anything being built in Britain—but Major Robert Mayo, technical adviser to Imperial, told him that such claims could not possibly be achieved because Americans were far behind British designers when it came to flying boats.

In the meantime Mayo kept urging development of his so-called Short-Mayo composite—two planes taking off one atop the other, the smaller plane then crossing the ocean alone. Of all the zany ideas advanced for crossing the Atlantic, this was to prove one of the most resilient.

Test flights of the Sikorsky and Martin flying boats, which soon followed, threw the British into a panic, for to a large extent the planes fulfilled their specifications. The Americans seemed able to begin transatlantic service at once, whereas the best British machine then extant had a range of less than a thousand miles and would run out of fuel halfway across.

It was at this point that negotiations with Pan Am for landing rights in Newfoundland and Ireland were broken off, and in addition, certain high government functionaries pushed Geddes and Woods-Humphery aside and attempted to take over Imperial's direction themselves. A series of meetings ensued, most chaired by director of Civil Aviation Sir Francis Shelmerdine, or else by Post Office head Sir Donald Banks. Woods-Humphery was sometimes not even invited to attend. Sir Francis and Sir Donald ordered work on the Short-Mayo composite expedited, and at the same time signed contracts for twenty-eight Empire flying boats at

£41,000 each—an enormous order for planes that existed only on drawing boards. (When Trippe ordered new equipment, his first order rarely exceeded three aircraft—he had contracted for only three S-42's, and only three Martins.) The Empire flying boats would be powered by four Pegasus 1,000-hp engines, and would weigh 45,000 pounds—a bit smaller than the Martins, which they somewhat resembled in looks, though not in performance.

Next Sir Francis and Sir Donald, together with a representative from Ireland, went to Montreal to meet a delegation of Canadians and to found the Atlantic Company, a transatlantic service between Britain and Canada that would freeze the Americans out altogether. The British would own 51 percent, Canada and Ireland would hold 24 1/2 percent each, and the Atlantic Company would be the chosen instrument of the British government in international aviation. The transatlantic terminal of the line would be Montreal, and the planes—which did not yet exist—would continue across Canada to Vancouver. New York, they hoped, would become a branch terminal at the end of a branch line.

From Montreal, at the beginning of December 1935, the Irish, Canadian and British negotiators went on to Washington to present their Atlantic Company to the Americans and to ask for the right to route their branch line over U.S. territory as far as New York. In exchange for this, because they owed Trippe a "square deal," they were willing to permit reciprocal flights to England by Pan American. A gentlemen's agreement —joint transatlantic service— existed between Geddes and Trippe, and the British meant to honor it, if possible.

Waiting for the Atlantic Company in Washington was the new Interdepartmental Committee on International Civil Aviation, appointed by President Roosevelt. It was staffed by men from State, Commerce, Justice, the Post Office and other departments, and was chaired by Assistant Secretary of State R. Walton Moore, a courtly, elderly gentleman, who, like his colleagues, knew almost nothing about international aviation.

Less than two weeks ago the *China Clipper* had crossed the Pacific on its maiden flight. Less than one week ago Trippe had submitted, via the State Department in Washington, his company's application to the British government for authority to operate between the United States and England, and between the United States and Bermuda. That is, Trippe, in working via the State Department, had at last conceded that he could not win these rights by himself. After seven years of personal diplomacy, negotiations on both sides had passed entirely into the hands of politicians.

How, Moore asked the Atlantic Company, could his committee certify Pan American, a private corporation bent on profit? Could not British landing rights be thrown open to any American company? The answer was no. The British knew Trippe and trusted him, and, in fact, were there to discharge a long-standing agreement with him. They didn't want just anyone flying the Atlantic. They wanted one company only, and they wanted to name it. It was a problem to which a legally sound solution was needed. This was done by issuing a press release asking all U.S. airline companies that were prepared to fly the Atlantic to attend the next day's meeting. Of course, only Trippe showed up. The Interdepartmental Committee still had no authority to certify Pan American as official representative of the United States and refused to do so, but it did agree to stipulate that it had no objections to Pan American. With this the British appeared satisfied, and as the meeting broke up it seemed possible that some kind of transatlantic service might begin in a few months.

Seven weeks later, on January 25, 1936, Trippe in New York and Woods-Humphery in London signed an agreement that divided the North Atlantic between them. Unfortunately, this agreement contained two provisions that would in the future cause no end of distress. First, neither party could begin service till the other was ready. Secondly, the agreement was exclusive: each party promised the other a "square deal" —they were in, everyone else was out. France and Germany, seeing themselves barred from British stepping-stones across the Atlantic, sent strong protests to London. Eddie Rickenbacker, representing Eastern Airlines, visited Croydon Aerodrome wanting information and a piece of the business.

Under such pressure as this, the politicians on both sides of the ocean began to question the agreement and to delay the necessary permits. Trippe still needed formal landing rights from Canada, Ireland, Bermuda and the British government. He also needed permission from the Portuguese to land in the Azores and Lisbon if he could ever hope to fly the southern route. Imperial needed a permit from the Department of Commerce in order to fly to New York. When the Imperial–Pan Am exclusivity clause began to be interpreted in Washington as a possible violation of the Sherman Antitrust Act, Trippe by telephone urged Woods-Humphery to hurry along the Canadian, Irish and British permits he needed, lest "the whole thing get into a mess."

The Germans went to London and asked permission to use Bermuda to make twelve experimental transatlantic flights with their catapult planes. They got nowhere. They went to Washington for permission to land on Long Island Sound, and it was accorded.

Months passed, and still the politicians argued and held back Trippe's permits. The Canadian politicians did not want New York as the terminus over Montreal. The U.S. Post Office warned Trippe that he was not going to get a transatlantic airmail contract because the Foreign Air Mail Act, Section 2244, p. 776, authorized the Postmaster General to award contracts only to the lowest responsible bidder. "It is the position of the Post Office," Trippe was informed, "that in view of this provision, a foreign airmail contract cannot be awarded under circumstances which do not permit an actual competition in the bidding. And by that I mean not merely legal freedom to anyone interested to come and bid, but a situation in which there are actually two or more persons interested and able to bid." The Post Office would take the position that no contract could be advertised until at least one other company was equipped to carry the mail and was in possession of all necessary British landing and traffic concessions.

In the fall of 1936 German catapult planes, carrying neither cargo nor passengers, duly arrived in Long Island Sound by air via Lisbon and the Azores, and with that the Atlantic had been crossed by a commercial company—more or less—at last. Round one to the Germans.

Trippe plodded doggedly on. He kept pressuring Washington, on the one hand, and Woods-Humphrey, on the other, for the permits he needed.

Meanwhile there were other preparations to be made. New York, its harbor frozen in winter, was no year-round seaplane base. Trippe would have to go south. After three months of negotiations, he reached agreement with the City of Baltimore, leasing ten acres of land for periods totaling twenty-five years. In exchange, the city agreed to build and pay for a great seaplane base: hangar, ramps and landing floats, office space —a vast expenditure. Baltimore, like Macao before it, exultantly saw itself in the role of a great ocean terminus, prosperous beyond all previous measure.

There was nothing Trippe could do now but wait. It was at this time that he and his wife first crossed the Pacific to Hong Kong, and from the Orient went around the world. Trippe enjoyed the scenery, or seemed to—as far as London, anyway. His meetings there gained nothing, and the Trippes, as Mr. and Mrs. Brown, crossed the South Atlantic and went home.

Christmas came. An entire year had gone by. There were still no permits from Britain, Canada, Bermuda or Ireland—not to mention Portugal, where Richard C. Long, the same amiable, rotund, energetic, resourceful, Portuguese-speaking businessman who had won Macao rights previously, had now been arguing for rights to the Azores for almost three and a half years. Portugal saw the Azores as indispensable forever. Somebody was going to make millions. Portugal wanted its share of these millions in advance.

On February 17, 1937, Trippe phoned Woods-Humphery to say that the American dirigible interests were now petitioning the government for equal rights on the North Atlantic. Three weeks later he phoned again to report that pressure from the press for a quick agreement was getting worse. Dirigibles. Press reports. Weak arguments, but perhaps the only ones that Trippe had left.

At last on February 22, 1937, the British Air Ministry issued Pan Am a permit for service to, through and away from the United Kingdom, Newfoundland and Bermuda. On March 5 a similar permit was signed in Canada, on March 25 in Bermuda, on April 13 in Ireland, on April 14 in Portugal.

At a ceremony in the office of the Secretary of Commerce in Washington on April 20, 1937, these British, Canadian, Irish and Bermuda permits were handed to Trippe. The Portuguese permit came separately, for it was a private agreement between Pan American and Portugal; it covered a period of twenty-five years, and contained another exclusivity clause. Portugal undertook for a period of fifteen years not to concede traffic rights between Portugal and North America to any other American entity unless the U.S. government nominated another carrier.

Bases had to be built fast, three of them along the eastern seaboard. In Baltimore a thousand men, twenty-five trucks, five steam shovels and a pile driver worked to convert a plot of choice harbor property into a combination flying-boat/landplane airdrome. Trucks carted soil and rock sufficient to raise the level of the field by six feet. Further south a similar scene existed at Charleston on the east bank of the Ashley River, site of the so-called southern transatlantic port—for use when even Baltimore might be iced in. In New York, after two years of discussions, $8 million had been allocated to build a new city-owned flying-boat/landplane airport at North Beach—later to be called LaGuardia Airport. Dredging was to begin at once, and facilities might be usable by the end of the year. In the meantime Trippe had ordered the improvement of a five-acre waterfront plot owned by the company in Port Washington, Long Island. This was the site of the defunct American Aeronautical Corporation, which had begun to construct an airplane factory there just before the 1929 stock market crash. The company went bankrupt, leaving behind a hangar, a ramp and some steelwork. Trippe had picked up the property for real estate value in 1933. It was going to be small, but it would do until city facilities at North Beach were ready.

Other bases were built. In Ireland between Foynes Island and Rynanna on the river Shannon lay a stretch of deep, open water about ten miles wide where flying boats could land. Mooring cables were laid and floats set up. A radio station was constructed, and meteorologists went to work. A new access road twice as wide as the old one and surfaced for heavy traffic was built.

At Shediac, in the Canadian province once called Acadia, a pier was built out into deep water. Plumbing was put in by which gasoline could be pumped out to the pier head, and from there into a flying boat's wings at the rate of a hundred gallons a minute. On a piece of rising ground the sixteen yellow-and-white masts of the adcock DF stood out in contrast to the dark green of the heavy pine forest that blanketed the rugged countryside.

Deep in the wilds of Newfoundland near the shores of Gander Lake a square mile of forest disappeared. Every single stump had to be dug out. Four runways were laid down, and woodsmen at the end of each cleared away more forest. Buildings went up: shops, hangars, offices, a hotel to house ninety passengers. At Gander Lake another huge crew worked on the marine air base. From Gander Lake it was nineteen hundred air miles to Shannon.

The northern route looked relatively easy, at least in summer. The problem was the southern route. The difficult place was going to be the Azores, and everyone knew it.

The Azores: nine islands adrift in the sea a thousand miles off the Portuguese coast. They were hilly, rocky, lava-based islands, and unlike the drowned summits of the Pacific, these were high; one of them, Pico, towered seven thousand feet above the waves. All were steep-sided, and there were no harbors. Nor, ashore, were there any significant stretches of flat land for a land airport for the future. In 1933 Trippe had sent Schildhauer there; he had found no water sheltered enough for flying boats. Lindbergh and his wife had followed later the same year at the end of their Greenland-Iceland explorations. Lindbergh's report was the same. More recently Trippe had sent a man named States Mead to study the pattern of seas and swells over a period of months. The harbor at Horta on Fayal island was the best spot the Azores offered, Mead reported. It was not, however, a harbor at all but rather a short passage of concave shoreline facing westward toward Pico about five miles away. Towering Pico, which might seem to shelter it to some extent, didn't; instead, heavy seas ran between the two islands. Between October 1 and April 1 sea swells off Horta exceeded three feet on thirty-five days out of each hundred, and two and a half feet on fifty-seven days out of each hundred. From such seas heavily laden flying boats would have great difficulty attaining enough speed to claw into the air. This promised long layovers in Horta waiting for smooth seas, and it might also mean accidents. It certainly meant additional expense, for special ship tenders would be needed. Pan Am engineers now designed them. One was a fifty-five-foot welded-steel tanker fitted with a ramp at the stern to which the bow of an aircraft could be tied. This tanker made it possible, on days when the seas off Horta itself were too rough, to service a flying boat around on the other side of the island. The second vessel was a fifty-foot tender for transporting passengers to shore. It was powerful enough also to execute rescue missions at sea in an emergency, and this seemed important because the Azores were not on regular steamship routes. Both tender and tanker were equipped with marine radio stations, direction finders and ship-to-shore telephones.

Horta itself was a primitive town of about seven thousand people. Around it was mostly barren rock, with some patchy vineyards and citrus groves. There was no hotel, though one could be built. Layovers there would probably be frequent, and passengers were not going to find them particularly exciting.

At Trippe's orders other preparations went forward. The Atlantic Division was formed, a hundred and thirteen men under Colonel J. Carroll Cone, former assistant director of Air Commerce in the U.S. Commerce Department. The operations manager would be Schildhauer, with McVitty as division engineer. Permanent schedules were set up, with each airline—Pan Am and Imperial—making one round trip per week, the crews to lay over during the three days at each end that it would take to turn the planes around. Pan Am forecasters studied North Atlantic weather records over the past forty-seven years, coordinating all surface reports, and then plotting averages by seasons, by months, by individual days. From these calculations upper-air conditions were estimated. Finally, as the bases along the routes were completed, actual upper-air observations were added in from Port Washington, Shediac, Gander, Iceland, Foynes and Southampton, Bermuda, Horta and Lisbon.

By late May 1937 all was ready for survey flights to begin.

30

The First Across

By now about a hundred and thirty-five airplanes had started out to cross the Atlantic. The craze had started in 1919. A three-plane U.S. Navy flotilla was first into the air, leaving Newfoundland on May 16; one of them the NC-4, piloted by A. C. Read, landed in Lisbon on the twenty-seventh after a long layover in the Azores. The other two went down short of the Azores, but their crews were saved. There were four other attempts from Newfoundland that year. Two crashed on takeoff, one crashed into the sea, and the fourth—a Vickers Vimy carrying John Alcock and A. W. Brown—made it to Ireland before crashing there.

Five years then passed while the skies stayed empty over the North Atlantic. In 1924 a single plane started out—and went down at sea. The next try—Fonck in the Sikorsky—came in 1926, and this produced the first two fatalities; in all there would be forty more men killed trying to cross the Atlantic before—with the start of World War II—the madness petered out.

The banner year was 1927, with nineteen flights. Lindbergh, of course, crossed alone all the way to Paris; two weeks later Clarence Chamberlin and Charles Levine flew to Germany, meaning that the entire Atlantic had now been crossed twice. Still takeoff followed takeoff all year. Nearly everybody else, however, crashed or aborted, and the death toll for 1927 alone was sixteen.

In the years that followed, the pace scarcely slowed down. Not all attempts were by small planes belonging to daring—and sometimes foolhardy—individualists. There was now a substantial sampling of "giant" flying boats representing nations.

The German DO-X made it. This twelve-engined monstrosity, built in 1929, held accommodations for sixty-six on a luxurious, shipboard scale, and its flight desk resembled the bridge of a ship, even to the huge round steering wheel. It even looked more like a ship than a plane, and once it had got off the ground with a hundred and sixty-nine people aboard. In May of 1932 it crossed the South Atlantic to Brazil, then flew island by island to New York, where it circled triumphantly over Manhattan. Fueling up, it headed back to Berlin via Newfoundland and the Azores. It barely made the Azores, and soon after reaching Berlin, its development was abandoned.

France's *Lieutenant de Vaisseau Paris* crossed, though only the South Atlantic, and only one way. Built according to plans and funds provided by the French Air Ministry, the six-engined, 37-ton machine made its way up the Caribbean to the United States, where it was scheduled to make an exhibition tour. A tropical storm caught it on the water at Pensacola, however, and wrecked it at its moorings. The tour was canceled; the crippled giant was taken apart, and it returned to France in pieces on a ship.

On July 1, 1933, Italian Air Minister General Balbo led a mass formation of twenty-four Savoia-Marchetti warplanes in formation via Holland, Ireland, Iceland, Labrador and Shediac to Montreal, Chicago and New York. These were twin-hulled aircraft that looked like catamarans with wings. Designed to carry bombs or torpedoes, not people and mail, they were powered by two engines mounted on a kind of scaffold above the middle of the wing, one behind the other, one prop pushing, the other pulling. Balbo had left Italy with twenty-five planes. One was wrecked in Holland, but the others made it across. Coming back, a second plane crashed in the Azores, killing the pilot; the remaining twenty-three made it home. So Balbo alone could be credited with forty-seven crossings of the Atlantic.

As the crossings and attempted crossings continued, the loss of life was appalling. Overall, only about ten planes, apart from Balbo's, got where they were going. Twenty-eight struck the opposite continent somewhere and landed or crash-landed, and it was fashionable, when speaking of all the rest who either were killed or disappeared, to remark that they "hadn't landed yet," or else that "they had not filed a position report in years."

This was the climate in the spring of 1937 as Pan Am and Imperial ventured out into the Atlantic for the first time. According to popular wisdom, the Atlantic was a deadly place, and that was why, the public thought, the decision had been made to fly out only partway at first—as far as Bermuda, which was about 770 air miles offshore.

In fact Bermuda was mandated by the "square deal" agreement, which still held. To Trippe's men over-ocean flying was nothing new, but Imperial had no over-ocean experience at all, nor even a long-range plane, and their vehicle, one of the first Empire-class flying boats off the assembly line, had reached Bermuda by ship.

The Pan American survey plane was another of those S-42's stripped of cabin furniture and crammed with fuel tanks. It was captained by Harold Gray, who was from Guttenberg, Ia., and who had started with Pan Am in 1929 flying trimotors from Brownsville, Tex., down into Mexico and back.

On May 25, 1937, the two planes—Pan Am's in New York, Imperial's in Bermuda—took off simultaneously. The square deal was being defended so fiercely that it had been arranged in advance that both flying boats would be in the air exactly the same length of time, even though the S-42 was much the faster of the two.

Four such survey flights were made, after which, on June 18, commercial service was inaugurated at the rate of one round trip per week per company. Pan Am provided maintenance and service at Port Washington, and Imperial in Bermuda.

At last came the Atlantic itself. On June 25 Gray flew to Shediac and back without landing. Two days after that he flew past Shediac to Gander, stayed overnight, then flew home. On July 3 he took off to go all the way. From Newfoundland he had enough fuel on board for 3,150 miles—enough to fly on past England, past Paris, past Rome, past the heel of the Italian boot and out into the middle of the Mediterranean. He estimated his flight time for his over-ocean leg to Ireland at 12 hours 30 minutes. Flying at an altitude of 10,000 feet, he got there three minutes early, coming down through a 5,000-foot wall of rain and mist to approach the river Shannon. Twenty-two star shots were made during the flight, three by Gray himself. During the night he and his crew never experienced total darkness. A light-gray glow filled the sky from the time the sun dropped behind them until it popped up again about four hours later. This twilight cast a slight haze through the infinity of the height above them, which actually helped the star sights, for it screened out the billions of little stars but not the major navigational fixes.

From Southampton the Caledonia flying boat of Imperial Airways had set out on the same day at the same time, but the headwinds high up were too strong for it, and out of Shannon it settled down close to the sea where it battled winds, rain, fog and pitch-black darkness for fifteen and a half hours, three hours longer than Gray, before landing in Newfoundland to refuel.

That was the start. In all, the British made five round trips across the Atlantic that summer, and Gray only three, one via the Azores and Lisbon.

In New York Van Dusen sent out reams of publicity designed to convince the world that the Atlantic was not dangerous, that three Pan Am flights were enough, that they were routine, and that they had been conducted for two purposes only: to test out upper-air weather by actually flying through it, and to give ground personnel at the various bases experience in handling the airplane. There had been no untoward events at all, Van Dusen insisted.

Indeed, this was true. The southern crossing had provided the only excitement Captain Gray was to experience. Upon reaching Lisbon, he found that the Portuguese had provided him with a mooring buoy big enough for a battleship. On it lay a hawser three inches in diameter, far too big to fit onto the mooring posts of a flying boat, and he had to hold the boat against the Tagus River current while smaller ropes were sent for.

The Atlantic had now been crossed by both companies, and along both routes, and it remained only to inaugurate regular service. Indeed, success looked so certain that Trippe entered at once into negotiations with the French, the Germans, the Spanish, the Danes and the Norwegians, lining up bases for a rapid expansion of service. He even talked to the Egyptians, and a letter to the managing director of Misr Air Work, the only private air-transport company in Egypt, read in part: "We have for some time been giving careful consideration to the extension of our Atlantic service through the Mediterranean to Egypt and have further considered (for your confidential information) future extension to connect our Atlantic and Pacific services in a round the world operation." When this letter was sent, Trippe's planes had not yet even touched France and had no permission to do so. But the pattern he set himself was a familiar one: Keep pushing, pushing, pushing. Always he was ready with the second step before having completed the first.

He began now to badger Woods-Humphery for a firm starting date for regular service: the two companies should start together. When would Woods-Humphery be ready to start?

Unfortunately, the answer was: Not soon. Imperial's five round-trip crossings so far had been achieved at unacceptable cost—the flying boats had been flown stripped, literally, to the bone. When John Leydon, an important Irish aviation official and a member of the Atlantic Company, had asked for passage on the first flying boat, Woods-Humphery had had to refuse him. Leydon wrote that he was aware that there was no cabin accommodation. He was "quite prepared to stand up or sit on the floor." Woods-Humphery had replied tersely that there was no floor. There was no way such Empire flying boats could ever fly the route commercially, and for the moment Woods-Humphery had nothing else. His hopes were pinned on aircraft still being built. Next year he would have a four-engined landplane, the De Havilland Albatross, and the Short-Mayo composite as well.

Trippe was only slightly better off. He, too, was waiting for the next year's planes, the new Boeings. The difference was that Trippe was ready to plunge ahead with hard plans on the strength of a manufacturer's promises, and to use S-42's in the interim. Woods-Humphery, a far more cautious man, was not. Now, to safeguard the prestige of British aviation, he stalled Trippe off.

All that summer the Germans again crossed the ocean to Long Island Sound, capturing headlines. They still carried no payload, but their success tarnished Trippe's image, dimmed his prestige, weakened his relationships in official Washington, and raised questions even among members of his own board of directors.

Trippe had scoffed at the Germans' catapult idea, and especially at the notion that a huge apron towed behind mother ships could calm the open sea sufficiently to permit safe landings by seaplanes. But in the summer of 1937 the Germans began pouring oil on the water too, and they made their system work.

There were two mother ships, the *Schwabenland,* which was a rebuilt freighter, and the *Friesenland,* which was built in Germany from the keel up as a catapult vessel. Each carried fifty-five officers and men, and the Germans stationed one near the Azores and the other on Long Island Sound. Two seaplanes were used. They were huge things, considering the fact that they had to be catapulted. Called the *Nordmeer* and the *Nordwind,* they had been built by Hamburger Flugzeugbau at Hamburg. Their wingspan was 80 feet, their length 64 feet, and they stood 19 feet 6 inches high on enormous twin floats, each of which was about two-thirds the size of the fuselage of the plane. Powered by four engines, these machines, which had a gross weight of 37,478 pounds—heavier than Trippe's S-42's—carried a crew of four, and a payload of only 880 pounds. They were blown down a 110-foot-long ship's catapult track by an explosion of cordite, accelerating from zero to 95 mph in two seconds at 4 1/2 g's. To take them into the air, and then to hold them there, required great skill from pilots. They were so heavily loaded that they had to be flown across the ocean for sixteen hours or more only a few feet above the wave tops, gaining the additional lift they needed from air flattened and compressed between water and wings.

Again Trippe phoned Woods-Humphery asking for a firm starting date. They had best move fast, he said. In addition to the Germans, other domestic American airlines were now after the transatlantic market. So were the shipping companies, especially American Export Line, which had decided to add aircraft to its fleet and had begun negotiations with France, Germany, Spain, Italy—all countries where its ships touched, and where it had friends. There had also been political developments in Washington that were bound to cause trouble for Pan Am.

But still Woods-Humphery stalled.

In Washington Congress had just enacted legislation giving birth to the Maritime Commission. Its chairman was the abrupt, abrasive, brilliant multimillionaire financier Joseph P. Kennedy, and Kennedy had appointed as his aviation consultant Grover Loening, one of the founding members of Trippe's board of directors, now an enemy of Trippe's. Surveys were being made, one of which calculated that there was a market for at least four thousand transatlantic air passengers per year, provided that the means to carry them existed, and suggested that in the future "large flying boats of 100,000 to 250,000 pounds and capable of carrying up to 150 passengers may well supersede highly expensive super-liners of the Queen Mary and Normandie class."

A second survey showed that a steamship used four or five times more horsepower per passenger than a flying boat; it concluded: "In view of the fact that aircraft have a definite place in overseas trade, and in view of the fact that there is a close relationship between shipping and air travel, it is urged that development of this new form of transport be lodged in the Maritime Commission."

Trippe did not like the sound of any of this, and he became extremely busy in Washington, where a second measure known as the "McCarran-Lee Bill for the Regulation of Air Commerce under the Interstate Commerce Commission" was awaiting passage. (The bill later became the 1938 Civil Aeronautics Act.) Recognizing the inevitability of regulation, Trippe wanted to be regulated by this bill, not by shipping interests. After weeks of careful work, he managed to have the following clause inserted into the McCarran-Lee bill: "If any person applying for certificate for foreign air transportation holds a contract, license, permit, concession, or franchise, which was in effect on the date of the passage of this part, permitting such transportation, the commission shall give preference to such holder over any other applicant." It was a grandfather clause. If it stayed in the bill and if the bill passed, and if he could avoid falling into the clutches of the Maritime Commission, then Trippe could keep every route he already had.

In the meantime the dangerous Loening composed a confidential memorandum for the Maritime Commission chairman which was all the more devastating to Trippe and to Pan American because it pretended to be so fair. Pan American was the only American carrier overseas, Loening wrote, because it had learned from the beginning to "ably and consistently present such a complicated and delicate foreign diplomatic situation—that the various departments in Washington were loath to mix in and the State Department in particular quite naturally welcomed the simplicity of having only one company's troubles to deal with. It was constantly represented that competition of any kind would ruin these imaginary delicate relations on attaining foreign flying rights and the able and persuasive Mr. Trippe successfully made it appear that only he could handle such delicate matters. To the foreigners Pan American has represented that they were the only authorized foreign airline in this country." The memo continued:

> Now add to this picture the fact that being the only foreign flying boat airline, Pan American gets all the ballyhoo, and has ably made use of it.
>
> Add further to this picture that the enormous mail and passenger revenue that has grown (although somewhat hidden) from the Miami–Havana–South American services has given Pan American a constant flow of literally millions of ready cash to expend on expansion and that during this period the company most honestly gave practically nothing to stockholders and officers, and never got mixed up in any Wall Street scandals for a Congressional Committee to shoot at. All to its great credit. But also a great talking point for a further monopoly.
>
> Add still further that during this time publicity and Washington relations were so adroitly and expertly handled that the greatest renown accrued to the company and all flaws were soft pedaled—so successfully for example that when in February and March 1936 not a single clipper was in the air on the entire system due to three fatal accidents in the South American Division and all kinds of operating troubles in the Pacific Division—practically no one knew about it. On such matters Mr. Trippe is adept at denying everything. . . .
>
> Pan American has successfully wound up official Washington on its little finger—and has a marvelous press in addition. It is now about to establish the completion of one of the most flagrant monopolies the government has ever had grow up under its nose. Transatlantic air commerce is about to be turned over in toto to this company, and added to the South American and Pacific domains which already make Pan American by far the largest airline in the world.
>
> Mr. Trippe has now signed an agreement with Imperial Airways providing for exclusive landing in England of only Pan American. Similar agreements are about to be concluded with Lufthansa and Air France. At the end of these Pan American with the assistance of the State Department and other departments will become the sole legal airline to carry the air commerce of the United States.

After castigating the "astute" Mr. Trippe's careful and diligent lobbying for passage of the McCarran-Lee Bill, Loening charged that if the McCarran-Lee Bill was enacted, the Maritime Commission's role would be obliterated and emasculated, and Pan American's monopoly throughout the world would henceforth be unassailable. "The only remaining source of assisting some other foreign air carrier to get started is in the Maritime Commission law," he concluded. "The American public doesn't want monopolies. Let it give Trippe and his wonderful airline the highest praise but not prohibit other Americans from having a chance to show what they can do."

Joseph P. Kennedy, chairman of the Maritime Commission, a heavy contributor to the presidential campaigns of Franklin D. Roosevelt and an acknowledged national political power, now summoned young Mr. Trippe to the Kennedy compound in Hyannis Port, Mass., for a talk. He was invited to stay for the weekend.

Trippe at this time kept a single-engined, single-pontoon Aeromarine that he used for commuting between the East River and his weekend home in East Hampton, Long Island. He climbed into this little plane, and he flew it across Long Island Sound and landed it on the water in front of the Kennedy mansion.

At first the meeting was cordial. While waiting for dinner to be served, Trippe was introduced to the four Kennedy sons—Joe Jr. and Jack, who were college boys; Bobby, who was twelve; and Teddy, who was only five. The adults and some of the kids sat in rockers on the porch. But the chairman of the Maritime Commission was not a man to waste time. It was his opinion, he said, that international aviation should be lodged in the Maritime Commission, and he expected that Trippe would testify before Congress to this effect. Did not Mr. Trippe agree with him?

Trippe said no, he did not.

"Why don't you think it over a few minutes," Joseph Kennedy suggested.

Trippe said he had already thought it over for a long time.

"I suggest you walk down to the end of the beach, and think it over," said Kennedy.

Trippe, curbing his temper, replied pleasantly that there was no need to walk down to the end of the beach. He was quite decided on the point.

In that case, said the millionaire to his guest, there was nothing further to discuss and there was no point in Mr. Trippe staying for the weekend. He had best leave at once. The two men stared at each other. Then Trippe went down the beach to the plane. The tide had gone out. The single pontoon was stuck on the beach.

While Rose Kennedy stood nearby, the older boys, Joe Jr. and Jack, helped Trippe turn it around so that it was pointed out toward open water. As Trippe pushed the starter the chairman of the Maritime Commission glared balefully from the veranda, his two smallest sons sitting in rockers beside him. Trippe taxied away and took off.

Joseph P. Kennedy was known to be an implacable enemy. Trippe, flying home, realized this. As Maritime Commission chairman, Kennedy represented the President in this matter. Probably that made the President an enemy too.

From then on, most news was bad. A rumor swept Washington and New York to the effect that Imperial had tied Trippe's hands so as to leave transatlantic passengers in the hands of the Cunard Line's *Queen Mary*. As the New Year, 1938, started, word came from Seattle that the new

Boeings, due before Christmas, had encountered design problems. They were not going to be ready that spring, and it was unlikely they would be ready even by summer. Then Musick went down off Pago Pago. A little later the *Hawaii Clipper* disappeared between Manila and Guam. In Washington there were congressional hearings by the House Committee on Merchant Marine and Fisheries. Congressmen called again for the North Atlantic to be opened up to all comers, and suggested that in signing his exclusive agreement with Woods-Humphery, Trippe was in violation of the Sherman Antitrust Act. Singled out was the clause by which Pan American and Imperial guaranteed each other "a square deal in the sense that this expression is interpreted by fair and reasonable-minded men."

And finally, American Export Lines had organized an airline to compete against Pan American across the Atlantic. Trippe met with American Export officials and offered them stock in Pan American in exchange for dropping their airline plans. They agreed, but the CAB promptly blocked the deal.

For the most part the men around Trippe got on with their jobs. Leuteritz went to Dublin for a four-nation conference at which an ocean-wide meteorological service was set up. The conference adopted Pan American's standard weather observations and reporting procedures, as well as Pan American's standard reporting forms. North Atlantic radio communication systems were coordinated. Again the standard Pan American forms and procedures were adopted, as well as the Pan American system that required a radio check every fifteen minutes and a position report from aircraft every thirty minutes.

Pan American engineers in conjunction with engineers from the Goodrich Tire and Rubber Company designed deicing equipment, and this was tested, installed and found effective. Wing deicers were mounted that extended the full length of the 118-foot wings of S-42's on the Bermuda run. They were in nine sections. Each section was expanded or contracted by means of five alternately inflating rubber tubes to which air was pumped. Similar deicing boots were installed on propellers and tail assemblies. Previously a pilot flying in winter in the northern latitudes could expect his plane to ice up almost every time he flew through a cloud.

And still other Pan Am engineers, together with pilots, shop superintendents, inspectors and flight engineers shuttled back and forth to Seattle to study the Boeings as they were built, and many of these people participated in the technical work done there. Most of all, their visits made possible the forecasting of maintenance needs and the development of highly stressed, very light mobile equipment for servicing the great flying boats—whenever they might be delivered.

31

The Correct Vehicle

The Boeings had been on order since the spring of 1936. Delivery had been promised for Christmas 1937. Now in mid-1938 none had been delivered. With two planes down in the Pacific, Trippe could not cross the Atlantic without the Boeings.

Even as the *China Clipper* had entered service in 1935 letters had gone out to the major manufacturers asking that designs be submitted for "the next step," a new long-range flying boat. The letters were signed by J. Franklin Gledhill, chief purchasing agent, whom Trippe had interposed between himself and the manufacturers. Gledhill was a marvelous haggler, as good as Trippe, perhaps better. Like most of Trippe's principal employees, he was allowed to run his own operation without interference, and was therefore the last word on most purchasing. However, Trippe reserved to himself the right to approve or disapprove the purchase of aircraft, and it was also Trippe who devised strategy.

In this case, Gledhill's letter had asked the manufacturers to submit their bids and their designs entirely on speculation—Pan Am would guarantee absolutely nothing for the months of work that would go into each presentation. Instead Gledhill (Trippe) promised a $50,000 first prize to whichever manufacturer submitted the winning design. There was no second prize. Pan American would be judge and jury in this contest, and perhaps would judge all submissions inadequate and award no prize at all. "I believe in tying the bag of oats out front," Trippe had said then, and also later, for he was a man who often employed pat phrases. In any case, the letter had gone out to the seven top aircraft manufacturers in the country.

In Baltimore this letter angered Glenn L. Martin. After furnishing the *China Clipper* and its two sister ships, he replied, he thought he deserved a better deal. He had manufactured those first three planes at a loss, expecting to make his profit on reorders, but there had been none. He thought he deserved now to be allowed to make a profit. He wanted to be allowed to improve the present design, or else to be granted a new contract on favorable terms. He was in business to make money, not to design new flying boats on speculation.

In Bridgeport, Conn., a similar reply was forthcoming from Sikorsky, though without the petulance. Sikorsky had got his reorders and had built ten S-42's. Now he was part of a conglomerate called United Aircraft, which also controlled Pratt and Whitney engines and Hamilton Standard Propellers; its chairman, Fred Rentschler, sat on the Pan American board of directors. Rentschler, originally a Pratt and Whitney man, and the force behind these mighty engines, backed Sikorsky. Trippe only shrugged. "Sikorsky refused to take his coat off," Trippe reported later. "Rentschler refused to take his coat off. Martin refused to take his coat off."

The one bidder was Boeing, which had recently designed the B-15 bomber for the Army Air Corps. The B-15 was not a success, and a few years later it would be succeeded by and incorporated into the B-17 Flying Fortress of World War II. In the meantime Boeing had a useless new bomber on its hands.

Two things about the B-15 were immediately apparent to Boeing officials. They had designed for it a splendid big new wing, which could be adapted to flying boats, and the 1,000-hp Wright engines that powered it could be adapted to flying-boat use also. The two principal variables in aircraft design: wing shape and power.

So Boeing decided to go into the modern flying-boat business, and delivery of six Boeing B-314's was promised, beginning in only seventeen months, an incredibly short time. With wing and engine work already done, there was hope that Boeing could deliver even sooner, and bonus clauses, like additional bags of oats, were written into the contract to make them hurry. Trippe appeared to have gotten a big new plane from a major manufacturer at maximum speed and minimum cost.

The Boeing agreement made Glenn Martin furious. Martin, then fifty, was an aging bachelor, who, when he needed advice, often sought out his mother. He never built another commercial flying boat, and only one other airliner, and he went to his grave claiming that Gledhill and Trippe had ruined him. Trippe replied then and later in more pat phrases: "We're businessmen. We can't have friends. We can't be in the position of according favors. We have to look at each deal on a cold-blooded business basis. We've made some enemies."

The Boeing-314, like the Martin before it, used sponsons, or sea wings, for lateral stability on the water, and there were no wing-tip pontoons. When it was first tested on Puget Sound—and these aircraft were launched like ships long before they flew—the angle and configuration of the sea wings were wrong, and the wind sent the right wing tip down into the water nearly as far as the outboard engine. Priester was there. He and Boeing officials watched aghast as the plane struggled against the wind to gain an even keel. The wind was blowing hard and the monstrous plane nearly capsized. It was as hair-raising an exhibition as any of the men assembled had ever watched. At last they managed to haul the plane out of the water, and there it forlornly sat while the sea wings and the weight distribution were adjusted. Later, new sea wings were mounted. They had more volume. Being set at a lower angle, they also rested deeper in the water. A long series of water tests ensued while deadlines passed and bonus clauses expired.

When at last the plane could float satisfactorily, it became necessary to test-fly it. Could anything else go wrong?

The B-15 had been a low-wing bomber, but flying-boat operations demanded a high-wing configuration to keep the propellers out of the water. So the B-15 wings had been mounted high on the new flying boat, where they looked fine, and a test pilot took the plane up to try it out. What no one knew was that too much dihedral had been put in the wings —they sloped upwards too much from the spine of the fuselage. This threw the plane's center of gravity so low that it could not be controlled in the air. The test pilot was up there over Seattle, and he could not turn the plane. It seemed willing to go in one direction only, straight ahead. In addition, its nose was corkscrewing through the air in what aviation men called a Dutch roll. The only way the pilot got the flying boat back to base was by manipulating the power of the engines from one side to the other. He managed to land safely. On the ground men stared at each other.

Back to the drawing board.

Months began to pass.

That summer of 1938 the transatlantic airways were crowded with planes, none of them Pan Am's. Most were German, though the French and British were up there too. To readers of headlines it seemed that Europeans once again dominated the North Atlantic, and in New York and Washington important men began to ask what had become of the fast-talking Mr. Trippe.

In England the Short-Mayo composite flew. The bottom half of the composite was an Empire flying boat similar to the Caledonia that, stripped even of its floorboards, had flown the Atlantic the year before.

The top half was a long-range seaplane called Mercury, whose four Napier engines developed 240 hp each. The Mercury's wingspan was 73 feet, its length 51 feet, its gross weight 14,000 pounds, and it supposedly had a range of 2,400 miles when taking off unaided. Launched in midair from the mother ship, it could carry double its original limit, 28,000 pounds gross, and this additional fuel gave it a range of over 6,000 miles. On July 20, all eight engines thundering, the piggy-back composite lifted off the Shannon River. Once aloft, Captain D. C. T. Bennett pushed the disengaging mechanism, and the Mercury under its own power pointed toward Montreal. There was a crew of two aboard—pilot and navigator —plus 1,000 pounds of mail, newsreels and freight, which made this the first revenue-producing commercial flight ever to cross the North Atlantic. The 2,715 miles were flown in 20 hours and 19 minutes. After unloading mailbags in Montreal, Bennett continued on the same day to New York in two hours and nine minutes more. It was a single isolated event —no payload went on to New York, and there was to be no second flight —though no one knew this at the time. All that the headlines reported was that the commercial race had been won—and it had been won by the British.

The mother ship was still in Ireland, and so for its return trip the Mercury took off alone, and Bennett flew it back via Newfoundland, the Azores and Lisbon to Southampton, 4,550 miles in 26 hours and one minute. A regular mail service might have been established by the British then and there, but this did not happen because the Air Ministry civil servants suddenly changed their minds about the Short-Mayo composite. They decided it was already obsolete. Instead of a second transatlantic mail flight, they sent it off for prestige purposes to fly nonstop from Scotland to Cape Town. It didn't quite make Cape Town, landing in Alexander Bay, South Africa, after 6,045 nonstop miles, 46 hours 6 minutes in the air at an average speed of 144 mph. This was the longest flight ever made by a seaplane.

For North Atlantic service the British Air Ministry had decided to rely on two other planes. One was the Cabot, a stretched version of last year's Empire flying boats; but the Cabot failed its tests, and its crossing was canceled. That left the second British hope, a big four-engined landplane made of wood and plastic, called the *Albatross,* but it broke in two in tests while landing in England.

The French crossed. Their route was from Biscarosse—their new seaplane base near Bordeaux—to Lisbon, then to Horta, where their flying boat—the same old *Lieutenant de Vaisseau Paris*—was delayed by heavy seas for six days, taking off for New York finally on August 30 and setting down on Long Island Sound the next day. The *Lieutenant de Vaisseau Paris* was a huge thing, and its six Hispano-Suiza water-cooled engines developed 5,340 hp, giving it a top speed of 162 mph and a cruising speed of 142 mph, but it was then about nine years old. It required a crew of eight, and when it took off on September 6 for the flight home, it was carrying 36,000 pounds of fuel. Its fuel load alone weighed more than a Pan American S-42. Even the French themselves conceded that this plane had no commercial possibilities at all.

Three years before, at the time that the Pacific route was opened, the *China Clipper* had seemed an exotic contraption. It was huge, sleek, and its nose and hull surfaces were corrugated like the heads of certain whales. In fact, a great flying whale was what it most resembled. But this year it was the foreigners who filled the sky with exotic aircraft and Pan American was nowhere to be seen.

Most ambitious of all were the Germans, who that summer made fourteen round-trip transatlantic flights, twenty-eight scheduled crossings in all, the entire operation carried out with a rigid adherence to timetables. Beginning on July 21, a single day after the British mail flight, the Germans crossed the Atlantic once each week until October, carrying mail. Lufthansa operated a Heinkel III, a twin-engined mail plane, from Berlin to Frankfurt to Marseille to Lisbon, where the mailbags were transferred to a Dornier DO-18 twin-engined flying boat for the flight to Horta. There the catapult planes took over, continuing to New York with no commercial payload. At first these were the *Nordmeer* and *Nordwind,* the same as last year, and they shuttled between the Azores and New York, arriving every Monday afternoon, departing every Monday evening, each catapult launching exactly on schedule, the service working like clockwork. Each plane laid over one week in New York with the crew living aboard the mother ship, *Friesenland,* which lay anchored in Long Island Sound. Late in the season a new seaplane, the *Nordstern,* appeared on the route. It had a straighter wing than its two predecessors, though still a gull wing, and a much higher speed, 175 mph to 157 mph, and it crossed from Horta to New York in 13 hours and 40 minutes, the fastest east–west crossing by a seaplane ever. Then it flew back again in 11 hours 53 minutes, another record.

These flights were stunning enough, but in the midst of them came the biggest surprise of all. In Berlin, with no advance publicity to speak of, a four-engined Focke-Wulf landplane took off for New York, where it landed nonstop after 24 hours 56 minutes of flight. The all-metal Focke-Wulf had a maximum cruising speed of 220 mph at 12,000 feet, and supposedly it could carry twenty-six passengers over distances up to 1,000 miles, and nine over distances of 2,500 miles. But it was not these specifications that stunned the aviation world. Rather, it was this much more significant fact: the Germans had moved away from flying boats, away from catapult planes—the Germans had turned to landplanes.

After a three-day layover the Focke-Wulf flew calmly back to Berlin in 19 hours 55 minutes. Trippe must have been glad to see the last of it, for it seemed to the public the correct Atlantic vehicle that everyone had sought for so long. It represented the future, and Trippe had nothing like it. Pan Am still did not even have the Boeings, nor could he be sure when they would be ready. The energetic Van Dusen put out press notices attempting to show that his company's absence on the North Atlantic this summer was normal and deliberate. After sixty million miles of overseas experience, including three million miles in the Pacific, Van Dusen wrote, Pan American had nothing further to learn out on the Atlantic. Fourteen complete ocean crews were trained and ready, and the 83,000-pound Boeings, Van Dusen bragged, would soon cross regularly with 10,000 pounds of commercial load—fifty passengers plus a ton of cargo. Six were on order, four for the Pacific, two for the Atlantic. They were almost ready, he declared, though, of course, they were not.

In Seattle tests continued. The Boeing that would not turn had had a single tail fin and rudder. This was ripped out. Dual fins and rudders were designed, manufactured and then mounted at either end of the horizontal stabilizer, and the plane was test-flown again. Still there was not enough directional stability and control. The center fin and rudder were put back in again. The third test flight—with three fins and rudders—was at last satisfactory. There was no more Dutch roll, and the plane could be steered.

However, the triple rudder and fin arrangement caused new difficulties in the horizontal stabilizer. The Boeing structural department installed strain gauges on it. These recorded 24 g's on landing, which meant still another redesign job to reinforce the stabilizer.

Now the plane floated and flew properly, but still it would not land properly. Each time it came down onto the water it bounded, skipped, porpoised. The Boeing test pilots, having grown up, so to speak, with the machine, devised methods to minimize this—they learned to chop the throttles just a second before touching the water.

After all this, a year late in delivery, the first Boeing was flown to San Francisco, where it was taken out for test flights over San Francisco Bay. William Cluthe, an experienced Pan Am flying-boat captain, was at the controls. Cluthe kept bouncing the flying boat off the water. He was embarrassed because he thought it was his fault. But no matter how he tried he couldn't make the hull stick without bouncing. Aboard were Leslie, now Pacific operations manager, and Wellwood Beall, the Boeing project engineer. Leslie took Beall back into the stern of the aircraft to tell him in a quiet voice that this "porpoising" simply wouldn't do. The airplane was unacceptable.

The pressures on Trippe were intense, and getting worse. During his frequent telephone conversations with Woods-Humphery he was now trying to alter certain clauses of the "exclusive" agreement the two men had signed, or else to abrogate the agreement entirely. In the American press, in the corridors and cloakrooms of Washington, charges of anti-trust violation had become ever more frequent. "Another SOS from Trippe," noted Woods-Humphery after one conversation, and he informed the Air Ministry that he could not leave Trippe open to prosecution. Something would have to be done to help: "I have not found Pan American guilty of a breach of faith so far, and I have been working with them for ten years."

At the Air Ministry these arguments had great weight. There could be a scandal in America, and possibly prosecution, and Imperial Airways would be dragged in. At length, the Air Ministry agreed to amend part of the agreement. Clauses relating to exclusivity, to square deals, would be eliminated. The result was that Pan Am, which still held its permits to set down in British bases along the route, was no longer bound—on paper—to wait until Imperial was ready before it began flights. It could start now on its own.

Trippe's exclusive agreement with Portugal remained a problem, however. On February 9, 1939, Trippe sent a letter to the new Civil Aeronautics Authority in which he agreed in the interests of American aviation to waive his exclusive rights, if so advised by the CAA. Although there was no immediate reply to this letter, its existence was publicized, and the antitrust mutterings died down for a while.

In England Woods-Humphery was forced to resign.

Priester flew out to San Francisco. Beall and Earl Ferguson, a Boeing test pilot, flew down from Seattle to give Pan Am pilots a cram course in how to land the Boeing. All learned to do it, more or less. Crews began to be checked out in it. There were no complaints. Leslie, Priester and the other engineers decided that perhaps their fears had been exaggerated. Since the pilots were not complaining, presumably they had learned to cope with the plane's poor landing characteristics.

But this was not the case. Instead, being jealous of their skill and being fearful that complaints about this flying boat might suggest their own inability to handle it, the pilots were simply keeping their mouths shut. It became just a matter of time before there would be an accident. The only question was: How serious would it be when it happened?

On March 3, 1939, having been flown nonstop to Washington, the first of the Boeings was christened the *Yankee Clipper* by Mrs. Franklin D. Roosevelt at Anacostia Naval Air Station. The President's wife was handed a gold-trimmed bottle containing not champagne but water gathered by Pan American from the Seven Seas—or so Van Dusen's publicity claimed—and this she cracked against the blunt nose of the largest airplane in the world. Water splashed over her face, white gloves, dark suit and hat, but she turned immediately to stand at attention for the national anthem. Also present on the official barge were Trippe, Postmaster General Farley, Air Corps General "Hap" Arnold, Rear Admiral George Pettengill, Chairman Edward J. Noble of the CAA, and Senator Josiah Bailey, who was chairman of the Senate Commerce Committee. The ceremony was broadcast live by NBC and CBS, and the nationwide audience heard Trippe describe the part his company had played in carrying on in world trade the tradition established by the hard-driving Yankee skippers in the days of the tall-masted sailing clippers. "Today America is ideally fitted by heritage, by ability and by the will of her people," Trippe said, "to maintain this leadership in world commerce, which the *Yankee Clipper* and her flying sister ships will soon set out to do. This same *Yankee Clipper* is to carry the American flag across aviation's last frontier —the Atlantic Ocean—to link the old world with the new."

Farley in his turn said, "To Pan American Airways—who had the courage, the vision and the determination to succeed where few would have had the enterprise to try—great credit is due."

Such praise came too late to save Trippe, who was about to be deposed by his own board of directors.

32

The Whitney
Takeover

Trippe was thirty-nine years old. For twelve years he had controlled absolutely the destiny of his company, which had grown to be a huge one. As of January 1, 1939, it served 54,072 route miles in 47 countries with 126 airliners and 145 ground radio stations. It had over 5,000 employees. Pan Am and its subsidiaries constituted by far the largest airline operation in the world.

As president and general manager, Trippe was and had always been subordinate to his board of directors. But this caused him no trouble, for he had handpicked these men himself, usually to fill some specific need. At the beginning most had been boyhood friends who brought in money, stayed awhile, then departed—men like Bill Rockefeller and Bill Vanderbilt or like John Hambleton, who was killed in the crash of a private plane. Such friends had never interfered with Trippe's running of the company. Later on, board members had been chosen because they represented shipping lines, railroad interests, aircraft factories or banks. Trippe was interested in presenting Pan Am to the world as a "community company" —the entire U.S. transportation industry should seem to be behind it. Three years before, at the time of his expansion into the Pacific, he had taken Donald Douglas, builder of the Douglas airliners, and Wallace Alexander, chairman of the Matson shipping line, on the board, and this to Trippe was ideal. Both were big transportation men, and in adding them he not only enhanced the prestige of his board but also neutralized two potential competing airlines. Now in 1939 Douglas had already resigned; Alexander, though still a director, seldom attended meetings.

To smother opposition was often one of Trippe's goals when inviting men to join his board, but prestige came first. Trippe's board members were busy men, rich men. They had weight. It was a board that tended to overawe not only potential competitors but also government agencies, including the Post Office and even Congress itself. It did not overawe Trippe, who used individual members as he needed them—when he needed a contact, for instance, or when he needed someone leaned on. On his instructions, minutes of meetings—especially directors' meetings —were kept brief and vague. There even were conferences at which Trippe sat with a wastebasket under his desk, and as he finished with each topic the papers relating to it went into the basket, so that at the end even the meeting itself left no record. It was as if it had never happened. All this had the effect of consolidating power not so much in Trippe's hands as in his head.

There had been rumblings against Trippe as early as 1928, when Richard Hoyt had been chairman of the board. Hoyt was said to have accused Trippe of excessive secrecy. The board had a right to know what Trippe was doing, Hoyt said. Hoyt at that time had been a power both at the Hayden, Stone investment house, and at Curtiss-Wright, and he was on the board not as a friend but as a result of Trippe's absorption of Hoyt's Atlantic, Gulf and Caribbean Airways, Inc. Hoyt had remained chairman until 1931 and a director until 1935, and he had possibly caused Trippe more trouble than any other director until now. Many times Hoyt had sought to control Trippe's expansionist plans. But on each occasion Trippe had had the votes to control Hoyt.

In the years since, Trippe's secretiveness had not diminished. He was obliged by company bylaws to seek board approval before carrying out certain decisions. Often he had done so. Sometimes he had convened his board only to have it approve action already taken. Disagreements had arisen. Always Trippe's persuasiveness—and his votes—had carried him through.

But at present the company was in poor financial shape—losing heavily in the Pacific, investing heavily in the Atlantic with no return as yet. Big loans had been needed. As a result, the board had become rather heavy with bankers.

On March 14, 1939, twelve days before the first transatlantic flight was to take place, a special meeting of the directors convened in the boardroom on the fifty-eighth floor of the Chrysler Building. Trippe walked in knowing there were problems, and probably knowing also that this time he could not talk his way past them. When the boardroom door opened again, the company's new chief executive was seen to be Cornelius Vanderbilt Whitney, who until now had shown himself entirely subservient to Trippe. He had seemed the last person in the world to threaten his power.

Whitney as chief executive? It was inconceivable, but it was true.

It was impossible to look at Sonny Whitney, who was then forty years old, without thinking of money. He stood as the living confluence of three of the mightiest fortunes in America—heir to the Payne money, the Whitney money and also the Vanderbilt money. His mother was Gertrude Vanderbilt, daughter of Cornelius Vanderbilt, granddaughter of the railroad baron known as Commodore Vanderbilt. On his father's side the wealth went back just as far and there was just as much of it. One great-grandfather, Henry B. Payne, had begun founding railroads as early as 1849. One of Henry's sons, Oliver Hazard Payne, had entered the new field of oil refining and later had consolidated with John D. Rockefeller; Hazard Payne also dominated both the American Tobacco Company and Tennessee Coal and Iron. He became wealthier than his father, so wealthy that he was accused of buying his father's way into the United States Senate, charges that were brought but never proved. A bachelor, he divided his wealth into portions of $12 million each and in his will left these portions to the children of his sisters, one of whom, Flora Payne, was married to the already ultrarich William Collins Whitney. William Collins Whitney controlled New York City utilities and was a power in Democratic politics. As Secretary of the Navy under Grover Cleveland, he went to Washington and there threw the most fabulous parties and balls the capital had yet seen. At his death he owned ten homes, which he kept fully staffed. He was the father of Harry Payne Whitney and the grandfather of Sonny Whitney.

Harry Payne Whitney, by investing heavily in silver, lead and copper mines in the western United States and Mexico, and by marrying Gertrude Vanderbilt, increased the family fortune. He was also a yachtsman and one of the few ten-goal polo players in the history of the sport; he hunted tigers in India and raced horses. One year his stable numbered more than two hundred thoroughbreds, which ran first in 272 races, second in 201 and third in 235.

This was the heritage of Sonny Whitney, who was born in New York City on February 20, 1899, making him just a few months older than Juan Terry Trippe. Sonny Whitney's boyhood home was a thousand-acre estate near Old Westbury, Long Island, a big red brick house on top of a hill that overlooked rolling green pastures to the south and forest land to the north. A 200-foot windmill tower supplied fresh water. The estate contained a stableful of horses, a good-size kennel, tennis courts, a swimming pool, of course, an indoor gymnasium with a bowling alley and a squash court. Sonny Whitney played with chums who lived on adjacent estates.

His summers were spent in a mansion in Newport, R.I., or else in the eighty-five-acre Whitney park in the Adirondacks. The Whitney New York town house was a brownstone mansion at 68th Street and Fifth

Avenue, one of the ten homes once owned by William C. Whitney. Sonny went to Miss Bowes School, then to Groton, where he went out for football, baseball and crew, took piano lessons, played the drums in the school band and rang the bells for the chapel tower. He was on the debating team also, and from then on, always enjoyed making speeches. Later, on behalf of Pan American, Juan Trippe used to let him give a great many. After Groton, Sonny went on to Yale, where all the male Paynes and Whitneys had been educated for several generations.

Here World War I intervened. His mother, Gertrude Vanderbilt Whitney, organized a volunteer nursing group and took it to France. Whitney's best pal, Tommy Hitchcock, joined the Lafayette Escadrille and went to France as a fighter pilot. Having conceived the idea that he wished to do likewise, the eighteen-year-old Sonny first enlisted in a summer training camp for boys, then went to Washington alone to enlist in the Signal Corps. He took flight training in Texas and after nine months was commissioned a second lieutenant. He stayed on there as an instructor, and never got overseas.

Back at Yale he majored in anthropology but was not much of a student. Being a tall, sturdy youth, he made the varsity crew. He liked girls and was seen with all sorts—society girls, chorus girls. During these years he knew Trippe slightly. Trippe was trying to make money with the *Yale Graphic.* Sonny was writing compositions for the Yale literary magazine. Trippe organized the Yale Flying Club and flew in intercollegiate races. Sonny did not join the club. He seemed to have lost interest in flying.

After graduation Trippe bought war-surplus planes, and organized Long Island Airways, while Sonny went to Europe on vacation on $2,000 handed him by his father. First he stayed with his chum Fred Prince in Dinard, France. Mornings they exercised ponies. Afternoons they played polo. Evenings they gambled in the casino. Heading on to Paris, Sonny explored the cabarets, dance halls, bistros and honky-tonks.

He went on to Budapest, where his uncle, Count Lazlo Sczechenyi, lived. This man was married to another Vanderbilt, his mother's sister. Sonny got off the Orient Express and was met by a yellow Rolls-Royce and taken to the family hunting lodge in a remote forest for some stag hunting. Back in Budapest, Uncle Lazlo gave gala parties for the elite of Hungary.

After his European holiday Sonny went to work in a Nevada silver mine owned by his father, beginning underground as a mucker, working his way up into the office from which he was sent to Sonora, Mexico, to an irrigation project backed by his father. There he met General Alvaro Obregón, governor of Sonora, who later became president of Mexico. This would prove to be a more important moment and meeting than Sonny realized at the time.

A year later he was installed in New York in a small Wall Street office, for his father thought it time he learned banking and high finance. Sonny was now twenty-six. One day he was called to his father's office. He went expecting a dressing-down, which was what he usually got from his father. Instead, Harry Payne Whitney declared that he was resigning from the boards of the Guaranty Trust Company, the Metropolitan Opera, the Museum of Natural History and the Metals Exploration Company. Sonny was to replace him on all these boards. His secretary would explain the details, said Harry Payne Whitney, dismissing his son. From the secretary's office Sonny overheard his father discussing the Sonora irrigation project. Harry Payne Whitney had put half a million into it but it had proved worthless, and now he ordered his certificates of ownership sold at once. Sonny, who had $7,000 in his bank account, rushed out, and unbeknown to his father, bought them over the counter for $3,150. Still saying nothing to his father, he caught a train to Arizona and crossed into Mexico, for he had conceived the notion of selling these "worthless" certificates to General Obregón. Bursting with pride, he did sell them— for $500,000, about what his father had paid for them in the first place. Harry Payne Whitney either set up this deal behind the scenes, or else died without knowing about it. In any case, his son never told him.

Sonny now had a small fortune in his own name. The money was there and had to be invested, and just then Trippe, who had already formed Eastern Air Transport, came to him with a scheme for consolidating with a group of New England investors and bidding for the New York–Boston airmail contract as Colonial Air Transport. Sonny handed Trippe $25,000.

In May 1927 Harry Payne Whitney's horse Whiskery was favored to win the Kentucky Derby. Harry Payne was present in Kentucky living in his private pullman car. Too nervous to watch the race, he asked his son to represent him, to accept the trophy and to make the victory speech. To seal this bargain, his father handed Sonny, who was then twenty-eight years old, $100 for lunch. Sonny went to the track, where he sat down with Ring Lardner and others. Although it was prohibition, scotch whiskey flowed, with the result that the befuddled Sonny missed the race entirely. Whiskery won. Sonny tried to find his way to the winner's circle but couldn't even find the track. No victory speech was made. The chauffeur got him back to the pullman car. By then he was sober enough to expect a showdown with his father, but Harry Payne, playing poker with pals, scarcely looked up from the game.

In New York at this time Trippe was trying to organize the Aviation Corporation of America. He was trying to raise $300,000. As soon as Sonny got back from the Derby, Trippe went to him. Bill Vanderbilt, Bill Rockefeller, John Hambleton and Trippe himself were putting up $25,000 each, Trippe said. Sonny put up nearly twice that much, $49,000, and became chairman of the board. Vanderbilt was named president, Hambleton vice president, and Rockefeller treasurer. Trippe was satisfied to be managing director because he also had authorization from the board to invest the company's capital in virtually any way he wished.

In later years Whitney was fond of calling himself the founder of Pan American Airways, sometimes adding that being a busy man, he had "put Juan Trippe in to run the company on a day-to-day basis."

Sonny acquired a wide reputation as a playboy. A dancer served him three times with the same paternity suit; he was at length exonerated, but only after having titillated millions of tabloid readers. He got married, divorced, remarried. He joined the Crusaders, a young man's group opposed to prohibition. Harry Payne Whitney, worried in advance about the family fortune, wrote out a will leaving most of Sonny's share in trust until the young man was thirty-five. During these years the straitlaced Juan and Betty Trippe did not see much of Sonny, which was fine with them, for they disapproved of him. Sonny was perhaps not even aware of this, merely considering Trippe a business friend rather than a social one: "We didn't live in the same community," he said once.

In October 1930 Harry Payne Whitney died suddenly, at age fifty-eight. It was years before the courts let go of most of the money. Sonny took over the racing stable, ran for Congress as a Democrat from the First Congressional District of Long Island (he was defeated) and bought paintings, including Renoir's famous *Femme au chapeau blanc.* Together with his cousin Jock Whitney, he financed on a fifty-fifty basis Selznick International Pictures. Producer David O. Selznick made *Little Lord Fauntleroy, A Star Is Born,* and *Nothing Sacred*—all successful films, except that no money was left over to pay off the Whitneys, who were now several million dollars down. Selznick came forward with *Gone With the Wind,* a best-selling book. Without bothering to read it, Sonny and Jock agreed to finance the film, a $4 million blockbuster. Sonny got divorced again and remarried again. He formed a polo team and wrested the national championship from Jock's team, the best in the country.

Sonny had been chairman of the board of Pan American since the frustrated Hoyt stepped down in 1931. During this time he had backed every one of Trippe's dreams. Sometimes he was the only support Trippe had. At one board meeting around 1934 Trippe requested some $3 million for expansion. The other board members shook their heads. Hoyt, who had remained as a director, was especially vociferous. He began to make a speech. Whitney, who was seated beside Trippe, had been out late the night before and had a terrible hangover. He sat with his face in his hands, listening to the dark muttering around the table. When Hoyt's speech ended, Sonny's head rose. "I'll take a million of that," he said.

Hoyt threw up his hands, the rest of the board caved in, and Trippe got his money. One Pan Am executive, commenting later, said, "Sonny had the money. He was willing to put up the money, and no one else was, and you couldn't argue with that."

Otherwise Sonny's contributions to the company were infrequent. He liked to go on inaugural flights. He liked to make speeches. Sometimes he liked to stand behind Trippe when important documents were signed.

But the company was his to take over if he wished. He held stock worth around $3 million—154,432 shares, more than 10 percent of all stock outstanding. His cousin Jock, also a board member, held an additional 56,400 shares.

At the beginning Trippe himself had been the biggest stockholder— he had owned as much as 25 percent of the company at one time, and had been granted additional stock since. But he had always sold most of it off for profit. He could not pay himself a high salary. Aviation was a regulated industry, almost a utility, and it was essential to give to the Congress and to the regulatory agencies the appearance of tightfisted financial policies. As a result, all Pan Am executive salaries were ridiculously low, Trippe's included. He paid himself only $17,500 a year. If he was a rich man, it was because he had regularly sold off most of his stock —a policy, unfortunately, that left him now owning only 18,000 shares.

The bankers—there were five of them on the board at the moment— had grown dissatisfied with Trippe's stewardship. Dividends had been due two months before, but the company had been unable to declare any, and it was now operating on deadline. Flights via Canton Island to Australia and New Zealand were about to start, making additional bank loans mandatory. However, because of the weakness of the company's financial position and the uncertainty of its future, it seemed doubtful that such loans would be accorded.

All these elements now came together: Whitney's ambition—or, as Trippe later suggested, his wife's; the board's dissatisfaction with Trippe; the board's need, whether real or imagined, to exert fiscal control over the company.

The special meeting was convened by Sonny Whitney, chairman. Out of fifteen directors only eight men, a bare quorum, filed into the boardroom. Trippe could have ended the meeting simply by walking out, but this was not his style and he did not do so. Present, in addition to the two Whitneys and Trippe, were Sloan Colt, Robert Lehman and E. O. McDonnell, who were bankers, plus Lyman Delano, who was a railroad man, and Sherman Fairchild, who manufactured both planes and aerial cameras. Since proxies were not permitted under New York State law, Whitney needed only five votes—three others besides himself and Jock —in order to assume control of the company, and he got them. Trippe was deposed. Chairman of the board Whitney became chief executive officer also. Next it was decided that the board's executive committee would be strengthened and would assume most of the functions of the board. As for Trippe, he was asked to remain as president, but henceforth he was to report to Whitney. The meeting ended. The men filed out. The minutes were written. They were as vague as always. No record was made of who voted for Trippe and who against.

The mechanics of the Whitney takeover were mysterious at the time, and remained so. Van Dusen, by his own account, discouraged press speculation. Contemporaneous press articles spoke of the "feud" between Whitney and Trippe, and were otherwise vague. Whitney later said, "They played up that Juan and I had disagreements. We did. We just put it to our board of directors, and they made the decision." Trippe refused to speak of the subject at all for years. When pressed by the author he said, "I handed it to him. He wanted it, and I handed it to him. When he tried to tell me what time to come in in the morning and what time to go home at night, that was the end of it. I took him in front of the board of directors and I said, 'Gentlemen, I think we have a resignation here.'" Later Trippe contended that Sloan Colt, a board member, had made the actual arrangements. Colt had advised Trippe that Whitney had various personal difficulties, and it would help him a lot if he could please be chief executive for a while. Trippe, according to Trippe, then allowed Whitney to become chief executive, and to take over the big office. According to Trippe, there was never any bad blood between the two of them, or between Trippe and the board, Trippe himself had felt no humiliation, Whitney had rarely come to the office or attempted to exercise the power, and Trippe himself had remained in active charge throughout. Trippe did admit that company morale during this period had been terrible, and he also said that Whitney had apologized to him later.

What is certain is that, once Whitney—or perhaps Colt—informed Trippe that Whitney was taking over, there was absolutely nothing Trippe could do about it. He had three possible courses of conduct. He could get involved in a proxy fight with Whitney, which he might lose, and which certainly would damage the company; he could resign from Pan Am altogether; or he could swallow his demotion and whatever emotion he felt, knowing that Whitney could not last, that the board would soon wish to give him his old job back. Since there was never any public outburst by Trippe of any kind, clearly he accepted the third of his options. Most likely Colt and/or other directors softened the blow by assuring Trippe that Whitney was taking over his job only temporarily.

Trippe's luxurious office occupied the corner of the fifty-eighth floor of the Chrysler Building. Into this office Whitney now moved. Trippe was assigned a smaller office at the opposite end of the building. His famous three-foot globe—he had been photographed beside it for dozens of newspapers and magazine articles—was then wheeled out of Whitney's office down the hall to Trippe's. Many of the other executives stood in their doorways watching—and musing perhaps on the vagaries of power —until the globe rolled by and disappeared into the small new office and the door closed behind it.

A man named Thomas Morgan, former chairman of the Curtiss-Wright Corporation, president and director of the Sperry Corporation, now was brought on the board. Morgan was a big man in aviation with experience in nearly all phases of the business: engineering, manufacturing, airline operation, corporate management and finance, and he was diplomat enough to have served three consecutive terms as president of the Aeronautical Chamber of Commerce. In addition, he had dealt previously with Trippe—it was he who had negotiated Curtiss-Wright's sale of China Airways to Trippe back in 1933.

Public relations chief Van Dusen was called in by Whitney and told to report to him from then on. Shortly afterwards Van Dusen was told by Morgan, in a vague way, what the trouble on the board was about— lack of candor and full disclosure by Trippe. Morgan also said that Whitney had insisted on handling public relations personally, and that Van Dusen should help him all he could.

Van Dusen's first job was to write a rather glowing press release about the new chief executive, and after that a similar glowing front-page article for the company magazine. It made Whitney sound twice the man Trippe had ever been. It also, inevitably, made Van Dusen sound like Whitney's man—and he would pay for this later.

The fifty-eighth floor of the Chrysler Building became an unhappy place to be. The other executives were forced, despite themselves, to take sides. There sat Whitney in the grand office on the southeast corner, with subordinates walking in and out. He told the press that he was disbanding his polo team—he was too busy. Conversely, he resumed active participation in horse racing after having retired his racing colors the year before.

Trippe, meanwhile, remained consigned to the small office formerly occupied by the corporate secretary and legal counsel, and from there he noted carefully who visited his former office and how often.

From the grand office, Whitney began to issue a series of directives. Among them was an executive memorandum ordering the operations committee—Whitney, Trippe, Rihl, Priester, Leuteritz, Chenea and Van Dusen—to meet in the boardroom each Monday and Friday at 10:30 A.M. At these meetings Whitney took to interrogating his executives, for he wanted to know what they were doing.

At each meeting Trippe sat stony-faced at the other end of the table, and for week after week he spoke not a single word. His silence had the effect of intimidating his former subordinates, who scarcely dared answer Whitney's questions.

Leuteritz had been in Colombia, and had missed the first meetings.

When he got home he received a phone call from vice president George Rihl, who wanted urgently to speak to him before the next one began. But Leuteritz's train broke down, and by the time he got to the office the meeting was under way.

Whitney asked Leuteritz to report on the situation in Colombia. Leuteritz was proud of what he had accomplished there these last few weeks, and began to regale his audience with all the succulent details. At the same time the radioman was aware of the rather heavy tension that had come upon the room.

When the meeting ended, Rihl pulled Leuteritz to one side. "I wanted to warn you," he said anxiously. "Why did you have to give Whitney all the details? Didn't you see Trippe's face?"

The months began to pass. Everyone felt the strain. No one knew what to do about it.

33

The Boeing Accident

On March 26, twelve days after the Whitney takeover, the *Yankee Clipper* had taken off under the command of Harold Gray for its inspection flight to Europe and return. Aboard was a crew of eleven, plus nine passengers, six of whom were technical observers representing the federal government. The other three men represented Boeing, Wright Aeronautical and Pan American. The giant flying boat proceeded via Horta, Lisbon, Biscarosse and Marseille, and then on to Southampton, where it laid over a week before starting home again via Foynes, Lisbon, Horta and Bermuda. The journey was totally without incident, except that the flying boat porpoised most times on landing.

After that, weeks began to pass while final preparations were made for the start of regular service, and while the company waited for the Civil Aeronautics Authority to hand down what was known as a "certificate of public convenience and necessity"—formal permission to carry passengers, property and mail between the United States and Europe.

However sullen he may have appeared in the corridors of the Chrysler Building, Trippe during this period was careful to keep intact via telephone his cordial relations with the British. Woods-Humphery was staying on in his job until the new power structure there settled down, and on May 5 Trippe telephoned him to report that "Washington" was pressing for the start of regular service to England as soon as possible. A few days later Trippe phoned again. The new company, American Export Airlines, was expected to start transatlantic survey flights soon, he said, and therefore he was obliged to press ahead with his own plans to cross

—much as he himself wanted to wait until Imperial was ready. The ideal situation would be for Pan Am and Imperial to begin jointly, exactly as they had started Bermuda service. But if Imperial still had no long-range planes, then Pan American, unfortunately, could wait no longer—Pan Am would have to start. With these phone conversations, Trippe let his British friends down as easily and as gradually as he could. He also maintained the illusion that in New York he was still in charge. In summaries as kept by Woods-Humphery, there is no indication that the British were even aware of Trippe's fall from grace.

But in the corridors of the Chrysler Building men could talk of little else. Lindbergh, who had returned now from his exile in England, had lunch with Trippe at the Cloud Club, and afterwards spent hours in the building, meeting old acquaintances, talking over company affairs—and trying to figure out exactly what had happened to Trippe. "I do not yet fully understand all of the details and will not attempt to set down the rumors on these pages," he wrote in his journal. "In many ways I am sorry to see this, for I like Juan and have always felt he had great ability." Lindbergh took no sides then or ever, and when next in the building he went to see Whitney. Sitting in the grand office, the two men were discussing the company's internal troubles when in walked Trippe. As Trippe sat down the subject abruptly changed to aircraft needs on the transatlantic route. Pan Am executives who knew Lindbergh well considered him an extremely cool individual, and now he merely observed the Trippe-Whitney relationship—he was not emotionally involved in what might happen to either of them.

May 20, 1939, was the twelfth anniversary of Lindbergh's solo flight to Paris, and to celebrate this date the New York World's Fair, which was then in progress, planned an elaborate Aviation Day program, part of which would be the departure of the *Yankee Clipper* on its first scheduled commercial transatlantic flight—to Lisbon and Marseille, not to England. At 1:08 P.M. the flying boat, loaded with 1,804 pounds of mail, cast off from its moorings and took to the air, flying out over the World's Fair grounds, circling in plain view above the thousands milling about below, while Captain Arthur E. LaPorte spoke by two-way radio telephone with government officials and aviation celebrities on the ground—the conversation was relayed to the listening crowds through loudspeakers hanging from trees. A laudatory telegram from President Roosevelt was read, after which LaPorte turned the Clipper's bow toward the Atlantic Ocean and the continent beyond. He stopped for six hours for fuel in the Azores, reached Lisbon, and the next day flew on to Marseille. On May 27 the Clipper, carrying 2,025 pounds of mail, landed back in Port Washington, and the first regularly scheduled commercial round-trip flight over the Atlantic was completed.

Regular passenger service, New York to Marseille, was announced for

June 28. A timetable was printed, and fares established: $375 one way, $675 round trip, and the first ticket was sold to W. J. Eck, who was from Washington, and who had applied for ticket No. 1 ten years before.

As the 3:00 P.M. takeoff neared on inaugural day a brass band played, and the quay was crowded with friends and well-wishers, with reporters and photographers, with messengers delivering flowers and telegrams to the travelers. Eck was there flashing his ticket, bragging that he had been offered $5,000 for it. Tickets and passports were examined. The baggage allowance was fifteen pounds per person. Baggage was weighed and checked.

When "All aboard" was called out, the twenty-two passengers walked down the long dock to the float to which the great flying boat was moored. Floating on Long Island Sound, it looked enormous, and to the taste of the day it looked incredibly sleek as well, though by any later standard it was not sleek at all. It had a bloated body and bloated wings. Its wings were so thick that they could and did contain companionways by which all four engines could be reached and serviced in flight. The idea of mid-ocean emergency servicing of engines had been Priester's, representing still another safety precaution that the cautious Dutchman had forced on the manufacturer.

The Boeing was the largest airplane then flying. Its propellers cut an arc 14 feet 10 inches in diameter. It had a maximum range of around 4,275 miles at 150 mph, and it could seat up to 74 passengers, or sleep 40 in berths. It had two decks, both carpeted, the upper deck being reserved exclusively for the crew. The lower deck contained five passenger compartments, plus a dining room seating fifteen people, plus a kind of honeymoon suite self-contained in the rear. There were separate dressing rooms for men and for women, each with its own toilet, and the gentlemen's toilet contained—for the first and last time in commercial aviation—twin urinals. From the faucets ran hot and cold water, though only in a trickle to conserve the small supply.

The Boeing was the first real transoceanic airliner, the first to combine adequate range and speed with a payload sufficient to make its operation economically viable. Apart from poor manners when landing, it was an excellent plane in every respect. Even when carrying its full load of 5,400 gallons of fuel, it could, under normal conditions, take off after a run across quiet water of around thirty seconds, or a bit more than half a mile.

Today normal procedure was being followed. The plane was held immediately above the water until an airspeed of 120 mph was attained. This signaled that full maneuverability on three engines was assured, and the engines, which had turned at the maximum 1,550 hp each at takeoff, were pulled back to 1,200 hp. Once the plane achieved an altitude of around 750 feet, the engines were again throttled back, and the plane now climbed at a speed of 126 mph using only 900 hp, or slightly more than half of what was available at full throttle.

As soon as the flying boat was out over the Atlantic the steward passed through handing out a passenger list, just as was done in those days on ocean liners, and everyone looked avidly to see who else was on board. Several passengers were members of the Pan Am board of directors. Sonny Whitney and his current wife were listed, and so was Betty Trippe, but not Trippe himself. Four days earlier he had gone across to England on the first mail flight along the northern route, because it coincided with Imperial's reciprocal first flight in the other direction. Let Chairman Whitney have the ceremonial ride. Trippe would take the business route, and would get his meetings done in London and Paris before Whitney got there.

With the Boeing in the air, Betty Trippe noted, the passengers moved about the spacious compartments, making acquaintance with one another and with the Boeing itself. The afternoon passed pleasantly. Many of the passengers played bridge. Others chatted or read. Officially there was no liquor on board—Priester was still death on liquor—but as dinnertime neared one of the passengers produced a bottle and began mixing cocktails. Betty Trippe, sipping hers, wondered if Pan Am would ever have to change its liquor policy in order to meet the competition of other airlines—in South America and Europe liquor was already being served aboard planes.

At last the steward announced dinner. The table was set with a white tablecloth, and the passengers found dinner as delicious and as beautifully served as in a restaurant. Afterwards Captain Sullivan, the same Rod Sullivan who had flown the first S-42 to Wake Island, came down from the flight deck to smoke a cigarette and chat with passengers.

The stewards began to make up berths, and the passengers went to bed. Betty Trippe found hers both larger and more comfortable than those on trains. She turned out the little light over her head, but was so excited she could not sleep. Her mind was filled with observations she must remember to tell Juan. She was a bit cold—they should carry more blankets on board, and the plane's heating should be more uniform. Was ice really so heavy that ice water couldn't be served at meals? Shouldn't the berths be made up before leaving to make it easier for the stewards? Because at eight thousand feet, the making up of a berth was strenuous work, and the stewards felt it. The air was somewhat rough. She looked out at a sky brilliant with stars—stars that seemed brighter and bigger than any she had ever seen before, as if the plane hung suspended in the sky among them while the clouds floated slowly by underneath.

Then it was morning and they were landing at Horta. Fifteen and a half hours had passed since takeoff. Open cars waited onshore, and they were driven about the island while the Boeing was refueled. There was a profusion of flowers; hydrangeas grew in hedges for miles on either side of the road between the fields. Windmills dotted the countryside, white sails turning slowly in the cool sea breeze.

Back on the quay, everyone was offered a Horta-made straw hat and a drink of port, and bunches of hydrangeas were presented to all the ladies. The refueling stop had lasted ninety minutes. The plane took off over bumpy water against a strong ground swell.

Seven hours later they were landing on the Tagus River at Lisbon. The passengers filed off the plane up the pier and into the customs and passenger building, which was an old chapel adjoining a mill at the edge of the river. From there they were driven through the streets to their hotel. The houses were pink and white and blue, and women moved along carrying baskets of vegetables on their heads. Donkeys carried milk from door to door, and oxcarts were being driven through the outlying streets.

Until recently their hotel, the Aviz, had been a palace—which it still resembled. It was a small, charming, luxurious place decorated in Louis XV style. There were only twenty bedrooms, which, of course, was more than big enough for the passenger loads of 1939. No one saw the Aviz as too small. It would serve transatlantic passengers only until the advent of "the next step."

The passengers were called next morning at 5:30 A.M. Breakfast was served en route to Marseille; at an altitude of ten thousand feet eggs and coffee took twelve minutes to boil. The stewards worked hard, then and always. They not only served all meals to the thirty-four people aboard —in addition to the twenty-two passengers there was a crew of twelve— but they also handled all baggage, made up berths, took charge of passports and landing papers in each country.

From Marseille Betty Trippe flew immediately to Paris to meet her husband and to wish him a happy birthday—he had turned forty at midnight a few days before when he was over the ocean between Newfoundland and Ireland. The men crossing with him, most of them government officials, had smuggled aboard a birthday cake, candles and champagne, and had thrown a party for him.

Afterwards Trippe had been busy. In Ireland he was received by Prime Minister Eamon De Valera, and in London by Prime Minister Neville Chamberlain. But not all his experiences had been pleasant ones. In London also, he had been summoned by U.S. Ambassador Joseph P. Kennedy, whom he had not seen since the aborted weekend at Hyannis Port two years before. Kennedy had decided to stage a bizarre ceremony designed both to glorify the American achievement and to humiliate the British for their failure. Hiring a theater and inviting enough prominent Britons to fill all the seats, Kennedy placed Trippe and his fellow transatlantic passengers on stage and then, taking the microphone, began not only to congratulate Trippe and Pan American but also to describe the simultaneous Imperial Airways flight that had got no farther than Ireland —a failure Kennedy laid to British incompetence and lack of American know-how. The ambassador's remarks did not please his British audience. People got up and began to leave. Trippe himself was mortified, and when Kennedy introduced him as the man who would elaborate on Imperial's failure, he tried to describe the unusually violent headwinds that had forced the British plane back. But people continued to walk out anyway.

Later he flew on to Paris for talks with Air France officials and to meet his wife, Whitney and the other directors who had come across on the southern route. In Paris there were social events, and these pleased Whitney and Betty Trippe much more than Trippe himself. One night Air France gave a dinner-dance at the famous three-star restaurant Maxim's. After dinner the party moved on to the Bal Tabarin, a Montmartre nightclub, where the floor show shocked both Trippes. The girls were practically nude.

The Pan Am people started home via the overnight train to Marseille, and they boarded their flying boat in the morning in a wind so strong that the plane was off the water in twenty-five seconds (in those days, and for some years to come, knowledgeable passengers always clocked the take-off runs of flying boats). Exhausted from the excitement and the nightclubbing, Betty Trippe fell asleep almost at once, but her husband woke her when the snow-capped Pyrenees began to sail past the window, for he wanted to share the spectacle with her.

At Lisbon, Portuguese officials threw a gala dinner for Trippe, not knowing that Whitney, who was also present, was now in charge, and early the next morning the party started to file aboard the Boeing once again. Just then a twin-engined flying boat, a Consolidated Catalina, came winging down over the river. They watched it land and taxi toward them. It bore the markings of American Export Airlines. This was the enemy, Pan American's new rival. The Export flying boat was too small to carry passengers economically, or even mail, and it was here only on a survey flight. Nonetheless, it had just crossed the ocean. It represented a threat to their company and perhaps to their very existence. It was a threat that needed to be stamped out. But how and by whom? Certain of the Pan Am people glanced around at Trippe, whose brain probably was churning, and at Whitney, whose brain probably was not.

Soon a more prosaic problem intervened. The Pan Am Boeing reached the Azores with a load of dirty dishes on board and not enough water to wash them in. Stewards staggered onto the quay carrying them in a basket, and customs officials objected, for it was not in the book to "import" dirty dishes and then "export" clean ones. It had never been done before. But finally agreement was reached, and two vital jobs were accomplished simultaneously. The dishes were successfully washed in the customs building, and the plane was successfully refueled.

Aloft again, dinner was served, including Portuguese sardines and other hors d'oeuvres, various French cheeses and champagne—Priester's ban on alcoholic beverages was already breaking down. Trippe sent for Captain Sullivan during dinner, asking him to come down from the flight deck so that the passengers could toast his health.

Hardly anyone aboard had ever flown at night before, and everyone was astonished at the beauty and clarity of the sky ten thousand feet up. Later, after passing through clouds, the plane came out into a star-studded sky with a full moon, and Betty Trippe thought it was like entering a brilliantly lit room.

The next day land was sighted below. Juan and Betty Trippe went aft for a better view. They picked out Montauk Point and followed the coast of Long Island down to Georgica Pond, and with this as a landmark, picked out their own East Hampton house on the dunes facing the ocean. Two of their children, Betsy and Charlie, and Trippe's mother waved up at them as they passed over. An hour later they were on the ground, having been to Europe and back in five and a half days—to Betty Trippe it seemed as if she was waking up from a dream to be back home so soon. The elapsed time from Lisbon to Port Washington had been twenty-six hours, two hours longer than the flight over. Passing quickly through customs, they climbed aboard their little blue Fairchild pontoon plane, and with Trippe at the controls, flew back part of the way they had come, setting down on Georgica Pond, then stepping ashore—with their fifteen pounds of baggage each—to embrace their children.

In her diary, Betty Trippe never addressed the question of the future of her husband, and it appears that he rarely if ever alluded to his problems in her presence. He had now thrown his planes across both oceans, and perhaps this seemed to him an immeasurably more difficult task than regaining control of the company.

Whitney had now been in command for four and a half months—and in command he remained. His meetings with the operations committee continued each Monday and Friday. Trippe attended, sat stony-faced, and did not speak, while the other men answered Whitney's questions and gave him their reports. Trippe, sitting in sullen silence, seemed to be daring Whitney to run the company without him. Whitney's reaction was a kind of acute embarrassment. At meetings he became increasingly ill at ease. He didn't know how to cope with Trippe's attitude. Soon the two men were no longer on speaking terms at all, which upset Whitney terribly.

The accident that might have been predicted now occurred.

The Boeing had proven a popular plane with passengers. The pilots also liked it—in the air. The difficulties were on the water. Not only was it clumsy to land, but at a taxi speed of around 20 mph the sponsons suddenly gave no stability because the water got sculpted from underneath them by the trough following the bow wave. That left nothing under them but air. One wing tip or the other would suddenly give a lurching drop. Pilots were regularly dunking their wing tips into the water. When this happened they pulled back fast on the power, and let the plane weathercock. The sponsons then took hold, and the plane could be taxied to the barge. Once it got there the pilots were careful to give the wings an extremely careful inspection for structural damage.

The pilots talked about the plane among themselves. By now all had worked out how to land it smoothly, or claimed they had. To land at a low trim angle was okay, they said, and to land at a high trim angle was okay. A low trim angle meant to come in flat and fast. A high trim angle meant to come in nose high and slow. Both of these were exaggerated landing techniques, but neither got penalized because of the construction of the plane. It was in between that a pilot got in trouble. The Boeing was a lady who reserved her worst manners for pilots who attempted to treat her correctly. It was only during "normal" landings that the machine bounced, skipped, porpoised.

In July Sullivan flew a load of newspaper publishers to Lisbon. Many were the same men who had accompanied Trippe on the festive first transpacific crossing. This time Trippe stayed home, and the most prominent company official on board was Priester, who did not have much to say to people like publishers.

It was on the trip back that the accident happened. Sullivan was one of those pilots who believed in the low-trim-angle approach when landing. A former chief petty officer trained by the Navy as an enlisted pilot, he was a rough man himself, and he had always been called a rough man with an airplane. To come in flat and fast was fine with him. His landings outward-bound at Horta and at Lisbon had been successful. His takeoff from Lisbon on the return flight had been successful also, and he reached Horta on schedule and brought the flying boat down for a landing meant to be as flat and fast as always.

The sea was rough, though not exceptionally so for Horta, and what happened next was blamed later on a "maverick swell." But if the Boeing had been a normal plane, and if Sullivan had been coming in slower and at a somewhat steeper angle—the normal angle for another plane—he might have been able to land without damage. But he was coming in very much faster, and he smashed head on into the so-called maverick swell. The plane bounced, shuddered, smacked the water a second time. The maverick swell was past, and Sullivan, finally in control of what he knew was a badly damaged airplane, taxied toward the special mooring tender, nosed up onto the ramp and watched as the Boeing was moored tight.

The bow had been staved in and the boat was taking water, but the passengers—the publishers—didn't know this, and they were disembarked and taken ashore. They had had too little experience with flying-boat landings to realize that anything unusual had happened, and no news reports of the accident ever appeared in the press.

Captain Sullivan inspected the damage. So did Priester. When the floorboards were taken up, it was seen that a number of bottom plates bulged inward, and the stringers that ran along these plates were spread. The main transverse frames of the hull, beams of specially extruded aluminum tubing built to take terrific strain, were bent also. Priester, surveying the damage, realized that this Boeing wasn't going anywhere for some time. The publishers were ashore at Horta, where there was nothing to do, and soon might begin asking embarrassing questions. The first job was to get them off the island; the second was to repair the Boeing; and the third, as Priester saw it, was to force the Boeing company to redesign its hull so that the boat would land properly.

But how do you repair structural damage to a huge flying boat in a primitive place like Horta where machinery of any kind is not available?

A message was sent to New York, and Captain Harold Gray arrived the next day at the controls of a second Boeing, bringing with him tools, gear and John Borger, one of the brightest of Priester's bright young engineers, and it was Borger who supervised actual repairs while Priester looked over his shoulder and gave advice. Men in diving helmets went under the flying boat with hammers and rivet guns and began trying to straighten and refasten loose plates. Inside the fuselage Borger rigged up timbers to keep the ruined beams from twisting further. A canvas sling was attached under the hull and the bilges pumped out, after which Borger poured in concrete, which both sealed the hull and solidified the timbers. Gray had flown the publishers home. Now the Boeing went back to New York with only its crew, Priester and Borger aboard.

Sullivan had been quite happy with the maverick-wave thesis, which might perhaps have satisfied Priester too, had not Gray arrived at Horta, noted the damage and realized how much worse the accident might have been. It was Gray who now stepped forward to denounce the plane's landing characteristics to Priester, and to demand that something be done.

Gray, chief pilot of the Atlantic Division, was then thirty-three years old, and he belonged to the second generation of airline pilots. Although only the tenth pilot hired by Pan American, he was much younger than Musick, Swinson, Fatt, Rowe, Sullivan and the others. He had not flown in World War I. He had never been a full-time barnstormer. Instead he had studied aeronautical engineering at two universities. He enjoyed theoretical research as much as flying and had done both before signing on, at the age of twenty-three, as a Pan Am pilot in Mexico.

It was Gray who did much of the practical testing that went into the earliest Pan Am experiments in blind flying. Later Priester sent him to Miami to teach these techniques to Swinson and Fatt, men ten years his senior. It was also Gray who had worked out the most economical long-range settings for the Ford trimotors, just as Musick had done for the S-42. When Priester established the rank of "master of ocean flying boats," the first man to pass all the tests and attain it was Harold Gray.

When a cerebral pilot like Gray complained about an airplane, he was listened to, and Priester now put enormous pressure on Boeing to correct the plane's faults. Boeing's method was to construct two models, and send them through extensive towing tests on Lake Washington. Later the models were taken to the testing tank at Langley Field, Va., where Gray and Boeing engineer George Schairer both rode the test rig. They simulated takeoffs and landings, and found it practically impossible to do either one properly.

Additional flaws were revealed. At certain speeds, spray from the hull damaged the sponsons' structure. At certain others the plane had no lateral stability whatever—this came as a complete surprise to Schairer, but Gray only laughed and remarked that the pilots had already learned to avoid those particular speeds.

The Boeing engineers had provided a kind of kit to make possible changes to the model. Various shapes, sizes and angles of sponsons could be tried out, and the shape of the hull could be altered by tying on blocks of wood. All kinds of hull and sponson configurations were now tried, including removal of sponsons altogether and the addition of wing-tip pontoons, but nothing worked until a block of wood was fastened in place that extended the hull step twenty inches further aft. Suddenly the model rode beautifully. The two men were amazed. It had been practically uncontrollable before; now it was docile during takeoffs and landings both. It was as simple as that.

A similar wooden block was now attached to an actual flying boat and a full range of tests carried out. The results were the same as those in the testing tank. The solution had been found.

After that, one by one the Boeings were brought in and the hull step extended aft the length of one frame, and from then on the Boeing B-314 was a pilot's dream.

In all, twelve Boeing flying boats were built. Only one was crashed— by Sullivan.

There had been talk in the past about grounding Sullivan. He was a big, bold, uncultivated, swashbuckling type, and definitely not Priester's kind of pilot. He liked to pour the coal to all four engines as soon as the mooring lines were cast off—thus spraying everybody. He was a show-off. In the air he would sometimes reach across and squeeze his copilot's forearm hard—so hard that he hurt him. The copilots all complained about it. No one ever understood why Musick had chosen him for those Pacific survey flights. They were not the same type of men at all.

But previous talk of grounding Sullivan had always come to nothing. He was an exceptionally skillful pilot, and most of the time he flew exactly as he was supposed to.

In 1943, coming in for a landing on the Tagus River in Lisbon at dusk, he apparently misjudged his altitude. He was on a shallow bank during his landing approach and he caught a wing tip in the river. The plane cartwheeled. Most of the crew and passengers perished, though not Sullivan. The crash was investigated, and its cause was determined to be pilot error. Sullivan had made a lazy man's approach, it was said, and he was forced to resign.

34

Trippe Returns

In September 1939, World War II broke out, and flying-boat service was pulled back to Lisbon on the southern route. Service on the northern route was at first pulled back to Ireland, and then closed altogether for a time.

Out of Lisbon business boomed. The passenger load was staggering. In the first two weeks of the war ten thousand Americans in Europe wanted to fly home. There were also forty thousand refugees in Portugal clamoring to get out. Mail loads were staggering also. For some trips there was so much mail that no passengers at all could be carried. Profits were suddenly so high that the board of directors approved the purchase of six more Boeings, making twelve in all.

In the Chrysler Building Whitney sent around a memo appointing Rihl a senior vice president reporting directly to him, and placing Rihl in charge of the New York office whenever Trippe might be absent—which made Trippe sound like an office manager. The same memo assigned Bixby, now a vice president, as director of the Atlantic, Pacific and Alaskan operations of the system.

Apart from such decisions as this, Whitney's leadership was invisible, and the company stagnated. Although there was a war on in Europe, and although American Export Airlines had just made three round-trip transatlantic flights, no long-range program had yet been thought out, much less implemented, with which to face either the war or the new rival—unless Trippe had something ready. But if he did, he was telling no one. Instead he sat balefully in his office, waiting for whatever was to happen.

In aviation circles rumors were rife: either he would get his old authority back or he would quit.

Morgan took over the executive committee, and began giving orders. Morgan was a competent man, and he was—with the possible exception of the Pratt and Whitney man, Rentschler—the only director possibly capable of running the airline; the bankers and the railroad and shipping men certainly couldn't.

But as Morgan tried to plan for the future he kept bumping into decisions and commitments Trippe had made previously, which Morgan had not known about and could not now undo. When he asked for information out of company records, he sometimes found that there were no company records. What he needed to know was all in Trippe's head. Morgan could solve scarcely a single problem on his own. To each one that arose there seemed only one course of action: ask Juan.

But Trippe remained remarkably uncommunicative. The entire company was at a standstill. It was November 28—Whitney had been in power then for eight and a half months—when Morgan became chairman of the executive committee. His brief effort to direct the company himself failed. "Juan had everything so snarled up nobody could ever untangle it," he said later. "He had the company in his pocket."

Whitney, meanwhile, was tiring of the chief-executive role. He lacked both the knowledge and the dynamism to run a company of this size. He was embarrassed at throwing his weight around. Executives who had backed him, even those who had been willing only to cooperate with him, saw that he was not going to be able to stick it out. The strain, clearly, was too much for him. He was going to leave, after which they would be exposed to whatever Trippe's wrath might be.

The traditional Christmas message, which went out to all employees, heralded the imminent transition of power. It was a rather joyous message this year—and it was signed not by Chairman Whitney but by President Trippe.

At year's end the company posted the biggest profit of its existence —the net after taxes came to $1,984,438.03, and this further consolidated Trippe's position. It was impossible to credit Whitney. It was profit that had really been earned years ago when, with foresight and daring, Trippe had first planned the transoceanic routes.

As for Whitney, it was clear to the board of directors that he could not run the company, and that furthermore he no longer wanted to. The only solution, Morgan told his fellow directors privately, was to put Trippe back in. Sonny Whitney agreed, and when the executive committee met on January 9, 1940, it was to recommend the necessary change in the bylaws that would designate the president—rather than the chairman— as chief executive officer. This resolution was adopted by the full board on January 23. The ten-and-a-half-month interregnum was over. Trippe moved back into the grand office, while Whitney went south on a long yachting vacation. Trippe's big globe was not rolled back down the hall; he had no intention of providing further dramatic entertainment of that nature. The globe went down in the freight elevator—a stage prop Trippe no longer needed or wanted—and from there to a museum. The time for stage props was now past. In a cold-blooded business one acted cold-bloodedly, or one did not survive.

Trippe's key job became to reestablish his control over the company. This meant that those who had served Whitney too enthusiastically would be punished, usually by being deprived of any further access to Trippe himself—which effectively removed most of their former authority. There would be no bloodbath. Bloodbaths were not Trippe's style. Among the chief victims were Van Dusen and Rihl. For his neutrality even Lindbergh would pay. But all this could wait. For now, Trippe needed these men.

But Comptroller J. H. Johnston, whom he did not need, suffered almost immediately. Johnston, the company's chief financial officer, had once been part of Florida Airways and had been taken over together with his airline in the very act of forming Pan American. In Key West he had kept the company books in a storefront office while Musick, Fatt and Swinson flew the Fokkers back and forth to Havana every day. Often he had crossed to Havana himself and had sold tickets out of his pockets to tourists he found in the Sevilla-Biltmore bar.

Trippe appears to have blamed Johnston not only for having supported Whitney, but also for having opposed certain of Trippe's financial expenditures well in advance of the takeover, thereby undermining him to some extent before the board.

Now Trippe called in Johnston's subordinate, John Woodbridge. "You're to be comptroller," Trippe said curtly.

When Woodbridge, out of loyalty to Johnston, tried to protest, Trippe cut him off: "There is no question about it. You are comptroller."

"What about Johnston?" asked Woodbridge.

"You take care of Johnston," said Trippe, with a wave of dismissal.

Later Woodbridge suggested to Trippe that Johnston be given the rank of assistant vice president, as this would soften the blow. Trippe agreed, providing Johnston was sent to some other office. He didn't want to see him around any more.

So Woodbridge sent his friend and former boss to Miami, where the ex–corporate comptroller became bookkeeper for the Latin-American Division. But sometimes it was necessary for Woodbridge to consult with Johnston in New York, and on one such occasion Johnston and Trippe happened to meet face to face in the hall. Summoning Woodbridge afterwards Trippe demanded, "What's Johnston doing here?" When Woodbridge attempted to explain, Trippe cut him off, saying "Get rid of him." Woodbridge pointed out that Johnston was due to retire in a few weeks. Trippe remained adamant, and Woodbridge was forced to fire Johnston, who died shortly afterwards. Woodbridge always referred to this as the company's "period of Gethsemane."

Others suffered also. Priester, named a vice president by Whitney, now found himself permanently out of favor with Trippe. So did Leuteritz. Trippe ordered subtle shiftings in his executive chain of command, effectively shunting aside both men. Though they remained chief engineer and chief communications engineer, respectively, their functions became largely advisory. They could no longer give orders to managers in the field. In a few years Leuteritz would quit in disgust. Priester would not, having no place else to go.

Strangely, Trippe seemed to bear no ill will toward Sonny Whitney. "Don't be unkind to Sonny," he advised a reporter later. "Sonny never wanted to be a businessman—and he didn't have to be."

Both Sonny and Jock Whitney told intimates that they were "getting out" of Pan American, and they began selling their stock. By Pearl Harbor day most of Sonny's was gone, and he resigned as chairman of the board and joined the Army Air Corps as a major. Though he lived to be over eighty, Sonny Whitney took no further interest in the affairs of the company he had helped found.

35

Trippe versus American Export Airlines

The company had drifted too long, and there were important jobs to be done. And so Trippe sent Rihl to South America to "delouse" SCADTA, the company's subsidiary in Colombia which had been founded by Germans, and which was to a large extent still staffed by them. This job was mandated by officials of the State and War departments. Colombia was the next country south of Panama, and with a war blazing in Europe, it made Washington nervous to imagine Germans in airplanes that close to the Canal.

Van Dusen went to Washington together with J. Carroll Cone, Mark McKee and Trippe himself, for the time had come to stop American Export Airlines, if possible, before it became powerful enough to compete on equal terms on the transatlantic run. Cone, who had been manager of the Atlantic Division, was needed for political reasons. He was a genial, glad-handing kind of man and a close friend of Senator John McClellan and Representative Orin Harris, both from Arkansas. McKee, who had just come on the Pan American board of directors, was chief executive of the Wisconsin and Michigan Steamship Company. He had shipping knowledge and shipping contacts.

There were at the time two principal American shipping lines: the United States Lines, which sailed to northern Europe, and American Export, which sailed to the Mediterranean and the Black Sea. Although during the thirties every contraption that could get off the ground seemed to attempt to fly the Atlantic, the United States Lines apparently took no notice of this phenomenon. It interested American Export very much, however, and the shipping company formed American Export Airlines, a wholly owned subsidiary, in April of 1937. The following year it bought a single Catalina flying boat. Again a long delay—eight months, this time—occurred. Then on May 9, 1939, American Export Airlines filed its application with the Civil Aeronautics Board for authority to engage in air transportation between New York and Marseille, New York and Southhampton, New York and Lisbon, and New York and Rome. With this application pending, Export and its lone plane that summer made three round-trip survey flights to Europe. Three of the crossings were via the northern route, three via the southern; Marseille was the most distant point attained. Pan American, with Whitney in charge, did not seem to react at all.

When World War II broke out, Export was obliged to file amendments to its CAB application. Most of Europe had become a war zone, and under the terms of the newly written Neutrality Act all of Export's proposed destinations were out of bounds except Lisbon. The second of these amendments was filed on October 23, and the next day, although Whitney was still in power, Pan American did react at last: its lawyers in Washington filed papers with the CAB by which it "sought leave to intervene" in the Export case—the polite legal phrase signaled a declaration of corporate warfare. As opening cannonades, Pan American's lawyers filed argument after argument with the CAB. Although many of them were later disallowed, all had to be answered by Export; the onslaught itself was so fierce that months were eaten up in the process, and this was supremely important because by the time the last response had been made, Trippe was back in power, had gathered his cohorts around him and was marching on Washington personally.

The CAB's open hearings began. To win certification, Export needed to prove that there was room across the Atlantic for more than one airline, and that competition between itself and Pan American would benefit everyone—the public, the American aeronautical industry and also the national defense. Furthermore, it would charge, failure to grant its own application would be tantamount to closing forever the door to competition by any American air carrier over the North Atlantic route.

In opposition, Pan American charged that Export had no planes, flight crews, operations base or money with which to fly the Atlantic on a commercial basis. All this was true. Export did have options on the Sikorsky S-44, Igor Sikorsky's newest (and last, as it turned out) four-engined flying boat, and proceedings were halted while Sikorsky himself was brought in to testify about what his new plane, which existed at this time only as an experimental Navy patrol plane, could do. It was only slightly larger than his S-42 of 1934, and its range and payload were only slightly better also. Sikorsky said it would provide sleeping accommodations for twelve passengers nonstop across the Atlantic, and Pan American countered by saying that its Boeings, with a stop at Horta, could sleep thirty-two, and that it would have twelve Boeings in all by the time the S-44 was flying. In addition, Pan American pointed out, Export's option on the S-44 had already expired. At this an Export lawyer jumped up claiming that an extension could be arranged.

As for the nonexistence of flight personnel or operations base, well, four of the six men who had made the three round-trip transatlantic survey flights were still with the company; and the mayor of New York had promised Export that facilities would be made available at North Beach Airport by the time Export was ready to commence service. As for money, Export admitted that three S-44 flying boats would cost over $1.7 million, with another $247,000 for spare engines, and that $391,460 for ground equipment was also needed. Although it did not have these funds in hand at the moment, it brought forth two witnesses from investment banks who testified that once the CAB had certified Export as a transatlantic carrier, money could be raised.

There were other more technical issues as well. Trippe and his men provided their lawyers with literally months of ammunition. But at last the hearings were concluded, after which oral arguments began and ended in their turn, only to be followed by formal briefs that were submitted and studied. On April 19 the "report of the examiner" was served on both parties. More days passed while exceptions were filed. On June 6—it was now thirteen months since Export had filed for its "certificate of convenience and necessity"—the CAB met to hear additional oral arguments from both parties. Five weeks after that, its findings came down in a document nearly forty printed pages long. This report had some splendid things to say about Pan American. "It does not appear that the quality of service rendered by intervener is at present inadequate in any respect." And again: "Intervener has pioneered the route here under consideration and is rendering efficient service within the limits of its facilities." But the bottom lines were these: "The record indicates that benefits to the public, in the shape of improved service resulting in advances from the industry, would be accelerated by competition between United States air carriers on the North Atlantic route . . . The saturation point of available air traffic on this route is not yet reached. The territory to be served through the termini of the transatlantic route is almost unlimited." As for Export's lack of money, bases, air crews and aircraft, the board professed to be satisfied with promises. Once certified, all these things would fall into Export's lap: "We find the applicant is fit, willing, and able properly to perform the transportation covered by the application . . . we are of the opinion that the inauguration of a second transatlantic service by a properly qualified United States air carrier is in the public interest."

Within hours President Roosevelt had affixed his signature to the decision, and American Export Airlines, the first non–Pan American overseas company, was in business—or seemed to be.

Trippe was furious. He had been defeated, as he saw it, not by logical arguments but by Roosevelt himself. Roosevelt the Dictator, he called him: Roosevelt favored shipping interests over Pan American, and always had; the CAB members were political appointees of Roosevelt—the President had put pressure on them, and they had voted his will.

Trippe was determined to go on fighting. He saw clearly Export's next moves—to go before Congress for airmail appropriations money and, simultaneously, to invade Pan Am terrain in Latin America. Trippe gathered Cone, Van Dusen, McKee and the lawyers around him to plot strategy.

Export, looking for a foothold in Latin America, had already begun negotiations with a Honduras-based airline known as TACA—Transportes Aéreos Centro-Americanos. TACA was owned by a New Zealander named Lowell Yerex, a kind of flying soldier of fortune, who had started with small secondhand planes, and gradually had linked the capital city of British Honduras with the six other Central American republics. Originally a charter operator, TACA still carried more freight than people. To some extent it had from the beginning paralleled Pan American services through Central America, but it did so in a third-class way, and Trippe had left it alone. It was not really competition.

But TACA, though it had no government subsidies to speak of, was shrewdly managed by Yerex, and it had grown into a prosperous enterprise. The year before, it had made a net profit of $196,000. It had also caught the eye of the executives of Export, and now Yerex, as a reward for years of hard work and enterprise, was about to be made a rich man. Export had agreed to buy him out for cash and stock totaling just under $2 million.

At this point the Pan Am "blitzkrieg"—so Yerex described it in sworn testimony later—struck Yerex and TACA.

36

Blitzkrieg against TACA

Of all the shadowy figures that peopled the early years of international aviation, Yerex was one of the most curious. At the time that the blitzkrieg struck him he owned about forty airplanes, plus all the radios, spare parts, rolling stock and shop gear that went with them, as well as landing fields and buildings in all seven republics. Unlike Juan Trippe, he had started with no capitalization at all and no wealthy friends, with the result that, also unlike Trippe, he still owned 80 percent of his business himself.

In 1931 Honduras, like most Central American countries, had almost no roads. The country was a mixture of impassable jungles and impassable mountains. Travel was by canoe where there were rivers, by mule where there were none. Yerex arrived there in a Stinson Jr. owned by a couple of other young men who wanted to start an airline; Yerex was the pilot. The Stinson Jr. could land in any meadow, and in the first thirty days of flying people and freight from meadow to meadow Yerex took in about $3,600 with the one plane. As time went on he secured an interest in the plane, and within a year had bought out his partners. A few months after that he bought a Stinson trimotor, his first. It was secondhand and in poor condition.

Yerex, four years older than Trippe, was born in Wellington, New Zealand, in 1895. His road to Central America had not been a straight one. He was brought to the United States at seven and grew up in Indiana, graduating from Valparaiso University there in 1916 with a bachelor of science degree. For a year he taught grade school in South

Hart, N.D. In 1917, being still a British subject, he joined the Royal Flying Corps. In combat over France he was shot down and taken prisoner by the Germans, and he served four months in a prison camp. When the war ended he returned to the United States and took a job as a private pilot for six months, transporting his employers throughout the country. At the end of that time he bought the plane, then two more planes, and he formed a company called Western Aviation, of which he was sole owner. He had two pilots working for him. This continued until 1925, by which time barnstorming was dead—in fact, the entire aviation business looked dead—and Yerex dissolved Western Aviation and became an automobile salesman. He had the Hudson and Essex agencies in Santa Fe, N.M. Yerex was a man who moved around a lot.

In June 1929, with aviation once again booming, Yerex found work with Southern Air Transport as a pilot and division manager working out of Amarillo, Tex. He stayed six months, then moved on to Torreón, Mexico, as pilot and operations manager for a small Mexican airline. It was from there that he drifted still farther south into Central America.

Yerex was an acquisitive man, as acquisitive as Trippe. From Honduras he began branching out, his tiny airline linking the various Central American capitals and from each of them radiating out into the mountains, into the bush. All around him were other tiny airlines owning one or two planes each. One by one he swallowed them up. He was careful to organize each as a national entity, though always under the same name: TACA. There was TACA of Guatemala, TACA of Nicaragua, TACA of Costa Rica and so forth. The overall holding company, which owned nothing except stock in the other companies, was based in Honduras, as was Yerex himself, who had a farm, a wife and three children there.

Central America at this time was being relentlessly exploited by major American corporations, and it was rich terrain for certain of them. It had an abundance of fruit, it had chicle, and it had mines, especially gold mines. The only problem was the lack of roads, which in the past had made certain plantations and certain mines unexploitable because there had been no way to bring in food, machinery or personnel. Now here was TACA filling this void to perfection. The fruit companies, the chicle companies and the mines were all able to expand. Business boomed for them, and so it boomed for Yerex too. Without ever attempting to raise capital, he kept expanding. He rarely took money out of the business. The aircraft he bought continued to be battered old ones. The airfields he used continued to be pastures. As a result, there were a great many accidents, most of them minor ones, particularly broken wheels and buckled undercarriages. One plane ran off a field onto a railroad track, and as workers were trying to lift it off before a train came, it broke in half. But other accidents were serious. One pilot flew into a mountain in fog. Another crash-landed off the coast; as the survivors sat on the tail waiting to be rescued by canoes, a passenger dove back into the plane for his suitcase, and when he came out towing it, he was taken, apparently, by a shark.

Despite the many planes destroyed, and the passengers occasionally killed, TACA had continued to prosper. This was because the value of the secondhand planes was small, as was the value of deceased passengers, for they were usually laborers from the plantations or mines. Most Central American liability laws limited damages to one-half the estimated earnings of the deceased over a ten-year period. Since the deceased were peons, $30,000 would cover a planeload.

It was Yerex's policy, TACA's policy, to keep fares extremely low. The existing air fares when Yerex first reached Central America were around fifty cents per mile. Under Yerex this dropped to ten cents a mile or even less, inasmuch as he instituted children's fares so that whole families of laborers and peasants could travel together. Some fares, for what had once been a five-day trek through roadless country (now reduced to 25 minutes' flying time), were as low as $3.75. Yerex later estimated that 85 percent of his passengers were natives and only about 15 percent Europeans, and he went on opening up the interiors of Central America to modern civilization. Children were able to go to school in the cities; the ill and the injured were able to reach hospitals in time. Letters and newspapers were being read in hours instead of weeks.

But most of his business was freight. Here, too, his sociological impact was enormous. Mines that had closed when surface veins petered out were opened up again, now that drills and dynamite could be brought in. One TACA plane was fitted out as a tanker, and tons of diesel fuel were suddenly available to power generators and heavy machinery. There was suddenly enough food to feed adequate manpower to make the mines work.

Near the gold mines of Nicaragua, where TACA built or improved five fields, a road and a bridge, towns of three to five thousand inhabitants sprang up, towns that existed solely on supplies brought in by TACA. Previously, to reach these mines from the Caribbean port of Puerto Cabezas, travelers went down the coast about fifty miles where a river debouched, then followed the river upcountry on a small schooner or barge, and then crossed Lake Nicaragua by launch, then took a fifty-mile train ride. It was a ten-day journey. Yerex's planes made the same trip in forty-five minutes, and the mines became viable again.

Similarly, the moribund chicle industry was revived. Chicle trees could be tapped only once every seven years, and plantations near existing landing fields had become exhausted. Yerex built four new fields in the jungles of the Petén region of northern Guatemala, though this required sending in engineers and laborers, not to mention supplies, on muleback to construct them, and his planes began bringing approximately two thousand tons of chicle per year out of those four new zones.

Yerex sometimes boasted that he ran the largest freight operation in the world, but it was an airline of short hops, of multiple landings and takeoffs. Planes that did not crash wore out fast. When they did, Yerex bought new ones—secondhand—and he continued to make a profit every single year. But his biggest profit was to come now as, having agreed to sell out to American Export Airlines, he waited for the papers to be signed.

Then began the blitzkrieg.

During the last eight years Pan American had watched Yerex closely, and a good many confidential memorandums originating in Central America had found their way to Trippe's desk in New York. Some contained supposedly secret information—one dated May 7, 1933, described Yerex's attempts to purchase bombing equipment on behalf of the Honduras government for $25,000. The memo judged that this gave him enormous clout with the Honduras generals. During these years Pan American was almost a state department unto itself, and it was vital to know such things.

Later memos gave the locations of Yerex's New York bank accounts and even his approximate bank balances.

Elton R. Silliman, called Tubby by his friends, was Pan American's "special representative" in Central America. He reported to Erwin Balluder, Western Division manager, who lived in Mexico City; Balluder reported to vice president Rihl in New York; and Rihl reported to Trippe.

So in Central America, Silliman counted as Trippe's eyes and ears. He had been there since 1932—about nine years, the first two and a half in El Salvador and after that in Guatemala. When asked on the witness stand later for a description of his duties, he replied, "I observe all phases of the company's business and interests in the territory and report them directly to the management; conduct all negotiations, officially and otherwise. In other words I represent the management in the field." In most of the Central American countries he held and exercised Pan American's power of attorney.

From time to time Silliman had called attention to Yerex and had urged that Pan Am take steps to stop TACA. But Trippe in New York had no interest in hauling Indian peasants in and out of the jungle, nor in hauling heavy machinery for gold prospectors and chicle farmers. Although some of Pan American's services paralleled some of TACA's, the two companies were aiming at different markets. TACA was perhaps the threat that Silliman in his memos claimed, but Trippe, during those periods when he chose to concentrate on Latin America at all, was not alarmed, and Silliman was not allowed to implement whatever schemes might have been churning in his head.

That Silliman was preoccupied with TACA seems clear. In a January

22, 1940, memo he reported that TACA had finally completed its "program of monopolization of all airlines operating in Central America and Panama," and he outlined which companies Yerex had just acquired and how. "I am fully aware of the company's attitude with respect to domestic operations in Central America," Silliman continued, "but despite this knowledge and in view of the dangerous inroads into our business now being experienced all the way between San Salvador and San Jose, I again recommend that serious thought be given to the formation of a Central American company dedicated principally to the transportation of freight . . . my impression is that an organization such as the one suggested above should be operated as a separate entity as nearly divorced as possible from Pan American Airways . . . I believe that we can obtain a fair volume of the chicle freight in Guatemala . . . and a fair share of the business both in Nicaragua and Costa Rica. TACA's control of practically all interior landing fields in Honduras would make it rather hard for us to do anything in that country . . ."

As the TACA threat grew stronger in Guatemala that spring, Silliman made contact with an American named Alfred Denby—known as Alfredo Denby there—a meat-packer who had served as bodyguard to dictator Jorge Ubico and who therefore had solid influence in the presidential palace. Denby reported that a new airline, if it was formed with himself as president, would have no difficulty becoming the only airline in the country. The two men held a number of conversations. Silliman apparently held conversations with men of a similar type in Nicaragua and Costa Rica as well.

By June, when negotiations between Yerex and American Export Airlines began, Silliman was ready, and the following month a coded telegram was en route from Balluder in Mexico City to Trippe in New York:

PAN AMERICAN AIRWAYS
       ATTN TRIPPE PUG
42 REFERENCE MY RECENT LETTER EDOEK YHKYS PTEHW RYFSA FOLLOWING FROM OUR IXCOT TAPPS QUOTE YHKYS PTEHW ADVISES ROLAF EXTREMELY ANXIOUS DIEKR OPWON WITH NUPUJ POSSIBLE EUGAC AND SUGGESTS SOMEONE DNOAM GUKOB EQAYP DIRECT ROLAF STOP UNDERSTAND IUHIL NOW MORE EYZAS PRUOG Y JBAR UNQUOTE TRUST WE MAY HAVE SOME INSTRUCTIONS THIS MATTER SHORTLY AS YHKYS PTEHW INSISTING UCEVZ AGOUF BE SIHIG GWOIZ THIS OMEXK
       PAN AMERICAN AIRWAYS BALLUDER

The translation read this way: "Reference my recent letter in connection with Denby Project following from our Guatemalan representative quote Denby advises president extremely anxious to close negotiations with least possible delay and suggests someone come empowered to deal direct president stop understand government now more determined to oust TACA unquote trust we may have some instructions this matter shortly as Denby insisting some agreement be reached before the end of this month. [Signed] Pan American Airways Balluder."

As an executive, Trippe then and always gave all of his attention to whatever project was on his mind at the moment; all the rest got short shrift. When he received the message, he ignored it. He had just been away from his office for most of a month in connection with the first transatlantic passenger flights and other things had piled up. And so two months passed. But on September 13 newspaper articles throughout Central America reported the imminent sale of TACA to American Export Airlines. Silliman sent the clippings to New York at once, where they were read by Rihl, who attached a memo and sent them in to Trippe.

There is no record of what happened next, of what instructions Trippe sent to Balluder in Mexico City or to Silliman in Guatemala. But the result of these instructions was the blitzkrieg against TACA which Yerex on the witness stand later described. This blitzkrieg was all the more devastating because Yerex was in New York negotiating with Export at the time. Ten years of long hours and high risk, of shrewdness, determination and stamina, were about to be rewarded. He was about to sign the contract that would make him rich.

In Central America TACA was like a feudal castle with its drawbridge open. Without Yerex it was more or less defenseless. The blitzkrieg occurred on almost all fronts simultaneously. On October 11, 1940, Aerovías de Guatemala was formed. Its chief executive officer was the meat-packer and ex–presidential bodyguard Alfredo Denby. Denby's capital money was a loan from a New York bank unsupported by collateral but co-signed by Pan Am. One of his "vice presidents" was Silliman. His rolling stock was a pair of fourteen-passenger Douglas DC-2's flown down from Compañía Mexicana, the wholly owned Pan American subsidiary to the north. The planes still bore the Mexicana logo on their fuselages, and they were operated by American crews. They were better aircraft than anything Yerex had, and this was only the start of the trouble. Aerovías began service within twenty-six days, something of a record for quick starts in airline service anywhere in the world. It secured most ground personnel by hiring men away from TACA: some radio operators, all agents, some mechanics, some station managers. Yerex came hurrying back from New York. He was already too late. His life work was being destroyed, and his deal with Export was contingent on his ability to deliver a viable airline. Although he held exclusive contracts from the Guatemalan government for the four fields he had built near the chicle plantations, Aerovías planes were already operating out of them. He listened to radio reports from his men on the scene. Bales of chicle consigned to TACA were being slung onto Aerovías planes by Aerovías employees. It was chicle that belonged to the Wrigley Importing Co. and to the Chicle Development Co. Shipments via Aerovías were not only not authorized, but in violation of signed contracts Yerex held. Nonetheless it was being done. His men at times put up resistance and there was violence. Men on both sides were carrying firearms.

In neighboring Costa Rica, Pan American offered the government a contract by which Pan Am would inaugurate local service instead of TACA. The newspapers there printed this news, together with the information that Pan Am's object was totally altruistic—the company would lose money, but wanted to do it in order to help the people of Costa Rica, and to help the country. As Yerex wryly commented later from the witness stand: "That kind of competition would be hard to meet." In Nicaragua an attempt to form a competing airline was being made by a man named Kennett, formerly a TACA vice president, and his connection with Pan American became public when, after his arrest on a gold-smuggling charge, Silliman interceded for him and a Pan American lawyer represented him. Another ex-TACA employee named Carl White, who headed the military aviation school in Honduras, gathered together three commercial aircraft and seemed on the verge of inaugurating a new airline also.

Throughout Central America new Pan American fares went into effect that cut ticket prices by up to 50 percent.

For three months Yerex raced back and forth trying to save TACA. The ironic thing was that the Pan American blitzkrieg was not even directed against Yerex or TACA but, rather, against American Export. On January 28, 1941, all Yerex's contracts in Guatemala—20 percent of his business—were canceled by government decree. This included not only his contracts with the chicle companies but also his leases on the four airfields he had constructed. After being ordered to get all his men, planes and equipment out of the country at once, he was authorized to make a maximum of three flights into the Petén region to bring out whatever equipment he could carry on the three trips. He got out most of it, but was forced to abandon the rest, including the buildings whose unamortized cost he estimated at $12,000. They weren't much, but they were his. Aerovías, moving in behind him, took them over, and later agreed to pay him $5,000.

In all the republics a press campaign seemed under way to discredit both TACA and Yerex. Yerex himself was pictured as a former revolutionary. New York knew better, and a Pan Am dossier stamped "Strictly confidential" described Yerex this way: "There appears to be no question as to the subject's integrity and moral standing. He is regarded as being thoroughly experienced in his particular field, and is familiar with conditions in Latin America. He bears a very good reputation in banking and business circles, is extremely energetic, and is a man of vision; he has been straight forward and honest in all of his business dealings. His financial condition is such that he is believed well able to take care of any reasonable credit arrangements which he may enter into."

To certain men at the State Department Trippe's attempt to destroy TACA seemed to constitute a serious diplomatic incident, and he was called in to explain, if he could, what he had done and why.

Trippe by this time was a highly experienced witness. He had testified scores of times before congressional committees and regulatory agencies. He was a man who always did his homework; he went into hearings in total possession of all pertinent facts, and sometimes when on the stand, he gave them. Usually he made a great effort to be ingratiating. If pressed for facts his listeners knew he knew, but which he did not wish to give, he didn't refuse to answer. Instead he would launch into what certain of his admiring employees called "gobbledygook," meaning that his sentences no longer tracked. His phrases would become so long and convoluted—subjects bearing only a distant relationship to their verbs, and verbs to their objects—that very soon no one had the faintest idea what he was talking about.

As a witness, Trippe also had a third mood; he sometimes became angry, and if this happened, he was likely to pay no attention to whichever company lawyer was whispering in his ear. Now, questioned by State Department officials about TACA, Trippe began speaking in his ingratiating, innocent, bewildered and then convoluted way. But when the officials pressed him, this third mood came upon him, and he explained that for many years he had been totally indifferent to Mr. Yerex's operation in Central America. Little local feeder airlines did not interest him in the slightest. Yerex, as far as he was concerned, could have stayed on in Central America forever conducting his little business. But once Yerex branched out, once he tied up with American Export, then suddenly he threatened competition destructive to Pan Am's entire Latin American Division. At that point he had to be competed against with all the force and determination that Pan American could muster. He could no longer be ignored. He had forced Trippe to take action against him.

Trippe then launched into a speech about international financiers, about secret agents prowling Central America in the service of foreign powers, about the importance of the Panama Canal. He alluded to mysterious plots and deals about which the State Department was unaware, and to threats to the national defense, which, this precarious year of our Lord 1941, was being safeguarded in some corners of the world not by the State Department but by Pan American. He believed all this himself or seemed to. The one thing that the State Department could rely on, he said, was that all of his company's actions were in the best interests of the United States of America. If State couldn't see this, then they were less well informed on dark Central American doings than they should be. A silence fell, while his interrogators attempted to regroup. Since when, interjected Trippe's counsel mildly, did the State Department have the authority to question the business tactics of a private American citizen abroad in peacetime?

End of interrogation.

Export, before its purchase of TACA could go forward, sought approval from the CAB, as was mandated by law, and formal hearings were opened. Trippe sent more lawyers before the board in this new case to argue for more months that approval should be denied. His principal—and ultimately successful—argument was the following. Under Section 408 (b) of the Civil Aeronautics Act, steamship companies were not allowed to purchase airlines. What Trippe was charging was that American Export Airlines, which had never yet flown a commercial mile, was not an airline at all but a steamship company. The CAB agreed with him, and the purchase of TACA was denied. The crowning achievement of Yerex's business life was not consummated.

Yerex attempted soon after to sell his diminished airline to Pan American. Conversations were held over a period of years, but at the end his offer was judged unattractive. He was told that he had nothing to sell that Pan American wanted.

Trippe versus the U.S. Government

Having blocked competition in Central America, it was now urgent to block it on the Atlantic, and there was very little time. Trippe flew at once to Lisbon to talk to Richard Long and Pedro Pinto Basto, his agents there. What was the best way to prevent the issuance of landing permits by Portugal to Export? Two years previously, Trippe had written his famous letter to the Civil Aeronautics Board offering to waive his exclusivity there. This letter had relieved immediate heat, and talk of monopoly and of prosecuting him under the antitrust statutes had disappeared.

But the board had never formally responded to Trippe's offer. Therefore his exclusive agreement with Portugal remained in force. Meantime the State Department had begun negotiating an air treaty with Portugal's National Air Council. A draft of such a treaty already existed. It would supersede Trippe's own agreement, and he was trying to figure out a way to stop Portugal and the United States from signing it. Suppose, Trippe asked Long, he should resurrect his two-year-old offer renouncing exclusivity; suppose as a result that the American government could be persuaded that an air treaty with Portugal really wasn't necessary, could be persuaded to stop all discussions regarding it, and at the same time withdraw, as unneeded, U.S. government support of Export. Suppose further that Export should be allowed now to negotiate its own rights. If all this could be brought about, Trippe asked Long, was there still some way to prevent Export from obtaining those rights altogether, or to delay them for at least a year?

Trippe was fighting for time. If he could keep Export's planes out of the sky long enough, the company's political and financial support might vanish. The hard-eyed men who backed Export were not visionaries like himself. They were not even aviation men. How much longer were they going to back an airline that existed only on paper before they cut their losses and walked away?

To Trippe's question Long replied with great caution. No doubt it would be easier to oppose Export in Portugal if Export had no support from the State Department. But the Portuguese might feel that Export still had the tacit backing of the American government, which, by forcing Pan Am to renounce exclusivity, had merely changed its method of showing support. In other words, said Long, the strong impression had been created in Portugal that the American government was anxious to see Export obtain landing rights, and if Trippe again renounced exclusivity, it would be most difficult to persuade the Portuguese government not to grant a permit to Export.

Trippe flew back to New York, and from there to Washington, where Van Dusen, McKee, Cone and the others had been busy in his absence. The House Appropriations Committee had been considering a bill entitled "Treasury and Post Office Department's Appropriation Bill, Fiscal Year 1942." The total appropriations involved mounted into the hundreds of millions of dollars, of which $1,299,736 was earmarked for the carrying of airmail by American Export Airlines on the New York–Lisbon run. Trippe's lobbyists were working hard against this clause. They had buttonholed congressmen, and had presented Pan Am's arguments against such an appropriation. They had brought forth handpicked experts willing to stand publicly behind Pan Am's position, including General Hugh S. Johnson, who had helped make the federal survey on transportation on which the Transportation Act was based. "There is little criticism of the marvelous pioneering work of Pan American," Johnson wrote in a document widely disseminated by Van Dusen. "No, the argument is neither bad service, high rates nor lack of full cooperation with the government. It is the word of evil omen in all American legislative deliberation, like the word 'unclean' in a country where there is leprosy. The word is 'monopoly.' It is the story of the railroads over again. Any kind of public service, such as transportation, has some elements of public helplessness— some aspect of monopoly." In dealing with the high-handed railroad barons, Johnson continued, the government had subsidized parallel railroads. The result was the "snarl and tangle of our inefficient and frequently bankrupt railroad web." This present air-route business, he continued, was an exactly similar case, and he urged that the errors of seventy years ago not be repeated. If the New York–Lisbon mail load was divided up between Pan American and Export, both companies would lose money. "Better one good line than two bad ones," Johnson concluded.

There were many other arguments that Trippe's men employed in their meetings with congressmen, and one was that Export was a monopoly too—it already had a monopoly of 90 percent of the traffic to Lisbon through the steamship lines of its parent company.

Trippe's lobbying was successful. The House Appropriations Committee cut Export's appropriations out of the bill, explaining in part: "The more companies the U.S. puts into foreign air operation on a heavily subsidized basis, the greater toll it will have to pay for maintaining a supremacy or holding its own. Distasteful as monopoly may be under ordinary conditions the facts remain that our foreign air operation is a monopoly, instituted, grown up and encouraged by the government with that knowledge, and developed into a successful and useful arm of our foreign trade."

But Export had lobbyists too, who managed to get the full House to argue the matter for two days. No congressman expressed himself as being in favor of monopoly. All praised competition, but the question kept recurring: What would this competition cost? Would they be justified in establishing an airmail service that was not needed for postal purposes, and paying for it three times the cost of Pan American's existing service?

The answer was no, and the Export appropriation remained cut from the bill, which was otherwise approved and sent on to the Senate.

Export, after four years, still had no planes flying, no viable airline, but it did have powerful friends, most of whom were infuriated by Trippe's constant, bitter and so far successful opposition. The State, War, Navy and Post Office departments all wanted a second airline to Europe, though for different reasons—meaning that they wanted the Export appropriations money back in the bill. Most of all, so did President Roosevelt. Some of Roosevelt's reasons were political. It made sense to him, as the champion of the New Deal, to oppose monopolies of whatever kind. In addition, he had pushed the Maritime Act, appointed Kennedy to head it and then seen the Maritime Act emasculated by Congress, who, listening to Trippe's arguments rather than to those of the White House, had chosen to pass the Civil Aeronautics Act. There were by this time bitter personal feelings between Trippe, a lifelong Republican, and the President. They knew each other—they had met often enough—and they were even distant cousins. Almost a century before, their families had been in the clipper-ship business together.

Under the Civil Aeronautics Act, the CAB was empowered to determine at any time whether current airmail rates paid to airlines were too high. If so, the board could ask that they be reduced. This was the board's —and the White House's—financial hold not only on Pan American but on all airlines. Now, even as Senate action pended, many of Pan American's original ten-year mail contracts were expiring; new CAB hearings became necessary. It was only a coincidence that they had to be held now —a fortunate coincidence for Trippe's enemies—and almost as soon as they opened it became clear that their object was to show that Pan American was guilty not only of inefficiency but also of false deals, fast deals, double deals and worse. The government's case was argued by Samuel Gates, a bright young CAB attorney, who had seized upon Pan American as a means of establishing his reputation in Washington.

More than 50 percent of Pan Am's operating revenue, or about $4 million a year, Gates charged in his opening statement, came from government airmail payments. This amount, Gates charged, was excessive, and he would prove it, and after that, it would be reduced. First Gates attempted to prove, partly by harassing witnesses, that the U.S. subsidy of Pan Am supported not only Pan Am itself but also all of its foreign affiliates and subsidiaries. Airmail subsidies were designed to guarantee airlines a "fair return" on investments. Therefore if Pan Am was making little profit in its own name but big profits on its subsidiaries, and if it was doing this by clever bookkeeping as a means of keeping its airmail subsidies high, then its actions were possibly criminal. But he failed to prove this.

Next Gates began to attack various of Pan Am's accounting methods. The chief witness over this sticky terrain was Comptroller John Woodbridge, who mostly handled himself very well. Although Gates scored points—and damaging newspaper headlines also—by seeming to prove inefficiency, he was in no way able to prove fraud.

Now Gates questioned Woodbridge about the activities of Trippe, Cone, Van Dusen and McKee in Washington. Were they not engaged in "legislative contact and counseling"? Woodbridge said he didn't know. He said Pan Am had paid no money to lobbyists during the last three years. Gates then pointed out that, although most members of the Pan Am board of directors were paid $100 per meeting attended, McKee was paid $12,000 a year plus expenses, and was in Washington all the time. In addition, a man named Ben Gray had been paid $4,500 in 1938 and $5,000 in 1940—and Gray was a registered lobbyist. What Gates was trying to show was that government subsidies were helping to pay for Pan Am's lobby, which in turn was used to squeeze additional subsidy money out of the same government.

After that, Gates began wandering further afield, and though he continued his aggressive cross-examination of witnesses, he seemed to be expending energy for very little profit. Most of the information elicited was so technical and inconclusive that official Washington lost interest. The newspaper reporters drifted away from the hearings even before they ended. Attorneys on both sides then retired to submit briefs, which the CAB examiner would take into consideration when writing his recommendation to the Civil Aeronautics Board. It was hard to estimate how many months would go by before any decision on the Pan Am mail subsidy—whether to reduce it or not—would be made.

In the meantime Trippe and Pan American had acquired a few more nasty headlines, a few more enemies. And Treasury and Post Office Appropriations Bill, H.R. 3205, had gone to the Senate Appropriations Committee, where Senator Kenneth McKellar, Democrat from Tennessee, proposed an amendment putting the Export appropriation money back in. Witnesses were called; nearly all testified that America needed Export on the New York–Lisbon run. The same dirty word "monopoly" was heard often. The witnesses were virtually unanimous in their support of Senator McKellar's amendment. Aircraft manufacturers wanted a second airline; Pan Am's monopoly was ruining them, they said, because Trippe, who had the only flying-boat airline, played them off one against the other, so that none made money. The War and Navy departments wanted a second airline as a backup on behalf of national defense. The State Department wanted the American flag to reach as many corners of the world as possible. Representatives of the Post Office and the Bureau of the Budget felt insulted that their judgment had been overruled and the money cut out. The Civil Aeronautics Board was, of course, in favor of Export, and the arguments by which it had awarded Export its certificate of convenience and necessity were hashed over once again.

But the star witness was Trippe, who chose to display the most ingratiating of his moods. He rebutted every argument advanced so far, and after doing so, he kept the issues simple. He reduced it to money, to figures any congressman could understand. American Export wanted a subsidy of $1.2 million. That didn't sound like much, but when amortized on a per trip basis, Export was proposing to charge the U. S. Treasury $21,000 per round trip to Lisbon. Trippe now offered to add the same number of round trips to Pan American's existing schedule for $9,000 each. Why pay $21,000 when you can get the same job done for $9,000? he asked the senators.

The committee retired to vote. The result was twelve to eleven against American Export. The appropriation was out of the bill. McKellar, defeated, left the hearings room muttering that Trippe was "the most brilliant witness I have ever seen."

News of their victory was relayed to Trippe and his cohorts, and a celebration began. But it was short-lived. After the committee had recessed, Republican Senator James J. Davis, of Pennsylvania, decided he wished to change his vote. Trippe himself always blamed Roosevelt personally for this. The committee was called back into session, a recount taken, and the original vote was reversed. Export was now the winner twelve votes to eleven.

And so the bill was reported out of committee and went before the entire Senate, where, after a brief debate, it was expected to be enacted into law.

To Trippe the matter had become a moral issue. The committee vote was irregular. He determined to reach as many senators as possible in advance of the Senate debate, and persuade them to vote the amendment down, and he and Cone, Van Dusen and McKee went to work. To every senator who seemed friendly Van Dusen handed a ream of fact sheets. Some of Trippe's strategy meetings were held in the Mayflower Hotel room of Senator Walter George, Democrat of Georgia, and it was decided that, on the floor of the Senate, Pan Am's fight would be led by Senator Millard Tydings, Democrat of Maryland. A column by Drew Pearson in the Washington *Times Herald* had previously identified Tydings as a close friend of Andrew Mellon's son-in-law, David K. E. Bruce, and Bruce as a large stockholder and former director of Pan American. Bruce was also a contributor to Tydings' campaign fund, and he was one of the officials of National Dairy Products, which was represented in Baltimore by Tydings' law firm.

Two years before, Trippe had invited Tydings' wife to christen the No. 3 Boeing as the *Atlantic Clipper,* a glamorous day for her. Her name and picture had appeared in all the papers.

The debate on the floor opened. "If there is to be a monopoly," said Senator Tydings to his peers, "I want to see Juan Terry Trippe, who is president of Pan American Airways, at the head of it. He is a very remarkable man. But that is the whole question: Do we want by this indirect method, by denying an appropriation, to establish a monopoly?" That was enough, Tydings judged, for a start, and he ceded the floor to Democratic Senator Joseph O'Mahoney, of Wyoming, who was against Trippe, against Pan American, against monopolies, and for Export. "The most extraordinary feature about this contest which has reverberated from one end of the capital to the other," said O'Mahoney, "is that a great organization, which has been the beneficiary of the largess of the Government of the United States, should be undertaking to prevent the Government of the United States from permitting another line to operate."

Next came Senator Josiah Bailey, Democrat of North Carolina. "The Pan American went out on its own capital," he orated, "at its own risk, under the leadership of this remarkable man. I know the senators always testified to Mr. Trippe's fine qualities and his great capacity. He is a young man. He was a poor man. He told me that he formed the Pan American with, as I recall, eleven other pilots. It was not one of these great monopolistic enterprises we so fear. It was a group of fine young men, most of whom had served in the World War as pilots and were looking for a chance to do something. They decided that the United States should be carrying passengers and mail across the Pacific and across the Atlantic.

The project grew. It was a success. It has become a great company. It had no competitors, I think mainly because no one dared to undertake the things Mr. Trippe dared to undertake." Senator Bailey went on to accuse Export of attempting to destroy foreign air transportation in order to maintain its own monopoly at sea. "What I am doing is not primarily in the interest of Pan American. It is in the interest of air transportation. It is in the interest of keeping the steamship companies and banking houses out of air transportation."

That was the first day, May 5, 1941. The debate was all going Trippe's way, and that night Postmaster General Frank C. Walker called Trippe on the phone and said, "If this debate goes on tomorrow, and if you and your directors continue this, you will be sued. Criminal antitrust charges will be brought."

For once Trippe was speechless.

"You be at my office before they convene tomorrow to tell me your answer," said the Postmaster General.

After a moment Trippe said, "But Congress decides this."

"You weren't born yesterday," rejoined the Postmaster General. Then he said in a milder voice, "I want you to tell your people to stop. You ought to think about this. As a friend, I thought I ought to tell you about it. Be at my office at eleven A.M."

It was nearly midnight when Trippe hung up the phone. He was sharing a hotel room with John Cooper, the middle-aged, excessively proper international lawyer, who was his vice president. Cooper in his pajamas paced up and down the room. "This is terrible," he told Trippe. "There has never been a scandal in your family or mine, and I think we should throw it in. Why don't we throw it in?"

Trippe was trying to think the matter out. He was, he said later, "so damn mad," but a criminal suit was no joke. They could put him in jail. The fact that the Postmaster General was so close to President Roosevelt made his threat even more serious. Probably Walker was closer to Roosevelt than any other Democratic politician. He had contributed to Roosevelt's campaigns as early as 1928, had served on the White House executive council—the so-called Super Cabinet—as early as 1933. He was thought of in Washington as "Assistant President." Obviously, he spoke now for Roosevelt himself, and Trippe was extremely concerned. If the federal government were to bring such a suit, it would be catastrophic for the company. It would wreck public confidence in the airline. Trippe was as worried about his company as he was about himself.

In the morning, even as Trippe approached Walker's office, debate continued on the floor of the Senate. "Originally it was said to be impossible to fly the Andes," intoned Senator Worth Clark, Idaho Democrat. "Pan American did it, so they had a monopoly on flying the Andes . . . it was said to be impossible to fly the Pacific but Pan American did it and they had a monopoly on the Pacific . . . so this monopoly has grown up I think perhaps not in the way monopolies ordinarily grow up, by financial manipulation, but by doing something that nobody else would do."

Senator Pat McCarran, Nevada Democrat, had also listened closely to Trippe's and Van Dusen's arguments, and had accepted most of them. "There is not enough traffic in this situation to warrant two lines being subsidized by the American Treasury," he said.

Meanwhile Trippe waited outside the office of Postmaster General Walker. By then he had made his decision, and when the secretary showed him in, he told Walker, "You give me a lot of credit—to think that I can stop this debate. But I can't do it."

"You sit out there in the anteroom another five minutes," said the Postmaster General grimly. "Then come back and see if you don't change your mind."

In the anteroom Trippe stood brooding. On his answer seemed to depend his own future, and the future of his airline as well.

"Well?" inquired the Postmaster General when the two men again stood face to face.

"No," said Trippe.

For a third day Senate debate continued. Senator O'Mahoney argued that if the Senate should now defeat the amendment, then the Senate would be reversing the policy that had been adopted by the official board (the CAB) appointed for that purpose by Congress itself. This would be to establish a new policy.

"Transatlantic air traffic is just in its infancy," O'Mahoney pleaded. "It is foolish to contend that there is not enough business for two lines. There is enough business for more. All one has to do is to read the story of the expansion of air traffic in the continental United States to know that it grows by leaps and bounds. I venture to say that, come peace, which we all pray may come some day soon, the traffic by air across the Atlantic will be sufficient to require daily trips."

O'Mahoney spoke a long time. "We have here what I believe to be an artful attempt, not clearly understood by members of Congress, on the part of one line to secure complete and permanent domination of the airways of the world . . . if the recommendation of this committee is defeated it will be a decision by the members of this body that they want to raise Pan American—an industrial, exclusive, monopolistic empire— above the authority of the Civil Aeronautics Board."

Senator O'Mahoney's plaintive voice rose with renewed emotion. "Why should this line which has been the beneficiary of the largest of the people of the United States," he demanded, "undertake to oppose a policy of Congress and the Civil Aeronautics Authority? Because it seeks, as I verily believe, to dominate the air traffic of the world . . . ninety

STAKING OUT THE WORLD

Trippe and his famous globe, about 1939. He used to stretch string between two points and then measure the string, and after that he would translate inches into a flying boat's hours in the air.

Trippe and chief engineer Andre Priester in 1929.

THE FIRST YEAR

The Fokker Trimotor, named General Machado (opposite top) after the Cuban dictator, was the company's first plane, shown here on October 28, 1927, when service between Key West and Havana was formally opened. Pilot Edwin Musick is at extreme right. When the "huge" airliner crashed at sea almost a year later, having missed the entire peninsula of Florida, Hugo Leuteritz (above) survived. In his hospital bed the radioman designed the loop antenna (right), with which he proposed to make such navigational errors impossible in future. But his loop direction finder, or DF, looked so flimsy that the pilots did not believe in it, and they continued to resist both it and him. It could be aimed like a gun at incoming radio signals up to 100 miles away, thus determining a plane's bearing.

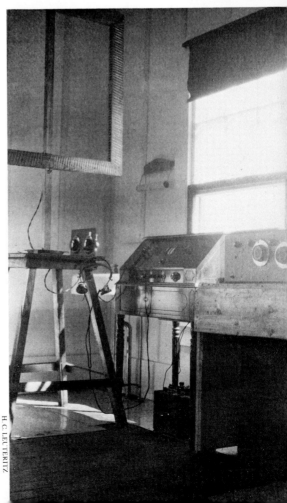

THE S-38

It could carry eight passengers in what was then considered great comfort, and cruise at 105 miles an hour, which was then considered great speed. Its range was about 300 miles. At right Charles and Anne Lindbergh, and Betty and Juan Trippe, are shown standing beside an S-38 in September 1929 during the first airmail run from the United States to the South American continent.

LINDBERGH

He was everybody's hero, the most famous young man in the world, and his every flight was news. His contribution to Trippe's company cannot be overdescribed. He opened up new routes, caused a million headlines—and millions of dollars' worth of free publicity—and even helped design the planes like the S-40 (right), the first of Pan Am's four-engined flying boats. The S-40 was an amphibian also, but its four Pratt and Whitney Hornets had developed 575 hp each, and gave it a range of around 800 miles. Its wingspan was 114 feet, its length 76 feet 8 inches, and fully loaded it weighed 34,600 pounds. It could carry up to forty passengers in its teak-lined nautical cabins. It is shown here landing at Pan Am's new international seaplane base at Miami around 1931.

THE ROUTE TO CHINA

A base had to be built on Wake Island, an uninhabited coral atoll. There was no anchorage, and the supply ship had to stand to offshore, while barges brought gear ashore in tumultuous seas (left). Inside the lagoon the surface of the water was appropriately calm, but hundreds of coral heads just beneath made landings by flying boats impossible. The coral heads were blasted out one by one by Bill Mullahey, twenty-four, a Columbia University swimmer whose only gear was a pair of marine goggles—swim fins, face mask, snorkel and scuba tank had not yet been invented. The Pacific was crossed with the aid of many specialists, none more vital than Mullahey. Other specialists erected adcock direction finders (lower left) on Wake, and indeed at each base all the way across, so that pilots in the air could home in on what were for the most part excruciatingly tiny targets.

Below is the S-42 piloted by Musick as it reached Pearl Harbor for the first time on April 17, 1935. Note the "ground" crew in the one-piece bathing suits of the day preparing to haul the flying boat out of the water.

THE CHINA CLIPPER
To the massed crowds that watched it take off for the Orient, the China Clipper
seemed as futuristic in design as a space capsule, and its goal seemed just as incalcu-
lably distant. The unfinished Golden Gate Bridge seemed a symbol of the uncom-
pleted world behind it as it set off into the future. To people who had never seen
them, and who never expected to see them, even the bases where it would touch down
seemed exotic—particularly Wake Island, more than 4,000 miles out into the vast
Pacific. An entire village now existed on Wake, every nail, every stick, every drop of
fuel, even—at first—every drop of fresh water having been shipped in from the main-
land. Wake itself had contributed nothing except 12 feet of sand above high tide, not
even shade, for its scattered shrubs were too low. But those travelers who henceforth
would cross the Pacific by air would spend the night in a modern hotel lobby, as
shown in upper right about 1937.

THE CELEBRATIONS
When Musick reached Manila, so many harbor craft crowded around that he feared
for the safety of his ship—the flying boats, to the men who piloted them, were always
"ships," not airplanes. Two years later Musick reached Auckland, and stepped into
the wildest celebration yet, his last before his plane exploded over Pago Pago.

CHINA

It was William Langhorne Bond (right) who presided over the Chinese National Aviation Corporation during most of its profitable, dangerous life. Shown below is the famous "DC-2½," only one of the airline's many bizarre triumphs. When a CNAC DC-3 lost most of its right wing in a Japanese air attack, the only possible replacement was the spare wing of the DC-2. Bond ordered it flown in from 800 miles away, it was fastened into place, and the aircraft flew successfully back to safety.

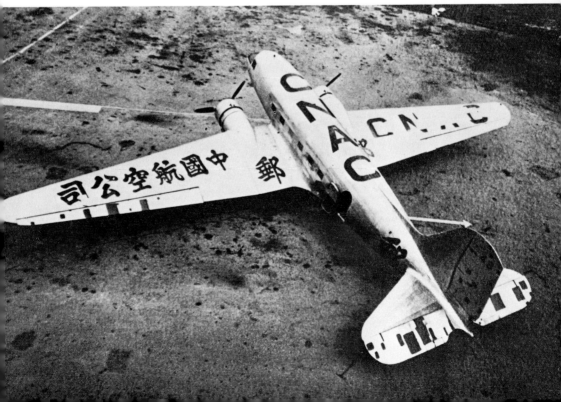

BIG BUSINESS

The once tiny airline had become the world's biggest and most famous. Passengers (left) are shown boarding across one of the sea wings, or sponsons, that had caused so much trouble when the Boeings first entered service in 1939. At war's end landplanes supplanted the romantic flying boats everywhere in the world, and all eleven surviving Boeings were scrapped. The Pan Am Building (above) built astride Park Avenue in the early sixties, was the biggest commercial office building in history, Trippe's personal monument in a way. It will survive longer than any flying boat.

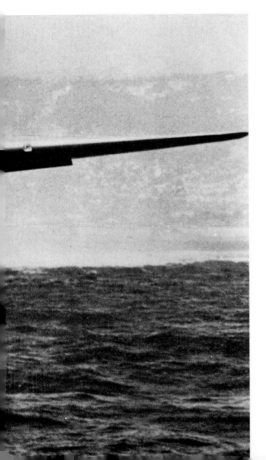

THE NEXT STEP

Having brought the world into the Jet Age with the Boeing 707, having forced through the Jumbo 747 as well, having reigned forty-one years, Trippe abruptly stepped down on May 7, 1968, and was photographed with the successors he had chosen: Harold Gray (left), the new chairman of the board, and Najeeb Halaby, the new president and, ultimately, Gray's successor.

million dollars have been paid in airmail pay to the Pan American. What has that done for Pan American?" O'Mahoney began to cite profit figures, and the bottom line by his reckoning was "a balance of $31,781,668.63 which has been added to the assets of this international giant because a generous people have supported it in its operation."

But immediately Senator John Danaher, Connecticut Democrat, countered with a long speech of his own. "Our nation has recognized the possibilities, and for years has given its support to the airports of Pan American. Only recently have some interests appeared who would now undertake to ask us to subsidize a new line to drive the Pan American out of business."

Senator Gerald Nye, North Dakota Republican, concurred: "For four years the officials of American Export Lines, which now argues that Pan American Airways has a monopoly on air transportation across the Atlantic, have been striving with all their might to accomplish legislation that would give American Export Lines a monopoly—not only a continuation of the monopoly that now enjoys an oceangoing commerce but a monopoly as well in air transportation." Nye saw a dire future if Export got the money. Export would not be content with a single trip per week across the Atlantic. "It will not be contented until it can have it all; and when it has all the air carrying rights between New York and Portugal it will have a 100 percent monopoly on all carrying facilities across the Atlantic."

Next the senators began to argue about money—Trippe's offer to add extra round trips at $9,000 each, as opposed to Export's best price, $21,000. It was a subject that left little room for oratory. It was cut and dried. It seemed to turn a complex issue into a matter of simple arithmetic.

Senator Arthur Vandenberg rose: "Mr. President, I ask for the yeas and nays."

The last three days had been tense ones for Trippe. If the Senate vote backed Export, he could reasonably expect to face federal antitrust prosecution. Only if the Senate voted in his favor was he safe. Then the people of the United States through their elected representatives would seem to have condoned his action and no one would dare prosecute him. Postmaster General Walker would be impotent to act. President Roosevelt would be impotent to act.

In the Senate the votes were counted, and the result was announced. The matter of appropriating $1.2 million for American Export Airlines was defeated 44 votes to 35. Trippe had stood against most of the executive branch of the government of the United States of America and he had won. A difference of only five votes would have settled it the other way.

Export now had no planes, no bases, no crews, no landing rights in

Portugal—and no airmail appropriation money. Nor was antitrust prosecution brought against Trippe. He waited a few weeks, and nothing happened.

Trippe imagined he had disposed of Export forever, but he hadn't. Later he would have to try to defeat it still again.

Part IV
WAR

38
China

War came first to China National Aviation Corporation.

In the summer of 1937 savage fighting broke out between Chinese and Japanese troops in the north. On August 14 Japanese planes bombed Shanghai. Official casualties were 1,740 killed, 1,873 wounded —atrocities committed by bombing from the air were new, and the Shanghai disaster was the most awful the world had yet known. To cart away the bodies and the pieces of bodies, it took, reportedly, three dozen trucks.

CNAC pilot Charles L. Sharp, at the controls of an airliner loaded with Ministry of Finance bank notes, was en route that very day to Shanghai. When he landed at an intermediate stop for fuel, military officers commandeered the plane. They stowed bomb racks and machine guns aboard, and ordered Sharp to fly to Hangchow. CNAC was a commercial airline, Sharp said, and not subject to the orders of Chinese officers. He himself was an American citizen forbidden by American law from taking part in foreign military action. But guns came out—at gunpoint Sharp flew the cargo to Hangchow as ordered.

A Chinese Air Force colonel, Lem Wei-Shing, was installed as managing director of CNAC. He seized most of the remaining planes, fired the Americans and replaced them with Chinese Air Force pilots and crews.

In New York Trippe's reaction was to send for CNAC's William Langhorne Bond, who happened to be on home leave in Virginia at the time. Bond took a train to New York and they met in a restaurant for lunch. Since Bond was vice president, a director and operations manager of

CNAC, Trippe asked what he thought Pan American's response in China should be.

Bond was then forty-four years old, six years older than Trippe. His friends called him Bondy. He had never intended to become an airline executive. At the time of Lindbergh's solo flight in 1927, Bond had been running a gravel plant in Miamitown, Ohio. He was thirty-four and had never been up in an airplane. Excited by the Lindbergh achievement, he had bought a ride with a barnstorming pilot, then had begun to take flying lessons. He had also changed jobs. George Westervelt, a relative by marriage, was general manager of a Curtiss-Wright subsidiary in Baltimore. Bond went to him for work and was hired. But when the stock market crashed, the Baltimore factory was stripped of machinery and abandoned. Bond was allowed to stay on at reduced pay as a kind of caretaker, and he expected to be fired any day.

Westervelt, meanwhile, was ordered to China to try to salvage China Airways Federal, Curtiss-Wright's floundering airline. Once in China one of Westervelt's first acts was to request that Bond be sent out to help him. Bond knew nothing about airline operations or China, but it was a job, it was $500 a month, and it was close to aviation.

He reached Shanghai on March 17, 1931. Morale, he found, was defeatist, and the airline was deteriorating fast. Bond called the Americans together and lectured them about their attitude. They were to begin treating the Chinese decently, he said, and they were also to keep their own personal lives sober and conservative, so that potential passengers would not be afraid to fly with them.

Next Bond began studying the operations of the airline. He saw ways to trim waste and increase efficiency; morale rose and China Airways Federal began to function.

Before Bond had been in China a year, however, the Japanese attacked in the north and Westervelt ordered operations suspended. Bond, who was in Nanking, rejected the order, wiring Westervelt: "Consider it imperative we keep this line running stop its future depends on it stop I'm not being insubordinate but believe your decision was merely for our safety stop we are coming through stop."

No sooner did Westervelt return to New York, leaving Bond in charge, than the military demanded that boxes of machine-gun bullets be flown from Shanghai to Peking. Bond rejected this order also, arguing that the airline enjoyed a nonbelligerent status, that Japanese fighter planes so far had left the airliners alone. Were a few boxes of ammunition more important to China than the continued safe operation of the airline? He held fast, and again won his point.

A government aviation commission ordered him to transfer the company's head office to remote Chengtu—the equivalent, perhaps, of trying to run a Pacific-coast airline from Bangor, Me. Again he did nothing. It ordered him to qualify Chinese pilots in the airliners within six months, and at the same time to write out all purchase orders in Chinese. Bond was both a persuasive man and a stubborn one, and after arguing against these incredible orders, he simply waited them out until they were rescinded.

As resources dwindled, Curtiss-Wright refused to invest additional capital to buy the new aircraft that were so desperately needed. Bond kept the airline running anyway. Chinese dignitaries continued to pressure him to hire this man, fire that one. Always he resisted. In one case the pressure came from K. C. Huang, chairman of the airline's board, who gave Bond a formal order. Bond stood his ground: operational control of the airline rested with the Americans, he said, and he suggested they go to Chiang Kai-shek himself—let the Generalissimo decide. This, Bond guessed, the European-educated Huang could not do, for he did not speak Chinese, and to converse with Chiang Kai-shek through an interpreter meant loss of face. Bond was right. Refusing to push the matter, Huang said he would defer to Bond's judgment.

Bond, who had never been in China before, wended his way day by day through the Chinese labyrinth. Indeed, he seems to have fallen in love with China and its people, and, of course, he was already in love with "his" airline.

When Pan American bought out Curtiss-Wright in 1933 and infused into it new men, new aircraft and new money, this resulted at first only in more setbacks. New contracts with the Chinese had to be negotiated; the two Pan Am S-38 amphibians crashed. Harold Bixby came out from New York and was nominally Bond's superior, but Bixby's job was to sign deals in Macao, Hong Kong and Manila, as well as in China, and he was frequently absent. CNAC was still Bond's airline to run, and now there began to be progress. By the time Bond went on home leave in the summer of 1937 the company had in operation or on order eighteen planes. There were thirty-four pilots and copilots. China being larger in land area than the United States, this may not sound like much, but the twenty major cities of the country had been linked up for the first time in history. Mail moved. Influential Chinese moved. The planes were all obsolescent, but four were twin-engined 160-mph Douglas DC-2's able to carry fourteen passengers—in 1937 only the DC-3 was superior to commercial landplanes. Company morale was excellent. There had been no recent passenger fatalities, and there even was money in the bank, some money, not much—$15,000.

Now in August 1937, even as Japanese armies ravaged China, even as a heavy-handed Chinese Air Force colonel ravaged CNAC, Bond sat in a New York restaurant listening to Juan Trippe. Bond wanted to be in China, not here, but he was a courtly Virginia gentleman, and this thought did not show. Trippe, on the surface, could be courtly too. It was, at first, a very polite lunch. Then Bond realized that Trippe's mind was already made up. Trippe wanted to close down Bond's airline and to fly as many planes as possible to safety in Manila. He wanted to freeze whatever CNAC funds could be frozen, to save what could be saved until the war was over.

Bond, marshaling his arguments carefully, replied that until the war had developed further and more was known, he thought they should hang on in China and continue operations as normally as would prove consistent with safety. The Chinese would fight it out for a long time, possibly years, Bond said.

Trippe scoffed at this notion. Years? Impossible. He shook his head.

Bond replied stubbornly, "The Chinese desperately need our service now. If we do not help now, Pan Am's future in China will be seriously injured, possibly finished."

The two men argued. Both were extremely polite but each defended his position with more and more stubbornness. Though the luncheon continued, neither man saw what he was eating. After six years Bond thought he knew China, and he tried to explain China to Trippe, who would not listen. Trippe knew the airline business better than Bond.

The only important thing to Bond was to get back to China as soon as possible, and he finally said so.

Again Trippe shook his head. There was no need for Bond to go back there. Bixby was on the scene and could close CNAC down well enough by himself.

"I must go back," said Bond.

"No," said Trippe, who had a new and better job in mind for Bond. The company was opening a line to New Zealand very soon, and he was putting Bond in charge and sending him there. The luncheon broke up, and the two men walked silently through the streets. Trippe was going back to his desk and Bond went with him. When they stepped off the elevator on the Pan Am floor, Trippe strode into his own office without further comment. Stubbornly Bond followed him in.

"Mr. Trippe," Bond said, "I would like to go to New Zealand, where I can have my wife and family, but my job is in China and I must go back."

Trippe was staring down at something on his desk. He never looked up. "Go on, go on," he said with a wave of his hand.

Unsure of what he meant, Bond walked out and took the next flight out of New York to San Francisco, and from there boarded a Clipper to Hong Kong. The Martin flying boat made the usual overnight stops: Honolulu, Midway, Wake, Guam, Manila, Hong Kong. The trip took eight days, and Bond was amazed, as always, to have traveled so far so fast. Three or four years previously the same trip would have taken over a month. Chief pilot Allison was waiting at the pier as Bond came off the flying boat in Hong Kong. Allison said that the Chinese Air Force had the airplanes. To Bond this was the worst news yet. CNAC no longer existed, and his Virginia courtliness at last broke down. Angrily Bond told Allison that he should have got the planes, and as much equipment as possible, out to Hong Kong; it was his fault if the planes were lost.

The next day Bixby and all of the American pilots and crews from Shanghai arrived in Hong Kong by boat. CNAC was finished, said Bixby. It wasn't finished, said Bond, it could be saved. "How?" demanded Bixby. Bond answered that he did not know, but that he had to make the try. As with Yerex in Central America, as with Trippe himself in New York, something incredible had happened to Bond. His airline had become himself—the two were indistinguishable one from the other. He had become totally dependent on CNAC and was perhaps not capable of living without it. For two days Bixby and Bond argued. Bond wanted to go to Hankow, where Air Force Colonel Lem now presided over CNAC. That was the place to try to get the airline back. He would figure out what to do when he got there.

Bixby threw up his hands. "Oppose any and all types of military flying," he advised Bond, "and—and keep yourself in the clear."

With that the two men flew off in opposite directions. Bixby went to Manila, where the transpacific telephone line ended, to try to place the CNAC pilots elsewhere in the Pan American system. Chilie Vaughn began flying a Sikorsky S-42 on the Manila–Hong Kong leg of the transpacific route; Sharp and Hugh Woods were placed with Panagra. That is, even as Bond reached Hankow, the essence of his airline—its pilots— evaporated behind his back.

Bond's first interview with Colonel Lem was fruitless. CNAC was now a military transport system, Lem said, but Bond was certainly welcome to stay on as operations manager. This offer Bond refused. The two men bowed politely to each other and parted.

Bond decided that, for a while, he would do nothing at all. He would simply wait. The Chinese Air Force, he was certain, would be unable to run the airline. In a month or so Lem would see this. All of China would see it. Once operations had broken down, the government would recognize that CNAC had been infinitely more valuable to China as a nonmilitary, commercial airline with active American participation.

For a time the airline staggered on. CNAC's supervisory personnel had all been American, and their half-trained Chinese subordinates attempted to run departments. Chinese copilots now served as captains. Lem himself was no airline executive. Very soon the planes ceased to run on time. Often they did not run at all.

Now Bond sought an audience with Dr. H. H. Kung, prime minister of China. CNAC was being ruined by the military, Bond told him. China needed the Americans back. Dr. Kung was unresponsive, and the interview got nowhere. Leaving him, Bond went to the minister of communications—who would not see him. He did see the vice minister, who was even colder than Dr. Kung. Bond went to Shanghai, where he hoped to talk to T.V. Soong, who was probably the second most powerful man in China. Soong, formerly minister of finance, was chairman of the Bank of China. Educated at Vanderbilt, Columbia and Harvard, he was also head of the so-called Soong dynasty. The oldest of his three sisters had been the wife of the late Sun Yat-sen, the father of modern China. The other two were married to Prime Minister Kung and to Generalissimo Chiang Kai-shek.

M. Y. Tong, Soong's right-hand man, was Bond's closest Chinese friend. Often they had lunched together, played tennis and deck tennis together.

In Shanghai Bond asked Tong for an audience with Soong, but Tong refused, saying that Soong had too many burdens and China was at war. Furthermore, Soong had already made it clear that he did not want to help Pan American again. Bond insisted that he was asking for help not for Pan Am but for CNAC, which was China's airline, and which was urgently needed by China. "I'm not asking for much," Bond pleaded. "Just get Colonel Lem and the Air Force out of CNAC and keep them out. Install a Chinese civilian as managing director. Let the Americans run the operation. If they do not do a good job, put the Americans out again. If they do a good job but China is still angry at the end of the war, put the Americans out then."

Bond brought forth his final argument. Pan Am was an important company and Trippe was an important man. Trippe was on a presidential advisory board, and Pan Am—Trippe—was the best connection China had with the American government apart from the embassy itself. "Don't lose this contact," Bond pleaded.

For a moment Tong said nothing. The two old friends looked at each other. Then Tong asked Bond to put his thoughts in a memo Tong would give to Soong.

Bond's memo was ready the next morning. He had made two copies. The original he gave to Tong to give to Soong. The copy, after much thought, he sent to Soong's sister Madame Chiang Kai-shek. There seemed nothing more Bond could do, and he sat down to wait for whatever might happen.

When nothing happened, Bond went to Nanking and sought an audience with W. H. Donald, an Australian who was financial adviser to Chiang Kai-shek, and who was possibly the most important foreigner in China. Nanking was under tremendous pressure. The city was being bombed every day and the Japanese army was at its gates. Bond asked Donald if Madame Chiang had received Bond's memo. Yes, Donald answered, and showed it to Bond—Madame Chiang had given it to him for study.

So Bond made the same appeal to Donald, adding that CNAC would do no military flying and CNAC itself would be the sole judge of what was military. "If we can get that, the Americans will come back," Bond promised. Donald said that he would see what could be done.

Escaping from Nanking on one of the last riverboats before the city fell, Bond made his way to Hankow to meet Bixby. But Hankow was threatened also, and Bixby made reservations for them both to escape from China. They would have to fly to Chungking and Chengtu, continuing from there by railroad to Hanoi. But Bond refused to go. He would stay on in China, he said. Bixby shook his head sadly, and flew out alone.

In Hankow Bond waited until at last Donald contacted him. Bond was to submit the names of three Chinese who would be acceptable to him as managing director of CNAC.

A few days later the military was summarily ejected from CNAC, and one of Bond's choices, CNAC's former business manager P. Y. Wong, was appointed by the government to replace Colonel Lem. CNAC was again Bond's airline to run if he could. He made his way to Hong Kong, then flew to Manila to tell Bixby.

Bixby was pleased, but his face soon clouded over. Trippe, he knew, did not want Pan American involved in a Sino-Japanese war. He wanted CNAC closed down.

"Our next hurdle," Bixby told Bond, "is J.T.T. He isn't going to like it." And he placed a telephone call to New York.

Bond had a possible solution. "Tell him," he said, "that I am resigning from Pan Am and going to work for CNAC."

When the transpacific call came through, Bixby confronted Trippe with Bond's decision. To remove all risk of embarrassment to Pan Am, Bond would resign. He would run CNAC—would safeguard Pan American's investment—for as long as China could hold out.

Trippe's first reaction was to demand a written resignation from Bond. Whatever happened, Pan American must not seem tied to CNAC. Trippe would send a written acceptance of this resignation.

Next Bond heard Bixby say, "Bondy has made one request and I am making it a condition. He wants Pan American to continue his company life insurance at ten thousand dollars, as it will be impossible for him to get any other."

In New York, ten thousand miles away, Trippe agreed to this condition.

Bixby said, "One thing more, which Bondy has not requested, but again I am making it a condition. Anything that Pan Am does by way of incentive pay or stock-purchase plans for its executives, Bondy will be included, just as if he were still on the payroll."

Trippe agreed to this too, and the phone call ended.

Bond flew back to China. Within four months he had coaxed back many of the pilots and CNAC was in operation again. The airline's routes kept changing as the Japanese Army swallowed up vast chunks of terrain. Peking, Shanghai, Hangchow all fell and were dropped as stations. Soon, except for Hong Kong, the Japanese held every seaport. Chiang Kai-shek moved the seat of government to Chungking, about nine hundred miles inland, and CNAC began to fly there from Hong Kong via Canton, and this service was the government's last link with the outside world. Planes now were always filled as diplomats and journalists shuttled in and out, as Chinese dignitaries flew to the United States to beg for aid. Cargo holds were full too: mail, dispatches, newspapers, medicines—vital commodities to a nation at war.

For CNAC the price was high and would go higher. Hugh Woods, piloting a DC-2 named *Kweilin* bound for Chungking with a full load of fourteen passengers aboard, was at six thousand feet, only a few minutes out of Hong Kong, when he sighted a patrol of Japanese pursuit planes. He had noted such patrols before—all the pilots had—but there had been no attacks. These planes, too, flew away, and Woods could not see them any more. Suddenly they were not only back but swooping down on him. Machine-gun bullets smashed through into the cockpit. Woods began spiraling downwards as tightly as he could. Bullets shattered the instrument panel. Flat paddy fields surrounded by dikes rose up to meet him, and a short distance off was a river. Woods shut down both engines and bellied in on the river. Machine-gun bullets were still striking the plane. Woods shouted to his two crewmen to get the passengers out. Caught by the current, the plane was being swept down the middle of the river. There was an emergency hatch over Woods's head and he squirmed through it and into the river. The Japanese planes continued their attack, spraying machine-gun bullets at the plane and at Woods. Woods was trying to swim to shore against the five-knot current. Each time the planes returned he dived underwater. He reached shore exhausted, and began to vomit. It was close to an hour, he said, before he could stand erect. The half-submerged plane, history's first unarmed airliner shot down by hostile fighter planes, was floating downstream. Inside it nine people were dead from bullet wounds, and five others died in the aftermath. There were three survivors, including Woods.

The U.S. State Department protested to Japan, which answered that the aircraft in question was Chinese and, therefore, none of the State Department's business.

Bond dragged the river for the *Kweilin,* found it, lifted it out and ordered it repaired, for CNAC could not afford the loss of a single plane. From then on there were no more daylight flights into or out of Hong Kong. Hong Kong was served only at night or in bad weather—and the other cities as well; this procedure, added to the existing hazards, made flying in China as dangerous as any men had ever done. Weather reports were no longer available, and Japanese technicians blocked navigation by jamming the radio beams. There was nothing to navigate by at all. In a blacked-out country there were not even any lighted cities on the ground. Every flight became an exploit, and certain of them were vital to China: for instance, when Japanese troops encircled Hankow, trapping Chiang Kai-shek and other high-ranking government officials in the city, Sharp, flying a DC-2, got them out.

But too many other flights ended in tragedy. A Ford trimotor crashed into a mountain near Kian. A DC-2 struck another in southern Hunan. Walter Kent, a thirty-two-year-old redheaded pilot from Louisiana, took off from Chungking for Hong Kong in the reconditioned *Kweilin*. His wife and three-year-old son were in Hong Kong to be evacuated to the United States the following day, and he wanted to say good-bye. But the *Kweilin* was an unlucky aircraft. Again it was caught by Japanese fighters. Kent dived for the ground to escape them, landing on a small emergency field near Changyi. He was taxiing rapidly into the safety of the trees as the Japanese began their strafing runs. On the first pass a 20-millimeter shell caught Kent in the back. He died instantly. The *Kweilin* was on fire. Crew and passengers—thirteen people in all—sprang from the blazing plane and ran for the trees. Eight were killed and two wounded by the strafing planes.

This time even Bond's great faith was shaken. "I don't know what the answer to all of this is," he wrote chief pilot Allison. "I wish there was some way I could get out of this. I feel I have done my part. I have a wife and child and if you saw Kitsi on her way home she probably told you we're expecting another. That is, if her constant worry about me out here doesn't cause a mishap. Well, it is no use to worry about it. If I don't like my job I can quit and if I haven't guts enough to quit I had better stop talking about it."

Pilot Woods, who had survived the first Japanese air attack on CNAC, now was caught by fighter planes a second time. He managed to land and to evacuate crew and passengers, and then he could only watch as the Japanese planes savagely attacked the empty airliner on the ground. They shot it full of holes and blew off its right wing.

Bond, desperate for aircraft, again moved to salvage the ruined plane. Though there was no spare DC-3 wing in all of China, Hong Kong did have an extra wing for a DC-2. Would a DC-3 fly with a DC-2 wing on one side? Bond didn't know. No one knew. Was it possible to airlift such a wing lashed to the fuselage of another plane into an emergency landing field 860 miles away? Pilot Harold Sweet volunteered to make the try, and the flight began. Sweet, taking off with two wings outstretched and a third folded back against his side, was apprehensive. What would be the aerodynamic effect of the third wing? To his surprise, the effect was negligible, though the flight was slower, of course, and he spent some six hours in the air, all of it watching out for Japanese patrols. When he landed, the spare DC-2 wing was attached to the stub of the DC-3 wing, after which Woods and Sweet walked around the odd-looking plane, asking each other aerodynamic questions that could not be answered on the ground. Would this thing fly?

Woods took off and flew the DC-2 1/2 back to Hong Kong. The only abnormality was having to use full aileron tab setting because of the unbalanced lift between the two wings. His safe arrival at Hong Kong was a signal for great joy, partly because the plane had been saved, partly because his achievement seemed a tribute to man's ingenuity and to man's tenacity, even in the face of man's madness.

The Japanese armies, meanwhile, conquered more and more cities, more and more terrain. But they failed to kill China, and they failed to kill CNAC. The indomitable Bond was still there. His airline was still in place. Every day his planes still flew.

39

"Delousing" SCADTA

At the beginning of 1939, as World War II moved inexorably closer, a special joint planning commission set up by the War Department decided where and how the attack on the United States would come. Their findings, as submitted on April 21 to Secretary of War Henry Stimson, focused on South America and on the Panama Canal. In 1939 the Panama Canal was considered America's most sacred, most vital possession, for it permitted the Navy's battleships to change oceans at will; to threaten the canal was to threaten the American way of life. After the canal was neutralized—either by sabotage or sneak attack—German and Italian troops massed in Africa would be ferried across to Brazil via the Dakar–Natal bulge, a distance of only about nineteen hundred miles, with the German Navy securing the flanks and beachheads. The African bulge, the military planners pointed out, was defended only by men with spears, and the Brazilian bulge was defended only by the Brazilian "Army"—a few thousand men. Once Brazilian bases were secured, three thousand bombers would be ferried across, and the German/Italian forces would proceed north to the Caribbean, and then island by island toward Washington.

To this dire scenario the War Department planners attached an additional sobering note: political and economic penetration of South America had already begun. There were at this time about two million first- and second-generation Germans in South America, and an even larger number of first- and second-generation Italians—as opposed to only twenty-three thousand Americans. The Germans and Italians had for the most part acquired local citizenship, had learned the local language and ran local businesses—as opposed to the Americans who ran branch offices of hated American corporations. In addition, eight Axis-owned or Axis-influenced airlines operated in South America—Condor in Brazil, Lufthansa in Peru, SEDTA in Ecuador, LATI in Brazil, LAB in Bolivia, Varig in Brazil, Corporación Sudamericana in Argentina and SCADTA in Colombia; these airlines flew a total of more than sixteen thousand route miles. As for the Colombian airline, SCADTA, its routes took it within two hours' flying time of the Panama Canal, and its pilots and management were not only German but in some cases Luftwaffe-trained. It seemed, therefore, an immediate and extremely serious treat to U.S. security.

What the military planners did not know, at least not at first, was that SCADTA was secretly owned by Pan American. In 1931 Trippe had concluded a deal with SCADTA's principal owner and chief executive, Peter Paul von Bauer, an Austrian national. Von Bauer was still the airline's chief executive, and he still voted Pan American's stock—ostensibly in his own name—under instructions from Trippe. That American ownership of SCADTA had remained clandestine all this time testified principally to just how close-mouthed Trippe could be. But his genius for secrecy was about to prove costly.

The military planners returned their focus to the Brazilian bulge. A base ought to be built at Natal from which to bomb the invasion fleet. It would slow the enemy down and it would have to be seized before any substantial troop landings could take place.

But Natal in 1939 was no easy place to get to, and so the planners decided that intermediate bases would be essential in order to move men, planes and equipment down there. In August 1939 Admiral Harold R. Stark, chief of naval operations, asked the State Department to contact various Latin American republics about the possibility of implanting American bases on their sovereign territory for the purpose of defending the Caribbean and the canal; toward the end of summer the State Department actually sent men out to begin such negotiations.

On September 1 the Germans invaded Poland and World War II began. The War Plans Division now began to push for the development of two separate air routes to the Brazilian bulge. These men were looking at their globes exactly as Trippe had once done. Their principal route would proceed from Miami directly south to Cuba and from there to Puerto Rico, Martinique, Trinidad and Dutch Guiana, and then around the northeast shoulder of Brazil to Natal. The secondary route would proceed from Texas down through Mexico, Central America and across Panama to Colombia, intercepting the primary route at Trinidad, swinging east there along the Venezuelan and Brazilian coasts to the bulge. In November 1939 Delos Emmons, commanding general of General Headquarters Air Force, even led an exploratory flight of bombers to Natal. Emmons's report made clear that by using Pan American's existing airfields the Army could fly medium and heavy bombers, but not smaller aircraft, to the bulge. A series of intermediary air bases would have to be built. The generals wanted to take over Pan American's bases, and also build new ones. But who was to build these bases?

This was not a question generals could answer, and for the time being the politicians refused to address it. The so-called phony war now existed in Europe. For almost a year the opposing armies faced each other across their guns; day after day neither side attacked and scarcely a shot was fired.

The War Plans Division continued to construct mental air bases by the score along the perimeters of countries which the United States did not own and which were not at war. But not a yard of runway was laid. The only cry of alarm even dimly perceived by Washington politicians was that note about the German airline in Colombia, SCADTA, whose routes reached perilously close to the Panama Canal. A chain of bases did not yet interest the politicians, but something would have to be done about SCADTA.

Colombia in 1939 was a vast and mostly empty country. It stood at the northern end of the Andes chain, which, shortly after crossing the Colombian border, divided into three separate ridges all pointing northward like the tines of a fork. The three tines divided the country into four zones —which was why SCADTA had been so successful there. Until the advent of airplanes—SCADTA's airplanes—in 1919, there had been no way to cross the country from one side to the other at all, for the three ridges towered as high as eighteen thousand feet. The principal inland cities, Bogotá, Cali and Medellín had been mostly inaccessible to one another, for they were tucked into the valleys between the tines, and they were inaccessible to the coastal cities as well, for all were at substantial altitudes—Bogotá, the capital, was at 8,400 feet. To get up there from Barranquilla on the north coast had been virtually impossible during some seasons of the year, and at the best of times had required up to two weeks' travel by launch up the tumultuous Magdalena River—with plenty of portages around rapids. That is, Colombia had been made-to-order terrain even for the rickety aircraft of 1919. Still, the adventurous young Germans who founded SCADTA had not prospered until Von Bauer joined them in 1922. It was Von Bauer who had built the airline up to a point of such stability and profitability that he was able in 1931 to sell Trippe just under 85 percent of its stock for over $1.1 million.

Supposedly, it was Von Bauer who demanded that this deal be kept secret, because he was a national hero in Colombia, he intended to go on living there, and he even intended to go on running "his" airline as before. His position in Colombia, he is supposed to have said, would be totally undermined if word got out that he had sold the nation's prize airline to the hated gringos.

Secrecy, as always, was congenial to Trippe, and he had agreed to Von Bauer's terms. Pan American had forced him to buy only American aircraft, had prevented him from expanding outside of Colombia, but had otherwise left him alone. SCADTA had turned into one of Trippe's most brilliant decisions. Every year since its acquisition it had earned a profit. It had been supervised by Balluder in Mexico City, and had required little or no attention from Trippe. The SCADTA problem having been solved, he had gone on to other matters.

Von Bauer had gone on hiring German pilots, German executives. The airline's working language continued to be not Spanish but German.

Trippe always reminded people later—after the hysteria started in 1939—that he had informed the State Department from the beginning that Pan American owned SCADTA. The Secretary of State in 1931 had been Frank B. Kellogg; Von Bauer later stated that Kellogg was "one of the small number of persons who knew." The then Assistant Secretary of State, Francis White, testified in 1940 that he had been told also. Trippe often claimed that he had even informed U.S. Post Office officials, but a 1931 letter to the Postmaster General giving full disclosure of the SCADTA acquisition was apparently never sent, for the original and carbon, stapled together, were found in Trippe's files many years later. As for Pan American stockholders, they were informed in the 1931 annual report only that "your company in March acquired a substantial interest in SCADTA." In Colombia itself no one, apparently, had knowledge of the secret deal, and all Colombians, from peons to president, still regarded SCADTA as the national airline—and even, given the country's geography, as a national treasure.

But a secret of such magnitude could not be kept forever. In Washington only Pan American's "substantial interest" in SCADTA was known, but in 1939, when the State Department became interested and began to ask pointed questions (What did "substantial" mean?), the secret could no longer be kept at all. With war looming, Trippe was obliged to tell his questioners what they wished to know. Yes, for all practical purposes Pan American owned SCADTA outright.

Certain State Department officials appear to have received this news —that Pan American for eight years had allowed Germans to fly that close to the Panama Canal—with outrage, one of them being Spruille Braden, the new American ambassador to Colombia. Braden was a bull-like man with a bullhorn of a voice that could be heard all the way to Washington. It was he who turned SCADTA into a national issue.

Braden, five years older than Trippe, was from Elkhorn, Mont., the son of the founder of the Braden Copper Company. Trained as a mining engineer, he had taken his father's fortune into the copper mines in the

Andes and had increased it. At thirty-nine, having earned a second fortune of his own, he had entered the diplomatic service in Chile, and now, five years later, he was ambassador to Colombia. He was a big, energetic man with a heavy face and a double chin. At Yale he had played water polo and football, and at forty-five he still swam and played handball as he tried, but failed, to stay in shape. He collected antique handwrought South American silver and rare books. He had a Chilean wife and six children. He was considered, and considered himself, a "crusading Democratic ambassador." It was written of him, and certainly this seemed to be his own belief, that in Colombia he stood alone against Nazi activities there, that he alone was charged with short-circuiting Nazi designs on the Panama Canal through SCADTA.

Braden had arrived in Colombia in 1938, only the year before. He had been there long enough to realize that SCADTA's pilots all spoke German, and only long enough to study the country's geography and to people it with goblins. Tucked into those three ridges of mountains, he saw, were innumerable secluded valleys. Farther to the south stretched a vast, virtually uninhabited plateau. For all anyone knew, the SCADTA pilots had already scraped out a runway in there somewhere, had constructed bombs or smuggled in bombs. A sneak attack by SCADTA planes and pilots operating off one or another of these hidden runways could wipe out the Panama Canal with a single stroke.

In 1939, two years in advance of the Japanese sneak attack on Pearl Harbor, this notion may have sounded far-fetched even to Braden. He needed an ally, and he soon found one—General David Stone, commandant of the Canal Zone. Braden and Stone began flooding Washington —State Department and War Department both—with messages. They wanted the Germans removed from Colombia at once, by armed force if necessary.

Learning that SCADTA was actually owned by Pan American, Braden was better able to focus his demands. It was Pan Am's job, he charged, to rid the hemisphere of the Nazi threat he had brought to light. When nothing immediately happened, he accused the company and Trippe of being Nazi sympathizers and of coddling the enemy. He fell just short of accusing them publicly of treason.

"Bull in a china shop," Trippe snorted.

Nonetheless, the pressure to act was there and Braden's charges were so serious that Trippe did not want them repeated. Pan American would have to do something, but what? The company could not simply march into Colombia, fire everybody and take over.

For one thing, most of the Germans, including the recently naturalized Von Bauer, were also Colombians, and were protected by Colombian law. For another, no one in Colombia even knew Pan American owned SCADTA. To take over might enrage the country. Because of the

bizarre Colombian geography, SCADTA was perhaps more vital to Colombia than any other airline to any other country. It was more than vital
—it was also popular. Its pilots constituted the Air Force reserve. Some
of its officers were national heroes, and one, Colonel Herbert Boy, had
had a town named after him. Von Bauer himself held the Grand Cross
of the Order of Boyaca, Colombia's most exalted distinction. A statue of
Von Krohm, a SCADTA pioneer, stood in a public square.

Braden's pressure ought to have been responded to in a planned,
measured way, but Trippe was not in control of Pan American that year
—Whitney was. And so piecemeal steps were taken that satisfied no one.

The first job, obviously, was to inform President Eduardo Santos of
Colombia that SCADTA didn't own SCADTA, that Pan American did.
David Grant, a lawyer who had negotiated many of the company's Latin
American contracts, and who was listed on the company's masthead as
foreign counsel, was sent to Bogotá to do this.

On the scheduled day Grant chanced to meet Colonel Boy in a Bogotá
restaurant. Boy, a German citizen who was also a colonel in the Colombian Air Force, was SCADTA's Bogotá representative. The two old
friends lunched together. When Grant remarked that he had an appointment with the president later, Boy replied that he did too.

They shared a taxi to the presidential palace, where President Santos
greeted them both in the presidential anteroom. He was about to take
Boy first when Grant spoke up, saying he had an important disclosure to
make which admitted of no delay. The president, unsuspecting, ushered
Grant into his office.

In the anteroom Boy waited. As Grant and Santos came out, Boy rose
expectantly to his feet. Santos looked stunned. "SCADTA is owned by
Pan American," he mumbled.

The two men stared at each other. "Tell Von Bauer," muttered Santos to Boy, "that I consider his naturalization a scrap of paper."

Boy himself resigned from SCADTA in protest.

For a time Pan American took no further steps. Ambassador Braden
read this as foot-dragging, and he began to meet with President Santos.
He wanted all the Germans fired from SCADTA. Santos refused—and
continued to refuse. SCADTA employed about 150 Germans out of a
total force of some 800. These people had done no wrong, Santos kept
saying, and to release them would be to disrupt the country's transportation system. There was no way to do it under Colombian law.

It was at this point that war broke out in Europe. Under steadily
increasing pressure from Washington, Whitney sent Rihl to Colombia to
see what, if anything, could be done about the Germans. Santos told Rihl
exactly what he had so often told Braden: the republic of Colombia owed
much to SCADTA, and he would not allow Pan Am to throw its German
employees out of work. When Rihl reported this conversation to Braden,

the ambassador promised to call on the president yet again. Rihl and Braden then drew up a program—it later became known as Plan A—whereby native Colombians and Americans would be placed in SCADTA in key technical positions ostensibly as observers.

Throughout the winter of 1939-40 Colombian newspapers continued to play down the German threat and to eulogize SCADTA as a Colombian institution. The Colombian minister of war told Von Bauer: "The Government has never believed that SCADTA is carrying on, or may in future carry on, activities which might constitute a menace to the so called 'Good Neighbor' policy." As late as January 1940 President Santos wrote that he hoped SCADTA would hold on to "the German technical element which, by its ties in Colombia, its competence and experience, constitutes a real guarantee for the company."

But by May Pan American had twenty-two technical men in Colombia keeping a vigil over suspect persons. The full contingent of German employees was still on hand also.

One of the Pan Am technical men was Spanish-speaking Bill Del Valle. Earlier that year Del Valle, an engineer serving as Pan American's representative to the Boeing factory in Seattle, had received a telephone call summoning him to New York. When he got there he was told to go back home to Seattle, pack and proceed from Seattle to Colombia by circuitous, non–Pan American channels. He was to keep his movements absolutely secret, even from his wife. When he got to Barranquilla, he was to check into the Del Prado Hotel, where further instructions would be waiting.

On January 20 Del Valle left Seattle, and made his way successively to Mexico City, to Guatemala, and to Cristóbal in Panama, where he acquired a visa for Colombia. On January 31 he checked into the Del Prado Hotel in Barranquilla, and there tore open an envelope containing the instructions that awaited him. They were brief, and they were also rather surprising. He was to keep to himself. He was to make no contact with Pan American people until he received further instructions. These, when they came, were also surprising. He was to go to Bogotá, check into the Victoria Hotel, and then proceed to the American embassy for a meeting with the ambassador.

This meeting took place in Braden's office. Present also were Rihl, John Steele and Hank Shea from Pan American. The setting was highly dramatic. Although it was early afternoon, Braden had all his drapes drawn. Illumination came from candles burning on the grand piano in the corner.

Braden spoke with great intensity. The Germans were planning to blow up the Panama Canal, he said, and the problem was to prevent this from happening, while at the same time preparing for the permanent "delousing" of SCADTA. In the guttering candlelight Del Valle glanced around at all the other faces. He was trying to figure out who this ambassador was and what the rest of them were doing here.

Del Valle's own function was made clear to him. He was about to be appointed assistant superintendent of maintenance and he would go on the SCADTA payroll. He would continue to live in the Del Prado Hotel in Barranquilla. He would work for the Germans by day and for the Americans by night.

He began to imagine himself a rather important spy. He would start by making an inspection trip of the entire SCADTA system. His cover story was that he was familiarizing himself with his new job; but his real purpose was to determine what the Germans were doing and which ones were essential to the smooth functioning of the airline.

Del Valle rode out over the line with Wilhelm Schnurbusch, SCADTA's chief engineer. Schnurbusch had received Del Valle with great cordiality, remarking only that his men had been doing a good job and he didn't see what this was all about. Del Valle gave a vague answer, kept his eyes open, and three days later was back in Barranquilla writing out his first report. Later he made a second inspection trip and still found no evidence of Nazis or Nazi plots. From then on he occupied an office at the seaplane base, did maintenance work and waited, though he didn't know what for.

In New York, meanwhile, Trippe, who was now back in full control, was attempting with great difficulty to resist pressure from the War and State departments to invade Colombia, fire all the Germans and take over all of SCADTA at once. Trippe wanted to tread softly, and he gave his reasons, but he was scarcely being listened to.

There were legal, commercial and political problems, and Trippe alone seems to have thought all of them out. Before Pan American could take outright control of SCADTA, there ought to be a directors' meeting. It ought to include the 15 percent minority stockholders, who were mostly Colombians. Pan Am's ownership of SCADTA was represented by share certificates with no one's name on them deposited in a lockbox at the National City Bank. Voting rights were tied to these certificates. They ought to be physically brought from New York to Colombia and displayed there. A takeover of this magnitude was sure to arouse substantial opposition, and only strict legality could minimize it.

The commercial problems were even more complex. Any abrupt takeover risked bankrupting SCADTA—with the attendant loss of Pan American's 85 percent investment—because there were not enough American pilots and technical men trained and on the scene to run the airline. It might simply cease to exist. In addition, any takeover was going to be costly. Under Colombian law it would be necessary to pay off the contract of each man fired, and to pay him in addition a *cesantía*—a month's pay for each year worked. German pilots and their families would have to be repatriated to Germany. American replacements would have to be flown in on expensive contracts. They would have to be paid approximately triple what German pilots earned.

The political problems were also substantial. Americans were disliked, even hated, in Colombia, largely because of their conduct at the beginning of the century. In order to win "freedom" for the northernmost Colombian province, the Americans had fomented a trumped-up revolution there. Once the "revolution" was successful, the Americans had formed the province into a republic known as Panama, had made their deal with the new nation and had cut their canal through it. All this had not been forgotten in Colombia. An abrupt takeover of SCADTA now might seem distressingly similar. An angry government might revoke SCADTA's operating concessions, or even expropriate it. An aroused citizenry might march on the airfields; the result could be violence, the wholesale destruction of SCADTA's properties and planes, and perhaps loss of life.

Trippe kept trying in meetings to calm the heavy voices. He kept saying, "We are looking for results, not a fight." Whatever was done had to be worked out carefully in advance, and no one was ready with a plan but himself.

What he had conceived—the eventual Plan B—was complex. It brought together a great many disparate elements, and its success or failure depended on faultless timing and absolute secrecy. Trippe thought it would work because it seemed to him legally, politically and commercially sound, as well as strategically sound. If all went well there would be no time for opposition to form. There would be no time for any of its targets even to react.

The first part of the plan was to create in Colombian aviation circles a climate as favorable to Pan American as possible. To this end Trippe began to send in new DC-3's, the best and fastest commercial airliners then flying, to replace obsolescent units of the SCADTA fleet. In a few weeks SCADTA service was dramatically upgraded—courtesy of Pan American.

The second part was to send Steele scouring the United States for former airline personnel who happened to be at large and were willing to sign contracts to go to Colombia. By mid-May Steele had rounded up a great number and brought them to New York, where they waited, muttering among themselves, "What's it all about?"

The third part began on the morning of May 14, 1940, when Trippe, Rihl and Tom Morgan, who still served as chairman of the Pan American executive committee, met in New York with Braden and Thomas Burke, chief of the Division of Inter-American Communications of the Department of State. Trippe told Burke and Braden that "Plan B" existed and was ready to go, and that it provided for the "simultaneous separation" from SCADTA of 14 pilots, 12 flight mechanics/radio operators, 42 mechanics, 10 airport managers and 7 radiomen—85 Germans in all. Without giving any details at all, Trippe stated that Plan B could be implemented within thirty days. He said he had drawn it up "on the assumption that current developments in Europe might require, in the opinion of the United States Government officials concerned, a more far-reaching program than that covered by Plan A, which is currently being carried out." But again Trippe argued for caution. Not only did he demand orders from Washington before putting Plan B into effect, but he also made it clear that he would not proceed unless President Santos in Colombia concurred.

Braden asserted that Santos would interpose no objection. What he meant was that the climate—in Colombia and in the world—had changed. World War II had begun, Germany was the enemy, and Santos, after two years of pressure from Washington, was now thoroughly cowed. Braden would see to Santos; he hoped there would be no delay in Pan American's proceeding with Plan B.

Trippe now brought up still another delicate subject: money. To remove the Germans from SCADTA was going to cost about $250,000. Such an action was not commercially justifiable. It would seriously affect SCADTA's financial position, and even though Pan American controlled SCADTA, there was an appreciable Colombian minority whose interests had to be protected. It was these interests that Trippe was defending now. Who was going to pay the $250,000?

The men around the table fenced carefully. Burke stated that the State Department would submit a confidential letter to the CAB, setting forth these expenses incurred "in the interest of the national defense of the United States"; the CAB would then give consideration to these costs the next time a Pan American subsidy rate was decided.

That meeting was followed by a regular meeting of the Pan Am executive committee. Again Trippe spoke of money. He would not move until the executive committee voted him the $250,000. Of course, it quickly did so.

When the executive committee met again ten days later, Trippe stated that the president of Colombia had given his permission for Plan B, and that full approval had also been granted by the United States Department of State. Plan B was therefore to proceed.

The phone call from New York to Del Valle in Colombia came on a Saturday in late May: Del Valle was to proceed to New York as quickly as possible. A room was being held for him in the Lexington Hotel. He flew all day and all night, and on Sunday morning at the Chrysler Building he began interviewing the people John Steele had rounded up. He personally hired about thirty-five of them. Only three spoke Spanish.

The problem now became to smuggle these people into Colombia without the SCADTA Germans suspecting they were there, for secrecy must be maintained to the very last instant if Plan B was to work. But Trippe had thought out in advance even this detail. A Boeing Stratoliner, the world's first four-engined pressurized landplane, had just been delivered; two more were to follow. When it took off for Colombia on June 3, supposedly on a gala introductory flight and tour of South American capitals, it carried all the pilots and technicians that Del Valle and others had hired. The plane landed at Barranquilla first, and then at Bogotá, and during the civic celebrations that ensued, pilots and technicians sneaked away from the airports and were hidden in the various hotels.

George Rihl was in Colombia and in charge. Secretaries were hired and put behind desks in hotel rooms, where they began to type out letters of dismissal in Spanish for eighty-five German employees of SCADTA. At two o'clock in the afternoon of June 12 all was ready and Rihl sent out word by code. At 5:00 P.M. that day Plan B was to go into operation simultaneously at every SCADTA airport and office in the country.

Del Valle contacted the German technicians who worked directly for him. He ordered all to report to his office at the Barranquilla seaplane base for a late-afternoon maintenance meeting. When the men had gathered, Del Valle even allowed technical discussion to start, but at the stroke of five he stood up. He was not at ease with what he was about to do, and so began to make a speech. This was war, he said. He was not personally responsible for any of this—and he began handing around the letters of dismissal and the severance paychecks. The assembled Germans were stunned. There were tears in the eyes of many among them, and several began protesting that they were Colombians, this was their country, they had done nothing to deserve such treatment. Nonetheless, Colombian troops had already taken up positions around SCADTA installations throughout the country. The Germans were not allowed even to return to their desks or workshops to gather personal effects. All were forced to leave the premises at once.

The next morning the American pilots and technicians stepped directly into the jobs for which they had been hired, SCADTA resumed service without losing a single day, and Rihl sent a coded message to Trippe: "Plan B successful."

40

The Airport Development Program

No sooner was the SCADTA matter settled than Trippe received a phone call from President Roosevelt, who summoned him to Washington on a matter, the President said, of even graver importance to national security. Thus began a series of meetings attended by Roosevelt, Secretary of War Stimson and a number of generals who were not then household names but soon would be.

Trippe came alone to the first of these meetings, and to the next in company with Graham Grosvenor, a Pan Am board member and vice president. Then, because he did not like what Roosevelt proposed, Trippe stepped back and sent Grosvenor by himself to the rest of them.

At the start of these meetings Trippe knew nothing about the projected German/Italian invasion of the United States as worked out by the joint planning commission in 1939. He did not know that an interdepartmental committee, called specifically to consider how to build a chain of air bases south to Brazil, had already worked out and carefully considered four alternative plans: (1) create a government agency to build them under the Civil Aeronautics Authority; (2) make Pan American build them; (3) establish a private corporation to build them; or (4) let contracts to at least twenty different Latin American governments to build the airports themselves.

The State Department was against Plan 2. It did not want Pan American involved in these bases in any way. State—in fact, all of Washington at this time—wanted to weaken the Pan American monopoly, not strengthen it. To have Pan American build bases to Brazil at government expense would indeed be a fine thing for national security, but it would also present the Pan Am octopus with a string of paved airports ready for commercial use which it could exploit once the war ended—or even immediately, since there was no war down there now and might never be. But unfortunately for State, the other three plans were all impractical. Plan 1 required a new law expanding the powers of the Civil Aeronautics Authority—and Congress might not pass such a law. Plan 3 required the formation from scratch of an enormous new private corporation. Plan 4 depended on the War Department conducting successful negotiations with twenty Latin American governments, all of whom would be fighting to maintain national sovereignty in the face of War Department pressure. And so the interdepartmental committee voted that the bases should be built by Pan Am. There were no dissents. Even State voted yes in the name of national defense.

Arguments for the chain of bases were much stronger now, for the Nazis had already conquered France and thus controlled not only Dakar in French Senegal on the African bulge, but also Martinique and Guadeloupe, the French Caribbean islands, and French Guiana on the northern coast of South America. In addition, the Germans had all the satellite airlines—less SCADTA—already operating in South America. This German threat to the hemispheres could only be checked, it seemed, by building the long-proposed chain of bases. It became Roosevelt's job to persuade Trippe to accept the job as builder, even as he signed American Export Airline's permit to Lisbon—for the Pan Am–Export fight was going on at that very time, and FDR meant to tip victory toward Export if he could.

The War Department, Roosevelt told Trippe, was asking Pan American for twenty-five land airports and nine seaplane bases in fourteen countries to start with. Pan American should do it as quickly as possible and as cheaply—the amount of money available was only $12 million. Above all, it must be done secretly. The United States was technically neutral, and public opinion was preponderantly isolationist. A foreign construction program sponsored by the War Department and costing $12 million would be extremely unpopular with U.S. voters, not to mention the people in Latin America.

Trippe was stupefied by Roosevelt's request, and at first refused it. Pan Am was not a construction company. It was not an arm of the War Department, either. It could not get involved in this plan except at tremendous risk both to itself and to its subsidiaries. The airports in Brazil would have to be built by Panair do Brasil, the ones in Mexico by Compañía Mexicana and so forth. For nationals of those countries to build airports for the U.S. War Department could be construed as treason. If word got out—and given the magnitude of the project, word could hardly not get out—Pan Am's operating concessions could be revoked, its local subsidiaries could be expropriated: Pan American's whole Latin American system could be destroyed.

Roosevelt and the War Department pleaded: all they were asking was that Pan American superimpose paved airports on its own airway, which already existed. But this, Trippe saw at once, was not what they were asking at all. They were asking for extra airports, for extra radio and meteorological equipment, and for the placing of vast stocks of aviation fuel.

How could such a plan possibly be kept secret? Trippe demanded. He was assured that only half a dozen men in Washington would know anything about it, but to Trippe this was an absurd statement. By July 10 there had already been a leak—the Washington *Post* reported most details of the plan even though the War Department and Pan American had only just begun talking. Nor could Congress vote $12 million secretly, said Trippe, but he was assured that the money would come out of the secret fund that Congress had recently authorized the President to use at his own discretion. There would not even be any governmental supervision of what Pan Am did with this $12 million; no auditing by government accountants would be necessary. This seemed to Trippe still another reason not to take the job; it left him open to charges of mishandling funds, of criminal misconduct, once the war was over.

About five weeks passed during which Trippe remained adamant and pressure from Stimson, Roosevelt and the generals never ceased.

Even as he tried to judge the weight of these pressures, Trippe was gearing up to defeat Export in the House and Senate, and to blitzkrieg Export's attempt to buy TACA—moves that he knew would be unpopular. If he built the airports he could win back some of that popularity—except that no one would know. There was no money in the airport job at all. As a commercial enterprise, Pan Am's object was profit, but none could be taken because the airports were needed for national security. He would have to donate his company's services. On the other hand, the company would inherit twenty-five landplane airports just as the change from flying boats to landplanes was to be made. Trippe did not know what to do. It was a terrible decision to be forced to make.

As he brooded, other people and problems fought for his time. He needed a new Atlantic Division manager; he also needed some way to beat winter weather on the Atlantic. England, blockaded by Nazi U-boats, and having no long-range aircraft of its own, wanted desperately to buy three of Pan Am's Boeing flying boats. Did Trippe want to sell any Boeings, and if so, at what price? On August 30, 1940, a contract for three Boeings was signed with the British. Trippe had paid $804,925.75 per flying boat. His price to Britain was $1,035,400 each. Britain was not his country; business was business and a profit of more than $600,000 went into the bank to cover overhead, maintenance and other such charges.

To help solve the Atlantic problem he called in young John Leslie, division operations manager in San Francisco, and offered him the job of Atlantic Division manager. Leslie, thirty-five, had just built a new house near Walnut Creek in California. He had a wife and three children, and every weekend they had been driving out to watch their house take shape. Even as the wallpaper was going up in the dining room, Leslie had been called to President Trippe's office in New York.

Trippe might simply have sent this young man, or any other employee, his marching orders. But when it came to moving executives around the world, this was not Trippe's style. Decorum—good manners—was called for; this cost nothing except Trippe's time, and did not in any case alter the final result.

It was past six o'clock at night, customarily the hour when Trippe conducted such business, and young Leslie across the desk, owner of a not-quite-finished house in California, was both elated and appalled.

"Mr. Trippe," he said, "can anybody really live like a human being in the New York area?"

Trippe gravely assured him it was possible. The Atlantic Division was the place for Leslie, Trippe said firmly and dismissed him. Trippe was not the man to imagine the next act in the Leslie family's personal drama—Jean Leslie sitting for an hour in her new kitchen, not yet used, weeping silently. That was Leslie's problem, not Trippe's.

Next, Trippe turned his attention to his New York–Lisbon route in winter. The fact that Leslie would run the division did not necessarily give him the right to make major decisions. Most major decisions anywhere in the world Trippe reserved for himself. Return flights out of Lisbon were often delayed in mid-ocean because of violent swells at Horta. Some even had to be canceled because of extremely strong westerly winds and unflyable mid-ocean storms covering areas too wide to detour. Still others were flown, but with very little payload aboard. Of twenty-five westbound crossings scheduled during the three winter months of 1940, only fourteen had been completed.

Now the winter of 1940–41 approached, and a way to circumvent these storms and winds had to be found. But what? Trippe stared at his maps awhile, then ordered Long in Lisbon to negotiate for landing rights in Bolama in Portuguese Guinea, West Africa. Thus did a new transatlantic route come into existence: Lisbon to New York via West Africa and Brazil. It was 4,085 miles longer than the direct route, but the prevailing winds that far south were favorable; there was no ice; and the cost of stopovers and extra fuel would be offset by the increased payload—passengers and mail—that could be moved. Trippe was opting for tailwinds in both directions. It was the same decision Columbus had once made. Trippe's Clippers, four hundred and fifty years later, would be following the route of Columbus's caravels.

Meanwhile he was being constantly harried by Washington. What about those Latin American airports? Would he build them or not? "The immediate conclusion of the PAA contract," wrote Chief of Staff General George Marshall to Secretary of War Stimson, "is now more essential to our national defense than any other single matter."

Eventually Trippe capitulated. He would accept the risk—and the work. He would build the airports, twenty-five of them, spaced approximately four hundred and fifty miles apart. He formed a new company called Pan American Airports, put vice president Grosvenor in charge, and the program lurched into motion.

The first job was to set up an organization. Evan Young, another vice president, was charged with foreign negotiations. Andrew Lewis would design the airports. L. L. Odell, who had supervised Wake and Midway, was superintendent of construction. Headquarters was New York, with division offices in Brownsville, Mexico City and Natal. Thirteen months later the United States would be at war. Although no one could be certain war would start, everyone understood that there was not much time. The bases were to form a shield, a kind of barrier reef extending from Miami to Brazil, behind which the United States could stand safe.

The contract with the War Department was signed on November 2. In New York Grosvenor, Young, Lewis and Odell, often working far into the night, drew up detailed plans for twenty-five individual projects, and a week and a day following the signing of the contract, local meetings were held in Brownsville, Miami, Mexico City and Rio.

The first order, as new people were brought into the program, was secrecy. Local executives were warned that the airports must be made to appear part of Pan American's normal commercial expansion. Each was to seem a single, local project. No one was to know there were twenty-four others, or that the chain of airports was more than five thousand miles long. Each subordinate executive was given sufficient information to enable him to accomplish his own job—and no more—and he was ordered to keep his own subordinates as much in the dark as possible.

The project was subdivided into parts: permission from the host government had to be requested; land had to be found and negotiated for; men had to be hired and transported to the sites; machines had to be found and transported to the sites; camps had to be built to house workers, and arrangements made to feed them.

Negotiations with host governments came first. These were conducted according to strict rules laid down by Trippe, who, after fourteen years of empire building, had developed an instinct for handling negotiations that seemed to the men around him both unerring and uncanny. Trippe now wanted an "expression of sympathy" from each government. Negotiators were to seek this at the outset, and were not to proceed until they got it. Trippe believed one should never negotiate seriously until the other party had committed itself to a stake in the outcome of the negotiations. The host governments were about to obtain free airports and had to be made in some way to pay for them—else they would not value the airports highly and might interfere with them. Since they were not going to pay money, what they should pay was "sympathy." Specifically, this could be shown by the elimination of customs duties on machinery imported in order to build each airport and on equipment to be installed there. Taxes could be eliminated on fuel and lubricants, and on the airport terrain itself. If duties and taxes by law could not be waived, then the government must be made to contract to maintain the airport or to build access roads to it, or to supply electricity for the navigational beacons, or to agree to provide police protection for the field when it was built.

But an "expression of sympathy" of some kind or another had to be pledged.

Every government was different. Guatemala, where Alfredo Denby now ran Aerovías de Guatemala and where Silliman was still on duty, was an efficient dictatorship. Nicaragua, the Dominican Republic and Cuba were dictatorships too, but less well run. Somoza in Nicaragua and Trujillo in the Dominican Republic were particularly unpredictable. In Trujillo's domain the obvious place to build the airport was at San Pedro de Macorís, which was flat, but Trujillo wanted it at Miraflores amid solid rock hills. Miraflores or nowhere, he decreed. In Nicaragua Somoza wanted the new airfield in the backyard of his presidential palace—in order, as one disgruntled negotiator put it, "to make a quick getaway, if necessary." The president also wanted a 10,000-foot runway, no one knew why. Until he got what he wanted, he not only would not sign the authorization but could rarely even be found. Somoza was one of the few who appeared to realize that the U.S. Treasury was footing the bill.

In Brazil, where Dr. Cauby Araujo, who was president of Panair do Brasil, negotiated directly with President Getulio Vargas, no one suspected the U.S. government involvement, even though the required "expression of sympathy" was not forthcoming until the State Department leaned on Vargas. Later, when news finally leaked out, Cauby Araujo was arrested and imprisoned, and it was expected that he would be shot for treason. After a year behind bars he was tried and acquitted.

Negotiations with landowners took even longer than with governments, partly because of bizarre Latin American land laws. In Cuba, for instance, original land grants had been made not along straight lines but in circles, which inevitably resulted in overlapping plots and multiple ownership. One plot had eleven claimants. Another was owned by two families, each with five daughters, one of whom, owning three fortieths of a one-half interest, refused to sell, merely to spite the rest of her family.

At Tapachula, Mexico, a Japanese landowner refused to move. It was arranged to have him dragged off his land by the Mexican militia. At Bahia, Brazil, the only suitable land was the existing grass field, but it was owned by Air France. Panair was asked to pay all of Air France's overdue taxes before building, and negotiations lasted eleven months. Even at Amapá, an uninhabited tract of Amazon jungle, there were problems. The future landing strip was owned by a certain Assaid Sfair, who was on hand, and his brothers, who were in Syria and who did not trust Assaid to represent them—the sale of their land, they wrote, would have to wait until the war ended. This land was finally expropriated.

In the United States men proved hard to find. The peacetime draft and the defense complex had begun to sweep clean every available source of manpower. The company's division offices in California, New Orleans, Brownsville and Miami were asked to hire heavy-equipment operators, electricians and draftsmen, but too few were found and the search was forced inland to places where Pan American did not operate: Colorado, Nevada, Alabama.

In the past the company had carefully screened its employees, and also, before shipping them abroad, had indoctrinated them in local mores and the local language. There wasn't time for that now—which promised a far higher than normal rate of mental and physical breakdowns later on. The ratio of natives to U.S. citizens would be three hundred to one. Many natives would be convicts, and almost none would speak English. Some would be peasants who had never before seen a piece of construction machinery. With such laborers these unscreened, unindoctrinated Americans would have to cope.

To find and transport the machinery itself proved equally difficult. Delivery to a pier somewhere took up to two and a half months. To get machines on board the rare small freighters that moved down toward Latin America usually meant another two months. The earliest airport work began with oxcarts instead of trucks, mules instead of tractors, with men grubbing out rocks and tree stumps with hoes.

Nor did such woes end when a ship at last docked. To move machinery out to sites was sometimes as major a job as building the airport itself. Often local bridges had to be reinforced before earth-moving machines could go on them. At Natal, Brazil, where one of the most crucial airports was to be constructed, the new machines were marooned twelve miles away until a paved access road could be constructed through sand dunes. To stabilize the dunes, thousands of pineapple plants had to be embedded in their slopes. The most isolated airport was Amapá, situated ten miles inland up a tributary of the Amazon. Leading to it were no roads whatsoever, and the river itself was unusable because it was alternately a rushing torrent and a mud flat, depending on the tides. Until a landing strip had been grubbed out by hand, no heavy equipment at all could be got in there—nor generators, nor fuel. Food was moved upriver by canoe, and then was carried in on men's backs over a trail hacked from the jungle by machetes. But since there was no electricity, there was also no refrigeration, and in damp tropical heat the food went bad fast. One solution was to drive cattle into Amapá alive, slaughtering them as needed. However, every time heavy rains fell, supply trains did not get through, forcing workers to live on rice and beans for weeks on end.

Where there was no gear, foremen improvised. At one site there were not even spades, so spades were made up out of discarded sheet iron and saplings. At another, treads for a motor grader were made out of wood. They lasted about a week, after which new ones had to be carved. Elsewhere a stone crusher was manufactured out of abandoned trolley rails, and asphalt was laid by hand and tramped flat by bare feet because there was no paving machine. Almost everywhere tropical rains caused enormous delays. Seventeen labor camps were set up, all seventeen in the malaria belt. Always the natives were taught the rudiments of sanitation; nevertheless washrooms were scorned, vitamin tablets went unused, purified water was not drunk. At San José, Guatemala, the malaria rate was 100 percent for natives and whites alike. At Amapá 400 of the 795 laborers were absent daily because of malaria. Among supervisory personnel mental breakdowns became almost as frequent as physical ones. These men were suffering from diseases for which there was no inoculation. At Paramaribo, Dutch Guiana, the supervising engineer, overwhelmed, more and more frequently "was seen in town, rather than at the field, and usually intoxicated."

With America's entrance into World War II now only a few weeks away, not one airport had been completed. The hemisphere's protective shield was not in place. The War Plans and G-4 divisions of the general staff made known their impatience. In September 1941 the War Department registered a formal complaint with Pan American: progress was "unsatisfactory."

Trippe replaced Grosvenor with Samuel Pryor, who had been a classmate at Yale. When in trouble, Trippe almost always turned to Yale men. Pryor, then forty-three, was vice president of the Southern Wheel Company; he was also assistant to the president of American Brake Shoe & Foundry. On the side he was a Republican national committeeman from Connecticut, meaning he had friends in Washington and could perhaps call in a favor if Trippe needed one.

41
Africa

In June of 1941 Trippe had accepted an invitation to give the annual Wilbur Wright Memorial lecture, a prestigious event in aviation circles, before the Royal Aeronautical Society in London. To get there he first flew to Lisbon in one of his own Boeing flying boats. Lisbon was still neutral, its streets still brightly lit. At the airport Italian and German airliners landed and took off. For the final leg to London, Trippe boarded a KLM landplane, whose pilot, as soon as he left Portuguese airspace, swung far out to sea and stayed in clouds as much as possible.

The lecture took place in an underground room at the Air Ministry in front of a huge map of the world. Outside in the night London was being bombed. Trippe could hear the muffled thud of bombs as he spoke. His subject was long-distance flight, and when he finished, high-ranking RAF officers crowded around him. General Rommel's panzers were at large in the Sahara at that time; they threatened Egypt and the Suez Canal, and had cut British troops off from their sources of supply. Could Trippe think of a way to supply those desert troops, the air officers asked. He began a second lecture, using the map on the wall. He showed how to fly south to Liberia in long-range flying boats, and from there across the Sahara and the Sudan via an airway that could be set up.

Trippe then went back to his hotel and up to the roof to watch the bombing. Handkerchief bombs, caught in the searchlights, drifted slowly down toward Hyde Park. Except for searchlights raking the sky, the city was blacked out, and a man he couldn't see tapped Trippe on the shoulder and said, "The Prime Minister asks that you join him for dinner."

It was eleven o'clock at night. "I've already had my dinner," said Trippe. "So has the Prime Minister. And I know when I'm being kidded."

"I have his car downstairs," said the messenger. "The hotel manager can confirm it for you."

Trippe was driven to No. 10 Downing Street and shown into a room where Winston Churchill sat before a log fire. Churchill wanted to know about the route to Cairo. The two men dined at a bridge table; it was Churchill's first dinner that evening, Trippe's second. They washed the food down with a good deal of scotch and soda. Churchill sent for maps. He wanted Trippe to explain how an air route to Cairo could be set up. Then sixty-six, Churchill was a heavy drinker, and Trippe, aged forty-two, could drink a good deal, too, and never show it. For two hours the two men talked and drank. Churchill said he would cable Roosevelt about this. The route to Cairo must be set up as soon as possible. Trippe should expect to hear from Roosevelt as soon as he landed in New York.

Trippe caught the KLM flight back to Lisbon, and rode his Clipper the rest of the way—an exhausting journey even for a man of Trippe's constitution. Waiting at the dock was a Marine Corps officer, who escorted him at once to another plane, and he was flown to Washington. A few minutes after landing, he was ushered into the Oval Office. "What did you tell the Prime Minister?" asked President Roosevelt from his wheelchair.

Roosevelt had a number of so-called anonymous assistants to whom he delegated presidential authority. When Trippe had finished his story, Roosevelt turned him over to one of them, James Forrestal, who would later serve as Secretary of the Navy and afterwards as the Nation's first Secretary of Defense. Trippe was to set up the trans-African route as soon as possible. He was to tell Forrestal how much money he needed and what further action was to be taken, and he was to make preparations to ferry lend-lease aircraft across to the British in Africa as well. Trippe realized that he was being handed a chance to penetrate Africa.

Carefully compartmentalizing his business as always, he incorporated Pan American Airways–Africa Ltd. on July 15 and Pan American Air Ferries on July 24. To head Air Ferries he brought in Dave Ingalls, still another former Yale classmate. John Steele rounded up pilots—retired airline pilots, crop dusters, any pilot he could find—and the first trickle of lend-lease planes began moving south through the chain of half-finished Latin American air bases to Natal, and then making the hop across the South Atlantic.

To head Pan American–Africa Trippe named Franklin Gledhill, his chief purchasing agent. The ace haggler, detached from office duty in New York, was now responsible, in effect, for the entire African continent, not one foot of which he had ever seen before. Gledhill, who was also a Yale man, would have to lay out a route to Cairo that would cross

Africa at its broadest point. It would be more than four thousand miles long. About ten bases would have to be constructed, a number of them in spots that were among the most inhospitable in the world. To inspect his new domain, Gledhill flew an average of twenty-five hundred miles per day for thirty consecutive days. He flew over jungles, over low mountains, across country as stark as any on earth. He planned bases in Takoradi and Accra in what would later be known as Ghana; in Kano and Maiduguri in northern Nigeria; at Fort Lamy in Chad; in El Geteina, El Fasher and Khartoum in the Sudan. He hired four hundred Americans and countless natives, and these men worked mostly in choking dust and in temperatures often above 120 degrees Fahrenheit. At El Fasher one day the temperature was 158 degrees. Runways were extended or built from scratch. Adcock masts rose. Aviation gasoline was brought in, sometimes on the backs of camels at the rate of thirty-five gallons per beast. There were no governments or landowners to negotiate with in this desolate land, and Gledhill had his route in operation by October 18— less than four months after Trippe's conversations with Churchill and Roosevelt. The British in Africa were not even totally cooperative, and one high official, Air Marshal Arthur Tedder, once termed Pan American–Africa Ltd. a naked grab by Pan Am for postwar air routes.

The more Trippe watched his new African empire take shape, the more he realized it was improperly anchored on the west coast. Portuguese Guinea and British Gambia were both too close to Dakar. The Germans could send Messerschmitts from Dakar and shoot down whatever flew out of either place. In addition, his African inroads were military ones only. If he meant to stay on after the war, he had best make a commercial penetration also.

From British Gambia a surveying team was sent out to find a better, safer landfall on the African bulge. At the same time Trippe applied to the Civil Aeronautics Board for a certificate of convenience and necessity for a route to Leopoldville in the Belgian Congo; if he could get this far, then after the war the whole of the rich southern portion of Africa would lie open to him. The CAB held hearings, but it was difficult by now to tell which projects had the War Department behind them, and which had only Trippe. The CAB hearings were partly open, partly secret—as if the examiner couldn't tell, either—and the certificate was awarded with unusual haste. Trippe even persuaded the government to buy the Boeing that would be used on the route, and then to lease it back to him. His argument was that the plane, by entering the war zone, had just become uninsurable. But Pan American never insured its planes; the company carried its own insurance by holding back fixed sums each year as a so-called crash reserve. There was understandable criticism of the arrangement, which Trippe answered by claiming that he had sold the Boeing at depreciated value, rather than replacement value, and had therefore come out the loser. A few weeks later, when the United States entered the war, he would sell all his Boeings to the government, and lease them back, on the same basis.

Meanwhile, up and down the west African coast the search continued for the new base that was needed. About eight hundred miles south of Vichy-controlled Dakar, what appeared to be a lake was spotted behind the coastal dunes. It wasn't really a lake but, rather, a bay almost entirely cut off from the sea. It would prove to be twelve miles long and five miles across at its widest point, and it looked, from the air, like the calm water needed for year-round flying-boat operations. A scout named Karl Lueder, traveling first by ship and then through the surf by rowboat, went in there and signaled that this place—it was called Fishermen's Lake— looked as good from the ground as from the air.

On November 20, 1941, the *Capetown Clipper,* under the command of Captain Harold Gray, put down on Fishermen's Lake for the first time and glided to a stop on the water. Division manager Leslie and his assistant division manager Ed McVitty were carried ashore on the shoulders of Liberian natives, and into the high grass where the deadly green mamba snake was not unknown. Young Leslie from his high perch looked all around. Grass was all he could see. Northwest of the lake, he knew, were swamps running four and a half miles to the nearest native village; east and north were thick jungles; in the west and south curved the low coast jungles and the dunes. Leslie saw where the dock would go to which the flying boats would tie up and where the cantonment would be built. He peered out toward higher ground where the grass would be cleared and a paved runway laid down.

When he was set down on his feet, he and McVitty made their way to the mission on the edge of the lake to talk to the Episcopal minister Harvey Simmons and his wife. Father Simmons had a small motor launch. Leslie and McVitty began to tour the rather large lake, checking depths, looking for subsurface obstructions, making absolutely certain that the decision Leslie had to make would be the correct one. By radio Leslie sent a message to New York: Fishermen's Lake was the anchor base the company sought.

At that moment two loaded freighters were already at sea. One carried thirty construction men, and the other contained the masts, prefabricated buildings, tanks, generators and machinery necessary to build a base. These ships had been bound for Bathurst in British Gambia. Leslie now requested that both be diverted to Fishermen's Lake; then he climbed aboard the flying boat and took off for home. As the Clipper rose off the lake Leslie looked down and wondered what life would be like for the men who would live there.

A few weeks later the first of the two freighters hove to offshore, and thirty settlers, all men, waded up onto the beach and in through the bush to the edge of the lake. There was no one there but Father and Mrs. Simmons, but the missionaries greeted them warmly and gave them a meal. They slept in tents under mosquito nettings. They built eight houses, each containing seven double rooms and a bathroom, with screened-in porches running completely around the outside. They, and the men who followed, built a mess hall, a recreation hall, storage buildings, a hospital and laundry. They built a control tower, an adcock, a marine runway and then a land one.

On December 6, 1941, the first airmail flight to Leopoldville, in the Belgian Congo, was inaugurated. This seemed so important—surely the most important event of that weekend—that Van Dusen himself was aboard, and on his portable typewriter he even began to tap out a breezy and informative open letter to his friends in the press.

Upon reaching Leopoldville, the flying boat was moored on the Congo itself at the edge of Stanley Pool—not a particularly safe anchorage. The river was full of submerged rocks and sandbars, and three hundred yards below the town the Congo poured over the crest of a tremendous cataract, the first of many. From upriver floating islands frequently appeared, tangles of thick jungle growth that moved rapidly downstream. Often they were bigger than flying boats, and they swept along whatever got caught in their way, disappearing a few seconds later over the cataract.

Everyone in Leopoldville, it seemed, was out to wave the *Capetown Clipper* off to the United States with its cargo of first covers. The Belgian, Free French, British and American officials were all there, resplendent in their starched whites and tropical hats. A military band played. American flags fluttered from nearly every flagpole in the town.

42

The Day of Infamy

On December 7, 1941, Trippe was sick in bed with the flu. His phone rang. It was Secretary of the Navy Frank Knox, who told him that Pearl Harbor, Manila and Hong Kong had been bombed, and were even now under attack by elements of the Japanese Navy and Air Force. Destruction had been great. The United States must consider itself at war.

Trippe got dressed and went down to the Chrysler Building. Since it was a Sunday, the lobby, as he waited for the elevator, was empty. Harold Bixby came in and waited beside him. Bixby was shaken. He judged, correctly, that the attack had been a terrible blow, that the United States had been caught way off balance. He had been in China and had already seen war with the Japanese at first hand. There was no way of knowing which way this war would go or how long it would take. Trippe, however, was cheerful. He was full of confidence about the country, and about Pan American. There would be a lot of work to do. They would all have to take their coats off.

Bixby mentioned the stock options both men held. Their options ran out on December 31. They would have to exercise them or not exercise them in the face of today's events, in the face of a future that had become terribly uncertain. Trippe smiled and shook his head. He had every intention of exercising his own options, he said. And, in fact, three weeks later he did so, acquiring all fifty thousand of the shares available to him. They cost him $750,000.

Bixby was wrong to feel as gloomy as he did, Trippe said, as the elevator lifted them to the fifty-eighth floor. He then went into his office to try to learn how many of his flying boats the Japanese might already have destroyed, and how many others were still in danger.

At the moment of the first Japanese attack three flying boats were in the air over the Pacific, and a fourth was on the water. The one in the most immediate danger was the *Anzac Clipper,* Captain H. Lanier Turner commanding, which would reach Pearl Harbor in about an hour with a crew of ten and seventeen passengers aboard. It was breakfast time. Passengers were waking up and moving toward tables set in the Clipper's lounge. They sipped coffee and orange juice. San Francisco was behind them and the semitropical islands just ahead. Several paused to set their watches to island time—vacation time for most of them—8:30 A.M. Japanese planes even then were swarming over Pearl Harbor, and the huge lumbering Boeing was flying right into them.

On the Clipper's upper deck, radio officer W. H. Bell took the message that had just been flashed to him and strode forward to the cockpit. The Japanese were attacking Pearl Harbor. All Clipper captains had carried sealed orders for weeks, and Turner ripped his open now, scanned the various contingencies and saw that he was ordered to divert to Hilo Bay on the big island of Hawaii, about 150 miles south of Pearl Harbor. Turner estimated that it would take him close to two hours to get there. By the standards of modern war, his flying boat was a slow, exceedingly easy target, and not only was there at least one Japanese carrier task force just over the horizon, but Japanese planes were ravaging Pearl an hour due west. He banked gently south. Passengers were told nothing. Unwarned, and therefore unalarmed, they continued to sip orange juice and daydream of vacation.

Not until the flying boat was on the water at Hilo did Turner call his passengers into the lounge. He gave them the news. Honolulu had been attacked. The Clipper would be refueled here at Hilo and flown back to San Francisco as soon as possible. Passengers were welcome to ride back with him if they chose to, Turner said. Or else they could stay here and make their own way to Honolulu or Maui or wherever they were going.

All opted to stay in the islands. In solemn silence they trooped off the Clipper and moved into the streets of the town to look for rooms in hotels, while Turner and his crew began the lengthy tasks of servicing and refueling the flying boat. There was no ground crew and no pressure fuel pumps, and gasoline was poured by hand, as in the old days.

That night the Clipper was still not ready to go, which meant staying over all the next day, for Turner dared not take off in the daytime lest a Japanese patrol find him. Takeoff came Monday night in radio silence into absolute darkness. The *Anzac Clipper* reached San Francisco eighteen hours later. It disgorged eleven weary men with bloodshot eyes who had not shaved or slept in a bed in seventy-two hours.

Early on Pearl Harbor Sunday Captain John Hamilton, thirty-four, lifted the *Philippine Clipper,* a Martin M-130, off the lagoon at Wake bound for Guam. Hamilton was a chunky man with a seventeen-inch collar. His nickname was Ham. He had learned to fly in the Navy, and after being discharged into the depression, he had taken whatever flying jobs he could get. For a time he sowed rice from the air for ten cents an acre, carrying eight hundred pounds of rice in the front cockpit. He had been a Pan Am pilot since 1932—nine years.

On board today was a military mission commanded by a colonel headed for the Far East. There was also a single Flying Tiger fighter pilot going back to work in China. Cargo consisted almost entirely of tires for the Flying Tigers' P-40's.

Hamilton had been in the air about thirty minutes when the Wake tower ordered him to return.

"What for?" Hamilton radioed.

The answer came back: "Pearl Harbor's been attacked."

Hamilton, too, ripped open his sealed orders and read the contingencies. His primary job, he saw, was to evacuate Pan Am personnel from Wake.

After dumping three thousand pounds of gas, Hamilton landed back on the Wake lagoon. From the pier he went directly to the radio shack. The radio operator was talking to Guam, which was under attack. Hamilton heard the Guam operator call, "There went the hotel." The man's final report was, "That one landed too close. I'm signing off."

So Hamilton knew he couldn't go on to Guam. He had to go back the way he came.

The other arm of the Wake hairpin had been paved into an airstrip earlier that year, and there was now a Marine Corps fighter squadron on the island: twelve Grumman Wildcat fighter planes. Hamilton drove around to the Marines' side, where he conferred with Commander W. S. Cunningham and Major James Devereux. They wanted him to take his flying boat out on patrol with a squadron of fighter planes. Hamilton's job would be to navigate the patrol out far enough to find any Japanese warships that might be in the vicinity, and then to navigate it back, for if they got out of sight of Wake the fighter planes risked not being able to find it again. Hamilton agreed to the patrol but imposed terms. Though there was very little fuel on Wake, he demanded enough to reach Midway, plus four hours' extra for the patrol.

The result was that the *Philippine Clipper* was floating there low in the water, all tanks filled to the brim with high-octane fuel, when Japanese attack planes came in over the lagoon an hour later. The noise of their engines, bombs and machine guns drowned out the roar of the surf. Hamilton's passengers were in the hotel. Hamilton himself had been on the pier watching the refueling, and he had just started back to the hotel with station manager John B. Cooke. Both men heard the planes coming. Cooke looked up and said, "Hey, there are some B-17's."

"They are not," said Hamilton.

The two men stood watching, stupefied. The planes, two formations of nine, came straight in. The first group hit the airstrip on the opposite arm of the hairpin. The second kept coming straight at Hamilton. A spray of bullets started in from the lagoon, kicking up water, then sand. Some ditches that had been dug for storm drains stood open nearby. Hamilton and Cooke went diving in as bullets blew sand all over them. The planes were gone, then came back. Bombs fell. Peering over the edge of his ditch, Hamilton watched a gas dump blow up. He saw bombs falling toward the *Philippine Clipper.* The dock disappeared and a mighty explosion of water obscured everything.

Hamilton stood up and started to climb out of the ditch, but the planes came back, and he dived back down again. He heard a second gas dump blow. He stood up and shook the sand off himself. The hotel, he saw, had been hit and was on fire. He listened, but could hear nothing except the pounding surf. The whole island seemed to be on fire. He ran down the pier toward the *Philippine Clipper.* It was still there, rocking on the now turbulent lagoon. Hamilton skirted holes in the pier, and jumped on board. There were bullet holes in the fuselage. He looked up at the ceiling and could see sky. He judged there were about sixty bullet holes, but the engines did not seem to have been hit. There was no leakage from fuel tanks that he could see. He sniffed but could not smell gasoline. A second man jumped on board—flight engineer T. E. Barnett. The two men checked the plane over as well as they could—amazingly, it seemed flyable.

The island's adcock had been destroyed. Hamilton looked around for the direction-finder masts. They were down. To get back to Honolulu he would have to find Midway first, and the adcock here was not going to be able to direct him outbound. Was the one at Midway still standing? During the next hour his men moved through the flying boat, stripping it not only of mail and cargo, but also of every passenger amenity that would come loose and could be thrown overboard.

According to his orders, Hamilton was to burn the plane's papers, and also the mail, for it would contain military secrets of value to the Japanese. His own papers blazed easily enough, but the mailbags would require a bonfire, for which Hamilton did not have time. He left the mail to be burned by the Marines, and began to herd his passengers and Pan Am island personnel on board. Three hours had passed since the Japanese attack. Hamilton, with sixty people on board, two of them badly wounded, taxied the overloaded flying boat out onto the too short Wake lagoon, opened all four throttles as far as they would go, and prayed that the flying boat would lift off. It did not do so. He came to the end of the lagoon and the machine was still stuck to the water. He made a second run, but the result was the same. He turned the flying boat around for a third try. This time all sixty people on board scarcely dared to breathe. Hamilton was jockeying the plane, trying to break it loose from the water. At last it lifted, leveled for a second, then began to lift further. It cleared the brush on the opposite side of the lagoon, and Hamilton pointed it toward Midway.

What he didn't know was that the Japanese warships were even then moving into position to shell Midway. The Midway adcock was about to be blown to bits also. Hamilton was flying from one pinpoint in the Pacific Ocean to another with no radio direction finder to help him.

In the air in full daylight, Hamilton stayed down close to the water so that Japanese attack planes, if any, could not see him easily. He flew at an altitude of twenty-five feet until at last it got dark, whereupon he went up high and opened up on the radio to anyone who might hear him, reading off the names of all those aboard and announcing his intentions: he was trying to make Midway, and after that, Hawaii. It was now pitch-dark over the desolate waste of the central Pacific. The flight was totally dependent upon celestial navigation. Every time navigator J. A. Hurtsky would take a star sight, Hamilton would take one too, each checking against the other.

Midway was easier to find than they had expected, because it was on fire. Hamilton turned on all his lights, so as not to get shot down, came down low and made a visual pass over the lagoon. It was a mess. Small craft were adrift everywhere. He could see them in the reflection of the flames.

The buoy lights were dark, but it didn't matter—it was impossible to use the normal marine runway anyway, because of the small craft. Hamilton put the flying boat down as far to the edge of the lagoon as he could, feeling for the water. Once down he taxied in darkness to where he imagined the Pan American barge must be, found it and tied up. He jumped ashore, and ordered his flying boat refueled at once. Midway had just come through a shelling, he was told. Excited personnel there wanted to know whatever Hamilton could tell them, but he knew little. Wake was finished. He was trying to make it to Hawaii.

In an hour and a half he was in the air again, flying toward Hawaii. Soon it began to be light. When at last he could see the island of Oahu ahead, Hamilton opened up on his radio, asking where to land. Though ready to go on to Hilo, he was told to come on in to Pearl Harbor. As he landed the destruction he saw around him was unbelievable. Fires were still blazing. Columns of smoke rose into a sky that was otherwise crystal clear, and he could see the masts of sunken ships.

The Pan Am side of the harbor had not been touched. Hamilton's passengers disembarked and walked numbly up the pier. Most were dressed in shorts and sneakers—the standard Wake Island uniform. Harry Eldridge, the Pearl Harbor station manager, was handing out whiskey to each man as he stepped ashore.

That was Monday, December 8. Hamilton went to bed. He had been flying, or refueling, or navigating, or dodging Japanese bullets for over thirty-six hours without a break.

Two days later he flew the *Philippine Clipper* from Pearl Harbor back to San Francisco, a flight that was, he reported later, "like any other we had ever made, with the exception that we maintained radio silence."

William Langhorne Bond that year lived in a house on a hill in Hong Kong overlooking Repulse Bay. On December 5, two days earlier, Trippe had publicly re-recognized Pan Am's affiliation with CNAC and Bond. Bond was once again a Pan Am vice president in good standing, but he didn't yet know it.

The early-morning telephone call woke him out of a sound sleep. It was December 7 in Hawaii but December 8 here. Bond looked out the window and it was still dark. It was a local call from Fred S. Ralph, captain of the *Hong Kong Clipper*. This plane was an elderly—six-year-old—S-42 that its crew called Myrtle. Myrtle flew the shuttle service between Manila and Hong Kong on the final leg of the transpacific air route. Now Ralph told Bond that he had just received confusing instructions. Manila had radioed him to stay where he was, but the Hong Kong authorities were urging him to get out of Hong Kong fast. What did this mean and what should he do?

Bond, still half asleep, judged that something catastrophic had happened or was about to happen, but he had no idea what. Ralph's passengers would be safe enough here, he reasoned, for Hong Kong was a free port. But if the Japanese had decided upon aggressive action against the United States in the Pacific, then the plane itself, being under American registry, was subject to attack; since the Japanese Army already surrounded Hong Kong, this attack might come at any moment.

Bond ordered Ralph to fly Myrtle to the presumed safety of Manila at once. Hanging up, Bond rushed upstairs to dress, but the phone rang again. The Japanese, Ralph told him excitedly, had just bombed Pearl Harbor and Manila. A state of war existed. Bond ordered Ralph to fly Myrtle out of Hong Kong as quickly as possible. Bond was sending a CNAC pilot to guide him inland to a lake Bond knew of near Kunming where she would be safe for a while.

Bond jumped into his car and sped across Hong Kong Island toward the ferry that would take him over to Kowloon, site of the airport, and the marine air station as well. Air-raid sirens were already wailing as Bond skidded to a stop in front of the ferry. But it had been shut down. He ran along the banks trying to hire a boatman to take him across. None would. Finally, with the help of a Canadian officer and three soldiers, he crossed in a commandeered sampan.

He did not witness the attack on Myrtle, but Ralph did. Japanese bombers had come in, wave after wave of them, ignoring Myrtle at first. They had pounded Kai-tek Airport, digging craters in the runways. They had strafed every CNAC plane standing on the field, destroying five, and had blown off part of the roof of the hangar. Then they had turned toward Myrtle riding gently on the waves. Ralph and his men saw them coming. There were passengers on the dock too. People started diving into the water, Ralph among them. The Japanese planes came low, machine guns spitting. Ralph, crouched behind a concrete pier, counted six dives directly on the *Hong Kong Clipper*. After the seventh it was ablaze. He stood there in water up to his waist, watching it burn.

After receiving Ralph's report Bond went to the airport, where he found his men pushing two DC-3's and one DC-2 off the field. There were no trees to hide them under, for the field was rimmed with vegetable gardens. Into the vegetable gardens went the three airliners spaced about three hundred yards apart, and the men spent the next two hours camouflaging them with mud and straw.

Bond was trying to organize and save what was left of his airline without any accurate knowledge of the state of the world, and he was interrupted by constant air raids. To move between the airport and Hong Kong was for the moment virtually impossible. There were no taxis; the ferry was shut down; and the Hong Kong police decided to require a kind of passport for moving back and forth. Bond believed the Japanese would move into Hong Kong within forty-eight hours, perhaps sooner. He had to collect his pilots and personnel, his spare parts and supplies, and also as many important Chinese and foreigners as he could find. CNAC was evacuating: he was moving it inland. He had not carried the airline this far to lose it now.

He watched one air raid from inside the airport gatekeeper's shack, which had been sandbagged. Anti-aircraft guns hammered just outside. The Japanese planes came in high. Bond listened to the swish of falling bombs, the closest hitting about three hundred yards away.

When the air raid ended, Bond raced for his hangar. A bomb had come through the roof, had pierced the aileron of a parked plane, and had shattered on the concrete floor without exploding. The hangar reeked of picric acid. The acid got on Bond's shoes and clothing, which turned yellow. He gagged on the fumes, and exited coughing, clutching his throat.

There were new shell craters all over the runway, and Bond ordered a crew to fill them in. A phone call came through to him. It was from H. H. Kung, the former Prime Minister who was now finance minister. He wanted Bond to evacuate his wife, one of the Soong sisters and sister-in-law to Chiang Kai-shek, from Hong Kong. If you hoped to go on operating in China, this type of request got priority. Over the next several hours Bond scoured Hong Kong trying to find Madame Kung, and when he found her, had difficulty persuading her to leave. She wanted to stay because she imagined that British warships would turn up any minute and blow the Japanese back to Tokyo.

When darkness fell, Bond began to send his planes out one by one, all of them heavily loaded. The first DC-3 took off at 7:00 P.M. for Namyung, only two hundred miles north but beyond the encircling Japanese lines. Fifteen minutes later the second DC-3 took off, and after that a DC-2. All three planes carried CNAC and Pan Am staff, families and equipment. Diplomats and Chinese officials would come next. Bond had told all these people to wait in the Peninsula Hotel in downtown Kowloon. Included were two Chinese from the Central Bank, two from the currency stabilization board, and others of similar rank. Bond was saving the men he thought most valuable to China.

In three hours the first of the planes was back, landing with all of its cabin lights on as protection against nervous anti-aircraft batteries. It had to be refueled by hand—a painfully slow process—for the gasoline-truck operators had fled. Bond, his throat raw from the acid fumes he had inhaled, paced nervously in the darkness, coughing constantly. Then the plane was reloaded and was off again, and a second was coming in to land.

At 5:30 A.M. the exhausted Bond found a bed in the Peninsula Hotel. He had injured his leg in the course of the day, but had no idea how. It was swollen and throbbing, and he could barely walk. His throat was worse and he lay awake coughing. When an air-raid alarm sounded, he stayed in bed, too tired to move. Bombs fell, followed by the all clear, followed almost immediately by another alarm. It was useless to try to sleep, so he got up, ate breakfast, crossed to Hong Kong and arranged for the company's vital records and funds to be trucked to the airport at once. When he got back to the airport, he found that the British were about to blow it up, and he was obliged to run this way and that, pleading with officials not to do so. It took hours to persuade them to leave a narrow strip of runway so that CNAC planes could continue their evacuation flights.

There were still many officials he had not been able to find, and all the rest of the day he tried to contact them. His advice was the same to all: Move to the Peninsula Hotel in Kowloon; be ready to leave the moment we send for you.

That night additional flights went out in total darkness, each one heavily loaded. Bond's cough was worse, so was his leg, and he became so groggy that sometimes he did not make sense. But still he stayed at his post.

It was time now to get out himself, and he boarded a DC-2 that took him to Chungking. After he had landed he sat down with his operations manager and his chief pilot, and began organizing evacuation flights for the following night. Only as dawn came did Bond begin looking for a bed. He had been awake and on duty for fifty-three hours. When he undressed, he saw that his foot and ankle, as he wrote later, "were as black as your hat and my leg was yellow."

By the time Hong Kong fell on the fourth day, Bond had been able to evacuate some 275 people. He had saved all of his crews, much of his spare parts, and all of his planes that were still able to fly. CNAC was still alive, though barely, like China itself.

The *Pacific Clipper,* Captain Robert Ford commanding a crew of ten, was in the air between New Caledonia and New Zealand when the Pearl Harbor war flash was received. At once Ford silenced the radio, posted watches in the navigator's blister in the roof of the Boeing, altered his course by fifty miles, and got out his .38-caliber revolver. But nothing happened, and two hours later he was landing normally at Auckland.

Ford, who was thirty-five years old, went directly to the U.S. consulate to wait for whatever instructions New York would send him. During the next seven days scores and scores of messages piled up, all of them in code, one of them perhaps for him, but he could not find out because the decoding clerks were overwhelmed. Many cables kept coming out garbled. Ford, watching, realized that the bottleneck, these early days of the war, was in consulates like this all over the world as too few clerks attempted to decode too many messages too fast. Ford did not have to be told how valuable his Boeing flying boat had suddenly become. Only twelve existed; only nine were still in the hands of the United States, and they were the only long-range, heavy-payload aircraft in the world. But his route back to San Francisco had already been cut off by the Japanese, whose aircraft carriers were at large in the Pacific. Manila and Wake, he learned, were under siege; Midway and Guam were partially out of commission. Canton Island—the most vital link in the New Zealand–San Francisco route—had been evacuated of Pan American personnel.

Ford's orders, when they came, were to try to get home the long way around. For Ford it was an awesome assignment. If he wanted to save himself, his crew and his flying boat, he had a 23,000-mile flight ahead of him. He would have to plot out his own route, pick unknown harbors to set down in, and find his own fuel once he got there. Servicing would be limited to the men and tools on board. There would be no navigational aids, no weather forecasts.

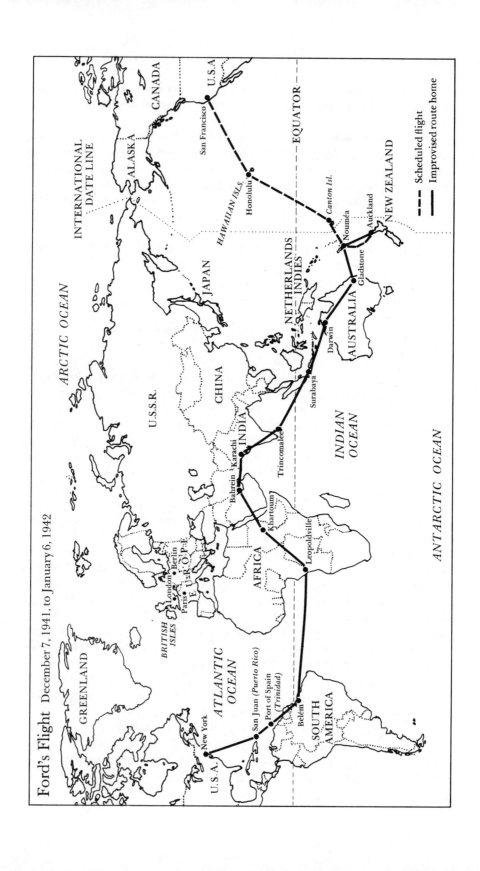

Ford's Flight December 7, 1941, to January 6, 1942

ARCTIC OCEAN

GREENLAND

CANADA

U.S.A.

ALASKA

INTERNATIONAL DATE LINE

San Francisco

JAPAN

U.S.S.R.

CHINA

Honolulu

HAWAIIAN ISLS.

EQUATOR

Canton Isl.

Nouméa

Auckland

NEW ZEALAND

NETHERLANDS INDIES

Gladstone

Darwin

AUSTRALIA

Surabaya

INDIA

Karachi

Bahrein

Trincomalee

INDIAN OCEAN

ANTARCTIC OCEAN

Khartoum

Leopoldville

AFRICA

London
Paris
Berlin

E·U·R·O·P·E

BRITISH ISLES

ATLANTIC OCEAN

New York

U.S.A.

San Juan (Puerto Rico)
Port of Spain (Trinidad)

Belém

SOUTH AMERICA

Scheduled flight
Improvised route home

Attached to the Pan American station at Auckland was Bill Mullahey, former dynamiter of the Wake Island lagoon. It was Mullahey who gathered together all the maps, charts and schoolboy geography books he could find, and who huddled with Ford to plot the possible route home of a lone plane with no ground support. It would be the first round-the-world flight by a commercial plane, and the first by any plane following a route near the equator. It represented as dangerous a flight as Ford had ever contemplated.

Additional orders arrived. His first stop must be Nouméa, in New Caledonia, an eight-hour flight partway back the way he had come. He was to pick up company personnel there and fly them to safety in Australia, and after that, to keep going for as long as he could.

At 10:00 P.M. on December 15 the flight home started. Completely blacked out and in total radio silence, Ford flew through the night, coming in for his landing at Nouméa just as dawn was rising over the Pacific. The unexpected flying boat woke up the town. Ford gave company people there one hour to get packed—one small bag apiece. He took aboard twenty-two men, women and children and all the gas he could carry, and immediately took off again. The next stop, six and a half hours later, was Gladstone, Australia. As soon as all the passengers had been off-loaded, Ford sent crew members through the town looking for 100-octane gas but they could find none, and at last they went to bed. At 6:00 A.M. the next morning the flying boat, with its tanks one third empty, took off for Darwin across the Australian continent, more than eleven hours away. All day Ford looked down on land—not water—beneath his hull. If something went wrong it would be impossible to land safely. A belly landing would wreck the plane; even if they all survived, their flight home would be over. All day Ford never saw a major lake or river.

Darwin, he saw when he had landed, was in a state of war hysteria. All women were to be evacuated within twenty-four hours. Air raids were expected momentarily. There were drunks either fighting or passed out in the streets. It was a night of terrific thunderstorms. On the harbor the flying boat was being gassed up even as sheets of lightning split open the sky.

It was 2:00 A.M. before refueling was completed and the men got to bed. Four hours later Ford took off for Surabaya in the Dutch East Indies. As the sun came up he looked down on thatched-roof villages, and navigated from island to island, guarding total radio silence. Suddenly, as he neared Surabaya, a fighter plane rose to meet him—and then three more. All four moved into position to blast the Boeing out of the sky. These were British fighter pilots, and they began calling the ground for instructions. They wanted to shoot the Boeing down; their voices could be heard as they discussed it. Ford's radio operator, John Poindexter, was trying to communicate with them, but was not getting through. Ford, cursing the camouflage he had ordered painted on in Auckland, could only fly straight ahead and wait.

The ground station asked if the flying boat bore identifying marks. After a moment's hesitation, one of the fighters closed in overhead. The pilot radioed that he could discern part of an American flag on the top of the wing.

"Stay on her tail," ordered the ground. "If she gets even a little way off the normal course, shoot her out of the sky."

Later in the officers' mess Ford and his crew chatted with these pilots. The young pilots, after several recent air raids, had gone up eager to shoot something down. The Boeing had been very, very lucky.

Ford wanted no repetition of this. The world was tense, and no one between here and Europe had ever seen a Boeing flying boat before. He was worried about itchy trigger fingers. He wanted messages sent ahead. He wanted everyone to know he was coming. He wanted to buy 100-octane aviation fuel also, but there was none on Java, only automobile gas. Having no choice, he took it, though the next leg of the journey would be the longest flight any of them had ever made, almost twenty-one hours across the Indian Ocean to Ceylon.

On the afternoon of December 21 Ford ordered the anchor hauled up, and he turned the flying boat into the wind, all four engines roaring. He used his last tank of aviation fuel on takeoff, then switched to auto gas. Very soon the engines started to pop and spit.

All afternoon the Boeing flew west, crossing the Java Sea, passing through the Sunda Strait. Below now in the night was the Bay of Bengal. Ford worried about his engines, and he worried about missing Ceylon altogether. If he got lost over India, he might run out of fuel before he could sort himself out. He had no charts. All he had was the latitude and longitude of his destination. So he stayed beneath scud and broken clouds, looking for lights for as long as the night lasted, looking for land after that. He was so low that he flew right over the top of a Japanese submarine. Its crew was on deck enjoying the fresh air. As the Japanese ran for their deck gun, Ford added full power and pointed his nose up toward clouds. The engines knocked and missed. The clouds approached too slowly, but at last the flying boat disappeared into them and was safe. A little later Ford spied Ceylon ahead, and then he was over Trincomalee, where no Boeing had ever landed before, and he was trying to pick out a path amid the harbor craft.

For one day following this nearly 21-hour flight, Ford and his crew rested. On Christmas Eve, about two thousand pounds overloaded with aviation fuel and with engines still knocking, they took off for Karachi, and thirty-four minutes out of Ceylon No. 3 engine blew, with oil pouring back over the wing. Ford threw the plane into a 180-degree turn, returned and landed. Once safe in the harbor he and copilot John Henry Mack looked at each other. That engine had lasted them all the way across the Indian Ocean plus only 34 minutes. Their "safe" 21-hour crossing had been that close.

Ford's flight engineers, Swede Rothe and Jocko Parish, tore down No. 3 engine. When they came to No. 6 cylinder, they found that ten of the sixteen studs holding the cylinder on had broken off. The studs themselves could be replaced from spares, but the job could not be done without a special tool, and they did not have it. Parish went across the harbor to a British warship, borrowed some cold rolled steel and the warship's lathe, made the tool he needed, and went back to the flying boat and to work. Repairs took the rest of Christmas Eve and all of Christmas Day. On December 26 Ford lifted the flying boat off Trincomalee harbor for the second time. The plane climbed so slowly in the still dawn air that fourth officer John Steers thought he could almost feel the palm fronds brushing the bottom of the hull.

All that day they flew across India, past terraced gardens, past a castle on top of a mountain, past villages and lakes and eroded country, landing about 4:00 P.M. in Karachi, where they went to the Carleton Hotel and soaked in deep tubs. Afterwards they changed a piston in one engine, took on 3,100 gallons of fuel, and on December 28 flew along the northern coast of the Gulf of Oman, then across the Persian Gulf to Bahrain, only 8 hours 9 minutes in the air—no problem, an easy day. Ford thought Bahrain the hottest and dampest place he had ever been to. When he came out of the hotel in the early morning, the gutters were running with dew as though from a shower of rain. But he was more concerned about his engines. Again there had been no high-octane fuel. Again he had been forced to top up with automobile gasoline.

In addition, having been denied permission to overfly Arabia, he had been obliged to file a flight plan skirting the entire peninsula, adding hundreds of miles to today's journey. However, as soon as he had taken off and climbed above a solid undercast, he steered straight across the Arabian Desert, navigating by the sun only. The undercast broke just as he overflew the Great Mosque at Mecca. At ten thousand feet the engines were popping and sputtering, but they kept pulling. Later Ford steered out across the Red Sea, and then into the Anglo-Egyptian Sudan. Late in the afternoon the Nile came into view. He followed it to where the Blue and the White Nile met. The river looked filthy and yellow. He put down on the water below Khartoum and went ashore, leaving his two engineers to check over all four engines as best they could.

But later, as Ford roared down the Nile on takeoff, part of an exhaust stack blew off No. 1 engine. Although the flying boat gained altitude, this made No. 1 very much noisier than the others, and it constituted a fire hazard as well. But there were no spare flying-boat parts in Khartoum, no way to repair it if they landed. Grimly Ford pointed the Boeing south-west toward Leopoldville and the Congo, and kept on going. Below now was rolling open country with a few native villages from time to time, and some rocky ranges of low hills. Then the country turned into jungle, and navigation was by dead reckoning, Ford and his navigator trying to match rivers to their maps. The Congo was coffee-colored when they saw it. It looked sluggish, but wasn't. Ford, as soon as he landed, felt the flying boat caught in a six-knot current. That was late New Year's Day. He opened the hatch and stepped out into a moist blanket of heat.

The next morning he and his crew were back on board early. They had taken on 5,100 gallons of aviation fuel weighing some 33,660 pounds. The day was hot. Not only was the temperature very high, but there was no wind—and just downstream began the cataracts. A worried Ford revved his engines as high as they could go, and headed downstream. He would have to drive the Boeing downstream, taking advantage of the six-knot current but heading straight for the cataracts, hoping to lift off out of this glassy calm before going over the edge. But the flying boat was so heavily loaded that it would not lift. An average takeoff would have lasted thirty seconds. This one took ninety-one. Just before entering the rapids, the hull broke contact with the river—barely. Ford held the throt-tles wide open because beyond the cataracts came the gorges of the Congo—a new problem. The flying boat was so heavy that Ford couldn't make it climb. It was down in the gorges. The wings were deformed from the overload of fuel and the ailerons wouldn't move, and Ford was skid-ding all of his turns. To hold the engines wide open any longer than a minute was to risk burning them out, but three minutes had now gone by, and still Ford couldn't throttle back. Still he held full power until at last the Boeing had cleared the gorges and begun to climb.

After dropping back to cruising power, Ford listened to his engines for a while. They sounded all right, so he pointed the nose of the Boeing due west toward the South Atlantic and Brazil.

All through the afternoon and night the Boeing droned on, and at about ten the next morning those aboard her sighted the coast of South America far ahead. It was nearly noon when they landed. They had been in the air 23 hours and 35 minutes and had covered 3,100 nautical miles.

For four hours the Boeing lay on the water at Natal. It was refueled, and the exhaust stack on No. 1 engine was wired back in place. Two men in rubber suits and oxygen masks went through the plane spraying it with insecticides, and when Ford and his crew came back on board, all their maps and petty cash—the currency of the various nations passed through en route—were missing. They took off. The repaired exhaust stack blew off immediately, and No. 1 engine hammered all the rest of the way north to Trinidad, where they landed about 3:00 A.M. the next day, after 13 hours and 52 minutes from Natal—a total of more than 40 hours of steady going from Leopoldville. In Trinidad, feeling they were almost home, they went to bed. Most of them slept around the clock.

Then they filed back on board for the final leg of the first flight around the world by men who had not started out to do so. New York was still nearly 16 hours away.

At six minutes to six on the bitter-cold following morning, January 6, 1942, the control officer on duty at LaGuardia field was shocked into instant alertness by the voice that came over his loudspeaker, by nineteen words that announced one of the epic achievements in the history of aviation. It was Ford's voice, and it pronounced in matter-of-fact tones the following message: *"Pacific Clipper,* inbound from Auckland, New Zealand, Captain Ford reporting. Due arrive Pan American Marine Terminal LaGuardia seven minutes."

When it landed, water splashed up onto the Boeing's wings and froze solid. The hawser on the buoy was like a chunk of ice. But Captain Ford and the *Pacific Clipper* had made it home.

43

Loyalty

Lindbergh, upon his return to the United States in 1939, had become an isolationist. He had warned against the entry of the United States into the war in Europe. He had become a speechmaker, a writer of treatises. He had denounced President Roosevelt, whose policies, he said, would lead to war. He had argued that Britain, faced with the might of the German Air Force, should be allowed to sink. The boyish hero of the past, the flyer who had once engaged in a pillow fight with Juan Trippe, had become a bit shrill. Lindbergh now took himself extremely seriously indeed.

He had lived too long in England, he said. He seemed to consider the British aircraft industry and most British aviation people incompetent. Whereas in Germany, which he had also toured, he had seen and put his hands on Messerschmitt 109's. He had been received by Göring while photographers' flashbulbs exploded—one photo showed the beloved couple, Charles and Anne, standing in Göring's library. They and the fat general are in the background. On a table in the foreground, occupying most of the photo, is a picture of Hitler. Of course, all this was carefully staged by the Germans, who had used Lindbergh—without his consent —for their own purposes. But the photos existed.

Lindbergh, following the attack on Pearl Harbor, had been among the first to rush forward to offer his services to his country. The trouble was, no one wanted him. He made a trip to Washington, where he was interviewed by Secretary of War Stimson. Stimson moved him along to Assistant Secretary Robert Lovett and to Henry ("Hap") Arnold, commanding general of the U.S. Army Air Corps. His country having been attacked, Lindbergh said, he wanted to serve in an important job in the Army Air Corps. Stimson, Lovett and Arnold were polite to him. All three suggested that in view of his public stance these last few years, it would probably be impossible for Lindbergh, as a member of the armed forces, to give himself wholeheartedly to the war effort, and to the service of his commander in chief, President Roosevelt.

If he wanted to help, Lindbergh realized, if he wanted an important job, he had nowhere to turn but to Pan American. He would have to see Trippe.

But he didn't go to Trippe directly. Instead, he turned to Trippe's vice president, Harold Bixby, who was also in Washington at the time. He invited Bixby, the former president of the St. Louis Chamber of Commerce and the principal backer of *The Spirit of St. Louis,* to supper, and after they had dined, Lindbergh brought up the subject that was on his mind: he wanted to contribute to the war effort by becoming actively associated again with Pan American in some major way. Bixby's reaction was enthusiastic. There were many places where Lindbergh could help, he said. But he did not offer to intercede with Trippe. When Bixby had gone, Lindbergh got out his diary: "The next move," he wrote, "is, of course, to contact Juan Trippe. Bix says Trippe will be in Washington in the morning."

All the next morning Lindbergh tried to get through to Trippe by telephone. Late in the afternoon Trippe finally called back. Although Lindbergh wanted to meet with him as soon as possible, Trippe suggested an appointment three days later in the Pan American offices in New York. That winter Lindbergh was living on Martha's Vineyard. It would mean laying over an extra day in New York. But it was the best appointment Lindbergh could get, so he took it. He then went out for a walk in the night air. The White House, he noted, was completely blacked out.

In Trippe's office three days later Lindbergh recounted his discussions with Stimson, Lovett and Arnold: the military didn't want him. His contribution to the war effort, he said, would have to be via the aviation industry and he wanted to work for Pan American.

Trippe seemed cordial. But before anything was done, he said, he probably ought to clear matters with the War Department and with the White House. Echoing Bixby, Trippe, too, claimed that there was much Lindbergh could contribute to Pan American. He expected to be talking to the President later in the week and so should be able to get an answer very soon. Trippe then asked a surprising question: Did Lindbergh think he should talk to Lord Halifax too—in other words, get British approval as well?

"By all means," answered Lindbergh, "if you get the opportunity."

The week dragged by. Finally at Martha's Vineyard Lindbergh's phone rang one evening, and it was Trippe. He said that "obstacles had been put in the way" of Lindbergh's taking an active role with Pan American. Trippe was again cordial, but also rather vague. He gave the impression that he did not wish to speak on the phone, and he suggested that Lindbergh drop in to see him "sometime next week."

Another trip down to New York for Lindbergh.

Eight days passed. At 10:00 A.M. on February 3, almost two months after the attack on Pearl Harbor, Lindbergh and Trippe again sat opposite each other in Trippe's office—the same big office in which Whitney had once sat. Lindbergh had chosen then to remain neutral. It was Trippe who chose to remain neutral now.

Trippe said he had talked to the War Department, and that "they" were quite willing for Lindbergh to resume active work for Pan American. Afterwards he had gone to the White House, where "they" were very angry with him for even bringing up Lindbergh's name. "They" did not want Lindbergh associated with Pan American in any capacity. Trippe seemed chagrined as he recounted this, or, at least, Lindbergh chose to think so. It was inadvisable, Trippe concluded, for Lindbergh to join Pan American at the present. Instead, they should "leave the door open" because who knew what the future might bring. Attitudes and conditions might change later on. They shook hands and Lindbergh walked out of Trippe's office.

Later Lindbergh went to work for Ford, who was building B-24 bombers, and then for United Aircraft, whose Pratt and Whitney engines powered more U.S. warplanes than any other, both corporations being at least as sensitive militarily as Pan Am, and perhaps more so. If in Washington "they" had really objected to his joining Pan Am, "they" were curiously mute afterwards. What seems clear is that Trippe, if he chose not to fight for Lindbergh, did so for reasons of his own. He was certainly not afraid to stand up to the White House to defend a man he believed in, as was proved by the case of Erwin Balluder.

Balluder was his manager for Latin America and Mexico. He had come with the company in 1929 with the takeover of Compañía Mexicana, and he had managed the division ever since. He was the man who had supervised Silliman in Central America; he had also supervised, to some extent, Von Bauer and SCADTA in Colombia.

In Colombia, without knowing it, Balluder had made an implacable enemy—Ambassador Spruille Braden. Braden, having become increasingly impatient with Trippe's reluctance to fire the Germans and to take over SCADTA, had gone so far as to accuse Trippe of German sympathies. Braden's eye also fell on Balluder, whom he called a German spy.

Balluder was born in the Virgin Islands of German parents in 1892. His father was a director of the Hamburg-American Shipping Line. Balluder, though an American citizen, was educated partly in the United States, and partly in Germany. He spoke German from childhood, and he continued to speak it occasionally in Mexico City, where he lived. Especially he liked to speak German to his wife, as if it were a secret language only they could understand. But suddenly most of the free world and Germany were at war (though the United States was still neutral), and a female journalist who had stayed with the Balluders as a house guest in Cuernavaca went on afterwards to the Canal Zone, where she denounced Balluder to Major General David Stone, the commandant there. Stone contacted his friend Ambassador Braden, and the two virulent patriots became determined to drive Balluder out of Latin America and out of Pan American.

Balluder had lately been moving through Mexico and Central America signing airport contracts; in addition to his post as division manager, he was also the principal local officer of Pan American Airports, Inc. He was in Venezuela when news reached him that he was thought to be a spy and therefore ought to be removed from his job.

Believing that the charges had originated with General Stone, Balluder wired Silliman in Guatemala to meet him in the Canal Zone—the heart of Silliman's territory—and he flew there himself. The two Pan American men called on General Stone on a Sunday. "I am an American citizen who stands in the confidence of our company," Balluder told Stone. "I have signed all the contracts to do with defense of Central America. It is true that I have a German background, but I am a good American. You say I am a German agent."

Stone became apologetic. Impressions were often misleading, he said, and he had a number of German friends who were completely loyal to the United States.

Balluder said that he was working for the United States in Mexico in a sensitive capacity, and that Stone's charges weakened Pan American and hurt national defense. He wanted a complete retraction, and pushed to get it.

"You have a president, Trippe, who is a traitor too," said Stone. "He should be brought up on charges for protecting Von Bauer."

"I have talked to you like a gentleman," said Balluder. "Now please shut up."

Braden pressured Trippe to fire Balluder. When Trippe did nothing, Braden went to the State Department and, ultimately, to President Roosevelt himself. Roosevelt sent for J. Edgar Hoover, who assigned FBI agents to investigate Balluder. An elderly "tourist" moved through Mexico City asking Balluder's friends how he felt about Jews. The FBI report that reached Roosevelt's desk advised that Balluder was a security risk. Roosevelt summoned Trippe and ordered him to get rid of Balluder.

Trippe called Balluder to New York—and left the division manager waiting outside his office door for days. This did not surprise Balluder, who had waited there before. Trippe's anteroom sometimes resembled a doctor's office, and once in the early thirties, after waiting weeks on a couch outside Trippe's office, Balluder and Dunten had had themselves photographed as if asleep on it; later they sent out this photo, together with a witty poem, as a Christmas card.

But this time as he waited, Balluder became more and more troubled. When Trippe went to Washington, Balluder followed him there. Pan Am had an office off Connecticut Avenue at that time, which was where Balluder at last managed to corner Trippe. Balluder by now was worried not only about his job but also about his daughter, who was ill in a San Antonio hospital facing surgery.

Trippe said, "Erwin, there is serious talk about you in Washington. You can't go back to Mexico."

Balluder said, "But, Juan, I have my family and my home in Mexico."

"Well, you can't go back as a Pan Am employee."

Balluder, so he said later, went faint. He had to lean against a door-jamb. He said, "But, Juan, I've been your servant for ten years. What's happened?"

Trippe would not say. The pressure from Roosevelt himself was not known to Balluder—he learned of it only later. Balluder still thought his principal enemy was General Stone.

"Don't deprive me of my title," he said. He was pleading with Trippe to support him against General Stone. "I signed a lot of contracts for Pan American. You have to support me."

Trippe demanded a written loyalty oath from Balluder, and once he got it he went back to Roosevelt and said he would not fire him. Finally Roosevelt conceded. If Trippe would agree to remove Balluder from Mexico, he would be satisfied, he said. And so Erwin Balluder moved to New York as a vice president, a rank he held until his retirement in 1965 at the age of seventy-three.

If Trippe had never done anything else for him, Balluder said when he learned what had happened, still he would be Trippe's servant forever because Trippe had stood up for him against the President.

44

The War Routes

The U.S. domestic airlines during the war were able to continue commercial service because their routes did not extend into war zones. But over half the Pan American system was converted immediately to military use.

The nine Boeings and the two Martins were painted a dull sea-gray, and inside them every passenger amenity was ripped out—the seats, the berths, even the floor. Commercial aviation would never know such luxury again. Transatlantic and transpacific crossings became shuttle flights —one pilot, Joe Hart, crossed the Atlantic twelve times in thirteen days. The great bloated flying boats were in the air an average of twelve hours a day every day, and all of them, except for the one Sullivan crashed in Lisbon, lasted the war out.

They carried priority passengers and priority cargo only. Admirals and generals flew, kings and queens of beleaguered nations flew—such as Wilhelmina of the Netherlands and George of Greece; film stars flew to entertain troops; and hundreds of that newest of American celebrities flew—the war correspondent. Roosevelt himself flew, becoming the first incumbent President ever taken aloft.

A Boeing took the President to and from the Casablanca Conference in 1943. This was an event of great secrecy. Dutch Schildhauer, who was back in the Navy, contacted Atlantic Division manager Leslie, a naval reserve lieutenant, who was at once activated as a lieutenant commander. Leslie gathered two flying boats and crews and brought them to Miami, where a mysterious Mr. Jones in his wheelchair was lifted aboard one

Boeing, followed by part of his retinue, while the rest of it boarded the other. Pilots and crews, recognizing their passenger, glanced at each other in shock. Leslie had told no one, not even Trippe. The pupil had outdone his master. Trippe didn't even know the two Boeings were gone. At the conclusion of the mission Commodore Leslie—as commander of a two-ship flotilla he was entitled to be addressed as Commodore—put away his naval uniform feeling inordinately pleased with himself, for no untoward event had marred the operation. Another Boeing once flew halfway around the world to take Stalin to a conference, but the Russian dictator did not show up.

Two days after Pearl Harbor a Boeing flew from New York to Calcutta, setting down on the Ganges amid the bridges and the floating corpses of animals with a cargo of tires for the Flying Tigers' P-40's in China. Lacking tires—Hamilton's load had been abandoned on Wake Island—some forty of these fighters were grounded at the time. From Calcutta the tires were transshipped inland via CNAC, and on Christmas Day in an action near Rangoon the Flying Tigers put all their P-40's in the air and shot down, it was claimed, twenty-six Japanese planes.

That was the first load of priority cargo flown. Some later loads were equally unusual: dust filters for General Montgomery's tank engines just before the Battle of El Alamein, without which there would have been no victory; cynogas A dust to put down a plague in China. Tons of ammunition were carried, as well as tons of mail to and from soldiers and sailors in combat. The biggest single Boeing mail load was 13,620 pounds, corresponding to about half a million letters.

An attempt was made to make Trippe a general. He was called to Washington by General Arnold, who spoke to him, the general said, as commander of the Army Air Corps and with the authority of the President, who wanted Trippe in uniform on active duty as head of an air-transport command. A number of domestic airlines would be drawn in and placed at Trippe's orders. Other airline executives were in uniform by now, and C. R. Smith, who headed American Airlines, was about to become a general. It had taken Arnold himself a whole career to make general, and Trippe would become one virtually overnight. It was a flattering offer, and Arnold, giver of this great boon, looked pleased with himself.

Trippe was then almost forty-three years old. His personality had long since hardened. He was not a man to take orders—but rather the one to give them. He gave Arnold his most ingratiating smile. He certainly wanted to help the war effort, he said, and he appreciated Arnold's most gracious offer. However, were he to accept it, he wasn't sure that this would be the best thing for the country, and he began to suggest that

Arnold's theories relating to a military air-transport system were perhaps not as sound as his own.

General Arnold was a choleric individual. He had high blood pressure, and now, as he realized that Trippe had refused him, he began to get red in the face. There was a war on, he snapped, and when he gave men jobs to do, he expected them to do them.

Trippe only smiled and continued his complicated and obfuscatory explanation as to how a military air-transport system ought to be organized.

Arnold's office had swinging louvered doors. They popped open and Major General Eisenhower strode in. He was leaving for Europe, he said, and he had stopped to bid General Arnold good-bye.

Eisenhower then made the mistake of mentioning the conversation that he had overheard in the corridor. Trippe had made some good points, Eisenhower said. General Arnold, furious, ordered both men out of his office.

So Trippe's military career ended before it began. Eisenhower's very nearly did also, for that day he was called to the White House by Harry Hopkins, the President's chief aide. Hopkins suggested that Eisenhower apologize to General Arnold. Eisenhower replied that he had nothing to apologize for, and left.

But a second message, this one from the President himself, called him back to the White House. Roosevelt, too, suggested that Eisenhower apologize to General Arnold in order to preserve good relations for the future. Finally Eisenhower said, "You are my commander in chief, and if you so order me, I will do it." Roosevelt looked across at Eisenhower for a long time. Finally—so Eisenhower later told Trippe—the President stuck out his hand saying, "You are my man to command our forces in Europe."

For most of the war Trippe's Atlantic, Pacific and Africa–Orient divisions operated in effect as military air-transport systems under contract to and orders from the War and Navy departments, which also supplied more and more planes. Always Trippe demanded contracts, and the legal language had to be perfect because enormous amounts of money were involved. In 1943 Pan American was paid more than $85 million by the government, at the same time grossing $35,550,168 on its surviving commercial routes, which were mostly in and to Latin America.

Much of the government money went to Pan American Airports, Inc., whose job had doubled overnight. The War Department now wanted not twenty-five but fifty airports built—and it wanted the original twenty-five done over as well. They had been designed to take planes no heavier than the DC-3 on runways 2,500 to 3,000 feet long. But runways twice that length were needed now, and the landing crust had to be twice as thick also, because the war had called forth transport planes with four engines instead of two, and the new bombers were even bigger and heavier. Flying Fortresses and B-24 Liberators landed fast and with tremendous wheel load. Single-seater fighter planes—and these, too, now moved toward the Brazil–Africa bulge and across the South Atlantic—rolled on two small wheels and landed with the impact of a twenty-ton truck. Furthermore, as the War Department distributed these planes all over the world via the bulge, whole flights of them now needed to set down on Latin American airports all at the same time. Additional taxiways and parking aprons were needed. Runways had to be widened so that in case of an accident planes still stacked up overhead could continue to land. There had to be alternate fields so that even bad weather could not stop the flow of warplanes toward the war zones. As a result, Yale-man Samuel Pryor's job burgeoned and his budget went from $12 million to $90 million. At its peak his program employed nearly 1,000 Americans, together with about 25,000 native laborers. Pryor himself proved a brilliant manager, and as success followed success the morale and efficiency of his men reached incredible heights.

No job stopped these people. Once they diverted a river that got in their way. Another time an out-of-gas B-24 landed on its belly on top of waist-high scrub in a kind of clearing in the Brazilian jungle. Apart from a cracked bombardier's window the plane was intact—though, of course, "hopelessly" lost to the war effort. The pilot, Lieutenant Felix Kershner, and his nine-man crew walked out. The men struggled through matted brush, floated their rubber life rafts down narrow, stump-filled streams, and at last came to a river which led to civilization. It had taken them eleven days.

An airport building gang from Belém decided to go in there and get the bomber out. In charge was Pan American Airports' engineer Mario de La Torre. William Moulton was the foreman of fifty-four handpicked laborers.

The first job was finding the B-24—it took a search plane four days to spot it. Then De La Torre, thirty-three years old, born in Ecuador but educated at the University of Maryland, plotted out a route into the jungle. By motor launches the safari started up the Acará River, then branched off into a tributary called the Turiaçu. After covering about a hundred and fifty miles, it reached a still smaller tributary too shallow for the launch, so the men piled into native canoes and paddled upstream fifteen miles more. There the canoes were beached, and the men struck inland on foot. A bushmaster, one of the deadliest snakes known, bit De La Torre on the left index finger. He shot off the end of his finger, and kept going.

It took the men four days to hack their way through to the "clearing" —apparently a former lake bed—where the B-24 lay on its belly on top of the brush. The entire clearing was carpeted with three-foot-high shrubs tangled in heavy grass. A 5,000-foot-long runway was staked out, and every shrub, every blade of grass within it marked for destruction. The men worked with machetes and hoes. They hacked at roots with the sides of shovels. Snakes were discovered and killed. Day after day in sweltering heat they grubbed their runway out of the jungle. Some suffered from malaria. All suffered from thirst. The nearest drinkable water was a small creek two miles away—too far. The native laborers cut off muriticia vines one yard at a time, upended them, and drank what little pure water they contained. They were kept going by food and supplies parachuted down by the Brazilian Air Force and also, as the runway took shape, by the sheer challenge of the thing—to get that bomber out of there. Once a cake of ice was dropped to them, and for a few hours they enjoyed the luxury of iced tea. At night, exhausted, they crept into their tents and were kept awake by the monkeys, who congregated by the hundreds and screamed until dawn.

Within two weeks enough of a runway had been grubbed out and leveled for a light plane to fly in with needed supplies. A week after that the entire mile-long landing strip had been pounded flat, and the B-24 had been jacked up, and then rolled to the end of the strip and turned around. On the morning of the twenty-second day pilot Kershner was in the cockpit gunning his engines. With a wave he started to roll forward. Engineers and laborers were all cheering. The giant bomber sped down the runway, and then was off the ground. It lifted above the trees at the edge of the clearing, waggled its wings and was gone. De La Torre, Moulton and the work gang were grinning and patting each other on the back. Then they gathered up their meager gear, packed their tents and started the long trek back to civilization.

Later on in the war a C-54 transport made a similar forced landing in the jungle, and another Airports' crew went in and got it out in much the same way.

In 1942 alone Pan American Air Ferries moved five hundred and forty bombers and transports through the Latin American bases and across to Africa, and military pilots ferried hundreds of planes more. In Africa itself the Africa–Orient Division transported tons of cargo first to the desert armies near Cairo and then, when that part of the war was won, it began flying most of it all the way to India, where CNAC planes and pilots took over for the ride across Burma and then over the Himalayas—the Hump —into China. The route from Miami to India was called the Cannonball Express, and considering its volume of traffic, it was remarkably accident-free. The Hump was where the danger lay, and it was the CNAC pilots who did the dirty job, and who paid the heavy price.

Bond's group was bigger now than it had been and also better equipped. Soon after Pearl Harbor the Flying Tigers—the celebrated gang of American mercenary pilots who had been harassing the Japanese since 1940—had been disbanded. Now some of their number joined the Army Air Corps, usually as lieutenants, and kept on with the job. Most went to work for CNAC as civilians at colonels' pay—but they earned it, for "work" meant going over the Hump.

The Japanese in Burma had cut the Burma Road, China's last surface link with the outside world. Future supplies, if any, would have to come in by air. It was Bond who plotted and opened the new, barely feasible route that for the rest of the war would serve as China's aerial lifeline. It ran from Chungking, the inland Chinese capital, south through Kunming to Calcutta, and the presence of Japanese fighter planes forced it to cross into Burma over the 10,000-foot-high eastern fringe of the Himalayas. This first route was difficult enough, but as the Japanese gobbled up more and more of Burma, Bond had to move it even farther west into even higher regions of the Himalayas. The aircraft used were still DC-3's and DC-2's. They were twin-engined, unpressurized machines, and, of course, they were unarmed. At high altitudes crews and priority passengers had to suck oxygen from bottles, and the planes were often unheated. Worse was the high mountain weather: clouds, heavy turbulence, ice. Clouds represented safety but also death—safety from Japanese patrols, death from hidden mountains. The pilots weighed the risks and—usually—sought the clouds. Successful forced landings were out of the question: below were jungles, mountains, then more jungles. Until late in the war there were no radio beams, airports were not lighted, and during the monsoon runways were frequently flooded. To keep China alive, pilots were obliged to fly in terrible weather, into hailstorms, into the monsoon. They developed their own safety rules, and one of them was this: runways were not unusable until standing water on them exceeded nine inches in depth.

The DC-3 had a standard gross load of 24,400 pounds. CNAC pilots consistently carried 27,000 pounds, sometimes more. Frequently there was no way to judge how heavy a load had been put aboard except by eye, and when the cargo was refugees this was impossible. On May 5, 1942, Moon Chin, an American-born Chinese pilot, left Chungking in a DC-3 carrying six passengers, one of them being Colonel Jimmy Doolittle, who, after leadng the famous "thirty seconds over Tokyo" raid, had crash-landed in China; he was now on his way out. At Myitkyina, Chin landed for fuel, but the Japanese were on the south side of the city, and the plane was surrounded by clamoring refugees. Chin stood at the door counting them as they came aboard. The normal passenger load of a DC-3 was 21 people. Doolittle was counting too. At 30 he became worried, and at 50 appalled. Still the refugees boarded. At 66 Chin slammed the hatch shut. Turning to the shaken Doolittle, Chin told him to calm down. He, Chin, knew how much a DC-3 could carry, and this one could carry 66. Taking off, he made Calcutta without incident, but when the plane was unloaded, 6 extra persons were found stowed away in the rear baggage compartment.

CNAC planes carried all kinds of freight, from bullets to jeeps, from medicines to dismantled road scrapers. And the planes were tough. One survived a Japanese air attack and landed safely with some three thousand bullet holes in it. The pilots were tougher still. They kept their planes flying by scavenging for spare parts and achieved legendary status among other pilots working out of India. The CNAC guys, it was said, would steal anything not nailed down.

But planes and crews were not indestructible. In the course of the war forty-six planes were lost, and twenty-five crews. Bond himself was a leader who worked beside his men, accepting the same risks they did, sometimes serving as copilot over the Hump. One day he was aboard a DC-3 out of Chungking on a flight to Calcutta. About sixty miles south of Kunming ice began to form on the wings and the pilot went higher, hoping to get above it. At 14,000 feet, with the mountains still ahead, the overcast was solid.

Ice began to form on the props, and every four or five minutes chunks would break loose and bang against the fuselage. The pilot went up higher yet but was still in clouds. Ice closed over the windows completely. It was like being in a training plane with the hood down. The plane's heating system failed. It was by then 25 degrees below zero both outside and inside. The engines were working perfectly, but the compass was out. They were flying a radio beam from India, picked up by a direction-finding loop on the top of the fuselage. The radio operator had to keep cranking the loop by hand to prevent it from freezing solid in one spot. Hour after hour they flew on.

At 20,800 feet, half frozen, they were as high as the plane would climb. They were on course according to the DF loop, but knew they were bucking tremendous winds outside and were over the Himalayas in the region of 20,000-foot peaks. If ice was still forming, then sooner or later its weight would bring them down. By the brightness outside his frosted window Bond could tell they were flying in and out of the tops of clouds. He wanted to check the wings for ice, but couldn't see out. When he tried pumping up the window deicer spray, the pressure got so high that the alcohol leaked out. This he rubbed on the inside of the window, but it failed to melt the glaze, and the intense cold plus the rapid evaporation of the alcohol nearly took his fingers off. Finally, by holding his bare palm on the side window, he thawed out enough glass to glimpse one engine and part of the wing. He noted ice on the engine cowling and on the wing itself, but it did not seem to be getting thicker. Although they had no idea how far they had come, whether they were past the mountains or still in them, the pilot began to let down through the soup. They struck no mountain, and when the cabin thermometer rose to zero degree, Bond felt like cheering.

This flight took place in January 1943, a month in which, because of bad weather, only 225 flights were made over the Hump. But as winter gave way to spring and summer, flight totals got steadily better: 551 round trips in August and 561 in September. By February 1944 the total was up to 645 round trips, by October to 942, and by November to 1,068. There were other problems. Chinese military authorities again sought to take over CNAC; Bond again fought them off. General "Vinegar Joe" Stilwell sought the same takeover, for he was outraged that American pilots in his theater of war flew outside of his control. Bond resisted Stilwell and won also. CNAC, of course, was earning money for its services, dollars from the United States and so-called CN dollars from Chiang Kai-shek's China, and Bond carefully hoarded both. Despite soaring inflation, he managed to pay his Chinese expenses in Chinese currency, while sending his dollars to Pan American for investment in U.S. banks, thus accruing a fund with which to rebuild CNAC after the war. Altogether, CNAC planes flew the Hump more than eighty thousand times between April 1942 and September 1945. Almost single-handedly CNAC kept China alive. Almost single-handedly Bond kept CNAC alive.

As the war wound down there was time to hand out medals. Bond got none, nor did Trippe, but the Medal for Merit, the nation's highest civilian decoration—the equivalent for a civilian of the Medal of Honor—was awarded to Samuel Pryor, Trippe's former Yale classmate, for building the fifty airports. Pryor was gratified, of course, but also concerned. He was worried about Trippe. How would Trippe take it? Unwilling to take any chances, Pryor arranged to have his own award both held up and kept secret while he scurried around Washington arguing that Trippe deserved a Medal for Merit too. He was Trippe's vice president, a job he liked and wanted to keep, and so for three months he lobbied. Ultimately he was successful. Trippe was called to Washington and the Medal for Merit was pinned on his chest by the Secretary of War. Trippe was inordinately pleased, and for the rest of his life the framed citation hung on the wall of his office and he frequently pointed it out to visitors. A discreet three months later Pryor stepped forward and claimed his own Medal for Merit.

As for Bond, though he loved China, he had grown ever more pessimistic about its future, and he had flown home to convey this pessimism first to Bixby and then to Trippe (everybody seemed to find Bixby easier to approach than Trippe himself). Bond wanted Pan American to renegotiate its contract with the Chinese. Pan Am ought to sell out most of its share to the Chinese government, retaining only a token 10 percent ownership, he said. Bixby allowed himself to be persuaded by Bond's arguments and long experience in China, and sent him on to meet Trippe for dinner, in the Pan Am House on F Street in Washington. But Bond found Trippe optimistic. The war had hardened CNAC like steel, Trippe told him. Air crews and ground staff had worked splendidly and would continue to do so. There even was a substantial cash reserve for postwar expansion—Bond had seen to it. Trippe, like many others, believed that from now on China would be a strong and unified country and its future, like CNAC's, looked limitless. CNAC could be expected to earn substantial profits, he said, and Pan American deserved to share in them.

Across the table Bond shook his head. There would be no peace in China, he told Trippe. The Communists were stronger than anyone knew, stronger than Chiang Kai-shek, whose government was morally and financially bankrupt. China, Bond pointed out, had been printing money all through the war with nothing behind it. The exchange rate in U.S. dollars, which had been three to one at the start, was five hundred to one now. "Sell out," Bond urged Trippe, "before the Communists take over and we lose everything." The Chiang government, Bond thought, would be glad to negotiate such a contract, and could pay Pan Am out of the cash Chiang himself had stashed in New York banks.

But Trippe only smiled, and repeated his own predictions as if Bond had not heard them the first time: China's future now was limitless; CNAC had become a profit-making airline; Pan Am deserved its share of future profits. Bond stared at his plate, then remarked that Trippe was no doubt correct in his judgment and he himself was wrong. And certainly Trippe's opinion should prevail. However, Bond himself would feel criminally disloyal to Pan Am if he did not to the limit of his ability oppose Trippe's decision. Therefore he had no recourse but to offer his resignation. No one talked to Trippe this way any more, and Bond knew this, or at least sensed it, and he seems to have expected Trippe to react coldly and probably angrily. For a moment the two men only stared at each other.

If Bond felt that strongly about it, Trippe said at last, he would defer to Bond's judgment. Bond was to return to China and negotiate a new contract that would reduce Pan American's interest as low as possible.

The postwar world in all its bewildering complexity was suddenly there, and had to be faced. Trippe was obliged to predict the future—and prepare contingency plans—for many countries. He was wrong about China, but right nearly everywhere else.

Before Pearl Harbor he had already extended his airline to sixty-two countries or colonies, most of them islands and banana republics, and to five continents, some of which it touched only barely—Europe only at Lisbon; Africa only at the west-coast landfall and Leopoldville; Asia only at Hong Kong and Singapore. There were only four U.S. terminals: Brownsville, San Francisco, New York and Miami. Though the greatest international airline in the world, the company's weight was still preponderantly in Latin America. Gross revenues in 1941 had been $39 million, and net profit a respectable $3,361,252. In 1945, a year of part peace, part war, gross revenues had come to $68 million, and net profit only to $7,565,580—of this, $4,460,036 resulted from the deal Bond was able to strike with the Chiang government, which reduced Pan American's participation in CNAC to 20 percent. In other words, Pan Am did not make much money out of the war, whereas the domestic airlines made a fortune. And in the most important respect of all—Trippe considered it most important, anyway—the company had lost tremendous ground because exclusivity was gone. Pan American had flown more than ninety million miles for the U.S. government, double the total of all other U.S. airlines put together. However, twenty-one of the others had managed to some degree to operate abroad—United Airlines to Australia, Eastern to Brazil, Northeast to Iceland, Northwest to Alaska. American had successfully invaded Mexico and had crossed regularly to Europe as well. TWA —at the time the initials stood for Transcontinental and Western Air— had served Europe also, and was pondering a change of name to Trans-World. American Export, after losing TACA and the mail contract, had looked dead in 1941, but the war had exhumed the corpse in 1942, and the company had operated across the Atlantic—to the United Kingdom only—ever since.

Trippe had thwarted competition wherever he could, but was restricted because he could not afford to seem to be endangering the war effort. He had prevented American Export from flying to Lisbon—a neutral country; his exclusive agreement there was still in force, and he did not choose to abrogate it. Braniff Airways, a small regional carrier serving the Southwest, had organized a Mexican subsidiary and had attempted to inaugurate service by using Mexican facilities owned either by Pan American or by its wholly owned subsidiary Compañía Mexicana. On its inaugural flight between Mexico City and Mérida, the Braniff plane was allowed to land at Veracruz, but it was denied permission to taxi to the Mexicana terminal or to refuel. Its employees were not permitted on the premises, and its passengers were not allowed access to the terminal building. This impasse ended when a Mexican military force crashed through the locked gate and led Braniff's gasoline truck onto the field. When the flight reached Mérida, Braniff's reception was similar, or perhaps worse—the passengers left the field by climbing through a fence. The irate Tom Braniff phoned Trippe, or so he later testified in Washington under oath, and was told at first that Compañía Mexicana was responsible and there was nothing Trippe could do about it. When Braniff continued to complain, Trippe told him that Compañía Mexicana's actions had been quite right, and that this was Pan American policy. If Braniff intended to invade Pan American territory and to compete directly with Pan American service, he could not very well expect Pan American to offer active cooperation.

But elsewhere in the world Trippe could do little more than watch other people's planes land and take off. Long before the war ended, the Pan American monopoly abroad looked irretrievably shattered.

That so many domestic airlines learned to fly the oceans was the work of a single man, Air Corps Chief of Staff General Arnold. Arnold wanted as many airlines as possible operating overseas, both now and after the war, and his motives were at least partly patriotic. To depend upon a single international airline was militarily unsound. The more companies that served foreign routes, the better prepared the Army would be now and in the future to react to military emergencies. Arnold had taken it upon himself, in effect, to decide postwar civilian air policy. Although he would not control this policy when the war ended, he did now, and he had unilaterally determined that the Pan American overseas monopoly should end. It seems likely that his motives were also at least partly personal. There were reasons why he should feel animosity toward Trippe.

In the first place, it had been Arnold himself, then a major, who had once sketched out air routes to Latin America and had taken preliminary steps to resign from the Army and to form an airline called Pan American. But he had not resigned from the Army, and the airline he had once conjured up had been controlled by Juan Trippe since 1927.

In 1940 he and Trippe had flown to England together. They had stood on the hotel roof watching the bombing together. Then the messenger had come summoning Trippe to a meeting with Prime Minister Churchill. It was Trippe who had dined alone with Churchill, not Air Corps Chief of Staff Arnold.

Then in 1942 Arnold had attempted to conscript Trippe into the Air Corps as head of what became the Air Transport Command and Trippe had refused him. Arnold had conscripted C. R. Smith of American Airlines instead, and afterwards had promoted him (ultimately to major general), praised him and decorated him on every possible occasion. The new policy Arnold was now trying to dictate would not only cut Trippe down to size, but would also aid Arnold's friend Smith.

And so in mid-1943 Arnold had called a secret meeting in Washington to which he invited all U.S. airlines, Pan American included. To these assembled men Arnold explained his concept of postwar air policy, and he "ordered" them (in 1943 Arnold was a peremptory man) to form a committee to assure free worldwide competition among airlines after the war.

There followed a conference at which representatives of seventeen domestic airlines decided that Arnold was right, and most of them determined then and there to file applications with the CAB for postwar international air routes. They also voted to contribute to a fund that would total $250,000, and this money would be used to advance their cause. Lastly, they published a statement of policy, and it was blunt. There could be no rational basis, it read, for permitting air transport outside the United States to be "left to the withering influence of monopoly."

Trippe managed to talk William Patterson, president of United Airlines, into not joining the committee, but he had no other success, and there remained sixteen airlines grouped against him, making it very clear to Washington, and to the CAB, where political weight lay. Inevitably the CAB announced publicly that it would entertain applications for international routes from any and all airlines interested. The previous official policy, which had always favored Pan American, was over.

Trippe's attitude toward overseas competition had not changed. To him, the common enemy was the foreigners. His principal postwar job would be to reestablish his company's "chosen instrument" status—no matter what the cost—and by the time the war ended he had taken preliminary steps. As was usual with Trippe, he saw a number of different paths toward his goal, and although some seemed contradictory, he was nonetheless energetically, and also secretly, already embarked on all of them.

Part V

THE NEW WORLD

45

The Community Company

Trippe's first move after the Washington conference had been to sit down at his rolltop desk—on the Pan Am floors of the Chrysler Building this wretched old desk was as much a symbol of Trippe's power as the huge globe used to be—and after that to light up one of the cheap cigars he favored at the time. Then he had begun to rough out a plan so audacious that it would, if successful, wipe out all of his adversaries at once—the sixteen domestics that wished to compete against him, and General Arnold too.

By September 20, 1943, the forty-four-year-old aviation tycoon had a first draft, and he ordered it printed up into a ten-page pamphlet entitled: A PLAN FOR THE CONSOLIDATION OF ALL AMERICAN-FLAG OVERSEAS AND FOREIGN AIR TRANSPORT OPERATIONS.

What he had written was nothing more nor less than a new bill, one he intended to put before Congress himself, one that would outrage, seduce and divide official Washington for the next four years. Trippe seemed to know this in advance. His bill read well. Its message pleased him. Once it had been enacted the competing domestic airlines would disappear from foreign skies, and monopoly—though of a slightly different type—would again hold sway.

Every other major trading nation, the pamphlet/"law" read, concentrated its strength behind a single "chosen instrument" airline. America in the postwar world must do the same. American companies competing against each other in foreign countries would be obliged to vie for the favor of the foreign governments to the detriment of their own best interests. The U.S. government would not be able to support any one of them. The foreigners, meanwhile, would be heavily subsidized by their own governments, and would engage in practices inimical to the Americans. For instance, the foreigners would feed all traffic generated in their countries into their own airlines. In America the many airlines were at odds, and they would feed their traffic into whatever foreign-flag airlines fed them back, not caring how this might hurt competing American-flag airlines, and not caring either how much it might add to America's balance of payments deficits.

To combat the foreign threat, America must have a single chosen instrument too. All who knew Trippe well were convinced he sincerely believed in America. They were convinced also that to him America and Pan American were the same. What was best for the one was best for the other.

How then was this American-flag airline—the pamphlet called it a "consolidation"—to be achieved?

In 1943 only three airlines regularly operated abroad on a commercial, as opposed to a military, basis: Pan American, Panagra and American Export. The first of the steps Trippe proposed was that these three companies be consolidated. The result, at the option of Congress, would be either (a) a new company or (b) Pan American.

Once this was effected, the consolidated company would issue around $200 million worth of common stock, one quarter of it to the three component airlines (Pan American, Panagra and Export) in proportion to their actual assets; and the remaining three quarters, in proportions to be worked out later, to the rest of the American transportation industry—the domestic airlines, the railroads, the shipping lines, even the bus lines. The result would be a "Community Company" (Trippe's phrase)—one company, and only one, operating overseas; the other airlines would own shares in it, and would cease any competing activities at once.

To encourage the domestic carriers to remain permanent participants in the Community Company, it would be made onerous for them to sell out. They would have to agree that if they desired to sell, they must first offer their stock to the company itself at book value or at the issue price, whichever was greater. The company would have thirty days in which to buy. If it did not buy, then the stockholder would have sixty days in which to sell the stock elsewhere—after which the Community Company would get a second crack at it, presumably at a lower price.

Many who studied his pamphlet thought that this was one of Trippe's most cunning strokes, for it seemed to ensure that the Community Company—which surely would resemble Pan Am, which might even be Pan Am—would eventually own all its own stock itself.

The operations of the company, the pamphlet continued, would be split into divisions, and each division would enjoy autonomy. Facilities for engineering research would be maintained, and a postwar aircraft-procurement program would begin at once. (Pan Am, under Trippe, had been split into autonomous divisions that came together only at the top of the Chrysler Building; Pan Am had an engineering research department; Pan Am was already preparing plans for postwar aircraft procurement.)

Another interesting provision was this: the Community Company would be authorized to enter into ten-year operating agreements with the domestic airlines for equipment and personnel interchange. Was this a means, Trippe's critics asked, by which the company would eventually be able to take over control of one or more of the domestic airlines?

During the ensuing weeks Trippe refined his plan and shaped the language exactly the way he wanted it. It remained only to get it written as a bill, and after that to ram it through Congress—and partly this would be the job of a woman named Anne Archibald.

Apart from his wife, Trippe displayed little interest in women. At dinner parties he avoided even conversing with them, and no one ever saw him look at a woman with prurient interest. Therefore it sometimes seemed strange that a woman ran his Washington office.

In 1943 assistant vice president Archibald was fifty or thereabouts, older than Trippe. She was a smooth-talking, hardheaded lady who wore a mink coat, flamboyant hats and, usually, an orchid corsage. Her refrigerator was sometimes too stuffed with orchids to take in food, and some of her friends referred to her as "little orchid Annie." Dimpled, red-haired, she gave a surface impression—it was dead wrong—of middle-aged frivolity.

Mrs. Archibald was born Anne Marie Monahan in Boston, and in the twenties was the wife of a Marine fighter pilot, Captain Robert Archibald, who commanded a detachment in Nicaragua. When Archibald was killed in a crash in 1928, his young widow went to Washington, where Trippe later hired her as a secretary in his Washington office. Mrs. Archibald took one look at the drab, conventional office and decided to redecorate it. The next time Trippe turned up there the place was filled with flowers and birds. Macaws from Central America screeched at him from ornate cages, and a dozen canaries added to the din. A man wearing a tailcoat, striped trousers, stock and white carnation served as receptionist. Such flair for showmanship might have been expected to sour Trippe's attitude toward Anne Archibald. It did not. Trippe, after all, was a showman too, with a keener sense for public relations than almost anyone else. By 1939 Mrs. Archibald had reached the rank of assistant vice president, the highest she was to attain, and she was one of the few Pan Am executives who could get through to Trippe on the telephone at any time. In Washington she exercised control over the company's sumptuous and somewhat mysterious "house on F Street," and also over the suite of rooms that the company leased in the Statler Hotel.

Supposedly, Pan American had the biggest, most complex, and strongest political machine that ever hit Washington. Perhaps this was true when Trippe and his men from New York came down for special projects. But the rest of the time the "political machine" was Anne Archibald. It was she who handled the essential day-to-day contacts with the CAB, the Post Office, the State, War and Navy departments and the foreign embassies. Every day she visited or received influential people, often at dinner parties. Her contacts and friendships were widespread, for the young officers who had served with her husband were now admirals and generals—even important politicians. Everyone liked her. She smiled a lot, and it was said of her that she never lied. A CAB official once said of her: "She knows instinctively who to call for what, how much to say and not to say. She's direct, disarming and, in her thinking, very masculine. She cinches a deal not by weeping on your shoulder but by knowing the facts better than anyone else."

Mrs. Archibald was now one of those who helped reach senators and congressmen likely to be sympathetic to the proposed Community Company law. With Pan American Airports winding up its labors, Samuel Pryor, Republican national committeeman from Connecticut, was available to help also.

Many senators had shown themselves friendly to Trippe and to Trippe's causes in the past, particularly during the battle to vote down American Export's airmail expropriation three years before. Most notable among them had been Democrats Josiah Bailey from North Carolina and Pat McCarran from Nevada, and Republican Owen Brewster from Maine. Brewster had been especially charmed by Trippe, and was about to fall even more closely under his influence.

The "All American-Flag Line" bill was introduced in the Senate by McCarran as S.1950 in mid-1944, and Trippe was called to an executive session of the Commerce Committee's Subcommittee on Aviation. He testified for four and a half days—four hundred printed pages. Others testified also, with the result that the original bill was rewritten and was reintroduced some months later under another name. Now designated S.326, it was usually referred to as the McCarran bill, for its principal sponsor was again Senator McCarran.

Public hearings conducted by the Subcommittee on Aviation began on March 19, and ended on May 4, 1945—seven weeks. Trippe, when called to testify, began by noting that he had no prepared statement to read but instead had brought with him maps, charts and graphs; he used these to "prove" that overseas air transport constituted only 18 percent of the total potential U.S. aviation market. The domestic airlines, that is, held 82 percent of the market, which made them much stronger than himself. He then pointed out that there had been approximately 31 different applicants for U.S. international routes during the past year or so, including 14 domestic airlines. If the 18 percent were divided by the 31 applicants, or even by the 14 domestic applicants, this meant such a small percentage of business for each that all would fail.

The 18 percent figure was central to Trippe's theme, and all day he kept returning to it, hammering the percentage home. American Airlines, largest of the domestics, had now made application to take over American Export Airlines and to expand overseas. Such a combination, he said, would control not only the largest single share of the domestic business but approximately half of the transatlantic business as well, giving the combination 23 1/2 percent of the total forecasted American Flag business. This left only 13 1/2 percent in the international field to Pan American, even if it were certificated for all remaining international routes. Although Pan Am was bigger, richer and more successful than any domestic airline, Trippe was trying to picture himself almost as a small boy threatened by a bully, and so far he was succeeding quite well.

The transatlantic route, he declared, constituted 50 percent of the total international traffic available. His company had submitted to the CAB detailed traffic estimates and statistics which predicted that the total postwar transatlantic traffic during the six off-season months could be carried by only eight aircraft, and that three more aircraft could handle the extra summer business as well. A mere six round-trip flights per day would suffice for peak summer business. The total estimated postwar traffic would come to only 440,000 passengers a year.

Next Trippe began to talk about fares. It was vital to get them down, he said. Heretofore foreign travel had been restricted mostly to upper-income groups. First-class steamship travel cost from $175 to $185 one way, a figure Trippe was hoping to beat as soon as the big new planes came in, provided labor costs did not rise and provided competition did not drive him to the wall. In fact, Trippe was hoping to reduce costs to four cents a mile, or even to $100—perhaps even less—for a one-way flight to Europe. "But that cannot be achieved unless the American share of the traffic can be concentrated in one carrier," he said. "As I pointed out before, if the American share of the traffic is concentrated in one carrier you still have far less traffic than would be carried by the largest of our domestic lines. We would not have any so called Octopus, or huge operation."

How much, Chairman Bailey interjected, would a monopoly such as Trippe advocated be worth: "How much could you sell out at if you had a monopoly?"

There were those who thought later that Trippe's true genius as a witness was his ability to provide obfuscatory answers to questions he did not like. Looking Senator Bailey straight in the eye, he replied, "It all depends, of course, Mr. Chairman, on what type of regulation the U.S. monopoly is conducted under. I would think, in general, if a united company is set up it would be so regulated by the government that the value of the investment by the stockholders would at all times fairly represent their investment."

Trippe then added, "The position of our company has been greatly misunderstood during the past several years," and he read into the record part of a speech to the thirtieth National Foreign Trade Convention the year before: "Our government should now formulate a national policy with respect to international air transport. In reaching a decision the government should not consider the position of any one airline or any group of airlines. The problem is too big for that. It is a national problem affecting the future, at home and abroad, of all American transportation. It will affect the future jobs and livelihood of millions of Americans. It will affect our foreign trade. It will even affect our national defense. The policy must only be determined by what is best for our country as a whole." After a moment Trippe now added: "Every effort should be made to create a corporate structure that will make it impossible for any one carrier or group of carriers or any individual or small group of individuals to control the Community Company."

Did he mean this? His opponents were accusing him of trying to set up a monopoly he himself would control. Who was right?

This Community Company, Senator Bailey suggested, was the only way for the United States to meet the threat of the foreign monopolies. "Isn't that your theory?" he asked Trippe.

"That is correct," Trippe answered, and he added a short speech. "I believe our stockholders will be better off in the long run and I am confident that our nation will be better off now and in the long run. I believe our board of directors—in my personal view—ought to be congratulated for what I believe is a very unselfish approach to this problem, a willingness to have the company, if so decided by our government, go out of existence—all in the interest of setting up a stronger pattern under which American Flag Air Transport in the international field can be handled."

There was a momentary silence, as if to let committee members ponder these two ponderous details. Pan Am, the mightiest airline in the world, was willing to go out of business. Trippe had actually pushed his scheme through his own board of directors, a group of supposedly hardheaded businessmen, some of whom had brought Pan American into existence eighteen years previously and had lavished on it all care and attention ever since. How had Trippe managed to get their approval? Were his motives and the motives of his board members really so altruistic? Or was there, hidden somewhere in the language of the proposed bill, the certainty that Trippe and Pan Am would reap either control or some sort of enormous profit?

Would Pan American be dissolved? asked Chairman Bailey.

"It might well be dissolved, as would also be the case with the other present international carriers," Trippe answered. "However, it might be decided to use one of the existing international air carriers as the new corporate vehicle." Such decisions as this, Trippe pointed out, would be left for the CAB to decide.

Opponents of the bill—and there were many—were charging that this Community Company bill was at the very least a power grab by Trippe personally, because there was no one else in the country competent to head such a monopoly. And so Senator Bailey turned to this subject: "I believe that it is a sort of law in this universe that somebody has to head up everything," he said. "If you distribute 100,000 shares of stock in anything in the United States, somebody has to head that up."

Trippe: "Here you would have, it seems to me, a board of directors representing the transportation brains of the country—"

Chairman Bailey interrupted. "You have got to head up that crowd in order to elect a board of directors."

Trippe: "Would not the public and each class of carrier elect so many directors, and the board would then meet, elect a management and determine policies?"

Bailey persisted: "Somebody would have to head that up."

"That is correct. No doubt a slate or several slates for that matter would be submitted to the stockholders—the stockholders of the present three international airlines, Pan American, American Export, and Pan American Grace Airways—perhaps some 25,000 in all."

Bailey pursued him: "Take an illustration from our American political structure. You have fifty million voters in America. It takes two political parties to head them up. We would never elect a president if we didn't have somebody to head up those voters."

Trippe: "Yes, sir, that is correct. Now, Mr. Chairman, are there any other questions that you or Senator Brewster desire to ask me?"

Chairman Bailey: "I have no further questions."

Perhaps it was then that Trippe lost Bailey, who heretofore had favored the bill. From the transcript, there is no way to be sure. The hearings went on, and most witnesses who filed before the committee—including representatives from the State, War, Navy and Justice departments—opposed Trippe's bill. If the threat of competition was removed through the establishment of a government-approved monopoly, it was argued, then this monopoly might become less aggressive, less efficient. It was desirable to have a second or third American Flag company flying overseas to serve as yardsticks to test the efficiency of the first. In addition, it was feared that a single company might tend to drift into government ownership. In a field as dynamic as international air transportation, it would be a mistake now to legislate on such restrictive lines.

Finally, public hearings were adjourned, and more than eight weeks elapsed while the subcommittee report was prepared and submitted to the full Commerce Committee, which announced that it would vote on the bill on July 6.

If this vote had been scheduled, say, a week earlier, it might have had a different outcome. As it happened, it was heavily influenced by CAB decisions in the so-called North Atlantic Routes Case announced only the day before. This case involved applications by Export and TWA to break the Pan American monopoly on the North Atlantic by acquiring new routes for themselves. It involved Pan Am's own application for most of these same routes. Finally, it involved the proposed takeover of Export by C. R. Smith's American Airlines, the largest domestic carrier.

Why the CAB chose July 5 to rule—its decision had been pending since the previous year—was never made clear. But one of Trippe's most vocal opponents in the Community Company hearings had been this same CAB. In any case, the ruling came down. The acquisition of American Export by American Airlines was approved, and new routes across the Atlantic were dealt out. Transcontinental and Western Air got Paris, Rome, Lisbon, Switzerland and Greece, plus stops through the Middle East and into India as far as Ceylon. Export, soon to be owned by American Airlines, got the United Kingdom, Holland, Northern Germany, Scandinavia, the Baltic States, Poland and Russia. Pan American got London, Brussels, Marseille (rather than Paris), Southern Germany, Austria, most countries of Eastern Europe, Turkey, Lebanon, Iraq, Iran, Afghanistan and Northern India. The route across the Balkans into the Middle East, which now would have to be served, was neither desired nor economic.

To Trippe July 5 was a black day, not only in itself, but also because of the way it affected July 6. When the Commerce Committee sat down on July 6 to vote on the Community Company bill, many senators felt that public policy had already been decided. The CAB ruling had made bill S.326 moot. A vote was taken nonetheless. The result was ten to ten, and among those voting against the bill was Chairman Bailey himself. The tie vote meant that S.326 would not be reported out onto the Senate floor for debate and possible enactment into law.

Refusing to see Trippe, Anne Archibald, Pryor or anyone else representing Pan American, Bailey went home to North Carolina. The frustrated Trippe decided to send Senator Owen Brewster, who was beginning to be known derisively as "the Senator from Pan Am," down there to talk to Bailey and to try to change his vote. According to Pryor, Trippe did this against Pryor's advice and the result was to make Bailey furious and turn him against Pan American permanently. He now wrote three letters. Not only did he send copies of each to President Truman, but he made them public, and they would haunt Trippe and his company for years to come.

The first went to Senator McCarran: "In rejecting your bill the committee by a tie vote confirmed the existing law providing for the exercise of discretion by the Civil Aeronautics Board. We function quite as effectively in rejecting legislation as in passing it. . . ."

The second went to Senator Theodore Bilbo (Democrat, Mississippi). Any new proposals on the bill, it noted, would be "as we used to say in Mississippi and North Carolina, the same old coon with another ring around his tail." There was no chance of Community Company legislation going through, Bailey wrote. "I know that the Pan American people are desperately in earnest to preserve their monopoly of transoceanic transportation under the American flag. Some of the members of the committee are evidently devoted to the idea of one company operation in transoceanic service, and they have a reasonably good argument. The only trouble with their argument is that the American policy is quite to the contrary. It is impressive to me that every department to which the bill was referred reported against it.

"I do not think that there is any doubt that the legislation before us would operate so as to give Mr. Trippe and his associates the American flag monopoly which they seek."

And the third letter went to Senator George Radcliffe (Democrat, Maryland). "I know a great deal about Pan American activities," Bailey wrote. "I am not unfriendly with its officials. I think they are wrong in their attitude. I do not think they can possibly succeed in changing the law now.

"I thought very favorably of the one company idea myself at one time, but I could not resist the representations of the several departments to which the bill was submitted, nor could I avoid the conclusion that Mr. Trippe of the Pan American was governed very largely by his own selfish interest, and that he was entirely too active. Some of these days I may tell you what I know of his activities.

"Mr. Trippe made the impression upon me of a man living under the conviction that he had a divine call to operate and control American aviation in the transoceanic field. I do not think so at all."

If Senator Bailey thought that the Community Company idea was forever dead, then he did not know Trippe as well as he thought.

A ten-to-ten vote to Trippe was no deathblow. The bill was still there. Congress would reconvene in the fall. Votes could be changed. Trippe only needed to change one.

46

High Stakes

In the meantime there were other roads to the desired end, and Trippe pursued them. The Community Company, he announced, was where America's best interests lay, but if public policy were to be confirmed in a different direction, in the proliferation of domestic airlines in foreign skies, then it was only fitting that these airlines share their routes with him in exchange. It was only fitting that Pan Am be allowed for the first time to enter deep into its own country and compete with its competitors at home. And he filed for the U.S. routes he wanted, routes that the domestics immediately claimed would devastate their business. At the same time he launched a massive advertising and publicity campaign to help him get what he wanted.

By 1945 Pan Am had, or soon would have, thirteen terminal cities: Boston, New York, Philadelphia, Baltimore-Washington and Miami; Seattle, San Francisco and Los Angeles; Detroit, Chicago, New Orleans and Houston. What Trippe proposed now was "merely" to link them all up with high-speed nonstop service. This would not endanger the other airlines, only complement them, he declared, for all still preferred multiple-stop service. They weren't even offering the long-range flights that had been Pan Am's specialty for nearly two decades, and that he, Trippe, was offering now. If accorded the new routes he sought, he would fly San Francisco to New York in five and a half hours, cutting seven hours off the present best scheduled time. He would fly New York to Miami in two hours and thirty minutes, with no time-wasting intermediate stops at places such as Norfolk, Charleston or Jacksonville.

To his competitors the intent of his plan seemed transparent. It wasn't just domestic routes he was after. He was promising competition they could not match. By invading his terrain they had invited him onto theirs.

Trippe frightened people because he thought out every step so carefully and so far in advance. He boxed people in. Eventually they would be able to move only in whatever direction he wanted them to go. He would fly the routes in his fast, radical new planes that were even now on order, and that Pan Am would own and put into service long before any other airline would—extraordinary new planes that would fly so high that storms could not impede them, planes that would carry so many people that he would be able to cut fares to 15 percent under what other airlines were charging.

Trippe filed for his new express routes, and all seventeen airlines objected, including even United, which alone had stood beside Trippe in the Community Company case. Formal interventions before the CAB were entered by those eleven airlines that felt most threatened. The hearings were going to be longer and more bitter than anyone had imagined—except for Trippe perhaps.

However, he seemed confident about the eventual outcome. If the domestic airlines were now to be permitted to operate abroad, he told his stockholders, this justified the assumption that Pan American would be permitted to operate inside the United States, a potential market five times greater than the overseas one. "Your system is, therefore, aggressively pressing its application for authority to operate domestic express routes to link its international gateways. The Civil Aeronautics Board has sanctioned early hearings on this application."

"Aggressively" was perhaps too weak a word. Trippe's public relations men became active, trying to stir up support in all thirteen gateway cities that the new routes would link. Trippe's ads appeared and made startling reading, for they described what the new planes could do.

There were two types on order: the Consolidated Vultee-37 and the Republic Rainbow. The CV-37 would be powered by six pusher propeller engines and would carry 204 passengers over three thousand miles nonstop. It was huge for the time. Its tail would stand as high as a five-story building, and the "footprint" of one main tire would be approximately ten feet square during landing impact. The four-engined Rainbow was smaller—it would carry only 46 passengers—but was much faster, with a top speed of 450 mph. It would have transcontinental nonstop range also, and furthermore it would fly at forty thousand feet, nearly twice as high as any commercial airliner had ever flown before.

The CV-37 would be the largest and most capacious airliner ever built, the ads read, and the Rainbow would be the fastest and highest flying. Trippe's ads made his competitors look bad. Why was he always getting these spectacular planes, while the other airlines were not?

Almost immediately C. R. Smith of American announced that his company, too, was ordering the Rainbow. He would take twenty, to Pan Am's six. But Pan Am would get delivery first, would put the plane in service first, would reap all that publicity, all that new business first.

Even as it began, the battle over the domestic routes was narrowing somewhat, becoming focused on these new planes. If Pan Am got them before anyone else, and if they met their specifications, then the nonstop service the company wished to offer the nation was so extraordinary that its petition to the CAB almost certainly could not be denied.

To represent Pan Am at the hearings, Trippe selected John Leslie. Leslie, the first of Priester's bright young men, was now almost forty and a brand-new vice president. He was a compactly built man, bespectacled, with prematurely snow-white hair. He had graduated not from Yale but from Princeton, which to Trippe was almost as good, and afterwards from M.I.T. Though trained as an engineer, he had shown a genius for administration, and as Atlantic Division manager during the war his decisions had been impeccable.

The divisions were considered almost fiefdoms inside the company; their managers were thought of as viceroys. But not one of them could even transfer a plane without Trippe's signature on the order. Similarly, Leslie could not go into these CAB hearings without clearing his arguments with Trippe first.

Leslie, as he considered what direction his testimony should take, began to cast about for a central theme that would stand up under the hammering from other airlines that he was sure to get. Presently he thought he had found one.

A man named Robert Young had recently taken control of the New York Central Railroad, and he had ambitions to inaugurate through passenger service from New York all the way to San Francisco—at that time all passengers were obliged to change trains at Chicago. A cow or a pig, Young had noted, could ride the same train coast to coast, but a human being could not, and this idea became Young's tag line in a series of New York Central ads. Were pigs better than people?

The same thought could be made to serve Pan Am's case, Leslie decided. Why should a man from New Zealand en route to London be obliged to step off Pan American in San Francisco, change airlines to New York, then get back on Pan Am again to cross the Atlantic? It was a menace to the man's baggage, which often got lost; to his nerves as connections were missed; to his pocketbook, since it was uneconomic; and even to his sanity, since it didn't make sense. This, Leslie judged, was the theme he needed, and he addressed himself to the company's advertising agency and asked for sample ads to be drawn up that would reflect the unfairness of it all. The message should be that Pan Am and its passengers were sure being treated dirty. As soon as the ads were ready, Leslie gathered them up and went in to see Trippe.

Trippe cut him off sharply. "No, no, no, John. That's the worst thing you could possibly do. You're to go in there and talk about the great service we can give the public, the new service, the better service, the new fast airplanes." So the strategic decision from the start was Trippe's, not Leslie's. Leslie's sketches went into the wastebasket. To Trippe they had represented a complaint, even an alibi. They were not Trippe's style.

Even as Leslie composed the new positive approach that Trippe wanted, Trippe himself cast about for the means by which he could merge with one or more of the major domestic airlines. Merger was still another avenue by which he sought his undeviating goal, which might better be defined as total domination of the sky rather than as monopoly, or simple bigness. He was already the biggest, and his size would only grow in the postwar world. Total operating revenue for 1945, partly a war year, would show Pan Am at $67,791,000; American Airlines at $51,408,000; United Airlines at $39,348,000; and TWA at $33,672,000. In route miles the disproportion was even greater: Pan Am at 93,076 miles; TWA at 26,732; and American Airlines, including its new foreign subsidiary American Overseas Airlines, only 19,177. Trippe now considered attempting to merge with all of the above, and with other airlines as well.

As all these simultaneously launched plans went forward, it was Trippe personally who arranged for the one preeminent ingredient—money—without which all would fail. He needed money, lots of money, if he was to pay for the new planes and routes, buy out or merge with competitors, and/or control any eventual Community Company. And he didn't have any.

Fortunately, he had begun thinking about this a long time ago and had taken certain steps.

Trippe had no money because he had plowed such wartime profits as there had been into the acquisition of substantial interests in nine more Latin American local airlines, and in the installation of night-flying facilities throughout the Latin American network. He had not been able to buy any new planes.

Not that these profits had amounted to very much. On the $90 million spent by Pan American Airports, no profit at all had been taken. The company's other wartime services had been conducted at cost plus 4 percent, and this "profit" had fallen steadily throughout the war from $6.9 million in 1941 to $1.6 million in 1944, a year in which American had netted $4.4 million, and TWA $2.8 million.

The company had not even been able to profit very much in terms of publicity, since most of its wartime work—Roosevelt's flight to Casablanca could stand as a perfect example—had been top secret. This was ironic because Trippe never in his life underestimated the value of publicity and public relations. A company's image was much more than what made passengers buy tickets. It was also what made banks willing to lend money, and individual investors willing to buy stock.

The amount of money Trippe judged he needed for postwar expansion was staggering—at least $25 million.

In the past he personally had raised a heavy proportion of Pan American's new capital as it was needed. It was his practice each time to place blocks of shares where he wanted them, and nowhere else. For instance, after winning the several airmail-route contracts in 1928 and 1929, he wrote more than a hundred letters to U.S. firms doing business in Latin America, trying to persuade each to buy into Pan American, and about seventy-six of these companies did subscribe to a total of almost $3 million. Trippe was trying to expand Pan Am's capital structure of $534,-000 to around $6 million. Most of the rest of the needed new capital came in a single $2,875,000 sale to Frederick Rentschler, whose United Aircraft and Transport Corporation bought 50,000 shares of stock at $57.50 a share on April 15, 1929, at which time it was selling on the open market at $62—this was stock that had sold originally at $15 per share. In succeeding years Trippe attracted other companies—Ford, General Motors, Curtiss-Wright—and they bought stock, though never in amounts as big as Rentschler did. Trippe's argument was always the same. Pan American represented America, and it was the job of the entire American transportation industry to back America's international airline. He was selling these men on helping him put the American flag around the world, an argument they liked. When he needed money—and he needed it constantly, two or three million dollars every year—he was always able to get it.

But now he wanted nearly ten times as much as he had ever asked for at one time before—far too much to raise by writing letters. Nor could he go to banks for it because he could not back up such a huge loan: not with wartime profits—relatively speaking, there had been none—and not with still-secret wartime achievements either. In the past he might have gone to a rich individual, like Sonny Whitney. But Sonny had departed, and even had he been there he could not have supplied $25 million. Where, then, was Trippe to get the money? At this time the $2.8 million Rentschler sale was still the biggest single sum he had ever raised.

There was an additional complication. He didn't need the money for as long as the war lasted, since there was nothing, under wartime restrictions, that he could buy with it—certainly not new planes or competing U.S. airlines. Nor did he even want it right now. He was not the man to pay high interest charges while the money sat there doing nothing.

What he wanted was a guarantee of the money in the fall of 1944 so that he could enter into negotiations with aircraft manufacturers at once, and plan the rest of his expansion right now. Ultimately this would allow him to enter the postwar world months ahead of other airlines. He didn't want the actual cash until mid-1945, when, he guessed, the war would end. However, he didn't want to pay any fee for this guarantee, or even for the $25 million itself.

Wall Street, could it have looked into his head, would have considered him mad. First of all, $25 million represented more than the value of all stock marketed in the United States in the entire year of 1942. It represented the biggest single deal anywhere going back probably to the twenties. Nor had any individual, company, investment bank or syndicate of investment banks, as far as anyone could remember, ever agreed to a deal that tied up that much cash that many months in advance. And he didn't even want to pay any fee. The normal underwriter's fees in such instances would amount to about $1 million. Clearly, Trippe was trying to structure the unstructurable. There were rules to high finance, and they were inflexible. Trippe was dreaming. What he wanted was unattainable, self-contradictory, impossible.

Nonetheless, he conceived of a way not only to float $25 million of new stock, but also if it did not sell, to guarantee himself that much money anyway.

With regular banking channels closed, and other former sources of financing closed also, Trippe for the first time reached outside the Yale Club/Wall Street orbit in which he himself by background and training felt most comfortable. Knowing full well the danger, and despite serious misgivings of his own, he began to negotiate with a man named Floyd Odlum, the most notorious financial speculator of the day. He asked Odlum to back his stock offering; any shares not sold to the public Odlum would buy himself.

Odlum was then fifty-two years old, seven years older than Trippe. He was a small, slender man, bald, with piercing eyes behind horn-rimmed spectacles. As early as 1935 he had been listed as one of the thirty men and families who "ran America," and an angry congressman once equated him with J. P. Morgan, claiming that, between them, Odlum and Morgan controlled American industry.

Odlum was not a Yale man. Born in Michigan, he grew up in Colorado, and one of his early jobs was as a newspaper reporter. After taking a law degree, he came to New York and began to make money. He started as a merger specialist in a major law firm, and there learned how to buy up hundreds of millions of dollars of subsidiary companies. But he soon branched out on his own. With a net capital of $39,600, he formed what became the Atlas Corporation, and within two years he had multiplied his company's net worth seventeen times. Four years after that, on the eve of the 1929 stock market crash, the Atlas Corporation had total assets of about $6 million.

Within a few months financiers would begin diving out of Wall Street windows. Odlum would not be one of them. He was only thirty-seven, but shrewder than nearly everyone, and in the summer of 1929 he sold off about half his holdings and put the cash aside. Then he issued $9 million of new stock, sold it to investors and put that cash aside also. He now had $14 million cash, and beginning in the spring of 1930 he walked up and down Wall Street buying up, at a fraction of their real value, companies that were about to go under. These companies he then immediately and quite legally gutted, selling off as much of each company's liquid assets as he could, using the proceeds to buy up more companies. He worked fourteen to sixteen hours a day, chain-smoked, and had nervous indigestion. Wall Street learned a new war song: "Little investment company don't you cry, Atlas will get you by and by." Odlum was sometimes described as the only man in the country who had got rich during the depression.

When in 1933 President Roosevelt took office and an upturn began, Odlum got still richer, for he began selling off some of his holdings as fast as he could, in order to put the money into large-scale financing. He went into the Greyhound Bus Lines, into Madison Square Garden, into New York's Bonwit Teller department store. He went into manufacturing companies and real estate. He took over Paramount Pictures, and he came to control the Curtiss-Wright Corporation. Soon Atlas had assets of more than $100 million and Odlum himself sat on the boards of corporations in many fields: banking, railroads, utilities, oil, mining. He dealt with other multimillionaires—Paul Getty, Howard Hughes, Joseph P. Kennedy—on a first-name basis, and he thought like most of them. He wanted government to get out of big business, and to stay out. He was in favor of hard work and against the five-day workweek: "What are you going to do with the extra two days? Just get into trouble. People are not trained for leisure."

He had a certain style. He once made a business call to London which lasted ninety-five minutes and cost $1,425. He kept a mansion on a ranch in Indian Palms, in California. He had an Olympic-size swimming pool in front of the house and sometimes conducted directors' meetings in the pool. Directors were asked for their votes while treading water, and a secretary at poolside took down minutes in shorthand.

There were those who called Odlum clever, or sharp, or perspicacious. Others merely called him ruthless. He wore a careless, almost indolent face at times, and his nickname was "the farmer." He could look guileless and bland, and his smile could seem complacent. But behind the horn-rimmed glasses his blue eyes could go cold and hard, and when he moved, he moved fast, knowing precisely where he was going.

His second wife was Jacqueline Cochran, the aviatrix, whom he married in 1936. She had been one of the first and most famous of the female air racers, had set records for speed, distance and altitude flying, and had won the Bendix Trophy. During the war she had organized the women's Air Force Service Pilots to ferry aircraft to England. Trippe later said he met Odlum through Miss Cochran. But by 1944 Odlum had been a major force in aviation securities for some time, and he had controlled Curtiss-Wright since 1940, so the two might have met almost anywhere. What is certain is that Trippe knew exactly who and what Odlum was. He went to him anyway.

Odlum had $25 million available because a stock market boom had started in April 1942, more than two years ago. Immediately he had begun converting much of his Atlas holdings into cash, and he had been sitting on this cash ever since, waiting for an opportunity such as Trippe was proposing.

In asking Odlum to underwrite a $25 million stock offering, Trippe was inviting the speculator in dangerously close. Pan American at this time was worth only about twice as much as the sum Trippe wanted—approximately $50 million—and the risk was clear. If the stock didn't sell, and if Odlum got stuck with many shares, then he might use them to take over the company. He had done it before often enough, and perhaps the old Wall Street war song even rang in Trippe's ears: ". . . don't you cry, Atlas will get you by and by."

Negotiations began. Trippe had to structure, in effect, two deals at once, one with Odlum as underwriter and one with the potential customers of the new shares. Of course, the two deals were related. If he could conceive of a stock issue so sweet that it would, as Wall Street describes a sellout, "go out the window," then Odlum would not have to buy up unbought shares and Trippe would avoid his tentacles. And so he structured the stock issue first. At the next stockholders' meeting he would ask permission to split Pan Am stock two for one, and also for permission to issue new shares. When these shares were issued next summer, eight or nine months from now, Trippe would attach a warrant to each that would permit purchasers to buy a second share at $18 at any time within two and a half years—in effect, a two-and-a-half-year $18 option. Since Pan Am shares were selling for about $34 now, he calculated that each share after the split would be worth about $17. But next summer the war would be over and the price almost certainly would rise. Although the $18 warrant price was fixed during the Trippe-Odlum negotiations in the fall of 1944, the offering price of the new stock was not. The Pan Am board of directors would decide that at the last minute in mid-1945.

To sweeten stocks with warrants was not a new idea with Trippe, but in the past a buyer usually got one warrant for each four or five shares bought. So Trippe's bait would be better than what was normally offered. Furthermore, he would be virtually forcing purchasers to subscribe to the additional share in order to protect their equity in Pan Am from dilution.

What Trippe now needed from Odlum was a $25 million guarantee

—any stock not bought by subscribers would be absorbed by the Atlas Corporation. Trippe was asking Odlum to accept this considerable risk, but for it he didn't want to pay money. He wanted to pay with paper. He wanted to pay Odlum with warrants also.

Odlum was agreeable. If the stock boomed, as the speculator believed it would, then his profit would be considerable. In addition, this profit would be taxed as capital gains. The question then became how many warrants Odlum was to get in exchange for his guarantee.

The two men stared across the desk at each other, and for weeks they haggled over this detail and others, at last agreeing that Atlas would receive warrants for the purchase of 500,000 shares (or 400,000 if the offering price per unit was more than $18, or 600,000 if the offering price per unit was under $14).

With that the risk had suddenly shifted back to Trippe. Suppose stockholders left many shares unbought? These, underwritten by Atlas, would now belong to Atlas, in addition to the half-million warrants. Atlas —that is, Odlum—would own perhaps a quarter of Pan Am stock, perhaps more. The feared speculator would be in a position to take over the company. Trippe's own holdings at this time amounted to only 30,413 shares.

So Trippe haggled some more. If the stock issue failed to sell out, if Atlas got stuck with many unbought shares, these would have to be subtracted from the half-million warrants. Furthermore, however many shares Atlas might wind up with, Odlum was obliged to dispose of all but 200,000 in secondary distributions, or by distribution to Atlas stockholders. A maximum of 200,000 shares could be retained by Odlum/Atlas personally.

Trippe kept pushing new and stronger defenses around his position. Pending Atlas's disposition of any excess stock, said stock was to be deposited in escrow, and was to be voted with the prevailing majority— that is, in effect it was not to be voted at all. In making secondary distributions of stock, Atlas was not knowingly to sell more than 4,000 shares to any single purchaser, nor more than 4,000 warrants either.

Trippe, cautious to the last, also demanded the right to cancel this underwriting agreement at any time prior to the stock offering. Odlum agreed to the cancellation clause but attached conditions. He had a habit of removing his glasses from time to time. It was like removing a mask —the indolent farmer disappeared, and his opponent looked into the contained, hard face of the most successful speculator in the world. For each month that the agreement ran prior to cancellation, Odlum specified, cash equal to one-third of 1 percent of the maximum amount of Atlas's commitment would have to be paid to him.

Negotiations halted while Trippe calculated how much money this could cost his company. It was now November 1944 and the offering would probably occur next July. One-third of 1 percent of $25 million equaled $83,333 a month. If the agreement ran seven months, and Trippe then canceled, he would have to pay nearly $600,000. Well, that was high, but he doubted the situation would ever occur.

Odlum pushed harder still. Or, in lieu of such payment—at Odlum's option—Pan Am would be required to sell to Atlas for investment, at $16 per share, 25,000 shares of stock for each month that the underwriting agreement lasted.

The maximum limit must be 100,000 such shares, Trippe insisted. Odlum agreed, and they shook hands on it. The deal was made.

Trippe kept going over details in his mind. He had made no mistake that he could discern. He had the promise he needed. On the strength of it the new planes could be ordered. He felt quite relieved. He had just got up from the highest-stakes poker game of his life against, reputedly, the world's sharpest player, and he had held his own. And he had paid for what he needed—as so often in the past—with paper, not with money.

On December 5 the contracts were signed, and the news was made public. Pan Am stock that day sold for 33 7/8.

Three months later, the stock price having dropped to 25 3/4, Pan Am stockholders at a special meeting in Jersey City approved Trippe's two-for-one stock split and, after that, his agreement with Odlum. The date was February 23, 1945. More than 73 percent of the company's stock was represented at the meeting, and fewer than one-half of 1 percent cast dissenting votes. Trippe entered into immediate negotiations with Consolidated-Vultee for the CV-37, and ordered Van Dusen's publicity department to put out notices describing these "wings of tomorrow."

Meanwhile, with war news good, all stocks began to boom and aviation stocks boomed bigger than most. In March in Europe, American troops crossed the Rhine into Germany, and in the Pacific Iwo Jima fell. In April Okinawa was taken, and on May 4 the German armies began surrendering. About then first-quarter airline statistics were published. Domestic airlines were seen to be up 74 percent over the same period the year before, and the Wall Street boom accelerated. Pan American stock shot up to $28, little lower than before the two-for-one split.

And Floyd Odlum, if the existing agreement went through, would get warrants for 400,000 of these shares at $18 per share. The man's profit would be around $4 million—as compared to the $1 million fee that a syndicate of investment banks would have charged.

Trippe attempted to renegotiate his agreement with Odlum. Again they sat across a table from one another. Odlum's glasses came off more and more frequently. Trippe stared more and more often into the speculator's cold naked eyes.

It was now June. The war was nearly over, and the $25 million was urgently needed. The offering to stockholders was only a few days away.

Would Odlum make concessions, or not? A $4 million profit was out of the question.

But Trippe was well and truly hooked, and Odlum knew it. True, he did have his cancellation clause. What he did not have, Odlum believed, was time enough to exercise it. If the deal fell through now at the last second, this would startle the financial community, make Pan Am's other bankers and creditors suspicious, and it would hurt the company's credit at least to the extent that new financing would become much more expensive to do. In addition, it would depress the price of the stock. And so Odlum held firm. He would concede virtually nothing.

This seemed to leave Trippe with only two options. To go through with the deal, paying Odlum's enormous profit, or else cancel it, in which case Odlum would collect a lesser but still enormous profit from the cancellation clause. But if Trippe canceled Odlum, where else was he to get the money he had to have?

The executive committee of Trippe's board of directors met. To Trippe this was the moment of truth. With his board members already in session, he left the room, went back to his office and phoned Odlum. The Atlas Corporation must make further concessions, or Trippe would cancel.

To Odlum, Trippe's threats were pure bluff. He could not be taken seriously. Cancel now? Impossible. Odlum, considering Trippe a beaten man, refused.

Trippe hung up, stood there a moment, then placed a call to Elisha Walker, managing partner of the Kuhn Loeb bank. Walker—Yale, 1900 —was one of the most distinguished bankers in the country. He was, of course, totally trustworthy. To Walker, Trippe proposed much the same deal as the one already in force with Odlum. But there were major differences. Instead of paying Kuhn Loeb and any associated investment banks in warrants—that is, in paper—Trippe would pay underwriting fees totaling just under $1 million. And the sum of money he wanted now was not $25 million but, given the increased market value of Pan American stock, $43 million. But he had to have Kuhn Loeb's decision almost instantly.

An instant decision on a matter of $43 million? It was possible, said Trippe persuasively, because the deal was already structured. It existed on paper in proper legal language; Kuhn Loeb had only to sign it. Odlum's lawyers and Trippe's lawyers had both been over it carefully. In addition, Kuhn Loeb would not have to guarantee the money eight months in advance as Odlum had done—the stock offering was now only a week away.

The Kuhn Loeb partner replied that he was leaving at once for Trippe's office and would be there by 5:30 P.M.

Trippe returned to the boardroom. He told his fellow members what was happening, and they sat there waiting. The air was so charged, Trippe said later, "that you could cut it with a knife. That afternoon was the most critical afternoon in the history of our company." It was also critical in the history of Trippe. If Elisha Walker refused him, then he was stuck with Odlum. He would seem naïve, bested by the master speculator. He would also seem rash—why had he gone to Odlum in the first place? The conservative-businessman image he had been trying to project would be lost, probably for good.

Precisely at five-thirty the door opened and in walked Elisha Walker. Trippe gave him the Odlum deal to read.

"Will you do this thing?" asked Trippe, when the banker had put it down.

"I will take the responsibility for it," said Walker. They worked out final details, and when this was done, shook hands on it.

As soon as the meeting ended, Trippe phoned Odlum. The deal was off, he informed the speculator. "We can't do business with you." Odlum said, "What? Let me come up to your office." Trippe said, "It's too late," and hung up.

That was June 25. The next day Trippe had Walker's commitment in writing.

Kuhn Loeb put together a syndicate of seventeen other investment banks, and on July 3, with Pan Am stock selling at 25 3/4, the offering, 2,043,261 shares, went on sale at $21.50 per unit. Pan Am was a tightly held company with most stock held in big blocks. As of December 31, 1944, there had been only 13,623 stockholders. These stockholders, and others, promptly bought more than 94 percent of the rights offered, leaving less than 6 percent to be taken up by the underwriters. The Kuhn Loeb syndicate kept $993,203 in fees, and handed Trippe $43 million in new equity capital.

Odlum had exercised his cancellation-clause option on June 30. He bought 100,000 shares at $16 per share, and got warrants for 50,000 more at $21.50, and this amounted to a paper profit of around $1.3 million. But Trippe, with $43 million in new capital and a potential total of $80 million if all the warrants were taken up, was able to gloss this over at the next stockholders' meeting by pointing out that the deal had enabled the company to place orders for new planes. Odlum's paper profit was therefore a reasonable fee for such an important service. The company had paid nothing, after all, in cash.

The deal itself was talked about on Wall Street for a long time afterwards. Such a successful sale of stock, insiders claimed, would have been spectacular even in the wild closing days of the 1920's. In mid-1945 there were simply no words to describe it.

From then on Trippe was regarded on the street as a financial wizard, and in the future, even though sums needed would be even larger ($269 million at the start of the Jet Age, $550 million when ordering the 747's), he would never again have much difficulty arranging the financing that he and Pan American needed.

Odlum's reputation in no way suffered from his defeat—if that's what it was—by Trippe. His outstanding career continued. He was the money behind the Atlas missile which later started man on the way to the moon —when government funding was cut back in the 1950's, Odlum coerced the Atlas board of directors into pumping corporate funds into the program's research and development. He did this for three years until at last the government again backed the Atlas program itself.

But from then on, if Odlum's name came up Trippe would dismiss the subject curtly. "Odlum? He was nothing but a speculator."

47

The Hearings

It may have appeared that with the needed money in hand, Trippe now could almost do what he liked. This was not the case. Pending in the Senate was a revised Community Company bill, and pending before the CAB was his application for domestic routes, and for some twenty months Trippe waited for one body or the other, or both, to take decisive action, but nothing happened. Instead the CAB began ruling on applications by domestic carriers for routes overseas, certificating Northwest Airlines to the Orient, Eastern to the Caribbean, Braniff into Latin America. These lines and others now would oppose any Community Company bill more vigorously than ever. Similarly, the CAB had been busily dealing out to others the domestic routes Pan American had applied for. John Leslie, who would represent the company at the hearings, had had his arguments prepared for months, but had been obliged to revise them constantly as the situation changed. The original application in March 1945 had been based on a number of facts which no longer obtained—that only Pan American could offer the new planes, that certain of the routes were served by only one carrier, or were not even served at all.

High up in the Chrysler Building, Trippe, Leslie and the others waited out the frustrating months. Only in the company's distant outposts could action sometimes be taken. When Braniff attempted to inaugurate its newly awarded route to Havana, Pan American denied permission to use its airport facilities there just as it had done in Mexico earlier. Braniff could use the landing strip only. Braniff tried to build its own terminal, but could not get permission to build a taxi strip connecting it to the runway. So Braniff's service to Havana was blocked. Elsewhere in Latin America, it was charged publicly, airport and runway lights were from time to time extinguished while competing planes were circling overhead. This was alleged to have happened to a Braniff plane at Veracruz, Mexico, and to a Union Southern charter plane at Ciudad Trujillo, Dominican Republic. In the latter case, it was alleged, but not proven, that even the radio calls of the incoming plane were ignored. Supposedly it took the protest and threats of a Jesuit priest waiting to board the plane to get the lights put back on and radio communication established. At other airports, Pan American charged competitors exorbitant landing fees, or demanded that permission to land be obtained from division headquarters in Miami far in advance of the scheduled flights—so far in advance that it became practically impossible for competitors to provide flexible schedules, or to change them to meet passenger demand.

Trippe later denied responsibility for most of this, and indeed may have given no such orders. His divisions were still being run as personal fiefdoms by the men in charge, and the Latin American fiefdom was held by Wilbur Morrison, the most independent of all Trippe's top executives. Morrison was not deterred by the good manners that sometimes weighed down the corporate Yale men. Born in Hallsville, Tex., in 1901, he was a semipro baseball player who went to Mexico at eighteen to work in the Tampico oil fields. His job consisted of delivering payrolls throughout a hundred-mile area infested by bandits. For a year and a half the young adventurer moved through his territory on horseback or by launch or by car, and the bandits never took a payroll away from him. In 1921, when Morrison was twenty, some barnstormers came in with a plane—the safest method yet for delivering payrolls—but the bandits began to wait in ambush in the brush at each airfield's edge. It was Morrison who devised a method of dropping payrolls like bombs out of the air. He had a special bag made up to carry the payrolls, which were all in gold coins, and he sat in the back seat of the open-cockpit plane dropping the gold into the center of the oil camps. By 1923, after four years on the job, Morrison was known as the oldest living oil-company paymaster. Leaving the oilfields, he began to deal in automobile tires, and then entered the prosperous but dangerous business of plugging wild gas wells in oil fields. In 1928 he went to work for Compañía Mexicana as traffic manager under Erwin Balluder. When Balluder was forced out of Latin America in 1941 by charges of Nazi sympathies, Morrison took over the division, and he was still in charge there. If he wanted something, whether from subordinates or from superiors in the Chrysler Building, he was known as a man who would snarl until he got it. No one had any hold on him except Trippe, who apparently admired him and chose most often not to try to control him.

Attempts by the Latin American division to block competition on the new routes were unsuccessful. The only effect was another flood of anti–Pan American publicity.

About this time occurred a second setback. Pan American's domestic-routes case still hung heavily on the spectacular service that the new planes would provide, especially the 204-passenger Consolidated Vultee-37 and the 450-mph Republic Rainbow. But the six-engined CV-37, the largest plane ever built till that time, proved to gulp fuel in unacceptable quantities. Although a military version later served for many years as the Strategic Air Command's B-36, the manufacturers could never meet the fuel-consumption specifications that would have made the plane commercially viable. Three planes did remain on order as hearings on the domestic-routes case at last opened, but it was already clear that the model was a failure, and Leslie was obliged once again to revise his arguments, dropping the CV-37 and focusing attention as much as he could on the Rainbow.

The CAB domestic-routes hearings, which lasted from November 1946 to January 1947, consumed thirty-six working days and amounted to 5,582 pages of testimony. Leslie himself was on the stand five days. He made all of the intellectual arguments that Trippe had ordained and none of the emotional ones that he himself had thought more powerful. He also insisted throughout, as instructed by Trippe, that Pan American would accept no limitations on the nature of the traffic that it would be allowed to carry on these routes; it must be allowed to carry local domestic passengers as well as through international passengers.

Leslie was an able man and an articulate one, and made a superb witness. The new routes sought, he said, would offer Americans improved service from coast to coast and from border to border. Americans proceeding overseas would no longer need to change airlines. Pan Am's existing system would be strengthened, and this was important to the United States. At present 52.7 percent of Pan American's route mileage, though vital to American trade and prestige, was thinly traveled. Income from the domestic routes, if Pan American was permitted to fly them, would help the company keep up these "national interest" routes overseas.

On some of the routes sought, he said, there was no competition at all, even though far more traffic was carried than on many of Pan American's international segments. "It is perfectly absurd that there should be more competition on thin traffic lines abroad than on heavy traffic runs at home." Pan American did not propose to compete with the entire domestic industry—only against a few major carriers on a few specific routes. The potential of the domestic market was enormous, far larger than the domestic airlines would admit or apparently even believed, and there was no evidence that Pan American would cause any of them any substantial injury. Pan Am was proposing long-range operations only, something wholly new. The public would get better service, because Pan American would be "free of the temptation of making intermediate stops." Furthermore, his company's proposed fair reduction to four cents per passenger mile would be a competitive spur to the entire industry to lower fares across the board.

Leslie next pointed out how much money Pan American was already spending on new aircraft, and how much more it was ready to spend on additional units if accorded domestic routes. The domestic airlines, he charged, had been too conservative from an engineering standpoint in backing newer, bigger, faster planes, as Pan American had done since the early thirties.

Cross-examination then began, and for the next four days Leslie was interrogated by men representing TWA, United, American—eleven different airlines in all—plus men from the Post Office Department. He was like one man standing against a seventeen-man team, one man obliged to throw the same pitch to batter after batter. Day after day they belabored him. The most caustic probably was Smythe Gambrell, attorney for Eastern Airlines, who charged that Pan Am's advertising campaign was a blatant attempt to develop public support for services it was not sure it would be authorized to provide. Leslie answered that this advertising campaign was merely intelligent merchandising. Pan Am meant only to place "on the counter" for public inspection those airplanes, flight times and fares that it proposed to offer the nation if permitted by the CAB to do so. Gambrell then accused Pan American of posing as "a transportation Messiah." In real or pretended outrage he held up copies of Pan Am newspapers ads, until Leslie told him facetiously that these ads had been placed only as a service to opposing counsel.

Previously witnesses representing the gateway cities Pan Am hoped to serve had testified in favor of the company's application. Now Gambrell produced evidence indicating that certain of these witnesses had been flown to the hearings by Pan Am at Pan Am's expense. This was no crime, but Gambrell made it sound like one, and it seemed to weaken Pan Am's position. Finally CAB examiner William J. Madden, who presided over the hearings, suggested that Gambrell become less argumentative. Once Gambrell turned to him inquiring, "Why does he [Leslie] have to give me an ornery answer?"

"You're inviting it," said the examiner.

Leslie was on the defensive throughout.

To Leslie, and to Trippe as well, the most surprising opposition was that of the Post Office Department, which announced itself against the award of domestic routes to Pan American on the grounds that this would divert mail from the domestic carriers, upset current mail subsidies, and, astonishingly, not significantly increase the speed at which the mail was moved.

Apart from the gateway cities, no one else intervened on Pan American's behalf except for Panagra, which it half owned, with the result that the arguments of the massed interveners seemed to overwhelm Pan Am's case. The more than thirteen thousand miles of domestic routes that Pan Am wanted would be worth, the interveners charged, a minimum of $100 million to the company. The smaller airlines would be unable to compete against the octopus—indeed, no one would be able to compete against it. Pan American would "skim the cream" off the entire domestic market.

The hearings closed. The lawyers went home to write briefs, which would be presented some two months later. The domestic interveners and the Post Office carefully buttressed positions already marked out during the hearings. The Pan American brief, two printed booklets totaling more than a hundred and fifty pages in length, at last presented certain of the emotional arguments that Leslie had been forbidden to articulate on the witness stand: that Pan Am was not being treated fairly. Its burdens in international operations were outlined, as was the amount and degree of the competition it faced. Foreign-flag airlines were paying their pilots and mechanics less than half the amount of Pan American salaries. They were also heavily subsidized by their governments. As for domestic airlines now competing with Pan Am abroad, they also had significant advantages, for they could feed passengers directly into their own planes, could move planes about the country more easily, had fewer thin routes, could group maintenance facilities to effect savings and costs, and could even afford ticket agencies in interior cities, which Pan American could not do. None of this was fair. Clearly, the brief declared, the award of domestic routes would give Pan American "the strength required for the proper performance of its international assignments."

But there was a rebuttal to this argument and the interveners in their briefs made it. Even with traffic now being diverted away from Pan American, even as the company sought to compete without domestic routes of any kind, it was still the biggest and most prosperous, and in the first seven months of 1947 had flown 158.5 million revenue passenger miles, as compared to 113 million for TWA and 101 million for American Overseas.

This left untouched only a single one of Pan American's principal arguments: it was the one Trippe had always counted his weightiest. The company still proposed to offer spectacularly improved service, namely, the 450-mph Republic Rainbow, a prototype of which would soon be rolled out of its hangar to begin tests.

The months began to pass. All waited for the CAB examiner's report to be made public and to be forwarded to the board for final decision.

The forces massed against Trippe were led mostly by airline presidents, and they didn't like him. There were reasons for this aside from their basic fear of his power. For instance, most of Trippe's peers were careful to attend important ATA (Air Transport Association) and IATA (International Air Transport Association) meetings. Trippe counted himself too busy, and so sent someone else, usually Leslie. Naturally, the others became convinced he considered himself more important than they and too good to meet with them.

Three other tycoons were now emerging in the airline business: Edward Rickenbacker of Eastern, William Patterson of United and C. R. Smith of American. Rickenbacker was born in 1890; Patterson, Smith and Trippe all in 1899. Rickenbacker, formerly a race-car driver, had shot down twenty-six German planes and balloons in World War I. He and some associates had bought Eastern in 1938. Though he had left school at twelve and was not by nature a businessman, Captain Eddie had run it ever since. Patterson had begun his business career by working fifteen years in a San Francisco bank, after which he went to the Boeing Airplane Company as assistant to the president. Later he became president of Boeing Air Transport, and in 1934, when Boeing and three other lines amalgamated, he became president of the new company, United Airlines. Patterson, an administrative genius, was slight, quiet, rather colorless.

Only Smith, it seemed, had the stature—the powerful personality, the business acumen, even the physical size—to stand up to Trippe. The chairman of American Airlines was born Cyrus Rowlett Smith in Minerva, Tex., on a different side of the tracks from Trippe. The oldest of seven children, Smith had gone to work at the age of nine after his father ran out on the family. By the time he was sixteen C. R., as he was known, had worked his way up to bookkeeper and part-time teller in a bank in Whitney, Tex. By nineteen the bookkeeper was earning $200 a month in a cotton mill, good money for 1919. At twenty-one he at last enrolled in college—the School of Business Administration and Law at Texas University. When he graduated he was twenty-five, and he took a job as a junior clerk in an accounting firm. He did not fly or yearn to. Moving to the Texas-Louisiana Power Company, he rose to become assistant treasurer, just as the company purchased Texas Air Transport, an airmail line flying between Dallas/Fort Worth, Brownsville and Houston. Young Smith was put in as manager of the airline, for there was nobody else and he was a hard worker. By then Pan American Airways had been flying for a full year, and twenty-nine-year-old Juan Trippe was already on his way to becoming an aviation tycoon.

In Texas twenty-nine-year-old C. R. Smith took flying lessons and got his air transport pilot's license. After a while, various small airlines began to consolidate around him, and a new corporation was formed called Southern Air Transport. At first he was treasurer of this firm, being a good bookkeeper, and later became vice president. Southern Air Transport, still growing, became American Airways in 1930, and Smith, as vice president of the new company, was put in charge of its southern division. A sprawling network of badly connected routes, American Airways was losing money, and when its Post Office mail contracts were canceled in 1934, the entire company had to be reorganized, reappearing later that same year as American Airlines, with C. R. Smith as president. The thirty-five-year-old bookkeeper eliminated crisscrossing and duplication in routes, and brought in up-to-date airplanes that were standardized as much as possible in order to reduce costs and confusion in maintenance. American Airlines began to prosper.

In April 1942 Smith entered the Air Corps, taking the job Trippe turned down. As Chief of Staff of the Air Transport Command, he rose to the rank of major general and won the Distinguished Service Medal, with a citation from General Arnold that called him "one of the world's greatest contributors to the development of military and global air transportation." He also got the Legion of Merit, the Air Medal and a number of other citations.

Back at American Airlines, he was elected to the newly created position of chairman of the board of a company employing ten thousand people, four thousand of whom he was said to know personally. He was tall, square-jawed and slow-spoken, and appeared easygoing, which he was not. Divorced, he lived alone in a twelve-room mansion on an estate on Long Island, the interior of which, according to one description, resembled "the great American Southwest wing of a natural history museum." On the walls hung paintings of Western landscapes. There were wood carvings of cowboys and horses, as well as stuffed animal heads and Navajo rugs, and the phonograph often blared cowboy songs.

Now early in 1947, with the revised Community Company bill pending, with Pan Am's domestic-routes case pending, with Trippe trying to merge with or buy out other airlines, including Smith's own, this hard, shrewd Texan studied his options and discovered a way, he thought, to stop Trippe on every count. His strategy centered on the Republic Rainbows—six ordered by Trippe, twenty by himself—and he took a careful look at Republic Aviation, the company building them.

Republic, he saw, had contracted with the Air Force to build a great number of F-84 jet fighter planes, but production problems had been encountered and the contract was running late. Republic had mounted a second project to build private planes that would cost $5,000 each or less and would sell like cars. But this, too, had hit snags.

The Rainbow program was approximately on schedule. A prototype already existed, and Pan American's chief pilot, Scott Flower, had flown a demonstration flight with Trippe and certain of his executives aboard. The plane promised to be highly successful—as fast as the Comet jet airliner the British were planning and with far more range. In fact, if the Rainbow got built, very likely the British Comet would not be.

Republic was counting on the Rainbow—on the twenty-six firm orders from American and Pan Am. Trippe was counting on it—its superior performance would influence the domestic-routes decision, and also would put such heavy pressure on his domestic rivals overseas that they might cease to fight the Community Company bill or give up their overseas routes, or both. Smith wanted the Rainbow too—it was 100 mph faster than anything promised for the next ten years—but he could live without it provided no one else got it.

He began to consider canceling his twenty orders. If he did so, it seemed probable that Republic would abort the entire project. An assembly line was expensive, and Republic did not have the resources to build only six planes for Trippe. If he canceled, a beautiful, promising plane would never get built. If he canceled, it would seriously embarrass Trippe.

On February 20, 1947, Smith canceled.

As expected, Republic immediately aborted. Although Trippe moved quickly, picking up his option for six more planes, giving Republic twelve firm orders in all, this was not enough to save the project. Pan Am was obliged to notify the CAB that it would not be able to fly the plane on any domestic routes it might eventually be accorded; new briefs had to be written and filed—amending a good many arguments made previously.

The examiner still had not filed his report.

Meanwhile the Community Company bill, wearing new raiment, was back before Congress for—literally—the twelfth time. This year five different but similar versions would be considered by both houses. There were four bills submitted by four different representatives in the House, and one bill in the Senate—S. 987—introduced by Senator Brewster and backed by Senators White, McCarran and McMahon. Trippe could be seductive when he chose; he had seduced all these men. His point of view had become theirs. They, too, believed in and would fight for a single airline representing the American flag around the world.

The 1945 version of the bill, McCarran's bill, had provided for the issuance of $200 million in stock, with no more than one-fourth of this stock to go to any one company. The following year, faced with charges that Trippe could easily control such a company, McCarran had revised the bill to limit to 2 percent the total capital stock that could be held by any one individual or company. Since, obviously, around 40 percent of the assets would come from Pan American, this meant that Pan Am's major stockholders would have to sell off most of their holdings.

Now, in 1947, the stock percentages had been shifted around again. Railroads, shipping lines and domestic airlines were each guaranteed important participation, and the ownership limit by any one individual or company was raised to 3 percent. Otherwise it was much the same bill as before. In May hearings in the Senate began, and the House waited to see what the Senate would do.

Trippe himself testified for two days, and he began by reading into the record part of Senator McCarran's report on the ten-to-ten vote of two years before. Although this report presented arguments both for and against the bill, nonetheless the several paragraphs favorable to Trippe, to Pan American and to the nobility of the idea itself were all that he read aloud.

Suggesting that the remainder of McCarran's report merely be inserted in the record—where the unfavorable parts would lie buried, possibly unread by anyone—Trippe attempted to proceed to other arguments. But Senator Edwin C. Johnson (Democrat, Colorado) jumped up flourishing the three letters Senator Bailey had written from North Carolina and demanding that these, too, be read into the record. Only then did Trippe's testimony continue.

Now Trippe broke out maps and charts once again, and he launched into the same arguments as the last time. The words in many cases were the same. Even the maps and charts may have been the same. "We are confident from the nineteen years experience that we have had in international air transport," he said, "that the best interests of our company would be served by unification; the long range interest of stockholders, not only in Pan American but in other American flag operations that operate abroad, will also be best served by unification. Frankly, I think it is a patriotic and fine decision that has been reached unanimously by our directors in favor of unification; even though they know that by doing so a great many of them, far more than half of our directors, will eliminate themselves from jobs as directors. The same thing applies to the management. Because as I will point out later on in my statement, no officer of Pan American—take for example our vice presidents, many of whom have devoted fifteen years to this business—has any assurance of what a future board of directors representing this united company is going to do, and whether he has an opportunity to continue in this business or not. I think that from their point of view—and I speak for our vice presidents and all our directors—it is a grand gesture on their part to authorize me to come down here and place our company on record as favoring unification, even though the company as now constituted goes out of business."

Again this speech left the assembled multitude nonplussed. What exactly was he saying, and why? Was he really offering to go out of business? If so, how had he got his directors to agree to it?

In Washington Trippe's reputation had come to seem awesome and the principal adjective applied to him was "smart." He was so smart that at times ordinary men could not cope with him. Congressional reports repeatedly used words like "exceedingly able" or "astute" to describe him. Was he now simply so incredibly smart that he had somehow concealed within this bill the means of regaining control of this Community Company as soon as all competitors had been absorbed into it? It didn't seem possible, and yet—

The persistent Trippe continued. "We, who perhaps as much as any other American flag company, perhaps more than any other American flag company, have a right to stay in business and carry on in this field, nevertheless appreciate that we can't if we have a unified operation. It is obviously impossible for Pan American to be again designated to represent the United States in overseas air transport. Therefore, we say that it is our desire to turn over our assets, our business, everything we have, to a unified company, on the basis that the Civil Aeronautics Board will assay the proper value of that business."

What did this statement mean? Were Trippe and his associates out to make a financial killing? Perhaps they hoped to sell out for what the CAB said their business was worth and retire as rich men. But Trippe himself was only forty-eight years old and already a rich man, and no one who knew him could imagine his giving up the company which he had created, and to which his entire being seemed devoted.

As if he had heard their unspoken questions, Trippe continued: "It has been said that this bill, with the changes that we have suggested, would still somehow permit Pan American to control the initial set up of the new board. I am convinced, gentlemen, that after you have heard the rest of my testimony and consider the suggestions that we make for amending the bill, you will agree that it effectively precludes any opportunity for Pan American or anyone connected with Pan American to control the unified company."

What he was saying, under the circumstances, did not make any sense at all. It was incomprehensible that he would do this. Unless he was operating out of motives of pure patriotism? But no one was that patriotic.

Opponents of the bill, during the past three years, had had ample time to muster arguments against it. These had been printed in a booklet entitled *The New Monopoly Aviation Bill,* and as soon as Trippe's testimony ended, the booklet was inserted into the record.

The booklet was part fact, part allegation, part supposition, part projection. The Community Company bill itself was long and complicated, and from it the booklet served up a rather frightening hash. Domestic airlines would have to trade in their international holdings for stock in the new Community Company, but the shipping lines and railroads would have to put up cash, perhaps $100 million. The shipping companies had money because of the war, but the railroads were in bad shape and wouldn't be able to participate. As for the CAB, which was at present a small judicial agency, its first job would be to operate as a sales office to attempt to get the 140 or more steamship companies and the 100 or more railroads to invest $100 million. This wasn't going to work. The government would also be faced with up to $25 million a year in subsidies and the CAB would have to administer that—the CAB was about to inherit tremendous responsibility and power over a $200 million company. Obviously, all Pan Am stockholders would become stockholders in this company and would have an excellent chance of electing their old Pan Am directors to manage it. Pan Am, once the Community Company was formed, would have six months in which to dispose of its excess stock over the 3 percent statutory limit, which no doubt it would place with groups favorable to it. Either Pan Am would control the new company or else there would be 17 domestic airlines, 100 railroads and 100 shipping lines jockeying for agreement, and this would result in incredible confusion and probably in economic sabotage.

There was much more, a good deal of it undocumented and even malicious. "Pan American practically ran their own State Department when they were the chosen instrument company in South America," the booklet charged. "The results were almost disastrous." During the war, Pan Am had "failed miserably." If the Community Company was approved, competition would be eliminated, aircraft suppliers would suffer, quality and frequency of foreign travel could suffer, whereas "right now we are on top."

Next came the long parade of witnesses. Patterson of United was still in favor, and so testified. John M. Franklin, president of the United States Lines, also testified in favor. Nearly everyone else was against: Cabinet secretaries, airline presidents. Such legislation, they maintained, was contrary to basic American principles, ignored the challenge of competition, and was alien to our nation's foreign policy. Croil Hunter, president of Northwest Airlines, averred that no one management could successfully operate a company that big, adding: "Mr. Trippe states that the directors and officers of Pan American Airways are unanimous in support of this legislation although they are aware that their company would go out of business. Does it seem reasonable, or, frankly, does it seem to make sense that a man who has devoted his entire business career over twenty years to building a great organization, and the officers and directors of that organization, would recommend that their company go out of business unless they were attempting to do one of two things—or probably both —to sell out to the government at a good price, and/or under the mess and confusion that this legislation would create, wind up in control of the consolidated company?"

On Monday, June 2, C. R. Smith took the stand, and he fenced repeatedly with committee chairman Brewster, the so-called senator from Pan Am.

Smith: "Now this persistent knocking on monopoly's door, this annual reappearance of Mr. Trippe in new clothing, is interesting."

Brewster: "I might make the point that it is the same old clothing."

Smith: "We welcome the opportunity of telling you about our business, about its problems, and about the need for your continued interest. But it does take up a good deal of your time and ours. If we could spend more time on the line, and in the offices and shops, giving to the business the detailed attention which it requires and deserves, if we could spend less time and effort preparing ourselves to meet Mr. Trippe's annual foray, we would be better equipped to compete with the foreign operations. We would, in the long run, be less dependent upon the appropriations which you gentlemen might authorize. We believe that we would be much better off, and that United States international air transportation would be better off, if more of our time could be devoted to the operation of our business and less time to Mr. Trippe's ambitions."

The final witness was Senator McCarran himself. "I am arguing for the principle," he began. "I do not desire that Pan American Airways or any other line shall control the Community Company. If the language now in the bill is not adequate to protect against such control, then let us rewrite the language. The Congress has experts who can write the language to do the will of Congress.

"How long will we continue to overlook, in our blindness, the fact that our real competition comes from over the seas, and that we must unite our efforts to meet that competition or go down before it? Even today—and it will be increasingly true in the years to come—air travel is the keystone of a country's transportation network. If we wish to increase our prosperity through foreign trade, we must have an international airline system capable of doing the job.

"Mr. Chairman, my name is on this bill, and I am naturally interested in the implication, which has been made here, that the bill never should have been introduced. Mr. Chairman, more than half of the witnesses who have testified against this bill have told the committee it is an un-American proposal because it is opposed to the theory of regulated competition. The trouble with that logic is that we do not have regulated competition in international air transportation today. Competition can be regulated only where all competing factors are subject to regulation. But we are not regulating, and we cannot regulate, the competition between American flag carriers and their foreign competitors. The real competition in the field of international air transportation is between nations, not between companies. That is a fact and not a theory. It is a fact which must be recognized. We cannot regulate that competition; we can only meet it. It is only plain old-fashioned American common sense to meet that competition with a united front. International aviation under the American flag stands today at the same crossroads where, decades ago, international shipping under the American flag took the wrong turn. This time, for the sake of our national welfare, we must choose wisely."

There the Senate hearings ended, and debate shifted to the four bills in the House, where the same witnesses trooped in and the same arguments were heard. Eventually votes were taken in both places, and the result was the same in both places. The Community Company bills were soundly defeated, all of them. The concept at that point looked utterly dead, without hope of resuscitation, to everyone except Trippe.

Trippe, though disappointed, was unwilling to give up. As he saw it, the bill had excited passionate responses. It was still there. It loomed over Congress. It still had the redoubtable Senator Brewster behind it, and also the highly respected Senator McCarran. Trippe might still get it enacted. Subordinates close to him urged him to forget it, but he would not do so. A number of these people believed his motive to be purely patriotic; others did not know what to think. All realized that he simply could not be talked out of it.

The bill might have reappeared again the next year, except that Senator Brewster was also head of the Senate's War Investigating Committee and less than two months later he launched an investigation into the wartime contracts of Howard Hughes—an investigation that ruined both Brewster and the future chances of Trippe's bill. Hughes had built the HK-1, the so-called Spruce Goose, a gigantic 200-ton wooden flying boat which had got off the water only once and otherwise did not fly, and which had become something of a national scandal.

It had been clear during the Community Company hearings that Brewster had treated Trippe gently, while at the same time interrogating opponents of the bill with increasing aggressiveness. He seemed to have hitched his political star to Juan Trippe and no one knew why—including Trippe, so he said. Obviously, Brewster believed in the bill himself. Even so, his positive response had seemed exaggerated.

Now with Howard Hughes on the stand, Brewster's relationship with Trippe came back to haunt him. He had been badgering Hughes, who also owned 78 percent of TWA, about the Spruce Goose contract. Under oath, Hughes suddenly accused the senator of having threatened him with this investigation months ago unless he agreed both to merge TWA with Pan American and to support the Community Company bill. He and Brewster had met in Brewster's suite in Washington's Mayflower Hotel, Hughes charged on the witness stand, and there Brewster had "in so many words told me . . . that if I would merge TWA with Pan American World Airways and go along with the Community Company, that there would be no further hearings in the investigation." This created an uproar, but Hughes was not finished yet, and he added additional charges which Trippe later denied absolutely. Once during a meeting with Trippe, Hughes said, he had asked if Trippe could get Brewster off his back. Trippe had promised to ask Brewster to hold up the investigation. Trippe had talked about Brewster, testified Hughes, as though Brewster worked for him.

The Hughes investigation collapsed almost instantly, to be replaced by charges of misconduct against Senator Brewster. The embattled senator denied all wrongdoing. He did admit to having accepted "hospitality" from Pan American, including a number of free rides around the country in Trippe's executive airplane. Brewster's political career ended then and there. He was soundly defeated in the next election.

Back on the Pan American floors of the Chrysler Building, Trippe's subordinates were astonished to realize that Trippe seemed personally undaunted by any of this. He had lost the Community Company case before Congress, and the prognosis in the domestics-routes case was unfavorable. But there were no recriminations. He blamed nobody. His subordinates were forced to conclude that he was simply a very good loser. He seemed by his attitude to be saying to them, Well, that's over, what will our next move be?

Few who worked for him saw any future practicable moves at all, apart from trying to make the best of the suddenly overcrowded international skies. But Trippe saw many possibilities, for he seemed perpetually to ask himself the question: Two or three or five years from now, what will I wish I had done?

There were the possible mergers. Trippe that year seemed ready to merge with almost anybody, but he particularly wanted TWA or American Overseas or both, for these were his principal rivals abroad. To absorb TWA he would have to get together with the mysterious Hughes, a reclusive multimillionaire. Just to get to see Hughes was difficult. Trippe was obliged to send a message to him via Noah Dietrich, executive vice president of the Hughes Tool Company. Sometime later Hughes telephoned Trippe to arrange a meeting in New York. Though a date was decided upon, Hughes canceled it at the last minute.

Later the two men did meet in Washington. Trippe tried to talk about the possible sale of TWA, but Hughes wanted only to know why Trippe supported this Community Company idea. After several hours Trippe had gained nothing except an appointment for a second meeting with Hughes in New York, but Hughes broke this date too. How about a meeting in St. Louis? Trippe suggested. Hughes agreed, but when Trippe's plane was over St. Louis, Hughes changed the site to Houston by radio. Trippe ordered his pilot to fly to Houston, but when they got there Hughes again changed the site. He suggested that Trippe meet him on the Mexican border in a place where neither would be recognized, namely, an abandoned airport where he had a cottage built precisely for such meetings. Trippe flew there in his executive plane, accompanied by his twelve-year-old son, Charlie, and at last found Hughes. Trippe talked about buying out or merging with the overseas end of TWA, but Hughes seemed to want to merge the entire TWA operation.

Hughes had his balance sheets and statements available. So did Trippe. They spent much of the day discussing the relative value of the companies. Trippe said the exchange should be based on net worth. Hughes felt that the overseas part alone of TWA was more valuable than Pan American, practically twice as valuable, in fact.

Suddenly Hughes jumped up, said he had a date in Los Angeles, and walked out. Left behind, Trippe and Dietrich continued to converse, but the negotiations, if that's what they were, got nowhere. The following morning about 10:00 A.M. Hughes was back, and negotiations were resumed, but Hughes's figures, to Trippe, were no more reasonable, and presently the talks were terminated. It was impossible to do business with this man, Trippe thought. Trippe's own plane came back to get him, and he flew back to New York.

Trippe and/or subordinates began to meet with other airline presidents, with G. T. Baker of National, and even with Patterson of United. Most meetings took place secretly in hotels, and were quickly broken off by the other parties on the grounds that Trippe thought too little of their airlines and too highly of his own.

The late forties was a time of depression in the airline business. The big profits of only a year or so ago had vanished and many lines were running in the red. To Trippe, all those he had approached so far had seemed ripe for the takeover, but all had resisted him, so he turned to the biggest domestic of them all. He began to meet with C. R. Smith of American.

Smith was a hard, proud man, but also a realistic one. He had counted on his foreign division, American Overseas Airlines, for profits, but there were none. Instead, AOA had proven a drain on the company. In the last few years the gruff-voiced Texan had discovered the truth of something Trippe had always maintained: running a domestic airline was akin to running a railroad; running an international airline was akin to running a shipping line. (Smith, Trippe sometimes chortled, had been the first, apart from himself, to see this.) The former bookkeeper wanted to get out of overseas operations and Trippe was happy to oblige. A deal was struck. For $17,450,000 AOA would sell its planes, routes and logo to Pan Am. In December 1948 the papers were signed, and they went forward to the CAB, which would hold hearings and then either approve or disapprove of the sale.

In advance of these hearings a good deal of lobbying ensued, most of it carried on by Sam Pryor, a far less controversial figure than Trippe. The congenial Pryor managed to sell Secretary of State George Marshall on the merger during several luncheons at Marshall's house in Virginia, after which he flew to San Francisco to convince Attorney General J. Howard

McGrath in a hotel room during a conference of Democratic politicians there. Although the CAB later turned down the merger, President Truman, influenced by Marshall and McGrath, reversed this decision and approved it. Pan Am got one DC-3, four DC4's, seven Constellations and eight Stratocruisers. It also got, for the first time, Paris and Rome, and the following year, reflecting all this, its traffic factor jumped 21 percent.

Nothing else that pleased Trippe or helped his airline came out of Washington that year or for a long time to come. The CAB examiner's report had come down in the domestic-routes case. It recommended that the company be accorded only one of the many routes sought, New York–Miami, and that even this route should be heavily restricted, and that all other routes be denied.

"It is readily apparent that Pan American is proposing to enter the most lucrative sections of the domestic air transportation market," the report noted, and added, "There are no instances in which Pan American would add a new service, all of the route segments in its pattern being already served by at least one carrier, while the great majority are served by two or more carriers." As for the promised fast new aircraft, the Rainbow would never be built, and the planes that would replace it, such as the Constellation, were far less spectacular. "There is no basis whatever for a conclusion that the operation of such aircraft by Pan American will result in higher speeds and lesser scheduled times than their use by the domestic carriers."

This report was forwarded to the CAB, which at length disallowed even the New York–Miami award, arguing that the advantages of allowing Pan American into its own country did not outweigh the disadvantages —the harm that the colossus might do to the more fragile domestics around it. This decision, too, might have been overturned by Truman but in fact it was not, and there was no other appeal. The President signed his approval, giving the document the force of law. Pan Am's petition for domestic routes was denied. The case was closed.

It was, John Leslie commented later, a complete and utter defeat for himself, for Trippe, for Pan American, without any redeeming features whatever.

48

The Plan to Save China

By June of 1947, having taken delivery of new, long-range Lockheed Constellations equipped with berths, it was possible for Trippe to fulfill a dream now twenty or more years old—to inaugurate commercial round-the-world service by a single airline, his own.

As with so many past first flights, this one was planned as a gala journey with Trippe and many of his publisher friends aboard. The departure ceremony was presided over by New York Mayor William O'Dwyer, and the Clipper *America* was escorted out to sea for a distance of a hundred and fifty miles by fourteen U.S. Army P-51 Mustangs, and four Navy Corsairs.

In London Trippe and the publishers took tea with Prime Minister Clement Attlee, and a bewildering array of dignitaries met their plane in all the cities that followed: Istanbul, Calcutta, Bangkok, Manila. Nothing remarkable happened until the party reached China, where Trippe became involved in a strange and singular episode.

At Shanghai Trippe and his guests boarded a CNAC DC-3 for a side trip to Nanking, where they were received at the presidential palace by Generalissimo and Madame Chiang Kai-shek. Madame Chiang, one of the Soong sisters, spoke fluent English, of course, but the Generalissimo did not; he and Trippe exchanged translated pleasantries. If either man was particularly impressed, it did not show. The reception ended, and Trippe and the publishers were soon back in Shanghai in their hotel.

Trippe was sharing a room with Roy Howard, publisher of the Scripps-Howard newspapers, and that night after dinner, while Howard was soaking in a hot tub, there came a knock on the door. Opening it, Trippe found himself facing Finance Minister Chang Kia Ngau, who was considered one of the most important men in China. The Finance Minister, yet another American-educated member of the Chinese hierarchy, apologized to Trippe for his intrusion. Having come alone and unannounced, he said, he had been obliged to come up by the freight elevator —had he been seen, it would have cost him a considerable loss of face. Quickly he informed Trippe that in the morning there would be a taxi out front with a red O on the windshield which would take him across town to a certain building. He was to go down through the basement of this building, cross through the garden in back and enter the rear of Chang's sister's house. There, he said, they would discuss "the plan." Then he bowed and vanished. Howard had got out of the tub, and the perplexed Trippe told him what had happened. Immediately the publisher invited himself along, but Trippe shook his head. He would go alone.

The next morning Trippe went downstairs, half believing the whole thing was a hoax. But just as he had been told, the taxicab with the red O on the windshield was standing at the curb, and it carried Trippe across the city. When he had made his way through the basement, through the garden and into the rear of the house, he found the Finance Minister waiting for him. Again Chang referred to "the plan." He wanted Trippe to take it back to Washington and deliver it verbally to President Truman. It was a plan to save China from the Communists. Without its implementation, all of China might be lost.

Trippe, listening with increasing attention, could hardly believe what he heard.

There were five parts to the plan. Nothing was in writing. The details were complicated, and he was trying to get them straight in his head. What Trippe understood was the following:

1. Chiang Kai-shek would accept an American high commissioner who would, in effect, rule China, as General MacArthur currently ruled Japan.

2. All taxes and all means of raising money within China would be eliminated except for a salt tax to collect sufficient money to keep local police forces in place. The combined police forces would not exceed three-eighths of 1 percent of the population, and therefore could not grow into an army. Government revenues would be raised entirely from customs duties, and this customs service would be administered by Americans just as in the old days Chinese customs had been run by the English. These funds, instead of being rifled by petty politicians, would remain intact and would be sufficient to run the government.

3. The United States would loan China about $200 million in silver, half of which would be used to buy up paper currency currently in circulation. With this single stroke there would be a sound value of exchange between

the people in the cities and the farmers on whom they depended for food. The other half of the bullion would back new paper currency as it was issued.

4. The United States would provide 2,000 army officers who would train an army of about half a million Chinese troops. Chiang Kai-shek's present 5-million-man army was largely a slave-labor force. This army would be disbanded, and the men would be given land expropriated from the warlords.

5. Seed and fertilizer for this new land would be provided by the United States.

No one must know of the plan except President Truman—and Mr. Trippe, of course. It would be political death for Chiang to propose the plan himself. President Truman must seem to impose it on him. If this happened, then Chiang could and would accept it, and China would be saved.

China knew Trippe and trusted him, Chang said. It was Trippe's job to carry the plan direct to Truman and persuade him to accept it.

With the currency stabilized, Trippe thought, and with a trained army of half a million men to fight the Communists, China might indeed be saved. But the Finance Minister wanted Trippe to deliver his plan verbally to President Truman. Trippe shook his head. "I can't do it—take back a verbal report. Why haven't you referred this to the American ambassador?" The answer was that the Chinese saw Trippe as a bigger man than the ambassador; they believed him to have immediate access to President Truman. Trippe again shook his head: it wasn't in writing—he couldn't do it.

Takeoff for Tokyo was scheduled for seven-fifteen the next morning. Trippe and Roy Howard, though awake early, were not yet dressed when a knock came at the door. Trippe opened it, and in walked the Finance Minister. "My car will take you to the airport," he told Trippe.

A motorcycle escort waited outside. The publishers were apportioned among a number of cars, and Trippe rode with the Finance Minister, who was silent. But once the car had driven out onto the tarmac and up to the waiting Pan American Constellation, Chang suddenly asked to be shown the inside of the plane. Trippe was agreeable. The crew members were already in the cockpit, going through their preflight checklist, and Trippe introduced the captain and first officer. But the Finance Minister seemed to have no interest in the cockpit or the pilots, nor was he impressed by the interior décor Trippe was so proud of. He did, however, want to see the men's room. Trippe opened the door to show it to him and Chang said, "Come in here, I want to talk to you." The two men stepped into the lavatory, and the Finance Minister pushed the door closed. They were standing almost nose to nose, and the tall, burly Trippe could barely stand upright.

"I've been up to Nanking," the Finance Minister said hurriedly. "We have put the plan in writing, and the Generalissimo has signed it, and here it is." He thrust the document at Trippe. Trippe received it almost with distaste; affairs of state should not be conducted in toilets. He looked it over and saw that part of it was in English, part in Chinese.

The Finance Minister pointed to the signature. "That is the Generalissimo's signature. The whole thing is top-secret. You must deliver the document personally to President Truman."

Trippe stared at the signature that he could not read. After a moment he said, "Won't you sign too?" Neither man had a pen. Leaving Chang, Trippe went forward to borrow a pen from the captain. Back in the lavatory, Chang put the document down on the washstand and signed it.

A moment later both men came out of the little room, Trippe clutching the plan designed to save China from a Communist takeover. Chang bowed, hurried down the steps of the plane and was gone. The plane took off for Tokyo. For a while Trippe stared out the window. The top-secret document, he said later, was burning a hole in his pocket.

He sat down beside Paul Patterson, publisher of the Baltimore *Sun,* and gave him the document to read. According to Trippe's description, "Patterson's hat nearly blew off."

Trippe owed nothing to Chiang Kai-shek or Chang Kia Ngau or China, not even secrecy. His loyalties were to himself, to Pan American and to the United States. He was trying to evaluate the document and to plot his own course of action.

"Do you think this is as important as I do?" asked Trippe.

"Yes, I do," said Patterson.

In Tokyo Trippe met privately with General MacArthur, whom he had first known years ago in Manila. MacArthur began to praise this first round-the-world flight, but Trippe interrupted by bringing forth the Finance Minister's document and thrusting it into MacArthur's hands.

MacArthur read it again, and then again.

"What do you think of the military part of it?" asked Trippe.

"Mr. Trippe," said MacArthur, "I've got enough military equipment here and on the islands to handle such a project. I wouldn't even have to go to Congress for appropriations. They've only got a single-track railroad across Manchuria. The military part is sound. Mr. Trippe, this can be the American century in China."

"General," said Trippe, "would you take the job as high commissioner?"

After a moment MacArthur replied, "I would. This job would be the most important job an American could do. I would rather do it than run for President." Then he added in a different tone of voice, "But I don't think I'm going to be asked."

"Why not?"

The answer was that President Truman feared MacArthur as a rival for the presidency in 1948 and would do nothing to enhance his prestige.

MacArthur said, "There are three men I would like you to take this to. They know my views. Vandenberg, Taft and Dewey. All three will want to use their efforts to help if you fail with Truman." Arthur Vandenberg and Robert Taft were leading Republican senators. Thomas Dewey was the Republican governor of New York who had run against Roosevelt for President in 1944, and who would run against Truman in the next election year.

As the Pan American Constellation set down for fuel on Wake, Trippe was still brooding about the plan, and about what his own next moves should be. He was a lifelong Republican with no great respect for President Truman, and on his own actions might depend the future of China.

Together with the publishers, he toured ravaged Wake, and this distracted him for a time, for he remembered the way he had seen it in the days when the *China Clipper* used to set down there. On December 23, 1941, after two weeks of almost constant bombardment, more than eleven hundred Japanese troops had swarmed ashore and had overrun the island. By then hardly a structure was standing. Immediately the Japanese had fortified their prize, not realizing that the island was so isolated that U.S. strategists could and would ignore it. Year after year Wake's Japanese garrison waited for the invasion that never came, and for supply ships that never came either. Tokyo was two thousand miles away across seas infested by U.S. submarines, and indeed by entire U.S. naval task forces. Wake could not be supplied by cargo planes—until very late in the war the only cargo planes in the world capable of reaching it belonged to Juan Trippe. And Japanese freighters that tried to sail there were sunk in appalling numbers. Finally the cost of trying to feed the Wake garrison was seen by Tokyo as too great; no more ships were sent out and the Japanese garrison commenced slowly, and then precipitously, to starve to death. Troops died by the hundreds. Now, touring the island, Trippe and the publishers saw that there were mass graves everywhere.

Since the previous year Pan American planes had begun once more to transit the Pacific, and Wake Island was again a refueling station. But the Pan American Hotel, Trippe had decided, would not be rebuilt. The day of the luxurious flying boats was over forever. The new modern airliners, carrying sixty or so people at two hundred miles an hour, would simply put down here to refuel, and then take off again.

Some of the publishers asked Trippe what would happen to Wake in the postwar world. Trippe said, and the publishers agreed, that Wake

Island had only grown in strategic importance. Doubtless, it would be a major factor in transpacific aviation until the end of time.

Once the Constellation was airborne, Trippe began again to brood about China and the plan. He had a personal stake in what would happen to China—Pan Am still owned 20 percent of CNAC—but this hardly seemed to matter. The important thing was that he believed the plan was sound. This meant it was his job to sell it to the Truman administration.

On June 30 the fourteen-day inaugural round-the-world flight terminated in New York. Trippe took his document and went to Washington, where he huddled with Samuel Pryor and tried to decide how to proceed. Trippe told Pryor he could sell the plan to the Truman administration within a week and he had come prepared to stay for that length of time.

He decided that his first meeting should be with Senator Vandenberg, as MacArthur had advised, and Pryor arranged it. On a hot July night Trippe and Pryor sat with the senator on the little porch off his apartment in the Wardman Park Hotel until three-thirty in the morning. The chairman of the Senate Foreign Relations Committee complained that he had virtually lost contact with Secretary of State Marshall. The Republicans were trying to keep Nationalist China alive, he complained, but Truman was against Chiang Kai-shek and his wife, and seemed willing to let China go to the Communists. Truman wasn't interested in advice from Republicans such as himself.

Vandenberg, and the Republicans, Trippe realized, were not going to be any help. The next day he decided to go directly to Secretary of State Marshall. They sat at a small round table at the end of the Secretary's desk. Marshall read the document, and at Trippe's urging, the two men went to the White House and were ushered into the Oval Office. "Mr. President," Marshall said, "you have a very important decision to make."

Vandenberg had promised that the Senate Foreign Relations Committee would approve the plan if it got that far, and General Marshall seemed impressed by it also. But Truman, Trippe saw, was highly skeptical. To Truman, Chiang Kai-shek was a thief who had diverted hundreds of millions of dollars of lend-lease aid to his own pocket. At that meeting and others that week Trippe sought to change the President's mind. He failed.

After a time Truman did appoint General Albert Wedemeyer to go to China to survey the situation there. Wedemeyer was gone some months, and after his return to Washington additional weeks passed while he wrote his report.

The Republicans were waiting for this report: Vandenberg might hold committee hearings, airing the Chang plan; the Senate might debate the matter; public opinion might be enlisted. But the report was stamped top-secret. The outraged Republicans could not get even a look at it. It became a political cause célèbre, with angry charges flying back and forth well into the beginning of the following year, 1948. By then China was almost gone.

By then, too, Trippe's own interest in China had focused once again on CNAC, whose route structure was shrinking fast as province after province fell into Communist hands. When Chiang Kai-shek in January 1949 transferred his seat of government—meaning his gold, his silver, his foreign exchange and himself—to Taiwan, Trippe sent Bixby to China to see if CNAC could be saved. "The corrupt Nationalist Government of China," Bixby wrote back, "disunited, inefficient, wholly lacking in any support from the people is on the way out. It is only a matter of time." Bixby's recommendation was "that we sell out as soon as possible for as much as we can get."

Having suffered two heart attacks and not yet fully recovered from the second of them, Bond was in New York at this time. No sooner had Bixby returned from China than the cautious Trippe, wanting a second opinion, sent Bond out on the same mission.

Upon arrival in Hong Kong, Bond found all CNAC flights suspended, for the Hong Kong government had proclaimed a state of emergency and had requisitioned all CNAC facilities. Bond began negotiating patiently, and soon managed to get a few CNAC flights into the air. Meanwhile, Canton had fallen without a shot fired, and Bond became convinced that China would have, and in fact already did have, a Communist government. Bond now wrote a series of reports back to the Chrysler Building: "The Generalissimo apparently hopes that World War III will break out soon and that through the following world-wide confusion he will regain power. A very pious hope. Failing in this, he apparently hopes to imitate Hitler and bring all China crashing down with him. In this he is already failing very rapidly. His people are more realistic. They prefer Strauss to Wagner."

To the Chinese staff of CNAC, Bond had returned as savior. These people wanted Bond's advice—they wanted him to tell them which way to jump. Should they hold the airline together and hand it over to the Communists intact? Or should they escape with it to Taiwan? Most of these employees had families in Mainland China. Bond urged caution. He was not their savior. Pan American owned only 20 percent of CNAC and could decide nothing for them. "All I can do now," Bond wrote New York, "is to prevent silly actions and overly zealous people who would like to lead the rush to the bandwagon. And also be prepared to do whatever is possible when the bottom falls out of the present situation. That exciting event is coming, I believe."

On November 9, C. Y. Liu, managing director of CNAC, defected to the Communists, taking with him ten (out of fifty-six) CNAC airliners, together with their crews, to Peking. "I dislike to be even close to such a double cross," Bond reported. "As you know, I am convinced that the National Government is finished and should be. I have served them to the best of my ability and I owe them nothing. But I would not have been a party to this defection. C. Y. Liu owed much loyalty to the central government. He had been one of the fair-haired boys in the government for thirty years. However, for thirty years he has been the kind of Chinese official that caused the collapse of China, so I guess little else could be expected of him."

In the week following this defection CNAC's Chinese staff at Hong Kong took physical possession of the remaining aircraft in the name of the Communist government in Peking—the employees went out onto the apron and stood guard around each plane. The Nationalist government in Taiwan responded by appointing a new managing director and by withdrawing the air-worthiness certificates of the aircraft—which caused the Hong Kong authorities to declare the planes improperly registered and therefore grounded, and they sent more guards out onto the airport apron to stand around the guards already there.

In New York Pan American went to court to freeze CNAC's assets in American banks.

Bond, feeling inexpressively sad, flew home to New York.

There was only one way for the Nationalist government, as majority stockholder, to unblock the airline's frozen dollar assets, and that was to buy out Pan American's 20 percent share. Negotiations began in November 1949 and lasted most of the month. T. V. Soong represented China; Bond and a company lawyer spoke for Pan American. Most negotiating sessions took place in Soong's luxuriously appointed apartment on Fifth Avenue overlooking Central Park. Bond had his instructions from Trippe. CNAC's assets had recently been appraised, and 20 percent of these assets came to just under $2 million. This was to be Bond's asking price.

Soong's first firm offer was $1 million. Bond said he could not even take such an offer back to Trippe. After much haggling, Soong agreed on a purchase price of $1.25 million, adding, "Tell Mr. Trippe I wouldn't give that to him—not to anybody else in the world, Bondy, but you."

This sum was approved by Trippe, who instructed the lawyer to draw up an agreement for signature that very afternoon. With contract in hand, Bond returned to Soong's apartment, where both men signed. Soong then observed that the contract required approval by the directors and shareholders of CNAC in Hong Kong. Bond said he knew this, and would fly to San Francisco at once to catch the next Clipper to China. That was the day of Trippe's annual Christmas party for his executives. On the Pan Am floors of the Chrysler Building, invitations to this party were much prized. But Bond, already en route to China, would miss it this year. He left San Francisco on December 24, and passed through Honolulu on

Christmas Day. When he reached Hong Kong the Chinese directors were already assembled. They wanted the board meeting held at once, but Bond refused. He was waiting for notification from New York that Soong's check had cleared.

At last, on December 31, 1949, the board meeting was held, Bond cast his vote, and CNAC, the airline that he had virtually created and had kept in the air for so many years, ceased to exist.

To the realistic Trippe, CNAC's demise caused little emotion. He was merely pleased to have his money, for now he could count Pan American's Chinese venture as having been successful from every point of view. It had generated prestige, goodwill and money in almost equal amounts. Although the first two qualities were impossible to measure accurately, money was not. Pan American's original investment in China Airways Federal had been $84,000 in Pan American stock. There had been repeated capital investments, of course, but in sixteen years under Pan American's control, CNAC had earned a net profit of approximately $3.87 million. When Bond sold most of Pan Am's shares in 1945, this had netted an additional $2.9 million. And now he had managed to sell the remaining shares for $1.25 million more. To Trippe, CNAC had been one of the best investments Pan Am had ever made.

Bond was proud of all this, of course, but he was a sentimental man. With CNAC gone, he had little further interest in the airline business, and the next year, aged fifty-seven, he left it forever, retiring to his farm in Warrenton, Va.

49

The Jets

Lindbergh was a complex man, and those who worked on the Pan Am floors of the Chrysler Building, Trippe included, came to know him intimately without ever getting to know him well. There were many Lindberghs: the celebrity, the technical consultant, the daredevil, the writer, the conservationist.

What it meant to be the first Lindbergh, the international celebrity, the man *Time* magazine once called "the most cherished citizen since Theodore Roosevelt," was known by every Pan Am executive who ever went out to lunch with him. Once in an elevator Trippe watched other passengers become so caught up in a frenzy of wanting to touch Lindbergh that by the time the doors opened on the fifty-eighth floor they had torn the left sleeve off his coat. Lindbergh was polite and good-natured about it, but all that day in technical meetings there was Lindbergh with his sleeve torn off.

A number of Pan Am executives, trying to describe him, would begin by saying, "The man is absolutely fearless." Whether this was true or not, they believed it, and they had evidence. In his early twenties Lindbergh had been a wing walker and stuntman in aerial acrobatic shows. As an air cadet he had survived a midair collision, parachuting to safety. In the eleven months preceding his flight to Paris he had been obliged to bail out of stricken mail planes three more times, once from an altitude of only 350 feet. During one of his descents, the empty plane turned back and narrowly missed him. Once, landing, he dislocated his shoulder. Another time he came down on top of a barbed-wire fence. His flight to Paris was, obviously, as risky a venture as existed in 1927. The kind of flying Lindbergh had grown up with and fallen in love with was an epic game for epic men, and no aviator of that early period expected to live very long. Lindbergh once said that if he could survive ten years before he was killed, this would more than equal any ordinary lifetime.

Most daredevils who survive get over their taste for danger, and Lindbergh might have, except that war came and he went to work for Pratt and Whitney. In the South Pacific P&W engines powered Air Corps and Navy fighter planes, and in time Lindbergh was sent there to observe how the engines performed. He was only a consultant and he was still a civilian, but he climbed into the cockpit of a Navy F-4U Corsair and flew twenty-five missions in combat, followed by twenty-five more in the Army's Lockheed P-38. He was forty-two years old. He didn't have to fly in combat, and technically should not have done so. According to the Geneva Convention, his conduct was illegal. But he flew into skies crowded with Japanese Zeros, shot one of them down, and was nearly shot down himself by another—a wing man saved him.

But the daredevil and the technician were always inextricably fused. Lindbergh's principal achievement in the South Pacific had nothing to do with dogfights; rather, it was the teaching of Pan American long-range flight techniques to fighter pilots, who, thanks to the settings he showed them, suddenly had enough range to reach previously unattainable targets, and to hang over them until each job was done.

From the South Pacific, still working as a consultant to Pratt and Whitney, Lindbergh was attached to a technical group sent into collapsing Germany. The group's mission was to seek out German developments in weaponry that might yet turn up in Japan. The U.S. high command believed that communication between Germany and Japan was still possible by submarine.

Lindbergh himself was looking for German jets. He knew that the Germans had had very short-ranged jet fighters in combat in the final days of the war, and he toured the ruined and abandoned factories looking for them. He found not only jet engines but aircraft with swept-back wings. He found Willy Messerschmitt living in a cow barn next to his house, which was occupied by American troops. Through an interpreter, Messerschmitt told Lindbergh that could he have kept going, he would have built a transoceanic passenger jet within four years. Lindbergh sent a cable to Pratt and Whitney, requesting that engineers be brought over to study and evaluate all this.

Back in the United States, Lindbergh went immediately to Trippe and Priester. It was the Dutch chief engineer who asked him the more probing questions. Trippe's principal reaction was enthusiasm. "Trippe was immediately open to it," Lindbergh reported later. Coincidentally, without a word spoken, Lindbergh was forgiven by Trippe for all past transgressions, real or imagined. He rejoined Pan American as technical consultant, his old role, and from then on was in on every stage of jet development.

Trippe had seemed certain at once that the jets were the wave of the future, but Lindbergh was not so sure. There had been many false starts in the aviation business—the Zeppelins had been one, and the autogyro another. Both had proven impractical, and perhaps the jets would too.

On August 13, 1945, Trippe wrote a letter to the Army Air Forces that introduced Philip B. Taylor as a consulting engineer assigned by Pan American to look into developments in jet propulsion. Taylor would need access and cooperation, and Trippe was asking the Army Air Forces to supply both.

From October to December of 1945 Taylor toured the jet world, which at the time extended from the small San Diego factory of the Solar Aircraft Co. to the German Air Ministry in Munich. However, it was the British, Taylor soon reported, who were out in front. British factories had not been flattened. Government subsidies were firmly in place, and jet development was proceeding apace.

By February 1947 the British had turbojet engines in production, and the world's first jet airliner, the four-engined Comet, was taking shape. There was at that time not a single jet engine or plane under development in the United States.

Events now began to move somewhat quickly. Pratt and Whitney obtained a license to manufacture the Rolls-Royce Nene jet engine, and from that starting point began to develop jet engines of its own.

In November 1949 Wellwood Beall, Boeing's vice president for engineering and sales, sent Trippe a letter in which he called attention to jet progress in Britain. Boeing's extensive military experience, wrote Beall, provided the company with the technical know-how needed to design and manufacture "an outstanding type" of jet airliner. "All we need for an immediate go ahead is a customer."

Trippe was not yet the customer Beall was looking for, and neither was any other airline. The projected jets had no range, and it was said that they had no future as commercial transport because a fuel emergency began the moment a jet plane took off.

That same year Britain's Comet prototype flew for the first time. It reached an altitude of 40,000 feet, flew at close to 400 miles an hour, promised to carry 40 passengers, and was incredibly sleek and beautiful in appearance. But it had no range.

In the United States, where no jet airliner was yet even in the design stage, Boeing began to build a high-wing, high-speed bomber for the Air Force. This plane, designated the B-47, had long thin wings swept back at a futuristic angle. Its engines dangled from four pods underneath these wings, which were so slender and fragile that they flapped in flight. The fuselage was a long, narrow needle, and though a huge machine when compared to previous bombers, the B-47 carried a crew of two or three.

Though no airliner, the B-47 represented the solution to a number of big-jet design problems, including the two principal ones, how to build a high-speed wing and how to mount jet engines. High speed meant a wing that could approach the sound barrier without loss of lift, or increase in drag, or excessive vibration. Mounting the engines in pods beneath the wings was considered an excellent safety factor. If an engine disintegrated in flight, as jets were prone to do, its pieces were unlikely to take the tail off or to damage the structural integrity of the wing.

But from a commercial standpoint many more problems remained unsolved. There was no room in the needle of the fuselage for people. The noise that the thing made was unacceptable and would pose political problems around every commercial airport in the world. Stopping this plane, once it had touched down, was a chancy business, for its brakes couldn't hold it, and there was no way yet to throw jet engines into reverse. The only solution Boeing could come up with was to pop a parachute out the tail. A commercial airliner would have to be a good deal more docile than this B-47.

On December 22, 1951, the *Baxter Report,* a confidential stock market newsletter, described the coming "jet revolution." Airline securities were "vulnerable," and holders were advised to sell. It was going to cost around $40 million to build a single experimental jet transport, and not a single airline had this much money.

On the last day of 1951 British Overseas Airways Corporation, the successor to Imperial, took delivery of its first Comet. Lindbergh had gone to England to study it closely. The Comet, he reported, was not the next step. It was too small to be economic and too short-ranged.

In July 1952 Pan Am engineer John Borger, after a visit to the Boeing, Douglas and Lockheed factories, sent a memo to vice president and chief purchasing agent Gledhill: "Mr. Priester has asked that I summarize the following information for you and Mr. Trippe." Douglas had fifty to seventy-five engineers working on its DC-8 project. The design was going forward. A mock-up had been built, and the cockpit section was nearly complete. A fuselage shell had been constructed. Even before deciding on optimum fuselage size, Douglas had run into structural and aerodynamic trouble. Borger was not happy with what he had seen. (American and United Airlines men had visited the factory a week before Borger and they had not been happy either.) Borger had been hoping for a bigger airplane. He wanted the fuselage tube 144 inches in diameter, for this would permit six-abreast seating. He wanted a plane that could carry at least 65 passengers from London to New York at 500 mph.

At Lockheed, Borger wrote, engineers were working on a 70-passenger, 530-mph plane whose fuselage diameter was only 130 inches. That meant five-abreast seating maximum. In Seattle a Boeing prototype was actually being built. Bill Allen, president of Boeing, was going way out on a limb. He was going to invest a minimum of $15 million to build a plane that possibly no airline would buy.

Lindbergh in his turn made visits to Lockheed and Douglas, where he talked to engineers about planes that would fly like rockets at 6,000 mph. Back in New York he had lunch with Trippe, Leslie and Harold Gray. The time had come, Lindbergh told them, when they could have any speed they wanted, as long as they disregarded economy. It was possible right now to send mail carrying rockets across the Atlantic in half an hour. The problem was no longer technical but economic. What Pan Am had to do was make a study of exactly what speed was practical at what cost.

By September of 1952 the jet airliners had become inevitable. Chief engineer Priester sent Trippe two memos spaced a week apart. The British were about to put Comets on their North Atlantic route. The plane would require one stop eastbound and two stops westbound, but still would be three to five hours faster than Pan American's Strato-cruisers. The double-decker Stratocruiser was quite possibly the most comfortable airplane ever built, but the world now was thinking almost exclusively in terms of speed, noted Priester. Pan American would have to take immediate steps to counteract the Comet's advantage.

Priester's second memo described the Boeing 707 prototype. The oval-shaped fuselage was to measure 164 inches in height but only 132 in width, the same as the Stratocruiser. That is, it would offer five-abreast seating at most. Furthermore, it would not be a truly nonstop transatlantic airplane. Although most days it could make London without refueling, almost always one stop would be required coming back against the prevailing winds. Boeing planned to submit more engineering data in about a month, Priester concluded, and mock-up construction was already under way.

To be safe, Trippe ordered three Comets. It was the first foreign design he had ordered since the early Fokker trimotors.

Nearly everyone else saw the jet as a rich man's airplane. It would offer well-heeled patrons extra speed at extra prices—a super-first-class premium ride. Trippe was one of the few who saw the Jet Age as a way to bring costs down. The tourist fare had just come in, forced through unilaterally by Trippe, after a four-year fight that had disrupted IATA traffic conferences in many parts of the world. Marketing figures since were unequivocal: the tourist fare was an enormous success. Transatlantic travel was up 30 percent over the same period the year before. The jets, as Trippe saw it, had to carry on in this tradition. They must transport a cabinful of passengers at the same cost or less per seat mile than previous airplanes. Since they would cost over $3 million per plane, they would have to carry many more passengers than any previous aircraft, and would have to cross the ocean nonstop. Otherwise they simply would not be economical. To Trippe the Comet was a failure before it ever entered service and he had ordered three planes only to cover himself. He doubted Pan Am would ever fly them.

And the fact was that this Boeing jet prototype, according to all the reports Trippe had read so far, was a failure also.

Meanwhile the turboprop engine had been developed, and airlines were lining up to buy Lockheed Electras and British Viscounts. The earliest delivery was promised for 1955, and this became an eagerly awaited date, for turboprops were swifter, more economical, less noisy and more comfortable than any previous airliner.

Only Pan American among major airlines determined to avoid this stage completely. A high percentage of senior Pan Am executives were engineers, and they were unanimous in what they thought about propellers—propellers were at the root of an enormous percentage of mechanical breakdowns. No one wanted anything further to do with them. Pan Am would wait as long as necessary, and then go straight to jets.

Priester, Gledhill, Leslie, Kauffman, Borger—they were all engineers. Trippe was not—not technically, anyway—but in meetings he grasped instantly whatever he was told, no matter how technical it might be, and the most complicated of memos and reports did not have to be explained to him. Everyone knew by now that Trippe was Pan Am's best financial man, but as one of his subordinates said later, "Trippe was also one of the company's best engineers."

A crucial stage now approached. The too small Boeing prototype was to be powered by Pratt and Whitney J-57 engines, a power plant one-third greater than anything that had come before, but still too small to cross the ocean nonstop.

At the Pratt and Whitney factory in Hartford, Conn., the J-57 was mounted on girders on a test-bed, running hour after hour, the noise and thrust being diverted up through the ceiling, through baffles, and out into the sky. In a glass-enclosed room men sat monitoring instruments. From time to time Pan Am engineers flew to Hartford in the executive plane and stood in the control room, watching the dials over the other men's shoulders, feeling the power of the engines through the glass. From time to time Pratt and Whitney tore these test engines down and measured the components for wear. When an engine burned a bearing or threw a blade, the Pan Am engineers knew about it; Pratt and Whitney hid nothing.

The Pan Am engineers tended to travel in pairs—Borger and Kauffman, Kauffman and Gledhill, Kauffman and Lindbergh. It was Borger who, around December 1953, became aware of an advanced version of the J-57—designated the J-75—and he signaled this in a confidential memo to Gledhill. To Borger this was just another technical memo to a superior. He had no idea of the importance it would soon assume, and neither did Gledhill. Borger accorded the new engine only a few lines. His principal worry was the proposed gross takeoff weight of the Boeing prototype—225,000 pounds—which made for runway requirements that were "excessive and probably impractical." Such a plane, Borger judged, would require an 8,500-foot runway on a 59-degree day, and 9,300 feet on an 80-degree day, and could barely be accommodated by the two most important airports in the Pan Am system. The longest runway at Idlewild (later JFK) Airport was 9,500 feet, and the longest at London was 9,570 feet. At its maximum weight the plane could rise only to 30,000 feet on an ordinary day, and if fitted with additional fuel tanks couldn't even get that high. This would be reflected in reduced range; at some lower altitude the plane would use up the fuel even faster.

The Boeing prototype, Borger's memo continued, was still too narrow to hold six-abreast seating, but to increase its body width by even ten inches meant an increase of 430 pounds in weight, plus an additional 193 pounds in payload lost due to increased drag, and to this should be added about 70 pounds for each extra passenger chair and attachments. To make the fuselage ten feet longer would be to make it also 1,518 pounds heavier, plus 1,050 pounds' payload loss due to increased drag. Such a plane would also cruise four knots slower. Borger, concentrating on the configuration of the Boeing prototype, was trying to figure out a way to make the plane big enough to hold six seats abreast. "Whether the full ten feet increase in length could be justified for a transocean airplane can be determined only after study of the range payload picture. This in turn depends upon a more adequate appraisal of the weight empty picture. It has been difficult to obtain weights from Boeing, and what we have appears quite optimistic."

In July 1954 the prototype flew, but it still had no buyers. Shortly after that Boeing announced that it was ready to enter production, and it sent around a memo describing the type of contract it was hoping to land, adding, "Boeing believes that the time has arrived to commence negotiations on such a contract." Boeing was thinking very big. If it could get 50 orders, the planes would cost $4.25 million each; 70 orders would mean only $3.8 million per plane, and 100 orders would drop this figure to $3.6 million.

Trippe sent Gledhill and Kauffman to Seattle to look the Boeing prototype over, and Wellwood Beall took them up for a ride. There was no soundproofing inside the fuselage; nonetheless both men felt it was a fantastic improvement over piston planes. When they got back to New York, Gledhill went alone to see Trippe. Trippe didn't like big meetings, and a big meeting to Trippe was three men. As he got older he was becoming more and more reclusive. Most of his employees, even his top executives, were afraid of him—not because he might shout at them or fire them, for he rarely did either, but because he was such a forceful personality that he was immune to ordinary feelings for others. He might, if displeased, simply ring down a curtain between himself and the offender. From then on he might refuse to return phone calls, refuse access to himself. This would be to withdraw from the offender all authority. It would be in business terms a cold-blooded execution.

But Trippe in a certain sense was afraid of his executives too, and he much preferred to meet with Gledhill alone. Both men were the same age, both had been to Yale, both smoked cigars. Also, Gledhill, though in no sense a confidant, was the closest subordinate to Trippe in terms of personal friendship—insofar as anyone was personally friends with Trippe.

Trippe was excited by Gledhill's report, but he wanted Pan American's interest in jets kept secret from other Pan Am employees, from other airlines and from the press.

He now sent Kauffman and Gledhill to the Douglas factory in Santa Monica to talk to Donald Douglas, and after that to the nearby Lockheed factory to talk to Courtland Gross. He wanted these men to know that he had decided to switch to jets as soon as a viable plane was offered him. He wanted them to compete with Boeing for his business.

But Donald Douglas at first refused. His DC-7 line was selling briskly. It would be the last major four-engined propeller airliner ever built, but Douglas did not know this, and he had orders for it carrying well into 1957. The newest version, the DC-7C, was a Pan American idea. Pressure from Pan Am had forced Douglas only the year before to lengthen the DC-7 wings by ten feet and to stretch the fuselage four feet in length. The result was a 20 percent increase in fuel capacity, plus engines placed five feet further outboard on each side, thereby reducing propeller vibration. The DC-7C could accommodate 91 tourist-class passengers, and was the first plane that could at last cross the Atlantic nonstop in all weather. Donald Douglas knew he had something good in this plane. Why should he allow himself to be pressured into a race for jet orders? He told Kauffman and Gledhill that a jet program would not be economic, and he mentioned a recent study by the Rand Corporation which seemed to prove that jet engines burned too much fuel, and that long-range jet aircraft could not be built.

"I've had an analysis made of that," Kauffman told him, and he handed over some documents. "Why don't you have your engineers make their own analysis."

Douglas found that his engineers were anxious to build the plane and that their own data coincided with Pan Am's. And so the Douglas Co., though far behind Boeing in development, decided to compete for Trippe's custom. The DC-8 program, little more than an intellectual exercise until now, would move forward with all prudent speed.

Kauffman and Gledhill went on to Lockheed, where they informed

President Gross of the status of their negotiations with Boeing and with Douglas. Would Gross like to build a jet also? Gross declined. Two factories competing was enough, he said. If Lockheed joined, this would reduce everyone's chances from fifty-fifty to one in three. Too much was at stake. He could not take the risk.

At this stage it was entirely possible that Douglas would build a prototype to match Boeing's, and that most airlines would refuse to buy either one. Apart from Trippe, the aviation world was terrified of jets. No sooner had the beautiful British Comets entered service than three units were damaged in runway accidents, and three others exploded in the air killing everyone. The Comet was currently grounded. Comet engineers —all engineers designing jet airframes and engines—had been working in unknown terrain. Jets flew at least a third again as high as propeller planes, which meant strengthening cabins against forces about which little was still known. One of the wrecked Comets had been fished off the bottom of the Mediterranean Sea—or parts of it had been—and it had been deduced that a small crack had formed in a window frame from pressure stress. When the plane hit turbulent air, the flexing of its wings and fuselage turned this crack instantly into a rip several feet long, after which the 450-mph wind outside tore the plane apart.

Commercially the jets seemed to promise disaster also. Airports for them did not exist. Fuel to feed them did not exist, nor tractors to tow them, nor staircases to get passengers on and off them, nor hangars in which to overhaul their voracious engines every six hundred hours.

To enter the Jet Age was to step into the unknown. The few who had done so thus far had moved with extreme caution, but most had lost everything anyway. Certainly the British had. Now here came Trippe. One day, as far as Boeing and Douglas were concerned, he wasn't there at all, and the next he had moved staff engineers into their factories, and there were frequent visits also by Gledhill, Kauffman, Borger, Lindbergh and by Trippe himself. But they still weren't certain he would buy, and he was at the moment their only customer.

Trippe had already made up his mind that he would buy nothing less than a true transatlantic jet, which neither the Boeing nor the Douglas design was, nor would he buy a plane less profitable to operate than the DC-7C. When the studies from his marketing people came in, this latter detail resolved itself into six-abreast seating—both designs seated five abreast—and into four extra rows of seats as well. In other words, the proposed airframes were not big enough, and the proposed Pratt and Whitney engines were not powerful enough, and so Trippe decided he would force all three manufacturers to build him something better.

His method, when negotiating, was always to state his eventual goal at the start, though usually he did this in such an ingratiating manner that the men across the table from him scarcely took him seriously. Such as:

"I sure hope you'll see your way clear to giving us a ship"—Trippe always spoke of "ships," not planes—"that can cross the ocean nonstop." Or else, depending upon his audience: "I sure hope you'll find a way to stretch your design enough to fit in four extra rows of seats."

He knew as well as anyone that the J-57 was not a transatlantic engine. He knew that to stretch a fuselage could mean redesigning the wings and tail, and could cost millions of dollars. The Boeing, Douglas, and Pratt and Whitney negotiators knew he knew these things. He was asking for the impossible and therefore, they thought, would be satisfied with much less. They began to make minor concessions, and each time, though never retreating from his original demands, Trippe appeared overjoyed. Relations between Pan American and the manufacturers had never seemed warmer and more relaxed.

In the spring of 1955, after six months of negotiations, Douglas submitted designs for the DC-8. Essentially it was the same plane Boeing had already built. It was too small, and had no nonstop transatlantic capability. Although Donald Douglas had won authorization from his board of directors to build the DC-8, provided he got fifty firm orders from airlines, he got none at all now. Trippe, who sometimes seemed close to signing, did not do so and neither did anyone else.

To the men from Douglas, Boeing, and Pratt and Whitney each contact with Trippe was frustrating. Always he would seem pleased with whatever was shown him. Always he would smile ingratiatingly, then add, "I sure hope you will see your way clear to—"

The bigger plane. The transatlantic plane. Both objectives still seemed impossible. Surely Trippe must realize this. He was ignoring Sikorsky's argument about going one step at a time. He was asking for two steps, or even three—right now. It was uneconomic, and also dangerous. The British had gone several steps at once and three Comets had exploded.

Still negotiations continued. Trippe and his engineers would fly to Seattle or Santa Monica, or else the West Coast people would come to the Chrysler Building. Often, once meetings had ended, Trippe would keep his executives there, arguing past dinnertime, sometimes past midnight, until, as Lindbergh once put it, "your mind almost didn't work well any more." Some meetings were conducted on Donald Douglas's yacht off the Southern California coast. At Boeing there was sometimes a blackboard in the room, and Trippe, Lindbergh, Gledhill, Kauffman and Borger would run quick calculations on it to measure proposed changes. At each meeting Trippe was pleasantly insistent.

"Let's think about engines that are around the corner," Trippe would urge the airframe manufacturers. "Let's build the airplane big, even if we have to fly it light the first couple of years. Bigger engines will come. If we build it too small, the airplane will be obsolete in a few years."

Boeing and Douglas held firm, and at last announced that they had frozen their designs. But Trippe on the long-distance telephone was as insistent as ever. The wider and longer fuselage could be made to work, he told Boeing and Douglas. More power could be squeezed out of the existing J-57 engine by going to water injection. Four thousand pounds of water injected into the engines during takeoff would serve to cool them, and it would also be slung out the back, adding a great mass of thrust. But water injection only posed new problems. The water had to be absolutely pure so as not to corrode the engine's working parts, and it had to be treated with antifreeze lest it become ice. And, of course, it added 4,000 pounds of weight to each already heavily loaded plane. Despite Trippe's pressure, both manufacturers remained firm.

Trippe understood perfectly well that he was the most important potential customer to each. If he bought, not only would domestic airlines have to follow suit, but so would all the foreign airlines against whom Pan Am competed. But Boeing's position was strong also. The prototype, even with five-abreast seating and no transatlantic range, was a reasonably successful airplane. If Trippe backed off, some domestic airline, to whom range was less important, might take it. Or the Air Force might take it as an aerial tanker. Boeing, with one airplane built, had already invested millions. It was totally committed. To change course now was out of the question.

Douglas, meanwhile, had built nothing. Its plan was to go directly from blueprints to finished airplane when and if it got the orders. Since blueprints were easier to alter than a tooled-up production line, Trippe and his engineers concentrated all their energies on Douglas. So many engineering meetings and negotiating sessions now took place that it began to appear that Pan American favored the Douglas design over the Boeing prototype, and would buy the Douglas blueprints rather than the existing Boeing airplane—a decision that seemed logical to both manufacturers. It was as if Douglas had always expected to win the competition, and Boeing to lose it. Douglas, after all, was number one in the world in commercial aircraft. Since the war its DC-4, DC-6 and DC-7 designs had all been moneymakers. Boeing, meanwhile, had concentrated on building bombers for the Air Force. Since the last flying boat, it had built only one successful commercial model, the Stratocruiser, a derivative of the B-29 Super Fortress that had dropped the atom bombs on Japan. The B-29 fuselage had been swollen to create double-decker room for passengers, who were offered berths, seven-course meals, vintage champagne and presents—orchids and perfume for the ladies, cigars for the men. There were five cabin attendants for a maximum of 47 passengers, there was a downstairs bar, and two- or four-occupant staterooms could be hired in the forward section of the plane. This had been Boeing's only contribution to postwar tourism, a "modern" version of the luxury of the flying-boat era, a luxuriously appointed bomber.

Emotional factors had begun more and more to influence these negotiations. Douglas was calmly confident. Boeing, commercially speaking, had a corporate inferiority complex. Trippe, noting the timbre of these men's voices and the look in their eyes, added such details into his equations and continued to play one against the other. Of course, Trippe had emotional weaknesses of his own, pride above all. Having been first across the Pacific, first across the Atlantic and first around the world, he wanted now to be the first to introduce jets worldwide—it was honor and prestige that could be converted immediately into commercial dollars. The trouble was, Trippe's emotions were kept so strongly in check that neither Boeing nor Douglas was ever able to exploit them.

With Trippe apparently planning to buy from Douglas, Boeing at last cracked, and agreed to broaden the fuselage of its prototype and to splice in extra length, which would increase seating capacity from 100 to 147, the most that the existing design would permit. Having made this enormous and enormously expensive concession, Boeing waited for Trippe's reaction.

Trippe was very pleased, but still not satisfied. He thought the plane could be stretched still a bit more, he said, and of course he still wanted that additional range, and he thought Boeing could manage both if only it would agree to switch from the J-57 engine, which powered the prototype, to Pratt and Whitney's experimental J-75. This was the first time he had even mentioned this bigger engine, which was the one Borger had learned of almost two years ago, when Pratt and Whitney had begun developing it for fighter planes under an Air Force contract. The J-75 was still on the secret list. Nonetheless, two hundred or more people outside of Pratt and Whitney knew of its existence—including much of the airline industry. But it was two years or more away from Air Force use, and at least eight years away from development to airline standards. Its durability and reliability—and even its total potential power output—were unknown. Eventually the Air Force, which could afford to do so, would employ it almost on an experimental basis. For an airline to attempt to fly it was to risk a series of engine failures that might be catastrophic in nature. It was not so much crashes that would become inevitable as the grounding of whole fleets of airliners while malfunctioning components were redesigned.

Boeing would have nothing to do with Trippe's latest far-fetched idea. The fact was that the big engine was on the Air Force secret list. Trippe thought he could get it released, but perhaps this was not true. It was untested, meaning that no reasonable men would design a plane around it, and, lastly, to employ it would mean further enlarging Boeing's fuselage and wingspan, and restressing the wings—in other words, a complete redesign of the existing airplane.

Abandoning Boeing, Trippe addressed himself to Douglas. In Santa Monica a meeting was held involving about twenty men: the chief executive officers of both companies, plus retinues of engineers on both sides. There Trippe suggested that Donald Douglas have his men design a new plane around the J-75. Not very long ago Douglas had built the DC-2, he said. It carried 14 passengers. A year later had come the DC-3, which was basically the same plane, except that it now carried 21. The difference between 14 passengers and 21 was the difference between success and failure. With DC-3's an airline could make money, and something like eleven thousand units had been built. The DC-3 was the most famous and successful airliner of all time. The situation today was comparable, Trippe explained patiently. Douglas was offering him the DC-2, when the DC-3 was the plane he wanted to buy. If they would agree to redesign their DC-8 around the J-75 engine—

Douglas and his engineers were polite to him, but their answer was firm. It was no.

Undaunted, Trippe took his retinue to the Pratt and Whitney factory in Hartford for a series of conferences with Fred Rentschler, Bill Gwinn, Luke Hobbs and others. To get the J-75 released from the secret list was a technicality only, Trippe began. That was not the problem. The problem was the engine itself. He would need about a hundred and twenty of them to go into his transatlantic jets.

Rentschler and the others knew very well that no such transatlantic jet existed.

The Pan Am engineers had studied the J-75. It promised a radical drop in fuel consumption because it was the first really high compression engine—compression ratios would be on the order of twelve to one. It would be built of new metals and therefore would support higher and more efficient temperatures. The J-57 at 10,000 pounds' thrust had already offered a third more power than any engine preceding it. The J-75 might be half again more powerful, for its promised thrust at a runway temperature of 59 degrees Fahrenheit would be around 15,800 pounds.

When negotiating with Boeing and Douglas for increased seating capacity, Trippe had been firmly backed by Kauffman, Borger and the rest of the engineers. But in pushing now for the J-75, he was operating on his own. His staff had given him the numbers to back the bigger fuselages. They had no such numbers for this experimental engine and were not advising him. No one was advising him.

How fast could he have these engines? Trippe asked Rentschler. Of all the men Trippe was negotiating with, it was Rentschler who knew him best. The Pratt and Whitney chairman had bought fifty thousand shares of Pan Am stock in April of 1929, the first big capital Trippe had ever raised; and the older man had sat on the Pan Am board of directors for many years after that. Now he said that he doubted any civilian market existed for the J-75. Boeing and Douglas both had fully designed aircraft, and Trippe should buy one or the other.

Trippe said stubbornly, "We are not going to take an airplane that can't do the Atlantic nonstop."

When Trippe had departed, Rentschler conferred with Gwinn, Hobbs and other subordinates. Until now jet engines had been notorious for their short life, and this one would have to fly day and night. Intervals between overhauls had to be high; otherwise the engine made no economic sense. If it should keep breaking down, this expense would have to be borne mostly by the engine company, according to the guarantee clauses Trippe would certainly insist upon. And there was no "high time" on any of the prototype J-75's as yet. The temperatures had to be pushed way up, and the engines had to run at those temperatures for a long time before anyone could be sure of them. No one knew how they would behave. Pratt and Whitney was still trying to learn about the new high-temperature metals that had gone into them.

Rentschler returned to Trippe and repeated that full-scale production of the J-75 was out of the question at this time. Trippe said, "Oh, you're being too conservative now. Look what a wonderful job the J-57's are doing for the Air Force."

Rentschler said, "We just don't know, this is a bigger animal, we haven't flown it yet."

Rentschler, like Boeing, also had a perfectly acceptable product to sell—the smaller J-57—which had been tested, proven and was already in production. That was the product he wanted to sell.

But Trippe continued to press by telephone. His arguments were incessant, unchanging, his voice monotonous. Every time Rentschler picked up the phone it was Trippe again. Eventually Rentschler agreed to a "final" meeting at lunch in the Cloud Club atop the Chrysler Building, where Rentschler gave Trippe his company's "final" decision: the J-75 was at least two years away—"two years too late to affect the design of the first jets"—and Trippe could not have it. He had best buy what Boeing and Douglas were offering. The Pratt and Whitney decision was unequivocal.

Trippe simply refused to accept it. According to Lindbergh, this was a typical Trippe technique—the man had an amazing ability to throw a deadlocked situation back into flux. Both sides should adjourn for two weeks and think the thing through again, Trippe said. Rentschler and his associates were astonished by this response. They glanced at each other around the table.

During the ensuing two weeks Trippe made contact with Rolls-Royce in England. Rolls-Royce had a jet engine coming along that supposedly had transatlantic capability. How soon could Trippe have this engine and at what price? Word filtered back to Hartford, exactly as Trippe had intended, that Pan American was now negotiating with Rolls-Royce, that Pan Am had decided to buy the engines it needed in England. It was no longer considering Pratt and Whitney engines at all because the J-57 was too small and the J-75 not available.

In Hartford, Rentschler went into immediate conference with his top aides. Was the J-75 really out of the question? Did Trippe really mean to buy from Rolls-Royce? The only certain answer was that P&W could not afford to let the first American jets fly on British engines. Rentschler and his men began to discuss their J-57—it had been flying in the Air Force's B-52's for some time, and had proven reliable and durable beyond the expectations of everyone. The company had learned a great deal since developing it, and the J-75 was basically only a bigger version of the same thing. The new engine couldn't be that much more brittle than the old one. They could stay within the same temperature limits. They didn't have to push the state of the art of temperature at all. It was only a bigger airflow engine, basically. They knew well enough how to handle the bigger shafts and bearings and blades. The vibration characteristics of the new engine were, of course, still largely unknown. Although the higher temperatures it had been designed for had not been obtained, even at lower temperatures it was at least a third again more powerful than the J-57.

Rentschler was still agonizing when Trippe phoned to ask for another meeting. He had a new proposition, he said. Again they lunched at the Cloud Club. If Pratt and Whitney would push those engines through, Trippe said, then Pan Am would buy them at a quarter of a million dollars apiece. Never mind what Boeing or Douglas decided to do. Rentschler had a customer and it was Trippe. Whether or not he ever got a plane to hang them on, Trippe would buy 120 engines, plus spares, outright.

Rentschler took Trippe's new proposition back to Hartford and conferred again with his closest aides. If he said no, this would push Trippe into the arms of Rolls-Royce, or so it seemed, for the Rolls-Royce reputation at this time was so awesome that the company could sell almost anything, even engines still on the drawing board. The management side of Pratt and Whitney was delighted with Trippe's offer. The technical side was not. If the engine failed, if Pratt and Whitney was obliged to replace or rebuild great numbers of them, the company could go bankrupt. The technical men thought this would not happen. But they were not sure.

The decision was made by Rentschler himself. Pratt and Whitney, he told Trippe, would sell him the engines he wanted and give the appropriate guarantees as well. The J-75 would be ready by the summer of 1959.

Trippe, once again putting the bag of oats out front, ordered a contract drawn up incorporating bonus clauses if P&W could deliver even earlier than that.

Some of the men around Trippe were amazed at the situation that now existed. Each of the untested big engines would cost $225,000—when the bonus clauses and spares were added in, Trippe's total order came to around $40 million. The gambler seemed to have gambled everything. He now owned $40 million worth of jet engines, and no planes. Suppose Boeing and Douglas still refused to build airframes to hold them?

Trippe flew to the West Coast, and he went to Boeing first. He had to have planes that would match his engines, he said. "If you won't build the plane I want, then I will find someone who will."

Allen, Boeing's president, had been trained as a lawyer, not as a pilot. He had grown into an extremely astute businessman. He knew how to read balance sheets, and also how to read the strengths and weaknesses of men who sat across his desk. He tried now to read Trippe. Trippe was trying to force Boeing to scrap the prototype 707 and to go to the work and expense of an entirely new design. Was he bluffing or not?

Deciding that he was, Allen refused to budge. The 707 prototype was there, and Trippe could take it or leave it.

Trippe went on to Douglas, and made the same statements. If Douglas would not build a plane around Trippe's big engines, then Trippe would find someone who would: "Even if I have to go abroad."

Now Donald Douglas was forced to weigh the same factors as Allen did. Trippe owned $40 million worth of engines. To have bought them seemed almost irrational, except that it tipped the negotiation in Trippe's favor because he could no longer back down. If Douglas wanted his business, then it was Douglas who would have to back down.

The DC-8 still existed only on paper. To change the design to fit the J-75's would be expensive, but it could be done.

Douglas folded. A bigger DC-8 would be redesigned around the J-75's. At once Trippe ordered twenty-four of these planes. He also asked that the deal be kept secret a short time longer, but he did not say why.

His reason was that he had thought of a way to force the big plane out of Boeing too, and the first part of his plan was to go back to Seattle, where he agreed to buy twenty-one of the small 707's with the small engines. No one at Boeing knew about the Douglas order. They thought they had all of Trippe's business—and on their terms, too. Trippe looked into a good many smirking faces that wouldn't be smirking much longer, he believed.

Back in New York, he arranged for a consortium of insurance companies to put up the money he needed. Pan American's total outlay would be $269 million, and the insurance consortium underwrote the first $60 million of this, sufficient long-term capital to permit commercial bank credit. Sales of Pan American's existing propeller-plane fleet would complete the financing of the jets.

A short time later the Boeing and Douglas contracts were ready and Trippe signed them the same day. Both manufacturers still imagined that they had cornered all of Trippe's business and both were in for a surprise, particularly Boeing; Trippe was reasonably certain that within a few days Boeing would be begging him to be allowed to build the big plane.

As it happened, the International Air Transport Association was meeting at New York's Waldorf-Astoria Hotel that week and Trippe made the welcoming speech to the delegates, who were the presidents and managing directors of the world's airlines. "The tourist plane and the bombing plane," Trippe told them, "have for years been racing each other to a photo finish. In my opinion, however, the tourist plane, if allowed to move forward unshackled by political boundaries and economic restrictions, will win this race between education and catastrophe. Mass travel by air may prove to be more significant to world destiny than the atom bomb."

Trippe also threw a party for the IATA executive committee in his Gracie Square apartment overlooking the East River. The date was October 13, 1955. The president of Pan American moved through the crowded room shaking hands, flashing his most ingratiating smile, mentioning here and there in the most casual kind of way that he had just bought forty-five jet airliners, and that the news was even now being released to the papers.

As his guests grasped the import of this, whole corners of the room fell abruptly silent. The Jet Age had just come upon them. Public acceptance was an unknown factor. Bewildering technical complexities lay ahead. Billions of dollars in new capital would have to be raised.

There was also a second, unspoken detail, one they began only dimly to comprehend. For the last several years Trippe had been slowing down his orders of propeller airplanes. Knowing he was about to bring on the Jet Age, he had ordered no turboprops. He had ordered no Super Constellations. He had ordered, relatively speaking, only a handful of DC-7C's, and these were largely amortized. Whereas they were stuck with whole fleets of brand-new, unamortized propeller planes. These would become obsolete the moment the jets started flying, and would have to be dumped. Nearly every other airline was in for a financial bath, and Trippe was the cause of it.

For most of the guests Trippe's party had just turned sour. Many left early, returned to their hotels and booked immediate flights to Seattle and Santa Monica. The rush to reserve places on the production lines was on.

The following morning William Allen of Boeing and his executives met to discuss Trippe's deal with Douglas, having read of it in the papers. Douglas had won the bigger of the two orders, 25 planes against 21, more than $160 million as against less than $100 million. More important, Douglas was about to corner the market in big new long-range jets. The foreign airlines would all go to Douglas, not Boeing, and a major part of the domestics' orders would go to Douglas as well. Commercially speaking, the Boeing 707—as it stood—was doomed before it ever entered service.

Allen phoned Trippe, offering to redesign the 707, and it was agreed that the Boeing–Pan Am contract would be renegotiated. Trippe would take six of the smaller 707's, inasmuch as Boeing was tooled up to turn them out reasonably quickly. These would suffice—with refueling stops —to open service on the North Atlantic months before anyone else did, and afterwards they could serve in Latin America. But, in addition, Boeing would build seventeen units of a bigger model that would be ten feet longer, carry 24 extra passengers—and be powered by the J-75. Trippe then hung the bag of oats out in front of Allen, offering to pay a premium of a quarter of a million dollars per month per plane for delivery in advance of the contract date: "I would pay a million dollars gladly to get those out three months ahead of time."

Trippe felt exceedingly pleased with himself, and this pleasure was evident whenever he repeated this story in later years. First he had forced Douglas to build the big jet, "something they wouldn't even talk about six months before," and then Boeing, "which they had claimed was impossible." He said this almost with a chortle, then added, "I spent a year raising that thing to a commercial airplane." But there were those afterwards who accused Trippe of having made an insane gamble with his stockholders' money. He had placed these orders totaling $269 million on a net income for the previous year (1954) of $10.4 million. Trippe responded that he had acted as a conservative businessman at every stage of his career, including this one: "With Long Island Airways, I didn't even resign my job with Lee, Higginson until I had my airplanes. In many of the other steps we weren't committed until we had the airmail contracts. There is no question that when we ordered the jets, people thought we were crazy. But if they had known how much we knew about jets, how much work had gone into the study of jets, they would not have thought that way. It was the least radical of things we had done. It was far less risky than ordering those four engine flying boats back in '33 and '34. Jets were not a risk either from the money side or the flying side. We had planned it for years and years in advance when nobody else was even thinking about it. That's the difference."

The first of the smaller Boeings was delivered in mid-1958, and the inaugural VIP flight was laid on for October 19—New York to Brussels.

The plane was fitted out like a club car, with eighty-four seats. There were ceremonies, speeches, TV and radio coverage—all in the manner of the first flight of the *China Clipper* twenty-three years before.

The jets were an immediate financial success. During the first quarter of the following year 33,400 passengers were carried on jets, a 90.8 percent seat occupancy, an all-time high. In the first five years of the Jet Age overseas traffic doubled, and in 1963 the company's net income after taxes was $33,568,000 on operating revenues, not including affiliated companies, of over half a billion dollars.

50

Priester
Demoted

In the beginning the company was two men: Trippe and Priester. But employees out in the way stations rarely saw Trippe. Some never saw him in their whole careers. To all these people the company was Priester. It was he who had made the rules they flew by and lived by, and who enforced them—all too often in person. Even in the forties and early fifties he would turn up in hangars and maintenance shops without warning, often early on Sunday mornings, introduce himself in his funny accent and, like a Prussian drill sergeant, search for dust by rubbing his fingers along windowsills. If he saw a toolbox that was well kept, he would remember who owned it and keep him in mind for promotion. The mechanics caught on—everyone caught on—and the men began to concentrate on their appearance and on the material they worked with. It made for increased efficiency in the long run.

At every station he inspected there were local executives who complained. "Why don't you let us know when you are coming?" they would ask him.

"Dot's no vay to inshpect," Priester would reply. "You boys vould alvays polish up if you knew I vas coming."

The chief engineer became, possibly, the most revered figure in the aviation industry in America. He had no children, and had no life except for his company and his planes, and his insistence on cleanliness, efficiency, discipline and safety spread industry-wide.

Thirty and forty years later men could still remember their first meeting with Priester. William Masland, a pilot, met him on a day when the top of the Chrysler Building was hidden in overcast. Masland was there to ask for a job. From Priester's outer office he could hear the wind whistling up the elevator shafts like organ pipes. At last the nervous young pilot was shown in. Priester sat at a desk. There was a window to either side of his head. He sat in semidarkness, and nothing showed of his face but what looked to Masland like a pair of large yellow eyes. Masland was totally intimidated, especially when Priester remained silent for so long that Masland himself began to babble. But Priester did hire him.

Masland also remembered sitting beside Priester once during an emergency drill in one of the early S-42's. When the order came to don life jackets, the chief engineer carefully read the instructions stenciled on his jacket, and as carefully put it on backwards. Shortly afterwards jackets appeared that could not be put on backwards, and Masland always imagined that this was Priester's work.

The chief engineer's authority, new men learned, was total. He would tolerate no insubordination, nor even the hint of it. In the early thirties he appointed John Leslie, who was then twenty-five years old, to be division engineer in Brazil. The eager young man took courses in Portuguese to ready himself for his new assignment, then made the long journey to Brazil, where a revolution was in progress— a man was shot dead right in front of him. He was trying to cope with his new job, and with the revolution, and doing well, he thought, when Priester came down and abruptly placed an older man above him. Crushed, Leslie asked Priester: Why? The question nearly cost him his career. Priester ordered him to pack his bags and leave Brazil on the next boat.

But, later, Priester nominated Leslie as division engineer in San Francisco. Before leaving for his new post, Leslie stopped in to ask Priester if he had any advice to give. Priester thought about this for a time, then said, "Always be fair, John."

No one who left Priester's employ for a better job was ever accepted back. The men who worked for him he drove hard, and he drove the aircraft manufacturers harder, and if any single man could be held responsible for the gigantic strides the aircraft manufacturers made between 1927 and 1955, that man was Priester.

As Pan American grew, Trippe himself grew—he learned to cope with vast amounts of capital, to walk with bankers, foreign dignitaries and Presidents of the United States, and to keep aloof from the everyday running of the airline. But some of the executives around him did not grow with the company, or at least so Trippe became convinced, and these he superseded with others. For instance, in Washington Anne Archibald was gradually superseded by Pryor.

Another who did not grow, or not enough to suit Trippe, was Andre

A. Priester. With the pioneering phase over, management had to buckle down and run the company as a business, but Priester's ideas were in conflict with this. He was still focused on all his former values—particularly discipline and safety. The new engineers and pilots were different men from the original grease monkeys and barnstormers, and Priester's idea of discipline often seemed to them only petty tyranny. The new aircraft engines and operating systems became more and more reliable, to the point where Priester's old margins of safety became unnecessary. It was Priester who had forced through the companionways in the wings of the Boeing flying boats, and even though Trippe bragged of this in his speeches in those years, he had resented it from the first and, in private, railed against it constantly. He was enough of an engineer to know that it wasn't really necessary, that it increased weight enormously and made the flying boats somewhat slower and less efficient than they ought to have been.

On the whole, Trippe was intensely loyal to the men who had helped him found the company. One early employee who had risen to the rank of vice president and general traffic manager had a drinking problem and often did not come to work. But Trippe tolerated him for years, before at last forcing him to retire.

However, Trippe's impatience with Priester continued to increase as the company entered still another new phase following World War II. Pan American had grown so vast that Trippe reorganized it, and the various divisions became virtually separate entities. New York would still be responsible for staff work, for policy, for providing the planes and for route structure. Otherwise each division manager was to run his own show.

The division managers were delighted, and certain of them promptly became tyrants in their turn. But at headquarters, Priester—and also Leuteritz—felt betrayed. Formerly their word had been law anywhere out on the line. Now they could only advise.

Leuteritz went to see Trippe for "clarification."

"It looks to me that from now on I have the same responsibility but no authority," said the chief communications engineer. "Suppose I want to introduce something into a division on an experimental basis. Do I simply do it, as in the past? Or do I have to clear it through the division manager?"

Trippe told him he would have to clear it.

What about inspection trips into a division?

These would have to be cleared too.

And communications budgets for each division?

These too, Trippe said.

After a similar interview with Trippe, Priester appeared in Leuteritz's office and sat down heavily in a chair. With Priester there were always long silences, but now after a moment he said, "Hugo, vot are dey trying to do to us?"

Leuteritz said, "Andre, they are forcing us to sit back and look at this thing from a distance. We can't do a damn thing about it."

The chief engineer, who was then in his mid-fifties, said, "I can't vork dat vay," and he started to cry.

Leuteritz said, "Andre, Andre, forget it. That's what he wants. Don't go getting upset about it."

But Priester remained upset, and everyone in the company knew this. He kept badgering Trippe to change his mind.

Though bereft of his old authority, Priester continued to make surprise inspections on Sundays, to poke around hangars and toolboxes. When something displeased him, he would complain to Trippe. More and more Trippe tended to put him off, saying, "Make a report."

More and more Priester seemed to him arbitrary, uncommercial, unrealistic. Airline flying had become an established art. It was no longer up to Priester to determine safety limits. The government made such decisions and the manufacturers complied. Sometimes Priester, dissatisfied, would suggest higher margins. "Andre," Trippe would say, his patience growing thinner every year, "we can't be out in front of the entire aviation industry on these things."

Leuteritz left the company. He could date his fall from favor from the time of the Whitney takeover. He had not sided with Whitney—only accepted him; but this had apparently cost him heavily. "There were those of us who cared more about PAA and the USA than about JTT," he said once. In any case, in 1946 he resigned to head up an aviation electronics firm.

By the start of the fifties Priester no longer had much influence on actual airline operations. Though still vice president and chief engineer, he had no direct access to Trippe, who used secretaries to keep him away. The men he had trained began now to attain his own level. Leslie was a vice president and on the board of directors. Kauffman and Borger would soon be vice presidents too. By 1953 the company had grown so huge as to overflow its Chrysler Building floors, and new quarters were rented in Long Island City, to which the engineering department was moved en masse—except Priester. Trippe, for unknown reasons, had chosen that moment to demote him, leaving him the rank of chief engineer but stripping him of his vice presidency. Priester was sixty-two years old and near enough to retirement so that this seemed to many people an act of needless cruelty on Trippe's part.

Priester's main function became to serve as chairman of the Pan Am technical committee, which consisted of Lindbergh and Philip B. Taylor, plus (ex officio) Gledhill and Willis Lipscomb. A new organizational chart was printed up and Priester's technical committee, though attached by direct line to Trippe, was shown at the absolute bottom of the chart.

At the same time Kauffman, having been elected assistant vice president, Engineering, was ordered to report not to Priester but to Gledhill. Unwilling or afraid to approach Trippe, Priester went to Kauffman, whom he had formed and who was sixteen years his junior, and asked why Trippe had done this to him.

To Kauffman the reason seemed clear enough: Priester created resistance—he wouldn't hesitate to argue with Trippe. But Kauffman tried to soften the blow by answering, "Andre, you're an elder statesman now. It's quite normal in American business for a man like yourself to go into a policy role when nearing retirement age. I'm sure Trippe just doesn't want to burden you any more with the day-to-day running of the company."

From then on, Kauffman was careful to spend a couple of hours a week with Priester, keeping his former mentor informed on what was happening in the engineering department across the river. For months Priester suffered in silence, and his secretary, Mona Cooper, suffered with him. Afterwards she always referred to this as the period "when we were alone, when the engineering department moved away from us."

The aviation world was surprised by Priester's demotion. The chief engineer, to many, seemed as much the personification of Pan American as Trippe himself. Gledhill heard the most criticism since he moved about the country more than Trippe did, though Trippe heard his share. Both men were obliged to answer the same question: What did Priester do to merit demotion?

Priester got up the nerve to face Trippe directly. "Why did you do this to me?" he asked.

Even Trippe was not equal to such pressures as this. He hadn't meant anything by it, he protested. But if Andre was really so upset, then of course he'd reinstate him as vice president.

One day Priester came into his office and said to Mona Cooper, "They have made me vice president again." The young woman, smiling happily, patted him on the back. It was the first and last time she had been able to show her affection for him in a physical way.

Priester did not live long after that. He died in Paris on November 28, 1955, while chairing an IATA technical committee meeting. He was sixty-four years old.

51

The Tycoon

In Washington, even before the first jets flew, a new investigation of Pan American had been conducted by a congressional committee headed by Representative Emanuel Celler of New York. In addition, a civil antitrust suit brought by the Department of Justice had complained that Panagra, Pan American and W. R. Grace & Co. were engaged in a conspiracy to monopolize air commerce between the United States and South America. The Grace, Pan Am and Panagra lawyers would manage to stall this case for years, but the end result was already foreseen: the signing of a consent decree, the unloading of Panagra's planes, installations and routes at a poor price, and the disappearance of the name from the skies.

In 1956 Celler was chairman of the antitrust subcommittee of the House Judiciary Committee. Nine years had passed since the last Community Company hearings. Trippe had kept a low profile during most of those years, and now, though obliged to serve as chief witness in defense of his company, he seemed to be attempting to remain inconspicuous even on the witness stand. Smiling ingratiatingly throughout, he spoke whenever possible in obfuscatory sentences. Though his interrogation by Celler and others was at times accusatory, he stood up under it, unperturbed. As soon as he stepped down, one witness after another mounted the stand to accuse him and/or his airline of dark deeds, many of them old ones, such as turning off landing lights in Latin America ten or more years before.

Ultimately the subcommittee report described how Trippe had built up his company from a 90-mile airline into a monolith nearly a thousand times greater in asset value—and still growing. In the last ten years alone the company's route mileage had increased by 14,549, more than 30 percent. By comparison, the total route mileage of TWA overseas was still only 13,416 miles and of Northwest Airlines only 13,044. (Both, of course, had domestic routes as well.) In any case, Pan American's recent growth alone exceeded the total overseas mileage of the next two biggest U.S. overseas airlines. Pan American in 1956 served 111 cities, TWA only 26. Although fourteen U.S. airlines now operated overseas, Pan American flew 54.4 percent of all overseas route mileage flown by U.S. airlines, and carried about 59 percent of the passengers and 60 percent of the air freight. Its capital investment amounted to 67 percent of the international industry total; TWA's capital investment was 11 percent.

It was also the largest U.S. company engaged in air transportation in terms of assets, the committee reported, adding that no statistics adequately reflected the extent of its economic power, for it also owned or controlled forty-nine affiliated companies or associations around the world, of which twelve were airlines, and frequently it used its affiliates to pressure its competitors. Although Pan American's growth and success was due in part to strong management, to the expanding nature of the industry, and to federal subsidies, yet, the committee charged, its dominant position had also been achieved "through the operation of a number of other factors such as sharp business practices."

After noting "the vision and acumen of its president, Juan Terry Trippe, and of the able men with whom he has surrounded himself," the committee named some of these sharp business practices: agreements with foreign governments to exclude competitors, agreements to divide territory, mergers, refusal of facilities to competitors, excessive lobbying. Trippe later protested that these "sharp" business practices were normal ones for every American company doing business abroad. But his protests had little impact.

No antitrust proceedings were ever initiated as a result of these hearings, and it was possible for Trippe to claim later that they had done no damage. But they had. Guilt or innocence had not really been established. Only the charges themselves had been established. The word "monopoly," the phrase "sharp business practices," had now been heard too many times. The company was scarred by them like wood from hammer-blows, and would wear these scars for a long time.

With the exception of the separate Panagra case, there was no need for the Celler subcommittee or anyone else to press Trippe to divest himself of his many affiliated airlines. Historical forces were at work that even Trippe could not stop. One by one nearly every country, even the so-called banana republics, announced plans to nationalize "their airline" and they began buying out Pan Am's interest. Usually this was done by installments—as money changed hands, the governments' holdings grew, and Pan Am's diminished, until at last each airline had been completely nationalized: Compañía Cubana in 1954, Middle East Airlines in 1955, Aeronaves de Mexico in 1959, Panair do Brasil in 1961. Panair was an especially sad case, for in 1965, now totally owned by Brazil, it went bankrupt and disappeared.

But through all this, Trippe's empire only grew, for he had begun to mold Pan American into a conglomerate.

The U.S. Air Force, envisioning a new kind of warfare in the future, had long ago begun developing long-distance guided missiles. They came in all sizes, ranges and destructive capability, but all had one thing in common: they had to be tested, which meant that they had to be tracked en route. The Air Force wanted to shoot them up from Cape Canaveral in Florida and send them down into the South Atlantic over distances of up to about six thousand miles. In 1953 a prospectus was let to potential civilian contractors asking for bids to build and man a string of tracking stations extending from Florida to Capetown, South Africa. One of these prospectuses landed on Trippe's desk. He brooded for a while, then called in Leslie, who, as administrative vice president, sat in the adjoining office. Leslie had seen the prospectus, and he, like Trippe, realized that Pan Am had been solicited for much the same reasons that the company had been asked to build the wartime airports through Latin America—it knew how to negotiate with foreign governments and how to build bases.

Trippe said to Leslie, "What do you think, do you think we ought to go into this? It's a pretty far outreach for us. Should we divert that much manpower and that much capital to do it?"

Leslie said, "Emphatically yes. We do have a peculiar expertise, and we owe that to our country if they need it, or think they need it. In addition, I see great advantages for Pan American. First of all, it's within our general scope of business, we can do as good or better a job than any other bidder, and it will expand our revenue base and our personnel base —it will give new opportunities to people already on our payroll, and it will permit us to employ additional people of very high training. On the one hand we'll gain new people to infuse into our own organization, and on the other we'll give new opportunities to those who are already in our organization. And finally, we'll get abreast of a new and rapidly developing technology. It's an absolute natural for us. Of course we have to bid. Let's go."

And so the Guided Missile Range Division was formed. It involved hiring some two thousand men and, eventually, the expenditure of $100 million in government money per year. Later its name was changed to the Aerospace Services Division. In addition to the South Atlantic project, it also operated the Churchill Rocket Research Range in Canada on the western shores of Hudson Bay and the Nuclear Rocket Development Station at Jackass Flats, Nev., and it performed the engineering support services in connection with the Apollo moon landing. At its peak the division employed seven thousand people, and it earned substantial profits every year.

The Business Jets Division, on the other hand, was born full-blown in Trippe's mind. In the fifties he saw corporate airplanes begin to proliferate. When Trippe climbed out of his converted B-23 on business trips, he noted parked all around him corporate planes representing ESSO, General Motors, U.S. Steel. Corporate jets would come next, Trippe reasoned, and this translated into a loss of some of Pan Am's business. Probably a third or more seats on every flight were taken by businessmen traveling for major corporations. These men would begin to travel by corporate jet, and Trippe was confronted with two choices: he could either lose them by default, together with the contacts and special relationships that such business represented, or else he could provide a new service that might accentuate the trend but that would keep the client and provide a profit to Pan Am. Trippe's solution was to sign a contract with the Dassault factory in France, which was then building a small jet known as the Mystère 20. For this plane Pan Am engineers drew up entirely new specifications: turbofan engines in place of turbojets, dual wheel landing gears in place of single wheels, and an executive configuration seating eight inside. These improvements and others were added until the Mystère, now conforming to airline standards, was renamed the Falcon and imported by Pan American into the United States in great numbers. Trippe's sales message, as his Business Jets Division began to market these corporate planes, was this: If you don't find it convenient to ride Pan Am schedules, then use our airports and airplanes. Each time a Falcon was sold, Pan Am offered to train pilots for it, and after that it could be maintained and refueled at Pan Am facilities at airports all over the world. In this way the Business Jets Division retained the interest, the loyalty and the liaison with big corporations which Trippe considered part of his company's lifeblood.

In New York a big new building began to be promoted. It would go up at the foot of Park Avenue, just north of Grand Central Terminal, and would straddle the New York Central tracks underneath. It would be the biggest corporate office building ever built, and its prospectus began to circulate. Its principal promoter was an American named Erwin Wolfson, who now sought a single tenant who would agree to lease a number of floors, and Wolfson sent a man to one of Trippe's subordinates to ask, "How do we get Pan American into this building?"

The subordinate was easy to approach. Trippe was not, and everyone knew it. He had become, with the passing of the years, ever more reclusive. An intermediary was needed, the subordinate said, someone Trippe knew or knew of, a man equal in rank to himself. This did not mean Wolfson. Trippe would never have heard of Wolfson. If approached by Wolfson, Trippe would be polite, and no more, and he would pass him off to some subordinate.

The name Henry Brunie was mentioned. Brunie was president of a major New York savings bank. Trippe would know Brunie, the subordinate judged, and would consider him an equal: "I can't think of anybody better."

So Brunie wrote Trippe a letter describing the projected building. In due time Trippe phoned him. He had some questions for Brunie, but he refused to talk to Wolfson. He refused to talk to anyone in the real estate or building business.

Brunie relayed this disheartening news to Wolfson, and the two men decided that Brunie should phone Trippe again and urge him to reconsider. Eventually Trippe did agree to meet Wolfson, and he arranged to keep the Cloud Club atop the Chrysler Building open after hours on the appointed day. He and Wolfson arrived and departed separately and talked in an otherwise empty room. Trippe warned Wolfson that if news of this meeting leaked, negotiations would cease at once.

The next meeting was arranged by Trippe, who called Wolfson on a private line before the real estate operator's switchboard was open. Trippe would come that night after hours to look at a scale model of the building. After that there were dozens of meetings between Trippe and Wolfson, and between small staffs working for both sides. To accommodate Trippe's insistence on secrecy, Wolfson's files relating to their negotiations were identified as "Project X." Pan American was identified as "Prince Albert." Trippe himself was labeled "the traveler."

The building, for which Walter Gropius and Pietro Belluschi acted as design consultants, was rather severely modern in appearance, and later would arouse howls of protest from conservative New Yorkers. But Trippe liked it—with reservations. He wanted it turned 90 degrees on its axis, and he wanted the price brought way down. He also wanted the Pan Am name and logo in lights in letters thirty feet high on all four sides at the roof. He wanted to pay rent that was at least a third less per square footage than the going rate. He wanted equity in the building, and he intended from the start to buy up shares as they became available until at last he would own it all. Negotiations over these and other details lasted months. Trippe won most of his points, not all. The rooftop letters and logo were scaled down from thirty feet to fifteen, for instance. But at length Pan Am signed a lease committing it to rental payments totaling $117 million over the next twenty-five years. It was the largest lease ever written for Manhattan office space. It was a document 100 pages long. It guaranteed that the building would be built, and seemed to promise also that Pan Am would very soon own it all.

John B. Gates, Yale '31, Yale Law '34, was an executive with Russell Burdsall & Ward, the largest manufacturer of nuts and bolts in the world. He was also one of Trippe's golfing partners. They had met on a golf course in Greenwich, Conn., where both had homes, in 1948. Because both also had homes in Bermuda, they soon began to play together there as well, and this association lasted for the next nine years. There were two other members of their regular foursome: Jim Linen, who was president of Time Inc., and Frank Pace, head of General Dynamics. Pace had the use of the General Dynamics plane, and Trippe had the Pan Am B-23, and on any given day the four men might play at the Round Hill Club in Greenwich, the Maidstone Club at East Hampton, at a course on Block Island or wherever else they happened to fancy. Of the four the best golfer was Gates. He was at least six strokes better than Trippe, who had a twelve handicap at this time. Trippe was fairly short off the tee, but most often his balls traveled dead straight. He had no great shots that Gates could see, but no bad ones either. As a golfing partner, Trippe was fun. Before, during and after the game he laughed a lot. He would be delighted to talk politics or business, but only if someone else brought up such weighty subjects. Otherwise on a golf course Trippe talked golf. He seemed entirely lighthearted, and he loved the game. There were times when his plane or Pace's plane would land the four men and their wives at Bermuda or Hobe Sound at four-thirty in the afternoon, and Trippe would hurry the men off the plane saying, "I think we can squeeze in eighteen holes before we have to meet the girls for dinner." And then the next day he would want the same men to join him for thirty-six holes more.

Gates also was active as a fund-raiser for Yale, as was Trippe. But late in 1956 his company asked him to cut down on his Yale activities and devote more time to business, and he was obliged to ask to be replaced as chairman of the Yale Alumni Fund.

Learning this, Trippe promptly asked Gates to join Pan Am as vice president for Finance, at a salary below what Gates was receiving at the manufacturing company. When Gates balked, Trippe spoke persuasively about what a fine opportunity this was for Gates, how he couldn't turn Pan Am down. Gates later found out two things: that Trippe never offered top dollar when hiring anyone, and that there was no such job as vice president, Finance.

Instead, as soon as Gates came to work for him, Trippe summoned him to his office for a short speech. Pan Am, Trippe told his new vice president, was interested in charities. The company's officers were urged to take part in fund-raising as much as possible. And he, Trippe, certainly hoped Gates would resume the chairmanship of the Yale Alumni Fund.

Had Trippe hired him just for that, Gates asked himself?

His first assignment was to get down to Washington to help Pryor lobby for a law then under consideration that would relieve the airlines from capital-gains taxes as their propeller-plane fleets were sold to make room for jets. Gates was in Washington for most of three months, and with all the other airlines also backing this bill, it passed.

Gates then returned to New York to his nonexistent job as vice president, Finance. The airline, he saw, already had a comptroller, who was Woodbridge, and a treasurer, who was Bob Ferguson, and in any case its chief financial officer was Trippe himself—to Gates, a financial genius. Trippe knew when to borrow money, when to use convertible debentures. He always knew far ahead exactly how much money he would need, and when. He had an amazing ability to guess at interest rates in advance, and almost invariably managed to borrow when rates were low, and to raise capital in some other way when they were high. He certainly didn't need Gates as V.P. Finance. For a time Gates merely hung around, enduring the suspicious stares of executives who felt their own positions threatened. With nothing to do, he grew increasingly despondent.

One day Trippe summoned Gates again. The jets were going to shrink the world by half, Trippe told him. "John, we are going to see the day when an overseas flight is just like getting on a train for Washington. No advance booking. No reservations. People will just go out to the airport and get on a plane to Paris, or Istanbul." The jets would open up new routes, new cities, and would land in places where no decent hotels existed. Before Pan Am's travel base could expand, there would have to be hotels where tourists and businessmen would want to stop, where they could drink the water and eat the food. Trippe wanted now to develop a chain of such hotels extending outward into every way-stop where the company might touch down, and he wanted Gates to do this job for him.

Pan American already had a hotel chain. Called Intercontinental Hotels, it was the proud owner of three major hotels and nine lesser ones that Gates, upon inspection, would categorize as fleabags. Trippe wanted this chain expanded to eighty or ninety grand hotels, perhaps more. "I'll bet you everything will fall into place," Trippe told Gates confidently. He wanted the hotels to be financed partly by the Export-Import bank, partly by local governments. Pan Am—or Intercontinental—would make a "modest" investment of around 10 percent as a gesture of good faith and would assume the management contract.

And so the new chief executive officer of Intercontinental Hotels Corp. began trying to make Trippe's dream a reality. But there were handicaps Trippe hadn't mentioned in advance. One was that Gates would have to find the money himself—10 percent of the cost of each hotel—because any money to which Pan Am had access was needed by

Trippe to buy planes. Nor was Gates permitted to use the Pan Am name to find credit or back loans. But despite a thousand other problems, Gates's hotels did begin to rise in thirty-seven countries on five continents.

To play golf with Trippe and to work for him were, Gates found, entirely different things, for now he saw even more of Trippe's unusual energy and much less of the warm personal friendship of the past. Like the division managers, Gates had autonomy—up to a point. But he had to prepare detailed project plans for Trippe's approval for each hotel, and these Trippe pored over, and he no more respected Gates's time than any other employee's. One Christmas Eve Gates did not get out of Trippe's office until nine-thirty at night. On another day he was due at his daughter's graduation at eleven in the morning, and Trippe knew this. Trippe called him in at ten o'clock, and Gates missed the graduation. He was, by then, not particularly surprised. Trippe, once he fastened on a problem, could not be got off it, and in the process he became absolutely oblivious to consideration for other people. A typical example occurred just before the nationalization in 1960 of the Havana Intercontinental by Castro. On New Year's Eve 1959 Gates flew from Havana, where he had been negotiating with Castro's officials, to the Cotton Bay Club on Eleuthera, a club Trippe had founded by selling shares to his friends, including Gates. Gates's wife and the Trippes waited for dinner and a party, and when Gates arrived, he presented Trippe with a Castro beard and cap that he claimed Castro had given him "from the dictator of one island to the dictator of another." When the party broke up, the two couples walked along the path toward their houses. They were bidding each other good night and Happy New Year when Trippe suddenly said, "John, let me have five minutes." He had begun, Gates realized, to think of the lost Havana hotel, and he now started what amounted to a full-scale business conference on the subject then and there. As the wives tapped their feet impatiently, Trippe kept saying, "Just give me five minutes more," and he kept all three standing on the path in the moonlight from just past midnight until three o'clock in the morning.

Hotels, missile ranges, business jets, a midtown office building, the mightiest international airline in the world. There was Trippe in the sixties sitting all alone atop a billion-dollar conglomerate. In 1964 Pan Am was flying to Europe 214 times a week, up from 170 flights in 1958 in propeller planes carrying half as many people. The following year there were 258 flights a week to Europe—and 152 across the Pacific. In 1966 traffic went up another 25 percent. The planes now touched down in 118 cities, and the net profit was $132 million.

The early years of the company had been characterized by Trippe's enormous drive, by his demand that the impossible be accomplished, by the short deadlines he gave out that kept his entire organization on its toes. But by now Pan Am was so vast that he had become isolated: no one could reach him that he did not want to see. He was not easily accessible even to his closest subordinates—they sometimes waited days or even weeks to see him—and when the meeting at length took place, it was to discuss Trippe's agenda, not theirs. "Divide and rule" was the method by which many chief executives operated—Trippe, too, at the beginning. But from the middle years on, it had been true no longer—Trippe ruled without any question at all.

Usually he reached the office each morning somewhat late—around nine-thirty. On the whole he concentrated on one problem at a time and he worked at it until his mind had exhausted the subject. He was capable of working right through lunch, working until midnight if necessary, and sometimes even past midnight. Meetings occasionally lasted until one-thirty in the morning. Lunch, when he took it at all, was never a social occasion. A social occasion to Trippe was his annual Christmas party for his executives. Once a year was enough.

The Christmas party was held at the Trippes' Gracie Square apartment. Middle-management executives who received invitations congratulated themselves for weeks. To be invited at all was step one in penetrating Trippe's inner circle. Step two was the day Betty Trippe added at the bottom of the invitation: "And plan to stay for dinner." At these Christmas parties Trippe was friendly and informal. At other gatherings he and Betty stood at the head of a receiving line. Trippe was poor at names, and he counted on Betty beside him to identify each individual who approached.

Each Monday the systems operating committee—Trippe and six or seven other men—convened for lunch. At these meetings a man could speak out freely. Opinions were not restricted to a man's own department. The mood was affable and Trippe did not impose himself. Usually these luncheons lasted till 3:00 P.M., but sometimes, if Trippe became immersed in a problem, the pots of coffee would come until it turned dark outside.

At meetings Trippe sometimes seemed to take pleasure in asking the wrong person the wrong question. He would deliberately hand out work assignments unrelated to a man's specialty—ask Marketing vice president Lipscomb to solve an engineering problem; order Operations vice president John Shannon to prepare a public relations program. No one objected to such assignments in Trippe's presence, because once the meeting broke up, the men would sort out the assignments among themselves.

Sometimes a decision would be needed that his subordinates judged only Trippe could make. They would bring him the problem, but he would be focused on something else and never get to it. Days might go by with still no word from Trippe. Finally one of the others would make the decision for him—a perfectly valid decision, though rather late. Many times one of them would urge Trippe to attend a specific meeting: "Only you can decide. You've got to be there." Trippe would agree—then not show up.

If anyone asked him for a raise, Trippe would get irritated. Salaries remained extremely low compared with those in other industries, but on management levels there was little turnover. And one of Trippe's achievements was that he managed to run a vast and successful corporation with minimum overhead. Of course all these men got stock options, and as business boomed, some of them became—on paper at least—rich men. There were also bonus lists each year—down to as little as $300 on the lowest levels.

Those close to Trippe saw him as a man of great rectitude according to his own standards, which were those of the 1920's. He believed in ethics not only for its own sake but also because it was good business. The businessman who can't be trusted, he believed, soon finds that no one will deal with him. As a businessman he was extremely tough, of course, and although some of his tactics might have seemed unattractive to later generations, they were perfectly ethical according to the customs in force during Trippe's early and mature years. On a personal level he didn't believe in misbehavior of any kind, and especially not in womanizing, in sexual liberation. He was almost a prude. He counted himself and was counted by others as a gentleman—as gentlemen were reckoned when he left Yale.

Trippe seemed almost like a king, for he had a court of nobles grouped tightly around him and their various ranks in the hierarchy were ordained, usually by not so subtle means, by him alone. Vice presidents learned to study the roster of officers every time a company report was published. There were ten or more of them, and Trippe moved their names up and down as the whim struck him. Those closest to the top— closest to Trippe's own name—had his favor, and in exactly the order they appeared. They studied the seating arrangements at company dinners too, because they knew he entered banquet rooms a few minutes early to put the place cards exactly where he wanted them. In an agony of suspense they would circle the table looking for their names. The men beside him were being rewarded and the men farthest away punished— in public.

52

The Biggest Gamble

Trippe's jets were flying, and business boomed. It was time for another "next step." Though in his sixties, Trippe looked younger, and his energy and enthusiasm had not flagged. What was the next step to be? He was as eager to make it happen as he had been as a young man.

A supersonic airliner perhaps? A British-French government consortium planned one that would be called the Concorde; it would cross the ocean in three and a half hours, but would take ten years to build. There were plans for an American supersonic transport also, a project so expensive that only the U.S. government could afford it. President Kennedy, who had received conflicting advice, would have to decide whether to back the project or not, and he sent a man named Najeeb Halaby to tell Trippe not to buy the foreign supersonic until he had made up his mind. Halaby, as head of the Federal Aviation Administration, held virtual Cabinet rank.

Trippe, too, had received conflicting advice. Lindbergh, for one, was strongly against supersonic jets on environmental grounds. Their noise figured to turn airport environs into wastelands, and for all anyone knew, they might destroy the ozone layer above the earth. Lindbergh was against them on economic grounds also. To get such a plane through the sound barrier its fuselage would have to be built in the shape of a pencil. That meant too few passengers and too much energy consumed per pound of payload.

Lindbergh had at last been invited by Trippe to be on the board of directors. The hero, now in his sixties, had become somewhat gloomy in recent years. He told intimates he was no longer certain that the airplane had been such a good thing. It had destroyed cities, cultures and hundreds of thousands of people, and now this proliferation of air travel had begun to seem to him only the aimless coming and going of too many people for no very good reason. The machine itself had become too technical, too complex, too expensive. It was responsible for too much noise, too much commotion, too much pollution. To Lindbergh, the supersonic project, known everywhere now as the SST, would only make a bad situation worse.

But to Trippe, even as he approached what ordinary men considered retirement age, nothing was impracticable, and if the SST was to be the next step, then he wanted to be the man who would bring it on. He knew President Kennedy was wavering and might withdraw funding from the American SST, and so Trippe decided to force the President's hand. When Kennedy promised a decision for the Monday following Memorial Day 1963, Trippe optioned three Concordes from the British-French consortium, and arranged for this news to be made public the day before.

Kennedy was forced to announce that the United States, too, would build a supersonic transport, but he was furious and he sent Halaby back to Trippe to demand an explanation. Twice he phoned Halaby while Halaby stood in Trippe's office. "Tell Mr. Trippe we will not forget this," Kennedy said.

Trippe arranged to be elected chairman of the board, a rank that had stood empty since Sonny Whitney departed at the start of World War II. At the same time, he made Harold Gray president—Gray, who had joined the company as a twenty-three-year-old pilot in 1929, who had moved steadily upward since: chief pilot on the Atlantic, vice president of the Pacific-Alaska and then the Atlantic divisions. Trippe was still chief executive officer. He still kept all major decisions for himself. Nonetheless, Gray was now widely seen as Trippe's heir apparent.

In the meantime business and tourist travel were increasing at such a rate that existing airline fleets couldn't handle the load, nor could most airports. Even the air lanes high overhead—the most efficient altitude for all these jets was about 33,000 feet—were becoming overcrowded. A solution to this traffic jam was needed, Trippe saw, and this could not be the SST because its day was still too far off.

Trippe was among the first to realize that the "next step" was perhaps not the SST at all but, rather, a giant jet that would carry at least double the two hundred or so passengers now being crammed aboard the 707's and DC-8's. Perhaps a plane could be built to carry a thousand people —at last a veritable ocean liner of the air.

Next occurred a major breakthrough in jet-engine design. The earlier jet engines had sent columns of superheated thrust straight out the back to bore holes in the sky. The new refinement was called the by-pass or fan-jet. Part of the thrust was used to turn gears which operated a second fan in front of the original one. The front fan became a kind of propeller whirling inside the cowling, and some of the thrust it created was sent down vents along the side of the engine—as air rather than as jet thrust —so that both ordinary air and superheated air intermingled and shot out the back not only with enormous volume but also with a significant expansion of the diameter, and therefore the efficiency, of the exiting column of thrust. In fact, the engine designers now had the best of both worlds. The forward cowled fan was acting as a propeller, and exerting more pull as a propeller than was provided by push from the jet-engine exhaust. These new engines were fatter but shorter than the old ones. They gave enormous power in a relatively compact package, and they made possible the gigantic ocean liner of an airplane that Trippe now determined to force on the world.

The Air Force at this time had sponsored competition for a giant military cargo plane. Boeing, Douglas and Lockheed were all competitors. The plane would be called the C-5, and would be able to carry massive military hardware out of short, unimproved airfields. As a civilian airliner, the C-5 would be useless, but whichever company won the contract would have solved most of the design problems inherent in the jumbo jet airliner Trippe wanted to see made. He thought the winner would be Douglas, and on the day the contract was to be awarded he actually had Gledhill at the Douglas plant in California prepared to sign preliminary agreements for a civilian version. When the winner was not Douglas but Lockheed, Trippe immediately telephoned Lockheed's Courtland Gross and attempted to start negotiations for a civilian derivative of the C-5 that very day. But he had enough problems just building the military version, Gross said. When his staff had cleared up some of these, he would call Trippe back. Lockheed did build the C-5, came close to bankruptcy in the process, and Gross never did call Trippe back. Meanwhile negotiations had begun with Douglas and Boeing. Declining to build any jumbo jet, Douglas elected instead to stretch the DC-8. To Trippe, stretching an existing plane could not be a next step. Boeing offered alternative suggestions also. Stretching the 707 was one; double-decking it was another.

No, said Trippe, and a number of three-way conferences ensued between Boeing, Pratt and Whitney, and Pan American. How much weight could the new engines lift? How many people could a practical airframe contain? How many orders was Pan Am willing to guarantee? The shape and size of the new airliner began to take form, and Boeing designated it the 747. On December 22, 1965, Boeing President Allen and Pan Am Chairman Trippe signed a statement of their intentions. Boeing would build the 747, and Pan American would buy and operate twenty-five of them.

The risks for both sides were enormous. To manufacture planes that huge, Boeing would first have to construct a factory big enough to encompass them. It would be one of the largest, perhaps the very largest, building in the world. A location for it was picked out alongside Paine Field, formerly a World War II military base, near Everett, Wash. To feed 747 material into this factory—indeed to build the factory itself—Boeing would have to lay a rail spur from the main line in Seattle and design and construct special cars big enough to hold the components—some of them enormous—that would be manufactured by subcontractors. At the end of the spur lay a short steep grade. Boeing would have to bring in special locomotives that could climb that grade into the factory. Boeing's total commitment would exceed $2 billion, and if the plane failed, Boeing would be bankrupt.

Pan American would likely be bankrupt too, for the total cost of the twenty-five planes it had agreed to buy would come to about $550 million. Nor could it put off payment until the planes were ready four years hence. Boeing demanded a down payment of 2.5 percent upon signing the contract—plus increasingly high installment payments that, six months before the scheduled delivery of the first aircraft and perhaps ten months before the first scheduled revenue mile was flown, would amount to around $250 million. All this would be paid before the plane was even certified by the Federal Aeronautics Administration to carry passengers.

The new plane was to have a range of 5,100 miles with a full load of 400 passengers. It was to fly at just under the speed of sound, and be able to take off in 8,000 feet on a hot day on any airport that was able to handle ordinary jet airliners. It was to cruise above 35,000 feet—high above the currently overcrowded passenger lanes. The arrangement also assured Trippe that Pan American would take delivery of most of its planes before other airlines received any. Obviously, Pan Am could not assimilate all twenty-five at once; in any case, Trippe wanted a few to go to Air France, Alitalia and Japan Airlines fairly quickly, for these were the national monopolies that controlled the most lucrative destinations that Pan Am served: if they attempted to block the 747 as too heavy or too noisy, this would be a disaster for Pan Am. Thinking far into the future as always, Trippe wanted these national monopolies to join him, not fight him. As for his American competitors, he wanted them to take delivery as close to last as possible, and this was agreed to.

And so public announcement was made. It was full of superlatives about the plane, but Trippe had ordered that it mention money too—the $550 million constituted the largest single undertaking ever carried out by a commercial company. Of all his accomplishments over the past nearly forty years, Trippe seemed proudest of his ability to raise these enormous amounts of money, repeatedly to finance new fleets. The most interesting part of the Pan American story, he told people often enough, was not the technical, geographical, political or heroic parts but, rather, the financial one.

Suddenly—from Trippe's point of view—disaster struck. In the face of steel shortages, in the face of inflation fears due to the burgeoning Vietnam war, President Johnson announced an austerity program during which big business was to curtail all its programs. No new plants were to be built, nor major new projects undertaken.

Trippe phoned the White House and asked for an appointment with the President but was refused. He phoned again and again, but the answer did not change. In recent years no President had ever refused to see him and he was both offended and outraged.

Johnson had convoked a regular meeting of his business advisory council, of which Trippe was a member. Trippe went to Washington and on the appointed day entered the East Room of the White House where the fifty business leaders sat stiffly on straight-backed chairs. Johnson and his Cabinet came into the room. Trippe was now in Johnson's presence, but still had no appointment with him.

As the meeting began, Johnson defended his new anti-inflation program. There could be no further expansion of the economy, he said. These men were not awed by Johnson, and all around the room they were shaking their heads. One of them interrupted to say that he had commitments to his employees and to his stockholders. He needed a new plant, and he intended to build it unless there was legislation to the contrary. A second businessman said the same. A third tried to soften the mood with a wisecrack. Johnson stood up and angrily adjourned the meeting. In heavy silence the business council members filed out the door.

Now was no time to accost the President on the same subject, but Trippe had no choice, and he hung back. Nearby stood Bill Martin, head of the Federal Reserve Board, who also was not leaving. Since he was less brash than Trippe, this meant that he was waiting for Johnson to be free, and that Johnson knew this and had agreed to a meeting in advance.

Like a general accurately assaying the terrain, Trippe approached Martin and said, "Will you let me have your appointment with the President? What I have to say to him is vital to the well being of the country. With the approval of the President, of course."

So Martin stepped aside—what else could he do?—and Johnson, turning, found himself face to face with Trippe.

Judging that he had about fifteen minutes to make his case, Trippe made every word count. He described the 747 project, spoke of the new engines, of the new wing shape, of projected sales to every foreign airline, of balance-of-payments deficits that such sales would redress, of the plane's vast troop-carrying capabilities in time of war, of the states whose employment picture would be enhanced if the plane was built. This amounted to many more arguments than Johnson could comprehend, much less cope with, in fifteen minutes. "Who else knows about this?" he asked, meaning who else in the White House or Cabinet.

"No one but you, Mr. President," said Trippe in a manner that could best be described as humble, for he perceived immediately that he had won, and could afford to be humble.

Johnson, after thinking a moment, said, "Be here tomorrow morning at ten A.M. My car will be waiting for you."

When Trippe reached the White House the following morning, the President's car drove him across the river to the Pentagon. Secretary of Defense Robert McNamara was standing in the doorway. "What the hell is this?" he said. "The Chief told me to clear everything. This has never happened before."

For the next two hours Trippe elaborated on the arguments presented to the President the night before: the new engines, the shape of the wing, the troop-carrying possibilities. McNamara had a slide rule on his desk and sometimes made calculations, checking out the numbers Trippe gave him. From time to time McNamara injected questions. What about the Lockheed C-5? Why couldn't that serve as an airliner? Why was the 747 needed at all? Trippe gave a lecture on the economics of the C-5, noting its extravagant costs per passenger carried, per cargo ton carried. Only the Air Force could afford to fly it. As an airliner it would be an economic catastrophe. In addition, it was so constructed that it could not be evacuated within the ninety seconds stipulated by the Federal Aeronautics Authority. In other respects also, its safety margins were too small. As a commercial airliner it would never get certified.

Trippe was so convincing that McNamara muttered, "I've wasted five hundred million dollars of the taxpayers' money."

Trippe was obliged to backtrack. No, he hadn't, the C-5 would be a wonderful military aircraft; it had short-field takeoff capability; McNamara had done exactly the right thing in sponsoring it. But the 747 was what the airlines needed, what the United States needed to enhance its balance-of-payments picture abroad, and it needed to go ahead now.

At length McNamara announced that he and Trippe would drive back to the White House to see the President at once.

"That seems to me a waste of your time, and the President's time," he told McNamara. "My time is not important here. But if you were still in industry, you would get on the phone with him right now, and tell him."

For a moment McNamara only stared at Trippe. Then he sat down and began to write a letter.

"You're not going to write him a letter?" said Trippe.

McNamara said, "You just sit down there and I'll be with you in a moment."

When the letter was finished, McNamara and Trippe were driven to the White House and promptly ushered into the Oval Office. It was then about twelve-thirty in the afternoon. McNamara handed Johnson the letter he had just written. Johnson, at his desk, read it several times. Then, standing up, he tore it to shreds. "That's what I think of your letter," he told McNamara. "Do you know what was in that letter?" he asked Trippe.

Trippe said he did not.

"That was the Secretary's letter of resignation," said Johnson.

Now McNamara did most of the talking. From time to time Johnson turned to Trippe to ask for details on load factors, economics, the locations of the plants of the various subcontractors. After approximately thirty minutes Johnson called in an aide and said, "I want word sent to the Boeing Company that work on the 747 is to go forward."

And so the 747 was saved for whatever future it might have. Would it bring the vast profits Trippe was predicting? Or the economic ruin which, considering its cost, seemed the only other possible outcome? Trippe's career had encompassed all of commercial aviation in the United States, and the elapsed period, forty years, was brief enough for him to have kept its entire history in his head. One constant during all of that period could not be denied: new planes almost never met their specifications. If this one didn't, then what?

According to contract, the 747's maximum weight empty would be 274,094 pounds. But it soon became clear that the Boeing engineers had badly underestimated the weight of their design, and after only a year's gestation, the 747 had swollen to 308,924 pounds, meaning a payload reduction of more than 10 percent. Boeing blamed Pan Am for adding frills, and Pan Am blamed Boeing for misjudging structural weights. Unfortunately, the plane's weight would swell still further.

Trippe had appointed retired U.S.A.F. General Lawrence Kuter to head his 747 project team. The rest of the team was composed of some old names—vice president (Engineering) Sanford Kauffman, chief engineer John Borger—and also some new ones, including Howard Blackwell, the new vice president for Purchasing, who had replaced the retired Gledhill. Trippe himself stayed aloof from the project for the time being.

A year and a half after Trippe and Allen signed their agreement specifying a takeoff gross weight of 550,000 pounds, that weight had grown to 710,000 pounds—the plane would not be able to lift a full payload off the ground, nor reach its operating altitude, nor manage its predicted maximum range. It would be the economic disaster that everyone for so long had so greatly feared.

From then on the two sides negotiated almost continually. Pan Am wanted Boeing to reduce weight, however costly this might be. Boeing could redesign, which would cost time and money; or employ new—and fabulously expensive—light metals. Boeing wanted Pan Am to accept reduced performance, to delay the entire project until more powerful engines were available from Pratt and Whitney, or to accept a fifth engine in the tail of the plane.

These earliest negotiations got nowhere, and General Kuter went to President Harold Gray and begged him to ask Trippe to intervene in the negotiations directly. Perhaps Trippe could get Pratt and Whitney to upgrade its engine or could get Boeing to absorb the tremendous costs of a major redesign.

After talking to Bill Gwinn, who now headed Pratt and Whitney, Trippe became convinced that not only was the engine favored by Boeing too small, but so was the "improved" version of the same engine that his own team favored. He decided he wanted an even more powerful engine than that, though such an engine existed only in the earliest stages of development, and he did not believe, or else chose to ignore, that the monstrous engine he favored also needed a bigger nacelle to ride in, and that such a nacelle would require major redesign of the 747 wing, engine mounting and landing gear. The "state of the art," Trippe decided, was adequate to produce such an engine in one year and nine months. Told that the cost of producing such an engine so quickly would be around a quarter of a billion dollars extra, Trippe never flinched. If he could get the plane he wanted, he was willing enough to pay premiums.

Next Trippe went to Boeing, where he began to talk of his own vision of what the 747 ought to be. He was no longer interested in the 747 as conceived and not yet built. He wanted Boeing to drop that design and go at once to an advanced 747B that would employ the new engines that did not yet exist. Somehow he managed to communicate his own enthusiasm to the Boeing engineers, who actually began to work out designs for the new plane that Trippe was talking about. They put in thousands of hours of work, as if such a plane could actually be built—right now. It couldn't be, and most of that work was wasted, though not all—for some spin-off did reappear in the original 747 as it began at last to be built.

The main thing Trippe communicated both to Pratt and Whitney and to Boeing was Pan Am's dissatisfaction with what was happening. Was this his only objective all the time? No one knew except Trippe, who kept secrets even from his own team. But throughout the industry his reputation as a negotiator was by now so formidable that men tended to read hidden meanings into every word he spoke, and even into his silences.

Each time Trippe personally entered the negotiations he was briefed by General Kuter and his staff, and sometimes he was furnished with status reports and engineering specifications. No one ever knew what he did with these briefings and reports, nor even if he made use of them. Once he and Mrs. Trippe spent a week with Mr. and Mrs. Allen fishing in Alaskan waters from the Boeing yacht. Another time the Allens stayed with the Trippes at the Cotton Bay Club in Eleuthera. Trippe never told

Kuter or anyone else what he had said to Allen, nor Allen to him, nor whether he had showed the studies and position reports, and he never wrote anything down, either before or after one of these meetings. As Kuter later noted: "His ability to disclaim in private what his staff had proposed in conferences was a negotiating weapon he cherished. He reserved the right, and frequently exercised it, to redirect the subjects under discussion into new and unexpected directions."

Most of the negotiations revolved around ways to reduce weight. For instance, the heavy triple-slotted landing flaps could be replaced by lighter conventional double-slotted flaps. But this would produce a much faster takeoff and landing speed which would require longer runways and probably fewer passengers. It was also possible to soup up the engines, but at what cost? and who should pay this cost, Pan Am or Boeing?

Almost all of these problems ultimately became economic. Boeing was not going to be able to meet its specifications at the price that Pan Am had agreed to pay. The two sides were at loggerheads, and Wall Street and the press knew it. Boeing and Pan Am common stock both began to fall, and this was blamed on the burgeoning problems of the 747. Concessions were made on both sides. Week by week the 747 design closed in on its original specifications, but never, it soon became clear, would it attain them completely.

The 747 was not going to fly as high as promised, nor as far, nor as fast, nor would it carry as many people. But there was no turning back now.

Meanwhile Trippe brooded from time to time about who was to succeed him. There were men in the Pan Am hierarchy who had seemed possibilities at times. The trouble was that most of them had started with the company almost as early as Trippe himself, and they were his own age —he was now in his late sixties. Even President Gray was nearly sixty-two.

He had thought about the succession off and on for years, and his first choice had been John Leslie, who had caught his eye in the mid-forties, and had gone on the board of directors in 1950. But Leslie had been stricken by an especially virulent form of polio; he had returned to work but had been in a wheelchair ever since.

In 1955 Assistant Secretary of the Air Force Roger Lewis had attracted Trippe and after resigning he had gone to work for Pan Am. For years Lewis had appeared to be the heir apparent, but in 1962 he had left Pan Am to head General Dynamics.

Next Trippe had appeared to fasten on Najeeb Halaby, whom he had met under adverse circumstances at the time Trippe had optioned the Concorde SST. Trippe had been tremendously impressed with Halaby at that time—in some ways Trippe was impressed rather easily—because the man had received two phone calls from the White House while standing at Trippe's desk.

Trippe was a man who admired success, and Halaby, in Trippe's mind, was successful. Trippe always had to have the best: the best aircraft, the best lawyers, the best routes, the best publicity. And the best executives.

In any case, on the night in 1965 that Halaby retired from government service, Trippe had phoned him at home to say, "I've prepared a definite offer of employment as a senior officer of Pan Am and I'm putting it in the mail." Halaby was disappointed in this offer when it came. The salary seemed low to him.

For weeks the two men met, played golf together, talked it over. The salary offer remained low but not the promise that seemed to go with it. Trippe allowed Halaby to conclude that Trippe wanted him at Pan Am as a potential successor. There was no telling how long a wait this might entail. Some people said that Trippe's retirement would be in a coffin. But once he told Halaby that he was absolutely determined to retire "in a year or so."

Halaby signed on as a vice president—Harold Gray was still president —and began to wait for the great day, whenever that might be.

53

The Great Day

A stockholders' meeting was scheduled for May 7, 1968. That morning Trippe rose at his normal hour. He breakfasted normally, saying little. He was almost sixty-nine years old. Downstairs his driver waited behind the wheel of the Chrysler. He got in, and the car started down Park Avenue in heavy traffic. Some forty blocks ahead rose the façade of the fifty-seven-story building that blocked off the avenue, and indeed most of the skyline of the city. It was still the largest commercial office building in the world, and it bore, in giant letters on its roof, the name of the company he had founded: Pan Am.

He got out of his car. An express elevator whisked him nonstop to his office on the forty-sixth floor. However undramatic the day may have seemed to him so far, there were special jobs that now had to be done.

He pushed a button on his desk. "Would you come in, please, Miss Clair." Kathleen Clair was his personal secretary.

"Miss Clair," he said when she stood before his desk, "I just want you to know that today I'm retiring as chairman, and Mr. Gray will be taking over."

Miss Clair's immediate response was an emotional one. She had been with him for eighteen years, and tears came to her eyes.

Later she would realize that he had arranged the details of his retirement so secretly that they had been accomplished entirely without the knowledge of his personal secretary, herself. How had he done that?

If Trippe was moved by Miss Clair's tears, it did not show. Nor did he seem affected when, at two-fifteen, in the Windsor Ballroom of the

Commodore Hotel he looked out over rows of stockholders, about eight hundred people in all. Pan Am stewardesses in powder-blue uniforms moved up and down the aisles handing out company literature. He rapped for order, and in a low, droning voice began to read a 45-minute stockholders' report: the net loss was four cents a share for the first quarter of 1968, but operating revenues had increased 15.6 percent, while operating expenses were up 22.6 percent. The statistics and the details followed in mind-numbing progression.

Trippe's bombshell announcement came almost at the end. Pan Am's board of directors would meet later that day, he said, adding, "At that meeting I plan to nominate President Harold Gray to succeed me as chairman and chief executive officer of our company." Trippe did not pause for effect, but continued to read from the report.

In the audience there was at first no reaction. People didn't realize what had just been said. Then, after a moment, came a smattering of applause. No one knew whether the moment called for applause or not, and Trippe's announcement had come as a total surprise. The few reporters present were wide awake now, for this routine meeting had just transformed itself into one of the biggest business stories of the decade: Juan Terry Trippe, the first aviation tycoon in history—and the last—was stepping down.

The story that had started forty-one years previously with virtually nothing—a plane, a pilot and a single 90-mile run from Key West to Havana—was over. Trippe was leaving behind him a billion-dollar, worldwide conglomerate. Pan Am alone had 40,000 employees, and spent $31 million a year just on advertising. Its fleet numbered 143 multiengined jets, with a billion and a half dollars' worth of planes on order. In addition, it had its hotels, its business jets, its airports, its midtown skyscraper—and all the rest.

In the entire world there had been only three other aviation tycoons, all of them Americans: Patterson of United, Smith of American and Rickenbacker of Eastern. All three took control in the early or middle thirties —much later than Trippe—and all retired before him: Rickenbacker in 1963, Patterson in 1966 and Smith in January 1968, only four months ago. Though these were big men in aviation history, none ever matched Trippe's scope, as Smith once grudgingly admitted. "Trippe was number one in the whole transport industry."

At his retirement, Trippe was many times a millionaire, but had little in the way of possessions to show for it. He held nine honorary degrees extending from the University of Miami to the University of Alaska, from the University of California to Yale. No other American civilian had been decorated by as many foreign governments as Trippe, who held medals from eighteen countries—some of which had been discreetly solicited by subordinates.

As soon as today's stockholders' meeting broke up, the board of directors convened. There Trippe formally announced his own retirement, and recommended Harold Gray to replace him. To replace Gray as president, Trippe named Halaby. These were his recommendations to the board. He was asking them and telling them at the same time.

Most board members were important men in their own right: Charles Francis Adams, chairman of Raytheon; Robert B. Anderson, a former Secretary of the Treasury; Norman Chandler, chairman of the Los Angeles *Times Mirror;* Donald K. David, former dean of the Harvard Business School; investment banker Robert Lehman; Charles Lindbergh; James Rockefeller, chairman of the First National City Bank; Arthur Watson of IBM, who would later serve as ambassador to Paris; and Cyrus Vance, later to become Secretary of State. These men voted Trippe's slate. They voted Gray chairman, and Halaby president. They voted a new title for Trippe: chairman emeritus. He said he would remain a member of the board of directors. He said he would remain a member of the board's executive committee also.

When the meeting broke up, Trippe led Gray into the big office at the southwest corner of the forty-sixth floor. Gray should take over the office as is, Trippe instructed him. He should take over even Trippe's desk. There was no need for Gray to bring any of his own furniture in or to move any of Trippe's furniture out.

As the now ex-chairman Trippe left for home that night, Miss Clair and the other women stood in the hall in such a way that he had to walk past each of them. They had tears in their eyes. When he got home he told his wife how touched he had been: "They were so nice to me," he said.

The next morning Trippe moved into a smaller office in the back. There was no vacation. He continued to come to work every day.

But some months later he did take his wife on a trip around the world. In Singapore they watched part of a golf tournament. They spent two days in Kashmir. They stopped in Lahore. The Khyber Pass was decked out in fall colors when they went through it by car. They visited Afghanistan for the first time. They spent some days in London, then flew home.

In his absence Harold Gray had removed some of Trippe's furniture and had replaced it with his own.

And Pan Am had begun to lose money.

There were those who imagined that the Trippe saga wasn't over yet.

54

Epilogue

And then Trippe did something that no one who knew him would have believed possible. He ceased to impose himself upon the company. Although he still attended most board meetings, he did not attempt to exert his will. He was available for consultation; otherwise he kept his thoughts to himself. His suffering, if he suffered, did not show.

In 1969 Pan Am lost $26 million, and the next year $49 million. After that the disaster only got worse. The public press blamed Trippe, asserting that he had seen the future and had got out before it struck. No one else had seen the future, but Trippe was smarter than everybody else, always had been. The future being clear to him, he had run off, leaving poor Gray in the path of the avalanche. This explained his "mysterious" retirement at "only" sixty-eight, when everyone had already decided he would die atop Pan Am—the airline and the building both.

It was a charge of cowardice against a man who had never shown cowardice before, but however much it may have rankled, Trippe did not respond.

Problems faced by Gray and, after him, Halaby, became desperate ones. The company was paying out $29 million a quarter on the 747, and the plane being built was less than the one contracted for. But this was almost the least of anyone's worries.

All through the sixties overseas air traffic had increased at close to 25 percent per year. Marketing projections at the time the 747 was conceived had pointed to continued growth. The projections were the best available.

But traffic stagnated even as Trippe moved into the back office, and in the following year growth all but disappeared—even as the 747's arrived offering two and a half times more empty seats. The new management did not file for reduced tariffs to fill them. Then came the start of an unforeseen two-year recession, during which the travel dollar simply fell off. But there were complicating factors also, increased competition being one of them. New international routes had come up; Pan Am had bid. The CAB had dealt them out elsewhere, every one, until there were now 13 domestic and foreign airlines competing across the Pacific, 23 in Central and South America, and 29 across the North Atlantic. The company's share of overseas traffic, which had once stood at 100 percent, and most recently at 20 percent, began its dive toward the floor, leveling off only after it hit 7.5 percent. The ruinous competition Trippe had predicted at the time of the Community Company bill had at last come true. A few domestic routes might have offset this. Though Pan Am continued to apply for one or another from time to time, none was ever awarded, and it remained the only airline in the world without a country of its own. Was Pan Am still paying for the resentment Trippe had aroused decades ago? There were those who thought so.

On top of the recession, the increased competition and the unfavorable CAB decisions rode Pan Am's monumental debt: almost $600 million for the 747's Trippe and his board had ordered; over $100 million for the new Kennedy Airport Terminal Building—grandly called Pan Am's World Port—which Gray had sponsored; and around $200 million for eight extra 747's, for which Halaby was responsible. It came to almost a billion dollars owed, and some of this money had had to be borrowed at near-usurious rates, 11 percent. With good management, and in the illimitable future that Trippe had always believed in and counted on, such a huge debt might have been, in the normal course of business, regularly amortized. But suddenly the world—and the future—were cramped, and that debt was rising faster than the company could pay it off. Gray cut two thousand employees from the payroll. It scarcely helped at all, and he did not have time to try much else.

Gray, replacing Trippe, was thought of as, formerly, the company's most skilled pilot, and after that as a good manager. He had done a superb job with the Atlantic Division, which he had headed as the first jets came in. He was thought of as an engineer also, and thought of himself as one. He attended marketing and operations meetings with slide rule in hand so that he could check out cost projections and other such details as they were given him. An associate once called him "a man of a hundred and ten percent integrity—as a person who trusts a slide rule should be." He was also a cold man, colder even than Trippe.

Trippe had thought automatically in political terms: How would people react, who could influence whom? But Gray hated politics, and public relations as well, and although usually he followed the advice of public relations vice president Willis Player, he did so with great discomfort. He didn't believe any of it was necessary, he told Player once: "All we have to do is be good, and people will recognize it."

Gray had the extremely orderly mind typical of an engineer. But he was not gifted in taking into account human, emotional reactions, even of passengers. If an idea, no matter what it was, didn't work out in numbers, it was a bad idea. One example was his attitude toward charter service. Many top Pan Am executives pleaded with him to take the company into the charter business; for a short period this could have been done, and at the very least, new avenues of potential profit might have opened up. Gray rejected the proposal out of hand. "We would have to carry all those flight crews in the winter," he said. This was perfectly correct, though it didn't exactly exhaust the situation.

This was the man Trippe had left behind him, and who now tried to fill the throne. He lasted eighteen months. During most of his reign he was undergoing cobalt treatments for what proved to be terminal lymph-gland cancer.

He was succeeded by Halaby. Although Trippe still sat on the board and the executive committee, his role now in the election of Halaby to replace Gray was not a dominant one.

Halaby was or had been many things, most of them laudable and even, in combination, rather rare: a lawyer, a Navy test pilot, a John F. Kennedy Democrat, a high-ranking federal official with, presumably, important Washington contacts, important Washington influence. He was handsome, charming, and played a good game of golf.

Unfortunately, at the time he joined Pan Am, he had known nothing about the airline business. Trippe had at first used him in Washington for lobbying, and had then stuck him in charge of the Business Jets Division. Under Gray his duties had expanded. He had headed the committee studying the option on eight additional 747's—the first twenty-five had not yet been received—and had recommended their purchase, saying that Pan Am had never had a time of overcapacity and never would have. Later Halaby blamed these eight extra monsters, which almost broke the company's back, on Gray. In truth, the decision had been Gray's and the board's, but the recommendation had been Halaby's.

In November 1969 President Halaby became chief executive officer, and he personally test-flew one of the prototype 747's over Seattle. With Boeing and Pan Am executives aboard, he wrung it out like a fighter plane: dives, stalls, violent pull-ups that made the whole plane shudder and shake, the huge wings flapping twelve feet up and down. His conclusion: this was the safest, most comfortable, most magnificently built plane in history. In the years since, the truth of his judgment has been amply demonstrated, and nearly every aviation figure has agreed with him. But at the time a different situation prevailed. The 747 had already become an object of controversy, and no one wanted to hear how great it was. Rumors abounded. Planes that crossed the 747's turbulent wake would be sent cartwheeling to destruction; in the event of an emergency it could never be evacuated in time; its engines "ovalized" and were unsafe.

There was some truth in the last charge; the engines did tend to change shape with use. Pratt and Whitney found a solution and redesigned, but this was expensive and took time. Boeing was producing planes faster than Pratt and Whitney could produce engines. The engineless planes piled up outside the factory and became known as 747 gliders. Pan Am should have had most of its planes in service twelve months before most of its rivals, and it did get the first few, but after that everyone got them more or less at once. That was one commercial advantage lost. Another had disappeared during gestation when the design had come in so much overweight; the promised extra speed, range and payload would not be recaptured until the bigger new engines were ready in two to three years' time. And finally the new plane was plagued by minor bugs, such as stereo systems that broke down in flight; passengers, already aware of past troubles and rumors, did not at first like the plane at all. They did not flock to it, and every day the monsters took off closer to empty than full.

The company's deficit for 1971 was again stupendous—$46 million—making a total of $121 million lost during the first three post-Trippe years. Halaby in panic began firing executives, in most cases bringing in outsiders to replace them. Many of these outsiders were not airline men, and knew no more about running Pan Am than Halaby did. In his first seventeen months Halaby changed seventeen of the company's top twenty-three officers. Although he called this "pumping in new blood," others saw it as a bloodbath—"a series of actions without causes," was the way one executive described it. Even Halaby later admitted to its failure: "We never really did have a team. We didn't even have unity born of fear as Trippe had inspired."

The board of directors was still Trippe's board. Some of these men were present or former Pan Am executives—the so-called "inside directors"—and the rest were men like Don Kendall of Pepsico and Arthur Watson of IBM—the outside directors. Kendall appears to have been one of the leaders in the move to oust Halaby. There is no evidence that Trippe organized any cabal. Even Halaby never said he did. All that's certain is that Trippe was consulted and that he, too, wanted Halaby gone.

Shortly before this, former Air Force Brigadier General William Seawell, a big, white-haired man, fifty-three years old, had been elected president and chief operating officer under Halaby. Seawell, a West Pointer who had graduated also from Harvard Law School, had been a highly decorated World War II bomber pilot, who afterwards had moved steadily upwards in rank until he served as commandant of the Air Force Academy. Resigning after twenty-two years' service, he had held a number of aviation jobs, including those of senior vice president (Operations) for American Airlines and president of Rolls-Royce Aero Engines, Inc., of North America.

Seawell was interviewed for the job of Pan Am president by a committee of directors; Trippe was not on that committee. When he joined Pan Am on December 1, 1971, Seawell had never met Trippe. Nor at subsequent board meetings during the next four months did Trippe ever seem to him a dominant figure. During that time, Seawell later learned, the board had been actively searching for a replacement for Halaby; another man had actually been approached. Halaby apparently was aware of this search.

On March 22, 1972, Chairman Halaby called to order his final board meeting: "Seawell sat at my left and tough old Juan Trippe at my right, both expectantly silent while I talked." Halaby made a plea for the continued confidence of the board. When he finished, he and all inside directors, including Seawell, were asked to leave the room.

It was Director Cyrus Vance who came to Seawell and asked him to take the job of chairman. Trippe's hand in this decision, if it existed, was invisible.

That was not the end of the company's travail. Losses for 1972 were also huge—$33 million. Seawell began to reduce the tariff structure and to abandon unprofitable routes—all of the Caribbean, for instance—and to cut the personnel roster almost in half. But the Mideast oil embargo caused fuel prices to skyrocket; the company lost $26 million in 1973 and $81.7 million in 1974. Seawell traded off routes with TWA, abandoning Paris and Rome but gaining exclusivity in Germany. Deficits continued. Seawell considered declaring bankruptcy. Not until 1977, after eight straight years of losses totaling $319.4 million, did Pan Am post a profit. Slowly, ever so slowly. Seawell's drastic tactics had turned the situation around. He had saved the airline, at least for now.

Trippe, meanwhile, had stayed on the board until 1975, when, aged seventy-six, he formally retired. Seawell then invited him to continue to attend board meetings and also to continue to sit at Seawell's right hand; the invitation pleased the old man, and he mentioned it proudly to all who would listen. Thereafter, even as he passed eighty, he rarely missed a meeting. His sight and hearing dimmed, he was very stooped, and he would sit there beside Seawell for however long each board meeting lasted and never say a word.

Out in the Pacific, Wake Island, whose existence Trippe had discovered in the New York Public Library almost fifty years previously, had gone through almost as many cycles since World War II as Trippe's airline did.

After the war Wake's position in the middle of the vast ocean had seemed ever more strategic. Therefore its runway was extended to 9,800 feet, and a passenger terminal worthy of a medium-sized American city was completed—all this at U.S. government expense. Many other buildings were erected—even a church. The Federal Aviation Administration was assigned to maintain and operate the airport; it kept up the roads, the commissary, the mess hall, the police and fire services, even a school through the ninth grade. The Coast Guard set up a loran station. The Weather Bureau sent men and instruments—this was the only weather station for a million or more square miles.

The Korean War confirmed the opinion that Wake's role was imperishable. Pan Am's Korean airlift planes set down on the island by the thousands. Also, it was to Wake that President Truman flew to meet General MacArthur, supreme commander of the United Nations' forces.

That war ended, and Wake still dominated the thoughts of men contemplating the Pacific. A transpacific telephone cable was laid via Wake. A Marine Corps memorial was erected there, and also a stele in memory of the Japanese troops who had suffered and died on Wake in far greater numbers than the Marines. The two memorials were no more than a hundred yards apart.

Airliners grew bigger and faster, and many now overflew Wake altogether.

Still another war: Vietnam. Another airlift to the Far East. About three thousand support people lived on Wake, which afterwards served as a staging area for Vietnamese refugees. Some two dozen children were born there.

By now aircraft had been built with such tremendous range that they could leap from San Francisco to Tokyo—and even much farther —without refueling. Almost unnoticed, other dramatic changes had occurred in the world. Navigational gear had been perfected to the point where Wake's radio beam—Leuteritz's DF—was no longer necessary. Weather could now be forecast from satellites, and a single satellite could "see" far more square miles of empty ocean than could instruments clustered on Wake. Passenger-ship travel across the Pacific had all but disappeared, meaning that there was little need for a mid-ocean Coast Guard station.

Gradually the Wake complement diminished. Federal Aviation Authority personnel went home. The Coast Guard sailed away. The U.S. Air Force sent six men and took over the island.

A small work force arrived from Japan and dug up the bodies of 786 Japanese soldiers. The remains were trucked to the ruined foundation of the old Pan Am Hotel, and there cremated and the ashes flown home to

Japan. A week later a U.S. Marine demolition expert arrived to explode still another bomb newly uncovered on a beach.

Mail and fresh vegetables for the tiny garrison came in by plane once a week. So did cassette television programs, and occasionally a movie. The commanding officer was, normally, an Air Force major. Wake was a hardship post. Term of duty was one year. Military regulations and logic applied. Wives and children were not allowed.

There was a quality of remoteness about the island that went beyond its location. Wake was past tense. Most of its buildings were boarded up. Eventually they would disintegrate. The former golf driving range, long unmowed, was now defunct. The former outdoor movie theater, called the Windy Palace, was defunct also. On the beaches the defunct pillboxes were being absorbed bit by bit into the sand.

Wake Island had erupted from the ocean floor who knew how many eons ago. Trippe had given it sudden extraordinary fame. Now its usefulness had ended, or nearly so, and its status was changing, or changed. The rather small island had evolved into little more than a rather large monument—one that commemorated more than anything else the hour of the hundreds of men who had first put it to use, the hour of the Pan Am flying boats, the hour when the Pacific was spanned for the first time by air, the hour of the vision and ambition of Juan Trippe. Unlike most monuments, this one would be visited in future by very few persons, and perhaps in time by no one at all. No matter, it was there, and would remain there, and its status as monument would last for as long as aviation had impact on the affairs of men.

Pan Am's
Generation of Capital

The following tables and explanatory notes were prepared by Donald Thomson, Pan Am treasurer at the time of his retirement in 1976. The figures were obtained from published reports and internal company reports. Because of changes in reporting methods over the years, there are some minor inconsistencies in the funds statements.

CONSOLIDATED SOURCE AND APPLICATION OF FUNDS STATEMENT

PAN AMERICAN WORLD AIRWAYS, INC.

(IN THOUSANDS)

	1928 1929	1930 1939	1940 1949	1950 1959	1960 1969	Total
Working capital at beginning of year	$	$ 1,600	$ 100	$ 20,100	$ 28,500	
SOURCE OF FUNDS during year						
Earnings (loss)	(300)	8,600	33,700	83,900	321,300	447,200
Noncash transactions						
Depreciation and amortization	900	18,400	75,800	232,300	708,200	1,035,600
Deferred federal income taxes				8,800	103,300	112,100
Self insurance reserve			3,600		8,500	12,100
Book value property sold or retired		1,900		18,600	155,400	175,900
Sale of common stock	6,700	11,300	51,500		14,100	83,600
Increase (decrease) long-term debt		2,200	32,800	165,500	200,200	400,700
Debentures				47,000	440,400	487,400
Total sources	7,300	42,400	197,400	556,100	1,951,400	2,754,600
APPLICATION OF FUNDS during year						
Purchase property and equipment	4,300	28,500	142,500	363,300	1,394,300	1,932,900
Advances on purchase contracts, net	100	1,100	(1,200)	123,800	298,400	422,200
Dividends		4,300	16,300	43,100	79,100	142,800
Deferred jet preoperating costs				9,000	50,900	59,900
Investments and advances to subsidiaries and associated companies, net	500	300	8,200	17,200	16,600	42,800
Increase in equity unconsolidated subs					17,500	17,500
Other, net	800	9,700	11,600	(8,700)	7,600	21,000
Total funds applied	5,700	43,900	177,400	547,700	1,864,400	2,639,100
NET INCREASE during year	1,600	(1,500)	20,000	8,400	87,000	115,500
Working capital at end of year	$ 1,600	$ 100	$ 20,100	$ 28,500	$115,500	$115,500

CONSOLIDATED SOURCE AND APPLICATION OF FUNDS STATEMENT
PAN AMERICAN WORLD AIRWAYS, INC.
(IN THOUSANDS)

	1930	1931	1932	1933	1934	1935	1936	1937	1938	1939	Total
Working capital at beginning of year	$ 1,600	$ 900	$ 2,200	$ 1,400	$ 1,400	$ 1,900	$ 2,800	$ 1,600	$ (200)	$(1,300)	$ 1,600
SOURCE OF FUNDS during year											
Earnings (loss)	(300)	100	700	900	1,000	1,200	1,000	1,900	100	2,000	8,600
Noncash transactions											
Depreciation and amortization	1,500	1,300	1,100	700	2,200	2,300	2,300	1,700	2,700	2,600	18,400
Deferred federal income taxes											
Self insurance reserve											
Book value property sold or retired					300	200	200	300	700	200	1,900
Sale of common stock	3,300	2,700	500	2,500		300	1,600	200	200		11,300
Increase (decrease) long-term debt								1,500	(500)	1,200	2,200
Debentures											
Total sources	4,500	4,100	2,300	4,100	3,500	4,000	5,100	5,600	3,200	6,000	42,400
APPLICATION OF FUNDS during year											
Purchase property and equipment	3,800	1,400	1,100	400	1,200	4,000	3,800	4,200	1,700	6,900	28,500
Advances on purchase contracts, net	(100)		1,500	3,900	(900)	(3,800)	200	800	100	(600)	1,100
Dividends					300	800	1,100	1,000	1,100		4,300
Deferred jet preoperating costs											
Investments and advances to subsidiaries and associated companies, net	500	(500)	400	300				(100)	100	(400)	300
Increase in equity unconsolidated subs											
Other, net	1,000	1,900	100	(500)	2,400	2,100	1,200	1,500	1,300	(1,300)	9,700
Total funds applied	5,200	2,800	3,100	4,100	3,000	3,100	6,300	7,400	4,300	4,600	43,900
NET INCREASE during year	(700)	1,300	(800)		500	900	(1,200)	(1,800)	(1,100)	1,400	(1,500)
Working capital at end of year	$ 900	$2,200	$ 1,400	$ 1,400	$ 1,900	$ 2,800	$ 1,600	$ (200)	$(1,300)	$ 100	$ 100

CONSOLIDATED SOURCE AND APPLICATION OF FUNDS STATEMENT
PAN AMERICAN WORLD AIRWAYS, INC.
(IN THOUSANDS)

	1940	1941	1942	1943	1944	1945	1946	1947	1948	1949	Total
Working capital at beginning of year	$ 100	$ 5,200	$ 3,900	$ 7,900	$12,700	$10,700	$19,400	$19,800	$13,800	$11,700	$ 100
SOURCE OF FUNDS during year											
Earnings (loss)	2,300	3,400	3,800	1,900	1,600	7,600	3,000	3,000	4,600	2,500	33,700
Noncash transactions											
Depreciation and amortization	3,800	5,400	3,700	3,000	3,200	4,100	8,100	14,800	13,200	16,500	75,800
Deferred federal income taxes	1,100	1,600	500	300	100						3,600
Self insurance reserve											
Book value property sold or retired											
Sale of common stock	6,300	600		700		43,900					51,500
Increase (decrease) long-term debt	1,400	(3,600)					18,000	(11,000)	18,000	10,000	32,800
Debentures											
Total sources	14,900	7,400	8,000	5,900	4,900	55,600	29,100	6,800	35,800	29,000	197,400
APPLICATION OF FUNDS during year											
Purchase property and equipment	4,800	3,500	5,200	4,600	4,100	6,700	41,200	14,200	18,200	40,000	142,500
Advances on purchase contracts, net	2,600	3,600	(1,300)	(6,100)	500	24,700	(15,100)	(2,900)	15,700	(22,900)	(1,200)
Dividends		1,900	1,900	2,000	2,000	2,500	1,500	1,500	1,500	1,500	16,300
Deferred jet preoperating costs											
Investments and advances to subsidiaries and associated companies, net	100	100		200	(300)	3,200	4,700	1,100	700	(1,600)	8,200
Increase in equity unconsolidated subs											
Other, net	2,300	(400)	(1,800)	400	600	9,800	(3,600)	(1,100)	1,800	3,600	11,600
Total funds applied	9,800	8,700	4,000	1,100	6,900	46,900	28,700	12,800	37,900	20,600	177,400
NET INCREASE during year	5,100	(1,300)	4,000	4,800	(2,000)	8,700	400	(6,000)	(2,100)	8,400	20,000
Working capital at end of year	$ 5,200	$ 3,900	$ 7,900	$12,700	$10,700	$19,400	$19,800	$13,800	$11,700	$20,100	$20,100

CONSOLIDATED SOURCE AND APPLICATION OF FUNDS STATEMENT
PAN AMERICAN WORLD AIRWAYS, INC.
(IN THOUSANDS)

	1950	1951	1952	1953	1954	1955	1956	1957	1958	1959	Total
Working capital at beginning of year	$20,100	$22,200	$17,500	$7,400	$17,200	$9,800	$23,800	$12,100	$7,500	$42,000	$20,100
SOURCE OF FUNDS during year											
Earnings (loss)	4,100	6,500	6,700	10,800	10,400	10,200	14,200	8,200	5,100	7,700	83,900
Noncash transactions											
Depreciation and amortization	17,700	16,800	17,300	18,400	18,900	18,700	22,200	34,200	31,300	36,800	232,300
Deferred federal income taxes							3,100	4,600	100	1,000	8,800
Self insurance reserve					2,500	3,500	2,100	1,700	4,300	4,500	18,600
Book value property sold or retired											
Sale of common stock											
Increase (decrease) long-term debt	5,300	(12,500)		15,400	(14,800)	24,900	24,500	3,400	77,900	41,400	165,500
Debentures										47,000	47,000
Total sources	27,100	10,800	24,000	44,600	17,000	57,300	66,100	52,100	118,700	138,400	556,100
APPLICATION OF FUNDS during year											
Purchase property and equipment	17,400	7,000	35,900	26,600	26,700	19,600	51,000	33,300	39,900	105,900	363,300
Advances on purchase contracts, net	500	5,200	2,100	200	(2,600)	15,500	14,600	19,400	34,600	34,300	123,800
Dividends	3,100	3,100	3,100	4,000	4,900	4,900	4,900	4,900	4,900	5,300	43,100
Deferred jet preoperating costs									1,500	7,500	9,000
Investments and advances to subsidiaries and associated companies, net	1,200	(100)	3,700	(700)	700	1,300		4,400	700	6,000	17,200
Increase in equity unconsolidated subs											
Other, net	2,800	300	(10,700)	4,700	(5,300)	2,000	7,300	(5,300)*	2,600	(7,100)	(8,700)
Total funds applied	25,000	15,500	34,100	34,800	24,400	43,300	77,800	56,700	84,200	151,900	547,700
NET INCREASE during year	2,100	(4,700)	(10,100)	9,800	(7,400)	14,000	(11,700)	(4,600)	34,500	(13,500)	8,400
Working capital at end of year	$22,200	$17,500	$7,400	$17,200	$9,800	$23,800	$12,100	$7,500	$42,000	$28,500	$28,500

*Includes reclassification of flight-equipment expendable parts to current assets to conform to revised Uniform System of Accounts of the Civil Aeronautics Board.

CONSOLIDATED SOURCE AND APPLICATION OF FUNDS STATEMENT

PAN AMERICAN WORLD AIRWAYS, INC.

(IN THOUSANDS)

	1960	1961	1962	1963	1964	1965	1966	1967	1968	1969	Total
Working capital at beginning of year	$28,500	$31,600	$53,900	$50,000	$20,200	$ 3,800	$33,600	$97,100	$74,900	$103,500	$28,500
SOURCE OF FUNDS during year											
Earnings (loss)	7,100	8,900	15,000	33,600	37,100	52,100	83,700	60,500	49,200	(25,900)	321,300
Noncash transactions											
Depreciation and amortization	50,200	59,100	58,300	56,300	54,100	60,900	70,300	88,300	104,500	106,200	708,200
Deferred federal income taxes	6,400	1,400	2,000	18,100	6,300	6,200	18,100	8,200	22,900	13,700	103,300
Self insurance reserve	7,400	1,100									8,500
Book value property sold or retired	3,700	19,000	14,200	15,700	6,900	8,400	7,700	15,500	50,500	13,800	155,400
Sale of common stock	200	300				1,400	1,300	1,700	3,300	5,900	14,100
Increase (decrease) long-term debt	69,800	(26,300)	(29,700)	(74,300)	17,200	58,100	(13,300)	158,800	66,400	(26,500)	200,200
Debentures					60,400		175,000		30,000	175,000	440,400
Total sources	144,800	63,500	59,800	49,400	182,000	187,100	342,800	333,000	331,000	262,200	1,951,400
APPLICATION OF FUNDS during year											
Purchase property and equipment	123,000	25,200	55,700	31,400	108,900	143,100	227,500	275,700	160,100	243,700	1,394,300
Advances on purchase contracts, net	4,100	10,700	6,500	24,800	80,500	(800)	34,600	47,200	110,300	(19,400)	298,500
Dividends	5,300	5,300	5,300	7,200	6,300	8,600	9,300	11,500	13,400	6,800	79,000
Deferred jet preoperating costs	12,000	2,900	2,000	3,800	2,300	400	3,800	5,200	15,800	2,700	50,900
Investments and advances to subsidiaries and associated companies, net	3,200	(15,300)	3,400	1,600	1,500	400	800	900	3,000	17,100	16,600
Increase in equity unconsolidated subs	(200)	100	(200)	(300)	500	1,500	1,000	11,100	1,700	2,300	17,500
Other, net	(5,700)	12,300	(9,000)	10,700	(1,600)	4,100	2,300	3,600	(6,100)		7,600
Total funds applied	141,700	41,200	63,700	79,200	198,400	157,300	279,300	355,200	298,200	253,200	1,864,400
NET INCREASE during year	3,100	22,300	(3,900)	(29,800)	(16,400)	29,800	63,500	(22,200)	28,600	12,000	87,000
Working capital at end of year	$31,600	$53,900	$50,000	$20,200	$ 3,800	$33,600	$97,100	$74,900	$103,500	$115,500	$115,500

PAN AM'S GENERATION OF CAPITAL:
EXPLANATORY NOTES

1928—Aviation Corporation of the Americas was organized in Delaware on June 23. Four days later it acquired all the assets of Aviation Corporation of America and of Atlantic, Gulf and Caribbean Airways, Inc., including all outstanding stock of Pan American Airways, Inc. Only a little more than half of the 90,000 shares in the corporation had been subscribed for at that date, and it was found necessary to extend the date for receiving subscriptions, first to July 2 and subsequently to July 17, 1928. Considerable efforts by the officers of the corporation were required to cause this stock to be taken up.

1929—On January 23 the capital stock (3,000 shares at $50 each) of Compañía Mexicana was acquired in exchange for 16,665 shares of the corporation stock, plus warrants entitling the holders to subscribe to 5,500 shares of the stock of Pan American Airways Corporation at a price of $15 per share on or before June 30, 1933.

1930—Whereas, on December 31, 1929, the corporation's cash balance amounted to $750,514 against current liabilities of $246,084. by March 31, 1930, its cash had been reduced to $306,000 against liabilities of $164,000. A substantial influx of capital was therefore urgently needed. Loan applications were made to numerous New York banks. All such banks declined. Finally, in order to secure working funds, notes of the corporation aggregating as high as $900,000 were endorsed by J. T. Trippe, and co-endorsed by C. V. Whitney. This bank indebtedness was retired in December 1931.

1931—On September 15 the second and final payment was made for assets acquired from NYRBA through the issuance of 24,184 shares of Pan American Airways Corporation stock. The entire consideration, 62,-572.2 shares of stock at a contract price of $65.62, meant that Pan Am could claim payment of $4,106,300 for the NYRBA assets. Since NYRBA had outstanding bearer warrants, it was necessary to issue to the holders of these warrants new warrants entitling them to subscribe to 50,380 shares of Pan American Airways Corporation stock at $91.875 per share, these warrants to be exercised by June 1, 1934. To prevent possible dilution of their interest, similar warrants were issued to the existing stockholders of Pan American Airways. The value of the Pan American stock on September 15, 1931, was $48.75 per share, and at no time thereafter prior to the expiration of the warrants did the market value exceed $58.50 per share. Hence, none of the warrants were exercised.

1939—Until 1937 the needed funds were provided from newly issued stock, reinvestment of earnings and cash throw-off from depreciation charges. However, with the expansion of the company and the need to acquire larger aircraft, these sources did not provide sufficient capital, and the company had to look elsewhere, even though the balance sheets and earnings records did not entitle the company to much credit. To buy the Boeings needed for the Atlantic operation, funds were finally obtained by issuing equipment trust notes somewhat similar to the railroad trust issues. On January 3, 1939, Pan American Airways Equipment Trust Certificates, bearing dividends at the rate of 4 percent per annum, were issued under a trust agreement between Pan American Aviation Supply Corporation, vendor; The New York Trust Company, trustee; and Pan American Airways Company, which was the issuer of the certificates. The Equipment Trust was set up to provide approximately 70 percent of the aggregate price ($5 million) of six Boeing-314 flying boats, and three Boeing-307 Strato-Clippers. These certificates were paid off in less than three years.

1940—A financing program was successfully concluded through the issuance of 525,931 additional shares of company stock through an underwriting group headed by G. M. D. Murphy & Co. and by Lehman Brothers. This new stock provided $6.3 million. These new funds were needed not only to acquire aircraft but to provide capital, which at the end of 1939 stood at only $100,000.

1945—About $43 million of new equity capital was obtained by a July 3 stock offering, as related in Chapter 46.

1946—The company arranged a $40 million standby credit with a group of twenty-eight banks headed by the National City Bank of New York, the Guaranty Trust Company, Chase National Bank and New York Trust Company as agent. The company had an option of converting all, or any part of, the funds borrowed into a term loan for an additional four years. Borrowing under this credit amounted to $18 million by December 31, 1946, and to $32 million as of April 30, 1947. By December 31, 1947, the amount borrowed under the credit agreement was reduced to $8 million with the help of substantial payments for mail service for the four years from 1944 to 1947.

1949—On February 1 the company entered into a new four-year standby credit agreement with the same group of banks. This agreement permitted borrowing of up to $50 million contingent with respect to $10 million of the borrowing upon the acquisition of American Overseas Airlines.

The agreement was renegotiated, and on September 20, 1949, the company entered into a new $59 million four-year standby agreement with a group of thirty banks. Under its terms, borrowing in excess of $40 million was to be held for use subject to acquisition of the assets and business of American Overseas Airlines.

1953—In October Pan Am mail pay was segregated into service pay mail and subsidy mail pay. The Post Office Department commenced paying for U.S. mail at rates fixed by the Civil Aeronautics Board, which would make its judgment based upon need. The company had been paid subsidy from the date of enactment of the Civil Aeronautics Act of 1938 and would continue on subsidy through and including September 30, 1956. Subsidy mail pay played an important part in furnishing the company with operating funds. In 1930 it was 57.9 percent of total revenue; in 1935, 29.6 percent; and in 1940, 8.6 percent. In 1956 it had dropped to 2.5 percent.

1955—The first phase in the financing of the jet fleet took place in May, when the company entered into a long-term credit arrangement, the first of its kind in the airline industry, with a group of eighteen life insurance agencies headed by Metropolitan Life and the Prudential. The total credit was $60 million. Amortization payments were scheduled to begin in 1966.

1956—In December the company obtained a supplemental long-term credit of $30 million with a group again headed by the Metropolitan and Prudential. Amortization payments were also to begin in 1966.

1958—But these borrowings were still not enough, and arrangements were made with thirty-nine banks to provide for revolving long-term credit of $130 million against which the company could borrow or reborrow, in whole or in part, through June 30, 1961.

1959—Early in the year the board of directors, after reviewing the company's heavy financial commitments, determined that a debt issue could be sold for advantage, and in August Pan Am offered to stockholders $47 million of 4 7/8 percent convertible debentures due August 1, 1979. The debentures were convertible into company stock at $30 per share.

1960—In August the company arranged with the eleven insurance companies for an additional long-term credit of $50 million. Proceeds of this borrowing were used to repay short-term bank borrowings. Repayment on this supplemental credit was due to commence in 1967.

1964—Pan Am again turned to the public market and in January sold an issue of $60.4 million of twenty-year 4 1/2 percent debentures convertible into common stock at $58.50 per share. The large increase in equity during 1964 reflected the conversion of a substantial amount of the 4 7/8 percent debentures by holders who wanted to hold stock so as to obtain rights to subscribe to the 4 1/2 percent debentures. Senior long-term debt was reduced, and subordinated convertible debt was increased. Since lenders considered subordinated convertible airline debentures as being substantially equivalent to equity, the replacement of a part of the senior debt with convertible debentures strengthened the company's balance sheet considerably, and enabled the company to roll over its institutional borrowing, totaling $140 million, so that no amortization payments would be required for these loans until 1976. These made available $93.5 million for a period of ten years at an average interest rate of 4.85 percent per annum.

1965—Pan Am arranged a new $100 million revolving credit agreement extending to February 1968 with thirty-six U.S. commercial banks. The company could borrow and repay as its needs dictated. At the end of the year the composition of capital structure consisted of: senior debt, $200 million; convertible debentures, $80.4 million; capitalized value of aircraft leases, $70 million; equity, $275.2 million. The ratio of long-term debt, including subordinated convertible debentures and capitalized leases, was 1.3 to one.

1966—The years 1966 to 1969 would require a capital outlay of $1.08 billion, an average of $270 million annually in order to pay for the newly ordered 747's. The average capital outlay for the years 1962 to 1965 had been $112.5 million, and for the 1954–57 period immediately preceding the Jet Age, it had been $44.2 million. As part of the orderly program devised to secure the needed financing, Pan Am stock was again split two for one. This served to widen the market for the stock, and it was followed by a 33 1/3 percent dividend increase. The company also concluded a $100 million twenty-five-year loan agreement with thirty-four institutional investors at an interest rate of 5 1/4 per annum.

1966—The company concluded a $180 million twenty-five-year loan agreement at an interest rate of 6.5 percent with fifty institutional investors. This financing was not a complete success, as only $162.1 million was finally obtained.

1968—In April Pan Am renegotiated its 1965 revolving credit agreement with thirty-eight U.S. commercial banks. The principal amount was increased from $150 million to $300 million. The end of the revolving period was extended to March 31, 1972, and final maturity to March 30, 1973.

1969—During the years 1966, 1968 and 1969, the company obtained $380 million from three successful public subordinated convertible debentures including a $30 million issue which was marketed by the Pan American Overseas Capital Corporation. By the end of 1969 the company's senior debt was $400.7 million, and subordinated debentures $410.3 million, not including capitalized leases. The ratio between debt and equity was 1.75 to one. Working capital was $115.5 million.

Bibliography

Arnold, Henry H. *Global Mission.* New York: Harper & Bros., 1949

Beaty, David. *The Water Jump.* New York: Harper & Row, 1976.

Becker, Beril. *Dreams and Realities of the Conquest of the Skies.* New York: Atheneum, 1967.

Bennett, William Edward. *Atlantic Highway.* New York: John Day Co., 1962.

Bixby, Harold M. "Top Side Ricksha." Unpublished ms., 1938.

Blair, Charles F. *Red Ball in the Sky.* New York: Random House, 1969.

Bonney, Walter T. *The Heritage of Kitty Hawk.* New York: W. W. Norton, 1962.

Boy, Herbert. *Una Historia Con Alas.* Madrid, 1955; Bogotá, 1963.

Brock, Horace. *Flying the Oceans.* Lunenburg, Vt.: Stinehouse Press, 1979.

Buchanan, Lamont. *The Flying Years.* New York: Putnam, 1953.

Calitri, Princine. *Harry A. Bruno, Public Relations Pioneer.* Minneapolis: T. S. Denison & Co., Inc., 1968.

Conn, Stetson, and Fairchild, Byron. *The Framework of Hemisphere Defense.* Washington, D.C.: Office of the Chief of Military History, Department of the Army, 1960–64.

Davies, R. E. G. *A History of the World's Airlines.* London: Oxford University Press, 1964.

Glines, Carroll. *The Saga of the Air Mail.* Princeton, N.J.: D. Van Nostrand Co., 1967.

Grooch, William Steven. *From Crate to Clipper—with Captain Musick, Pioneer Pilot.* New York: Longmans Green & Co., 1939.

———. *Skyway to Asia.* New York: Longmans Green & Co., 1936.

———. *Winged Highway.* New York: Longmans Green & Co., 1938.

Halaby, Najeeb E. *Crosswinds.* Garden City, N.Y.: Doubleday, 1978.

Hamlen, Joseph. *Flight Fever.* Garden City, N.Y.: Doubleday, 1971.

Harris, Sherwood. *The First to Fly—Aviation's Pioneer Days.* New York: Simon & Schuster, 1970.

Higham, Robin. *Britain's Imperial Air Routes 1918–1939*. Hamden, Conn.: The Shoestring Press, 1960.

Howard, Frank. *The Conquest of the Air*. New York: Random House, 1972.

Hudson, Kenneth. *Air Travel: A Social History*. Totowa, N.J.: Rowman & Littlefield, 1972.

Jablonski, Edward. *Atlantic Fever*. New York: Macmillan Company, 1972.

Josephson, Matthew. *Empire of the Air*. New York: Harcourt, Brace & Company, 1944.

Kelly, Charles J., Jr. *The Sky's the Limit—The History of the Airlines*. New York: Coward-McCann, Inc., 1963.

Kuter, Laurence S. *The Great Gamble: The Boeing 747*. University: University of Alabama Press, 1973.

Leary, William M., Jr. *The Dragon's Wings*. Athens: University of Georgia Press, 1976.

Leslie, John C. Unpublished ms, 1970–75.

Lindbergh, Anne Morrow. *The Flower and the Nettle: Diaries and Letters 1936–1939*. New York: Harcourt Brace Jovanovich, 1973.

———. *Hour of Gold, Hour of Lead: Diaries and Letters, 1929–1932*. New York: Harcourt Brace Jovanovich, 1973.

———. *Listen! the Wind*. New York: Harcourt Brace, 1938.

———. *North to the Orient*. New York: Harcourt Brace, 1935.

Lindbergh, Charles Augustus. *An Autobiography of Values*. New York: Harcourt Brace Jovanovich, 1978.

———. *The Spirit of St. Louis*. New York: Charles Scribner's Sons, 1953.

———. *The Wartime Journals of Charles A. Lindbergh*. New York: Harcourt Brace Jovanovich, 1970.

———. *We*. New York and London: G. P. Putnam's Sons, 1927.

Loening, Grover. *Our Wings Grow Faster*. Garden City, N.Y.: Doubleday, Doran & Company, Inc., 1935.

———. *Takeoff into Greatness*. New York: G. P. Putnam's Sons, 1978.

Mansfield, Harold. *Vision: A Saga of the Sky*. New York: Duell, Sloan & Pearce, 1956.

Morris, Lloyd, and Smith, Kendall. *Ceiling Unlimited*. New York: Macmillan Company, 1953.

Newton, Wesley. *Aviation in the Relations of the United States and Latin America, 1916–1929*. University Microfilms, Ann Arbor, Mich., 1971. Ph.D. thesis, The University of Alabama, 1964. This thesis was published by the University of Miami Press in 1978 under the title *The Perilous Sky: Evolution of United States Diplomacy Towards Latin America, 1919–31*.

O'Neill, Ralph A., with Joseph F. Hood. *A Dream of Eagles*. Boston: Houghton Mifflin Company, 1973.

Pudney, John. *The Seven Skies: A Study of B.O.A.C. and Its Forerunner since 1919*. London: Putnam, 1959.

Rae, John B. *Climb to Greatness: The American Aircraft Industry 1920–1960*. Cambridge, Mass., and London: MIT Press, 1968.

Ray, Deborah W., "The Airport Development Program of World War II in South American and the Caribbean." Thesis, New York University, 1973.

Roseberry, C. R. *The Challenging Skies.* Garden City, N. Y.: Doubleday & Company, Inc., 1966.

Rowe, Basil. *Under My Wings.* Indianapolis, Ind.: Bobbs-Merrill Company, Inc., 1956.

Sikorsky, Igor. *The Story of the Winged S.* London, 1939.

Smith, Henry Ladd. *Airways Abroad, The Story of American World Air Routes.* Madison: University of Wisconsin Press, 1950.

Smith, Richard K. *First Across!* Annapolis, Md.: Naval Institute Press, 1973.

Solberg, Carl, *Conquest of the Air.* Boston: Little, Brown, 1979.

Spenser, Francis A. *Air Mail Payment and the Government.* The Brookings Institute, Washington, D.C., 1941.

St. John Turner, P. *Pictorial history of Pan American World Airways.* Shepperton, Middlesex: Ian Allan Ltd., 1973.

Straszheim, Mahlon R. *The International Airline Industry.* The Brookings Institute, Washington, D.C., 1969.

Thayer, Frederick C. *Air Transport Policy and National Security: A Political, Economic and Military Analysis.* Chapel Hill: University of North Carolina Press, 1965.

Van de Water, Frederick F. *The Real McCoy.* Garden City, N.Y.: Doubleday Doran, 1931.

Weathers, Bynum. E., Jr. *A Study of the Methods Employed in the Acquisition of Air Bases in Latin America for the Army Air Forces in World War II.* University Microfilms, Ann Arbor, Mich., 1971. Ph.D. thesis, Denver University.

Whitney, C. V. *High Peaks.* Lexington: University Press of Kentucky, 1977.

Wings Over Asia. 4 vols. Chinese National Aviation Association Foundation, 1971–76.

Wright, Vic, as told to Richard, Thruelsen. "Early Bird." Unpublished ms.

Source Notes

Wherever possible, research for this book was restricted to primary sources: original letters and memos, diaries, contracts and agreements, etc.; transcripts of CAB and congressional hearings, transcripts of radio transmissions during flights, transcripts of inaugural-flight radio broadcasts, and also taped conversations between participants; logs kept by crew members; contemporary summaries of phone conversations; company histories prepared as exhibits to accompany CAB rate and route applications; proxy statements and annual reports to stockholders; books and articles, whether published or unpublished, written by the participants themselves; and about three hundred interviews conducted by the author between April 1976 and August 1979. The author also traveled about 40,000 miles in all, both to interview subjects and to look at the aircraft factories, flying-boat bases and other sites described in this book, the most isolated point reached being Wake Island. Except for newspaper reports of actual events and certain background information, secondary sources were used either sparingly or not at all.

There is no previous large-scale history of Pan American, and no previous biography of any kind, not even a full-length magazine profile, of Juan Trippe. This is not surprising. The Pan Am and Trippe stories are so inextricably entangled that no writer could write the one without at the same time writing the other, and Trippe, until now, always refused to cooperate—not only with outside writers but even with at least one he hired himself. About 1957, with Trippe's approval, a journalist named

Wolfgang Langewiesche, who then worked for the *Reader's Digest,* was contracted by Pan American to prepare a company history, and for most of the next ten years he traveled the system, interviewing the men who had played key roles, especially those who had been there at the begin- ning. But Trippe held veto power over this project, and no book was ever written. Langewiesche did, however, leave behind extensive notes of his interviews. Certain of these—especially in the cases of men who had since died—proved valuable to the author.

Two histories of Pan American and its aerial conquest of the world have appeared in print. The first began as a five-part *Saturday Evening Post* serial entitled "Columbus of the Airways." Written by Matthew Joseph- son, it ran from August 14 to September 11, 1943, and was republished the following year under the title *Empire of the Air.* Josephson's view of the company, 227 pages long in book form, is a superficial one, not much better than a rewrite of *New York Times* headlines and Pan Am house organs. There is no portrait of Trippe, nor indeed of any other executive or pilot. There is no internal evidence that Josephson had ready access to Trippe, and certainly he had no access to company activities that Trippe counted confidential—and Trippe in 1943 counted nearly every- thing confidential. There is no bibliography or appendix, and sources are not given.

A second book called *Pictorial History of Pan American World Airways* appeared in England in 1973, written by P. St. John Turner. Again the text, 160 pages in length, confines itself to surface information. The appendix gives no sources. Again the author had no access to Trippe nor to other Pan Am executives.

The Trippe/Pan American story is such an important one that surely there would have been other books besides these had not Trippe, until now, chosen to remain silent. The author can give no explanation as to why, beginning at age seventy-six, he at last agreed to speak. But before submitting to around fifty interviews over a three-year period, he did impose terms. He formed the Pan American Foundation with himself at the head of it, and this foundation acquired the ownership of a great many relevant files and documents collected over the last several years by retired Pan Am vice president John Leslie. The author was obliged to sign a contract with this foundation, giving him access to these files and to Trippe; in exchange, it was stipulated that Trippe's foundation would receive a percentage of the book's royalties. Full editorial control rested with the author.

If the complete Pan American story has not been told before, nonetheless parts of it were written down often enough over the years by men who were there. The most frequent authors were pilots. There were Charles and Anne Lindbergh, of course, who, between them, published six books important to this study: Charles's *The Spirit of St. Louis, The Wartime Journals* and *An Autobiography of Values;* Anne's *North to the Orient, Listen! the Wind* and *Hour of Gold, Hour of Lead.* In addition, pilots Basil Rowe, Charles Blair, Horace Brock and Ralph O'Neill published one book each; and pilot William Grooch published three. There were a substantial number of unpublished manuscripts also: by the pilot Marius Lodeson; by the pilot Vic Wright as told to Richard Thruelsen; and by company vice presidents Harold M. Bixby and John C. Leslie. However much these unpublished manuscripts may have lacked in literary expertise, each contributed important details by eyewitnesses that otherwise would have been lost. Three unpublished diaries of inaugural flights written by Betty Trippe and made available to the author by her also proved invaluable.

Only two women, Betty Trippe and Anne Lindbergh, were interviewed at any length in the course of the author's research; Pan American, for the most part, was as much a male preserve as the Marine Corps. Among the subjects of the author's interviews the following were the most important and the most generous with their time, and the author acknowledges with gratitude their help: John C. Leslie, who joined the company in 1929 and retired as vice president and member of the board of directors in 1970; Hugo C. Leuteritz, chief communications engineer, 1929–46; Sanford Kauffman, who joined in 1929 and retired as vice president (Engineering) in 1972; Samuel Pryor, who joined as vice president in 1941 and retired in 1965 as vice president and member of the board of directors; John Shannon, who joined from NYRBA in 1930 and still serves as vice president (Operations) in 1969; John B. Gates, who joined Pan Am as vice president (Finance) in 1957 and retired as chief executive of the Intercontinental Hotels Corp. in 1971, but who remains on the board of directors to this day; John Woodbridge, who joined in 1929 and retired as treasurer in 1970; John Borger, who joined the Wake Island expedition in 1935 and still serves as vice president–chief engineer in 1979; C. H. (Dutch) Schildhauer, who joined the company in 1931, went back into the Navy at the start of World War II and did not return; Donald Thomson, who joined Pan Am in 1932 and retired as treasurer in 1976; Willis Player, who joined in 1946 and who still serves as vice president and assistant to the president; and William Seawell, who joined Pan Am as president in 1971 and who is currently chairman of the board. Other sources are identified as they appear in the notes below.

Throughout the notes the abbreviation PAF (followed by a file number) refers to the Pan American Foundation Archives. Books cited are listed in the Bibliography.

Part I
A YOUNG MAN PLANS
1 · The Island

Wake Island: The description is from the author's visit March 14–15, 1978. Transportation in and out was via military C-141 jet transport from Hawaii, Wake at that time being served by a single round-trip flight per week.

No coves or inlets: Maps of the island seem to show some, but they cannot be reached from the open sea because of the reef.

Typhoons every fifteen years: The first recorded typhoon struck Wake in late Oct. 1940; it devastated the vegetation and the Pan Am compound, but there were no fatalities. The next one, typhoon "Olive," struck Sept. 16, 1952, with 170-mph winds. On Sept. 16, 1967, fifteen years later to the day, came typhoon "Sarah." Same winds, same destruction.

Buildings: There seemed to be about 100, a surprising number for such a small island. There were also a number of massive oil-storage tanks, whose rooftops dominated the skyline on the opposite side of the hairpin. At the time of the author's visit, about 190 people lived on the island, including six from the Air Force, six weather forecasters and about 175 employees of Kemtron International Inc., the company which held the contract for maintaining runways, roads and buildings. Most of the Kemtron employees were Filipino laborers earning under $2.50 an hour and obliged by contract to remain on the island one year without leaving. With the exception of six wives of supervisory personnel, there were no women and no children. Signs were posted warning personnel that surrounding waters were filled with vicious sharks; the lagoon was said to be filled with eels, occasional sharks and poisonous fish. Consequently, no one swam in the surf, and for the most part no one swam or snorkeled in the lagoon either. Although fish were sometimes caught from the bridge between Wake and Peale Island, no one ever dared eat them, and a fresh-fish dinner on Wake was unknown. The buddy system was mandatory even for strolling the beaches: solitary beachcombing was forbidden.

The Wake ramp: Normally the flying boats were serviced at the dock, spent the night on the water, and took off again the

following dawn. Unless major repairs were needed, the ramp was not used.

Wake discovered by Trippe: As will be seen later, passing ships had come upon the island from time to time over the centuries, and one or two had left records of their passage. But in 1930 the existence of the island was not general knowledge. It was at this time that Trippe, searching for island stepping-stones that would make a route across the Pacific, and unable to find the mid-Pacific island he needed on any map, began researching the earliest histories of transpacific navigation, and especially the logs of the clipper ships. He found mention of Wake. Once he knew it existed it was possible to locate the records of the men and ships who, however briefly, had actually been there. Trippe's research was described in interviews with the author on April 5 and June 21, 1978, and on April 4, 1979.

2 · Trippe

Trippe's first air race: Trippe to author, Aug. 25, 1976. In 1910–11 these were more flying demonstrations than races, for pilots could rarely get more than one plane into the air at a time.

Trippe goes to Marconi School: Trippe to author, Aug. 25, 1976; Trippe in interviews claimed that his father was not rich, only well-to-do; however, Trippe Sr. was a member of the stock exchange, had his own bank, kept a town house, a country home in East Hampton, and was listed in the Social Register (see *Saturday Evening Post,* Aug. 21, 1943, p. 40). As for the Puritan ethic, Trippe as a boy lived at 85th Street and Fifth Avenue and attended school at 49th Street and Fifth Avenue. Trolley fare was a nickel, but he used to walk home from school every day, because every nickel he saved his father would double—Trippe to author April 4, 1979.

Trippe to Curtiss Flying School: Trippe to author, April 5, 1978.

Yale team joins Marines: This was immediately after the Yale-Harvard game, won by Yale 14–0 with Trippe intercepting a pass inside his own thirty and running it back past midfield—New York *Herald,* Nov. 25, 1917. He described his training, his pranks and his choice of bombers over fighter planes ("I was already thinking of after the war") to author, Aug. 25, 1976.

Back to Yale: Trippe to author, Aug. 30, 1976.

Trippe's nicknames: In a letter to John Leslie dated Oct. 24, 1972, William Van Dusen mentions a *Fortune* magazine article in the early thirties which gave Trippe's childhood nickname as Wang, adding, "Trippe never got over that." References to Mummy are more numerous: *Today* magazine, Oct. 19, 1935 p. 5; *Life,* Oct. 20, 1941; *Time,* March 28, 1949, p. 86.

Trippe wins air race: The *Yale Graphic* of June 9, 1920, describes it. It took place on May 7 under the auspices of the U.S. Army, and the start was at Mitchell Field, Long Island. The planes were identical Jennies provided by the Army and assigned to the young pilots twenty-four hours in advance of the race so they could tune and adjust them as they liked. In author's interviews, Aug. 25, 1976, and April 4, 1979, Trippe said he believed that changing the dihedral had allowed the plane to "grasp more air." He added, "The first up could zoom the first pylon."

Trippe's inheritance: Trippe to author, April 4, 1979. Trippe said there was nothing much beyond his father's life insurance and the value of his seat on the stock exchange.

Rich friends: Trippe to author, April 5, 1978.

Forming Long Island Airways: Trippe to author, Aug. 30, 1976.

Letter from Robbins Sr.: Trippe to author, April 4, 1978.

Souping up the planes: Trippe to author, Aug. 25, and Sept. 1, 1976. The job was done in a garage in Astoria, N.Y., and Trippe, as he recounted the story, seemed extremely proud of it. Taking out the reduction gear meant that reverse propellers were necessary, and these were not so easy to find. In later interviews (April 5 and June 21, 1978, and April 4, 1979) Trippe added additional details. When the first plane was ready, he took two friends from Rockaway all the way to New London for the Yale-Harvard boat race. This was "unheard of." The plane was "extremely impressive on takeoff—And away we'd go. There was no FAA then to certify it as safe. Nobody checked to see if the wings would hold up." Then he added thoughtfully, "I learned a lot from that Hisso."

Trippe flies down Broadway: Trippe to author, Aug. 8, 1979.

Visiting United Fruit and other companies: Trippe to author, Sept. 1, 1976, and June 21, 1978—"At the end of six months I knew what United Fruit could do for the next ten years."

3 · Colonial Air Transport

Meets general manager for Honduras: Trippe to author Aug. 25, 1976. Trippe remembered the man's name as Dr. Pounds. In this same interview he described trucking the plane to the pier. In Honduras Pounds did arrange for the plane to carry airmail, the first in the Western Hemisphere, and the stamp used became known as the Black Maria (to philatelists it is today one of the most valuable stamps extant). In an interview on Sept. 1, 1976, Trippe described himself visiting Washington a year or two later in attempts to acquire airmail contracts, and meeting high-ranking officials, including Secretary of Commerce Herbert Hoover. Although Trippe was very young, all of these dignitaries were "very impressed with that Honduras thing. Nobody else had that."

Long Island Airways ends: Trippe to author, Feb. 17, 1978. Business got "worse and worse."

The Kelly bill: Trippe's roommates at Yale were Bud Scully and Alan Scaife, both from Pittsburgh, and he often spent holidays in Pittsburgh with these friends (Trippe to author, April 4, 1979). He also said that he met Congressman Kelly well before the first Kelly bill was passed, on Feb. 2, 1925, and actually helped write the bill. This is possible. What is certain is that he helped write the later bill in 1928.

Alaskan Air Transport: Trippe to author, April 5, 1978. "Eielson's hangar was a tent."

Plans for Siberia: Trippe to author, Aug. 30, 1976.

The Star Route contracts: Trippe to author, Aug. 30, 1976, and Feb. 17, 1978. According to Trippe the dog-team drivers petitioned the governor of the territory, claiming that if the plane crashed, all mail would be lost and the Post Office blamed. The Postmaster General then ruled there was no mention of airmail in the Star Route contracts, and that therefore airmail was not legal.

Eastern merges with Colonial: Most of the relevant documents survive in the Pan American Foundation archives. See PAF 20.04.00—Eastern Air Transport, and 20.13.00—Colonial Air Transport.

The voting trust: Trippe to author, April 5, 1978, and April 4, 1979. Trippe claimed he controlled the voting trust from the start, but this does not seem likely. Governor Trumbull was later replaced by Theodore Weicker, who lived in Greenwich and was a neighbor of Trippe's. Since he persuaded Weicker to invest in the company, it is possible that Trippe controlled the voting trust from that point on. Whittemore was the leader of the other side. Trumbull, the professional politician, apparently tried to straddle the fence most times.

Roster swells to 21: The quote is from a paper entitled "Colonial Air Transport, Inc." in PAF 20.13.00. Unsigned and undated, it sounds like Trippe and was found among his Colonial papers of 1926. Internal dating indicates it was written in Nov. 1926.

The trimotors: Letter from Trippe to Major Talbot Freeman, March 24, 1926—"The Fokker people have been after me these last few weeks for a first payment . . ." Trippe was asking Freeman to send a check for $6,250.

Trippe and Kelly: Trippe may in fact have met Kelly earlier than this (see previous note on the Kelly bill). What is certain is that he saw him frequently now. In the Feb. 17 and April 5, 1978, interviews Trippe described meeting Kelly through Scaife and Mellon—"Mellon fixed it up." The Scaifes were tin manufacturers, and Alan had married Sarah Mellon, Andrew's niece.

Trippe meets Lindbergh: From Trippe's Wings Club lecture May 20, 1977, p. 1. Anne Morrow Lindbergh discussed this lecture with the author on Maui, March 12, 1978, and remarked that her husband did not remember meeting Trippe this early.

Trippe escorts his sister: Letter from Trippe to Hambleton, Dec. 31, 1926.

The Key West–Havana route: It is first mentioned in the Oct. 15, 1925, stock agreement Trippe signed apportioning the stock in Eastern Air Transport.

The flight to Havana: Trippe to author, Aug. 30, 1976. Trippe quoted Fokker saying, "Come and see my toilet."

Also Van Dusen letter to Leslie, Nov. 15, 1972.

Hambleton: He was apparently Trippe's closest friend, and had he lived longer he might have played an important role in Pan American. Hambleton was born on Oct. 20, 1897, attended St. Paul's, then Harvard. His family had lived next to the Trippes on the Eastern Shore of Maryland for generations. Young John Hambleton learned to fly in 1916, sailed for France on Oct. 28, 1917, and won the Croix de Guerre and the Distinguished Service Cross in aerial combat. According to a letter which former Brigadier General Billy Mitchell wrote to the Baltimore *Sun* and which was published June 12, 1929, Hambleton was a great combat pilot. On one patrol the right body strut almost in front of his face was shot away, and shell fragments lodged in his head and shoulders. When he returned to civilian life, Hambleton went to work in the family bank in Baltimore. Later he was almost the only one of Trippe's rich young friends who actually worked for Pan American, as opposed merely to investing money, and he was Lindbergh's copilot when the route to the Panama Canal was opened in Feb. 1929. He was killed in the crash of a private plane in a flight from New York City to Wilmington, N.C., on June 8, 1929.

Boedecker quits flight: The dialogue is from Boedecker's letter to Lesley N. Forden dated "July 1967." No specific day is given.

Trippe in Cuba: Trippe to author, Aug. 30 and Sept. 1, 1976. Trippe, said he found a lawyer through a Yale classmate in Havana, and that this lawyer was the author of whatever document was eventually signed. There is no trace of this "simple two- or three-page letter" in the Pan Am archives.

Forced landing: Trippe to author, Aug. 30, 1976, and April 4, 1979. Trippe pointed out that the plane was owned by and under the control of Fokker. Therefore, when Fokker chose to disregard Boedecker's warnings, Trippe did not interfere. Trippe seems to have been an extremely fatalistic young man, as far as his own safety was concerned. The plane itself, according to Trippe, was on the reef for weeks before new engines came down. Afterwards it was sold to Ford, and was used by Richard Byrd to make the first flight over the North Pole.

4 · Fired

Single-engined planes: Letter from Trippe to Harris Whittemore, June 15, 1926. "There is a very good chance that the Post Office Department may insist upon our lighting our airways and purchasing a large number of single engine ships, as provided for in our contract, before permitting us to start on this route." Trippe thought that "our friends in National Air Transport may be indirectly responsible for this. The letter quoted in the text was addressed to Major Freeman, March 24, 1926.

Morrow intervenes: Trippe to Hambleton, June 19, 1926—"Mr. Morrow had evidently done some yeoman work on our behalf. There was no further talk of Colonial providing ten ships, nor even five."

Fokkers delayed: Trippe wrote Hambleton on June 18, 1926, that they were due September 1. The first was not delivered until December, and it seems to have been rejected by Colonial for technical reasons, and to have been returned to the factory for revisions.

Company too poor to telephone: Letter from Prof. Edward P. Warner to Trippe, June 23, 1926—"Of course we cannot afford indiscriminate use of the long distance telephone."

Raising more capital: Letter from Trippe to Freeman, March 24, 1926—"the matter of financing continues to be our greatest obstacle." Johnson's letter to Trippe refusing to invest was dated Sept. 7, 1926.

Money-raising techniques: Trippe to author, Feb. 17, 1978. In an April 4, 1979, interview Trippe claimed that only 5 percent of his time was spent raising money. Maybe so, but his letters of the period sound preoccupied with the subject.

Trippe judges himself too young: *Saturday Evening Post*, Aug. 21, 1943, p. 46. Trippe confirmed this to author, April 4, 1979.

O'Ryan hired: Sept. 13, 1926, letter from Trippe to Scaife—"I have persuaded General O'Ryan to join the company." In the April 4, 1979, interview with the author, Trippe said O'Ryan's only job was to call on banks and drum up airmail traffic—"He was a mail salesman."

Buffalo survey: Trippe's memo is dated Sept. 14, 1926.

Second trip to Buffalo: Unsigned memo, apparently by Trippe, dated Sept. 27, 1926, PAF 20.12.00.

Proposed meeting with Ford: Trippe to Satterfield, Nov. 4, 1926. The Ford Airline began carrying airmail on Feb. 15, 1926, and passengers on Aug. 26 of the same year. See *Airways*, Sept. 1926, p. 106.

Financing Buffalo Airlines: Trippe gave his presentation on Nov. 10. For the plan itself, see PAF 20.12.00—Buffalo Airlines.

Letters to aircraft factories: The letters to Fokker and Ford are both dated Dec. 8, 1926.

O'Ryan giving Trippe orders: Letter from O'Ryan to Trippe, Dec. 20, 1926—it begins "Dear Trippe," and is clearly the letter of a company president to a subordinate. It chides Trippe for disagreeing with O'Ryan's policies and for expressing this disagreement to the executive committee. Other letters show the same relationship, particularly Trippe's to Irving Bullard dated Jan. 18, 1927, in which Trippe describes his efforts to get O'Ryan to "consent" to entering the airmail bid Trippe favored.

Possible merger with National: Trippe to Hambleton, Dec. 2, 1926. This is the same letter in which Trippe states that he cannot agree to O'Ryan's policy.

Lobbying for support: Trippe to Hambleton, Dec. 2, 1926.

The Chicago airmail bids: Trippe to Bullard, Jan. 18, 1927—"I had spotted National's bid of $1.98 per pound the week previous."

All bids thrown out: Trippe to Bullard, Jan. 31, 1927.

Letter to Coonley: It was dated March 29, 1927. Trippe in the same letter writes: "In the past I have brought into the company all the additional revenue that we have received."

Cutthroat competition: The quote is from Trippe's letter to Satterfield, March 29, 1927.

Cost of operations: Trippe to Reginald Taylor, May 2, 1927. This same letter describes the "open break" with O'Ryan.

The voting trust votes: Trippe to author, Aug. 30, 1976, April 5, 1978, April 4, 1979. The voting trust at this time was composed of Trippe, Hambleton, William Rockefeller, Weicker, Bullard, Coonley and Whittemore. According to letters that Trippe wrote to Coonley dated March 29 and 30, 1927, Coonley himself was out of the country as the voting trust voted. In a letter he wrote to Lucius Robinson dated May 3, 1927, Trippe referred to having won a "large majority of the seven voting trustees." He names them, but lists William Harkness in place of Bullard. However, Bullard, who resigned on March 30, perhaps under protest, appears to have been the trustee of record when the vote in the Greenwich railroad station was taken. There is no contemporary record of who was present or how each man voted. If Coonley was absent, if Whittemore was the leader of the other side, and if Bullard resigned in protest on March 30, this would indicate that the winning side was composed of Trippe, Hambleton, Rockefeller and Weicker. The lawyer Robert Thach was probably present, because in the Aug. 30, 1976, interview with the author, Trippe said that he, Hambleton and Thach had flown to Washington after the vote. Even the date of the vote is not certain. In Trippe's March 29 letter to Coonley, he writes, "The bids closed at noon last Thursday." The meeting in the Greenwich railroad station that same day was evidently a brief one, for Trippe told the author on April 5, 1978, that even the minutes of this meeting had been drawn up in advance.

The flight to Washington: Trippe to author, Aug. 30, 1976, Feb. 17, 1978. Trippe did not pilot the plane himself because "I was the senior administrative officer of the company."

Rivals outraged: In the April 4, 1979, interview with the author, Trippe insisted that Trumbull, the politician, was not outraged at all, and that in fact he and Trippe met afterwards quite amicably. The legal point at issue was the tenure of the voting trust. Under Connecticut law, maximum tenure was seven years, but the Colonial voting trust was for ten. Trippe says that Trumbull was open-minded and that Trippe explained that the issue would take months to settle in the courts, but "We can settle it at once by putting it to a vote of the shareholders." The shareholders then met in the governor's mansion. According to the Leslie ms, Trippe resigned as vice president of Colonial Air Transport on April 30, 1927.

Trippe's courtship of Elizabeth Stettinius: Van Dusen to Leslie, Oct. 24, 1972. Van Dusen, who knew Trippe as early as 1928, described how badly Trippe wanted to get married.

Origin of the Stettinius family: Betty Trippe to author, March 6, 1978.

Origin of Trippe family: See *Life* magazine, Oct. 20, 1941. In the April 5, 1978, interview with the author, Trippe described how there were originally four Trippe brothers who left England at the same time. One went to Holland, one to New Zealand, one to Newfoundland and the fourth to Baltimore.

Betty and Juan play golf: Betty Trippe to author, March 6, 1978. This was probably in May 1925.

Marriage postponed: The family decision was made by Betty's mother and her brother Carrington, who was older by nine years. In a letter to the author dated April 3, 1979, Betty Trippe described how she and Juan walked up and down Park Avenue in the night explaining to each other how they could not get married for at least a year, promising each other that they would write regularly while she was abroad. At no time, Mrs. Trippe insisted, was there any doubt in either of their minds that they would eventually marry.

5 · *A New Company*

The rich young men: Trippe to author, Feb. 17, 1978—"I went to see them at their country houses." Most of these young men had backed Trippe before, but with the exception of Hambleton there is scarcely a trace of any of them in his letters. At the time that the New York–Chicago airmail contract was being decided, William Rockefeller was at sea off South Carolina on the yacht *Hirondelle*. He wrote Trippe asking to be informed which way the decision went. He was on his way south to Florida, so that Trippe, writing back, asked him to stop at Key West and look for a suitable airfield there. There is no record that he ever did so. Of the thirteen original investors, W. Averell Harriman and William Beckers put up $50,000 each, and Sonny Whitney $49,000. The lawyer Robert Thach, once a member of Trippe's squadron, invested $30,000, and Rockefeller, Vanderbilt, Hambleton and Trippe put up $25,000 each. Sherman Fairchild, Seymour Knox, Edward McDonnell and Ansley Sawyer each invested $5,000, and Grover Loening put up $1,000. Aviation Corporation was incorporated on June 2, 1927.

Trippe's authority: From the minutes of the July 12 directors' meeting.

The origins of Pan American Airways: Arnold describes his part in it in his autobiography, *Global Mission*, pp. 114-22. See also a seven-page typewritten document entitled "Pan American Airways Incorporated —History of its Promotion" up to Oct. 4, 1927, from Box T-37, Pan American corporate archives; *Fortune* magazine, April 1931 and April 1936. According to the Box T-37 document, Mason and Montgomery chased General Machado to Washington and back in April 1927; the same paper reports how fund-raising stopped while Mason got married.

Florida Airways: See PAF 20.05.00; also Davies, *History of the World's Airlines*. The Ford planes purchased by Florida Airways were original Stouts, not Trimotors. Florida Airways did have one signal success. In the late summer of 1926 a hurricane devastated southern Florida. In its aftermath a Miami bank sent to Jacksonville for $1 million in cash, but there seemed no way to get the money to Miami, for railroad tracks and roads were washed out in many places. The bank needed the money so badly that it agreed to have it flown down. The Jacksonville Bank made up a 59-pound package and drove it out under guard to the airfield, where Chenea waited beside the plane. By the time he landed in Miami it was sunset, and he could find no transport to take himself and the money into the city over the ruined roads. So he carried the million dollars to the bank on foot, with aching arms. When he arrived about midnight, he found all the bank's lights still on and the worried bank officials pacing the floor.

Paper to take to a bank: Letter from Van Dusen to Leslie, Nov. 15, 1972.

Original Trippe-Hoyt meeting: Trippe to author, April 4, 1979. According to Trippe, Curtiss-Wright intended to sell the land for a housing development. Trippe wanted it as an airport, but didn't want to pay out Colonial's money. He went before the city's board of estimate and tried to persuade the city to buy the land for an airport. He was told that the city had no money. So he went to Washington and, on behalf of the city, begged federal funds, then came back to New York, went before the board of estimate once more, reported that funds were now available, and persuaded the board to buy the land.

Hoyt as chairman: He did become chairman of Aviation Corporation of the Americas from June 26, 1928, to April 28, 1931. He remained a director until 1935, the year he died.

Chambers and Chenea meet Trippe: Trippe to author, April 4, 1979; see also notes of interview with Chenea, undated in PAF 30.10.08.

6 · First Flight

Trippe's intuitive vision: Anne Morrow Lindbergh to author, March 12, 1978.

Trippe as a negotiator: Van Dusen letter to Leslie, Oct. 24, 1972—"Negotiations with Juan never got any place very fast." The author also negotiated with Trippe for most of a year to assure his cooperation in the writing of this book, and had the same experience.

Montgomery back to Cuba: Box T-37, Archives, Pan American Airways Inc., history of its promotion up to Oct. 4, 1927.

Details of final agreement: From minutes of the board meetings of Oct. 11 and Oct. 13, 1927. Trippe's plan for the company's future activities was taken from the same minutes.

Pilot standing by: This was Musick.

The Key West Airport: Conditions there are partly described in the minutes of the Oct. 13 directors' meeting. Approximately $10,000 was appropriated for runway construction, and $18,000 for a hangar. See also Leslie ms, p. 34; and the 50th-anniversary issue of the Pan American Clipper house organ of Oct. 1977.

Trippe begs extension: *Saturday Evening Post*, Aug. 21, 1943, p. 28; confirmed to author, April 4, 1979.

Caldwell's flight: Whitbeck's friend knew that Caldwell had landed because a picture of Caldwell and his plane appeared in the Miami *Herald.* The plane was an FC-2 called *La Nina.* See Caldwell's account of his flight in PAF 50.03.05.

Official inauguration: From the account in the Key West *Citizen*, Oct. 26, 27, 28, 29, 1927.

Trippe's telegram to Paris: Betty Trippe to author, March 6, 1978.

7 · Priester

Wells replaced: Leuteritz to author, Sept. 22, 1978. Technically Wells was the number one Pan Am pilot in terms of seniority. According to Leuteritz, he checked out Cap Swinson in the F-7, two rides to Havana and back, after which Priester sent him packing. In New York Trippe kept him on, giving him jobs to do from time to time, and memos from him can be found in Trippe's correspondence file into the early thirties.

Captain Whitbeck: See *Aviation,* April 29, 1929.

Priester: Trippe to author, April 4, 1979 —"Priester was the first employee I hired." The profile on Priester that follows was put together from interviews with Leslie, Kauffman and Borger, all of whom worked for him; from Leuteritz and from Trippe; and also from various biographical sketches of him to be found in PAF 50.16.02. One of these was put together about 1957, two years after Priester's death, and it bears corrections by Mrs. Priester in ink in the margins.

Priester fails to solo: According to Leslie, Priester was too intellectual, too abstract and too uncoordinated ever to become a pilot. "He would be thinking of the breaker points moving back and forth a thousand times a minute instead of flying the plane. And he was no athlete."

The Philadelphia Exposition: This celebrated the 150th anniversary of the Declaration of Independence.

The Philadelphia Rapid Transit Airline: It owned three planes and carried 3,700 passengers without incident. See Davies, *A History of the World's Airlines.* The planes flew at an average speed of 87 mph. The company's ads boasted that the cabins were roomy with individual seats for eight passengers, plus the pilot "and his assistant." Windows afforded adequate ventilation; ordinary street clothing was all that was required; and the planes were equipped with lavatories. "An entrancing view of the countryside is possible from the windows, unobstructed by the plane's structure." Pilots were named and identified. Chief pilot Musick, it was written, already boasted thirteen years' flying experience.

Priester in Detroit: Letters from Priester to Trippe, Feb. 22, 1927, and from Trippe to Priester, Feb. 27, 1927.

Priester's memo: Handwritten, it is dated Nov. 1927. PAF 50.16.02.

Priester writes new operations manual: That Priester was its author was attested to by Leslie. The manual still exists.

The New York office: Van Dusen to Leslie, Oct. 11, 1972.

8 · Key West

The Key West airfield: See "Story of PAA's First Flight" in PAF 10.06.00. It was written in the winter of 1944 by George Dacy, a free lance, on assignment to the Pan Am Public Relations Department. Dacy interviewed all the surviving participants, including Caldwell. This is the company's "official" version.

Trippe's name misspelled: PAF 10.06,00 contains photostats of the manifest.

Salesmen aboard trains: Trippe to author, April 4, 1979; see also Miami *Herald,* April 28, 1978—Chenea's obituary (he was eighty-five).

Navigation errors between Havana and Key West: Leuteritz described them to the author, June 16, 1978. When a plane was due, the man Priester would usually mutter to was Leuteritz.

Swinson hired: Notes of interview with Swinson, no date, around 1957, PAF 30.-10.08.

Fatt hired: Notes of Fatt, Aug. 26, 1957, PAF 30.10.08. Fatt died April 5, 1973.

Disciplinary problems: Priester is remembered as a stiff, formal man who ruled the airline like a despot. Discipline was not the primary virtue but almost the only one, and he saw nearly every problem in terms of discipline. Note this excerpt from an early memo to Trippe: "The pilots and the mechanics are kept going by small advances. None of them are paid their full salaries, although several have been with us one month. We require them always to be on time at the job, and we should therefore be on time with the payments . . . the lack of regular payments will not help to preserve proper discipline."

Trippe meets Leuteritz: Trippe to author June 21, 1978—"I asked General Sarnoff [head of RCA] who was the best man he had, and he told me Leuteritz was." This was around 1925, when Trippe was still with Colonial, and Leuteritz was involved with

Trippe's attempt then to use radio for navigational purposes. These were ground triangular stations, and they were calibrated with the help of the Navy dirigible *Los Angeles.*

9 · Leuteritz

Leuteritz hikes to Fire Island: Leuteritz to author, March 9, 1978. The transmitting antenna there resembled the ribs of an umbrella. In the center a rotating transmitter made contact individually with one rib after another, as regularly as clockwork. The captain of a ship at sea would pick up the first signal, snap his stopwatch, and wait until the signal got as loud as it was going to get. At its loudest point he would snap his stopwatch again, then check a chart to find out what sector he was in. The chart gave him his approximate bearing from the station.

Leuteritz's early career: Leuteritz to author, March 9 and June 16, 1978. RCA had between eighty and a hundred men, one of them being Leuteritz, conducting research into the possible uses of radio.

The crash: Leuteritz's transmissions were monitored by the Marine radio station at Hialeah which prepared a verbatim transcript. This can be found in PAF 10.06.00.

Priester sends Swinson up: In fact he sent him up twice, Swinson landing once to report that he had been unable to spot the other plane.

Leuteritz sounding unworried: Notes of interview with Pippinger, dated Jan. 1959, PAF 30.10.08.

Fatt and Alfonso on the wing: Notes of interview with Fatt dated Aug. 26, 1957, PAF 30.10.08.

Ageton lost: The Aug. 16, 1928, *New York Times* report of the crash identified him as a chemist from Banford Avenue, Flushing, N.Y.

Fatt punches cameraman: Notes of interview with Fatt, Aug. 26, 1957, PAF 30.10.8.

Trippe hires Doremus & Co.: Van Dusen to Leslie, a tape-recorded conversation, Oct. 24, 1972. Formerly Trippe's public relations had been handled by Bruno and Blyth, which numbered as clients then and later most of the leading aviators of the day including Lindbergh, Chamberlain, Admiral Byrd, Wiley Post and others. The Van

Dusen quote is from a letter he wrote to Leslie dated Oct. 11, 1972.

The new loop: Sullinger took Leuteritz's sketches, procured the necessary wood and wire and built the loop himself. It was mounted and ready to go by the time Leuteritz was released from the hospital.

The new grid system: Letter from Leuteritz to author, June 27, 1978.

Leuteritz's desk: Leuteritz to author, June 16, 1978.

10 · West Indian Aerial Express

Trippe's dreams: In an interview with the author on April 27, 1979, Trippe pointed out that the U.S. government in the late twenties had committees meeting regularly to consider how to run overseas transport. First Coolidge and then Hoover were watching closely. The Europeans, principally Germany and France, had already established subsidiaries in South America—airmail crossed the South Atlantic by destroyer. The U.S. government committees and the two presidents all wanted to get a strong U.S. carrier in there. Trippe himself was going to South America first because it could be done in 1928, whereas no existing plane could cross the North Atlantic or the Pacific; but he maintains that he had his eye on both oceans from the start and never restricted his thinking to Latin America. The record bears this out.

The first Sikorsky: It was delivered Aug. 20, 1928, and cost $31,500.

West Indian's route: PAF 20.09.00 contains a number of memos from Roscoe Dunten to Trippe describing it.

Rowe profile: The best profile of Rowe is his book *Under My Wings.* See also *New Horizons,* Jan.–March 1946, and his obituary in *The New York Times,* Nov. 11, 1973. Rowe claimed that his original pilot's license was signed by Orville Wright and was No. 223.

The dirigible stunt: Rowe, p. 53.

Barnstorming ends: Rowe talks about it in a *New Horizons* profile dated Aug.–Sept.–Oct. 1943.

West Indian Aerial Express formed: See Rowe, p. 112; the various documents of incorporation are in PAF 20.09.00. Rowe describes heading north to buy new aircraft, and hiring Cy Caldwell, beginning on p. 113.

The company's organization: Dunten spelled it out in a letter to Trippe dated June 4, 1928.

The Foreign Air Mail Act: The minutes of a directors' meeting of Atlantic, Gulf and Caribbean on Dec. 16, 1927, mention the "Washington situation." The bill had already been introduced by Senator George Moses in the Senate and by Congressman Clyde Kelly in the House. It gave the Postmaster General absolute discretion in the awarding of contracts not necessarily to the lowest bidder but to the lowest responsible bidder capable of performing the contracted services. It was this same Atlantic, Gulf and Caribbean directors' meeting that ratified the ordering of the first Sikorsky amphibian for $31,500.

Dunten's proposal to Trippe: The June 4, 1928, letter.

Trippe's offer: Trippe to Dunten, June 25, 1928.

Trippe busy politically: In *Under My Wings*, Rowe, on p. 118, writes: "We realized too late that while we had been developing an airline in the West Indies, our competitors had been busy on the much more important job of developing a lobby in Washington." Trippe pointed out to the author on April 27, 1979, that there was nothing personal in the award of the route to Pan Am: "I had no personal ability beyond reading our balance sheets. We had a much stronger setup. When they saw those names . . ." Trippe seemed to be claiming that he did not lobby, but the record contradicts him. He was at all times very close to the men in Washington, especially those in the Post Office Department. On Feb. 17, 1934, Trippe even wrote to Harllee Branch, Second Assistant Postmaster General, offering to put someone from the Post Office on the Pan Am board of directors.

Trippe accompanied by Lindbergh: In interviews with the author on Aug. 30, 1976, Sept. 1, 1976, and May 9, 1979, Trippe described how he and Lindbergh testified before Congress to the effect that an amendment to the 1928 Foreign Air Mail Act was needed so that carriers—there was only one —could receive two dollars per mile for carrying 800 pounds of mail in *both* directions. The amended law was passed March 2, 1929. In other words, Lindbergh testified beside Trippe even before he signed his contract as a consultant with Pan American.

Trippe meets Lindbergh: Trippe to author, Aug. 30, 1976.

Lindbergh's recollection: Anne Morrow Lindbergh to author, March 12, 1978.

Subsequent meetings with Lindbergh: Leuteritz, after examining his files, wrote the author on June 27, 1978, that he had met Trippe and Lindbergh together in 1927 "when they came back from Washington prior to Slim's May flight." Trippe told the author on April 27, 1979, that he had arranged in advance to meet with Lindbergh on whatever day he came back from his transatlantic flight.

Trippe watches takeoff: Trippe to author, Aug. 30, 1976, April 27, 1979; there were also a number of interviews between the author and Trippe in May of 1977 as the 50th anniversary of the Lindbergh flight approached. According to Anne Lindbergh (March 12, 1978 interview), Lindbergh did not realize that Trippe was present at the takeoff. Trippe, according to Trippe, had watched the disastrous Fonck attempt to take off the year before—the plane crashed at the end of the runway, incinerating itself and two crewmen. So the chances are he did intend to watch every takeoff until someone made it.

Trippe and Lindbergh meet: Trippe to author, April 27, 1979. Trippe said he telephoned Lindbergh at the hotel of Raymond Orteig, who had put up the $25,000 prize. Probably Orteig was staying at the Brevoort Hotel, for Trippe's files contain an invitation to a breakfast there with Orteig and Lindbergh a few days later. Trippe remembered meeting Lindbergh the night of the ticker-tape parade, but the mayor's dinner for Lindbergh at the Commodore was on the following night and it seems likely that the meeting between the two men took place then. When Trippe told Lindbergh that he would not speak to him except through a lawyer "that impressed Lindbergh more than anything else," according to Trippe.

Date with Betty Stettinius: Mrs. Trippe to author, March 6, 1978. The meeting with Lindbergh was probably on June 15; Betty went abroad at the beginning of July, and she was still in Europe at the time of the first flight to Havana in late October.

Trippe's conversations with men of influence: Among the most important was Assistant Postmaster General Irving Glover, who told him, according to a June 21, 1978, interview with the author, that "A second company doesn't make sense. Foreigners may beat us." Trippe said he had talked to the Secretary of State and also to the Undersecretary of State.

Patriotic arguments: The PAF files, as well as Trippe's interviews with the author, are replete with these. On April 5, 1978, he described to the author the arguments he used to persuade U.S. authorities—the Departments of State and the Navy, and President Roosevelt himself—to annex Wake and Canton islands, the mid-Pacific bases he needed in the thirties. In the case of Wake he reported that he had "heard" that flights to Wake were planned by the Japanese. Canton lies far closer to Australia than to Central America, but he argued that "I always understood that Canton was one of the key defenses of the Panama Canal." As he reported these arguments and others he was not chortling. He evidently believed each of them himself, and certainly Washington was willing to believe them during those years preceding the outbreak of World War II. A Feb. 2, 1937, memo from Assistant Secretary of State Moore to President Roosevelt warns F.D.R. that "The other day Mr. J. T. Trippe, President of Pan American Airways, met with the committee and urged that unless the Germans and Dutch are to take charge to a large extent in South America, his company should be put in a position to establish several additional routes. I have in hand all of the data pertaining to that matter, and perhaps in the very near future, since quick action seems imperative, you may be able to see me with Mr. Harllee Branch at the Post Office Department."

Aviation Corporation buys West Indian: See the documents relating to the sale in PAF 20.09.00. The Dunten quote is from his letter to Trippe of June 6, 1928.

Trippe's men fly the line: Letter from Trippe to J. H. Johnston, acting division superintendent, Sept. 30, 1928. Trippe asked that a budget be made up. Rowe, on p. 120, mentions the presence of Pink Whiskers.

Rowe joins Pan Am: He was five feet four inches tall, weighed 140 pounds and was bald. He was number one pilot in seniority for the latter part of his career and he lived to be seventy-seven.

Dunten signs on: Letter from Trippe to Dunten, Aug. 25, 1928. Actually Trippe wrote to Dunten twice that day, the second letter being an employment contract at $10,000 per year which Dunten was to

countersign and return. Dunten committed suicide in 1934.

Trippe plans route: Letter from Trippe to Richard K. Mellon, Mellon National Bank, Pittsburgh, Aug. 31, 1928. Mellon had just become a stockholder and Trippe revealed that Pan Am's budget for the next six months contemplated capital investments totaling $1.25 million. "Inasmuch as a large part of our revenue is received from the United States government for transporting mail, and also inasmuch as our vouchers for such service are paid promptly on the tenth or the eleventh of the following month, we are able to reduce our working capital to a relatively small amount, and, therefore, we do not carry large balances in our checking accounts."

Contracts for ten years' duration: On Feb. 28, 1978, Trippe told the author: "We got Kelly to put up 10 year contracts." Trippe's argument had been that in order to attract capital investment, Pan Am would have to show investors a guaranteed stability at least over the next ten years. Otherwise no one would invest, and the airline companies would all fail.

New stock offered: Trippe to author, Feb. 28, 1978. "We went out and determined who we would invite in with us." The full story of the rapid expansion of capital is told in Chapter 46, "High Stakes," and in the Source Notes that accompany it.

Trippe a multimillionaire: Trippe's stockholdings over the years are discussed in the notes for Chapter 32, "The Whitney Takeover."

Steer clear of Trippe: Betty Trippe to author, March 6, 1978.

The wedding day: That Trippe turned up at the office on the morning of his wedding day was printed as fact in most of the early magazine articles about Pan Am, and Josephson repeats it in Empire of the Air when he describes the wedding, pp. 60–63. Trippe insisted to the author on April 27, 1979, and this was affirmed in a letter from Betty Trippe to the author written the previous day, that Trippe had not gone to work on his wedding day, but had played golf at Piping Rock with his best man and ushers. Since the wedding was in the late afternoon, perhaps he worked and golfed both.

The wedding trip: Trippe to author, Aug. 25, 1976, and April 6, 1978. With a chuckle he described how friends said the marriage wouldn't last: "That fellow won't even take her on a wedding trip."

Planning the trunk lines: In a letter to Richard Mellon dated Jan. 4, 1929, Trippe described how "Pan Am is developing rapidly. Both the Atlantic coastline and Florida West Coast Railroads are substantial stockholders in addition to several of the shipping lines operating in the Caribbean area and South America. A northern terminal has been moved from Key West to a large airport we have just constructed at Miami. Schedules have been increased until there are four trimotors leaving this airport daily, closely connecting with through trains from the northwest. Air mail tickets to any point on our line will soon be available at all airline ticket offices. We are pushing into Mexico. We expect to have operations underway by Feb. 1. A subsidiary company, Peruvian Airways Corporation, has been operating successfully since Sept. 13 at Peru. We expect shortly to extend service connecting with our present line at Colon to all the west-coast of South America. From this brief picture you can see that our situation is moving along in great shape." According to a legal document dated April 18, 1929, the board of directors of Aviation Corporation nullified the boards of all the subsidiary companies, consolidating all operations under "the unified control of the president of Pan American Airways Inc." Six days later Whitney, as chairman of the board, signed a document giving Trippe power of attorney "to represent the said Aviation Corporation of America before the government and all administrative authorities in each and every country of the world."

Compañía Mexicana: See PAF 20.14.00. Folder includes a brief history of the company, a profile of Rihl and various company financial statements.

The Brownsville–Canal Zone bids: Pan Am was awarded the contract on Feb. 16, 1929. Even then Pan Am could operate only by subterfuge. A special dispensation was obtained from the Mexican government by which Compañía Mexicana was permitted to employ Pan American planes and pilots to cross Mexican territory twice a week in both directions. As Irwin Balluder wrote in a letter dated Dec. 17, 1932: "There is no operation of Pan American Airways, Inc. in Mexico. It is the Compania Mexicana de Aviacion exclusively, operating in Mexico under the Mexican concession." This produced compromises. Service was supposed to start in Matamoros, Mexico, where there was no airport. For a number of years a Pan

American car crossed the Rio Grande to pick up the Mexican customs and immigration officials and bring them over to the Brownsville airport, where they cleared the flights that left every morning for the south and came back every afternoon. In 1933 the minister of communications canceled the work permits of the American pilots, so Balluder began to call them technical advisers instead of pilots, making them assistants to the Mexican copilots. For additional information on Compañía Mexicana, see CAB docket No. 525 et al.; and also Wesley Newton's The Perilous Sky.

Huff-Daland Dusters: The possible acquisition of this "airline" is mentioned in the minutes of the Atlantic, Gulf and Caribbean board of directors' meeting on Oct. 13, 1927, and it is mentioned again in the minutes of the Dec. 16, 1927, meeting.

SCADTA: The story is told in detail in Chapter 39, " 'Delousing' " SCADTA."

The Lindbergh Pan Am contract: It is described in the minutes of the July 17, 1929, directors' meeting. In the April 27, 1979, interview, Trippe told the author: "Lindbergh was quite a factor when he joined us. Because the public would go out to see him wherever he'd go." The report of the mobs crowding around Lindbergh at Miami is from the Miami Herald of Feb. 3, 1929. The headline read: FIVE THOUSAND WATCH LINDBERGH AT MIAMI AIRPORT.

Lindbergh's flight to the Canal Zone: It was described in the Miami Herald of Feb. 14, 1929, upon his return there. There is also a good account of it in the American Aviation Historical Society Journal, dated Spring 1961. The article's title is "Lindbergh Flies the Mail to Panama," and the author is Mitch Mayborn.

Lindbergh's telegram: It was dated Feb. 9, 1929.

The formation of Panagra: The relevant file is PAF 10.13.00.

11 · NYRBA

Grooch: He was not really a major character in the Pan Am saga, but he was there at the beginning and he wrote three books about it. The principal sources of this chapter are Grooch's Winged Highway and Ralph O'Neill's A Dream of Eagles. O'Neill, on p.

196, describes Grooch as a short, swarthy man of unprepossessing appearance, but with the best record of all Navy pilots—nearly 3,000 hours in flying boats. Grooch's own account of his interview with Priester, and his eventual signing on with NYRBA, is described by him on pp. 56–62.

O'Neill's point of view: See *A Dream of Eagles*, beginning on p. 115. According to O'Neill, the rumor that he had cracked his head open in Uruguay was spread by Richard Hoyt. According to the Leslie ms, Chapter II, p. 31, O'Neill's first idea had been to submit a bid of $1.95 per mile on behalf of a company he called Trimotor Safety Airways Inc. for U.S. Air Mail Contract FAM No. 9 between the Canal Zone and Chile. O'Neill was underbid by Panagra, and in any case had no organization or equipment with which to serve such a route. Having lost the west coast of South America, he then decided to try for the east coast, and he formed NYRBA.

O'Neill's S-38: O'Neill and Grooch both give accounts of this journey, O'Neill beginning on p. 141, and Grooch on p. 71.

O'Neill power-dives Copacabana Palace Hotel: *A Dream of Eagles*, p. 177.

The Lindberghs and the Trippes fly south: There are a number of extant accounts of this flight. Betty Trippe kept a diary, and Anne Lindbergh wrote letters during most of it; Mrs. Trippe's diary was made available to the author, and Mrs. Lindbergh's letters were later published in her *Hour of Gold, Hour of Lead.* In addition, the radio log as given out to the press Sept. 20–26, 1929, still exists in PAF 10.06.00.

Impressions of Trippe: Anne Morrow Lindbergh to author, March 12, 1978. She also remembered his "glaring white suit."

Lindbergh stands up to take pictures: Copilot Charles Lorber was flying the plane. Betty Trippe describes this in her diary, and Anne Lindbergh described it to the author in an interview on June 19, 1978. She said she wasn't scared when Lindbergh was out there in the slipstream: "He was the hero. I really didn't believe anything could happen to him. I was very young, and I was in love." She said she gasped to see him out there, but did not scold him when he came back.

Lindbergh kissed: Trippe's quote was made to the author in the course of the May 1977 interviews.

The Barranquilla lagoon: Betty Trippe and Anne Lindbergh both described it at the time, but it was not part of any log

given out by the Pan Am press department.

Trippe worried about modesty: Anne Lindbergh to author, March 12, 1978.

Lindbergh's revolver: It is mentioned in Betty Trippe's diary. In addition, it seems to have made an impression on Trippe himself, for he mentioned it during the course of the June 21, 1978, interview with the author. When asked whether he and Lindbergh shared the same vision, Trippe shook his head and said they did not. "Lindbergh was very conservative. For instance, on our trip to South America in 1929 he had a revolver with him."

Trippe never takes controls: Trippe to author, Feb. 28, 1978.

"The Trippes have been such fun": Anne Lindbergh, *Hour of Gold, Hour of Lead*, p. 97.

Consolidated Commodore: Much of what O'Neill has written in *A Dream of Eagles* must be discounted, for he was an intemperate man at the time, and the book was written some forty years later. But his impressions as he looked up at "giant" Commodores sound genuine.

The open cockpits: In fact Grooch had his way, and all the Commodores were delivered with closed cockpits.

Trippe and Mrs. Hoover: Trippe denied to the author April 29, 1979, that any such event as described by O'Neill ever took place. O'Neill's account is from *A Dream of Eagles*, pp. 201–2; in *Winged Highway*, Grooch describes the christening on p. 68, but omits mentioning the presence of Trippe. *The New York Times* account published on p. 18, col. IV, Oct. 4, 1929, notes that O'Neill did make a brief speech, and adds that "Every Central and South American government was represented at the ceremonies"—so possibly Trippe was there too. It is possible that O'Neill was at first pushed back by guards, then later allowed to mount the dais. In any case, this incident preyed upon his mind, and in a speech to the Clipper Pioneers in Oct. 1971 he again mentioned it, and again denounced Trippe.

The trip to South America: Grooch, *Winged Highway*, beginning on p. 71.

Grooch reports in South America: *Winged Highway*, p. 85.

O'Neill maligns Postmaster General Brown: In *A Dream of Eagles*, p. 227, O'Neill quotes a cable from Jim Rand, his principal backer—"Why are you pulling house down on our ears?"

Summer's dirty work: Summer was Pan

Am representative in Brazil, Argentina and Uruguay from 1929 on. Trippe insisted to author during April 29, 1979, interview that there was no dirty work of any kind at any time, and that none was ever necessary. On May 9 he phoned to reiterate this argument. As soon as NYRBA entered into mail contracts with Argentina and Brazil—and these were in place by Feb. 1930—the competition, to Trippe, was over. NYRBA now could never get the U.S. airmail contract down the east coast of South America. "O'Neill and his crowd had disqualified themselves. Those contracts were formal, and public, and they were made with sovereign states. We got copies of them as soon as they made them. There was no possibility that they could get out of them. After that we just let them stew in their own juice. We ignored them." Trippe also said that he never was worried about NYRBA, not for a single day. NYRBA was incorporated in April 1929, and the threat, therefore, was a short-lived one—ten months—if Trippe is to be believed.

O'Neill's first airmail flight: O'Neill claimed in A Dream of Eagles that he went seven nights without sleep. The description of the flight is put together from the Grooch and O'Neill accounts.

O'Neill fires pilots and Bevier: O'Neill, A Dream of Eagles, pp. 280–83.

12 · The Mad Cutthroat Struggle

O'Neill's plan: It is reiterated throughout his Dream of Eagles.

Extend every courtesy: A July 1, 1930, memo from E. E. Wyman (whose title was assistant to the president) to Trippe notes what these courtesies had been. On Sept. 16 and Jan. 18 Dunten had been instructed by telegram to "extend all courtesies" and "to continue the present policy of cooperation with NYRBA." On Feb. 19 Dunten had been informed by telegram that NYRBA was to be allowed landings and takeoffs without charge at Pan Am airports. In addition, Leuteritz had ordered radio facilities made available, though on a pay basis, and when a NYRBA plane cracked up off Paramaribo, Pan Am personnel had helped rescue passengers and the plane itself.

Grooch chases Commodore: Grooch, Winged Highway, p. 99.

The Battle of Montenegro: It took place on Lake Amapa, a NYRBA emergency base. Grooch mentions it on p. 97, O'Neill on p. 169, Josephson on pp. 74–75.

O'Neill's strategy: Having established a base at Buenos Aires, NYRBA's inaugural 142-mile flight to Montevideo took place on Aug. 26, 1929. Flights from Buenos Aires to Santiago began Aug. 19, and from Buenos Aires to La Paz, Bolivia, on Nov. 15. The first flight from Buenos Aires to Rio took place on Jan 15, 1930, and from Rio to Buenos Aires three weeks later, Feb. 7. By then the Pan Am system included some 12,-000 route miles. It covered all of the Caribbean, Mexico and Central America, and all of South America except the sector between Dutch Guiana and Buenos Aires. All six foreign airmail contracts awarded by the U.S. Post Office thus far had gone to Pan American.

The NYRBA airmail contracts: Financial information on NYRBA can be found in PAF 40.04.00. At the beginning of 1930 NYRBA had a cash balance of $662,000 against net current obligations of $168,000. Only five months later, on May 31, NYRBA was virtually insolvent, with only $16,000 in the bank against $99,000 of current obligations. It had already received an infusion of new capital totaling $1.4 million that year.

Brown sees little merit: He so testified before the so-called Black Committee (Senator Hugo Black, chairman). These hearings were held by the Special Committee on Investigation of the Air Mail and Ocean Mail Contracts, U. S. Senate, 73rd Cong., 2nd Sess. 1933. Brown's testimony begins on p. 2349.

NYRBA's foreign contracts: Trippe's principal argument, as he prepared to buy NYRBA out, was that NYRBA had removed itself from the field of possible bidders for U.S. airmail contracts by these improvident contracts it had entered into with Argentina, Uruguay and Brazil. It was bound under those agreements to fly the mails north at rates ranging downward from $10 per pound, and this was less than 50 percent of the rates fixed by the U.S. Post Office. To Trippe, these contracts made it absolutely impossible for NYRBA to bid competitively for the east-coast route. The award of the contract to NYRBA in the face of these contracts would have broken down the entire northbound rate structure for the west and north coasts of South America and for the West Indies, a rate structure from which the Post Office was directly profiting.

NYRBA losing money: PAF40.04.00.

O'Neill's speech to his directors: O'Neill, *A Dream of Eagles*, p. 296.

Trippe meets with MacCracken: On July 16, according to the minutes of the special meeting of the Pan Am Executive Committee, Trippe reported on the "results" of his negotiations with MacCracken to purchase NYRBA. The two of them met with Brown on July 22; the memo was signed by Mac-Cracken and countersigned by Trippe. Trippe, on April 29, 1979, said he did not remember any meeting with O'Neill in the hotel that morning.

Brown's absolute discretion: The relevant clauses in both the March 8, 1928, Foreign Air Mail Act, and the amended act of March 2, 1929, are identical: "In the award and interpretation of the contracts herein authorized, the decision of the Postmaster General shall be final, and not subject to review by any office or tribunal of the United States except by the president and the federal courts."

Trippe and Pierson meet on yacht: Trippe to author, April 5, 1978. Mac-Cracken was present, and Rand may have been there too. Trippe wrote the agreement out in longhand, and Pierson and Mac-Cracken signed it.

O'Neill's speech: O'Neill, *A Dream of Eagles*, p. 306. On Aug. 28, a notice went out to the stockholders over O'Neill's signature notifying them of a meeting to ratify the sale scheduled for Sept. 10. But by then ratification was a formality only.

Rihl hires Grooch: The Grooch material that follows is from his *Winged Highway*, pp. 111 ff. In making his way back to South America, Grooch went to Miami and begged a free ride from Dunten aboard Pan American.

The new uniforms: See Dunten's memo to his staff dated July 30, 1930; pilots were obliged to buy their own uniforms, but the company would see to it they got cut rates. Van Dusen discusses the first uniform in a letter to Leslie dated April 30, 1971. He claimed he and Priester worked out the first uniforms.

Priester's discipline: Leslie to author, Nov. 30, 1978; Kauffman to author, July 11, 1978. The story of Priester firing the steward came from Leuteritz, June 16, 1978. As for his letters upsetting his subordinates,

see Balluder's letter to Trippe, Jan. 9, 1930—"The same afternoon I had an opportunity to talk the matter over with Mr. Holcombe, who was successful in assuring me that Priester could not possibly be aware of the offensive tone of his letter, on account of his lack of control of his English." The postcard to his wife is in PAF 50.16.02.

Swinson tipped: Leuteritz to author, June 16, 1978.

Baby born: Notes of an interview with Pippinger, undated, about 1960, PAF 30.-10.08.

The aerial wedding: This is from a letter Mrs. Patterson addressed to Pan American Airways, attaching both a copy of her marriage license and a description of the Dec. 28, 1932, ceremony. Her letter was dated Nov. 20, 1972. There is no explanation as to why she chose to address a letter to the company, to no specific person, on that particular date.

The pilot anecdotes: These are fairly easy to cull from any of the writings about the pilots of those times. The Shorty Clark and Ed Schultz stories are from the Wright-Thruelsen ms, pp. 14, 16. It was Harold Bixby who used to describe the way Schultz would bark like a dog—he had once roomed with Schultz in Charleston, S.C.—as he ferried a Sikorsky flying boat south toward Miami. The Bancroft stories are from notes of an interview with Captain Hamilton in 1961, PAF 30.10.08. Pilots, as Lindbergh described it in a 1967 letter, were still part of the ground element when flying—not the air. They could sense the trees beneath their wings, or the wave tops. The cabins were not pressurized. High altitude was impossible to attain. When bucking the trade winds in the tropics, the early airliners would fly eight to ten feet off the water, for the trades blew at 35 mph or faster and would cut their speed by a third. Coming back, they would ride as high as 8,000 feet, letting the trades sweep them along. All planes carried survival gear, which meant not only life rafts, but also machetes, guns and snakebite serum.

"Pan Am was like a religion then": From notes of a interview with Lyle Warner in July 1958, PAF 30.10.08.

Pilots on the move: See Rowe, p. 140—"I didn't sleep in one bed very long."

Leuteritz's Christmas tree: Leuteritz to author, June 16, 1978.

The revolutions: Leuteritz described his 1930 trip to South America to the author,

June 16, 1978. He landed in revolutions in two countries, one after the other. The Cuban revolution was described to the author by Kauffman on July 16, 1978. The New York *Herald Tribune* reported the incident on Aug. 12, 1933, and Captain Terletzky's official report, dated Aug. 14, is in PAF 30.10.08.

13 · The First Clipper

Trippe planning the S-40's: Trippe described this to the author during the interviews of May 1977. Trippe had just come back from his combination business-honeymoon trip to the 1928 Berlin Air Show. He had traveled on luxurious ocean liners, and once ashore he had looked over a number of European airliners. These were all landplanes, but some were extremely luxurious by the standards of the day.

Sikorsky: The Sikorsky profile was put together from his own Wings Club lecture in New York on Nov. 16, 1964; from his Cierva Memorial Lecture entitled "Sixty Years in Flying," reprinted in the *Aeronautical Journal* of Nov. 1971; from his front-page *New York Times* obituary of Oct. 27, 1972, and from his book *The Story of the Winged S*, London, 1939.

Sikorsky loops Trippe: Trippe to author, April 29, 1979.

Sikorsky's dream: See "The Incredible Sikorsky Clippers," *Air Classics*, Aug. 1973.

The contract: PAF 30.07.10. This file includes also the specifications, and a good deal of the correspondence back and forth between Pan American and Sikorsky.

The Clipper name: Trippe to author, April 5, 1978.

The christening ceremony: *The New York Times*, Oct. 13, 1931.

The Pan American name: Trippe to author, Sept. 1, 1976—"We had a hell of a discussion about which was the best name, Aviation Corporation or Pan American." Van Dusen described these meetings to Leslie on Oct. 24, 1972, a tape-recorded conversation. According to Van Dusen, Trippe's first corporate signature was J. Terry Trippe, and he was also listed under that name in the Social Register.

Trippe's demeanor changes: By the end of 1929, being two years and two months old, Pan American was serving 28 countries, and its route structure totaled 12,265 miles; its sixty aircraft flew out of sixty airports and seaplane bases owned or operated by the company itself, and pilots aloft were navigated by 25 ground radio stations put into operation by Leuteritz. In 1929, 20,728 passengers were flown a total of 2,752,880 miles; 1929 was spoken of afterwards as the miracle year. But 1930 was almost as good —route mileage up to 18,021, overall traffic up 60 percent, passenger mileage up over 4.2 million, the fleet swollen to 111 units. Josephson, in *Empire of the Air*, p. 78, describes Trippe conducting himself with the dignity of a much older man. Anne Morrow Lindbergh described to the author on March 12, 1978, how Trippe's employees seemed to her to be afraid of him. Trippe's technique in Washington was described by Van Dusen to Leslie on Oct. 24, 1972: "Trippe had a wonderful technique. Trippe always knew everybody in Washington and you've heard him say, I'm sure, 'Well, my board this and my board that.' Often his board had no idea what the hell this was all about."

Trippe's methods with subordinates: Leuteritz described to the author on June 16, 1978, how Trippe would tear a page off a pad, and this would be orders to begin the next project. Mary Tay Pryor told the author on March 11, 1978, that Trippe was always careful to stay aloof from subordinates: "He would never shake hands with station people. He would walk through the crew like a general reviewing his troops and never shake hands. They respected him enormously. Most people in the office were afraid of him."

The Jan. 12, 1932, memo: It was from E. E. Wyman, whose title was assistant to the president, and it was addressed to the Caribbean Division manager in Miami relative to the pending visit of J. P. Hand and Major and Mrs. Mayo from Ford.

Part II
THE PACIFIC
14 · The Next Step

Swinson and Fatt refuse: Kauffman to author, July 11, 1978. According to Kauffman, Musick came to him for advice, "What shall I do?" Swinson remained for many years chief pilot of the Latin American Division and later was succeeded as chief pilot by Fatt.

Expanding their knowledge: See PAF 10.06.00. Included are a number of "certificate of proficiency" diplomas issued to Leo Terletzky. One, dated Sept. 13, 1934, attests to the pilot's proficiency in 21 subjects. Issued by International Correspondence Schools, it bears a number of signatures at the bottom, including Priester's. A second certificate dated Nov. 26, 1935, lists 12 more in which Terletzky had acquired "proficiency."

Swinson checks out Rowe: Notes of interview with Swinson, undated, about 1958, PAF 30.10.08.

Ten takeoffs and landings: Lindbergh made them Nov. 18, 1931, according to a Miami *Herald* report the following day.

The maiden flight of the S-40: From "The Incredible Sikorsky Clippers," by M.D. Class, in *Air Classics*, Vol. IX, No. 8 (Aug. 1972); conversation between Lindbergh and Sikorsky as per PAF 30.20.01. March 1959. In Nov. 1967 Lindbergh wrote a letter to Langewiesche in which he described his opposition to the design of the S-40.

Sikorsky decides on one step at a time: From his *Story of the Winged S*, pp. 202–3.

The flight itself: This account was pieced together from the Lindbergh-Sikorsky conversations of 1959, from Sikorsky's book, *The Story of the Winged S*, and from Class's article, "The Incredible Sikorsky Clippers." According to the Miami *Herald*, Nov. 26, 1931, when Lindbergh landed back at Miami at 6:28 there was only one oil flare illuminating the landing area. Sikorsky and Van Dusen were among the twenty-eight people aboard.

15 · Staking Out the World

Trippe's problems: Trippe to author, June 21, 1978—"We had three main jobs, Latin America, the Atlantic, and the Pacific." On April 29, 1979, Trippe pointed out that he had conceived Pan American from the beginning as an international airline, not a Latin American airline.

The 1925 statistics: The report quoted

was prepared by the Air Transport Engineering Corporation—Report No. 20. A second report, found like the first among Trippe's papers, was entitled "The Martin Report," and estimated ship traffic suitable for aviation at $250 million annually.

Trippe to the public library: Trippe to author, April 5 and June 21, 1978; April 4, 1979. He said he had begun to frequent the public library as early as his Long Island Airways days, when he was trying to research ground transportation and such shippers as United Fruit.

Arctic not insoluble: Trippe to author, June 21, 1978—"Ice in the north was no more unbeatable than the DF."

Trippe in Europe: He had letters of introduction to important Europeans signed by equally important Americans, including Assistant Secretary of the Navy Edward Warner and Assistant Secretary of Commerce William P. MacCracken. These survive in PAF 50.20.02.

The tripartite negotiations: Trippe to author, June 21, 1978. See also PAF 10.-04.02: this file contains the various drafts of the document itself. The final draft was 35 printed pages long and imposed penalties for noncompliance by any of the contracting parties. It also proposed to set up common funds.

Description of Trippe as a negotiator: Anne Morrow Lindbergh to author, March 12, 1978, and June 19, 1978. This was actually her husband's description of Trippe, repeated to her many times over the years. "Charles talked of these interminable meetings. Charles was intrigued by him. He was astonished at how artless Trippe seemed, and how he always got his own way."

New York Airways: The Pan Am-Imperial permit to operate to and from Bermuda was dated July 1, 1930, for a period up to April 1932, according to CAB docket No. 855 et al.—"History of the Transatlantic Air Services." A company document, dated Sept. 15, 1944, and written by George Wardman as a CAB exhibit, is to be found in PAF 20.17.00.

Trippe sends Winslow: Trippe to author, June 21, 1978. "History of the Transatlantic Air Services" describes the foundation of Boston and Maine Airways. On July 31, 1931, Pan Am was awarded Foreign Air Mail Route No. 12, and on the same date concluded an agreement between American Airways and Colonial Air Transport, whose territory this was. An order of the Post

Office Department was issued on Aug. 15 to amend the existing arrangement for Air Mail Route No. 1 (Colonial's New York–Boston route) and to recognize Pan American for the performance of service between Boston and Maine, and then on into Halifax.

Back to the library: Again the citations are Trippe's interviews with the author, April 5 and June 21, 1978, and April 4, 1979.

The vehicles: Trippe's files contain at least two long reports from those years, Air Transport Engineering Corps, Report No. 20, dated May 16, 1930; and a long memo from James McDonnell to Trippe, dated May 16, 1932. One of the earliest descriptions of the seadrome idea was reported in *Airways*, the air travel magazine, in Sept. 1926. The six-engined French flying boat, the *Lieutenant de Vaisseau Paris*, finally did cross the Atlantic in 1938. The German DO-X was built in 1929, and its gross weight was 100,000 pounds. The Boeing flying boat of ten years later was rated at 82,000 pounds.

Trippe's letter to the manufacturers: It was dated June 26, 1931. For the letter and the replies to it see PAF 30.07.17.

Lindbergh's plan: See Anne Lindbergh's *North to the Orient*. The quote "But she's crew," appears on p. 61.

bergh prior to the flight, some of them concerned with his radio, others with which route he should take, and whether he should overfly the Kurile Islands or go around them.

Lindbergh reports to Trippe: See "History of Pan American Air Services to and through Alaska," CAB docket No. 547 et al., Pacific certificate proceeding, New York, 1944, I, 3.

Trippe buys Alaska aviation companies: Pacific-Alaska was incorporated June 11, 1932, and it purchased Alaskan Airways Sept. 1, and Pacific International Oct. 15. The new Pan Am subsidiary thereby acquired 17 single-engined aircraft, together with assorted operating bases and equipment. Alaskan Airways had had forty employees, including five pilots, and it owned small frame hangars at Fairbanks, Anchorage and Nome. Pacific International had eight employees, two of them pilots, and one hangar at Anchorage. Each of these companies held eight Star Route mail contracts, which the new Pan Am subsidiary inherited.

Trippe negotiates with Amtorg: Trippe to author, April 5 and June 21, 27, 1978— "It didn't look like a big money route." He also testified before Congress on the subject a number of times, notably during the S-987 hearings of the mid-forties.

16 · North to the Orient

The Pan Am radio: Leuteritz to author, June 16, 1978; Anne Lindbergh to author, March 12, 1978. Leuteritz met with Anne Lindbergh at first, but most of her instruction came from subordinates.

The takeoff: *The New York Times*, July 28, 1931.

The flight: Details are from Anne Lindbergh's *North to the Orient*, and from Charles Lindbergh's report, "Survey Flights for Pan Am." See PAF 50.12.06,

Welcome to Japan: Japan's resistance to and resentment of United States "aggression" in the Pacific apparently dated from this flight. See papers relating to the "Foreign Relations of the United States and Japan, 1931–41," Department of State, Washington, D.C., 1943, I, 253. Trippe told the author in a June 27, 1978, interview, that there had been many meetings with Lind-

17 · China Airways

Clement Keys: M. Wright, "Builders of the Aviation Industry," *Scientific American*, March 1929; *Scientific American*, Sept. 1929; *World Work*, July 1925.

Robertson to China: Keys's principal goal in starting an airline in China seems to have been to open up a new market for selling Curtiss-Wright aircraft. For the most complete account of the early years of China Airways, see Leary, *The Dragon's Wings*. The Pan Am Foundation Archives also contains the 1958 master's degree thesis by Thomas B. Bartow, of the University of Hawaii, entitled "Early Transpacific Aviation 1930–1941"; and the 1943 senior thesis of Kenneth E. Folsom, of Princeton, entitled "The China National Aviation Corporation, an affiliated company of Pan American Airways System." See also *Wings Over Asia*, published by the Chinese National Aviation Association Foundation. Vol. III contains a long account of the early years by Chief Pilot Ernest Allison.

"If I want to invest a million dollars": The emissary to Keys was E. L. Sloniger, a pilot, and the quote is from his memoirs as supplied to Professor Leary.

"Extreme economy": Keys's letter to Price was dated Dec. 2, 1929.

Chiang jails Ott: The event took place in Dec. 1930 and was reported to the Department of State on Jan. 6, 1931, by F. P. Lockhart, the American consul at Hankow. The report is in State Department File 893.796.

Trippe meets Bixby: Trippe to author, May 16, 1979. Bixby's early dealings with Lindbergh are recounted in Lindbergh's *Spirit of St. Louis.* Bixby became ill in Japan, according to Trippe, because "they served him fish that was still flapping."

Trippe buys China Airways: PAF 10.-05.00—China National Aviation Corporation—contains a letter to Trippe signed by Cyril McNear, North American Aviation, Inc., 15 Exchange Place, Jersey City, N.J., dated April 1, 1932. Attached is a document entitled "History of China Airways Federal Inc.," and it outlines the company's contract with the Chinese government. "For our 45% of stock, we paid in all of the fixed assets of the company at book value, plus the development expense and losses to June 1, 1930 and in addition $25,000 in gold. For their 55% the Chinese Post Office delivered their total equipment, were credited with the development cost and losses from operations to June 1, 1930 and agreed to advance the company the equivalent of $700,-000." According to the contract, the airline's managing director should be Chinese, and a majority of the board should be Chinese. The operating management of the company was divided into three departments, Business (Chinese), Finance (joint Chinese and American, each with veto power) and Operations (American). Losses at this time were running at about $7,500 per month. Negotiations were still going on when Trippe sent Bixby out to China, and he advised Thomas Morgan, who was handling negotiations for the other side, in a Jan. 26, 1933, letter that "Pan Am's representatives" would not reach Shanghai until Feb. 11, 1933. Morgan wrote back on Feb. 1, 1933: "We did not look upon this as a friendly act." Morgan appears to have believed that Trippe intended to start a Mani-

la–Hong Kong line, and another line up the Chinese coast to Japan. "We are placed in a position of having no alternative except resistance in every way possible to your attempt to exploit this territory." The letter was addressed "Dear Mr. Trippe," although Trippe's letters to Morgan at this time are addressed "Dear Tom." On Feb. 7 Trippe sent Morgan an extremely conciliatory letter apologizing for any misunderstanding. Morgan would later serve on Pan Am's board of directors, and would become embroiled in Sonny Whitney's ouster of Trippe in 1939–40. On Feb. 20 Trippe wrote to Robert Payne, of Dillon, Reid and Company, setting out the terms of Pan Am's purchase of CNAC, and on March 28, 1933, Trippe's board of directors (of Aviation Corporation of the Americas) ratified the agreement with Intercontinent Aviation Inc. and North American Aviation Inc. (the Curtiss-Wright subsidiaries) whereby Pan Am bought 50,000 shares of CNAC. The price was 3,000 shares of Pan Am stock, plus an option to purchase 10,000 shares of Pan Am at $25 before March 31, 1935.

Bixby's inspection tour: Letter from Bixby to S. W. Morgan, Oct. 17, 1934. Morgan was president of Pacific American Airways, the Pan Am subsidiary holding jurisdiction at that time over CNAC. Bixby sets out all of the problems and equipment shortages, and Morgan replied, on Dec. 14, that Pan Am radio equipment could not be installed in planes purchased for and operated by CNAC because of the patent agreement under which this equipment was manufactured. At the same time, according to Morgan, Leuteritz had no confidence in any other radio system. Bixby also describes his feelings upon reaching China in his unpublished autobiography, "Top Side Ricksha," including the comment that a man riding a Loening had to tie his hat on when aloft even with the windows closed.

Bixby's trip to Chengtu: He describes it in "Top Side Ricksha," and Allison gives his version in *Wings Over Asia,* Vol. I, beginning on p. 40.

The Grooch expedition: Grooch describes it in his *Winged Highway,* pp. 168 ff.

The Canton postmaster: In "Top Side Ricksha," Bixby describes him as an Englishman.

No cumshaw paid: Trippe to author, May 16, 1979. He had discussed this subject in previous interviews, and usually his pride was obvious. Now he explained that he knew about cumshaw before sending Bixby there, and had in fact provided him with a letter—his formal orders, so to speak—to be shown to Chinese authorities if necessary. The point of this letter was that Bixby simply had no discretion on the subject. A single exchange of letters between Bixby and Trippe, each letter taking about a month in transit, then followed.

Rummel crashes: Grooch describes this crash in his *Winged Highway*, pp. 207–14.

Conditions worsen: Grooch, pp. 214–42. Nowhere, however, does Grooch mention his personal tragedy.

Bixby waits to see Trippe: Grooch, p. 243.

18 · *Europe via Greenland*

Trippe buys Iceland rights: CAB docket No. 855 et al.—"History of the Transatlantic Air Services," Exhibit No. PA 2. In March 1932 the Icelandic parliament passed a law authorizing the grant of a 75-year landing concession to Trans-American Airlines Corporation, a predecessor company of American Airlines. In July 1932, having earlier purchased an option for $5,000, Pan American acquired the concession at an additional cost of $50,000. This same docket describes the two scientific expeditions to Greenland. The house organ, *Pan American Air Ways*, also describes the expeditions in the July–Aug. 1933 issue.

Lindbergh's claim: He made this a number of times over the years. For instance, Leary quotes him in *The Dragon's Wings*, p. 72. In a letter to Langewiesche dated Nov. 19, 1967, he insisted that he always paid his own expenses. But he was also willing to admit that since he was a consultant to Pan Am, all data that he collected was inevitably made available to Pan Am.

Lindbergh's flight to Greenland and beyond: The description of this flight which follows has been put together from a number of sources. CAB docket No. 855 describes in some detail the function of the *Jelling*; Anne Lindbergh's long *National Geographic* article, dated Sept. 1934, describes the actual overflying of Greenland; her book *Listen! the Wind* concentrates on the latter part of the flight, from the Cape Verde Is-

lands home; and Lindbergh's report to Pan American entitled "Greenland–Iceland Transatlantic Route," dated May 1934, is a technical study of the feasibility of the route. Finally, the house organ, *Pan American Air Ways*, for Jan.–Feb. 1934, gives a long account of the entire flight under the headline "Flying Couple Back After Visit to Four Continents, 31 Countries."

19 · *The Long-Range DF*

Leuteritz and the adcock: The author discussed this work with Leuteritz on June 16 and Sept. 22, 1978, and Leuteritz elaborated on it in letters dated June 27 and Sept. 18, 1978.

Trippe gives Leuteritz money: Trippe to author, Aug. 30, 1976. He said he had given Leuteritz a million dollars in all for radio navigation research—"One million is what it cost; we had to have it."

Trippe fails to ask for progress reports: Trippe to author, May 16, 1979. He claimed it was not so much faith in Leuteritz as faith that some method or other of navigation could be found "if men would just take their coats off." At worst, his planes could fall back on celestial navigation. Trippe at this time did not know how difficult, and also how unreliable, celestial navigation aloft would prove to be.

Leuteritz paces off the ground: He said this was a potato farm, and the farmer was chiefly worried about whether radio waves striking the adcock posts would damage his potatoes.

20 · *A Switch to the Pacific*

Tripartite agreement falls apart: Aéropostale went bankrupt in 1931, and the government withdrew its subsidy. The remnants of the company became part of Air France when it was formed on Aug. 30, 1933. See Trippe's letter to Woods-Humphery, Sept. 19, 1931.

Winslow's cable: It was dated April 6,

1932. His negotiations in Newfoundland were described in great detail by Trippe to the Interdepartmental Committee Dec. 2, 1935, (the minutes are among the Walton Moore papers, Box 2, 1935, F.D.R. Library, Hyde Park) and are described also in a document entitled "History of Transatlantic Air Services," by George Wardman, dated Sept. 15, 1944, and found in PAF 30.10.06. Wardman, then a Pan Am employee, wrote it for use in various routes cases of the 1940's, but in a letter acknowledging his authorship wondered if it was ever used at all. Newfoundland negotiations were also described to the author by Trippe on June 21, 1978, and June 4, 1979. Newfoundland became a crown colony on Feb. 16, 1934.

Winslow's death: He resigned from Pan Am on July 11, 1932, but rejoined the company the following year. He was the first American pilot to shoot down a German plane in World War I, and he had lost his left arm and been taken prisoner when he was shot down in his turn. His wife had died on Feb. 26, 1932; they had three small sons. He was in Ottawa on behalf of Pan Am when, on Aug. 16, 1933, he tumbled from his third-floor hotel-room window, apparently a suicide.

Pacific-Alaska Airways: The company had now operated throughout an entire winter. Temperatures 40 to 70 degrees below zero had been registered. In cold so intense, no mechanic could work more than thirty seconds with bare hands, and men wore scarves over their mouths to protect their lungs. Engines were kept running between flights lest they freeze up solid and stop. Planes took off and landed on skis that could not be steered straight when taxiing. When new skis were designed in cast aluminum, they broke like glass. High alloy steel skis mounted on hydraulic shock absorbers worked better: when central ridges were extended partly back along the ski, they could even be steered on the ice. However, they still could not be braked, and a pilot, setting down, had no notion how far his plane might skid before it stopped because temperature, humidity and the reflection of the sun caused the ice surface to vary widely. The skis of parked planes tended to freeze solid to the ice. Men were forced to attach oil-soaked rags under each ski each time a plane was made to stand motionless for any time at all. In addition, massive heaters had to be invented, heaters for carburetors lest they ice up in flight and cause engine failure, heaters for cabins lest passengers arrive at their destination frozen stiff. With summer, conditions changed violently, but remained almost as uncomfortable. Temperatures rose above 80 degrees and brought swarms of mosquitoes, which could not be kept out of the planes. Air crews took to wearing gloves and protective face netting even in flight.

Amtorg agreement canceled: Trippe to author, April 5, 1978, June 21, 1978, May 16, 1979.

Trippe decides overnight to cross the Pacific: Trippe to author, June 21, 28, 1978. After Newfoundland became a crown colony, there had been a long telephone call between Trippe and Eric Geddes, who was chairman of Imperial. The connection was bad. The two men were shouting at each other to be heard. But there was nothing Geddes could do to countermand his government's decisions, and to help Trippe. "We had to go down the next morning with a plan of what to do," Trippe told the author. "The day after that the program for the Pacific went into high gear. The Pacific could be done. It was not as good economically for our company, or the U.S., or the world." Then he added, "This is a difficult world that we live in, isn't it?"

The budget study: Signed by Schildhauer, it was dated Sept. 24, 1934, and counted aviation gasoline at 20 cents a gallon, assigned a four-year obsolescence factor to each plane, and established a "crash reserve" of one-half plane per year. Crew salaries, according to the budget, were these: master pilot, $650 per month; first officer, $500; second officer, $400; third officer, $300. Sixteen mechanics would be needed at the San Francisco base and these would cost a total of $2,975 per month. A Pan Am secretary that year got paid $120 per month.

Schildhauer to Washington: Schildhauer to author, June 15, 1978.

Letters between State and Navy: Trippe wrote the Secretary of the Navy, Oct. 3, 1934, requesting a five-year lease on Wake Island with rights to renew for four additional five-year periods. On Dec. 29, 1934, Executive Order No. 6935 placed Wake under the control and jurisdiction of the Navy Department.

21 · The Public Decision

The S-42 conferences: Trippe to author during the May 1977 interviews; notes of conversation between Lindbergh and Sikorsky in March 1959, PAF 30.07.10.

Exchange of letters with Farley: Trippe's was dated Oct. 10, 1934, and Farley's Oct. 12.

Trippe to the West Coast: Trippe was corresponding with men such as J. L. Maddux of Inglewood, Calif., asking which men of influence he should meet with on the West Coast. On Aug. 1 Maddux wrote him suggesting five men in Los Angeles, four in San Francisco, one in Seattle and eight in Honolulu. The roster ends: "All of the men that are listed above are extremely wealthy and no doubt would be interested in the proposed line. I believe that these men are the keystones to the business of the islands, and that a careful selection among them should give us substantial support." Among the men named by Maddux are Alexander, Roth, Norman Chandler of the Los Angeles *Times*, Jim Dole of the pineapple Doles and Earl Thacker of the Hawaiian Trust Company. PAF 10.10.00 contains a memorandum of a meeting between Trippe, Alexander, Roth and Sutro on Nov. 19, 1934, including details of Trippe's stock offering to "the Hawaiian group."

Schildhauer to Midway: Schildhauer to author, June 15, 1978; letter from Kennedy to Trippe, Dec. 3, 1934, in which Kennedy adds a handwritten postscript to the effect that Schildhauer "called early this morning with your letter." A second letter from Kennedy to Trippe on Dec. 12 notes that Schildhauer departed for Midway "last evening."

Kennedy's hostility: Letter from Norman Chandler to Trippe, Dec. 22, 1934, noting that Kennedy "told me that he was meeting with you in Washington and that it did not look as though Pan American and Inter-Island would ever get together . . . he appeared to be quite perturbed about the whole situation and felt badly that Pan American had 'stolen his thunder.' He urged me not to tie in with Pan American in any way."

Schildhauer's findings: Schildhauer to author, June 15, 1978. The Honolulu *Star Bulletin* for Dec. 22, 1934, reports that Schildhauer had arrived back in Honolulu aboard the *Dickinson*.

Photos of Wake: The order from Navy Secretary Claude Swanson to the *Nitro* did not go out until early 1935.

22 · Practice Flights

Odell organizes expedition: The details are from a memo dated March 1, 1938, from Odell to P. E. D. Nagle on the subject of the Pacific expedition record. Nagle was a Pan Am executive in Washington. Odell's memo concluded: "I camped out in San Francisco supervising the ship loading and all installations by radio, from March 11 to July 19 when I returned to New York with the job completed, all construction forces being aboard ship homeward bound."

Description of the compound: Letter from Trippe to the director of naval intelligence, March 18, 1935; drawings of the proposed structures were attached.

Vague romantic longings: From Leslie's address to Phillips Exeter Academy assembly, Nov. 6, 1972: "Looking up at the steep black sides of that vessel in the foggy San Francisco night and realizing the indispensable part that it had to play in our forthcoming adventure, gave me a feeling of awe and a shiver of anticipation." The *North Haven*'s cargo is listed in CAB docket No. 851 et al., "History of the Transpacific Air Services to and through Hawaii," Aug. 12, 1944, Exhibit PA-2.

College boys hired: Among the laborers hired were recent M.I.T. graduates John Borger for Wake and Bill Taylor for Midway.

Trippe seeks Navy jurisdiction: Letter from Trippe to John Goldhammer, Commercial Pacific Cable Company, Jan. 11, 1935, asking the cable company to "join us in prevailing upon the government to undertake such a project"—the dredging of a channel into the Midway lagoon. The presidential order had been signed on Dec. 29, 1934. Trippe's contract with the Navy for Wake Island was dated March 12, 1935. Trippe apparently signed this contract on March 6, and Secretary Swanson six days later. Separate contracts were signed by both men for Midway and Guam at the same time.

The revised budget: It was dated March 1935 and covered 8,070 miles between San Francisco and Manila.

The competition: A letter from Secretary Swanson dated Nov. 23, 1934, informed Trippe that "another company" had requested permits and leases for the same islands that would permit "any commercial United States airline to use them for a given rental." Therefore the Navy Department favored this other company's request, rather than Pan Am's. The company in question was South Seas Commercial. Kennedy's plans were formally announced on March 15, 1935, eleven days after passage of the bill allocating $2 million for transpacific airmail. On March 23 Trippe wrote William Castle, Jr., in Washington that he was on his way to San Francisco to meet Kennedy to settle the misunderstanding.

No longer the public's darling: Ex–Postmaster General Brown's letter of July 7, 1931, to Eastern Air Transport had been printed in *The New York Times* of Feb. 15, 1934, as part of the Black Investigation revelations. It read in part: "I have stated frankly to the air mail operators that in the present state of the industry it did not seem the part of wisdom to invade each other's territory with competitive services, and that I did not believe that money paid for postal services should be used to set up services to injure competitors. In pursuance of this policy I suggested the abandonment by the Pan American Company in the domestic field in the United States . . . their field is the international service . . . consistently with this policy outlined, it would seem improper for any of our domestic operators to use mail pay to invade the particular field of the Pan American Company." In addition to Brown's letter, the *Times* printed testimony indicating that Brown consistently favored airlines with the strongest financial backing, using Post Office pressure to force mergers or to restrict certain airlines to particular areas, forcing the least solvent companies out of business or into marginal areas.

The range-stretched S-42: Crewman Harry Canaday mentioned the figure 4,500 pounds of fuel in cabin tanks in a tape-recorded conversation with Leslie on Dec. 9, 1974. Leslie, division engineer in the Pacific at the time, agreed with this figure. Schildhauer's original budget noted that the S-42 would consume 1,083 pounds of fuel per hour at 150 mph. This was, of course, an estimate. It would mean that range had been extended by four hours, not three, but as a commercial proposition a 25 percent reserve had to be included.

The Miami tests: Leslie to author, Aug. 24, 1978. Wright also describes the range stretching in "Early Bird," the unpublished manuscript he wrote with Richard Thruelsen, and he adds a good account of the Caribbean test flight.

Noonan: He left Pan American in 1937, and signed on as navigator for Amelia Earhart, who planned to fly around the world. The plane disappeared July 2, 1937, near Howland Island in the mid-Pacific. Numerous biographical sketches of Noonan appeared in the public press the next day. Both his personality and his methods as navigator were described in Canaday's conversation with Leslie, Dec. 9, 1974. Grooch also describes him in his *From Crate to Clipper*, beginning on p. 158: so does Wright's "Early Bird," pp. 48 ff. All these were men who flew with Noonan. The Acapulco anecdote is by Canaday: "You never ran into Musick but that he would say, have you seen Fred? Or, if there were a group of us sitting around, he would walk up: Has anybody seen Fred? You could just be absolutely certain that that was going to be the greeting. He was always concerned whether Fred would make it, you know. It was a variable." Grooch also mentions the Acapulco incident.

West Coast reception and continued training flights: From *Crate to Clipper* pp. 160 ff.

23 · To Hawaii Nonstop

Voyage of the *North Haven:* The expedition was headed by Grooch, whose book about it, *Skyway to Asia,* was published the next year. This was Grooch's last major assignment. He left the company intending to start an airline of his own in Mexico, and was killed in a crash there. His account of the colonization of Midway and Wake is the longest, but by no means the only one extant. The house organ *Pan American Air Ways* published a kind of running story with each issue. *Fortune* magazine for April 1936 gave a long account. Mullahey's arrival aboard ship was described by Kuhn in an interview (see PAF 30.10.08) in July 1958 and the quote is Kuhn's.

Musick's training flights, Musick studies navigation: Grooch, *From Crate to Clipper.*

Two directors resign: Betty Trippe notes this in her diary the following year as she and her husband started their trip around the world. One who resigned was Grover Loening. Since a number of directors came and went during that period, the name of the other could not be ascertained.

Dr. Lewis's offer: Trippe to author, May 16, 1979. He said that Lewis had "come to me as a friend." Trippe maintained the illusion of friendship to the end, thanking Dr. Lewis for his concern, treating the offer as if it had come from a friend rather than from a prestigious aviation official.

"Are you sure of your DF?": Leuteritz to author, June 16, 1978.

First flight to Honolulu: Wright, "Early Bird," pp. 61 ff.

Wind-driven fuel pump breaks: Canaday to Leslie, Dec. 9, 1974.

Flight back: Wright, "Early Bird," pp. 65 ff.; Grooch, *From Crate to Clipper*, pp. 170 ff.; Canaday to Leslie, Dec. 9, 1974. Both Wright and Canaday noted that the tanks were almost dry.

24 · Wake

Colonizing Wake: Grooch, *Skyway to Asia;* notes of interview with George Kuhn, July 1958; *Fortune* magazine, April 1936; assorted articles in the house organ, *Pan American Air Ways,* May, June, July, Aug. 1935; additional details can be found in Bicknell's letters to Leslie between Aug. 23 and Dec. 7, 1935. A number of the men who were boys on Wake Island attained high rank within the company. John Borger, a twenty-one-year-old M.I.T. graduate, later became vice president and chief engineer. Mullahey became director of the Central and South Pacific.

Howard's letter to Thacker, and Thacker's to Howard: Copies can be found in PAF 10.10.00.

Details occupy Trippe: The specifications and drawings of the atolls' structures were attached to a memo from Odell to Trippe dated July 22, 1935. Trippe's letter to the Secretary of the Navy was dated Oct. 22, 1935.

Sullivan's flight to Midway and Wake: An account appeared under Sullivan's by-line in *Pan American Air Ways,* July–Aug. 1935.

His landing: Canaday to Leslie, Dec. 9, 1974. He was comparing Musick with Sullivan—"unlike Rod Sullivan who manhandled the airplane—threw it around. He could do a good job but it was kind of uncomfortable the way he did it sometimes. But Musick was just as smooth as could be." On Aug. 29, 1972, Jack Tilton, a former Pan Am captain, told Ione Wright, wife of Vic Wright, in a tape-recorded conversation, of the first Wake landing. Tilton made only two trips with Sullivan, the first into Wake and the first into Guam. As for Wake: "Sully made our first landing, and just got stopped in time." The first scheduled Guam flight left San Francisco on Oct. 5 and reached Guam on Oct. 13, 1935.

25 · The China Clipper

The Martin flying boat commissioned: The acceptance ceremony and flight tests carrying political celebrities are described in news reports in the Baltimore *Sun* and *The New York Times* of Oct. 10, 1935.

Priester's methods: Kauffman to author, July 11, 1978. Van Dusen told Leslie in their Oct. 24, 1972, tape-recorded conversation that the multiple-crew idea was Priester's. Trippe was against it on the grounds of cost —too many people, too expensive. Priester went to Van Dusen, who went to *The New York Times* and got his friend Reg Cleveland to do an editorial praising the idea. The next morning Trippe called Van Dusen into his office and said, "That's my idea, I've been thinking of that for a long time."

"Thrill of danger": San Francisco *Chronicle,* Nov. 12. 1935.

Publicity bothers Musick: Grooch, *From Crate to Clipper,* p. 189.

Musick profile: Grooch, *From Crate to Clipper; Time* magazine cover story, Dec. 2, 1935; *New Horizons,* March 1944; *The New York Times,* Jan. 14, 1938. *The Real McCoy,* by Frederick F. Van de Water, deals with a major bootlegger from prohibition days. One of the photographs shows a man, who appears to be Musick, standing in the nose of a flying boat, and the text mentions that one of the pilots "called himself Music—we never knew his real name."

The takeoff and flight of the *China Clipper:* From the Nov. 23 edition of the San

Francisco *Chronicle, Examiner* and *News.* The official transcript of the ceremony was printed up by Van Dusen's office as a sort of magazine and was widely distributed at the time. The same publication includes the log of the *China Clipper.*

Japanese resentment: See papers relating to "The Foreign Relations of the United States and Japan, 1931–41," Department of State, Washington D.C., 1943, I, 253.

The attempted sabotage: Trippe to author, April 5, 1978; May 16, 1979. The attempted sabotage is mentioned also by Josephson, *Empire of the Air,* p. 123.

Wright ducks: From Vic Wright's report, *Flight Ops* (a Pan American publication), No. 6, Feb. 1975. "It had been our intention to fly over the bridge, but Musick quickly saw that with the engine cowl flaps open he wouldn't be able to get up enough speed to clear the wires, so he nosed the Clipper down at the last moment and went under the bridge cables, threading his way through the dangling construction wire. We all ducked and held our breaths until we were in the clear. I think the little planes must have been as surprised as we were, but they all followed us right through." The reference to Leslie's prematurely white hair is from his partially completed ms.

Van Dusen and the reporters: Van Dusen to Leslie, Oct. 24, 1972, a tape-recorded conversation. He also described how he wrote by-line stories for everybody on that crew, seven different stories per night.

26 · Life on the Atolls

Bicknell's account: From a series of letters he wrote to Leslie between Aug. 23 and Dec. 7, 1935. The first of these was the "Isle of Capri" letter, and the second, dated Sept. 6, was written from "The Island of Lost Souls." Many of these letters praised Mullahey and the Nov. 7 letter noted that the young man was paid only $100 a month. The Dec. 7 letter described how Bicknell was loading the Clippers without benefit of a scale, and also how the Secretary of War came ashore in a launch from a warship.

Life on Midway: From notes of PAF 30.-10.08 interview with Bill Newport, July 1958.

Musick aborts: The reports are in PAF 10.10.00, No. 2.

Priester and Montieth: Kauffman to author, July 11, 1978. Kauffman was aboard, and swears both that Monteith swallowed his cigar and that his footprints were on the ceiling. As for the typhoon itself, it had struck without warning because it had originated, as most typhoons did, in the Japanese mandated islands in the Southwest Pacific. Japanese weather service had developed a good reporting network and for some years weather data had gone out regularly from radio stations in the Bonin, Mariana, Caroline and Marshall Islands. But shortly after the Pan American transpacific flights began, the Japanese ceased broadcasting weather data in clear international code. The degree of resentment which the Japanese felt for all things American during the thirties cannot be exaggerated, and, of course, it led to the bombing of Pearl Harbor and to U.S. participation in World War II. In the early months of 1936 their weather reports continued to be broadcast regularly from their South Pacific bases, but in a code that was unintelligible to meteorologists. There was no purpose to this new code except to deny weather data to the hated Americans. It was Leuteritz, according to a June 16, 1978, interview with the author, who went to naval intelligence for help; presently John Cooke, an expert radioman trained by the Navy not only in meteorology but also in cryptography and in the Japanese language, was sent to Guam as Pan American's radio operator in charge. To everyone but Cooke the new Japanese weather code sounded like gibberish. "But I had recalled from my language training in Japanese," he noted later, "that occasionally, instead of one, meaning one tenth of the sky was covered with clouds, they would use the character 'ichi' which meant one. For the number two, meaning that two tenths of the sky was covered, they would use 'ni.' Once I got these things correlated to the right numbers it took about a week of days and nights trying to put the weather together with the Japanese characters, but we finally resolved it and started transmitting the weather reports from all these islands back into the small international numbers to our headquarters in Alameda and Honolulu." A vast area on the weather map of the world, which had gone blank, was blank no longer. The Japanese began to change the frequencies and hours of their transmissions, but this presented no great obstacle to Cooke, because at the end of each transmission they would indicate in code what the next one would be. When the day came when Cooke transferred back to the mainland, he successfully taught his techniques to his successors.

The *North Haven*'s second voyage to the atolls: Notes of interview with Kuhn, July 1958, PAF 30.10.08.

27 · *Trippe around the World*

Crowds stare at flying boats: Leslie to Canaday, a tape-recorded conversation, Dec. 9, 1974.

Hawaii Clipper christened: The house organ, *Pan American Air Ways*, for May–June 1936 gives a long account of the arrival of the *Hawaii Clipper* in Honolulu.

Trippe's Hong Kong strategy: *Macao Travel Talk*, Oct. 1977, reprinted translated excerpts from the *Voz de Macao*, the first dating from Sept. 6, 1935, and the last from April 28, 1941. It is clear from these excerpts, which cover more than two complete pages and describe not only the opening of a Pan Am office in Macao but every other detail designed to worry Hong Kong businessmen, exactly what Trippe's strategy was. For instance, the Sept. 7, 1935, *Voz de Macao* reported that Pan American was speeding up its preparations for the San Francisco–Honolulu–Manila–China service, and "the Hong Kong newspaper was not happy with Macao's selection as the company's terminal, claiming that Hong Kong should have been chosen as it could offer greater advantages and better facilities." Thereafter preparations in the harbor were described, as was the arrival of the flying boat that carried Trippe, his wife and the publishers the following fall. The *Voz de Macao* for Oct. 26, 1936, reported that "Captain J. T. Trippe, who flew the clipper to Macao, sent a message to the governor thanking him for 'the cordial reception and delightful tiffin.'" On Dec. 8 the *South China Morning Post* in Hong Kong reported the signing of a contract in Lisbon between the Portuguese government and Pan American for Macao to be the terminus of "this colossal and important American airline company," adding that "CNAC would soon link Macao to the internal Chinese air net-

work." The following April 6 the *Voz* printed a wire service report out of San Francisco saying that Macao was considered the best place in South China for Pan American's new air base with Hong Kong as an intermediary port. Bond, in a letter to Leslie dated Jan. 6, 1975, wrote: "It was never a question of Hong Kong not granting permission to Pan Am to land, Pan Am had never requested it of Hong Kong. A request may have been made in London but I never heard of it. I am sure Bix [Bixby] never requested it because it was essential that CNAC be there to meet Pan Am for the onward flight of passengers and mail to all parts of China." Bond also described an interview he gave to a British journalist who wanted to know what was wrong with Pan Am, and why Pan Am had "not applied for entrance to Hong Kong, the talk of Macao was incomprehensible." The day after this report was published, the British Consul General came to see Bond and asked the same questions.

Trippe takes publishers across the Pacific: There are two long accounts of this flight, one of them Betty Trippe's diary, nearly 100 pages in length, which she made available to the author; and the other a reprint of a three-installment article in the *Nashville Banner* magazine entitled "Wings Over the Orient" by James G. Stahlman, the paper's publisher. The articles appeared in the fall of 1935 and were reprinted in booklet form and distributed by Stahlman to his friends the following year. One point should be added to any description of the trip. After leaving each place, Betty Trippe invariably sat down in her seat aboard the plane and wrote thank-you notes to each and every person who had extended hospitality at the previous stop.

Bixby reorganizes CNAC: PAF 10.05.00 contains the minutes of the sixth annual meeting of the stockholders of China National Aviation Corporation in Shanghai, Sept. 7, 1935. There were five Chinese present, and five Americans. The company now had eleven planes, and had flown 5,516 passengers a total of 2.9 million kilometers the year before.

Trippes visit Lindberghs: Anne Lindbergh to author, March 12, 1978. There is no question that the Lindberghs were eager to see the Trippes, for they had trained their son Jon, then five years old, to look up at the sky anytime a plane flew overhead, and to remark for Trippe's benefit: "There goes one of those big, slow Imperial Airways planes." When Anne Lindbergh added that "the Trippes were not close friends," she was trying to describe something else: "Trippe did the right things, but he was not suave, he was very closed in, shy; Betty made up for his lack of closeness."

28 · New Zealand

Trippe's talks in London: Betty Trippe's diary alludes to them, but does not indicate that he ever explained to her what his exact problems were. But his negotiations for landing rights in New Zealand and Australia were part of his attempts to cross the Atlantic at the same time, as will be seen in the text and notes for Part III, "The Atlantic."

Trippe's strategy: Trippe to author, June 21, 1978; May 16, 1979. Trippe's version is supported by the Leslie ms, in the chapter entitled "Transpacific," pp. 33 ff.; and by letters from Trippe to Gatty, PAF 10.10.00, which are concerned not only with Gatty's negotiations in New Zealand, but with his selection of Pago Pago as the interim stop. Kingman Reef had been chosen before Oct. 28, 1935, the date of Trippe's letter to the Secretary of the Navy requesting permission to use it, and describing it.

The Imperial Air Conference: It ran through the closing days of Sept. 1936. Probably Australia could have been broken off from London also, but in later negotiations with Trippe's envoys it demanded reciprocal landing rights in Honolulu and California, rights that were beyond Trippe's powers to concede. The agreement eventually struck with New Zealand provided only that should a New Zealand airline ever request such landing concessions and be denied them, then the New Zealand government could cancel Pan American's permits if it chose to do so.

Trippe loses interest in the Pacific: The first memo quoted was from Leslie to Pacific Division manager Clarence Young, and it was dated Feb. 12, 1936. Leslie's request for information on a fourth airplane was dated Jan. 4, 1936. There were many other letters and memos back and forth in a similar vein, principally exchanges between Kauffman and McVitty, working for Priester in New York and Leslie in California. All were

marked "Personal," some were handwritten, and one from Kauffman was not only handwritten but on Yale Club stationery. Schildhauer's statement that "we have got to have more personnel" was included in a memo dated Dec. 4, 1936. Leslie's Jan. 4, 1936, memo to Young was not sent, and a carbon in Leslie's personal file bears the note in his handwriting: "All copies given to division manager, with suggestion he forward one to chief engineer personally, to be destroyed later."

Survey flight to New Zealand: Wright's "Early Bird" describes in detail how the cabin filled up with the odor of raw gas. Canaday mentions this also in his Dec. 9, 1974, tape-recorded conversation with Leslie. The official company version of this flight and those that followed it was published at great length in *Pan American Air Ways* the following month; the odor of raw gas was not mentioned, nor was Musick's string of curse words when he first saw Pago Pago. This version pretends to be a composite crew's log. A copy exists in PAF 10.10.00.

Fatt in Florida: Notes of interview with Fatt, Aug. 26, 1957, PAF 30.10.08. The Department of Commerce's order was dated Oct. 9, 1937.

Musick's meticulousness: His way of loaning cigarettes was described by Canaday to Leslie, Dec. 9, 1974; his habit of wiping off seat, yoke, throttles, and adjusting the crease of his trousers was described by flight mechanic John Donahue (see PAF 30.-10.08) in June 1957; Donahue had been flying with Musick since 1927.

The search: *The New York Times*, Jan. 13, 1938, 5:2. The *Times'* explanation of the crash appeared the following day, and it was this article that included a listing of the items found on the sea by the *Avocet*.

The memorials: The program that accompanied the memorial service in San Francisco also included an account of the service at sea by the captain of the *Matua*.

Canton Island: Like Wake, no one knew who owned Canton, nor, in the past, had anyone cared. Trippe found an obscure law relating to guano collectors. Guano—bird droppings—made good fertilizer, and to gather same, American captains had stopped at Canton from time to time in the past—which seemed by American law sufficient to prove American sovereignty over the uninhabited island. Trippe himself now formed a guano company; he called it Oceanic Nitrates Inc., and installed S. D. Robins, an old friend, as president. Keeping his personal ownership clandestine, he sent an expedition of radio and aviation technicians to Canton disguised as guano collectors. Learning of this, the British got to Canton in a warship almost simultaneously and claimed the island for the crown. At Trippe's request the U.S. Navy was called upon to defend the sacred right of Americans to gather guano on Canton. An American warship turned up; the two warships stood each other off. Eventually the minuscule sandbank of an island was partitioned. The British kept a "post office" at one end, and Pan American built a flying-boat base at the other.

Loening's telegram: It was dated Jan. 13, 1938, the day Musick's flying boat went down.

The *Hawaii Clipper:* It went down July 28. Priester wrote a report Aug. 2, 1938, stating that the flight as far as Guam, and even beyond, had been normal in every respect. The plane had been fueled for 2,600 miles, Guam being 1,589 miles from Manila. Position reports were received every thirty minutes in accordance with standard procedure until two o'clock in the afternoon Guam time. When contact with the Clipper could not be resumed, "an attempt was made to use the direction finder, but no signal could be heard from the aircraft," according to Priester. The last position of the aircraft was approximately 565 miles from Manila and about 300 miles east of the nearest island of the Philippines. Five long-range Army bombers, thirteen Navy vessels and two amphibians immediately joined the search. The U.S.S. *Meigs* did report finding a gasoline and oil stain on the water about 50 miles from the last reported position of the aircraft, but a laboratory examination failed to prove conclusively that the sample had come from the plane. No other wreckage was ever found. The captain of the *Hawaii Clipper* was Leo Terletzky.

The rumors: Trippe repeated them to the author at least three times, and at one time or another noted all of the details presented in the text. The dates of the interviews in which he returned to this subject were June 21 and 27, 1978, and May 16, 1979. He said that he had the story originally from Admiral J. T. Towers who joined Pan Am as a vice president after World War II. Every Japanese Zero examined by U.S. technicians during and after the war bore

the same serial number on their magnetos—the same serial number as the magneto on one of the engines of the *Hawaii Clipper,* said Tower to Trippe, according to Trippe. On Aug. 26, 1970, he told the story to a man named Harvey Katz, who made a memo of the conversation; this memo is to be found in PAF 10.10.00; and he also told it to Langewiesche in 1957.

Cork in the fuel line: Letter from Leslie to Ione Wright, Feb. 13, 1974.

The losses: *The New York Times* reported Oct. 11, 1938, 37:4, that Pan Am, applying to the CAB for "fair and reasonable rates for carrying air mail," had disclosed that it had been operating at tremendous losses from the beginning. Losses on the San Francisco-Hong Kong route were $474,858 for the first full year of operations and $373,523 for the first six months of 1938."

Part III
THE ATLANTIC
29 · The Obstacles

Atlantic cost: The $4 million figure was the cost of the first six Boeings at $668,000 each. The $1.5 million in out-of-pocket expenses was mentioned frequently in company publicity, and was listed in many of the documents. See "History of Transatlantic Air Services," dated Sept. 15, 1944, prepared by George Wardman for use in hearings before Congress and regulatory agencies—PAF 30.10.06.

Early history of Imperial: *The Water Jump,* by David Beaty, contains much British archival material dating from the early thirties. See also *A History of the World's Airlines,* by R. E. G. Davies; *The Seven Skies,* by John Pudney; and PAF 40.03.00.

Subsidies of foreign airlines: *Foreign Affairs,* April 1938, an article entitled "Atlantic Airways," by Edward P. Warner.

Planes engaged in regular air transport: From a letter written by Sir Eric Geddes to the *Daily Mail* in 1932 (Beaty, p. 109).

Trippe kept Woods-Humphery informed: Trippe to Woods-Humphery, Sept. 22, 1931. He gives specifications on the new Sikorsky S-40. The American aviation journals reported early that the S-42 would have a range of 2,500 miles and a payload of about 800 pounds. Major Robert Mayo believed that these figures were ridiculous, that a 1,200-mile range and a 400-pound payload was more like it (Beaty, p. 112).

Negotiations broken off: As described in Chapter 20, Trippe had been forced to turn to the Pacific. Geddes and Woods-Humphery were no longer in charge in London. Banks and Shelmerdine had begun making the major decisions. They decided to push the Short-Mayo composite in a meeting at the Air Ministry in London on Feb. 13, 1935. Only after the S-42 had made it to Hawaii did Shelmerdine promise £10,000 toward the design of three transatlantic flying boats. The twenty-eight Empire boats that had already been ordered were for use principally on the rest of the "all-red route."

Atlantic Company agreement: It was signed in Montreal on Dec. 2, 1935, the same day that Trippe appeared before the Interdepartmental Committee; he gave the history of his negotiations with the British in advance of their arrival in Washington. Summaries of the committee meetings, marked "Confidential" and stamped with Moore's seal, exist in the Walton Moore Papers (F.D.R. Library, Hyde Park), Box 2: "Interdepartmental Committee on International Civil Aviation 1935." The State Department press release of Dec. 4, 1935, read: "The Interdepartmental Committee has requested any American Airline Company that desires a hearing to communicate with its executive secretary." The British feelings about Trippe and Pan Am were explained in a letter from Imperial to Pan Am dated March 10, 1936.

Protests from France, Germany, Rickenbacker and others: Beaty, p. 97.

Lest "the whole thing get into a mess": From Woods-Humphery's summary of a telephone conversation with Trippe, PAF 40.-03.00. See also the Wardman document, and CAB docket No. 855, "History of the Transatlantic Services," an exhibit 49 printed pages long.

Post Office warns Trippe: The last page or pages of this document are missing. There is therefore no signature. See PAF 10.04.00.

Trippe's negotiations with Baltimore: The Baltimore Sun, Nov. 5, 1936. Glenn L. Martin, whose flying-boat factory was nearby, is quoted as saying that Baltimore now faces a golden opportunity of becoming a world airport.

Trippe's worried phone calls: Woods-Humphery's summaries are in PAF 40.03.-00. The British and Canadian permits had been signed, but Trippe still couldn't move without permits for Bermuda and Ireland.

Preparation of bases: On Feb. 7, 1937, Van Dusen began the practice of sending out letters nearly every week to a selected press mailing list. These became known as "Dear Senor" letters, for that's how most of them began, but occasionally Van Dusen changed his tempo by starting out with "Dear Monsieur." Van Dusen was a brilliant publicity man. The "Dear Senor" letters lasted until July 2, 1947. They are folksy, friendly and full of information. They made writing an article about Pan Am extremely simple. The series of letters that appeared during the spring and summer of 1937 described the construction of the bases in Baltimore, Charleston and LaGuardia, described the purchase and the improving of the company waterfront property in Port Washington, and then went on to describe the other bases all the way across: Foynes, Shediac, Gander. Subsequent letters described what the Pan Am weather and radiomen were doing. Once survey flights across the Atlantic began, Van Dusen described each of them in intimate, fascinating detail, even adding brief profiles of Captain Gray and J. Carroll Cone, the new Atlantic Division manager.

Schildhauer's Azores visit: Wardman's "History of Transatlantic Air Services," PAF 30.10.06. The Schildhauer and Lindbergh reports were also referred to in Trippe's letter to Richard Long, his agent in Portugal, dated July 6, 1934, which read in part: "The company must not be limited as to choice of landing places on any particular island or any islands or the vicinity thereof. The technical questions are difficult and we must be free from time to time to use such territorial waters of the Azores or landing places therein as the development of the service may indicate." Mead's report in the spring of 1938 read in part: "There does not exist in the archipelago a single locality which can be used permanently in all sea conditions. The predominant characteristics of the winter weather in the Azores are inconstancy and changeability. The studies carried out up to now indicate that the most promising areas are those in the vicinity of Fayal with a center in Horta Bay. It has been necessary to formulate plans under which the flying boats will not always use the same locality." Schildhauer's report had located the largest level area of land in the entire Azores that in any manner could be considered as a landing field. It was on the north shore of the island of Terceira. It wasn't long enough, and according to Schildhauer, "the possibilities of enlarging are remote without excess cost due to the lava formation." The two special tenders constructed for use in the Azores are described in CAB docket No. 855, which states also that Pan American was obliged to pay all costs of radio installations both at Horta and at Lisbon, since the Portuguese refused to do it, and after that, had to train Portuguese naval personnel as radio operators.

30 · The First Across

Flight attempts: Van Dusen gives figures for successes and failures over the North Atlantic in "Dear Senor" No. 14, May 17, 1937. Beaty's figures in *The Water Jump*, p. 75, differ slightly from Van Dusen's, and Jablonski's in *Atlantic Fever* differ again. Any figures of this nature must be taken as approximate. Beaty and Jablonski both give excellent accounts of all these flights. The flippant quotes about fliers who failed to make it are from Van Dusen's "Dear Senor" letter of May 17, 1937.

Survey flights to Bermuda and Europe: See CAB docket No. 855; "Dear Senor," July 26, 1937, and the Wardman ms (PAF 30.10.06). The exact elapsed time of the Caledonia in its first crossing from Foynes to Botwood was 15 hours 26 minutes. It was captained by A. S. Wilcockson, whose altitude of course varied. Most of the time he appears to have flown at about 1,000 feet.

Gray's flight: Van Dusen, the perfect PR man, apparently had asked Captain Gray to wire him details of the flight upon reaching the Azores and Lisbon. In any case, such a telegram exists dated Aug. 25, 1937, in PAF 10.04.00.

Trippe's letter to Egypt: Nov. 19, 1937.

Correspondence between Woods-Humphery and Leydon: Beaty, *The Water Jump*, pp. 30–31.

Trippe scoffs: Letter from Trippe to Woods-Humphery, PAF 10.03.00—"It will be interesting to see if this plan is feasible."

The German catapult ships: They were described in the company magazine, *Pan American Air Ways* in the June–July 1937 issue, and photos were printed in the Aug. issue. Details on the German system were widely reported in the press that summer, and again the following summer when the catapult flights resumed. Pan Am studied the system closely, and presumably sent men aboard the catapult ship anchored in Long Island Sound to collect additional data. Van Dusen collected and collated a good deal of this and sent it around to his friends in the press in a five-page summary dated Oct. 27, 1938.

The Merchant Marine Act of 1936: Out of it grew the Maritime Commission, an independent regulatory agency empowered to carry out a program to develop an American merchant marine through government aid. The Act eliminated subsidies in the form of ocean mail contracts, and provided, instead, outright subsidies based on differentials between foreign and domestic operating aid and construction cost. Joseph P. Kennedy, its first chairman, held the job only seventy-five days, but they were busy ones. He worked out a scheme for subsidizing shipping companies to the tune of $25 million a year. He also performed the remarkable job of settling the ship operators' claims against the government. In Dec. 1937 he was appointed ambassador to Great Britain, the first Catholic and the first American of Irish origin to hold this job.

The Maritime Commission surveys: PAF 10.03.00. Though unsigned, they are apparently Loening's work.

The grandfather clause: That summer Trippe bid on the airmail contract for the New York–Bermuda run. Instead of bidding $2 per mile, the maximum bid allowed by law, as he had most often done in Latin America, he bid the ridiculous sum of less than a thousandth of a cent per mile. His sole object was to win the contract before the Civil Aeronautics Act was passed. Once he had the route, the grandfather clause would guarantee it to him virtually in perpetuity. He could always renegotiate better terms later.

Loening's confidential memo: From F.D.R. Library at Hyde Park, President's official file 2875.

The Kennedy-Trippe meeting at Hyannis Port: Betty Trippe describes this in a footnote to her diary of the first passenger flight across the Atlantic to Lisbon in 1939; Trippe described it to the author on a number of occasions, first on Aug. 25, 1976, and most fully on Oct. 2, 1978.

Rumors that Imperial had tied Trippe's hands: They were fed by articles like the one in *The New York Times* on March 21, 1938, which read in part: "While little was said about it at the time, the British learned that their Empire boats, for which so much was claimed, did not have the range for the 1900 mile jump between Newfoundland and Ireland with a payload." The hearings by the House Committee on Merchant Marine and Fisheries took place during March 1938.

Trippe met with American Export officials: Agreement was reached Sept. 28, 1938, but was subsequently disapproved by the CAB under Section 412 of the Act of June 1938.

The conference in Ireland: Author's interview with Leuteritz, June 16, 1978; "Dear Senor" letter, April 1939; CAB docket No. 855. Details on the deicing equipment were given by Van Dusen in the "Dear Senor" letter of March 15, 1938. Visits by Pan Am technicians to Seattle are described in CAB docket No. 855.

31 · The Correct Vehicle

The contract with Boeing: It was signed July 21, 1936. It called for the manufacture of six flying boats, the first to be delivered Dec. 21, 1937, the others to be delivered every two months thereafter. Problems cropped up almost immediately, for a supplemental agreement was signed on Jan. 20, 1937, extending all delivery dates by three months.

Gledhill's letter: This tactic of making manufacturers compete for the contract continued many years. CAB docket No. 855, Appendix B, includes a sample letter from Gledhill. To the author's knowledge, this is the only such letter ever made public. The final clause, about the $50,000 prize, remained virtually unchanged year after year. Trippe's "bag of oats" phrase was one of his favorites and recurred often during author's interviews with him.

Martin's reaction: Kauffman to author, July 11, 1978; Leslie to author, Oct. 17, 1978. Leslie at this time was division engineer in San Francisco, making him the man charged with the smooth functioning of the Martin *China Clipper* and its two sister ships. Martin also wrote a petulant letter to Gledhill dated Jan. 24, 1940, stating that he had deserved better treatment from Pan Am. "Martin refused to take his coat off," said Trippe to author on June 21, 1978; this is another phrase the author heard often during interviews with Trippe; on June 27, 1978, he added that Rentschler had opted for military contracts instead.

Boeing incorporates the B-15: Leslie to author, Oct. 17, 1978; John Borger to author, Sept. 29, 1978. Borger by then was vice president and chief engineer— Priester's old job—but he had started with the company at the age of twenty-two, a newly graduated engineer from M.I.T., as a laborer on Wake Island. A good account of the development and problems of the Boeing-314 appears in *Vision*, a kind of biography of the Boeing Co., by Harold Mansfield, a former Boeing PR man.

Martin's claims against Trippe and Gledhill: Trippe to author May 14, 1977; Kauffman to author July 11, 1978.

The Boeing nearly capsizes: Leslie to author; also in letters to Leslie from Boeing's G. W. Taylor, Aug. 20, 1974; and from Wellwood Beall, Aug. 30, 1974. Beall had been Boeing's project engineer during the building of the B-314. Mansfield, in *Vision*, pp. 144–49, gives the date of the near capsizing as June 3, 1938.

The 1938 crossings of the Atlantic: From press reports, and from Van Dusen's long press-release resumé of the summer's activities, Oct. 27, 1938.

The familiarization flight of the first Boeing: The authority is Leslie, who was aboard.

Trippe's SOS: This is from Woods-Humphery's letter to Sir Donald Banks dated April 13, 1938. The reaction at the Air Ministry in London is from Beaty, *The Water Jump*, p. 131.

Priester flies to San Francisco: Beall to Leslie, Aug. 30, 1974; Schairer was an engineer who worked on the Boeing and eventually solved its porpoising problems.

Yankee Clipper christened: From press reports the following day.

32 · The Whitney Takeover

Statistics as of Jan. 1, 1939: From the annual report to stockholders.

Trippe and directors: Alexander was elected a director on May 21, 1936, and served until Nov. 22, 1939; Douglas was elected May 17, 1935, and served until Jan. 13, 1939. There were in an average year about ten board meetings. Board members who were also company executives were paid $100 per meeting. Outside directors were paid about $3,000 a year, but they also got a system pass, plus invitations to annual directors' flights and to other special flights each time a new route was opened up. Usually they found their own prestige enhanced also, for in the business community the Pan Am board was looked upon as a prestigious one. Prestige was the image Trippe was trying to project. In interviews with the author, Trippe spoke often and with pride of the boards he had put together: "We had the damndest Board—"

Trippe's wastebasket: Leslie to author, Oct. 17, 1978.

Hoyt's opposition: *Life* magazine, Oct. 20, 1941, p. 122. Hoyt's attempts to control Trippe's expenditures were described by Van Dusen in a tape-recorded conversation with Leslie, Oct. 24, 1972. Van Dusen also claimed that Trippe had ordered the Martin flying boats without seeking board approval first, though obliged by company bylaws to do so.

The March 14, 1939, directors' meeting: Unfortunately, the minutes tell little more than the names of the men present. Trippe's ouster by Whitney is reported in a single line.

Biographies of C. V. Whitney ancestors: From *The Dictionary of American Biography* (Scribner's, 1943); the background of Sonny Whitney himself is principally from his book, *High Peaks*. This 127-page autobiography, which supposedly describes the biggest moments and highest peaks of Whitney's life, makes little reference to his association with Pan American. His ten and a half months as chief executive are not mentioned. On p. 24, having described selling the "worthless" certificates for $500,000, Whitney adds, "With this windfall I founded Pan American Airways." The reference to putting Trippe in to run the company is from the author's interview with Whitney on Sept. 12, 1978.

Reputation as a playboy: The New York

World, Sept. 24, 1929, not only reported from Reno the dissolution of Whitney's first marriage to Marie Norton, but also referred to the million-dollar breach of promise and paternity suit previously brought by Evan Burrows Fontaine. A federal court jury completely exonerated Whitney in 1924. When Miss Fontaine reinstituted suit for a third time early in 1929, it was thrown out of court. The details of Harry Payne Whitney's will are from *The New York Times*, Nov. 6, 1930, and Oct. 13, 1936. The Trippes' disapproval of Whitney's life-style seemed evident from repeated comments the Trippes made about him during author's interviews.

Whitney as Trippe's only support: From Van Dusen's Oct. 24, 1972, conversation with Leslie. Van Dusen describes Whitney saying "I'll take a million." Whitney verified this to the author on Sept. 12, 1978.

Whitney's contributions to the company: When asked by the author, Whitney mentioned the inaugural flights and the speeches. A photo on his office wall at 230 Park Avenue showed an airmail-contract signing from the early thirties: Trippe, at a desk with a Post Office official, signs; Whitney stands behind Trippe's chair looking on.

The Pan Am financial situation in March 1939 is from a handwritten memo by Whitney to President Roosevelt which is in the F.D.R. Library at Hyde Park, President's personal file PPF-1840. Whitney had just authorized the expenditure of $200,000 to make a survey flight to Nouméa via Canton Island, and believed that additional loans were unlikely, according to this memo. That the bankers, especially board member Robert Lehman of Lehman Brothers, were behind the ouster of Trippe was suggested by Leuteritz to author, Sept. 22, 1978. Leuteritz was repeating what had been general hallway gossip at the time.

Whitney's stock: His memo to F.D.R. notes that there were about 4,000 stockholders averaging 350 shares each. In fact there were at the time 1,361,964 shares issued; the annual report for 1939, approximately nine months later, lists 5,802 stockholders. *The New York Times* for Aug. 19, 1938, reported that Whitney had bought an additional 15,000 shares the previous March, bringing his total holdings to 154,432 shares. Trippe's 18,000 shares were not even all in his own name, more than half being held in trust for his children. When the company was formed in 1927, half the stock (1,000 shares of founders' stock—see Trippe's letter to Robert Thach, June 28, 1927) had been held back to be distributed six months later to whichever of the founders contributed most to company development. At a 1928 stockholders' meeting Trippe was asked to leave the room, and in his absence the other directors voted him half of the held-back stock, or 25 percent of all shares outstanding. His salary year by year was a matter of public record. Year-end reports also showed that he regularly bought additional stock as part of an executive compensation plan which he had set up himself—all other executives on a policy-making level belonged to this plan—and that just as regularly he sold his stock off. According to Balluder (Balluder to Solberg, July 22, 1977), this was another bone of contention between him and the directors, who said it showed lack of confidence in the future of the company. Trippe is supposed to have replied that he believed in land, not stock, and land is what he regularly bought year by year: an enormous house built in 1888 on the dunes at East Hampton; a luxury apartment overlooking the East River in New York; a house in Bermuda; part of an island in the Bahamas; tracts in Liberia. A study of Trippe's sales of stock shows that his timing was often poor. For instance, he sold heavily just before the jet age began at the end of the fifties, only to see Pan Am's stock skyrocket almost at once.

The Trippe-Whitney office: Leuteritz to author, Sept. 22, 1978.

Trippe's globe: Notes of interview with Abe French, former Pan Am archivist, Oct. 1, 1959, PAF 30.10.08.

Morgan: He was elected to the board of directors on April 27, 1939. Trippe and Morgan had signed the China Airways contract on March 31, 1933. See notes to Chapter 17.

Van Dusen called in by Morgan and Whitney: Van Dusen to Leslie, Oct. 11, 1972.

Whitney disbands polo team: *The New York Times*, April 20, 1939. His entire stable of horses had been sold at auction on Nov. 7, 1937. On Oct. 15, 1938, he had announced plans to return to racing the following spring, and on April 6, 1939, *The New York Times* reported that the now chief executive of Pan Am had been named vice president of Belmont Park.

The mechanics of the takeover: Whitney

to author, Sept. 12, 1978; Trippe to author Feb. 28, 1978, Aug. 8, 15, 1979. One of the sparks that had ignited "the feud," according to Judge Henry Friendly (Friendly to Leslie, June 8, 1973) occurred during the acquisition by Pan Am of Cubana Airlines in 1932. In the period between the signing of the contract and the closing, Trippe was away from the office for some weeks. In his absence the sellers prevailed upon Whitney to sign a letter giving up what Trippe considered an important point. When Trippe returned, he was furious, and refused to allow the board of directors to ratify the letter. "I am sure this did not leave Whitney with very good feelings," wrote Friendly, who for many years was the company's chief legal officer, to Leslie on June 26, 1973. "Of course, the basic trouble was that Whitney had put up most of the money to buy Cubana in the first place." According to Friendly, Whitney began to resent Trippe at that time, this resentment grew, and it resulted seven years later, at a time when Trippe's influence with the board was low, in Whitney's seizure of control.

The climate on the fifty-eighth floor: Leuteritz to author, Sept. 22, 1978, Aug. 21, 1979. He mentioned specifically the operations committee meetings. Trippe conceded to the author Aug. 8 and 15, 1979, that it was his habit at these meetings to keep silent.

33 · The Boeing Accident

The March 26 survey flight: From the company's house organ, *Pan American Air Ways*, April 1939. The Clipper took off from and landed back at Baltimore. It was gone twenty-two days and covered 11,017 miles. Only three and a third days were spent in the air. The departure of the *Yankee Clipper* on May 20 is from press clippings from *The New York Times* and the New York *Herald Tribune* of May 21; also from *Pan American Air Ways*, May–June 1939.

Summaries of the Woods-Humphery–Trippe transatlantic telephone conversations: PAF 40.03.00.

Lindbergh's visits: From Lindbergh's *Wartime Journals*. See entries for May 23, Sept. 20, 21, 1939.

"Pan Am executives who knew Lindbergh": Leslie to author, Sept. 27, 1978.

The June 28 flight: Details, including the $5,000 offered for Eck's ticket, are from press reports the following day, from the June issue of the company magazine, *Pan American Air Ways*, and from the diary of Betty Trippe.

Priester responsible for the companionways in the wings: Author's interviews with Leslie and Trippe.

Boeing statistics: *Airpower*, Nov. 1977, pp. 20 ff.; *Aerospace* magazine, Jan. 1976, pp. 24 ff.; also, Trippe's Wilbur Wright Lecture as delivered in London, June 17, 1941.

Takeoff procedures: from Trippe's lecture in London.

Atmosphere and details aboard the June 28 flight: From Betty Trippe's diary. The diary also includes a description of her husband's trip to London, and the Ambassador Kennedy incident, the Paris revels, the phrase "practically nude," the landing of the Export plane and the washing of the dirty dishes.

Trippe's version of the Hyannis Port incident: Trippe to author, Aug. 25, 1976, Oct. 2, 1978, etc.

Whitney's committee meetings: Leuteritz to author, June 16 and Sept. 22, 1978.

Trippe and Whitney not speaking: Josephson, *Empire of the Air*, p. 138.

The accident to the Boeing: Interview with John Borger, Sept. 29, 1978.

The Boeing redesigned: Letter from G. W. Taylor of Boeing to Leslie, Aug. 20, 1974.

Gray's background: From company biographies, from press reports when he succeeded Trippe as chairman, from his obituary in *The New York Times*, and from Leslie, who described to the author Gray's experiments with the Ford trimotor. When Gray went to Miami to teach blind flying to Swinson and Fatt, he first had to coax these much older, much more experienced pilots into a cockpit, and then to pull a hood down over their heads. "You're not getting me in that thing," said Fatt. But later he agreed to be taught, and was such a natural and excellent pilot that he picked up blind flying at once.

Sullivan: Ironically, Van Dusen had chosen to profile him, elaborating on the dry company biography, in the Jan. 25, 1943, "Dear Senor" letter, less than a month before the Feb. 22 crash. Sullivan, from Hannibal, Mo., had been a Pan Am pilot since 1929.

34 · Trippe Returns

World War II: Germany invaded Poland on Sept. 1, 1939. The 40,000 refugees in Portugal and the 10,000 Americans in Europe are estimates widely reported at the time. For a fictional treatment see *The Night in Lisbon*, by Erich Maria Remarque (Harcourt, Brace & World, Inc., 1964). The frenzy was such that refugees attempted to bribe Pan Am employees for seats on the Clippers. Although rumors arose occasionally at the time, no case of bribe-taking ever proven. Estimates before service began of probable mail loads had ranged from 135,000 pounds eastbound to no more than 50,000 pounds westbound per year. But in 1940 the company carried 242,223 pounds eastbound, and 192,540 pounds westbound. Many flights from Lisbon took off carrying either no passengers or only a handful of priority passengers, all the rest of the payload being taken up by mail, the only commercial cargo carried.

Six additional Boeings: The price had now risen to over $800,000 each. The decision to buy them was announced by Whitney on Oct. 3, 1939, and the news was reported in *The New York Times* and the New York *Herald Tribune* the following day.

The Whitney memo: Executive system memorandum No. 48, Nov. 7, 1939.

Morgan elected to executive committee; The date was Nov. 14, 1939; he became chairman of the executive committee on Nov. 28. As an old man, Morgan used to invite Van Dusen to his apartment to talk about "the old days." Shortly before his death he wanted to discuss the Whitney-Trippe episode and his own attempts to run the company. "Juan had everything so snarled up nobody could ever untangle it," he told Van Dusen, who put his recollections down in a memo dated Oct. 11, 1972.

Trippe's Christmas message: It was printed on the front page of *Pan American Air Ways*, Dec. 1939.

Profits for 1939: From the annual report to the stockholders.

The Jan. 9 and Jan. 23, 1940, meetings: From the minutes. Trippe's globe was lodged for a time in Fort Slocum, and then he gave it to the Institute of the Aeronautical Sciences, which wanted to start a museum. At present it is housed in a glass case together with a wicker chair from an early Fokker trimotor, and an opened logbook by

Musick, in the Pan Am Terminal Building at
J.F.K. Airport.

Johnston fired: Leuteritz and Woodbridge interviews, Sept. 22, 1978, and Sept.
29, 1978. The 1940 annual report shows
Johnston in his new rank. The Trippe-
Woodbridge conversation and the rest of
the Johnston incident are from the Sept. 29
interview.

Leuteritz and Priester: Leuteritz to author, June 18, 1978. Jock Whitney resigned
from the Pan Am board on Feb. 25, 1942.

"Don't be unkind to Sonny": Trippe to
author, Feb. 28, 1978.

See testimony before the CAB dockets Nos.
238, 319 and 491. These are the three principal cases covering Export's application for
certificates of convenience and necessity to
operate on the North Atlantic, for approval
of its status as a subsidiary of American Export Lines, Inc., and for approval of its acquisition of TACA. In all three cases Pan
American intervened. Details concerning
the arguments of both parties are from the
transcripts of the hearings.

Trippe's reaction of fury: Trippe to author, Oct. 2, 1978: "I was mad."

Information on TACA: From CAB
docket No. 491; also, Davies, *A History of the
World's Airlines*, pp. 162–64, 330–31.

35 · *Trippe versus American Export Airlines*

Rihl to South America: "George Rihl
was the chief victim," said Judge Henry J.
Friendly to Leslie on June 8, 1973, a tape-
recorded conversation. "A friend of Whitney's from the PAA-CMA deal, Rihl was
caught in the Trippe-Whitney internecine
warfare," wrote Van Dusen to Leslie on
June 27, 1972. Leuteritz concurred in an
interview with author, Sept. 22, 1978. "Two
of my dear friends, J. Herbert Johnston, and
George Rihl, both devoted pioneers in their
respective fields, as well as William I. Van
Dusen, were caught up in the maelstrom,"
wrote Woodbridge to Leslie on June 24,
1974, adding, "I was directed to release
Johnston." Rihl was banished to South
America almost at once, and he stayed there
for a series of assignments. He was never
fired, but was rarely seen again in New York.
At the time of his retirement on Sept. 30,
1945, he was based in Brazil. Van Dusen
lasted as head of public relations until 1947,
but had no further access to Trippe. "When
I joined the company in 1946," said his
successor, Willis Player, to the author on
Jan. 11, 1979, "Van had almost no access to
Trippe at all, and the company had no public relations policy at all." Van Dusen died
on March 3, 1976.

Trippe, Van Dusen, Cone and McKee to
Washington: Woodbridge so testified before CAB examiner Brown in April 1941
during the CAB investigation into Pan Am
airmail pay.

Cone as politician: Leslie to author, Oct.
17, 1978.

History of American Export Airlines:

36 · *Blitzkrieg against TACA*

Lowell Yerex: See CAB docket No. 491.
Yerex's testimony begins on p. 346 and continues for most of 200 pages. He was on the
stand from April 29 to May 2, 1941, and in
the course of direct, cross and redirect ex-
aminations described in detail his own life,
the founding and operation of TACA, the
deal with American Export Airlines, and
then the blitzkrieg. For the "strictly confidential" memo describing Yerex's background and bank accounts, see PAF 50.25.-
02; the memo is dated Aug. 18, 1942, and is
unsigned.

Yerex's attempts to buy bombing equipment: Silliman's May 7, 1933, memo was
addressed to Evan Young, then Pan Am's
vice president in charge of the foreign department. Silliman's description of himself
is from CAB docket No. 491.

Silliman's Jan. 22, 1940, memo: It was
addressed to Balluder and a copy was sent
to Trippe on Jan. 29. At the top of the page
Trippe scrawled a note to his secretary:
"Hand to me if E. B. [Erwin Balluder]
should call in here this week."

Silliman's contacts with Denby: See his
own CAB testimony. Denby's background is
from testimony by Yerex and Silliman in the
same hearing. The coded telegram was
dated July 16, 1940. Although Balluder was
stationed in Mexico City, the telegram was
sent from Brownsville, Tex., which was the
U.S. terminal of the north–south line
through Mexico. The Rihl memo to Trippe
was dated Sept. 23.

The blitzkrieg: See Yerex's testimony, and the cross-examination of Silliman. At first only one DC-2 came down from Compañía Mexicana, but the second soon followed. Yerex testified to listening to radio reports from his outlying fields even as the bales of chicle already consigned to TACA were being loaded onto Aerovías planes. Reports on Silliman's activities in Costa Rica, Nicaragua and Honduras are from the same testimony. Silliman claimed on the stand that Kennett had nothing to do with Pan American, and that he had tried to help him only as a friend: "I would do it for anybody." Yerex testified that he had been extremely worried by White's activities, but no longer thought White intended to start a competing airline.

Pan American's cut-rate fares: These were on a standby basis. This appears to be the first introduction of cut-rate standby fares as opposed to full-fare reserved seats. However, once a standby passenger got on the plane he was allowed to ride all the way to the end of the line even if full-fare passengers appeared.

Trippe's appearance at the State Department: Josephson, *Empire of the Air*, pp. 175–76. The State Department got involved because, according to law, the CAB's responsibilities with respect to the foreign routes of the U.S. flag airlines are shared with the President, who must make the final determination, "and who does so with the advice of the State Department." Trippe verified the incident to author Aug. 8, 1979.

Trippe's techniques as a witness: Leslie to author, March 12, 1978. In addition, Trippe's techniques are clear to anyone who wishes to study transcripts of hearings at which he appeared.

TACA purchase denied: See CAB docket No. 491. The decision was dated Sept. 4, 1941. To some observers it appeared that Pan American had totally crushed Lowell Yerex. Not so. By the end of 1942 he appears to have come to the conclusion that Pan Am was stringing him along and would not buy him out. In 1943 he began to sell pieces of TACA to American investors, including TWA and the Pennsylvania Railroad. But he kept 54 percent of it himself, and attempted to spread his network wider by forming additional subsidiaries in Brazil, Venezuela, Colombia and even Paraguay. In May 1943 he founded British West Indian Airways (BWIA) and served as its first managing director.

37 · Trippe versus the U.S. Government

Trippe in Lisbon: His discussions with Long and Pinto Basto on Feb. 3–5, 1941, are summarized in a long memorandum dated Feb. 9 from Long to Bixby.

"Treasury and Post Office Department's Appropriation Bill, Fiscal Year 1942": the bill number was H.R. 3295. The General Johnson argument was reprinted in full by Van Dusen in the March 1941 issue of the company magazine, whose name had now been changed from *Pan American Air Ways* to *New Horizons*.

House debate: See the Congressional Record of Feb. 12, 1941: the debate starts on p. 927.

Trippe's relationship with Roosevelt: Trippe to author, April 5 and Oct. 2, 1978.

CAB hearings into Pan Am mail pay: These began in the late winter of 1941 and extended into the spring, except for a recess from March 25 to April 21 due to illnesses of certain of the participants. The results were handed down as Order No. 1913, Aug. 28, 1942. The young lawyer Gates did succeed in making a reputation for himself with this one case, or so he said in an Oct. 5, 1978, interview, but he did not succeed in getting Pan Am's mail pay drastically cut. Instead, a new formula of payment was worked out that both sides claimed to be satisfied with.

Senate hearings: From the Congressional Record, May 5–7, 1941. The vote comes on p. 3716. Reference to Senator Davis changing his vote in committee is made by Senator Tydings on p. 3703. Senator McKellar's description of Trippe as a witness is from *Life* magazine, Oct. 20, 1941, p. 124.

Meetings in hotel room of Senator George: Trippe to author, April 5, 1978. The Drew Pearson column ran in the Washington *Times Herald* and other papers on Sunday, Sept. 29, 1940. Mrs. Tydings, looking radiant, christened the *Atlantic Clipper* on April 25, 1939.

Trippe and Postmaster General Walker: Trippe to author, April 5, 1978, Oct. 2, 1978 and Aug. 8, 1979—"I was so damned mad." For additional information on Walker, see *Collier's*, July 6, 1935; *Newsweek*, Sept. 9, 1940; *The New York Times*, Sept. 1, 1940.

Part IV
WAR
38 · China

Sharp commandeered: Leary, *The Dragon's Wings*, p. 113.

Trippe summons Bond: Letter from Bond to Leslie, Jan. 6, 1975.

Bond's career: Letter from Bond to W. F. McCulloch, director of Benefits Administration, Pan American Airways, Nov. 27, 1972. Born Nov. 12, 1893, Bond was then seventy-nine years old, and he outlined his career to McCulloch as a means of applying for the benefits due him as a retired vice president with sixteen years' uninterrupted service. Apparently he was being credited with service only from 1941 to 1950, and he explained how, all during the Sino-Japanese War, he had been carried by the Pan Am Pension Plan with the concurrence of Trippe, even though, officially, he had resigned.

Bond reaches Shanghai: Letter from Bond to Leary, March 20, 1969.

Bond's telegram to Westervelt: A letter from Westervelt to Rieta Westervelt dated Jan. 28, 1932, quotes it.

Bond rejects meddling by Chinese: Leary, pp. 104–7.

Eighteen planes: There were four DC-2's, one S-43, two Douglas Dolphins, two Ford trimotors, four Loening amphibians and five Stinsons.

Bond and Trippe talk: Bond gives a 27-page handwritten account of the Chinese takeover of CNAC in a letter to Leslie dated Jan. 6, 1975. The dialogue is Bond's.

Pilots placed elsewhere: Charles S. Vaughn, in a letter to Leslie Oct. 12, 1972, describes how he himself was transferred to Manila in Sept. 1937.

Bond's attempts to get back CNAC: Bond to Leslie, Jan. 6, 1975.

Woods shot down: *Wings Over Asia*, Vol. IV, p. 45—the pilot's official report dated Hong Kong, Aug. 26, 1938.

Flying conditions in China: Leary, pp. 123–29.

Bond writes Allison: The date of the letter is Dec. 1, 1940.

The DC-2 1/2: *New Horizons*, Aug. 1941; "My Story of the DC-2 1/2" by Zygmund Soldinski, in *Wings Over Asia*, Vol. II, p. 47. Soldinski had gone out to China as chief mechanic in 1933 as part of the Grooch expedition.

39 · "Delousing" SCADTA

The Joint Planning Commission: See the University of Texas Ph.D. thesis "United States Diplomacy in the Caribbean during World War II," pp. 47–56, by Calvin Hines (University Microfilms, Ann Arbor, Mich., 1971). The thesis is fully documented. See also *The Framework of Hemisphere Defense*, by Stetson Conn and Byron Fairchild, which is also fully documented and is the official Army version.

The Axis-owned or influenced airlines: Condor was controlled by Lufthansa; it had a route system of over 8,000 miles and featured four-engined Focke-Wulf landplanes. LAB was owned by Germans who had adopted Bolivian citizenship. In Peru the airline, a Lufthansa subsidiary, was actually called Lufthansa. Corporación Sudamericana was organized by Argentine capital, but with help from the Italian government. The Italian LATI crossed the South Atlantic to Brazil. Varig used German equipment, and was staffed to a greater or lesser degree by Germans, but was wholly owned by Brazilians. SEDTA in Ecuador was managed by Fritz Hammer, who had also helped found SCADTA; in May 1940 Hammer proposed a route to the Galápagos Islands, which made no commercial sense at all, but did perhaps make military sense because the islands guarded the approaches to the Pacific side of the Panama Canal. SEDTA had been founded in 1937 with help from Lufthansa.

Admiral Stark's request: Stetson Conn and Byron Fairchild, *The United States Army in World War II*, series 12 (2 vols.), Washington, D.C., 1960–64, I, pp. 8–10. There was a plan to buy not only the Dutch West Indies but also Greenland, in case attack should come from the north. But in May 1939 the War Department held that neither was sufficiently valuable to warrant being purchased. In the spring of 1939 executive directives ordered the modernization of U.S. bases at San Juan and St. Thomas.

General Emmons's report: It went forward to the War Plans Division dated Dec. 7, 1939. A second report was sent forward by Lieutenant Colonel Robert Olds, who accompanied Emmons. Dated Dec. 1, 1939, it was addressed to the Commanding General, General Headquarters, Air Force. Both these reports can be found in War Plans Division file 4185-2.

Pan Am buys SCADTA: See "A Memorandum Of Fact Concerning The Relations

Of Pan American Airways With The Colombian Airlines SCADTA and its successor Avianca," which was prepared by Root, Clark, Buckner & Ballantine, Pan Am's then law firm, about 1941. This document can be found in Pan Am legal department files, Box 134L.

Trippe's secrecy: Trippe to author, Aug. 8, 1979—"I don't think even anyone at Pan Am knew about it." See the memo of closing, April 10, 1931. Von Bauer in a letter to Trippe, Aug. 8, 1930, stated that Kellogg knew the details of the sale. According to the Memorandum of Fact (p. 19), White's statement came in a conference with Trippe; the 1931 letter to Postmaster General Brown is dated April 28.

Profile of Braden: *Collier's*, Nov. 10, 1945; *Time*, Nov. 15, 1945. Trippe called Braden "a bull in a China shop" in conversation with the author on April 29, 1979.

Germans protected by Colombian law: For some time Pan American had been ordering Von Bauer to hire no more Germans. Vice President Evan Young wrote him to this effect on Aug. 7, 1939, and again on Oct. 30 of the same year. That Von Bauer would hire no more Germans was stated by George Rihl in a letter to him in Oct. 1939, according to a Rihl memo to Trippe dated May 7, 1940.

Santos informed: Colonel Boy's version of this is recorded in his autobiography, *Historia Con Alas*, published in Madrid in 1955.

Whitney sends Rihl to Colombia: Rihl memo dated Oct. 31, 1939.

SCADTA threat played down: The quote of the Colombian minister of war is from a letter to Von Bauer dated June 13, 1939. The Santos quote is from an undated memo that was apparently written in Jan. 1940.

Del Valle to Colombia: *New Horizons*, April 1941. See also notes of an interview with Del Valle in September 1957, PAF 30.-08.10. Del Valle, an engineer, had gone to work for Pan American in 1929.

Trippe's thoughts: Trippe to author, Apr. 29, 1979. See also the Memorandum of Fact.

The May 14, 1940, meeting: From the minutes of the regular meeting of the executive committee.

The May 24 meeting: From the minutes. After this meeting Trippe went to Washington, where he told a gathering of State, Army and Navy department officials the full details of Plan B. All in attendance then endorsed the plan. Trippe gave a full report on this conference to the executive committee of Pan Am on May 28.

The actual takeover: From the Memorandum of Fact.

40 · The Airport Development Program

Trippe's call from the White House: As in the case of the SCADTA takeover, a Memorandum of Fact was prepared by Pan Am on the Airport Development Program. But because the program itself was so secret, not only was the report never disseminated but it was never even edited, and it exists today in PAF 10.02.00 undated, variously paged, and with no author mentioned.

Grosvenor: He was born July 22, 1884, and died Oct. 28, 1943. He was an airline executive most of his working life, and at one time had been vice president of the Fairchild Aviation Corporation.

The planning behind ADP: Most of the memos relating to this can be found in War Plans Division file 4185, including a number of letters and memos back and forth between the Secretary of War and the Secretary of State. See Conn and Fairchild, *The Framework of Hemisphere Defense*, pp. 249 ff., for a good resumé of this planning. An interdepartmental conference on May 15, 1940, decided that the bases should be built by a new corporation, with Pan Am coming in afterwards to supply fuel and maintenance. But during conferences the following week the three other plans were considered also, and on June 10 a State Department letter presented the question to Roosevelt for decision. By July 1, according to a War Plans Division memo to the Chief of Staff (War Plans Division file 4113–22,) Roosevelt had authorized the Army to have Pan American build the bases with money from his emergency fund. Trippe places his meeting with Roosevelt on this subject in the first week of July 1940.

Boeings sold to England: See March 28, 1941, memo signed by Franklin Gledhill entitled "Status Sale Boeing 314-A flying boats to British Government."

Trippe promotes Leslie: Leslie to author, Aug. 7, 1978.

Lisbon–New York via Africa: See *New Horizons*, March 1941. Flight 262, Harold Gray commanding, left on Feb. 1 to Lisbon and on Feb. 6 returned home via Bolama, with Wendell Willkie, Trippe and Bixby among the passengers.

Marshall writes Stimson: Memo from Chief of Staff to the Secretary of War, Sept. 7, 1940.

Detailed plans: The fifteen land airports down the chain of islands to the Brazilian bulge were to be constructed for just over $4.3 million. The ten airports on Route No. 2—from Tampico down through Central America into Venezuela—were to be built for $3.2 million. The nine seaplane bases were budgeted at $1.4 million. The rest of the money was budgeted for the storing of fuel, the operation and maintenance of the airfields, and administrative and other expenses. That is, Grosvenor had $12 million to work with, but only $9 million to build with. For further details on the airport-development program, see the report dated Jan. 25, 1946, to the Undersecretary of War by Colonel Curtis G. Pratt et al., entitled "Construction of Certain Latin American and Caribbean Air Bases Built by the United States." See also two dissertations: "The Airport Development Program of World War II in South America and the Caribbean," by Deborah W. Ray, PAF 30.10.01; and "A Study of the Methods Employed in the Acquisition of Air Bases in Latin America for the Army Air Forces in World War II," by Bynum E. Weathers, Jr. Written in 1971, the latter dissertation contains a vast array of facts concerning most aspects of the program. If you want to know how many farmers and how many goats were displaced by the building of Coolidge Field in Antigua, this is the place to find out.

Cauby Araujo arrested: Pryor to Leslie, letter dated June 22, 1974. Trippe told the author Aug. 8, 1979, that only his own personal intervention saved Cauby Araujo from being shot. Later he was acquitted and released.

Paramaribo engineer seen drunk: Report of the American vice consul, June 3, 1941, from War Plans Division file 4113–109.

The shield not in place: The Secretary of War wrote Trippe, Sept. 19, 1941. Pryor had been hired the previous June.

41 · Africa

Trippe's lecture: The date was June 17, 1941; the title was "Ocean Air Transport." Trippe described to the author on Sept. 30 and Oct. 2, 1978, his flight across, the lecture room, and his second lecture about the Trans-African Airway. General Arnold was a passenger on the same flying boat across, and he also stood with Trippe on the roof watching the bombing when the messenger came summoning Trippe to No. 10 Downing Street. The description of Trippe's meeting with Churchill is also by Trippe, but it was common knowledge in the company at the time. Pryor described it in considerable detail to Leslie in a June 22, 1974, letter, and to the author on March 11, 1978. The airway was possible because certain small Imperial Airways bases already existed; these Pan Am would take over and expand. Not everything had to be built from scratch.

Gledhill: He was born in Jersey City on June 29, 1898, and graduated from Yale in 1923. He joined Pan Am in Jan. 1929 as general purchasing agent, became vice president in 1940 and a director in 1946. He had been working as a coal-mining engineer in Colorado when Trippe hired him. Gledhill was also a pilot, having served first with the U.S. Cavalry on the Mexican border in 1916, and after that transferring as a pilot to the air service when the United States entered World War I.

Pan Am–Africa: Again a Memorandum of Fact was written, this one in 1942. It was 36 pages long, and was distributed privately for reasons of military security. An additional account entitled "Pan American's War Service Story" covered much the same ground. It was prepared for the Office of War Information in 1943. A letter from Gledhill to Lieutenant Colonel James Douglas, Air Transport Command, dated Aug. 10, 1942, gave an account of the record of Pan American–ica to that point. In addition, there was a *Saturday Evening Post* article in the Nov. 22, 1941, issue entitled "America's New Lifeline to Africa."

Gledhill flies 2,500 miles per day: This is mentioned by Van Dusen in his "Dear Senor" letter of June 8, 1942. The figure sounds like an exaggeration, but Van Dusen was apparently there at the time, for he datelines his letter "Somewhere in Africa," and he begins it with not "Dear Senor" but "'Alo Mastah!" It is this same letter that records the 158-degree temperature at El Fasher.

The route to Leopoldville: See CAB docket No. 855 et al. Pan Am filed a 47-page exhibit called "History of the Transatlantic Services." The South Atlantic air route is described beginning on p. 38. The Boeing flying boat was transferred to the government in Sept. 1941.

Aircraft insurance: The annual reports show "reserves for self insured risk" $1.2 million in 1938, $1.5 million in 1939, $2,-409,153 in 1940, and $1,570,261 in 1941.

The Fishermen's Lake surveys: CAB docket No. 855 describes these also, as does Leslie in a letter to William R. Stanley dated June 25, 1975. Fishermen's Lake was surveyed from the air on July 11, 1941, and the ground expedition went in in September.

Leslie flies in: Leslie to author.

First flight to Leopoldville: This plane was in the air when Pearl Harbor was struck. It received orders to continue to Leopoldville, and it did so. Van Dusen's "Dear Senor" letter was dated Dec. 12, and was the first of these letters in which the salutation read "'Alo Mastah!" In this letter he describes the Congo River as it rushes past Leopoldville. A similar description occurs in CAB docket No. 855.

42 · The Day of Infamy

Trippe on Dec. 7: Trippe to author, Sept. 30 and Dec. 7, 1978.

Trippe's stock: The Pan Am board of directors voted Trippe a 50,000-share stock option in 1935 at $12.50 per share, the option to expire on Dec. 31, 1941. Trippe did exercise this option. In Jan. 1943 he sold these 50,000 shares at $25 per share, so his profit on that one transaction was nearly three-quarters of a million dollars. At that time he still held 45,000 shares in his own name and, with both Whitneys gone, was the single largest stockholder.

Trippe at his desk: He stayed there most of the night and took many calls from Washington, including one from Roosevelt, who phoned him from bed. The following morning a memo went to Roosevelt from Steven Early, a special assistant. It read: "The Postmaster General reports the following from Pan American Airways. Guam lost. One

S-42 lost. Gas at Guam and Wake destroyed. Clipper now probably on its way from Wake Island coming east toward San Francisco according to radio from captain of clipper two miles out of Wake Island."

The sealed orders: Radios were to be silenced, lights blacked out and headings changed. The captains' first responsibility was to their passengers. Mail was to be either safeguarded or destroyed. Pan Am personnel were to be evacuated from bases if possible.

Turner's flight: Described in *New Horizons*, Jan. 1942; also in Van Dusen's "Dear Senor" letter of Dec. 15, 1941, and in CAB docket No. 851 et al., exhibit PA-2, Aug. 12, 1944—a long account entitled "History of Transpacific Air Services to and through Hawaii."

Hamilton's flight: The above sources describe it also. CAB docket No. 851 notes that nine of Pan Am's 66-man staff on Wake were killed, and one man, Waldo Raugust, who was driving an ambulance and missed the plane, was later interned by the Japanese. The Midway adcock was shelled and destroyed at 10:00 P.M. that night, considerably before Hamilton got there. Additional details of Hamilton's flight came from his obituary in *Pan American Clipper*, May 15, 1968, and from notes of an interview with Hamilton in July 1958 in PAF 30.10.08.

Bond's story: Bond was a man who wrote very long letters, usually in his own hand, and most of what happened to him following the Japanese attack was reported in a letter to Bixby dated Dec. 17, 1941, and an edited version appeared in *New Horizons* in Feb. 1942. See also "The Evacuation of Hong Kong," by Roger Reynolds, in *Wings Over Asia*, Vol. II, p. 44.

Trippe re-recognizes CNAC: Letter from Trippe to Bond dated Dec. 5, 1941.

Myrtle destroyed: From *New Horizons*, Jan. 1942.

Ford's story: From Van Dusen's "Dear Senor" letter, Feb. 16, 1942; from an account in the *Daily News*, Jan. 7, 1942—the headline read "Pacific Clipper In." *New Horizons* printed a full account in the Jan. 1942 issue. But all these early accounts were heavily censored, and Ford's exact route was not given. However, Ford taped an account of his flight on April 27, 1974, and fourth officer John Steers contributed his log and diary of the flight. Ford's other crew members were John Henry Mack, first officer; Roderick Brown, second officer;

James Henriksen, third officer; John Poindexter, first radio officer; Oscar Henrickson, second radio officer; Homans "Swede" Rothe, first engineering officer; John "Jocko" Parish, second engineering officer; Barney Sawicki and Vern Edwards, stewards. According to Steers, after flying more than 30,000 miles almost without incident, Ford managed to run the flying boat aground while taxiing toward the New York dock. There was a moment of acute embarrassment, then Ford poured the coal to all four engines, and the Boeing came loose and was successfully moored. All the men aboard were flat broke, and Atlantic Division manager Leslie handed each of them $100 in cash.

02.05; and from notes of Carl Solberg's interview with Balluder on July 22, 1977. The remark "Spruille Braden was responsible for my persecution," was made to Solberg. The quotes regarding Trippe, which are ascribed to General Stone, were made by Balluder.

The loyalty oath: It still exists in Balluder's confidential file in the Pan Am Corporate Archives, as does Balluder's own contemporary account of his meetings with General Stone; his Jan. 21, 1940, letter to Trippe noting that his daughter was out of danger, and requesting permission to go back to work; and also summaries of Trippe's own meetings that same month with J. Edgar Hoover and other War Department and FBI officials.

43 · Loyalty

Lindbergh: All of this information is documented from the *Wartime Journals*, including the photograph of the Lindberghs and Göring with Hitler's picture on the table. Lindbergh began brooding about what to do on Dec. 12; he regrets having resigned his commission. On Dec. 30 Arnold released the contents of the letter Lindbergh sent him, offering his services. On Saturday, Jan. 10, Lindbergh was in Washington attempting to see General Arnold over the weekend. Arnold's secretary advised Lindbergh to contact Secretary of War Stimson directly, and Lindbergh got in to see him late in the afternoon of Jan. 12. Assistant Secretary Lovett sat in on part of the conference. Lindbergh met Arnold in Lovett's office the following day. On Jan. 15 Lindbergh had supper with Bixby, and the next day reached Trippe by telephone. The two men met in New York on Jan. 19, and Trippe's phone call reporting "obstacles" occurred Jan. 26. It was March 16 before Lindbergh made his connection with Ford. Ford made his offer to Lindbergh on March 24. The Willow Run plant was beginning to produce B-24 bombers, and Lindbergh began to help work the bugs out of this plane. By early 1943 he was also working as a consultant for United Aircraft, whose Vought-Sikorsky Division was making the Corsair fighter.

Balluder's story: From notes of interview with Balluder on Feb. 26, 1958, in PAF 50.-

44 · The War Routes

The Ocean crossings: Leslie described the interiors of the flying boats to the author on Feb. 16, 1979. Van Dusen notes Captain Hart's multiple crossings of the South Atlantic in his "Dear Senor" letter of March 31, 1943.

The Roosevelt flight: See *New Horizons*, Jan. 1943, and *Time* magazine, Feb. 1, 1943.

The company's war service: There are many accounts of this. *New Horizons* (Jan. 1943) describes the first year of the war; also, *Pan American's War Service Story* (1943), prepared for the Office of War Information. Also Pan American's "Worldwide War Service," forming part of CAB docket No. 5132, written in 1952.

Trippe, Arnold and Eisenhower: Trippe told this story to Leslie on Aug. 25, 1971, and Leslie wrote an aide-mémoire on it the following day. Trippe repeated the story to the author on Dec. 7, 1978. Trippe said he had learned Eisenhower's part of the story around 1950, while Eisenhower was president of Columbia University. Eisenhower and Trippe were riding in a car away from a campus ceremony both had attended.

The Airport development program expanded: See the Pratt report (cited in Chapter 40).

Rescuing the downed B-24: An excellent account of this appears in *New Horizons*, Nov. 1942.

The downed C-54: See *New Horizons*,

May 1944. The plane went down in the jungle in British Guiana. The clearing there was deep mud and there were alligators about. It took the crew fifty-five days before they could lay steel landing mats and get the plane out of there.

CNAC over the Hump: The work of CNAC is described in CAB docket No. 5132, and also in all of the various company accounts of its wartime service. Leary's *The Dragon's Wings* also contributes a fine account, and it is fully documented as well.

Doolittle's escape from China: The overloaded DC-3 story first appeared in *The New York Times* of April 26, 1943.

Bond's flight: Bond to Bixby, a letter dated Feb. 2, 1943.

The two Medals for Merit: Pryor's was dated April 15, 1946, and Trippe's July 18, 1946. The author has seen both citations and verified the dates. Pryor described lobbying in Trippe's behalf at an interview at his ranch on Maui on March 11, 1978. "He deserved it; I was only carrying out another man's ideas," said Pryor. Trippe's medal was presented to him by Secretary of War Robert Patterson probably in Sept. 1946—the Oct. 9, 1946, issue of *The Pan American Clipper—Atlantic Division* takes note of the presentation on the front page. Pryor's medal was presented—also by Patterson—on Nov. 2, 1946.

Bond urges Trippe to sell CNAC: Bond to Leary, June 3, 1968. Bond's conversations with Bixby and Trippe took place apparently in the early days of 1945. His earliest discussions with the Chinese began that April with Bond asking for reduction of Pan Am's interest to 10 percent on a five-year contract. Agreement was reached in December at 20 percent.

Domestics' wartime profits: Net profits for 1944, for example, show Pan Am at $1.6 million, American Airlines at $4.4 million, and TWA at $2.8 million.

Export blocked from Lisbon: Memo from Richard Long to Bixby regarding his conversations with Trippe in Lisbon. The memo is dated Feb. 9, 1941.

Braniff blocked: Tom Braniff himself made these charges on a number of occasions over the years, including his appearance before the House Antitrust Subcommittee of the Committee on the Judiciary in June 1955. His testimony can be found in the transcript, Vol. IV, pp. 2857–3001. Van Dusen answered a number of these charges in his Oct. 1, 1945, "Dear Senor" letter,

pointing out that what Braniff really was trying to do was to use Pan Am and Mexicana facilities, all of which were privately owned, without paying for them. He had permission only for "experimental flights" in Mexico anyway. According to Van Dusen, who was no doubt reflecting Trippe's views, Braniff was hoping to get himself established in Mexico at little or no cost to himself by using facilities for which Pan Am and Mexicana had paid hundreds of thousands of dollars. Naturally they refused to let him do it.

Arnold's policy: The "secret" meeting was noted by *Time* magazine, July 26, 1943, p. 43, under the headline "Sixteen Versus Pan Am." Later the sixteen published a booklet titled *The Airplane, an American Heritage, Its Worldwide Future Now Is in the Making.* It is this booklet which contains the statement of policy and the quote about "withering" monopoly. The booklet closes by listing the sixteen airlines that financed it—with United the only major domestic missing. The sixteen called themselves "The Airlines Committee For United States Air Policy," and the address given was 923 Sixteenth Street, N.W., Washington 6, D.C.

CAB announces: The CAB requested May 4, 1943, that U.S. airlines submit ideas on future international air policy. The airlines replied on May 18. A supplemental statement was submitted by them to the board on July 15.

Part V
THE NEW WORLD
45 · The Community Company

Trippe's plan: PAF 30.04.02. The document is marked Proof A.

Anne Archibald: "Mrs. Archie: Washington Wonder Woman," *Kiplinger* magazine, May 1948. She died Jan. 18, 1953, aged fifty-six.

The "All American-Flag Line" bill: For transcripts, summaries, decisions and other material relating to this and succeeding Chosen Instrument bills, see PAF 30.04.00.

CAB's North Atlantic routes decision: PAF 30.03.01.

Bailey refuses to see Trippe: Letter from Bailey to Senator Radcliffe, July 24, 1945. This letter was read into the record at the request of Senator Johnson on May 21, 1947, during what proved to be the final hearings before the Senate committee of the revised Community Company bill.

Trippe sends Brewster to see Bailey: Pryor to author, March 18, 1978.

46 · High Stakes

Trippe's reasoning: He spelled it out in his 1945 report to the stockholders.

Application filed with CAB: This is the Domestic Routes case. CAB docket No. 1803 contains testimony by many of Trippe's rivals.

The new planes: PAF 30.07.17. The CV-37 contract was signed Feb. 15, 1945, and the specifications were explicit. Gross takeoff weight would be 320,000 pounds. The guaranteed performance was 4,200 miles at 340 mph at 25,000 feet with 43,000 pounds of payload. The plane would be powered by six WAC T-35 turboprops generating approximately 5,000 horsepower at takeoff. The Rainbow contract was signed that same summer, and specified a gross weight of 113,250 pounds. It was to be powered by four turbo supercharged Pratt and Whitney Wasp Major engines producing 3,000 horsepower each.

Leslie's arguments: Leslie to author, Nov. 28, 1978.

Operating statistics for 1945: CAB docket No. 1803.

The financial climate of 1944–45: See *Time,* Dec. 18, 1944; *Fortune,* Oct. 1945. On p. 21 of the 1944 annual report under the head "Financing Postwar Expansion," Trippe explains most of the details of the underwriting by the Atlas Corporation.

Odlum: For portraits of Odlum see *Business Week,* May 10, 1933; Aug. 8, 1936; March 13, 1937; July 17, 1937. See also *Fortune,* Sept. 1935; *Look,* Dec. 2, 1941; *The New Yorker,* Aug. 26, 1933; *Saturday Evening Post,* July 10, 1937. Trippe himself was unable to remember how he had met Odlum.

Trippe writes 118 letters: Donald Thomson to author, Feb. 3, 1979. Trippe to author, Sept. 1, 1976: "We decided who we wanted to invite in." Details of the April 15, 1929, sale of stock to United Aircraft are from the minutes of a special meeting of the board of directors of Aviation Corporation

of the Americas the day before. According to the minutes, there were reasons why Trippe wanted United Aircraft. The company manufactured Pratt and Whitney engines and Hamilton standard propellers. In addition, in conjunction with the Boeing Airplane Company it ran Chicago–Pacific Coast and Seattle–Los Angeles airline routes. Not only was it in itself a major new aviation enterprise, but it had among its backers the National City Bank, which had branch offices all over Latin America. By acquiring United Aircraft, Trippe hoped he was also acquiring the goodwill and the influence of the National City Bank in Latin America, assets of incalculable value to Pan American. United Aircraft agreed not to sell Pan Am stock within two years; according to the standards by which time was measured by the infant aviation industry, this sounded permanent. The minutes also include Trippe's philosophy as of that date: "We should be owned as far as possible and as equally as possible by the substantial interests concerned with air transportation in the United States, and you will have observed from the course of our development how sound that conception was."

Negotiations with Odlum: *Wall Street Journal,* Dec. 6, 1944; *Time,* Dec. 18, 1944; *The New York Times,* Feb. 24, 1945; *Wall Street Journal,* Feb. 24, 1945; the deal itself is explained in the proxy statement of Feb. 23, 1945, Special Meeting of Stockholders.

Trippe cancels: *Fortune,* Oct. 1945; *Wall Street Journal,* July 20, 1945. Annual report, 1945; proxy statement, annual meeting of stockholders, July 18, 1946.

Trippe phones Elisha Walker: From the minutes of the executive committee of the board of directors' meeting, June 25, 1945. There were meetings nearly every day that week. Walker's letter to Trippe was dated June 25, and read to the executive committee by Trippe the next day. Walker specified that Kuhn Loeb would not get involved until Trippe had canceled his deal with Atlas. On the twenty-eighth Trippe accepted the Kuhn Loeb offer, and on July 2 he set the price of the stock.

Trippe's conversations with Odlum: Trippe to author, Dec. 7, 1978.

Odlum and Atlas missile: From a long profile on Odlum by Robert Wright, *The New York Times,* Jan. 28, 1973.

Trippe calls Odlum a speculator: Trippe to author, Dec. 7, 1978.

47 · The Hearings

Braniff blocked: Charges of this nature against Pan American were repeated frequently in CAB hearings and congressional investigations into the company's activities throughout the late forties and fifties. See, for instance, the transcript of the Antitrust Subcommittee of the House Committee on the Judiciary following the 1956 hearings, Vol. IV, pp. 2857–3001. The first mention of them goes back to 1945. See the North Atlantic Route Transfer case, CAB docket No. 3589.

Morrison: PAF 50.13.12.

CV-37 fails to meet specifications: Borger to author, Dec. 11, 1978.

The Domestic Routes case: For further details see CAB docket No. 1803; *American Aviation Daily*, Nov. 8, 12, 13, 14, 15, 18, 19, 20, 1946; "$100 Million Revenue at Stake in Pan American's Bid for Domestic Routes," *Wall Street Journal*, Nov. 2, 1946; and PAF 30.03.02. The hearings ended Jan. 10, 1947, and attorneys' briefs were filed March 10, 1947.

Trippe skips ATA and IATA meetings: Leslie to author.

Profile of W. A. Patterson: *Who's Who in America*, 1946–47; *Liberty*, Sept. 28, 1946; *National Cyclopedia of American Biography*, Vol. E, p. 300.

Profile of C. R. Smith: *Who's Who in America*, 1944–45; *Saturday Evening Post*, Feb. 1, 1941; *Current Biography*, 1945.

Republic's problems: Borger to author, Dec. 11, 1978. The twenty firm orders by American and the six from Pan American are mentioned frequently in testimony in CAB docket No. 1803. So is Smith's cancellation.

Trippe picks up option: Borger to author, Dec. 11, 1978.

Smith's cancellation of the Rainbow: The date, according to CAB Docket No. 1803, was Feb. 20, 1947.

Trippe's testimony: From the official transcript.

Trippe smarter than anybody: A typical example appears on p. 249 of the Celler committee hearings of 1956—"the Committee believes that Pan American's dominance of United States flag foreign and overseas air transportation is due in considerable measure to the vision and acumen of its president Juan Terry Trippe." During the TACA hearings of May 1941, Senator Tydings on the floor of the Senate

called Trippe "a very remarkable man."

The *New Monopoly Aviation Bill* booklet: The author or authors of this booklet are not given in the record.

Brewster's investigation of Hughes: A good summary appeared in *Aviation Week and Space Technology*, April 1, 1963, by L. L. Doty. Brewster was defeated in the 1952 election and died on Dec. 26, 1961.

Trippe a good loser: Leslie to author.

The Trippe-Hughes meetings: Trippe to author, Aug. 15, 1979. Doty gives a slightly different version.

The mergers: Doty, op. cit. Most of the details of Trippe's meetings with the airline presidents were described by Trippe, Hughes, Dietrich, TWA president Charles Tillinghast and others in testimony in the North Atlantic Route Transfer case, CAB docket No. 3589.

Pryor lobbies: Pryor to author, March 11–13, 1978.

48 · The Plan to Save China

Round-the-world flight: The Clipper *America* took off from New York at 1:15 P.M. June 17 and returned at 4:15 P.M. June 30. For details of the ceremonial aspects of the flight see PAF 30.23.00. The stops were Gander, Shannon, London, Istanbul, Dhahran, Karachi, Bangkok, Calcutta, Manila, Shanghai, Tokyo, Guam, Wake, Midway, Honolulu and San Francisco. Since this was a special flight, the Constellation was allowed to proceed to New York with a refueling stop at Chicago. The flight was under the command of Captain Hugh H. Gordon III between New York and Calcutta, and under Captain Gordon F. Maxwell between Calcutta and San Francisco. There were twenty-five newspaper and magazine publishers aboard.

Trippe's account of his meetings with Chang and "the plan": Trippe to author, Aug. 30, Sept. 1, 1976. Trippe's meeting with Chiang Kai-shek in Nanking is a matter of public record. All of the details of his meetings with Chang, and of his conversations with Howard, Patterson and General MacArthur, come from Trippe. However, in interviews given in Dec. 1957 (see PAF 50.-20.02) and to the author all of these details matched, even though the interviews took place some twenty years apart. In Hawaii on the return trip Sam Pryor came aboard and Trippe told Pryor all that had happened, and together the two men decided how to proceed in Washington. So Pryor counts, in effect, as a contemporaneous witness, and in interviews at his ranch on Maui on March 11, 12 and 13, 1978, he substantially verified Trippe's account. The entire story is also outlined in considerable detail in letters from Pryor to Leslie on April 9, 1974, and from Chang to Pryor on Feb. 4, 1976. In the latter letter Chang described himself in 1947 as governor of the Central Bank of China. He briefly outlines the financial aspects of "the plan," notes that "I was later told that Mr. Trippe read my proposal to his friends aboard the plane," and finally he blames General Wedemeyer for having modified the plan so as to include military aid. At the time of writing this letter, Chang was attached to the Hoover Institution on War, Revolution and Peace at Stanford University. He was eighty-seven years old. Neither General MacArthur nor General Wedemeyer in their memoirs mention "the plan."

The meetings in Washington: Trippe to author; Pryor to author.

Bixby's report: Bixby to Trippe, June 19, 1949.

Bond's report: Bond to Pan Am vice president J. T. Towers, Oct. 20, 1949.

Bond re Colonel Liu: Bond to Towers, Nov. 11, 1949.

Pan Am sells CNAC: Towers memorandum, "CNAC," Nov. 11–Dec. 30, 1949; Leary, pp. 221–22.

49 · The Jets

Description of Lindbergh: Trippe to author during May 1977 interviews; Kauffman to author, July 11, 1978; Leslie to author. Although Lindbergh once claimed that no one had ever torn off his coat, Trippe insisted to the author that he saw it happen. For Lindbergh's early life and career see *We* and *The Spirit of St. Louis.* Trippe's Wings Club lecture on May 20, 1977, the 50th anniversary of Lindbergh's flight, provides a good brief resumé of the hero's life. He was *Time* magazine's "Man of the Year" for 1927. Leslie, Trippe

and Kauffman all called him "fearless."

Lindbergh in the South Pacific: *The Wartime Journals,* pp. 785–930. He describes how he shot down a Japanese plane on July 28, 1944, and how he was almost shot down himself three days later. From July 4 on he had begun teaching the long-range settings to pilots.

Lindbergh in Germany: His *Wartime Journals,* pp. 931–1000. His first meeting with Messerschmidt was on May 21, 1945. He describes how two men were supposed to have left the Messerschmidt factory in Sept. or Oct. 1944 and traveled by submarine to Japan with drawings of the German jets.

Lindbergh sees Trippe and Priester: Notes of interview with Lindbergh, 1967, PAF 50.12.05.

Lindbergh in on every stage of jet development: Trippe to author, May 1967. Trippe reiterated this in his Wings Club lecture.

Taylor's reports: PAF 50.20.07. His San Diego report was dated Oct. 22, 1945, and his Munich report Dec. 9, 1945.

British jets in production: Letter from Kauffman to Trippe, Feb. 26, 1947.

Beall's letter: Addressed "Dear Juan," it was dated Nov. 1, 1949. For information on early jet development see PAF 30.07.18—"Procurement of jet aircraft."

The Boeing prototype: Letter from William Allen, Boeing president, to Trippe, Jan. 6, 1953. It included an invitation "to visit our Seattle factory whenever your itinerary will permit." Allen added that the prototype would be demonstrated to the airlines and to the armed forces in the fall of 1954, that it would be just a shell, without any airline interior, and that "I feel that the time has arrived when it would be worthwhile for you to pay us a visit."

Lindbergh lunches with Trippe, Leslie and Gray: Trippe to author, May 1977.

Priester's memos: They were dated Sept. 12 and Sept. 19, 1952.

Trippe orders Comets: Borger memo to Gledhill, Priester et al., March 17, 1953. The memo was chiefly concerned with the Comet's seat capacity. It wasn't going to be big enough. The company's 1952 annual report also announced that the Comets had been ordered.

The tourist fare: The decision was Trippe's, but the chief architect of the multitude of details involved was vice president Willis Lipscomb. Pan American's first "tourist fare" flight to London was scheduled in the first week of Dec. 1945. Passengers paid only $275 for their tickets, down from $572. But at that price the British Air Ministry refused to let the plane land in London, and the flight was first canceled and later rescheduled only as far as Shannon. See PAF 30.13.00.

In Sept. 1948 the tourist-fare concept was tried out between New York and San Juan, a route that required only the approval of the CAB. The one-way fare was $75, a 43.6 percent discount off the then prevailing fare. The planes used were DC-4's, whose seating capacity was increased from 44 to 61. Public reaction was overwhelmingly favorable. Planes were jammed. For $75 a good many indigent Puerto Rican laborers could afford to come to New York to seek work (or in many cases to wind up on welfare rolls), so to some extent Juan Trippe could be accused of changing the demographics of the city.

From 1945 on, international fare structures had been worked out in International Air Transport Association meetings, and almost simultaneously with the San Juan service Trippe began to send emissaries to IATA conferences to demand tourist fares across the Atlantic. But always such proposals were quickly voted down.

At virtually every IATA conference after that Pan American's representatives put forth new tourist-fare proposals. For a while Sabena voted in favor, but by May of 1950 even this feeble ally had been seduced over to the other side. In advocating tourist fares, Pan American was now alone.

Even the CAB was against tourist fares, and in fact urged that transatlantic fares be increased by $25.

Meanwhile a so-called open rate prevailed in the Western Hemisphere, and so the company was able to introduce tourist service to Rio and Buenos Aires effective March 1, 1949. The fare reduction was 17 percent. These flights proved extremely popular also.

Pan American continued to go it alone where possible, dropping New York–Bermuda fares by $50 in Oct. 1950, and making formal application to the CAB for limited, experimental tourist-class service to London. On May 4, 1951, the board for the first time gave formal support to the project. That same day the company circulated its proposal to IATA members, asking for consideration at the scheduled meeting five days later in Bermuda. Pan American was

proposing a one-way New York–London fare of $225, and a round trip of $405; there would be four round-trip tourist flights per week between New York and London, three between New York and Paris during the summer months, and two in each direction on each route between October and March. But in Bermuda, after days of heated discussion, there was still no agreement. Now for the first time Pan American threatened an "open rate"—rates of its own choosing—and in threatening this, Trippe was threatening chaos. But IATA's director general, Sir William Hildred, persuaded the delegates to return to the negotiating table, and an agreement close to the Pan Am proposal was reached.

But in Washington the CAB disapproved of this agreement because it contained frequency limitations (see letter dated July 31, 1951), and this effectively blocked the tourist fare once again.

The next IATA meeting of North Atlantic members was scheduled for London beginning Sept. 20, 1951, and here Pan American put forth new proposals: a maximum transatlantic one-way fare of $250 and a starting date of April 1, 1952. But the other carriers, trying to hold out as long as possible, voted instead to start in April 1953.

So the Pan Am delegate convened a press conference in London, spoke of "the disgusting and repetitious" performances of Pan American's opponents, and in effect called upon the public to force the tourist fares through.

Finally an IATA meeting was convened in Nice on Nov. 27, 1951, and tourist-class service was hammered out mostly on Pan American's terms to begin April 1, 1952. The delegates had no choice. It was clear now that Pan American would go it alone if agreement was not reached. In brief, the agreed-upon resolution covering North Atlantic service provided one-way tourist fare New York–London of $270, with an on-season round trip priced at $486, and an off-season round trip at $417. Seating configurations of the various airplanes then in use were stipulated, ranging from 40 seats in the earliest type of DC-4 to 77 seats in the DC-6B. The inaugural date was set for May 1, 1952. Succeeding IATA conferences merely extended the number of terminal cities. Trippe's dream of "fares for the average man" was at last a reality.

Propellers: Leslie to William P. Gwinn,

Sept. 4, 1974, a tape-recorded conversation —"We'd had a belly full."

Trippe as engineer: The quote is Borger's, from interview with author, Dec. 11, 1978. Leslie in a Feb. 28, 1978, interview said much the same: "Trippe was a very good technician. He was never lacking any capability in the field of aircraft engineering or flying or anything of the sort. He was not an engineer, but he was a very knowledgeable man."

Testing the J-57: Kauffman to author, Dec. 18, 1978.

Borger's memo: Dated Dec. 11, 1953.

The Boeing memo: Dated Oct. 1, 1954. It included the line: "Boeing has a sincere desire to produce such a jet transport for the airlines."

Kauffman and Gledhill ride the Boeing: Kauffman to author, Dec. 18, 1978.

Employees' fear of Trippe: This idea occurred repeatedly in the author's interviews with Anne Lindbergh, Kauffman, Leslie, John Shannon and John Gates. No one ever managed to articulate to the author's satisfaction exactly what this fear amounted to, but it had something to do with the impossibility of convincing Trippe of a point of view he did not wish to see. Executives who held an opposing point of view had to decide each time exactly how far they dared push it, each time trying to weigh their responsibility to their company and to themselves against the impenetrability of Trippe and their fear that he not only might not see their argument but would get angry.

Trippe excited by Gledhill's report: Kauffman to author Dec. 8, 1978.

First negotiations with Douglas: According to the 1955 annual report, Pan Am received its first DC-7B aircraft in 1955, and deliveries on the DC-7C were to begin in May of 1956. The annual report also explained the new plane's extra size and range. The final ten units of the DC-7C would go into service in 1957.

Early jet negotiations: "Pan American Details Jet Transport Needs," *Aviation Week*, March 16, 1953.

Trippe's arguments: Trippe to author, Sept. 1, 1976; June 21, 1978.

Stratocruiser a B-29 derivative: The company's Nov. 28, 1945, press release states that the Stratocruiser's wing is "the new Boeing-developed high performance wing that carried thousands of Superforts over the long Pacific wastes to bomb the Japanese and return."

Boeing's inferiority complex: According to the company's press release of Oct. 13, 1955, Boeing had built "well over a thousand of the 200,000 pound B-47 Stratojet medium bombers." According to Leslie, the Stratocruiser had been only a marginally successful plane, and Boeing's servicing of this plane had fallen short of airline needs. Douglas, on the other hand, had always been very strong on service.

Trippe asks for the J-75: Trippe to author, June 21, 1978—"I called Douglas, and I said, 'Don, you're six months behind. We have the big engine, how about increasing your wingspan a little.'" Gwinn explained to Leslie in their tape-recorded Sept. 4, 1974, conversation what the negotiations were like on the Pratt and Whitney side. "Secret" meant that the engines were ultimately sold, not only to Pan American but also to European airlines, with no exact dimensions, no specific details given out. Boeing did have these details, but Boeing was a military producer, and so it was all right.

Fear of catastrophic engine failures: Gwinn to Leslie. Gwinn also gave a good account of the development of these engines in his Wings Club lecture, May 16, 1973.

Twenty men meet in Santa Monica: Kauffman to author, Dec. 18, 1978.

Trippe supported by his engineers: Borger to author, Dec. 11, 1978—"We backed up his story."

Pratt and Whitney executives confer: According to Gwinn, "the computer really enabled us to make the advancement over the J-57. We could only have done it with a computer. There were never enough pads or papers or lead pencils and people to push them to compute it manually without a computer, particularly broadening the bands so that you could have more latitude on the throttle. There were 500 different designs and compressors that went through there before we settled on one." It was Gwinn who described the final meetings with Trippe, and also Rentschler's decision-making process. According to Gwinn, it was the last big decision Rentschler was to make, for he died in the spring of 1956.

The Rolls-Royce engine: It was called the Conway. According to Gwinn, Rolls-Royce had another advantage over Pratt and Whitney. It could give potential customers details and specifications of its engine, and Pratt and Whitney could not.

Men around Trippe amazed: Kauffman to author Dec. 18, 1978.

Trippe meets with Allen: Trippe to author, June 21, 1978; Allen to author, May 14, 1979. Allen conceded that he did not know about the Douglas order until he read about it in the papers. Douglas did not know about the Boeing order either—Douglas's Oct. 13 press release states: "Douglas is the first American plane produced to receive a firm order for this type of commercial jet airliner."

The financing: The two principal insurance companies involved were the Metropolitan and the Prudential. Trippe himself sat on the board of the Metropolitan, but excused himself when the board voted in favor of the deal—Trippe's conduct in matters of this kind was always almost religiously proper.

Trippe's IATA speech: He gave it on Oct. 18, 1955, five days after joint press releases were handed to the press by Boeing, Douglas, Pratt and Whitney, and Pan American.

Trippe's party: Trippe to author, Sept. 1, 1976.

Allen offers to redesign: Allen to author, May 14, 1979.

Trippe chortles: Trippe to author, Sept. 1, 1976.

The inaugural VIP flight: Gwinn described it to Leslie, Sept. 4, 1974.

Jet statistics: From the annual reports.

50 · Priester Demoted

Priester profile: PAF 50.16.02.

Masland meets Priester: Letter from Masland to Leslie, Nov. 30, 1975.

Priester sends Leslie home: Leslie to author, Feb. 21, 1978.

Trippe on Priester: Although Borger, Kauffman and Leslie, all of whom worked for Priester, spoke of him almost with reverence in interviews with the author, Trippe became noticeably reticent whenever Priester's name came up, and sometimes made uncomplimentary comments about him, claiming that Priester's contributions to the company were not nearly as important as other people seemed to think.

Vice president forced out: He retired "on doctor's orders" in June 1947.

Leuteritz questions Trippe: Leuteritz to author, June 16, 1978. Leuteritz also described Priester weeping and his own resignation from Pan Am.

Engineering department moves to Long Island City: Borger to author, Dec. 11, 1978. Executive system memorandum No. 127, June 30, 1953, shows Kauffman's election to the rank of assistant vice president for Engineering, reporting to Gledhill. Priester was appointed chairman of the technical committee on Aug. 1.

The new organizational chart: Kauffman to author, Dec. 18, 1978. Kauffman also described being careful to spend a couple of hours a week with Priester.

Aviation world shocked: Shannon to author, June 23, 1978. "Great pressure was put on Trippe to take Priester back." Borger, Kauffman and Leslie all attested to this also.

Priester's secretary's affection: Notes of interview with Mona Cooper, 1958, PAF 30.10.08.

51 · The Tycoon

Panagra antitrust suit: *Aviation Week*, June 25, 1954. In 1963 Pan Am and W. R. Grace & Co. applied to the CAB for approval of an agreement whereby Pan American would buy out Grace's 50 percent share. CAB approval was refused, however, and so Panagra was sold to Braniff Airways for $30 million on Dec. 29, 1966.

The Celler committee hearings: Trippe testified beginning June 14, 1956; his testimony begins on p. 2445 of the transcript.

The Guided Missile Range Division: PAF 10.07.00. It began to operate the Cape Kennedy test range in 1953.

The Business Jets Division: PAF 10.-04.00. It was formed in August 1963.

Pan Am Building: Negotiations between Trippe and Wolfson are described in *Fortune*, Dec. 1960; *Time*, March 15, 1963.

Leslie suggests Brunie: Leslie to author, Feb. 16, 1979.

Intercontinental Hotels: Gates to author, Aug. 25, 1978.

Trippe's habits as president/chairman of the board: A composite picture drawn from interviews with Leslie, Kauffman, Gates, Shannon and chief pilot Sam Miller.

It was Leslie who described the Christmas parties. Leslie, Kauffman and Shannon described the systems-operating-committee meetings. Leslie stated that a man could speak out freely; but Shannon said, "You didn't jump at an opportunity to tell Trippe he was wrong. I think he used people as sounding boards." Kauffman said, "One day he gave me a traffic problem." Leslie and Gates spoke of Trippe's penchant for low salaries, and Leslie and Shannon described the way names of vice presidents moved up and down the roster. Leslie was once listed second, and Shannon once got up to five, behind Trippe, Gray, Halaby and Lipscomb. Shannon described the place cards at company dinners. All agreed on the subject of Trippe's code of ethics, saying that he was old-fashioned and almost puritanical, always a gentleman, a man who played by Ivy League rules. Leslie once wrote down his own impressions of Trippe's personality, and this read in part: "Could be prudent, cautious, patient, evasive, and able to equivocate when he did not want to be pressured into a commitment—almost Asian in this respect—but rarely untruthful. Most of the calumny directed at him came from persons who had not thought and planned as far ahead as JTT and so were bested in a fair contest." It was Leslie who spoke of waiting days to see Trippe, who then concentrated on his own agenda, not Leslie's; and it was Gates who spoke of Trippe's habit of concentrating on one problem at a time—there were occasions when Trippe would summon Gates several times a day, after which, as Gates put it, "peace and quiet might reign for four or five months."

52 · The Biggest Gamble

Trippe meets Halaby: Halaby, *Crosswinds*, pp. 198 ff. Halaby goes on to describe taking phone calls from the President at Trippe's desk.

Lindbergh gloomy: Lindbergh, as he approached old age, had become an arch conservationist, and had made a number of public pronouncements on the subject. He was especially outspoken on the subject of the supersonic transport, which he was against. In the June 21, 1978, interview, Trippe admitted this; Lindbergh thought the end of the line had been reached. Trippe then added, "The end of the line has not been reached. It will never be reached. I felt that then, and I feel that today." Halaby quotes Lindbergh on this same subject on p. 204.

Trippe becomes chairman of the board: He announced his election to the newly created post and the election of Gray as president in July 1964. These corporate shifts and the booming airline business are reported in the 1964 annual report.

The breakthrough in engine design: General Kuter describes it in *The Great Gamble*, pp. 4 ff. He also describes the C-5 competition, Trippe's immediate effort to capitalize on it, and the early design work leading to the statement of intention signed by Allen and Trippe in December 1965.

Johnson's austerity program: Trippe to author, April 5, 6, 1978; June 21, 1978; Allen to author, May 14, 1979; McNamara to author, May 30, 1979. Allen said he was probably present at the business council meeting, but that Trippe had accosted Johnson alone without his knowledge. Later he and Trippe together conferred with subordinates of Johnson. Nor did Allen accompany Trippe to McNamara's office. McNamara denied that the letter Johnson tore up was his resignation—without, however, explaining what the letter was.

The 747's contract specifications: The Pan Am press release dated April 13, 1966, details many of them. The gestation problems of the aircraft are reported in brilliant detail by Kuter.

The succession: In separate interviews Willis Player and Betty Trippe both reported to the author that the first choice had been Leslie, and that former Assistant Secretary of the Air Force Roger Lewis had seemed the heir apparent for a number of years after that. That Trippe eventually focused on Halaby was proven by events. Halaby's credentials were impressive. Born in Dallas on Nov. 19, 1915, Halaby had graduated from Stanford University and Yale Law School. He had been a Navy test pilot in World War II, and a Deputy Assistant Secretary of Defense after that. Halaby discusses salary negotiations with Trippe in his *Crosswinds*, pp. 211 ff.

53 · The Great Day

Trippe's account: Trippe to author, April 5, 1978.

Miss Clair's account: Kathleen Clair to author, April 5, 1978.

The stockholders' meeting: The scene was described to the author by Willis Player on June 7, 1978; the statistics and Trippe's retirement announcements are from the minutes.

Pan Am 1968 statistics: From Player's press release accompanying Trippe's retirement.

Smith calls Trippe number one: Smith to Ann Crittenden, *The New York Times*, July 3, 1977, Sec. 3, p. 1.

Medals solicited: Pryor solicited the Medal for Merit, and under questioning, Leslie admitted that the same thing had been done by other subordinates a number of other times.

The directors' meeting: From the minutes.

Trippe escorts Gray into Gray's new office: Kathleen Clair to author April 5, 1978.

Women with tears in their eyes: Betty Trippe to author, April 5, 1978. According to Mrs. Trippe, Trippe came home greatly moved, saying, "They were so nice to me." Whereupon Mrs. Trippe phoned Miss Clair to thank her, saying, according to Miss Clair, "It's so wonderful what you girls did for him today."

Trippe returns from golf tournament: Kathleen Clair to author, April 5, 1978.

Epilogue

Trippe ceases to impose himself: Player to author, Jan. 11, 1979; Leslie to author, Feb. 17, 1979; Seawell to author, Jan. 11, 1979. Leslie was vice president and a director at the time; Player was vice president and the company's chief public relations officer. Seawell's testimony is partly hearsay, since he joined the company only in Dec. 1971.

Losses: From the company's annual reports to the CAB. The 1977 profit was $45 million.

Quarterly payments on the 747: See Kuter, pp. 52 ff.

Trippe blamed: See Halaby, p. 253; *Business Week*, June 26, 1971; "Pan Am submerges Trippe regime," *Aviation Week*, June 21, 1971.

Traffic levels off at 7.5 percent: "Bumpy Flying," by William M. Carley, in the *Wall Street Journal*, Jan. 10, 1979.

Domestic routes not accorded: Other "favors" also were not accorded. During the Halaby tenure the company sought to merge with Eastern Airlines, and merger talks were reopened once again with TWA. The CAB would not permit either.

Gray as chief executive: See Halaby, pp. 256–65; also, Player to author, Jan. 11, 1979, Leslie to author, Nov. 29, 1978. The quote about Gray's "110 percent integrity" is by Player. Gray died Dec. 24, 1972.

Gray's attitude toward charter service: Leslie to author, Nov. 29, 1978.

Halaby as chief executive: This is drawn principally from his book *Crosswinds*, supplemented by interviews with Leslie and Player who, admittedly, did not like him.

Problems with the 747: See Kuter, p. 79 ff.

Halaby fires executives: Again the source is Halaby himself (*Crosswinds*, pp. 261, 320).

Halaby ousted: "I had to ask him to leave," said Trippe to the author one day at lunch. Player described Trippe's role as that of "consultant rather than an activist."

Seawell hired: Seawell to author Jan. 11, 1979.

Trippe continues to attend board meetings: Seawell to author.

Wake Island after World War II: From a brochure prepared by the Federal Aviation Administration in March 1971; also from author's interviews on Wake. A demolition expert and also a technician to repair the Marine Corps Memorial were aboard the author's flight to Wake; the author heard the newly uncovered bomb or shell explode, and saw the smoke rise above the dunes. The remains of the 786 Japanese soldiers had been dug up and cremated approximately one week previously.

Index

ABOUT THE AUTHOR

ROBERT DALEY is the author of fifteen previous books, six of them novels, three of them picture books containing the author's own photographs. His articles, photographs and short stories have appeared in most major magazines, including *Esquire, Vogue, Playboy, Life, New York* magazine, *Reader's Digest* and *The New York Times Magazine,* and, abroad, in *Paris-Match.* His photographs have been exhibited in the Baltimore Museum, the Art Institute of Chicago and other galleries. His work has been translated into many languages, including Japanese, Portuguese and Dutch. Certain of his books have grown out of personal experience. His six years with the New York Football Giants resulted in *Only a Game,* the first serious pro football novel; and his six years as a *New York Times* foreign correspondent resulted in another novel, *The Whole Truth.* In 1971 and 1972 he served as a New York City deputy police commissioner; the nonfiction best seller *Target Blue* followed in 1973, the novel *To Kill A Cop* in 1976, and another nonfiction best seller, *Prince of The City,* in 1979.

Mr. Daley, who served in the Air Force during the Korean War, has had a continued interest in aviation, and devoted more than three years of research and writing to the making of *An American Saga.*

Mr. Daley and his French-born wife have three daughters and live in Connecticut.

	DATE DUE	
DEC 1 3 1986		
OCT 1 9 1982		
NOV 2 3 1982		
OCT 4 1986		
8 1988		
DEC 1 6 1988		